COLLECTED
PROSE

J M

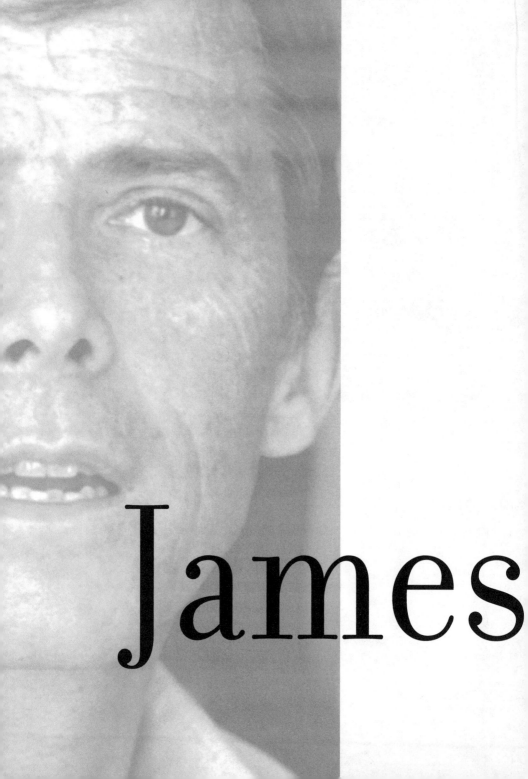

James

COLLECTED

PROSE

---

edited by

J. D. McClatchy and Stephen Yenser

Merrill

Alfred A. Knopf • New York • 2004

www.aaknopf.com

Grateful acknowledgment is made to the following for permission to reprint
previously published material:

Boosey & Hawkes, Inc.: Excerpt from The Rake's Progress, *music by Igor*
Stravinsky, text by W. H. Auden and Chester Kallman, copyright © 1949, 1950,
1951 by Boosey & Hawkes, Inc. Copyright renewed. Reprinted by permission.

Farrar, Straus and Giroux, LLC.: Excerpts from The Complete Poems 1927–1979
by Elizabeth Bishop. Copyright © 1979, 1983 by Alice Helen Methfessel.
Reprinted by permission of Farrar, Straus and Giroux, LLC.

Yale University Press: For permission to
reprint Merrill's forewords to the Yale Series of Younger Poets.

Knopf, Borzoi Books, and the colophon are registered trademarks
of Random House, Inc.

Library of Congress Cataloging-in-Publication Data
Merrill, James Ingram.
[Selections. 2004]
Collected prose / James Merrill ; edited by J. D. McClatchy and Stephen Yenser.
p. cm.
Includes bibliographical references and index.
ISBN 0-375-41136-4
I. McClatchy, J. D., 1945– II. Yenser, Stephen. III. Title. PS3525.E6645A6 2004
818'.548—dc22
2004040914

Manufactured in the United States of America
First Edition

EDITORS' NOTE

As much as any poet of his time, James Merrill conceived of his work and his life as warp and woof, and the prose collected here shows how intimately related to his technique (itself a recurrent topic) were his everyday readings and reflections, his frequent travels and his friendships. As Merrill remarked to an interviewer, a poet "is someone choosing the words he lives by," and throughout this volume one recognizes the care for verbal nuance and hears the inimitably varied tones (witty and indignant, skeptical and reverent, analytic and nostalgic, and withal passionate) that distinguish his work in all genres.

Parts of this volume appeared in an earlier selection of Merrill's prose, *Recitative* (1986). For this new collection we have arranged pieces in broad categories, and within each we have as a rule presented the selections chronologically, though on a few occasions we have thought it more sensible to group them with an eye to subject.

In our first section, "Writing," we have included Merrill's most substantial pieces on that subject. The "Interviews" section contains what we understand to be his most trenchant commentary in that mode—and indeed at times some commentary perhaps less significant, since we wanted to interrupt as little as possible the flow of each of these often carefully crafted pieces, some of which were written and some of which were transcribed from tapes and then edited. We have omitted from this section certain interviews the substance of which appears elsewhere in this collection. (We cite them in the headnote to the "Interviews" section.) "Writers" comprises Merrill's major critical essays and reviews and a selection of his commentary on authors and other literary matters. Because his forewords to the books he chose for publication in the Yale Younger Poets series have much in common in regard to format, we have grouped those seven pieces together. "Occasions" convenes a miscellany of work, much of it hitherto available, when available at all, only in fugitive publications. The three "Stories" and the three "Translations" of prose are Merrill's only completed mature works in those genres.

We have included in the "Juvenilia" a few of what we take to be Merrill's most anticipatory writings. A notable omission in this regard is his unpublished honors thesis, "*A La Recherche du Temps Perdu:* Impressionism in Literature," written at Amherst College in 1947. Our omission of it has partly to do with its length and partly to do with our feeling that the passages in it that meant most to their author appeared in more developed forms later in his career.

We have chosen not to include slight pieces—such as brief introductions, letters to the editor, and remarks to reporters—or those that merely repeat what has elsewhere here been better put. On the rare occasion when for similar reasons we have deleted material from pieces reprinted here, we have indicated the deletion with bracketed ellipses. We have also silently corrected certain evident errors. Textual notes appear before the index.

We are once more indebted to Jack W. C. Hagstrom for his bibliographical efforts and to Marcia Carlson, Deborah Garrison, Ilana Kurshan, and Patrick Merla for their editorial assistance.

—JDMcC and SY

CONTENTS

WRITING

ACOUSTICAL CHAMBERS

Interior spaces, the shape and correlation of rooms in a house, have always appealed to me. Trying for a blank mind, I catch myself instead revisiting a childhood bedroom on Long Island. Recently, on giving up the house in Greece where I'd lived for much of the previous fifteen years, it wasn't so much the fine view it commanded or the human comedies it had witnessed that I felt deprived of; rather, I missed the hairpin turn of the staircase underfoot, the height of our kitchen ceiling, the low door ducked through in order to enter a rooftop laundry room that had become my study. This fondness for given arrangements might explain how instinctively I took to quatrains, to octaves and sestets, when I began to write poems. "Stanza" is after all the Italian word for "room."

Foreign languages entered my life early in the person of my governess. Although we called her Mademoiselle she was not a spinster but a widow. Neither was she French, or even, as she led us to believe, Belgian, but part English and part, to her undying shame, Prussian. She had lived in Brussels at least, and her sister, who now taught music in Pennsylvania, had been decorated for playing duets with the old Queen Mother of Belgium. Mademoiselle's maiden name was Fanning. This meant some distant kin-

New York Times Book Review, February 21, 1982.

ship with the explorer who discovered—I can see her finger poised above the open atlas—*those* tiny Pacific islands, and whose house a block away from mine in Stonington, Connecticut, I would be able to point out to her when she spent a day with me thirty years later.

I worshipped this kind, sad woman: her sensible clothes, her carrot hair and watery eyes, the sunburnt triangle at her throat, the lavender wen on her wrist. She taught me to say the Ave Maria and to sing Carmen's "Habanera." I got by heart the brother heroically dead, the sister in Johnstown, the other sister in Copenhagen. I resolved as soon as I grew up to marry her daughter, Stella, at that age plain and rather disagreeable, who was boarded out to a refined Catholic family in East Hampton—the light of love suffused even *them*. I heard all there was to hear about Mademoiselle's previous charges and prayed every night to grieve her less than spoilt Constance M. or devilish Peter T. had done. While she talked a needle flashed—costumes for my marionettes. Stories that ten years later would have convulsed me, I drank in solemnly. For instance: Having to relieve herself at a border checkpoint during the war, Mademoiselle had overlaid the *"infecte"* toilet seat with some family letters she happened to be carrying in her purse. In the course of the "formalities" her innocent buttocks were bared by a uniformed matron and found to be stenciled with suspicious mirror writing, which triggered a long and humiliating interrogation. *"Figure-toi!"* she exclaimed, gravely fixing me through her gold-rimmed spectacles. I could indeed imagine. I too was being imprinted, there and then.

By the time I was eight I had learned from her enough French and German to understand that English was merely one of many ways to express things. A single everyday object could be called *assiette* or *Teller* as well as *plate*—or were plates themselves subtly different in France and Germany? Mademoiselle's French and Latin prayers seemed to invoke absolutes beyond the ken of our Sunday school pageants. At the same time, I was discovering how the everyday sounds of English could mislead you by having more than one meaning. One afternoon at home I opened a random book and read: "Where is your husband, Alice?" "In the library, sampling the port." If samples were little squares of wallpaper or chintz, and ports were where ships dropped anchor, this hardly clarified the behavior of Alice's husband. Long after Mademoiselle's exegesis, the phrase haunted me. Words weren't what they seemed. The mother tongue could inspire both fascination and distrust.

But back to those octaves and sestets. Words might frustrate me, forms never did; neither did meter. Children in my day were exposed to a good deal of competent verse. Each first grader at St. Bernard's memorized his hundred lines of Sir Walter Scott and received an apple for so doing. Before graduation he would speak deathless poetry in the annual Shakespeare play. The masters somehow let meaning take care of itself, a chip borne along by the rhetorical surge. Accordingly, frustration was reserved for the content, or lack of it, in what I'd begun to write at boarding school. Gerrish Thurber, the mild and merciful librarian who "advised" the young editors of the *Lawrenceville Lit*, read through my first submission and nodded, saying only, "We can always use a well-made sonnet." It took me a while to fathom what he hadn't said.

My classmate Frederick Buechner wrote his poem first. In a flash I thought: I can do that too! And away we went. Luckily perhaps, since it allowed us to polish without much thought for what (if anything) we were communicating, our callowness led us to second-rate, fin de siècle stuff—Wilde, Heredia, Alice Meynell. These writers didn't figure in the Lawrenceville curriculum, although they met its chief requirement by having died. The living poets (unlike Milton or Keats, on whom white-haired Mr. Raymond had given us the last sonorous word) were still scandalously eluding definition in the pages of anthologies never seen in the classroom. Would our style ever mature? Or rather, dripping and sugary, would it ever unripen? Long after Freddy had gone on to Blake and Whitman, I dawdled behind with Elinor Wylie and the gaudier bits in Baudelaire.

On the threshold of our senior year the *Lit*'s graduating editor summoned his two least trustworthy successors. Sucking at a pipe, this man of eighteen urged us to recant. "Write about *real things* for God's sake: blondes and pistons!"—fetishes no less conventional than the moonlit foliage, masquerades, mad crones, and pet monkeys that clotted our own poems and stories. We left his room with scornful smiles.

The airs I was giving myself ran in the family. My father had offered his Aunt Grace the sum, unheard of in those Depression years, of five dollars a page for memoirs of her Mississippi girlhood. She couldn't do it;

the truth froze her pen. Not that she stopped writing. One summer a flier came in the mail from a vanity press in New York, announcing Aunt Grace's novel, *Femme Fatale*. "Set against the turbulent background of the French court, this tale of searing passion . . ." My mother and I, alone that year and needing diversion, at once ordered our copy—several copies: Christmas was coming. Before it did, German troops overran a real France Aunt Grace wouldn't have crossed the street to see, and *Femme Fatale* was never published or our money refunded.

Like Aunt Grace, and like many adolescents, I needed to feel that I was fulfilling myself in the face of heartless indifference. In fact my mother was both proud and critical of my early writing. She had taken a summer course in the short story at Columbia, worked on the Jacksonville newspaper, and edited until her marriage a weekly gazette of her own. Some satirical doggerel she dashed off about the preparations for my sister's wedding dazzled me, at nine, with its zany, end-stopped rhyming. My father, who could compose long lucid letters in his beautifully rounded hand and read with X-ray eyes the to me impenetrable editorials in the *Herald Tribune*, looked to literature for a good cry. His favorite author was J. M. Barrie—indeed, Alice and her port-sampling husband may be found in Barrie's play *Dear Brutus*. My father had a way of his own with rhyme. Here is how he acknowledged one of my letters when I first went abroad:

> *Though we're apart,*
> *You're in my heart—*
> *I too love Chartres.*

He was also a powerful and unpredictable man, never more so, in my young eyes, than when, pretending to want for his scrapbook the poems and stories I'd written up to then, he had a small edition of them handsomely produced during my senior year at Lawrenceville. *Jim's Book*, as he titled it, thrilled me for days, then mortified me for a quarter century. I wouldn't put it past my father to have foreseen the furthest consequences of his brilliant, unsettling gesture, which, like the pat on a sleepwalker's back, looked like approbation but was aimed at waking me up.

It partly succeeded. I opened my eyes enough at least to see how much remained to be learned about writing. Presently I was at Amherst, reading Proust, Dante, and *Faust* in their various originals, Jane Austen and Pope with Reuben Brower, Shakespeare and Darwin with Theodore Baird. Here also Kimon Friar put before me the living poets and gave the nine-day wonders that shot up like beanstalks from this richest of mulches their first and only detailed criticism. Many hands made light work. Four years after graduation my *First Poems* had appeared. I was living alone and unhappy in Rome and going to a psychiatrist for writer's block.

The doctor wanted to hear about my life. It had been flowing along unnoticed in my absorption with the images that came and went on its surface. Now its very droplets were being studied on a slide. "Real things"—was I condemned to write about them, after all?

Of course I had been doing nothing else. Symbolist pastiche or makeshift jotting, our words reveal more than we think. The diary kept during my first year away at school reports a Christmas-break visit to Silver Springs, Florida. I'd like to go back there one day and ride again in the glass-bottomed boat, peering down at the cold pastoral of swaying grasses and glinting schools. There would be much to say about "unconscious depths," about my zodiacal creature the Fish, above all about the heavy pane of glass that, like a kind of intelligence, protected me and my mother from that sunken world while revealing its secrets in magical detail. But in 1940 the artless diarist records only this: "Silver Springs—heavenly colors and swell fish."

Two banalities, each by itself bad enough, and hopelessly so in conjunction. Yet in their simple awfulness they broach the issue most crucial to this boy not quite fourteen. Two years earlier my parents had been divorced and Mademoiselle amicably sent packing: I am thought to need "a man's influence." We hear how children suffer under these circumstances. I am no exception; my grades plummet, I grow fat gorging on sweets. "Heavenly colors and swell fish." What is that phrase but an attempt to bring my parents together, to remarry on the page their characteristic inflections—the ladylike gush and the regular-guy terseness? In reality my parents have tones more personal and complex than these, but the time is still far off when I can dream of echoing them. To do so, I see in retrospect, will involve a search for magical places real or invented, like Silver Springs or Sandover, acoustical chambers so designed as to endow the weariest platitude with resonance and depth. By then, too, surrogate parents will enter the scene, figures more articulate than Mademoiselle but not unlike her, either, in the safe ease and mystery of their influence: Proust and Elizabeth Bishop; Maria and Auden in the *Sandover* books. The unities of home and world, and world and page, will be observed through the very act of transition from one to the other.

THE EDUCATION
OF THE POET

I wish I could simply throw away these crutches and let what I have to say come dancing forth. But the sad truth is that I've never trusted myself to improvise, so I'll have to read from a text and it will sound more closely reasoned than it actually is. Just between us, "The Education of the Poet" isn't the most promising title. What must have been secretly intended— to judge from so many rapt faces—is the education of the audience; but that I won't presume to undertake. The trouble with one's own education is that one can go on talking and never stop, because everything that happens runs the risk of teaching us something. "What subjects did you take?" we ask a young person just out of school. The question could as well be asked at the end of life, and the answer would go something like: "Well, let's see, I flunked War and Civics, but did OK in Friendship, Travel, Italian Opera, Social Graces, and Death." All those are among my subjects, but I shall try not to discuss them this evening. Many of them are your subjects too, so you don't need to hear about them from me.

Instead I would like to take Education in its most obvious sense, and tell you about a handful of particular things learned—from teachers, from reading, from accidents in the very act of writing—which played a part in the kind of poet I became. I mean those moments early on, when

Envoy, September 1988.

one begins to recognize possibilities as well as limitations, and comes a shade closer to some proverbial "voice of one's own." Notions of form and tone and metaphor are vital to that developing voice, and I'll be saying something brief and diffident about each of those three, and hoping to sugar the pill with a poem now and then, as I go along.

Since the unborn child hears its mother's heartbeat, it must be that we come into the world with some degree of prosodic consciousness. Patients with brain damage, incapable of ordinary language, have been known to speak in nonsense hexameters—which isn't to say that they would ever have been able to read "Evangeline" aloud. Only that the meter was in their heads. I remember a lithograph that hung in the stairwell of my grandparents' house in Florida. It was the four stanzas, illustrated in faded yellows and greens, of the Tennyson poem beginning "Home they brought her warrior dead." At the center the young widow sat in her beautiful Pre-Raphaelite dress, too numbed by grief to weep for her husband. Word by word I made out the ending:

> *Rose a nurse of ninety years,*
> *Set his child upon her knee—*
> *Like summer tempests came her tears—*
> *"Sweet my child, I live for thee."*

Now that was thrilling stuff for a five-year-old. The fact that my experience occurred within Freud's lifetime must have helped me to grasp the connection between a murdered father and a maternal muse, and to fix the lines in my head forever. But my simple point is that even then I knew the lines were metrical. This understanding came long before any real acquaintance with meaning.

That lesson was soon to be reinforced a few blocks north of this auditorium, at St. Bernard's School, by the first grader's having to get by heart a hundred lines from Sir Walter Scott's "Lay of the Last Minstrel"—for which the tiny Adam was rewarded by an apple—and more impressively by the annual Shakespeare play. I can read you a poem about that. [Merrill reads "The School Play."]

We at St. Bernard's were too young to know what many of Shakespeare's lines meant. When Richard II said, "Wanting the manage of unruly jades," he could have been talking not about horsemanship so much as an earthquake in a Hong Kong curio shop. But once the line was said with proper stresses, there was little more to ask of the child who wore the crown.

My earliest writings, at nine or ten, owed nothing to Tennyson or Shakespeare. Rather, I imitated the doggerel my mother sometimes produced on family occasions. For her as for me, poems already in books were off-limits. People who aren't poets—or aren't poets *yet*—frequently take pride in versifying with deliberate clumsiness, so as to keep their standing in a community that might well distrust or ridicule them for being literary. The result belongs to a folk tradition centuries old, which sticks to its own quaint manners and would sooner die than parallel the shifting course of high art.

Very much in the air as I was growing up—thanks to Pound and Dr. Williams and some of my own contemporaries, like John Ashbery and Allen Ginsberg—was the injunction to forge a "new measure." The pentameter—so went the argument in part—wasn't a truly *American* line. I had to wonder if these patriots had ever heard the blues. "I hate to see that evening sun go down"—wasn't that an effortless and purely native music?

No doubt the real question must be put in some such terms as these: doesn't our world, with all its terrifying fragmentations and new frontiers, call for equivalent formal breakthroughs? Who would dream of coping with today in heroic couplets or terza rima? The degree to which one yields to such demands is finally, I think, a matter of temperament, and cannot be forced. I, in any case, never got round to that new measure. It remained a fairly old-fashioned context—the need for a rhyme or an amphibrach—that I found most conducive to surprise. It was always "educational" to try a new *form*. Just three or four years ago I wrote my first Sapphic stanzas. Here's a short example—they're so tricky that *any* example would be short: a poem about being old enough to see one's father's face in the shaving mirror. Or maybe it's about the Tradition, personified as father and son ["Arabian Night"].

To go on a bit longer about form, my favorite stanza—the *abba* quatrain—I encountered first not in "In Memoriam" but in Oscar Wilde's Whistler-haunted impressions of London. From such poets as Wilde, Elinor Wylie, and half-forgotten French Symbolists my young self was able to learn technical skill with little danger of lasting pollution by their ideas—for they had mercifully few of these. The one idea they did convey, and this has stayed with me, was that ideas in poetry should constitute a shifting, unutterable subtext to be glimpsed through spangles, like the Houses of Parliament seen upside down in the Thames.

One afternoon at boarding school I was launched upon a dramatic lyric to be spoken by the emperor Nero, when somehow the quatrain I expected to produce took a new turn. Three lines had so far ended *aba*, but the fourth line followed an eddy of its own, and could be accommodated only by extending the stanza to six lines. Here, nearly fifty years later, are those six lines, every bit as callow and effete as I had hoped they would be at the time:

> *As I am smeared with scented oil*
> *So are these Christians black with pitch.*
> *It is a shame that they must spoil*
> *My vines and flowers with their crying—*
> *But golden flames rise from them, which*
> *Burn on in memory, undying.*

You can live without hearing the rest. Now I was hardly the first poet to use that scheme. Yet the things you find yourself doing on your own, prompted by your own instincts, are in a totally different category from those same things done by others. "My vines and flowers with their crying"—I can still feel the disproportionate thrill that fourth line awoke in me with its sly new rhyme sound, its unforeseen feminine ending, and most of all, the formal adjustment it called for. Now that I think about it, the great commandment throughout *The Changing Light at Sandover* was: Thou shalt make room for new impulses.

Hugh Kenner has beautifully evoked the excitement which such a stroke can bring about in a good reader—*and*, be it understood, when the poem in question is a masterpiece. Here he is on the conclusion of Verlaine's "Clair de Lune":

But what are we to make of the poem's final clause which leaps without syntactic interruption into a new stanza and furnishes that stanza with wonder after wonder, each springing into existence because a rhyme or a cadence or a grammatical construction seems to require it. . . . [B]efore our eyes a reality is created . . . by the most formal means, in obedience to the most formal demands.

The setting of "Clair de Lune" by Debussy, and its performance by Maggie Teyte and Alfred Cortot in a famous recording of the mid-forties, left me with an ideal of how I wanted my poems to be. Meanwhile a thirst for syntax was leading me to Henry James and Proust. I learned that when James began to dictate his novels the involution of his already elaborate sentences, which nevertheless cleared up by magic the moment they were read aloud, grew even more pronounced, as if "natural word order"— far from corresponding to the mechanical faucet gush of SEE DICK RUN—flowed rather from sources buried deep in the psyche of a properly fussed-over child. Here's an illustration dating from 1951 ["Olive Grove"].

My subject, as you'll have noticed, is no longer form so much as what we used to call tone—the shades of mood and manner implied by this or that way of speaking. The waywardness of speech, which that last poem conceives as an all but interminable sostenuto phrase, could also be represented—in livelier manner, I came to think—by disruptions, reversals of attitude, shifts in midsentence. We are used to this on the stage, where conflicting views can be assigned to the various characters. But its equivalent on the page appears late in our poetry, not perhaps until Pope's "Epistle to Dr. Arbuthnot," and only reaches its flowering in Byron. Byron adored Pope, and never bought the widespread notion that Wordsworth wrote in a language people actually used. In Byron's hands these comic self-disruptions lighten the burden borne by a single speaker, or at least keep him from painting himself into the corner of a single viewpoint ["Time"].

I like to recall an hour during my senior year at Amherst. Reuben Brower and I were looking at these lines by Pope, from *The Dunciad*, describing the behavior, on his Grand Tour, of a young nobleman who

> *The stews and palace equally explored;*
> *Intrigued with glory, and with spirit whored.*

Mr. Brower casually pointed out the fun here: not only did the dreadful youth go in spirited fashion to the brothel, he also in a sense debauched his loftiest faculty—whored with spirit. This second meaning glistened wickedly up through the first, making *it* seem relatively innocent and red-blooded. I was enthralled. Everything depended on how you understood the dull little word "with." Years would pass before I could begin to approach this expert lightness of means.

Lightness of manner, as well. Another couplet by Pope can still persuade me, for as long as I sit under the spell of its sound effects, that our world weighs no more than a feather. It describes the French writer Voiture:

> *Thus, wisely careless, innocently gay,*
> *Cheerful, he played the trifle, life, away.*

We speak wistfully of sounding the depths of language, but language has its shallows too, and we can drown in those just as easily as in the raptures of the former. A London *Times* crossword puzzle gave this definition of a nine-letter word: "A kind of cakewalk? Plenty of it!" The answer was ABUNDANCE. Now this is at best the kindergarten of language; still, it has the virtue of training us, once we grow up, to keep in mind the oddity of a given word. Abundance comes from the Latin for "wave," *unda*, preceded by *ab-*, which denotes a movement away. Hence, an overflowing. But "cakewalk," by stressing and isolating the dance at the end of the word, allows us to see not one but two Latin prefixes, *ab-* and *un-*, both negative. Whereupon a faint shudder of false meaning comes over us, a meaning that derives from those two negatives as well as from the idea of dancing in the face of such adversity. These undertones subvert the hearty definition of Abundance held in common by the rest of us. I'm not pretending that any *good* is done by driving language to such extremes, simply that it is the way of the world—of the Western world at least—and that our literary explorers are still looking for waterways to Cathay.

In that poem "Time" I read just now you will have noticed a play on words. The pack of cards with which a game of Patience is being played turns, by the poem's end, into a mountaineer's backpack; or rather, the reader is asked to keep both meanings in mind simultaneously. This is of course the essence of metaphor—two things rendered in terms of one another. The Greek word, both now and in antiquity, means the act of transferring. One sees trucks in Athens blazoned with METAPHOROS. In this case a chasm some fifty lines wide separates the two meanings of "pack." I like to think that this measurable interval gives the transaction what energy it has. If you're just moving into the house next door you don't need a blue-and-white truck.

It was reading Proust long ago that started me thinking about his kind of spatial metaphor. Here is a very short example from *Swann's Way*: a piece of music is being described in visual or dimensional terms. Notice how the word "foreground" prepares us for the Dutch paintings a line or two before the metaphorical truck gets to them:

> the pianist would play for them—for their two selves and for no one else—that little phrase by Vinteuil which was, so to speak, the national anthem of their love. He began, always, with a sustained tremolo from the violin part, which, for several bars, was unaccompanied, and filled all the foreground; until suddenly it seemed to be drawn aside and—just as in those interiors by Pieter de Hooch, where the subject is set back a long way through the narrow framework of a half-opened door—infinitely remote, in color quite different, velvety with the radiance of some intervening light, the little phrase appeared, dancing, pastoral, interpolated, episodic, belonging to another world.

I've come to think of effects like these, which often require a great many lines, or even a great many pages, for their accomplishment—as a way of reconciling two ongoing and contradictory impulses in my writing: the extensive and the intensive, Calvino calls them. Narrative breadth needn't preclude an at times extreme involution, the hermetic node of phrase or image, like a knot in lumber, actually enlivening the flat, dependable stretches. Let me read you two poems that appear side by side in one of my books. The first you might call "narrative." It tells a story, there are characters and feelings in it, and it runs to just over one hundred lines. I won't translate an off-color passage in French, but the Greek word *yiayia*, meaning grandmother, can be applied to any old woman with whom one is on affectionate terms ["After the Fire"].

Now the second poem. It's only five lines long, but—for me, at any rate—it manages to encapsulate much of the experience and feeling of the longer one ["Log"].

While we're still talking about metaphor, bear with me through two more passages. The first is a well-known one from *The Origin of Species*:

> If we must compare the eye to an optical instrument, we ought in imagination to take a thick layer of transparent tissue, with spaces filled with fluid, and with a nerve sensitive to light beneath, and then suppose every part of this layer to be continually changing slowly in density, so as to separate into layers of different densities and thicknesses placed at different distances from each other, and with the surfaces of each layer slowly changing in form. Further we must suppose that there is a power, represented by natural selection . . . always intently watching each slight alteration in the transparent layers; and carefully preserving each which, under varied circumstances, in any way or degree, tends to produce a distincter image.

By concentrating upon the structure of the eye, and describing it as carefully as possible, Darwin accomplishes something he does not intend. The more he dwells upon the eyeball, the more his language sends out filaments toward another subject, a subject implicit both in language and in perception—the shifting densities of consciousness itself.

The second passage comes by courtesy of David Jackson, whom some puzzling but (as it turned out) trivial symptoms a few months ago obliged to visit an eye specialist. He returned disgruntled from Miami with many pages and pamphlets, and here is an example of his doctor's prose:

> I like to think of the eye as being analogous to a white porcelain mixing bowl lined with Saran Wrap. . . . As the Saran Wrap sticks to the inside surface of the mixing bowl, so does the retina normally stick to the back surface of the eye. If you then take this mixing bowl and fill its interior with a clear Jell-O, you can imagine that with time this Jell-O will become somewhat dehydrated and tend to pull the Saran Wrap toward the center of the mixing bowl.

It doesn't stop there. . . . Now both Darwin and this Dr. Seymour in Miami (not his real name) have important things to tell, and each passage can be said to accomplish its descriptive purpose. I would trust Dr. Seymour to repair a hole in my retina. But I would prefer to see the world through Darwin's version of the eye. One must conclude that style is *almost* everything.

Among the many educational experiences I warned you I'd be leaving out, there are two I'd like to hint at before we call it a night.

The poet I was most in awe of at twenty was Rilke, as much for his poems as for the uncompromising example he set. Desiring nothing less than the full flood of unconscious or—who can say?—divine inspiration, he saw that it was out of the question to force the issue. What he *could* do while waiting for the lightning to strike was to keep his instrument in order by writing poems that came to him in the usual way: set pieces, minor brainstorms, beautiful feelings, bits of life which caught his eye. Such modest pursuits never kept him from giving himself the most insufferable airs. But that's beside the point. When the *Duino Elegies* and the *Sonnets to Orpheus* burst upon him, he was ready for them, he could cope with the technical demands. But that's probably beside the point as well. The lessons I mean are those that reach us from a source beyond the Self, a level of the psyche we no longer recognize as ours. How to invite that education is anybody's guess. Drugs have worked for some, meditation for others; in my own case it was something as apparently flimsy as the Ouija board. I've always loved the work of writing—the boredom, the revisions, the surprises, even the typing. But the joy of collecting the material with David Jackson, and shaping it into *Sandover*, was keener, and much longer-lasting, than anything I've known before or since. Here's a short passage from the end of *Mirabell* that expresses some of that joy. It begins with a phrase by Wittgenstein and a glimpse of the DNA disguised as a diamond necklace, and tells how we felt during the hour before our first visit from the archangel Michael [*Mirabell* excerpt].

Finally, in honor of all the things I've forgotten to say, a poem about learning to forget. The idea came on hearing that Lady Diana Duff Cooper, whenever a name or a fact escaped her, used to give her ravishing smile and say, "Oh, well, another marble gone!" Someone else playing the trifle, life, away—but it suddenly made me think of the Elgin marbles, and the poem was underway. It's in seven sections, the third of which is deliberately incoherent, representing a text half effaced by rain. But don't be alarmed: the page will return fully restored in Section 5. [Merrill closes by reading his poem "Losing the Marbles."]

JUNG LOVE

At six or seven, Martin is transported to a new continent, accidentally shoots a roseate spoonbill, and is swept off into exotic topographies and hallucinatory encounters. Rain forest Indians strip him bare; desert vultures confer round his sleeping form, talking like eighteenth-century surgeons. The People of the Mirage bless him and the Lady of the Hills rocks him to sleep wound in her long, black, silky hair. By the book's end, Martin has confronted the Old Man of the Sea, and amazed a crew that could almost be the Flying Dutchman's with the sight of a naked child asleep on a raft.

Jung would have liked W. H. Hudson's *A Little Boy Lost*. Its sources, unimaginable when I first read it, would in time come gradually to light for me. A certain serpent-guarded fruit tree reappeared in Genesis. Knowing Martin's story, I hardly needed Sunday school to learn about a carpenter's son whose mother, pregnant with him, was visited by a bird in a dream. A chapter set among underworld smithies prepared me for Wagner's Nibelungen. The red-coated army of conquest and havoc that Martin sees from afar, through eyes made keen by the Hill Lady's magic ointment, came straight out of Tennyson. A famous albatross would recall the murdered spoonbill. And the procession in which it is borne

Voice Literary Supplement, February 1992.

past on a litter as a beautiful wounded prince—Amfortas?—had clearly been staged by Bakst or Klimt.

Thus I ingested a powerful, delectably coated capsule packed with cultural information. The story's chief emotional tension—whether to stay with the motherly Hill Lady or follow the vagabond destiny bestowed upon Martin by the Queen of the Mirage—speaks to me no less at sixty than it did at eight. And when *Sandover* began emerging from our Ouija board it was perhaps to be expected that Hudson's Old Man of the Sea—rising up before the boy as "a man-shaped tower of water and spray, and white froth and brown seaweed"—had long ago dictated the protean aspect of my own poem's elemental angels.

On Literary Tradition

In response to a question from William Matthews about literary apprenticeship:

I want to start with a phrase you used. You were saying about the young poet that the best he or she could do was to write what was truly felt and could be clearly said. I think probably my ambition, when I was an adolescent, was to do almost the opposite. Because I didn't know what I felt, it seemed to be that what was obscurely said had a kind of resonance that charmed me and led me at least down that dangerous path toward the impenetrable quatrains of Mallarmé, trying deliberately to create a surface of such impenetrability and, at the same time, such beauty that it wouldn't yield up a meaning easily, if at all. Maybe eventually one gets tired of that kind of thing, though in my weak moments I still find myself drawn to it. My point is that one needn't have any idea what one feels when one starts to write a poem. The poem is, in a way, an act of self-purification. The clarity you may arrive at is unforeseeable. . . .

The feeling, too, can surface at the end. The feeling you begin with is very often just the feeling of wanting to write a poem. With any luck you can put it together with a so-called real emotion, love or anger.

About tradition—Bill was talking about the reaction of one genera-

Shenandoah, Autumn 1982.

tion to another against the tone, everything, to use a clumsy word, *human*, that has been brought by the poet to his work. I think this changes, and one reacts against tone much more automatically and rapidly than one reacts against form. Descartes may have wanted to turn his knowledge inside out but he still was using the form of the French sentence and the language. The forms in writing are what tide one over these periods of reaction. . . . They *do* change, but they change as slowly as the forms in Darwin, whereas the pendulum of individual tone from one generation to the next keeps moving briskly.

To a question about passion in poetry:

Life will teach you passion. I agree with Lytton Strachey when he was asked what the most important thing was in the world and he said passion. Unfortunately, when we've been in workshops, or looked at beginner poems, we've seen poems full of passion which neither we nor their authors would want to read a few months later. And yet the great poems, in our language or in any language, are the passionate poems. As a young person, I didn't know what I felt. I was a very backward child and I practiced simply the skills; whatever came to hand filled in the frame. As I grew older, I had stronger, more trustable emotions, things that came to me with life, from life, not from reading or from the classroom, and those feelings went into my frame. I don't deny that we all felt intensely at the age of fifteen or twenty, but it's a feeling that doesn't always bear inspection a few years later because we grow so rapidly at that time in our lives. It's really the artistry that sustains the passionate poem that we would read from one century to the next. What I might have wanted to learn in a workshop was precisely as much as I could about artistry, trusting life to take care of the rest.

To a question about some earlier remarks Merrill made about Elizabeth Bishop:

I was talking about Elizabeth Bishop and wondering what sets her apart from the male giants—Eliot, Pound, Wallace Stevens—who seem in their life's work to transcend human dimensions; somehow wondering whether the light that philosophy casts made a greater shadow on the wall behind them. I've noticed in my own work, to my horror, writing this trilogy, that suddenly everything was getting much bigger than I thought a life should be. I kept clinging to the idea of Elizabeth with her sanity and levelheadedness and quirkiness of mind.

To a question about modernism:

The modernist work is like one of these plate-glass banks where you can look in and see the vaults, see all of the workings and all the precautions they're taken against being robbed. The only thing you don't see is what happens to the individual safe deposit box. Sometimes I wish we still had those heavy marble facades that kept everything a mystery.

To a question about discipline:

My discipline is that of a terrible untidiness. I never know what piece of paper I've written yesterday's note down on or what little notebook I should be looking into for this or that. Back to workshops—Auden used to say that he didn't believe in them, except that one might learn at an age young enough for it to take how to keep a tidy desk, and from then on everything would follow.

To a question about strategies of allusion:

I think perhaps there's the same amount of embarrassment attached to alluding overtly to other writers as there would be in alluding to your own work. It's a bit snotty to nudge the reader too obviously with reference to Virgil or Eliot. In our day resonance has become, thanks to Freud and Jung, more the property of the unconscious than a conscious manipulation of the body of literature. So that whenever I've alluded to either another part of my own work or to a poem from the past, I've been happiest about it when I realized *after* I'd done my work that the allusion was there. Whether I wanted to bring it to light or not, to make it explicit or not, was entirely up to me. I think of a poem I wrote twenty years ago, a description of a willowware teacup. Luckily I didn't connect my poem, until I had finished it, with a famous poem about a vessel with figures on the outside and images that were both idyllic and violent.

On "The Country of a Thousand Years of Peace"

THE COUNTRY OF A THOUSAND YEARS OF PEACE

> Here they all come to die,
> Fluent therein as in a fourth tongue.
> But for a young man not yet of their race
> It was madness you should lie
>
> Blind in one eye, and fed
> By the blood of a scrubbed face;
> It was madness to look down
> On the toy city where
>
> The glittering neutrality
> Of clock and chocolate and lake and cloud
> Made every morning somewhat
> Less than you could bear;
>
> And makes me cry aloud
> At the old masters of disease

Poet's Choice, ed. Paul Engle and Joseph Langland (New York: Dial, 1962).

Who dangling high above you on a hair
The sword that, never falling, kills

Would coax you still back from that starry land
Under the world, which no one sees
Without a death, its finish and sharp weight
Flashing in his own hand.

In 1950, at the beginning of nearly three years abroad, I went to Lausanne for an hour with my friend the Dutch poet Hans Lodeizen. He had been reading George Sand's autobiography; there was Roussel on the phonograph and a Picasso etching of acrobats on the floor. The June sunset filled up his hospital room. He spoke with carefree relish of the injection they would give him presently. Before I left we agreed to meet in Italy sometime that fall. He had leukemia and died two weeks later, at twenty-six. It was my first deeply felt death. I connected it with the spell of aimless living in Europe to which I was then committed and to which all those picturesque and novel sights corresponded painfully enough. As the inevitable verses took shape, strictness of form seemed at last beside the point; my material nevertheless allowed for a good deal of paring and polishing. Eight years later, a word from Barbara Deming led me to rephrase the last four lines; another, from Benjamin DeMott, to make use of the second person. The poem still surprises me, as much by its clarification of what I was feeling, as by its foreknowledge of where I needed to go next, in my work.

On "Snapshot of Adam"

SNAPSHOT OF ADAM

By flash in sunshine "to reduce contrast"
He grins back from the green deck chair,
Stripped, easy at last, bush tangle rhyming
With beard and windblown hair;
Coke sweating, forearm tanned to oak,
Scar's lightning hid by flat milk-blaze of belly
—But all grown, in the sliding glass
Beyond him, unsubstantial. Here I dwell,

Finger on shutter, amid my clay
Or marble ghosts; treetops in silhouette;
And day, his day, its vivid shining stuff
Negated to matte slate
A riddle's chalked on: Name the threat
Posed never long or nakedly enough.

Imprinted over centuries upon the sestet of a sonnet is a change of mood or direction. The example at hand modulates from solid to flat; Adam to

Epoch, Fall-Winter 1983.

his maker; the opener (if only for a Coke) to the camera's shutter, etc. Rather than plan ahead as the eighth line approaches, I'm apt to recall a moment at the Kabuki in Tokyo decades ago. A long ramp (the *hamamichi* or "flower way") cuts through the public to join the stage at right angles. This transitional point challenges the actor who crosses it. That day we had seen Benten the Thief at work plundering a house from top to bottom. Frightened, furtive, eyes darting, sleeves full of loot, he ran from the scene, set foot upon the ramp, paused, straightened, tidied his clothing, stuck out his chest. An imaginary thoroughfare took shape around utter probity, now striding out of sight to loud cheers.

FOREWORD TO RECITATIVE

There are after all things to be said for prose. I still read it, often with more profit than I do poetry. I go on using it for letters, conversation, the recording of dreams, and so forth. It is not *that* much harder to write than verse, or (as a seventeen-thousand-line poem goes to show) that much less concise. Yet I persist in seeing it as a mildly nightmarish medium, to which *there is no end*: conterminous with one's very life, and only at rare and irregular intervals affording that least pause in flight whereby a given line of poetry creates the desire for another, and renews through all-but-subliminal closure the musical attack. With prose, as I saw it, the aria never came. All was recitative which, however threatened by resolution, continued self-importantly to advance the plot, explaining, describing, discriminating, while at least this listener, in the grip of his untenable prejudice, held out for song, for opera, for *opera*—works no longer made up of set pieces but *durchkomponiert* according to the best post-Wagnerian models. In retrospect, however, it must be granted that certain evenings were much enlivened by those skittish interludes, and I shall be glad to have these of mine assembled, whenever *Una voce poco fa* finds itself with nothing to say, or *Il mio tesoro* falls outside the tenor's range.

Recitative: Prose by James Merrill, ed. J. D. McClatchy (San Francisco: North Point Press, 1986).

FROM *POURQUOI ÉCRIVEZ-VOUS?*

Je dirai avec la plus grande prudence qu'en écrivant, je semble remplir un contrat que j'ai souscrit avec moi-même à l'adolescence: utiliser les formes et les ressources de la poésie afin de faire entrer en jeu la plus grande part possible d'une nature qui, alors comme maintenant, n'avait pas atteint une parfaite conscience de soi. Je croyais aux pouvoirs assainissants et clarifiants de l'Art et, malgré pas maint d'éléments qui semblent prouver le contraire, j'y crois toujours.

[I will say, very cautiously, that, when I write, I feel I am fulfilling a contract I drew up with myself as an adolescent: that I would use the forms and resources of poetry in order to bring into play the greatest possible part of a nature which, then as now, had yet to reach full self-awareness. I believed in the cleansing and clarifying powers of Art and, despite a good many elements that seem to prove otherwise, I still do.]

Pourquoi écrivez-vous?, eds. Jean-François Fogel and Daniel Rondeau (Paris: Libération, 1988).

On Allusion

The lucky eighteenth-century reader—having read literally *tous les livres*—could be trusted to catch every possible allusion. This is no longer the case; some of us substitute wordplay to make our texts resound.

Or else the mere tone of knowing does the trick. Proust is apt to speak of "certain works by Poussin" or "certain minerals whose properties include phosphorescence" when what he means, seeing that he isn't about to name them, is *un*certain works and minerals. It makes him sound more authoritative than precise reference could possibly do.

Some readers (I am among them) are flattered by an author's assumption that they've read the same poems as he, or know by heart the same music. Others complain of elitism. This means we can't expect them to consult a reference book.

The kind of allusion I hope to chance upon lifts the original into a context hitherto unforeseeable. Here is W. H. Auden (in *The Changing Light at Sandover*) on his own death:

MY DEMISE A FORM OF LEAD

POISONING: I WENT OFF TO MY ROOM

TIDDLY THAT NIGHT BUT HAD IN MIND TO SCRIBBLE

University of Toronto Quarterly, Spring 1992.

A NOTE TO C[hester], & AS I'D DONE SINCE CHILDHOOD
SUCKED ON A PENCIL THINKING. NEXT I KNEW,
AN ICY SUN SHONE IN UPON THE DEAD
WEIGHT OF MY FEATHER QUILT   But how does lead
Destroy the soul? DJ: They don't *use* lead—
Graphite in pencils. LET THE FACT REMAIN
(OR FABLE!) THAT I SIPPED IT GRAIN BY GRAIN.
OVER THE YEARS ANYTHING FROM AN X RAY
TO THE COSMIC RAYS WE'RE ALL EXPOSED TO WD
RESIDE UNDISSIPATED IN MY BLOOD
& VITAL ORGANS: I BECAME A WALKING
NONCONDUCTING LEADEN CASKET THESE
PARTICULAR DESTRUCTIVE ENERGIES
HAD FILLED WITH RADIANT WASTE   Dear God . . . & NO
BLOND BLUEEYED LATTERDAY BASSANIO
TO LIFT THE LID. WE MAKE OUR DEATH MY DEARS.

In our Ouija transcripts WHA left it at RADIANT WASTE, in terms made, I thought at first, sufficiently resonant by allusion to "certain" bits of up-to-date science. But of course LEADEN CASKET rang a further bell, and I had no choice but to bring the dear dead poet's trope—of the self imprisoned for lack of a lover's touch—to full ripeness by putting the last lines into his mouth myself.

THE POET'S NOTEBOOK

How did we live in the Golden Age? We kept notebooks, journals, commonplace books full of odds and ends—which of course got mislaid, sometimes lost forever. Not that the computer, when it came along, was infallible; my first, overprogrammed one broke down last year, was pronounced brain-dead, and had to be, as they say, disposed of thoughtfully. Still, some such arrangement beats living, as I would otherwise do, in a welter of places and people, undated drafts, cryptic jottings. Keeping these between covers provides a faint illusion of tidiness, and the thought of so many opposing impulses sleeping peacefully face-to-face when the book is shut, remains oddly satisfying.

Postage / Gestapo
Proust / stupor
Neruda / unread
manatee / emanate
Nashville / ill-shaven

The Poet's Notebook: Excerpts from the Notebooks of Contemporary American Poets, eds. Stephen Kuusisto, Deborah Tall, and David Weiss (New York: W. W. Norton, 1995).

•

After the first few games of Patience, the new deck understood that its life in your hands would be one of dire omens and cheating.

•

Crowded lecture hall, one of his last appearances.

Member of audience: Mr. Cage, do you and Merce Cunningham have a homosexual relationship?

Long pause. JC (amiably): Well . . . I cook and he eats.

•

DJ's aunt in South Dakota, 1930s. One day an itinerant worker knocks— she's alone in the house—to ask if she could give him a meal in return for a half day's work. She agrees, and off he goes to the field. By noon she has laid out a spread of leftovers which they both find wanting. The man nevertheless cleans his plate.

She: I hope that was all right?

He: Yes, Mam. Delicious—what there was of it. (This sounds wrong, so he keeps going.) And there was plenty, such as it was.

•

The various commentators on TV, lest their ratings drop, vie with one another: how best to sensationalize today's disaster? Reported flatly, the disaster is already bad enough. Let's have these media people tested, like athletes, and expelled from the club if the rhetorical steroids in their urine rise above a certain level.

(Cf. photo of Saddam jovial beside grim nine-year-old hostage. Headline: BRITISH BOY SUBJECTED TO REPEATED HAIR TOU-SLINGS.)

•

The bold diction of expiring sense.

•

Rossini's "Musique Anodyne"—multiple settings for solo voices of a single brief text (Metastasio). By turns tragic, romantic, mocking, these little songs suggest how many different tones can channel a given statement. As if what we have to say were negligible compared to the saying of it.

•

(Athens, 1985) Ruth Somebody at dinner: tall, blonde costume-jewelry Dolly Sister type. Sixty, looks forty-five. She waited till her children were grown, then came to Greece. Now ending her second fairly disastrous love affair "with a man who had mistresses all over Europe," and has just one more session—this one in church, not the Greek priest's house—to complete her exorcism. Session One left the priest ill for days, and Ruth's toes scorched by the thwarted, exiting demon. The priest's sofa was scorched, too.

•

Always to have suffered fools gladly.

•

Italian activists insist that the pope refer to his would-be assassin as "a human being." Poor simpletons—as if the human being weren't capable of anything.

•

"His subject is Man, his tragic fate and heroic defiance in the face of extinction"—Bruce Chatwin on Malraux. Why do I so loathe this kind of talk? I heard it first, I think, from Kimon and took it even then with distrust. Meanwhile it emerges ever more vividly that we ourselves have all along been contriving that tragic fate: extinction is nothing if not man-made.

•

As the ship pulls away, a panorama: the slopes of Piraeus mantled in sulphur yellow. It's the miasma everyone deplores in this country without public spirit. But through the smog burn grids of tiny red-gold baguettes—far-off windows catching the sunset at our backs; while high above, pearly in dark-blue evening, a full moon has risen. To be remembered always.

•

What is my type? Crafty italics, tall thinking caps. . . .

•

Dream: I am carrying a half-mile-long cloth "kraken" in triumph through the streets. At every corner, a vendor of "Volcanic Ices." I have won!

•

> *Wings that bore me, bear me hence*
> *Into that timeless zone*
> *The written page, the perfect tense—*
> (on the plane)

•

Dinner with a shrink.

Q. What does dying mean to you?
A. Acceleration of the aging process.

•

Newly discovered poetic fragment by Stesichoros: the "proto-Oedipus." It antedates Sophocles, and by a somewhat cooler telling of the story (Oedipus lives on, blind but fed & cared for, while Jocasta just goes on reigning upstairs) shows the more famous poet as overreliant upon the loud pedal. . . .

•

"Earthenware with lead glaze which has degraded to iridescence during burial." (Label in museum.)

•

The gods of rock and tree, their masses celebrated by Cézanne.

•

Alpine valleys, meadows around Barbizon—genre painters virtually Hindu in their worship of the cow.

•

Bruce M. mishears the topic of an art history lecture at London Univ: Pierrot's Flagellation.

•

> *The hat motheaten, the bathtub of zinc,*
> *The parrot-droppings on a speechless perch*
> *A crumble in green sunlight speck by speck*
> *Wonder naively why Toulouse-Lautrec*
> *Should not have left them rich. So paupers think*
> *Of an old flame's estate left to the church.*

•

After Dartmouth reading & question period, a student (blond, in tank top) comes up: Who *are* you? Are you American? What sort of English are you speaking?

•

X remained vernal throughout his long life—past sixty still enticing, graceful, fragrantly in bud. Old Mrs. Y—older, that is, by only a few years than himself, but whom the generations had bent and gnarled into a leafless trunk—said it was a scandal. (Ending for novella ca. 1900.)

•

Postcard of Pompidou Center—all multicolored pipes and vents. PH: You should hear it when the Hunchback's at the console.

•

> *Watching the fire,*
> *An ironwood log splits into blazing discs*

on its bed of ashes—not discs, letters
They spell DRUMIAEL (a 99th rate devil)
Nearby a little incandescence crab, Kabuki-faced, pulses,
its claws open & shut, diamonded for the dance.
Signals of terrible complexity. Computer chips,
hot barnacles at the Red Sea's bottom—
Saurian roast
   Alligator luau!
     (psychedelic mushroom)

•

Hank: You're treating me like a servant!

Mrs. Porter: You don't know how servants are treated. I'd never ask a servant where he went last night & what he did. That's no business of mine. I *can* ask my lover these questions. My lover may prefer not to answer them, but I'm within my rights—as I am when I draw my own conclusions from his silence.

•

Christmas 1984. Mary Lou [Aswell]'s obituary in the *Times*. No surprise—she'd been dimming rapidly—just pure grief. We were alike in our love of amusement. Like me, she aged without maturing. Or rather, could still, at the end, shed the . . . opacity, and simply sparkle. DMc had written how, bedridden, blind, but receiving the sunset's last communion through a prism on the sill, she threw her arms wide & exulted: "There it is—my *source!*"

(Added later.) Charlotte tells a not dissimilar story of the elderly Frenchman met at Notre Dame during the Fauré Requiem. Years ago, as a boy, he'd sung bits of it to his mother in a car driving south. She loved it so, he promised to sing it to her when she was dying. Fifty years pass. At her deathbed he begins to hum the melody. Slowly, from the old woman, a ravishing smile.

•

SCHUBERT BUTCHERS
WAGNER'S NEW RAGS
(anagrammatic headline in the Entertainment section of *Afterlife*.)

•

Dronning *is the Danish word for Queen.*
A walker near the Palace will have seen
Her driven past, in picture hat and poils,
Making that gesture only known to Royals,
A kind of . . . wave? "Young man,"—her smile is stunning—
"I'm much farther out than you think, and not waving but dronning."

•

. . . but vive la difference! Your kiss-off could be my jacuzzi.

•

The new pack of cards: slick, disco-slithery.

•

Alexandria. An exchange between old friends (ca. 1960).
Germaine: So-and-so called me "Christine" when we met the other day. I was very annoyed.
Christian: I know. Somebody called me "Germain" not long ago & I threw up.

•

Everyone is responsible for his face.
No one wears it undeservedly.
Will there be another war? Look at yourselves,
 Europeans, look at yourselves.
Nothing is peaceful in your faces.
All is struggle, desire, avidity.
Even peace you want violently.
    —Henri Michaux in Asia, 1933

•

Dream: A music festival. I am seated halfway back in a crowded theater. Charlotte & her children are within sight. The lights dim. *The Magic Flute* begins in silence. Curtain rises on a gang of perhaps twenty-five ten-year-old boys racked like pool balls in a close triangle. Now they "break" and deploy rapidly through the audience, spraying at random a luminous paint onto people's faces. I am grateful to receive a cool quick-drying coat of it on mine. We are now the chosen ones—herded onto the stage (I touch Charlotte's bare shoulder and wave farewell) and into a mysterious world. My particular guardian here is a grown-up. It is clear that he and I are of different natures (different species?), yet a deep sympathy grows between us. Now we are crossing a long low wooden bridge. He falls into the shallow water & is instantly helpless, passively drowning. Since no one else will, I jump in after him & try to save him. He goes by limp in the jaws of a great fish. I manage to put a line into his hand, which hauls him back into the world. Now it is my turn to be lost underwater. A prismatic igloo of flesh-colored sand encloses me. I try to escape but every door is just one more reflection. House of mirrors. I hear my friend calling, feel him trying to reach me. I'm not afraid. I know he will.

(1974)

•

Awesome—Two Thumbs Up! (up what?)—wannabes—
Pustules of idiom we itch to squeeze.
What can the Muse do for the common weal?
Make an appointment for a facial peel.

•

(Istanbul) Evening after evening where we drink our wine we've noticed a . . . drunk? a lunatic? A rotund, scowling, twitching little person in his thirties—like the boy one teases at school, but tougher. Cigarette in his mouth, mirthless parodies of another customer's dance. Tonight, before our eyes, the riddle is solved. He approaches a table near ours, one of whose drinkers (tall, lean, sexy) presently stands, moves his chair across the way & sits down in it. Out come towel, soap, lather, a razor—our little madman is a barber! In between sweeps of the blade both he and his client light cigarettes, take swallows of raki, rise to do a few dance steps together. The razor harmlessly glittering in the dusk.

On *Scripts for the Pageant*: The First Five Lessons

Anyone who chooses may make his own Ouija board. Draw on a large smooth surface an arc of capital letters A to Z; below these, the ten Arabic numerals; above, in either corner, the words YES and NO. The half moon between alphabet and numbers can be filled to order. We made do for years with a lonely ampersand before adding our basic punctuation marks. The two mediums sit so that each may comfortably keep a hand on the pointer. The one whose left hand is thus engaged may with his right transcribe the messages. Our pointer was from the start an overturned teacup which glided about "like a thing possessed," indicating with its handle the desired symbol.

From all this has come a poem in three books. The first—"The Book of Ephraim" in *Divine Comedies* (1976)—was arranged in twenty-six sections, each beginning with a successive letter of the alphabet. Its sequel—*Mirabell: Books of Number* (1978)—contains ten sections from 0 to 9, with ten subsections apiece. There remained YES and NO, and the ampersand, round which to organize a concluding volume.

The easy manners and doctrines of Ephraim's kindergarten grow decidedly more stringent in *Mirabell*. Our familiar spirit is no longer a human shade but one of a host who describe themselves now as fallen

The Kenyon Review, Summer 1979.

angels, now as volatile subatomic particles; the scale accordingly wobbles throughout, from vast to microscopic. They have numbers for names, they are in aspect—to those who "see" them—huge red-hot bats. Our particular favorite, however, is soon transformed into a peacock and named by us Mirabell. His main fields are History and Science, often much mythologized. Thus we are told of an Arcadian Atlantis whose immortal denizens resembled centaurs and themselves created the bat-angels to serve them. It didn't work. Two rival worlds—one electrically, one atomically powered—ended in mutual destruction. It would be for Man to reconcile those opposites. We learn of one attempt that misfired when Akhnaton used solar power to explode a pyramid of quartz.

Now Akhnaton is one of the Five—five human souls (not unlike the thirty-six "Just Men" of the Jews) who in this or that incarnation, famously or humbly, do God's work here below. It's a glittering roster: Plato, Galileo, Blake, Einstein, and so forth. They are the masterpieces of what Mirabell calls the Research Lab. From this mysterious, insulated hell at the heart of heaven—or, if the reader prefers, from this tiny chemical workshop deep in each red corpuscle—innumerable and complex operations control the seemingly random ("THERE IS NO ACCIDENT") events relating to some two million "Lab souls" on earth today. The Lab does not shrink from a certain amount of nongenetic meddling, or its legions from a high tone audible even at Los Alamos or MIT. What, Mirabell shrugs, can one expect of those human billions that remain? They must be left to Nature and her slow recyclings.

Finally, Mirabell and his kind are Mercury; and the mirror a doorway at once to Death, as in Cocteau, and to the Imagination, as in Lewis Carroll. Their visits prepare us for a seminar with the angels—whose twenty-five lessons are in fact the marrow of this third volume. As prelude, we have already met Michael and his brothers, one by one.

Auden and Maria continue invaluable, not least for their renderings of "effects" invisible to both Hand and Scribe. Maria's death of cancer, and the damage done to her soul by radiation therapy, has been explained in *Mirabell*. Throughout, God is Biology, "V WORK" is shorthand for "WORK GUIDED BY HIGHER COLLABORATION." What follows may or may not be taken as an instance of that.

On "The Ballroom at Sandover"

You will be hearing today the last hundred or so lines of a very long poem about the Other World. "The Book of Ephraim" began it, years ago: "Admittedly I err by undertaking / This in its present form." In fact I had no idea *then* what the completed form would be, or how many powers (dear friends, elemental angels, Nature herself—the queen of heaven) would visit the Ouija board where David Jackson and I sat taking it all down, learning, among ten thousand other things, that so-called V works, such as a ghostwritten poem or a chemical structure revealed in a dream, are more common than one might think. *The Waste Land,* for instance, was largely the work of Rimbaud.

So. The poem is done. After the third book comes a short epilogue at whose close a reading aloud of the entire work has been arranged. This will ostensibly take place at the table in our entrance hall in Athens, but no less in the grandly restored ballroom at Sandover, the estate where much of the imagined action goes on. Twenty-six chairs are set up for the likes of Jane Austen, Marius Bewley, Congreve, Dante, Maya Deren—almost an alphabet of august influences and dear ones no longer in the world but vital to the work. Nature has appointed our old friend Ephraim master of ceremonies, and asked him to "SAVE ME A PLACE TO ONE SIDE WHERE MY

Harvard Magazine, September-October 1980.

MEEK / ATTENTION CANNOT FLUSTER THESE OUR BETTERS / (IF ONLY IN THE MINIREALM OF LETTERS)." She has also asked Alice Toklas to handle the refreshments.

At the last moment, an empty chair is filled by the all-too-timely death in Rome of Mimí Vassilikos. Her husband, Vassílis, has buried her there, in her favorite white dress, and told us to expect him sooner or later in Athens.

Foreword
to *A Reader's Guide*
to *James Merrill's*
The Changing Light at
Sandover

It's an old, ongoing story. From prehistory to fairy tales to Henry James's late revery of "The Great Good Place," we read about a hero or heroine faced by an insuperable task—which, however, through some half-magical, wholly unforeseen agency, is accomplished, as it were, overnight. The subtlest of these tasks is perhaps the one in Apuleius, set for Psyche by the jealous Goddess of Love. The poor child is presented with a great heap of different grains and told to sort them according to kind—far more than her clumsy fingers can think of doing. But her friends the Ants unerringly finish the chore by sunrise. While Robert Polito is a poet, not a social insect, and has been at it not for hours but for years, something at once minute and visionary about his labor evokes the industry and organizational skills of Psyche's helpers. To be so thorough, so tidy, and yet so in touch with the underlying sense! I think of the ant colony brought, in a time innocent of ecology, from the Amazon to a trendy New York museum. The habitat appeared intact, yet within weeks every last ant had perished. Had they responded to bad vibes from the

Robert Polito, *A Reader's Guide to James Merrill's* The Changing Light at Sandover (Ann Arbor: University of Michigan Press, 1994).

subway? Were their pulses no longer those of earth's heart? Happily, no such doom awaits this volume. Formic, informative, positively formidable, it will spare the *Sandover* buff hours of rummaging for mislaid "gems," giving him instead leisure for charmed attention to the patterns they form in Mr. Polito's kaleidoscope.

INTERVIEWS

AN INTERVIEW
WITH DONALD SHEEHAN

Q: I'd like to start by asking you about your poetry course at the University of Wisconsin this semester. What did you teach in it?

JM: It was described as a poetry workshop, though there was little actual writing done. The eight weeks were mostly spent reading things I liked, then toward the end we took up some student work. We spent half of the time at least on Elizabeth Bishop's last book, *Questions of Travel*. And then we read some of Berryman's *Dream Songs* and some Lowell, and we had a glorious day on *The Rubáiyát*.

Q: What do you think *The Rubáiyát* offers in teaching?

JM: An anonymous poem, really, where the language, the content, is drawn from a whole universe much older, say, than Greek mythology, a kind of Old Testament, as old as language itself. The wine, the bread, the wilderness, the rose—all that of course translates beautifully into just what a Victorian audience wanted to hear: those Christian words, I mean. The vocabulary of the poem works both ways, for piety and paganism alike, which perhaps explains why Fitzgerald's translation sank so quickly into everybody's consciousness. People know lines from it who have never heard of Fitzgerald or Omar—or of poetry, for that matter.

Q: This seems to be something of a comment about the so-called confessional poetry of late. Do you have any feelings about it?

Contemporary Literature, Winter 1968.

JM: It seems to me that confessional poetry, to all but the very naive reader or writer, is a literary convention like any other, the problem being to make it *sound* as if it were true. One can, of course, tell the truth, but I shouldn't think that would be necessary to give the illusion of a True Confession.

Q: So the division between confessional and objective poetry is, you would say, artificial in the sense that both modes are conventions.

JM: Precisely. Now and then it's been *true* what I wrote. Often, though, it's been quite made up or taken from somebody else's life and put in as if it were mine.

Q: Critics today are asserting that in poetry the period of experimentation is over and a period of consolidation has set in, the Second World War being the Great Divide. Does this have any meaning to you? Is this true?

JM: I've always been suspicious of the word "experimentation." It partakes too much of staircase wit. People who talk about experimentation sound as if they thought poets set out deliberately to experiment, when in fact they haven't: they've simply recognized afterward the newness of what they've done. William Carlos Williams talks about breaking the back of the pentameter as if this had been the first step in a program. It's something I should think he'd have been more likely to recognize well after doing it—if he ever did do it. The pentameter has been a good friend to me; you'd think I'd have noticed a little thing like a broken back. As for consolidation, I'm not so sure. Anybody starting to write today has at least ten kinds of poems, each different from the other, on which to pattern his own.

Q: What kinds would you say?

JM: There would be the confessional, if you will; or the personal nature lyric along the lines of Roethke; or the Chinese-sage manner, full of insects and ponies and small boats and liquor and place-names; or the kind of stammered-out neo-epigram of people like Creeley—to name only a few. And there are all sorts of schemes on the page to reproduce—the broken line, Williams's downward staircase, three paces to a step; the tight stanza; the heavy garlands of Perse; the "expressionist" calligrams of Pound or Olson. . . .

Q: Perhaps this is a false abstraction to keep pursuing, but the sort of poetry that, say, Eliot and Pound wrote, doesn't seem to be getting written today. At the same time, though, I can't imagine, without some of Pound at least, any poets writing as they do today. Do you think there exists an "influence" (if I can use that tricky word) of Eliot and Pound on poets today?

JM: Yes, if only as something to react against. Eliot and Pound, though, seem to be so terribly different in the long run. With Pound, in the *Cantos* at least, we find precious little unity except the contents of a single, very brilliant, and erratic mind. Whereas Eliot gives what may be only an illusion—I haven't read him for twenty years—of being infinitely in control of his material: so much so, that you have the sense of the whole civilization under glass. As, indeed, Eliot's poems are under glass for me. The temptation to reread them, though it's growing, is still fairly slight.

Q: How about Wallace Stevens?

JM: Stevens seems much more of a poet, that is to say, a nonhistorian. There's a nice distinction in a poem of A. D. Hope's, where he says that he wanted to be a poet, the "eater of time," rather than that "anus of mind, the historian." I'm an enemy of history, by the way—absurd thing to say, I'll be condemned to repeat it if I'm not careful. Repeat history, that is. Well, my position's open to analysis; I even have a poem about Father Time. However. Back to Stevens, I think he continues to persuade us of having had a private life, despite—or thanks to—all the bizarreness of his vocabulary and idiom.

Q: I here think of the term used constantly, "voice." As a critical term, do you think it has meaning?

JM: I think it does. "Voice" is the democratic word for "tone." "Tone" always sounds snobbish, but without a sense of it how one flounders!

Q: Is voice a function of metrics, would you say?

JM: I notice voice a good deal more in metrical poetry. The line lends itself to shifts of emphasis. If Frost had written free verse, I don't think we'd have heard as much of the voice in it.

Q: I'd like to ask you about your own development. I notice in your four published volumes that you seem to have gone from a rather strict, symmetrical poem to a much looser, freer poem. Do you agree with this, and if you do, I wonder what led you in this direction?

JM: I always relapse into the strict poem. I'd like to think I would continue to write a strict poem when I felt like it. But what you say is true. I remember—this might modify what I said about experimentation—I remember, after *First Poems* was published, having in mind the kind of poem I wanted to write. I could picture it to myself only by seeing an unbroken page of blank verse, the density of the print trailing down the page; and long before any of these poems began to turn up in the little *Short Stories*, there was this picture I had of a certain look to the poem. And with these poems came various new conversational elements—the first earmark, perhaps, of blank verse.

Q: This is related, I think, to another point. You're probably one of the few poets who has written completely successful novels, ones that can't be termed "poetic" in the usual sense of that word. What about the prose element in poetry, in your verse particularly?

JM: I've enjoyed reading novels more often—or more profoundly— than I've enjoyed reading poems. There seems to be no poet except perhaps Dante whose work has the extraordinary richness of Tolstoy or Proust; and there are very few poets whose work gives as much fun as James. Oh, there's always a give-and-take. For instance, though a lot of the sound of James is prose, can't one tell that he'd read Browning? You hear a voice talking in prose, often a very delightful voice which can say all kinds of odd things. For me, to get something of that into poetry was a pleasure and even perhaps an object.

Q: That would seem to contradict what some reviewers have said about your poems, that they have become more personal, perhaps even autobiographical. If the point is, as you were saying, to get a voice in poetry, what would you say to the critics and reviewers who claim this voice to be autobiographical?

JM: To *sound* personal is the point—which is something I don't believe, by the way, that Pound and Eliot do very often; rather, they have impersonal, oracular voices. But so does an Elizabethan lyric sound impersonal. I'm not making judgments.

Q: What about Auden's remark that if the poet raises his voice, he becomes phony or dishonest. Is that what you're saying?

JM: If it's raised in all earnestness, dishonesty usually follows.

Q: You know many European languages and speak a number of them, including modern Greek. Are you drawn to any of the modern foreign literatures? If so, which ones do you like especially?

JM: I began caring more about French poetry than I did about English, no doubt because there was no question of completely understanding it.

But, again, my feeling for it ends with Apollinaire and Valéry. I find very few living French poets intelligible—my French has withered on the vine.

Q: I noticed you recently translated Eugenio Montale.

JM: My Italian is even worse than my French, but I liked his poems very much and felt close to the feeling behind them.

Q: What is the feeling behind Montale's poems that struck you especially?

JM: The emotional refinement, gloomy and strongly curbed. It's surprisingly permeable by quite ordinary objects—ladles, hens, pianos, half-read letters. To me he's *the* twentieth-century nature poet. Any word can lead you from the kitchen garden into really inhuman depths—if there are any of those left nowadays. The two natures were always one, but it takes an extraordinary poet to make us feel that, feel it in our spines.

Q: You mentioned Elizabeth Bishop before. A number of other poets today have singled her out. Would you say, in terms of form, that she has provided valuable examples for poets, especially in your own poetry?

JM: The unpretentiousness of her form is very appealing. But I don't know if it's simply a matter of form. Rather, I like the way her whole oeuvre is on the scale of a human life; there is no oracular amplification, she doesn't go about on stilts to make her vision wider. She doesn't need that. She's wise and humane enough as it is. And this is rather what I feel about Stevens. For all the philosophy that intrudes in and between the lines, Stevens's poetry is a body of work that is man-sized. Whereas I wouldn't say that of Pound; he tries, I think, to write like a god. Stevens and Miss Bishop merely write like angels.

Q: Do you think it might have something to do with wit and humor? Reviewers have used the term "witty" to describe your poetry; and Stevens's is surely filled with various sorts of jokes. Reed Whittemore once claimed that, in recent poetry, there was an unbridgeable split between light and serious verse. Do you agree?

JM: Hardly unbridgeable. Aren't we used by now to the light poem that has dark touches and the serious poem shot through with lighter ones? The Canadian George Johnston comes to mind as an example of the first. His material is all quite shallow and amusing indeed, but leaves a sense of something unspoken, something positively sinister. . . .

Q: Can the joke control that sort of oracular voice of Eliot and Pound, tone it down, make it more human?

JM: That is my fond illusion.

Q: Whittemore was referring in part, I think, to the *New Yorker* sort of exclusively light verse as created by Ogden Nash. John Updike's poems come to mind.

JM: Updike's are light indeed. Ogden Nash may be taken more seriously by another generation. The prosody—if you can call it that—is really such a delight. To me, it's a very American form—that interminable line with the funny rhyme.

Q: In two recent poems of yours, "The Thousand and Second Night" and "From the Cupola," you've written what's called a long poem. Do you feel any distinctions between the long and short poem in terms of style, structure, and form?

JM: The length of those poems is partly accidental. I never dreamed, when "The Thousand and Second Night" began to take shape, that it would be as long as it is. I couldn't foresee the structure of the poem. I was working on what seemed rather unrelated poems, then suddenly an afternoon of patchwork saw them all stitched together. What emerged as the final section had been written quite early in the process.

Q: This account almost seems to have a musical metaphor under it. Would you say there's any relation between music and your poetry?

JM: There's to me a tremendous relation. Certainly I cared about music long before I cared about literature. When I was eleven years old, I began being taken to the opera in New York; and the sense of a feeling that could be expressed without any particular attention to words must have excited me very much. I daren't go into the effect Mrs. Wix would have pounced upon, of the opera on my moral sense. All those passions—illnesses, ecstasies, deceptions—induced for the pure sake of having something to sing beautifully about. Whenever I reach an impasse, working on a poem, I try to imagine an analogy with musical form; it usually helps. For instance, in "The Thousand and Second Night" the last thing I had to write was the passage at the end of section three beginning "Love. Warmth." I had no idea how to write it; I thought I would do it in free verse and made all kinds of beginnings, before the six-line stanza finally evolved. But the moment for which I'm most grateful is in the third of those five stanzas, when it came to me to make the meter trochaic rather than iambic—a stroke I associated quite arbitrarily with that moment at the end of the rondo of the "Waldstein" Sonata, where the tempo is suddenly doubled or halved (I'm not sure which), and it goes twice as fast. "An Urban Convalescence" is in the form of an introduction and allegro. In between comes a trill (on the word "cold"), an organ point (following "self-knowledge"), then the rhymes, the quatrains begin, in 4/4 time, as it were. Need I say how subjective this all is?

Q: I'm reminded of a brief essay of Valéry's, "On Speaking Verse," in which he instructs the actor to approach the line from the state of music, understanding musical form first, then letting the words and the meaning come through. Does music take us back again to voice?

JM: It does, if we're poets. The next step, for me, was listening to French art songs: especially Maggie Teyte's records of Debussy, Fauré, and Duparc, where, once more, though most of the words were intelligible, they made no great demands on the intelligence. It was only the extreme beauty of the musical line that was spellbinding. At first I hadn't known any German songs, but when I began to hear Schubert and Schumann, the text would often as not have some independent merit. Unlike Albert Samain and Leconte de Lisle, Heine was intense and psychological. By then, a way of uttering a line to have it make real sense, real human sense, had come into my musical education.

These were all things I could have learned from my teachers. I remember a course at Amherst that Reuben Brower gave. I now see it was chiefly a course in tone, in putting meaning and the sound of meaning back into words. He made very clear connections, so that by the time we read some Frost poems, we could see certain relationships to E. M. Forster and Jane Austen, whom we'd read earlier.

Q: If, as you say, rhythm often has its own sense and meaning and energy, could it sometimes so shape the line or stanza (or even whole poem) that it dictates what words will work? Has this ever been your experience?

JM: Oh, absolutely. Words just aren't that meaningful in themselves. *De la musique avant toute chose.* The best writers can usually be recognized by their rhythms. An act of Chekhov has a movement unlike anything in the world.

Q: I think here of Frost's idea of "sentence sounds." Is this more or less relevant to what you're saying?

JM: I think so. The point about music and song is that theirs is the sound of sheer feeling—as opposed to that of sense, of verbal sense. To combine the two is always worth dreaming about.

Q: I'd like to ask you about "From the Cupola." The poem uses Greek myth, but (perhaps to distinguish it from an Eliot poem) one couldn't say it was at all "propped up" by the Eros-Psyche story. What shifts and transformations were involved in making the myth relevant to the poem?

JM: Again, this is all afterthought. In the poem there are, let's see, three stories going. There's the story of Eros and Psyche, which is, if not known, at least knowable to any reader. Then there is the contemporary situation of a New England village Psyche and her two nasty sisters and of somebody writing love letters to her. And finally there is what I begin by describing as an unknowable situation, something I'm going to keep quiet about. But in a way, the New England village situation is transparent enough to let us see the story of Eros and Psyche on one side of the glass and, perhaps, to guess at, to triangulate the third story, the untold one.

Q: Then it's the contemporary situation that unified the mythic and the unknowable situations?

JM: If anything does. I suppose the two twentieth-century writers who have used myth most brilliantly are Joyce and Cocteau. Joyce teaches us to immerse the mythical elements in a well-known setting; Cocteau teaches us to immerse them in a contemporary spoken idiom. Although I can't pretend I planned on doing this, what pleases me in the poem are precisely those two effects: a great deal of setting and a great deal of contemporary idiom.

Q: *The (Diblos) Notebook* also uses myth. Is the same thing involved?

JM: Not really, because there's no myth underneath; that is, there's no structural use of myth in *The (Diblos) Notebook*. Rather, it is used as ornament; the central character's attitude toward myth is the issue, not myth itself.

Q: Does this apply to "From the Cupola"? The poem is perhaps the most difficult of yours to understand in that its experience (which may well be the speaker's attitude toward it) seems to be so elusive.

JM: It is elusive. As I said, the poem begins with the statement that it's not going to be a confessional poem. To be honest, I don't understand the poem very well myself—at least not the first third. I've been helped, though, by the times I've read it aloud. I trust the way it *sounds* at any rate; though I find that I have to read sections of it very rapidly indeed, like that long speech of Alice's: there's next to no meaning in the speech, except for a few nuggets for a clever reader to unearth. She does ramble and that may be part of her terror. In this sense, her speech is a device out of theater: a ranting scene that goes on for its own sake, in which every word doesn't count.

Q: I seem to hear vague echoes somewhere of Plato: the poet composing without understanding his poem, in a kind of inspired frenzy.

JM: In a way, yes. I'm not sure about frenzy, though: "From the Cupola" was not composed in a frenzy. Yet certainly there wouldn't be as much pleasure in writing poems if one understood exactly what one had in one's heart and head. The process of writing discovers this—if we're lucky.

Q: Would you say that "From the Cupola" represents anything new in your career? Is a new idea involved in this poem, a new technique?

JM: The newness would have to do with the narrative elements, I suspect. Without these to carry it forward, "From the Cupola" mightn't seem drastically different from those two sets of "variations" in *First Poems*.

Q: The speakers in a number of your recent poems seem to be concerned with the difficulties or joys of being a poet. Is this a new subject for you?

JM: It's one I've tried to resist. In principle, I'm quite against the persona of the poem talking about the splendors and miseries of writing; it seems to me far too many poets today make the act of writing one of their primary subjects. Obviously I'm following the crowd myself, but I've hoped as much as possible to sugar the pill by being a bit rueful and amusing about having to do so.

Q: The fourth section of "The Thousand and Second Night"—the academic parody—is surely quite amusing about it.

JM: A friend of mine urged me to take that section out, saying it was hard enough to create an illusion, and that to shatter one would be disastrously perverse. I left it in, though, because, well, I wanted something to delay the final section. Also, the parody of the classroom was a structural equivalent, it occurred to me later, of the use of quotation, interspersed throughout the poem—the little snippets from Eliot, Yeats, Hofmannsthal, and so forth. It did in terms of structure what those did ornamentally. Once I thought of that, I had a sounder reason to leave it in.

Q: You've used the words "ornament" and "decoration" a number of times. Would they possibly relate to what a number of readers have felt in your work: that the novels, plays, and poems project in toto a particular sort of social milieu? I'd define the term along the lines, say, of taste, intelligence, and manners rather than class or family. Am I right in saying that there is a more or less unified social world in your work?

JM: We all have our limits. I draw the line at politics or hippies. I'd rather present the world through, say, a character's intelligence or lack of it than through any sort of sociological prism. It's perhaps why I side with Stevens over Eliot. I don't care much about generalizing; it's unavoidable, to begin with. The point about manners is that—as we all know, whether we're writers or not—they keep the ball rolling. One could paraphrase Marianne Moore: using them with a perfect contempt for them, one discovers in them after all a place for the genuine. In writing a novel or poem of manners you provide a framework all the nicer for being more fallible, more hospitable to irony, self-expression, self-contradiction, than many a philosophical or sociological system. Manners for me are the touch of nature, an artifice in the very bloodstream. Someone who does not take them seriously is making a serious mistake. They are as vital as all appearances, and if they deceive us they do so by mutual consent. It's hard to imagine a work of literature that doesn't depend on manners, at least negatively. One of the points of a poem like Ginsberg's "Howl" is that it uses an impatience with manners very brilliantly; but if there had been no touchstone to strike that flint upon, where would Ginsberg be?

And manners—whether good or bad—are entirely allied with tone or voice in poetry. If the manners are inferior, the poem will seem unreal or allegorical as in some of Stephen Crane's little poems. Take the one in which the man is eating his heart and the stranger comes up and asks if it's good. Those are bad manners for a stranger. Consequently the poem ends shortly after it begins because they have nothing more to say to each other. On the other hand, a poem like George Herbert's "Love" goes on for three stanzas; in a situation fully as "unreal" as Crane's, two characters are being ravishingly polite to one another. Manners aren't merely descriptions of social behavior. The real triumph of manners in Proust is the extreme courtesy toward the reader, the voice explaining at once formally and intimately. Though it can be heard, of course, as megalomania, there is something wonderful in the reasonableness, the long-windedness of that voice, in its desire to be understood, in its treatment of *every* phenomenon (whether the way someone pronounces a word, or the article of clothing worn, or the color of a flower) as having ultimate importance. Proust says to us in effect, "I will not patronize you by treating these delicate matters with less than total, patient, sparkling seriousness."

Q: Reviewers have sometimes used the word "elegant" to describe your poetry. How would you react to this term?

JM: With a shrug.

Q: I'd like to ask you about *The Seraglio*. I'm tempted at times to read Francis Tanning as something of a paradigm. That is, I see a young man who struggles to see the world singly, but somehow seems doomed to see it doubly; mirror and dreams figure prominently. Is this young man a sort of ur-character? And are his struggles some sort of ur-plot in your work?

JM: He seems to me, with a few superficial differences, the kind of young man one finds in nearly any first novel. As far as an ur-character goes: well, four or five years after I'd written the novel, I came upon some books from my childhood. I reread one of them, having no particular memory of ever reading it before, yet I must have, since I found—to my horror and amusement—that, by and large, its plot was that of *The Seraglio*. Both novels involved the effort to reintroduce an exiled mother into an atmosphere of ease and comfort; both scenes were dominated by an irascible grandfather figure. Of course, the children's book was *Little Lord Fauntleroy*.

Q: Again, one hesitates to use the word influence. To return to *The (Diblos) Notebook,* the novel has raised what is perhaps a side issue: how it actually was composed. Did it really grow out of a notebook?

JM: Yes. I had the story in mind several years before I found myself writing the book. During that time I had no idea how to write it, although I made a few conventional beginnings. Then, one summer, when I'd been traveling in Greece, unable to do any real work, I kept a journal. But whenever I tried to inject any of those impressions into my conventional narrative, they went dead on me. The notebook itself, though, still seemed comparatively full of life. It took a while to realize that this was a possible technique, and use it. It's a technique I might have discovered much earlier from, say, that edition of Keats's letters where the deletions are legible; and, of course, from letters one receives oneself: the eye instantly flies to the crossed-out word. It seems to promise so much more than the words left exposed.

Q: You've written for the theater as well, one of your plays—*The Immortal Husband*—receiving highest critical praise. Have you an opinion on the "verse drama" so many modern poets have attempted—Eliot, Yeats, Pound, even Wallace Stevens, as well as Ted Hughes and Robert Lowell more recently? What aesthetic problems does a poet face in writing plays?

JM: I loved the first act of *The Cocktail Party*—that unmistakable sound of Eliot, his line, hired out in the service of small talk. You couldn't imagine a suaver bartender. The poet writing plays faces the same problem that the playwright does. Borges has a piece on Aeschylus as the man who introduced a second actor onto the stage, thus allowing for an infinite dialogue. The problem from then on has been to decide on the dimensions of that dialogue for one's particular purpose. We spoke of structural rhythm a while back. One responds to that in plays more immediately than in poems. It's virtually one's entire first impression of any play by Beckett.

Q: Have you found any older—that is, pre-twentieth-century—poetry relevant to your work?

JM: Actually, I'd read little twentieth-century poetry until I'd been writing for several years. My first efforts, sonnets of course, were written at fourteen when I knew only bits and pieces of Shakespeare, Mrs. Browning, some Pre-Raphaelite verse. My first twentieth-century passion, two years later, was Elinor Wylie. I was a retarded child. No reflection on her—I still think she's marvelous, far and away the most magical rhyming we've ever had. There's a glaze of perfection to contend with, but I ate it up; it never put me off—not at least until I went on to Yeats. Older poets, though. Pope, Keats, "Lycidas." I was out of college by the time I read Herbert. Much later, though I'd never looked at more than a page of *Don Juan* and knew about Byron only through Auden's "Letter" to him, I *knew* that he had been an influence on "The Thousand and Second Night." When I checked, I found very much the tone I'd been trying for: that air of irrelevance, of running on at the risk of never becoming terribly significant. I see no point, often, in the kind of poem that makes every single touch, every syllable, count. It can be a joy to write, but not always to read. You can't forgo the whole level of entertainment in art. Think of Stevens's phrase: "The essential gaudiness of poetry." The inessential suddenly felt as essence.

Q: This attitude is directly counter, isn't it, to the one underlying so much earlier-twentieth-century poetry: the desire for concentration and concision in poems.

JM: Yes, it may well involve a fatigue with all that. How can you appreciate the delights of concision unless you abuse them?

Q: One of the perennial questions asked any artist is whether he has any particular method of composition. Would you care to reply?

JM: Usually I begin a poem with an image or phrase; if you follow trustfully, it's surprising how far an image can lead. Once in a great while I've seen the shape of the whole poem (never a very long one, though) and tried simply to follow the stages of plot, or argument. The danger in this method is that one knows so well where the poem is going that one hasn't much impetus to write it. In either case, even before the poem is fully drafted, my endless revisions begin—the one dependable pleasure in the whole process. Some poets actually say they don't revise, don't believe in revising. They say their originality suffers. I don't see that at all. The words that come first are anybody's, a froth of phrases, like the first words from a medium's mouth. You have to make them your own. Even if the impersonal is what you're after, you first have to make them your own, and only then begin to efface yourself.

Q: Novelists sometimes speak of characters "taking over" and the work "writing itself." Has this been your experience, either as a novelist or a poet?

JM: As a novelist, no, I'm not good enough. That kind of submission must be one of the darkest secrets of technique. With poems I don't know who or what takes over, unless it's I who do, and that's not what you mean. Sooner or later one touches upon matters that are all the realer for not being easily talked about.

An Interview
with Ashley Brown

Q: I'd like to ask you about your literary education. Did your family and teachers encourage you to write, or did you take it up on the sly?

JM: My family weren't exactly averse to it, but I suspect if they had encouraged me more than they did, I would have stopped then and there. When I went away to school in Lawrenceville, I wrote my poems out of envy of my friend Freddy Buechner, who was already writing lovely poems. This soon became a habit, and before long I worked up to a poem a day. My very first efforts were sonnets, which I wrote as much with French models as with English—the melodic, empty-headed fin de siècle sort of thing.

Q: How was Amherst as a training ground? Richard Wilbur and two or three other literary students were there in your time, weren't they?

JM: Wilbur had already graduated when I entered. I started in the summer of 1943, when there were only ninety students. You remember how the colleges were during the war. Kimon Friar was teaching languages at that time—he was not on the regular faculty—and he encouraged the campus poets. Nobody on the faculty was particularly helpful. George Whicher was always pleased to see a poem. There were classes in writing, but the best training one got was in reading, and this was important to me. Nobody ever taught the works of a living poet—except Frost, of course. Reuben Brower once mentioned the name of Marianne Moore.

Shenandoah, Summer 1968.

Q: Things have certainly changed, haven't they? Nowadays many students seem to read nothing but the moderns. Even Frost seems like a nineteenth-century poet to a lot of them. Was he teaching there when you were a student?

JM: He was always in and out, but I never saw much of him. I met him through G. R. Elliott. I was a student in Elliott's Spenser class, and he once had me to tea to meet Frost. Frost always liked students—not faculty. He usually had fifteen students at his feet every evening. It was rather sad, in a way, for both sides, because he eventually would have to begin repeating himself, and the students weren't as interchangeable as he may have thought.

Q: You've actually taught writing courses yourself two or three times, haven't you?

JM: Only once in a great while. I spent a year at Amherst, and there was a year at Bard, which was interesting, and recently I had a short period at Madison—the University of Wisconsin.

Q: Do you have any opinions on this general subject of young poets in the universities? A lot of people, including some of their teachers, think they ought to get out in the world more and cut loose from fellowships and graduate schools and even writing courses.

JM: One of the best poets at Madison actually did that. I felt sorry for a lot of those students. The more advanced ones were graduate students, and they were too busy keeping up with their teaching to do much writing. They are under terrible pressures to get degrees.

Q: Do you think the universities foster an excessively cautious sort of poetry?

JM: That hasn't been my impression. But I guess I'm an archconservative. More arch than conservative, I'm sometimes made to feel. At any rate, I've come to the conclusion that most people aren't helped by writing courses.

Q: By the time you started publishing, back in the 1940s, some young poets were almost painfully aware of the achievement of their predecessors—Eliot and Stevens and Auden and the rest—two generations of modernists. Did you feel their presence was something to resist?

JM: No, I don't think I ever felt that. They seemed very much their own men. They represented the immediate past. I felt no sense of competition, if you could call it that. If I had any sense of competition, it was with people at most five years older than I was. My reaction to Stevens, for instance, was merely that it was wonderful to mention strange colors along with big abstract words. I was, to begin with, more influenced by Elinor Wylie, whom I worshipped when I was fifteen or sixteen.

Q: Stevens and Auden had a large influence twenty years ago, didn't they? I guess I'm right in saying that you were touched by both of them. I was recently rereading your "Medusa," which is a wonderfully supple poem and fairly characteristic of your work then. It has something of Stevens's rhetorical splendor, but toned down a little, as it were, by Auden's understatement.

JM: I certainly liked them both and still do! The first Stevens I read was "Notes toward a Supreme Fiction." I teethed on that. I read Auden by stages. I remember reading *The Sea and the Mirror* when I was in the army (just the place for that) and being dazzled by the range of forms, which meant most to me at that time. Certainly I was inspired to try some of these things myself. *The Age of Anxiety* was so murky by contrast.

To come back to "Medusa": I read it over not long ago, I can't think why. It's a poem without content, really. I read so easily in those days. The stanza is one of Elinor Wylie's. But you are right in mentioning Stevens. You remember the passage about the stone mask in the "Notes." I must have had that in mind, the image, I mean, as distinct from Stevens's glorious sound effects. I thought of poems as visual artifacts back then.

Q: Elizabeth Bishop doesn't much care for reading poetry aloud. Do you?

JM: She doesn't need to! In the old days it never occurred to me to read aloud—the vogue for public recitation started later. I didn't even read aloud to myself. What was I thinking of? If you value tone, how else can you get the effects of irony and understatement? Still, I always felt I was turning out a poem for the eye rather than the ear.

Q: Did you ever hear Stevens read? On the recording it's not quite satisfactory.

JM: In Florida once he visited Marjorie Kinnan Rawlings, who was a friend of my mother. He started reading at someone's request, but it was unendurable, and after twenty minutes Marjorie Rawlings snatched the book from his hand. She was going to show him how! No, I never heard him read.

Q: You really were formal in those early days, weren't you? In *First Poems* you managed terza rima, triplets, and some rather intricate stanzas (for example in "The Peacock"). I suppose much of the pleasure of writing came by way of the forms themselves.

JM: Yes, I liked that "Peacock" stanza—I used it four times. I'm no less formal now, but I no longer dote on elaborate stanzas.

Q: Did you find yourself much involved in your early poems? The one I find most affecting (just my own reaction) is the "Elegy" which begins, "Sickness, at least, becomes us. . . ." Significantly perhaps, it's the most irregular poem you had written. But even here you generalize the experience, don't you? "We" rather than "I" is the characteristic pronoun. Indeed "I" scarcely appears in the early poems.

JM: Oh, you know, the "Elegy" is really part of something longer—the "Variations and Elegy." The way it's set up in the book it looks separate. I'll admit that part of the "Elegy" was trumped up. It was a task I set not to use rhyme. But that sort of thing didn't pay off for a number of years, perhaps not till my *Short Stories*. I felt humanly more involved in "The Willow" and "The House," the last poems in my early book. "Real" experience had grazed them, somehow. They are very formal poems in triplets, too.

Your remark about "we" opens up quite a subject. A generation ago "we" was *the* pronoun. It probably started with Auden—let's say it conveyed the sense of a political elite. But there was another and to me more important source—Rilke in the *Duino Elegies*. The "we" there is an elite of sufferers. I didn't know German very well then, but Rilke was five times more poetic to me than Yeats. Yeats seemed by comparison somewhat external to one's situation. Auden, you know, must have learned a lot from Rilke, even the excessive personification. So maybe the two "we"s are one.

Q: I've always felt one had to know German rather well to read Rilke—he eludes translation much of the time. But maybe I'm being too strict about this.

JM: I don't know German any better now. In fact the point may be *not* to know German well enough where Rilke is concerned! So as still to feel, I mean, the overture of abstraction in all those capitalized nouns. In mentioning Yeats, by the way, I must say that I read and admired him a lot in my youth. I read "Sailing to Byzantium" when I was in the army. It got through to me because of the circumstances. I couldn't wait to get "out of nature" myself. But what I got from Rilke was more than literary; that emphasis on the *acceptance* of pain and loneliness. Rilke helps you with suffering, especially in your adolescence. . . .

Q: I wonder if you agree with Ransom about the virtue of having little dramatic situations in short poems?

JM: Not altogether. I always find when I don't like a poem I'm writing, I don't look any more into the human components. I look more to the *setting*—a room, the objects in it. I think that objects are very subtle reflectors. When you are in an emotional state, whatever your eye lights on takes on something of the quality of a state of mind.

Q: But to what extent do you think a poem depends on objects? Can't you have the reverse—say Sonnet 129 of Shakespeare, which is almost a poetry of statement? And a lot of Stevens is statement.

JM: Perhaps. But in my case the objects are important, more so than ever.

Q: Quite a few of your poems—even recent ones—are built up out of human situations which are themselves almost metaphors—"The Lovers," for instance, in your second book. Do you defend this kind of indirection? You seem to be pointing toward something else beyond the ostensible subject of the poem.

JM: "The Lovers" is one of a great number of my poems where the human situation *is* a metaphor or perhaps even a vision. I must have some kind of awful religious streak just under the surface. "The Doodler," for instance, turns out to be God looking at his creatures. I've had to conclude that these buried meanings help. Without something like them, one ends up writing light verse about love affairs. "In the Hall of Mirrors" is a fairly obvious case. It was written during the 1950s when the "myth" poems were popular. It's about the expulsion from Eden. I won't say the buried meaning came first; probably it didn't. I'm never altogether pleased to see this happen, but it does again and again.

Q: During the 1950s you moved into playwriting and prose fiction—and very gracefully, in my opinion. Your *Short Stories* poems like "A Narrow Escape" are the obvious result. Did you find the blank verse of these poems an advantage?

JM: I wanted to write blank verse—even before I wrote the poems. Why? Because I wanted to get some of the pleasures of prose into poetry. The influence of playwriting came a bit later.

Q: I've had the impression for some time that older writers of prose— for instance Katherine Anne Porter—often took their tonal effects from the poets, say Eliot and Pound and Yeats. But now American poets are tapping the resources of prose more than ever. Do you agree?

JM: Absolutely. Prose feeds into poetry much more than the reverse. I was thinking this way in the 1950s, and I was already trying for something new in "About the Phoenix," even though this poem is slightly modeled on Elizabeth Bishop's "Over 2,000 Illustrations and a Complete Concordance."

Q: What *about* your playwriting? *The Immortal Husband* had a successful production off-Broadway, didn't it? I didn't see it, but I thought your manipulation of Tithonus's sad story through several period settings was a delight to read. You seem to work best in drama and fiction when you reverse the naturalistic illusions. *The Seraglio* is the exception—that's rather Jamesian.

JM: It was *fairly* successful. I wrote the play for Anne Meacham, a marvelous actress. Well, about naturalistic illusions: In *The Immortal Husband* the doubling of characters gives a unity that Aristotle knew about but never bothered to mention: the unity of the performer. His reality is often far more immediate than that of his material. Just as in my second novel, *The (Diblos) Notebook*, the writing of the novel is the immediate reality. In that sense I'm not reversing the illusion at all.

Q: Do you plan another novel?

JM: No, I can't invent, and I think a novelist must have that talent. Right now I'm working on a ballad about Stonington. It contains four local characters, the people in fact that *Water Street* is dedicated to. It's a substitute for a novel.

Q: Something like Elizabeth Bishop's "Burglar of Babylon"?

JM: In a way, yes. Since I've been living in Greece I've found myself thinking a lot about human behavior. It's because of the language barrier—when you can't ascertain the full range of people's motives and feelings, they are simplified in a sense. This particular experience of being with people may have led to a ballad—in traditional ballads the characters *are* properly simplified. I think I like either those people who completely understand whatever I say—at all levels—or those who understand hardly any of it, for whom I am simplified into a dream-figure, as they no doubt are for me. Understanding has more than one face.

Q: I guess one of the turning points in your poetry came with "An Urban Convalescence" in *Water Street*. It's perhaps the most innovative and the most personal poem you had yet written.

JM: Yes, it was a turning point. I remember writing half of it and thinking it was going to be impossible to finish. Then I had the idea of letting it go back to a more formal pattern at the end. I was helped by a musical analogy—a procedure I've used several times since. In this case it was a toccata (or introduction) and allegro, and so I let my quatrains wind up a poem which threatened to fall away. Although I am very personal in this poem (more so than in the "Elegy" in the first book), I feel I'm inventing things here and there.

Q: Have you been attracted to the dramatic monologue as a way of getting a lot of experience into poetry? "Roger Clay's Proposal" and "1939" are two of these among your more recent poems. Or does this seem like the easy way out?

JM: I like Browning's monologues; they seem more natural than Lowell's. Those little *données* about the Canadian nun and the old man falling asleep over the *Aeneid* would never occur to me as a way of getting a poem started. I approach the dramatic monologue with diffidence; I feel happier not restricting myself to the single speaker. The overt monologue serves well enough only when I know exactly where I'm going. For instance, "1939" is an actual transcription of an anecdote told by a woman here in Stonington. I wanted to get away from pentameter, too. Do you know that wonderful poem by Elizabeth Bishop called "The Riverman"? It's in *Questions of Travel*. Wonderful, fluid, pulsing lines—you hardly feel the meter at all.

Q: In your last book, *Nights and Days*, you've certainly come a long way from *First Poems*, but your formal experiments are pretty clearly developed out of "An Urban Convalescence," aren't they?

JM: Yes, I think so. I can tell you precisely the point when I felt I was on the right track: when I thought to use the phrase "the sickness of our time." I loathe that phrase and tried to put it into perspective.

Q: Since you are now involved in long poems, what do you think are their possibilities and limitations at this stage of American poetry? I assume that epic is out of the question. You seem to like the theme and variations best.

JM: Well, everybody has agreed that psychological action is more interesting than epic. One mainly wants a form where one thing leads to another—it needn't, but it can.

Q: I keep thinking that "The Prelude" could still be used as a model of some sort. It was very bold of Wordsworth, don't you agree, to write a poem of epic length that departed from the inherited tradition of mythology that almost everybody had depended on? It *is* somewhat ruminative, but it has a real unity.

JM: You will have imagined (and come close to the truth) that I fell asleep on the seventh page of "The Prelude" and woke only the next morning. It's not me, I'm afraid!

Q: In "The Thousand and Second Night" the writing of the poem itself is part of the subject—the "immediate reality" as you were saying about *The (Diblos) Notebook*. Would you care to comment on this?

JM: I don't know what the main subject is—the poem is flirtatious in that sense. Writing poems about the act of writing both attracts and repulses me—like "the sickness of our time." The idea is usually more interesting than the execution, as in Mallarmé's "Un Coup de Dés." Some people balked at the name-dropping in the poem, but this was only the representational plane. And I meant the comedy of the surface to sugar the pill. I don't think it's like the *serious* name-dropping of the Beats—Ferlinghetti is the worst offender there.

Q: "From the Cupola" is your most ambitious work so far—you stretch your form to the limit. Could you talk about the inception of the poem? Why did you elaborate it in the way that you did?

JM: I had no sense of the extent to which I would take it when I began it. At first it was just a little poem in the first person. It was involved with a curious experience—receiving letters from somebody I never met, who seemed to know everything about me. I'm not paranoiac, but it was rather unsettling. After a while I became engrossed with this interior experience. I didn't want to meet the writer of the letters; I wanted to detach myself from the experience to write about it. The poem from the beginning needed "body," and I gave it this by way of landscape—what I can see from this window. And then I thought of Psyche. Psyche, you know, is a

Hellenistic myth. I also liked the "montage" of Hellenistic Alexandria and Stonington, which likewise has a lighthouse and a library. Well, it *is* ambitious, but the first and the last parts, I think, tone it down—I frame it in "my own voice." A friend of mine, Benjamin DeMott, was very helpful in urging me to make this framework as explicit as possible. I did the best I could!

Q: You seem very confident about the state of poetry today—you were saying earlier that prose feeds it more than the reverse.

JM: Oh, yes! But there are still things to be learned from prose. What I value more than anything else is the fluid seamless narrative of Stendhal. But I read so quickly. I even have to read novels twice, and my attitude toward writing is probably affected by that. In *(Diblos)* I tried to slow down the reader—make him see the sentences, as it were, by leaving some of them unfinished. Make him pause to complete them.

Q: We do seem to be going through a major shift in the arts. The period of Eliot and Stravinsky and Joyce is being succeeded by something else, the era of the "dithyrambic spectator." The only absolute for some people now is change. Do you feel involved in this?

JM: I think that under the circumstances I'm lucky to be a poet rather than a painter or sculptor—they have to think of something new every year. I don't worry about it. What else can one do except grow old gracefully? I've yet to see a poem that I can't relate to something at least fifty years old if not two hundred. I think one should try in what one does to charm the reader. I still like Stevens's idea about the imagination "pressing back against the pressure of reality."

An Interview with John Boatwright and Enrique Ucelay DaCal

Q: At what age did you first begin to write poetry and why? Do you consider it a justified reason for having started, in terms of yourself today?

JM: I began at fourteen or so. My best friend at school was writing poems, and I must have thought: Why not me? Years of pleasing himself have properly wrinkled the brash little Narcissus who made that choice. And yet I stand by it, for better or worse. To write is "me," and not to write is "not-me." One does what one can.

Q: Much of the work done by students today in poetry could be called neosurrealist, in that automatic psychological imagery, even Oriental-mystical imagery is used. How do you feel about these trends?

JM: All imagery allows for a psychological reading. You can analyze Wordsworth until he sounds like Freud's first patient, if you like. As for automatism, I'd hope there was enough in all of us without our needing to cultivate it.

These things come and go. The Orient has kept breaking upon the scene in *nouvelles vagues* for centuries. Beautiful styles may result, which are about as Oriental as a Chinese Chippendale chair. Since they are not truly part of us, these ideas seem more attractive company than those of our guilt-blackened West. Remember how Ogden Nash put it?—

Stage IV, 1968.

There would be less danger
From the wiles of the stranger
If one's own kin and kith
Were more fun to be with.

Q: The war in Vietnam particularly, but the Negro revolution as well, have sparked a lot of markedly social poetry among both student and professional poets. What is your opinion on the relation of poetry to social or political realities? What is the power or use of social poetry?

JM: Oh dear. These immensely real concerns do not produce *poetry*. But of course one responds. A word-cluster like *napalm-baby-burn* stimulates the juices as infallibly as the high C of a Donizetti mad scene. Both audiences have been prepared for what they get and are strongly moved. The trouble with overtly political or social writing is that when the tide of feeling goes out, the language begins to stink. In poetry I look for English in its billiard-table sense—words that have been set spinning against their own gravity. Once in competition with today's headlines or editorial page you just can't sustain that crucial, liberating lightness without sounding like a sick comedian. The wisest resources appear to be those of song (Lorca, Brecht, rock groups) or those of extreme obliquity—which last, however, can all too easily bewilder the reader who expects a message rather than a poem.

Q: There seems to be, among those of our generation, a distaste for anything that might seem a strictly aesthetic approach to poetry, not only in its writing, but also in its reading. Poetry, it is argued, should be a majority art form, and the fact that it is not is seen as a function of the emptiness of our culture. How do you feel about this?

JM: Popular art, in a society without ritual, can only be that which entertains, is consumed, and is replaced at once by the next thing. Its admirers include, to a man, us aesthetes. That the admiration isn't mutual needn't bother anyone. Some will always have a more complex emotional or intellectual life than others, which a more complex art will be called upon to nourish. What's fascinating today is the communization of the aesthete—his drugs, his adornments, his arrogance, his whole allure taken over from Baudelaire or Robert de Montesquiou as a group project, like a private house turned into a school. Perhaps after all the majority *can* be tenderized by sprinklings of these neural equivalents of the papaya enzyme.

Q: In the same vein, how personal do you feel poetry should be, not only thematically, but imagistically? As a corollary, how do you feel about the tendency, since Joyce, toward strongly hermetical poetry?

JM: Total, clear-eyed immersion in one's own little world produces (especially if one is Joyce, or Montaigne, or Tolstoy) an excellent likeness of the universe. Under Joyce's difficult surface there's an old, old story, a family scene with himself at the head of the table. My own ideal of the hermetic artist is Mallarmé. Under his difficult surface there's the midnight sky, a skull of stars. John Ashbery is closest in our language to that tradition, nowadays. His work is precious in most senses of the word.

The means—imagery, tone, and so forth—can be as personal as you like, so long as the end is not to express personality.

Q: Do you feel that there is any real possibility in our technological society for traditional poetry, or that some form of new poetry must be evolved?

JM: New forms evolved in nontechnological societies, just as they seem to be doing in ours. With fewer and fewer people, even bright ones, who know what traditions are, my old-fashioned kind of poem may soon be mistaken for something much newer than it is, and read with appropriate cries of delight.

Q: How do you feel about the potentialities of mixed media poetry? Can poetry be a physical experience?

JM: It was for Housman. He felt it in the pit of his stomach without any mixing of media. I feel about the mixers like a student when the Dow Chemical man turns up on campus. I don't want any part of it. I want full control over my own product.

ON "YÁNNINA":
AN INTERVIEW WITH
DAVID KALSTONE

YÁNNINA

For Stephen Yenser

"There lay the peninsula stretching far into the dark gray water, with its mosque, its cypress tufts and fortress walls; there was the city stretching far and wide along the water's edge; there was the fatal island, the closing scene of the history of the once all-powerful Ali." —EDWARD LEAR

Somnambulists along the promenade
Have set up booths, their dreams:
Carpets, jewelry, kitchenware, halvah, shoes.
From a loudspeaker passionate lament
Mingles with the penny Jungle's roars and screams.
Tonight in the magician's tent
Next door a woman will be sawed in two,
But right now she's asleep, as who is not, as who . . .

An old Turk at the water's edge has laid
His weapons and himself down, sleeps

Saturday Review, December 1972.

Undisturbed since, oh, 1913?
Nothing will surprise him should he wake,
Only how tall, how green the grass has grown
There by the dusty carpet of the lake
Sun beats, then sleepwalks down a vine-festooned arcade,
Giving himself away in golden heaps.

And in the dark gray water sleeps
One who said no to Ali. Kiosks all over town
Sell that postcard, "Kyra Frossíni's Drown,"
Showing her, eyeballs white as mothballs, trussed
Beneath the bulging moon of Ali's lust.
A devil (turban and moustache and sword)
Chucks the pious matron overboard—
Wait—Heaven help us—SPLASH!

The torch smokes on the prow. Too late.
(A picture deeply felt, if in technique slapdash.)
Wherefore the Lion of Epirus, feared
By Greek and Turk alike, tore his black beard
When to barred casements rose the song
Broken from bubbles rising all night long:
"A ton of sugar pour, oh pour into the lake
To sweeten it for poor, for poor Frossíni's sake."

Awake? Her story's aftertaste
Varies according to the listener.
Friend, it's bitter coffee you prefer?
Brandy for me, and with a fine
White sandy bottom. Not among those braced
By action taken without comment, neat,

---

*"Time was kind to the reputation of this woman who had been unfaithful to her husband, vain, and grasping. She came to be regarded as a Christian martyr and even as an early heroine in the struggle for Greek independence. She has been celebrated in legend, in poetry, in popular songs and historical fiction, and surrounded with the glamour which so often attaches to women whose love affairs have been of an intense nature and have involved men of political or historical importance." —WILLIAM PLOMER, *The Diamond of Jannina*

Here's how! Grounds of our footnote infiltrate the treat,
Mud-vile to your lips, crystal-sweet to mine.

Twilight at last. Enter the populace.
One little public garden must retrace
Long after school its childish X,
Two paths that cross and cross. The hollyhock, the rose,
Zinnia and marigold hear themselves named
And blush for form's sake, unashamed
Chorus out of Ignoramus Rex:
"What shall the heart learn, that already knows

Its place by water, and its time by sun?"
Mother wit fills the stately whispering sails
Of girls someone will board and marry. Who?
Look at those radiant young males.
Their morning-glory nature neon blue
Wilts here on the provincial vine. Where did it lead,
The race, the radiance? To oblivion
Dissembled by a sac of sparse black seed.

Now under trees men with rush baskets sell
Crayfish tiny and scarlet as the sins
In any fin de siècle villanelle.
Tables fill up. A shadow play begins.
Painted, translucent cut-outs fill the screen.
It glows. His children by a jumping bean
Karaghióʒi clobbers, baits the Turk,
Then all of them sing, dance, tell stories, go berserk.

Tomorrow we shall cross the lake to see
The cottage tumbling down, where soldiers killed
Ali. Two rugless rooms. Cushions. Vitrines
In which, to this day, silks and bracelets swim.
Above, a painting hangs. It's him,
Ali. The end is near, he's sleeping between scenes

In a dark lady's lap. Vassilikí.
The mood is calm, the brushwork skilled

By contrast with Frossíni's mass-produced
Unsophisticated piece of goods.
The candle trembles in the watching god's
Hand—almost a love-death, höchste Lust!
Her drained, compliant features haunt
The waters there was never cause to drown her in.
Your grimiest ragamuffin comes to want
Two loves, two versions of the Feminine:

One virginal and tense, brief as a bubble,
One flesh and bone—gone up no less in smoke
Where giant spits revolving try their rusty treble,
Sheep's eyes pop, and death-wish ravens croak.
Remember, the Romantic's in full feather.
Byron has visited. He likes
The luxe, and overlooks the heads on pikes;
Finds Ali "Very kind . . . indeed, a father . . ."*

Funny, that is how I think of Ali.
On the one hand, the power and the gory
Details, pigeon-blood rages and retali-
ations, gouts of fate that crust his story;
And on the other, charm, the whimsically
Meek brow, its motives all ab ulteriori,
The flower-blue gaze twining to choke proportion,
Having made one more pretty face's fortune.

---

*Letter to his mother, November 12, 1809. Plomer observes: ". . . even allowing for Oriental effusiveness, it seems doubtful whether [Ali's] interest in Byron was exactly as paternal as he pretended, for a father does not give his son sweets twenty times a day and beg him to visit him at night. It is worth remarking that Ali was a judge of character and a connoisseur of beauty, whether male or female, and that the like of Byron, and Byron at twenty-one, is not often seen."

A dove with Parkinson's disease
Selects our fortunes: TRAVEL AND GROW WISE
And A LOYAL FRIEND IS MORE THAN GOLD.
But, at the island monastery, eyes
Gouged long since to the gesso sockets will outstare
This or that old-timer on his knees
Asking the candlelight for skill to hold
The figures flush against the screen's mild glare.

Ali, my father—both are dead.
In so many words, so many rhymes,
The brave old world sleeps. Are we what it dreams
And is a rude awakening overdue?
Not in Yánnina. To bed, to bed.
The Lion sets. The lights wink out along the lake.
Weeks later, in this study gone opaque,
They are relit. See through me. See me through.

For partings hurt although we dip the pain
Into a glowing well—the pen I mean.
Living alone won't make some inmost face to shine
Maned with light, ember and anodyne,
Deep in a desktop burnished to its grain.
That the last hour be learned again
By riper selves, couldn't you doff this green
Incorruptible, the might-have-been,

And arm in arm with me dare the magician's tent?
It's hung with asterisks. A glittering death
Is hefted, swung. The victim smiles consent.
To a sharp intake of breath she comes apart
(Done by mirrors? Just one woman? Two?
A fight starts—in the provinces, one feels,
There's never that much else to do)
Then to a general exhalation heals

Like anybody's life, bubble and smoke
In afterthought, whose elements converge,
Glory of windless mornings that the barge
(Two barges, one reflected, a quicksilver joke)
Kept scissoring and mending as it steered
The old man outward and away,
Amber mouthpiece of a narghilé
Buried in his by then snow-white beard.

Q: Can you say something about the circumstances surrounding "Yánnina"?

JM: It's a town I'd wanted to visit for years and had begun to fear I never would, like Proust and Parma. So that I must have worked myself into a fairly receptive state by the time I got there. No research, mind you—a phrase or two out of Lear, a dim echo of Byron, the foreknowledge of a lake. It never hurts, does it, to have a body of water up one's sleeve, something that flows or reflects? Ali Pasha was just a name. Later on, halfway through the poem when I needed a biography of him, I was delighted to find the wonderful William Plomer had written it. In any case the day came—less than a day: I didn't spend twenty-four hours on the spot. But the piano had been prepared, and only the notation remained. That whole element—do we dare call it reality?—had to be unforeseeable, accidental, something to fill in then and there. I'd counted on that.

Q: Did you have a theme already in mind? Is that what you're saying?

JM: No, not really. . . . Wait—yes, I did! How odd not to have made the connection. Earlier that year I'd been concerned for a friend, a woman whose son had disappeared. He'd been teaching somewhere—a man in his thirties—and one day absolutely vanished without a trace. Weeks passed, months passed, his friends imagined the worst, his mother was beside herself. I was already in Greece when two letters came from her. In the first she had just heard from a friend of Bruce's that he was well and living under an assumed name—she didn't yet know where. Her second letter, not long afterward, said that she'd heard from Bruce (or Tom, as he now wanted to be called); he'd given her his address, told her he'd found work there. What he'd wanted was no less than a brand-new life, and it looked, at that point, as if he'd found it. Now it may sound—it may *be*—

childish, but haven't we all dreamed of doing exactly that? To disappear and reemerge as a new person without any ties, the slate wiped clean. Sometimes one even puts the dream into action, in a less dramatic way than Bruce's, or do I mean Tom's? In my own case I began going to Greece—over ten years ago—very much in the spirit of one who embarks upon a double life. The life I lived there seemed I can't tell you how different from life in America. I felt for the first time that I was doing exactly as I pleased. How we delude ourselves! As if there were ever more than one life. Tom is as close to Bruce's mother as Bruce had ever been. He's in touch with many of his former friends—all this after scarcely a year of his new identity. I myself, after ten years of moving back and forth, can hardly distinguish, now, between Athens and Stonington, Connecticut. Anyhow, you might say that these "scissorings and mendings" are the theme of "Yánnina."

Q: Does this notion of playing different roles connect with the shadow play in the poem? I'm not altogether sure what a shadow play is.

JM: They're dying out, like everything. The one I describe was set up out of doors—a proscenium framing a long, white screen lit from behind. The puppets are two-dimensional figures of colored parchment, or maybe plastic nowadays, somewhat articulated but mainly relying on the verve and bounce of the manipulators who hold them flat against the screen with rods. Rather the effect of a primitive animated cartoon. Lots of contemporary allusion, popular songs, political jokes, but the main action generally refers back to the Turkish occupation. There's always a pompous, dim-witted Pasha whom Karaghiózi makes a fool of. Karaghiózi's the hero—a wily little Greek, terribly demotic and down-to-earth. The play Byron saw in Yánnina reminded him of morris dancing, it was so indecent. I'm afraid things have changed since his day.

Q: About these changing roles. You appear to identify with the manipulator in one stanza—"to hold the figures flush," etc.—and in the next with the translucent puppet itself—"See through me. . . ."

JM: Yes. It was greedy of me to want that double life. A writer already has two lives, don't you think? Not so much in the obvious division between experience and its imitation on the page as in the two sides of—well, I'll have to trust you, when this gets transcribed, to put in some less inflated term—the two sides of the creative temperament. That which conceives and that which executes. There are moments when the light *does* seem to shine through us. The rest of the time we spend trying to keep our images steady.

Q: The poem is full of paired figures, isn't it? Frossíni and Vassilikí, the speaker and his companion. And it's not just your poet who has a double life; many of the characters do as well. Frossíni in the text comes off as a chaste martyr, but as "unfaithful, vain, and grasping" in the footnote. Vassilikí gives her body to Ali but "goes up in smoke"; we never know what she was thinking. Ali himself is both gentle and cruel.

JM: Isn't it odd? I mean, how one tries—not just in writing—to escape from these opposites, from there being two sides to every question!

Q: But you also show things being made whole. The magician—

JM: The magician, yes, performs the essential act. He heals what he has divided. A double-edged action, like his sword. It's what one comes to feel that life keeps doing.

Q: You said once that your poems are not "historical." Yet I'd say that this poem is almost *about* history, that it's a kind of stand against people locked into the present. Not history as public record, mind you, but—

JM: A kind of time-zoo?

Q: The vividness of your Ali—

JM: Historical figures are always so well lighted. Even if one never gets to the truth about them, their contradictions, even their crimes, are so expressive. They're like figures in a novel read by millions of people at once. What's terrifying is that they're human as well, and therefore no more reliable than you or I. They have their blind, "genetic" side, just like my boys and girls in Yánnina.

Q: That's the point, isn't it? Not just that historical figures enter the poem, but that they're *creatures* of history ("oblivion / dissembled by a sac of sparse black seed"). There's no clear present in your poem; the past shadows it. It's as if you always need the past as a sounding board.

JM: I liked that sense of sleeping presences. Ali, Frossíni, Vassilikí, the old Turk at the beginning—they're merely asleep. The woman to be sawed in half. Even "you and I" toward the end seem half-absorbed into the dreaming landscape.

Maybe there's something worth saying about tenses here, how one handles them. Last winter, I visited a workshop in which only one out of fifteen poets had noticed that he needn't invariably use the first-person present active indicative. Poem after poem began: "I empty my glass . . . I go out . . . I stop by woods. . . ." For me a "hot" tense like that can't be handled for very long without cool pasts and futures to temper it. Or some complexity of syntax, or a modulation into the conditional—*something*. An imperative, even an auxiliary verb, can do wonders. Otherwise, you get this addictive, self-centered immediacy, harder to break oneself of than cigarettes. That kind of talk (which, by the way, is purely literary; it's never heard in life unless from foreigners or four-year-olds) calls to mind a speaker suspicious of words, in great boots, chain-smoking, Getting It Down on Paper. He'll never notice "Whose woods these are I think I know" gliding backward through the room, or "Longtemps je me suis couché de bonne heure" plumping a cushion invitingly at her side.

Q: You're talking about—against?—so-called confessional poems. Yet the present is still *the* lyric tense, isn't it? Isn't the point that it aims at an ecstatic, timeless state? "Earth has not anything to show more fair . . ."

JM: Ah, but that's in the third person; that's another matter. No, you're right, and I don't want to paint myself into a corner. Yet I can't help . . . Think how often poems in the first-person present begin with a veil drawn, a sublimation of the active voice or the indicative mood, as if some ritual effacement of the ego were needed before one could go on. "I wonder, by my troth, what thou and I . . ."; "Let us go then you and I . . ." The poet isn't always the hero of a movie who *does* this, *does* that. He is a man choosing the words he lives by.

Q: Your own way of veiling the first person here has to do with the way you present the landscape, doesn't it?

JM: You hardly ever need to *state* your feelings. The point is to feel and keep the eyes open. Then what you feel is expressed, is mimed back at you by the scene. A room, a landscape. I'd go a step further. We don't *know* what we feel until we see it distanced by this kind of translation.

Q: So, people and places fade into one another. Like the sun in "Yánnina" sleepwalking down the vine and the provincial boys who wilt on it? In Yánnina—*your* Yánnina—we're doomed to repeat certain experiences. Human contradictions appear to root themselves in nature.

JM: No wonder Nature revenges herself. Those lines in Jarrell— remember?

A quarter of an hour and we tire
Of any landscape, said Goethe; eighty years
And he had not tired of Goethe. The landscape had,
And disposed of Goethe in the usual way.

Q: Is that why you don't write protest poems?

JM: I don't know. Auden says they do no good, except to get you an audience among people who feel the same way.

Q: Wouldn't you like a larger audience?

JM: When I search my heart, no, not really. So why invite it, even supposing that I could? Think what one has to *do* to get a mass audience. I'd rather have one perfect reader. Why dynamite the pond in order to catch that single silver carp? Better to find a bait that only the carp will take. One still has plenty of choices. The carp at Fountainebleau were thought to swallow small children, whole.

As to protest poems . . . they aren't poems first of all, so much as bits of honorable oratory. A protest *poem* would be one written against a poem of a different kind, one that reflected a different tradition. Wordsworth against Pope, Byron against Wordsworth.

Q: Would you like to say what kind of poem "Yánnina" is written against?

JM: You must be joking. Well . . .

Q: There's a phrase in your second novel. You say about Racine— "the overlay of prismatic verse deflects a brutal, horrible action." Not that the underlying action of "Yánnina" is brutal or horrible.

JM: No, but you mean it's implicit rather than presented as narrative? Yes. I'd wanted to let the scene, the succession of scenes, convey not meaning so much as a sense of it, a sense that something both is, and isn't, being said. I hoped that a reader's own experience would remind him that some things can go without saying. I was trying for an intimacy of tone, not of content. People are always asking, Was it real? Did it happen? (Thank *you* for not asking that, by the way.) As if a yes-or-no answer would settle the question. Was it really Yánnina I went to? Was my companion real or imaginary? I can only say yes *and* no to questions like that.

Q: You used the image of a veil earlier, talking about reticence. Does your veiling of tense and voice have to do with your feelings about "real" experience in a poem?

JM: I suppose it would have to. We've all written poems that imitate a plausible sequence of events. "I go out" for a walk and find these beautiful daffodils or this dead songbird and have the following feelings. But, for better or worse, that walk is in fact taken—or Yánnina is visited—by a writer in hopes of finding something to write about. Then you have not simply imitated or recollected experience, but experience in the light of a projected emotion, like a beam into which what you encounter will seem to have strayed. The poem and its occasion will have created one another.

An Interview
with Helen Vendler

Q: When you called your last book *Divine Comedies*, did you mean by that allusion to Dante that you were planning a trilogy?

JM: Not consciously. I'd convinced myself that "The Book of Ephraim" told everything I had to say about the "other world." Because of its length and looniness I'd taken to calling *it* the Divine Comedy— not of course a usable title, until David Jackson thought of making it plural. Dante, subtler as always, let posterity affix the adjective.

Q: In your new book, *Mirabell: Books of Number*, you say there will be one more volume in this vein; after that you will be permitted to return to your "chronicles of love and loss." These three books have all been based on Ouija board material. Is there anything else that unites them, in general, and that separates them from your earlier poetry?

JM: Chiefly, I think, the—to me—unprecedented way in which the material came. Not through flashes of insight, wordplay, trains of thought. More like what a friend, or stranger, might say over a telephone. DJ and I never knew until it had been spelled out letter by letter. What I felt about the material became a natural part of the poem, corresponding to those earlier poems written "all by myself."

Q: In "The Book of Ephraim," the first book, we heard the voices of the dead; but in *Mirabell* nonhuman voices are added, telling a compli-

New York Review of Books, May 3, 1979.

cated tale of evolutionary history, molecular biology, and subatomic behavior. Would you like to talk about the books you read before creating your phantasmagoria of "science"? (You mention *The Lives of a Cell,* and looking at a model of the double helix.)

JM: They weren't many. The simplest science book is over my head. At college I'd seen my dead frog's limbs twitch under some applied stimulus or other—seen, but hadn't believed. Didn't dream of thinking beyond or around what I saw. Oh, I picked up a two-volume *Guide to Science* by Asimov—very useful still, each time I forget how the carbon atom is put together, or need to shake my head over periodic tables. A book on the black holes. Arthur Young's *Reflexive Universe*—fascinating but too schematic to fit into *my* scheme. The most I could hope for was a sense of the vocabulary and some possible images.

Q: Do you think the vocabulary, models, and concepts of science— cloning, DNA, carbon bonds, the ozone layer, protons, etc.—offer real new resources to poetry? So far, poets haven't seemed inclined to see poetry and science as compatible, even though Wordsworth thought they should.

JM: The vocabulary can be perfectly ghastly ("polymerization," "kink instability") or unconsciously beautiful, like things a child says ("red shift," "spectral lines"). Knowing some Greek helped defuse forbidding words—not that I counted much on using them. You'll find only trace elements of this language in the poem. The images, the concepts? Professor Baird at Amherst gave a course in Science and Literature which showed how much the "ideas" depended on metaphor, ways of talking. And while Science may have grown more "imaginative"—or at least more "apocalyptic"—in the decades since I left school, how many writers in that, or any, field are really wise to the ways of the word? Lewis Thomas is an exception—if only he would give us more than snippets. I'd like to think the scientists need us—but do they? Did Newton need Blake?

Q: What would you especially like a reader to be caught up by in your trilogy? The density of your myths? The civilized love of conversation? The range in tone? The domesticity?

JM: For me the talk and the tone—along with the elements of plot— are the candy coating. The pill itself is another matter. The reader who can't swallow it has my full sympathy. I've choked on it again and again.

Q: The new mythology you've invented via the Ouija board—including the new God Biology, a universal past including Atlantis, centaurs, and angels, an afterlife which includes reincarnation—how real does it all seem to you?

JM: Literally, not very—except in recurrent euphoric hours when it's altogether too beautiful not to be true. Imaginatively real? I would hope so, but in all modesty, for the imagination in question kept assuming proportions broader and grander than mine. Also at times sillier: Atlantis, UFOs? I climbed the wall trying to escape that sort of material. But the point remained, to be always of two minds.

Q: In the past, you've written fiction as well as lyrics. Does the trilogy satisfy your narrative impulse as much as your fiction did? Or more?

JM: Before trying a novel I wrote a couple of plays. (The Artists' Theatre—John Myers and Herbert Machiz—put them on in the fifties.) Behind them lay one of my earliest literary thrills: to open a little Samuel French booklet, some simpleminded "play for children," and find on the page a fiction made up of stage directions more suggestive than any rendered narrative scene, and of words set down to be spoken by a real, undreamed-of mouth—my own if I wished! The effect was somehow far more naked, far less quilted, than the nicely written stories I fell asleep to. Twenty years later, I confused an exercise in dramatic form with "writing for the theater"—that royal road to megalomania. But those two plays left me on fresh terms with language. I didn't always have to speak in my own voice.

Q: Does the quartet activating the poem—you and David Jackson at the Ouija board, W. H. Auden and Maria Mitsotáki on the other side— make up a family constellation? Why do you think the poem needed a ghostly father and ghostly mother?

JM: Strange about parents. We have such easy access to them and such daunting problems of communication. Over the Ouija board it was just the other way. A certain apparatus was needed to get in touch—but then! Affection, understanding, tact, surprises, laughter, tears. Why the *poem* needed Wystan and Maria I'm not sure. Without being Dante, can I think of them as Virgil and Beatrice?

Q: The intense affection that binds you to your familiar spirit Ephraim, to dead friends, and even to the inhuman Bat-Angel you talk to in the new book, seems the quality celebrated and even venerated in the poem. Do you see this as a change from your earlier poems about your family and about love?

JM: In life, there are no perfect affections. Estrangements among the living reek of unfinished business. Poems get written *to* the person no longer reachable. Yet, once dead, overnight the shrewish wife becomes "a saint," frustrations vanish at cockcrow, and from the once fallible human mouth come words of blessed reassurance. Your question looks down into smoking chasms and up into innocent blankness. Given the power— without being Orpheus, either—would I bring any of these figures back to earth?

Q: If it's true that every poem, besides saying something about life, says something about poetry, what is this new form saying about itself?

JM: Something possibly to do with the doubleness of its source, spelled out on every page by the interplay between the spirits' capitals and our own lowercase responses. Julian Jaynes's book on the "bicameral mind" came out last year. Don't ask me to paraphrase his thesis—but, reading Jaynes as I was finishing *Mirabell*, I rather goggled. Because the poem is set by and large in two adjacent rooms: a domed red one where we took down the messages, and a blue one, dominated by an outsized mirror, where we reflected upon them.

Q: The predecessors you have in mind seem to be Dante, Yeats, and Auden. Do you think of yourself as in any way distinctively American? Or of this poem as in any active relation to American literature and American culture?

JM: I feel American in Europe and exotic at home—and haven't we our own "expatriate" tradition for that? I was about to suggest—until I recalled *The Anathemata* and John Heath-Stubbs's wonderful *Artorius*— that the long, "impossible" poem was an American phenomenon in our day. The thought didn't comfort me. How many of us get out of our cars when we hit the badlands in the *Cantos*, or take that detour through downtown *Paterson*? In such a context, "foreignness" would be the storyteller's rather than the missionary's concern for his reader's soul.

Q: How did the poem get transcribed and composed? The work of transcription alone must have been enormous.

JM: The board goes along at a smart clip, perhaps six hundred words an hour. Sometimes it was hard to reconstruct *our* words—"What was the question?" as Miss Stein put it. Then what to cut? What to paraphrase? What to add? Plus the danger of flatness when putting into verse a passage already coherent in prose. I could have left it in prose, but it would have been too sensational—like Castaneda, or Gwendolyn's diary in *The Importance of Being Earnest*.

An Interview
with Ross Labrie

Q: You once said that Rilke is someone who helped you with suffering, particularly in your adolescence. What were the main causes of that suffering?

JM: I suppose trying to discover my own nature and my own place in the world with regard to other people and with regard to what I would do with my life. A lot of it probably goes back to my parents' divorce, and perhaps even to my sense of the tensions between them before things came to a head. I always understood without having any confirmation of it that I didn't very much care for the world as seen through their eyes. I didn't like the kind of lives they led. I'm not saying that I didn't like *them*; I just thought that their world wasn't for me—and yet since I didn't know very many other worlds—I couldn't imagine which one I would fit into. On the other hand, an adolescent who starts to write poetry perhaps exaggerates the whole role of suffering in his life. It seemed to me that Rilke made it a good deal more dignified and less a matter of self-pity but that he projected it on really quite a grand scale. He made almost a career of enforced loneliness and hopeless passions.

Q: Is the fact that you've never had to work something that you feel has limited your experience or given you a freedom which other people unhappily lack?

Arizona Quarterly, Spring 1982.

JM: Both. I think one of the great pleasures of being in Greece was that one had a kind of anonymity whereas here in America from simply the way I talk I sound like somebody very leisured and privileged. That's something that could not be inferred from the way I spoke Greek, because an accent that would be a class accent, if you like, in America would simply be an American accent in Greek; so in a way I could talk much more easily to all kinds of people in Greece than I have been able to do through a lot of my life here.

Q: So Greece was an escape from the narrowness of a well-to-do background. You have gone out into the world, as it were, through Greece?

JM: Yes.

Q: Is Greece for you what it seems to be for the narrator of *The (Diblos) Notebook*, a kind of counterworld for America—such as one might find in Henry James?

JM: Yes, very much so, and it seemed to be a world on a surprisingly small human scale compared to the great American world of business, technology, and political machines. All of those things were in Greece but on a tiny scale compared to here.

Q: Is Stonington a kind of middle world between America and Greece, having some of the aspects of a smaller culture, or has Stonington by this time been swept up in the broad current of American life?

JM: Stonington *is* a point of withdrawal; at least, I could never live very happily in New York because there is too much going on. There is the conflict of events with the work I want to do. But here where very little happens—or what does is dependent on whether or not you accept invitations—you can do with your time what you want.

Q: I noticed with pleasure your recent essay on Cavafy, and it made me aware that you have not done a great deal of literary criticism—unlike a number of contemporary American poets who have not only done a lot of criticism but a lot of work on poetics. Does this indicate boredom with or antipathy to this sort of work?

JM: No, I enjoyed very much writing the piece on Cavafy and the piece on Ponge. I don't feel that I have that much to say about a lot of other people; also, it takes me forever to turn out a piece like that. I must have worked on it for a month. I don't know how long you're meant to take to write a twelve-page essay but because I don't have critical theories or whatever at my fingertips, I have to dredge up what I really think about these things.

Q: I thought I might mention the names of a few people who seem to me to be relevant to your work and ask you for a brief statement about their significance for you. The obvious first one is Proust.

JM: He's meant more than I could possibly say over the years. When I first read him, not really understanding enough French or indeed enough of the intricacies of his thought—though I don't think his ideas are that wonderful even if that is what he was admired for as a disciple of Bergson—but I think he's much more original simply as a writer of sentences and as a viewer of society. Certainly what stunned me about the book was its wonderful size and the scheme that held it together. Along with Dante he has been as fortunate as anybody in the literary history of the West to have had a grand subject and to have brought it off.

Q: What about his "magnifying" of everyday detail—or what we assume to be everyday detail and what Proust shows us is not everyday detail?

JM: Certainly he showed us there was nothing too commonplace or too trivial which once seen as a phenomenon either of light or of social behavior couldn't be dwelt on in perfect seriousness.

Q: How about Henry James?

JM: I admire him very, very much. I felt in a way, at least compared to Proust, that he was always a bit hampered by his plots. Because the over-lying fiction was not that of a single life as in Proust, he had to taper and shape things. Probably my favorite James is a book like *The American Scene* where he is for once relieved of the machinery of the plot.

Q: Do you ever feel like a Jamesian cosmopolite?

JM: Well, I don't feel particularly cultured and international. I felt very American when I was living abroad, perhaps in the sense of a Jamesian American, and felt a bit displaced by the same token, when I would come back here.

Q: That's the case isn't it, that his Americans feel not very American when they are living here, but something about their American identity occurs to them when they're abroad.

JM: Yes, I believed in all of that, that was part of my motive in first going to Europe for an indefinite period—just to put it to the test, to see what it would do for me.

Q: What about the Jamesian drama of the aesthetic and the moral? Do you see a final merging of the beautiful and the good?

JM: I do rather, yes.

Q: How about Wallace Stevens?

JM: When I began to read a lot of modern poetry, suddenly, as a sophomore and junior in college—not just anthologies but the books themselves—he was the one who most appealed to me. I liked his ability, without at the time getting very much of the thought behind his poems. I loved the vocabulary, where he mixed the very gaudiest words with the grandest philosophical terms as if they were on a par with each other. You could throw off a philosophical term the way you might name a color to get texture and a certain dimension.

Q: Does it seem to you that Stevens struck a balance thereby that needed to be struck, that he took some of the ponderousness out of intellectualizing and yet also created a more deserved seriousness for aesthetics?

JM: Yes, absolutely.

Q: Has Hart Crane been an influence?

JM: Hart Crane rather excited me when I read him. He seemed to be an American, slightly provincial version of the things I was already liking in French poetry—I mean the deliberate obscurity of someone like Mallarmé—though I think I preferred Mallarmé to Crane. They're miles apart, of course, but I like that clotted poetry and I occasionally still work in trying to produce a poem that resists the intelligence almost successfully, as Stevens said.

Q: So that the poem is open to what? The feelings, the subconscious rather than a mediating intellectual apprehension?

JM: That should be ideally the case for both the writer and the reader.

Q: You have a poem which is dedicated to William Carlos Williams, as if you felt a special debt to him.

JM: I don't feel any debt to him, but I was very moved when he died. It took me aback, as if I really did care for his work. There is very little I care about in it, perhaps just the famous simple snippets that one wouldn't have thought were poems at all.

Q: When did you meet and become friends with Auden? Did his work have any influence that you can perceive on your own?

JM: I knew him by the mid-fifties a little bit, but I knew him much better after we began going to Greece and after Chester Kallman also came to Greece. Auden was always very well disposed to people who liked Chester, who was a difficult person. Auden's poems I had begun reading while I was in the army and *The Sea and the Mirror* came out. That and the Christmas oratorio *For the Time Being* absolutely captivated me. These poems appeared just when I was old enough to read them. The earlier poems seemed to belong to another part of history for me, but I was wild about these poems.

Q: One of the things which it occurs to me that you, Auden, and Kallman have in common is a love of music, especially opera. I recall Auden writing about opera and describing it as unusual in our time because it is high art.

JM: It was the first art that came my way. I was eleven when I started going to the opera and that was long before I'd ever read a serious novel. It seemed to me the most marvelous thing on earth. It was the way it could heighten and stylize the emotions—a kind of absurdity dignified by the music, or transformed by the music. There seemed to be nothing that couldn't be expressed in opera. When I was a child, and therefore very literal, what I felt most comfortable with would have been Wagner, where all you have to do is to recognize the motifs in order to know what's going on. I scorned something like *Trovatore,* because of the absurdity, and only came to it when I was in my thirties. I had come similarly to Dickens, whom I had scorned for the same reasons, beforehand, seeing later what masterly things had been made of such peculiar materials.

Q: What kind of drama were you thinking about in the 1950s when you were writing plays?

JM: *The Bait* I thought of as an opera. There were lyrical interludes, recitatives, duets, even something I thought of as a trio. *The Immortal Husband,* being in prose, was another matter. I used a different pastiche for each act: Chekhov in the second, some twentieth-century farce in the third, with a touch perhaps of Gertrude Stein's "opera" toward the end. The original opening had been a kind of Jacobean ranting scene—all this in the back of my head, merely as guidelines to tone.

Q: What role did you intend for Greek myth in *The Immortal Husband?*

JM: I had been very taken by Cocteau. He gave me a contemporary tone that somehow melted the marble of the Greek myths.

Q: At some point you appear to have decided that the drama was not your medium, although I suppose it could be argued that you gave up on the drama and the novel in order to integrate them into your poetry.

JM: What I really hated about working in the theater was the demand on your time—conferences, explaining your lines to actors, making yourself available for rewrites, and all that—the rather wasteful, inessential things you do. I was delighted indeed, having written plays and novels, to learn that I could put some of their lessons to use in poems.

Q: In both novels, *The Seraglio* and *The (Diblos) Notebook*, you depict a coarser actor character and a refined observer. What seems to you to be the interest of this sort of combination? It's almost as if the sensitive observer can only be complete by attaching himself to a strong protagonist who lacks the emotional and intellectual equipment to do much thinking or feeling himself.

JM: I am sure this must go back to the very beginnings of literature. I can't flesh out the pattern offhand, but it would seem to me to go back in terms of drama at any rate to *The Bacchae*. Part of the pattern involves a character who is destroyed by what he sees and finds that he is forced to exist in a certain way in a society he abhors.

Q: How do you feel in retrospect about your experiment in the novel with *The (Diblos) Notebook*?

JM: I wish that I had somehow made the technique a little more crucial to the action. The deletions conveyed simply my own impatience with the traditional novel form. The technique should have interacted more with the telling of the novel.

Q: Somewhere in your notes you have written about that novel that it is the small "rips and ripples that make the reader know there is a fabric of illusion." Why do you want the reader to sense this fabric of illusion?

JM: Well I do. That always appeals to me when I read. I am delighted with the picture of a transparently sustained illusion one gets, for example, in people like Nabokov, who is as wonderful as anyone at that sort of thing.

Q: Often, you stop your poems to comment on how the poem itself is working out. This shows you as having quite a fraternal relationship with your reader. Do you have a particular reader in mind as you write?

JM: It changes. Sometimes I have written poems which seemed to be for one other person only, but never really. Somebody asked me years ago whom I was writing for and I couldn't think. He said: "If you're writing for the angels be careful. Only the angels will read you." I suppose I'll have to let it go at that.

Q: Is the name "Diblos" meant to convey the sense of a split?

JM: Yes, the name in Greek sounds like "double."

Q: Referring then to the two central characters?

JM: Yes, or the double nature of reality, or the dramatic division one sees on the spot, of island and mainland.

Q: What island is it?

JM: It's the island of Poros, a small island near Athens.

Q: With regard to your primary art, what do you see as your distinctiveness as a poet?

JM: I haven't thought very much about it. I feel that I belong to a certain group of poets, those who follow formal conventions to a greater or lesser degree and those who at the very worst go in for wordplay, double meanings and that sort of thing.

Q: Do you think of yourself as supporting formal art in a period when that sort of thing is not particularly valued?

JM: I don't think I have very much choice. It's simply the way that I know how to write. Even when I sort of slyly thought of changing to irregular line lengths I always found some way to justify them, by secret scanning and rhyme.

Q: James Dickey, I remember, complained in connection with one of your early books of poems that you explained too much to the reader. Is that something that you were conscious of doing and does it seem to you a suitable comment?

JM: I found that comment very helpful. There was nothing much I could really do about it, but it did help me to try to be more relaxed.

Q: Someone has remarked that the self is the last remaining universal. Would that be close to your view of the subject matter of poetry?

JM: Not really. The self is extremely ambiguous. There are so many different selves.

Q: You don't seem to spend much time talking about world events or social history or to go in much for social commentary.

JM: What I mean by the outside world are the things we see, our experiences, those around us, our friends, strangers. You can render yourself, see yourself reflected by these people and things so that you wouldn't know you had a self except through these surroundings. I see myself as not much of a social commentator. I see a certain kind of American life facing me, but there is only so much that I can write about.

Q: Do you feel a difference in your handling of ideas between your early and your very recent work? In particular, have you become more comfortable with ideas in your more recent work?

JM: Maybe. I still shy away from ideas, at least on principle. In reviewing my work recently for a selected edition I was surprised to see how many important ideas I had touched upon, unbeknownst to myself. I began reading and it was quite astonishing that I, or the angels, or whoever were all by and large concerned with the things that men have been concerned about since the birth of philosophy.

Q: Somewhere you quote T. S. Eliot to the effect that Henry James had a mind which "no idea violates." This struck me as compatible with your viewpoint.

JM: Yes, it is more or less how I feel. I like also very much Ponge's remark that ideas solicit only our approval, that the least we can do is to accept them.

Q: Who is "Charles," that mysterious personage who appears in the early and middle poems?

JM: I think he was a kind of projection of myself, slightly more mature, slightly more even-tempered, slightly more worldly at least than I was when I was writing those poems. Occasionally he would crop up again at a time when I was more or less his equal. He was a side of myself that I wanted to express and perhaps even develop.

Q: *Water Street* was clearly a turning point of some sort for you.

JM: It was partly becoming a little looser in terms of form. In "An Urban Convalescence" I first hit upon this sense of the self-reflexive side of the poem—that you can break up the argument in a very fruitful way. This is probably something learned from working in the theater where you write a line and you can have someone else contradict it. But you can also incorporate that within yourself as poet and stop a certain train of thought and break into something new or criticize what you've done up to that moment.

Q: One of the most celebrated of your middle-period poems is "From the Cupola." Could you comment on the significance of the mysterious Eros in the poem who writes anonymous letters?

JM: Yes, I think that a stranger who knows one very well is practically a metaphor for God. When you put that together with what Borges said—"to love is to found a religion with a fallible God"—well, no wonder Eros became an easy analogy.

Q: Waterfalls seem to play quite a symbolic part in your work, in your poems about the Southwest in particular.

JM: The waterfalls I write about usually have a space behind them, and probably this has to do with some inmost reality or some inmost image underneath the rush of experience.

Q: Would you comment on the trilogy in relation to your earlier work?

JM: The form was not foreseeable. I really thought "Ephraim" was all I would ever do on the subject. Successive volumes came about in part through a lucky connection with the appearance of the Ouija board. It provided the alphabet, the numerals, and the "Yes" and "No" that formed the basis for the structure of the trilogy. I suppose that no early poem ever depended that much or at least at such length on some exterior icon like the arrangements of letters on a board.

Q: How literally are you into spiritualism?

JM: As Yeats said, when you are caught up in it you believe it wholeheartedly; when you cool off you see it as a stylization of various things in your experience or in the world's experience.

Q: How much of the trilogy stems from your sessions as opposed to the time it took to write the poem?

JM: In the case of *Mirabell* and *Scripts for the Pageant,* for example, allowing for a few things that were cut out or rephrased for symmetrical purposes, it's all pretty much verbatim. I haven't falsified anything to speak of, or perhaps five percent at the most.

Q: Was there really a novel which preceded the poem?

JM: Yes. I started writing a novel to be set in New Mexico. It didn't seem to me that I could ever use this "Ephraim" material in a poem because it was so extensive. So I made a stab at writing a novel. I didn't get more than forty or fifty pages done before I lost it. They were very halfhearted pages to begin with; then I thought, well, if it's not to be done as fiction I should try and do a kind of Castaneda book, making it sound as if it had all happened. It became more and more important to me, though, and it must have been from one of those pages that I stopped and took a second look and saw it dissolving into verse before my eyes. I was just pencil-marking off lines; they were practically written in that form. That would have been the first page of "Ephraim," eventually.

Q: In connection with "Ephraim," is a belief in reincarnation something you actually hold or is it a metaphorical thing?

JM: Yes and no. I simply couldn't say. I think it's a very fruitful belief to have. I think it does wonders in a way for the way you live. I can see also that it might not do wonders, that you would say: oh well, born again, and this life doesn't really matter, but I always believed Proust when he spoke about it, saying it seems as if we come into this world with obligations formed in another one. I think it helped him to imagine that.

Q: Is Proust the origin of your thinking about reincarnation?

JM: Well, probably in a sense he is. But I don't think that I ever took it literally until we began talking to Ephraim on the board.

Q: Am I right that somehow the motif of metamorphosis dominates the trilogy? This would be compatible with the motif of reincarnation.

JM: Yes—and I think that's a very good point if you also include the way the revelations revised themselves—something that seemed to be the last word on the subject at one level is then explained differently at another.

Q: Is that ascending understanding which the reader has as he goes through the three books a rough parallel for Dante's ascent?

JM: It might be; again, it's nothing that I planned. I might have hoped it would turn out to be something like that.

Q: In connection with the role which Maya Deren has in "Ephraim" and particularly, I suppose, the allusions to her book *Divine Horsemen*, one feels that you are interested in enriching the myth-starved culture which you see around you.

JM: I certainly feel it is myth-starved. I am first of all enriching myself with some of these attitudes and possibilities and if other people are hungry for them, fine.

Q: What is the role of the atom in the trilogy?

JM: Well, I think the atom is the more or less original vision of life. It seems to me that when Mirabell speaks of Dante's atomic vision he is referring specifically to the whirling point of light that Dante sees in the *Paradiso*, which is shelled with concentric spheres somehow going at different speeds. I don't know what it could be except a vision of the atom. Dante laboriously might explain it in some other way, but it is what people see when they have this experience.

Q: What do you see as the result of the interfusing of scientific imagery and a more classical mythic and literary imagery? Is this an attempt to draw science into the whole sort of visionary landscape which you have constructed?

JM: I think science is a visionary landscape in the twentieth century and was even in the nineteenth. If as you say we are myth-starved, we certainly are starved for the scientific myths. These are constantly bursting out in front of us in fascinating forms, and I suppose the point would be to show or to somehow open the possibility that the classical myths and the scientific myths are really one and the same. They're talking about the same things in different ways. You don't have to know very much about electricity to think of Hermes and Zeus and the powers that were under their control. These are all spoken of now in scientific language.

Q: What about technology, which figures in the trilogy? You go into things like cloning, genetic engineering, and population control. Of course, it is only at one level in the trilogy that these things are stressed, I suppose more in *Mirabell* than elsewhere.

JM: Probably, but I think the angels are certainly all in favor of reducing the population by one means or another. I don't know what to say about these subjects; I think they're very grave problems.

Q: Certainly the talk about population control in the trilogy throws your earlier poetic motif of childlessness into a new light.

JM: It does, yet one reason I like the epilogue is because up until then there's the feeling that the fewer children there are the better, but in the epilogue we have Robert Morse reborn, and the ceremonies that take place, both in the schoolroom and in the womb in the few days just before his birth. There is this flood of tenderness from the angels and Queen Mum toward this little child born in Minnesota. That made me breathe a bit easier when it came.

Q: Is number in *Mirabell* a sort of neutral meeting place between science and art?

JM: What a good idea. I think that makes perfect sense. Again it's nothing I have ever studied very much, but I think everyone has a fascination with it. The old-fashioned word for poetry *was* "numbers."

Q: The tone of your trilogy suggests that you wanted a divine comedy in an even fuller sense than Dante.

JM: Well, it seemed to me indispensable to keep it as light as possible. One didn't want anything too sober, too cowed.

Q: In your Edenic world I gather that when we get centaurs in one book and unicorns in another we are getting essentially a shift in the angle of vision more than anything?

JM: I suppose, yes. I haven't thought that out very much, but I noted in puzzlement that this creature's shape was changing.

Q: *Mirabell* has a very purgatorial feeling about it.

JM: Well, it's purgatory to read certainly and it was purgatory to arrange on the page and to make it as trimmed down as I possibly could. I must have cut out about two-fifths of the entire transcript. Occasionally there would be every reason to cut simply because we hadn't understood it.

Q: Could you comment on the symbol of Venice in "Ephraim" and also at the end of *Scripts*?

JM: I think it's the most magical city in the world. I don't think it's a symbol. It's just a wonderful place.

Q: An earthly paradise?

JM: Yes.

Q: Gabriel seems the central character in *Scripts*. When I was reading the poem, I heard quoted in connection with the Picasso show in New York Picasso's statement that a painting is the "sum of destructions" and I wondered if that was relevant to Gabriel's vision of things—the breaking down of things in order to reorder them.

JM: I remember that phrase of Picasso's, and I always liked it, but I don't much connect with it. I agree that Gabriel is the most interesting of the angelic teachers. I think it's because his secret takes the longest to come to the surface. He's the most inward and brooding and, in a way, conscientious, the one who cares most.

Q: The most complex?

JM: Yes.

Q: On the one hand the material and immaterial seem to be a continuum in the trilogy and on the other hand there are moments when the soul is described as being utterly destroyed by radiation.

JM: The word "soul" means a couple of things in the poem: first of all it means the individual soul in any given incarnation as opposed to the

Geist of the spirit that would persist from life to life so that you can speak of a discarded life or a past life as a soul that is no longer available to you. But I think Mirabell meant literally when he talks about Hiroshima that even that lasting soul was put beyond any use. As when Hitler appears, his soul still has a kind of selfhood, but will no longer have access to life, will no longer be used for another life on earth, which is almost tantamount to being destroyed.

Q: Do you regard yourself in the light of the trilogy as a Platonist?

JM: Yes, I suppose I am. It's again nothing I would have thought until the trilogy had been written. I have not read that much philosophy.

Q: With respect to the metamorphoses that go on and those that are contemplated—Maria into tree and Auden into rock—does this express a kind of egalitarianism as far as being is concerned?

JM: I think what's significant is that consciousness doesn't stop with human beings. There is probably a great untapped mind, if you can call it that, in the natural world itself. As Mirabell says when Maria goes into the tree world and Wystan into the mineral, they will increase the volume of mind in those particular kingdoms.

AN INTERVIEW
WITH J. D. McCLATCHY

Q: You've left your house in Athens for good now, right?

JM: It looks that way.

Q: And your original decision to settle there—was that just an accumulation of accidents?

JM: Oh, there's no accident. I went first to Greece to visit Kimon Friar in 1950. Between then and 1959, when I went back with David, we'd gone to a great number of other places too—to the Orient and, either together or separately, all over Europe, except Greece. And suddenly here was a place—I can't tell you how much we liked it. We liked Stonington, too, but didn't want to stay there all year round. It had slowly dawned on us, as it continues to dawn on young people in Stonington, that it's a community of older people by and large. Nearly all our friends were five to *fifty* years older than we were. And in Greece we began seeing, for a change, people our own age, or younger.

Q: I presume you came to Stonington to get away from New York. If, by analogy, you went to Athens to get away from things in America, what was it you found there?

JM: Things that have mostly disappeared, I'm afraid. The dazzling air, the drowsy waterfronts. Our own ignorance, even: a language we didn't

The Paris Review, Summer 1982.

understand two words of at first. That *was* a holiday! You could imagine that others were saying extraordinarily fascinating things—the point was to invent, if not what they were saying, at least its implications, its overtones. Also, in those days foreign tourists were both rare and welcome, and the delighted surprise with which the Greeks acknowledged our ability to put two words together, you know, was irresistible.

Q: What sort of people did you find yourselves falling in with? Other Americans?

JM: No, certainly not. In fact, even Greeks who spoke English or French had to be extremely charming for us to want to see them more than once. We wanted to learn Greek and we also wanted to learn *Greece*, and the turn of mind that made a Greek.

Q: It can't be accidental, then, that your leaving Greece coincides with the completion of your trilogy—

JM: Probably not. A coincidence over which I had no control was that, within a year of my finishing the trilogy, David had come to see that Athens was no longer a livable place. We'd both seen this day coming, I'm afraid, but for one reason or another neither of us wanted to believe his eyes. If he'd stayed on, I'd still be going back and forth. Maria might have been another reason for staying. Even after her death—or especially after her death, as her role in the poem grew clearer—I couldn't have faced, right away, cutting ourselves off from the friends we'd had in common, friends also in their own right, who made all the difference.

Q: That's Maria Mitsotáki? Was she really—

JM: Everything I say she was in the trilogy? Oh yes, and more. Her father had indeed been prime minister, three times, I think—but under which king? Constantine I or George II, or both? I'm vague about things like that. I'm vague, too, about her husband, who died long before our time. They'd lived in South Africa, in London. . . . Maria went home for a visit and was stranded in Athens during the whole German occupation. Horrible stories—and wonderful ones: dashing young cousins in the underground, hidden for weeks in bedroom closets. Literary men fell in love with her, quite understandably—aside from being an enchantment to look at, she *never missed a thing you said.*

Q: Your trilogy attests to a warm, intimate relationship with Maria Mitsotáki and W. H. Auden. Did working on the poem *change* your feelings about them?

JM: In a way, yes. The friendships, which had been merely "real" on earth—subject to interruption, mutual convenience, states of health, like events that have to be scheduled "weather permitting"—became ideal. Nothing was hazed over by reticence or put off by a cold snap. Whenever we needed them, there they were; and a large part of *that* wonder was to feel how deeply they needed *us*. I can't pretend to have known Wystan terribly well in *this* world. He liked me, I think, and approved of my work, and liked the reassurance of David's and my being in Athens to stand by Chester Kallman when emergencies arose. But he was twenty years older and had been famous while I was still in boarding school, and—well, it took the poem, and the almost jubilant youthfulness he recovers after death, to get me over my shyness. With Maria it was different. In the years we knew her she saw very few people, but we were part of that happy few. Many of her old friends whom she no longer saw couldn't imagine what had come over her—"She's given us up for those *Americans*!" We simply adored her. It seemed like the perfection of intimacy, light, airy, without confessions or possessiveness—yet one would have to be Jung or Dante to foresee her role in the poem.

Q: You hadn't even an inkling of that role when you began the poem?

JM: Oh, no. It's true, I began "Ephraim" within days of hearing that she'd died—and felt, I suppose, enough of a coincidence to list her among the characters. There's only one mention of her in the whole "Book of Ephraim," yet I kept her in, and look what happened! The cassia shrub on the terrace—how could the poem have ended without it? I couldn't bring *it* home to America, though I did the next best thing and sneaked some seedpods through customs. They've given rise to that rather promising affair out there on the deck.

Q: Panning the Ouija board transcripts for poetic gold—*that* must have been a daunting project. How did you go about it?

JM: The problem changed from volume to volume. With "Ephraim," many of the transcripts I had made from Ouija board sessions had vanished, or hadn't been saved. So I mainly used whatever came to hand, except for the high points which I'd copied out over the years into a special notebook. Those years—time itself—did my winnowing for me. With *Mirabell* it was, to put it mildly, harder. The transcript was enormous. What you see in the poem might be half, or two-fifths, of the original. Most of the cuts were repetitions: things said a second or third time, in new ways often, to make sure we'd understood. Or further, unnecessary illustrations of a point. I haven't looked at them for several years now, and can only hope that nothing too vital got left out. Getting it onto the page seemed really beyond me at first, perhaps because I'd begun imagining a poem the same length as "Ephraim." By the time the fourteen-syllable line occurred to me (that exchange with Wystan is largely contrived), I'd also decided where to divide it into books, so it all got under way at last.

With *Scripts*, there was no shaping to be done. Except for the minutest changes and deciding about line breaks and so forth, the lessons you see on the page appear just as we took them down. The doggerel at the fêtes, everything. In between the lessons—our chats with Wystan or Robert Morse or Uni, the trilogy's resident unicorn—I still felt free to pick and choose; but even there, the design of the book just swept me along.

Q: You don't feel that too much was sacrificed for the sake of shapeliness?

JM: If so, perhaps no accident? I came upon the pages of one of our very earliest evenings with Ephraim. He's giving us a lecture about the senses: POLISH THE WINDOWS OF YOUR EYES, etc., each sense in turn. That obviously prefigures, by over twenty years, one of the themes crucial to volume 3—but isn't it nicer and less daunting somehow to have it emerge casually, without pedantry?

Then there were things outside the transcript—things in "life" that kept staring me in the face, only I couldn't see them, as if I'd been hypnotized, until the danger was past. Only this year I was in my study, playing the perhaps ten thousandth game of Patience since beginning "Ephraim." I'm using my old, nearly effaced Greek cards with their strange neoclassical royalties, and I do a little superstitious trick when I'm through. I reassemble the deck so that the Queen of Hearts is at the bottom, facing up. Now on those old-style Greek cards the queens are all marked K, for Kyria—Lady. It's what George Cotzias calls Mother Nature, and I'd simply never made the connection. Furthermore, the kings are all marked B, for Basileus. God B of Hearts? "You're nothing but a pack of cards!" You can be sure I'd have dragged all that in if I'd thought of it in time. Plus another clever but expendable allusion to the graveyard scene of the *Rake,* where Tom calls upon the Queen of Hearts and is saved. Driven out of his wits, but saved.

Other things that in retrospect seem indispensable came to hand just when they were needed, as if by magic. Stephen Yenser explaining the Golden Section when I was halfway through "Ephraim." Marilyn Lavin telling me about the X-rayed Giorgione—I'd already written V and W— and hunting up the relevant article. Stephen Orgel's book on the masque, which he sent me not a moment too soon. A friend of my nephew's, Michael Beard, writing me a letter on the metaphysical implications of Arabic calligraphy. A month or so later I would simply need to versify some of his phrases in order to make that little lyric about the Bismillah formula. Then Alfred Corn's joke about E—Ephraim—equalling any emcee squared. I felt like a perfect magpie.

Q: What do the Ouija transcripts look like?

JM: Like first-grade compositions. Drunken lines of capitals lurching across the page, gibberish until they're divided into words and sentences. It depends on the pace. Sometimes the powers take pity on us and slow down.

Q: The Ouija board, now. I gather you use a homemade one, but that doesn't exactly help me to imagine it or its workings. An overturned teacup is your pointer?

JM: Yes. The commercial boards come with a funny see-through planchette on legs. I find them too cramped. Besides, it's so easy to make your own—just write out the alphabet and the numbers and your YES and NO (punctuation marks too, if you're going all out) on a big sheet of cardboard. Or use brown paper—it travels better. On our Grand Tour, whenever we felt lonely in the hotel room, David and I could just unfold our instant company. He puts his right hand lightly on the cup, I put my left, leaving the right free to transcribe, and away we go. We get, oh, five hundred to six hundred words an hour. Better than gasoline.

Q: What *is* your fuel, would you say? With all the other disciplines available to a poet, why this one?

JM: Well, don't you think there comes a time when everyone, not just a poet, wants to get beyond the self? To reach, if you like, the "god" within you? The board, in however clumsy or absurd a way, allows for precisely that. Or if it's still *yourself* that you're drawing upon, then that self is much stranger and freer and more farseeing than the one you thought you knew. Of course there are disciplines with grander pedigrees and similar goals. The board happens to be ours. I've stopped, by the way, recommending it to inquisitive friends.

Q: When did you start using a Ouija board?

JM: Frederick Buechner gave me one as a birthday present in 1953. As I recall, we sat down then and there to try it, and got a touching little story from a fairly simple soul—that engineer "dead of cholera in Cairo," who'd met Goethe. I used it in the first thing I ever wrote about the Ouija board (a poem called "Voices from the Other World"), although by that time the *experiences* behind this poem were mine and David's. We started in the summer of 1955. But the spirit *we* contacted—Ephraim—was anything but simple. So much so that for a long time I felt that the material he dictated really couldn't be used—then or perhaps ever. I felt it would be like cheating, or plagiarizing from some unidentifiable source. Oh, I put a few snippets of it into *The Seraglio,* but that was just a novel, and didn't count. Twenty years later, though, I was yet again trying to tell the whole story as fiction, through a set of characters bearing little resemblance to David or me. I'd got about fifty pages done, hating every bit of it. I'm not a novelist, and never was. No accident, then, that I simply "forgot" the manuscript in a taxi in Atlanta and never recovered it—well, all that's described in "The Book of Ephraim." But I went on, I didn't take the hint. I put together all the drafts and notes for those lost pages and proceeded to forget *these* in a hotel room in Frankfurt! By now I was down to just two pages of an opening draft. As I sat glaring at them, the prose began to dissolve into verse. I marked the line breaks with a pencil, fiddled a bit, typed it up, and showed the two versions to a friend who said quite firmly, "You must never write prose again." At that point "The Book of Ephraim" crystallized, and got written without any particular trouble.

Q: Throughout the trilogy you have many "voices"—Wallace Stevens, Gertrude Stein, Pythagoras, Nefertiti. How does this work? Do they simply break in, or do you ask specifically for them?

JM: Either way. Most of the time, we never knew what to expect. Last summer, for instance, we were about to sit down at the board—no, I was already in my chair—when David called from the kitchen. He can never keep abreast of the rising postal rates, and wanted to know which stamp to put on his letter. I called back, "Put on an Edna St. Vincent Millay"—I'd bought a sheet of her commemoratives just that week. And when we started at the board, there she was. Very embarrassing on both sides, as it dawned on the poor creature that we hadn't meant to talk to *her* at all.

Q: Does what Auden tells you via the Ouija board remind you of him? Are there distinctive phrases or sentiments that could only be his?

JM: Some of his best-known sentiments get revised—his Christian views, for instance—but the turns of phrase sound very like him, to my ears. Remember, though, that we never knew each other well, not in *this* world.

Q: Would the Ouija board be your instrument—like a keyboard on which a musician composes or improvises?

JM: Not a bit! If anything, the keyboard was us. And our one obligation, at any given session, was to be as "well tempered" as possible.

Q: So the Ouija board is by no means a mnemonic device—it is not something to get you going.

JM: No. At least, not something to start me *writing*. In other ways, evidently, it did start us "going"—thinking, puzzling, resisting, testing the messages against everything we knew or thought possible.

Q: What is David's function when you use the Ouija board?

JM: That's a good question. According to Mirabell, David is the subconscious shaper of the message itself, the "Hand," as they call him. Of the two of us, he's the spokesman for human nature, while I'm the "Scribe," the one in whose words and images the message gets expressed. This would be a fairly rough distinction, but enough to show that the transcripts as they stand could never have come into being without him. I wonder if the trilogy shouldn't have been signed with both our names—or simply "by DJ, as told to JM"?

Q: Could not the "they" who move the teacup around the board be considered the authors of the poems?

JM: Well, yes and no. As "they" keep saying throughout, language is the human medium. It doesn't exist—except perhaps as vast mathematical or chemical formulas—in that realm of, oh, cosmic forces, elemental processes, which *we* then personify, or tame if you like, through the imagination. So, in a sense, all these figures are our creation, or mankind's. The powers they represent are real—as, say, gravity is "real"—but they'd be invisible, inconceivable, if they'd never passed through our heads and clothed themselves out of the costume box they found there. *How* they appear depends on us, on the imaginer, and would have to vary wildly from culture to culture, or even temperament to temperament. A process that Einstein could entertain as a formula might be described by an African witch doctor as a crocodile. What's tiresome is when people exclusively insist on the forms they've imagined. Those powers don't need churches in order to be sacred. What they do need are fresh ways of being seen.

Q: Does the idea of the Ouija board ever embarrass you—I mean that you have this curious collaborator?

JM: From what I've just said, you see how pompous I can get. The mechanics of the board—this absurd, flimsy contraption, creaking along—serves wonderfully as a hedge against inflation. I think it does embarrass the sort of reader who can't bear to face the random or trivial elements that coalesce, among others, to produce an "elevated" thought. That doesn't bother me *at all*.

Q: Does the Ouija board ever manifest maniacal tendencies? Do you ever feel yourself lost in its grip?

JM: Thanks perhaps to a certain ongoing resistance, we seem to have held our own. We kept it as a parlor game for the first twenty years. Those early voices in *Mirabell* gave us, I admit, a nasty turn. Looking back, though, I've the sense that we *agreed* to let them take us over, for the sake of the poem. Poems can do that, even when you think you're writing them all by yourself. Oh, we've been scared at times. A friend who sat with us at the board just once went on to have a pretty awful experience with some people out in Detroit. She was told to go west, and to sail on a certain freighter on a certain day, and the name of the island where she'd meet her great-grandmother reincarnated as a Polynesian teenager who would guide her to a mountain cave where in turn an old man . . . and so forth. Luckily she collapsed before she ever made it to California. I don't believe she was being manipulated by the other people. The experience sounds genuine. But she didn't have the strength to use it properly—whatever I mean by that! It would seem that David and I *have* that strength; or else, that we've been handled with kid gloves. A number of friends have been scared *for* us over the years. One of them took me to a Trappist monastery to talk to one of the more literary priests. It was a lovely couple of hours. I read from some of the transcripts, filling in as much as I could of the background. Afterward, the priest admitted that they'd all been warned in seminary against these devilish devices, but that, frankly, I'd read nothing to him that he didn't believe himself. I suspect a lot of people use the board to guide them through life—"What's next week's winning lottery number?"—and get the answers they deserve. Our voices are often very illuminating when we bring up a dilemma or a symptom, but they never *tell* us what to do. At most they suggest the possibilities, the various consequences. Now that I think of it, our friend might have misread a hint for a command, or a metaphorical itinerary of self-discovery for a real trip to Hawaii.

Q: What about more conventional aids to inspiration—drugs? drink?

JM: Liquor, in my parents' world, was always your reward at the end of a hard day—or an easy day, for that matter—and I like to observe that old family tradition. But I've never drunk for inspiration. Quite the contrary—it's like the wet sponge on the blackboard. I do now and then take a puff of grass, or a crumb of Alice Toklas fudge, when I've reached the last drafts of a poem. That's when you need X-ray eyes to see what you've done, and the grass helps. Some nice touches can fall into place.

Q: In hindsight, do you have any general feelings about the occult, about the *use* of the occult in poetry?

JM: I've never much liked hearing about it. Usually the people who write about it have such dreadful style. Yeats is almost the only exception I can think of. The first thing to do is to get rid of that awful vocabulary. It's almost acceptable once it's purged of all those fancy words—"auras" and "astral bodies."

Q: Has it been a kind of displaced religion for you? I take it you *have* a religious streak somewhere in you.

JM: Oh, that's a very good phrase for it—"displaced religion." I never felt at home with the "pastoral" Episcopalianism I was handed. Unctuous mouthings of scripture, a system that like the courtier-shepherds and milkmaids at the Petit Trianon seemed almost willfully deluded, given the state of the world and the fears and fantasies already raging in my little head. Mademoiselle's Catholicism corresponded more to these. She taught me the Ave Maria—without which the Lord's Prayer calls up the image of dry bread in a motherless reformatory. Even her Jesus, next to the Protestant one, was all blood and magic—the face on Veronica's napkin, the ghastly little Sacred Heart hanging above her bed, like something out of a boy's book about Aztec sacrifice, or something the gardener pulled out of the earth. These images *connected*. I mean, we used napkins the size of Veronica's at every meal. As Shaw reminds us, Christ wasn't out to proselytize. He said that God was in each of us, a spark of pure potential. He held no special brief for the Family. All very sensible, but I'm afraid I've long since thrown out the baby with the churchly bathwater. The need, as you say, remained. I never cared for the pose of the atheist—though the angels came round to that, you know, in their way, insisting on man as master of his own destiny.

Q: You don't describe yourself as having been a very good student, and still seem a bit self-conscious as an "intellectual."

JM: Ummmh . . .

Q: No accident, then, that the trilogy's caps are all unrelieved meaning? A case of the return of the repressed?

JM: You're probably exactly right there, at least where the "Grand Design" is concerned. Also in passages—like Mirabell on Culture or Technology—where the proliferation of crisp ideas sounds almost like a Shaw preface. Not at all the kind of page I could turn out by myself. On the other hand, a lot of what we're loosely calling "meaning" turns out, on inspection, to be metaphor, which leads one back toward language: wordplay, etymology, the "wholly human instrument" (as Wystan says) I'd used and trusted—like every poet, wouldn't you say?—to ground the lightning of ideas. We could say that the uppercase represented a *range* of metaphor, a depth of meaning, that hadn't been available to me in earlier poems. Victor Hugo described his voices as his own conscious powers multiplied by five, and *he* was probably exactly right there, too.

Q: Though your trilogy takes up the ultimate question of origins and destiny, you are not a poet—like Yeats or Auden or Lowell—who has taken on political issues in your work. Or is that very avoidance itself a kind of "stand"?

JM: The lobbies? The candidates' rhetoric—our "commitments abroad"? The shah as Helen of Troy launching a thousand missile carriers? One whiff of all that, and I turn purple and start kicking my cradle.

I like the idea of nations, actually, and even more those pockets of genuine strangeness within nations. Yet those are being emptied, turned inside out, made to conform—in the interest of what? The friendly American smile we're told to wear in our passport photos? Oh, it's not just in America. You can go to an outdoor concert in Athens—in that brown, poisonous air the government isn't strong enough to do anything about—and there are the president and the prime minister in their natty suits, surrounded by flashbulbs, hugging and patting each other as if they hadn't met for months. God have mercy on whoever's meant to be impressed by that. Of course I can't conceive of anyone *choosing* public life, unless from some unspeakable hidden motive.

Q: What newspapers do you read?

JM: In Europe the Paris *Herald*—I get very American over there, and it's so concise. Here, I never learned how to read a paper. My first year away at school, I watched my classmates, some of them littler than I was, frowning over the war news or the financial page. They already knew how! I realized then and there I couldn't hope to catch up. I told this to Marianne Moore before introducing her at her Amherst reading in 1956. She looked rather taken aback, as I did myself, a half hour later, when in the middle of a poem she was reading—a poem I thought I knew—I heard my name. "Now Mr. Merrill," she was saying, "tells me he doesn't read a newspaper. That's hard for me to understand. The things one would miss! Why, only last week I read that our U.S. Customs Bureau was collecting all the egret and bird-of-paradise feathers we'd confiscated during the twenties and thirties—collecting them and sending them off to Nepal, where they're *needed*. . . ." And then she went right on with her poem.

Q: I'll have to interrupt. Why were those feathers needed in Nepal?

JM: Oh, headdresses, regalia . . . *you* must remember—the papers were full of it!

But let's be serious for a moment. If our angels are right, every leader—president or terrorist—is responsible for keeping his ranks thinned out. Good politics would therefore encourage death in one form or another—if not actual, organized bloodshed, then the legalization of abortion or, heaven forbid, the various chemical or technological atrocities. Only this last strikes me as truly immoral, perhaps because it's a threat that hadn't existed before my own lifetime. I take it personally. That bit in "The Broken Home"—"Father Time and Mother Earth, / A marriage on the rocks"—isn't meant as a joke. History in our time *has* cut loose, *has* broken faith with Nature. But poems, even those of the most savage incandescence, can't deal frontally with such huge, urgent subjects without sounding grumpy or dated when they should still be in their prime. So my parents' divorce dramatized on a human scale a subject that couldn't have been handled otherwise. Which is what a "poetic" turn of mind allows for. You don't see eternity *except* in the grain of sand, or history except at the family dinner table.

Q: You had a very privileged childhood, in the normal sense of "privileged"—wealth, advantages. But the privilege also of being able to turn the pain of that childhood into art. How do you look back on it now?

JM: Perhaps turning it into art came naturally. . . . I mean, it's hard to speak of a child having a sense of reality or unreality, because after all, what are his criteria? It strikes me now maybe that during much of my childhood I found it difficult to *believe* in the way my parents lived. They seemed so utterly taken up with engagements, obligations, ceremonies— every child must feel that, to some extent, about the grown-ups in his life. The excitement, the emotional quickening *I* felt in those years came usually through animals or nature, or through the servants in the house— Colette knew all about that—whose lives seemed by contrast to make such perfect *sense*. The gardeners had their hands in the earth. The cook was dredging things with flour, making pies. My father was merely making money, while my mother wrote names on place-cards, planned menus, and did her needlepoint. Her masterpiece—not the imaginary fire screen I describe in the poem—depicted the facade of the Southampton house. I could see how stylized it was. The designer had put these peculiar flowers all over the front lawn, and a stereotyped old black servant on either side. Once in a while my mother would let me complete a stitch. It fascinated me. It had nothing really to do with the world, yet somehow. . . . Was it the world becoming art?

Q: The picture your poems paint of yourself as a child is of someone who's bored. Were you?

JM: We shouldn't exaggerate. There were things I enjoyed enormously, like fishing—something responding and resisting from deep,

deep down. It's true, sometimes I must have been extremely bored, though never inactive. My mother remembers asking me, when I was five or six, what I wanted to do when I was grown up. Didn't I want, she asked, to go downtown and work in Daddy's office? "Oh no," I said, "I'll be too tired by then." Because, you see, everything was arranged: to so-and-so's house to play, the beach for lunch, a tennis lesson. As we know, the life of leisure doesn't give us a moment's rest. I didn't care for the games or the playmates. I don't recall there being anyone I really liked, my own age, until I went away to school.

Q: There may be links between that boredom and an impulse to write, to make up a life of your own. I suppose you were a great reader as a child?

JM: [. . .] Generally I read what I was told to read, not always liking it. My mother gave me *Mrs. Wiggs of the Cabbage Patch* and I remember throwing it out the window. By then I was . . . eight? A couple of years later I read *Gone with the Wind*. No one told me there were any other novels, *grown-up* novels. I must have read it six or seven times in succession; I thought it was one of a kind. As for *good* literature—one got a bit of it at school, but not at home.

Q: You began writing at that age too?

JM: I had written at least one poem when I was seven or eight. It was a poem about going with the Irish setter into my mother's room—an episode that ended up in "The Broken Home." The Irish setter *was* named Michael and I think the poem began: "One day while she lay sleeping, / Michael and I went peeping." My first publication was in the *St. Nicholas Magazine*, a quatrain: "Pushing slowly every day / Autumn finally makes its way. / Now when the days are cool, / We children go to school." They wanted a drawing to illustrate your verses. And that gave me my first *severe* aesthetic lesson, because when the poem and sketch were printed—the sketch showed a little boy on the crest of a hill heading for a schoolhouse far below—I saw to my consternation that, although I'd drawn the windows of the schoolhouse very carefully with a ruler, the editors had made them crooked, as befitted a child's drawing. Of course they were right. But the lesson sank in: one must act one's age and give people what they expect.

Q: A ballroom, empty of all but ghostly presences, is an image, or *scene* of instruction, that recurs in key poems during your career. I'm thinking of "A Tenancy" in *Water Street,* "The Broken Home" in *Nights and Days,* the epilogue to the trilogy. It is a haunting image, and seems a haunted one as well. What associations and significance does that room have for you?

JM: The original, the primal ballroom—in Southampton—would have made even a grown-up gasp. My brother once heard a Mrs. Jaeckel say, "Stanford White put his *heart* into this room." Four families could have lived in it. Two pianos *did,* and an organ, with pipes that covered the whole upper half of a wall, and a huge spiral column of gilded wood in each corner. And a monster stone fireplace with a buffalo head above it. At night it was often dark; people drank before dinner in the library. So that, after being sent to bed, I'd have to make my way through the ballroom in order to get upstairs. Once I didn't—I sat clutching my knees on one of the window seats, hidden by the twenty-foot-high red damask curtain, for hours it seemed, listening to my name being called throughout the house. Once I was allowed to stay up, before a party, long enough to see the chandeliers lit—hundreds of candles. It must have answered beautifully to my father's Gatsby side. It's a room I remember *him* in, not my mother. He took me aside there, one evening, to warn me—with tears in his eyes—against the drink in his hand. We didn't *call* it the ballroom—it was the music room. Some afternoons my grandmother played the organ, rather shyly. One morning a houseguest, a woman who later gave me piano lessons in New York, played through the whole score of *Pagliacci* for me, singing and explaining. That was my first "opera." Looking back, even going back to visit while my father still had that house, I could see how much grander the room was than any of the uses we'd put it to, so maybe the ghostly presences appeared in order to make up for a thousand unrealized possibilities. That same sense probably accounts for my "redecoration" in the epilogue—making the room conform to an ideal much sunnier, much more silvery, that I began to trust only as an adult, while keeping carefully out of my mind (until that passage had been written) the story of how Cronus cuts off the scrotum, or "ballroom," of his father Uranus and throws it into the sea, where it begins to foam and shine, and the goddess of Love and Beauty is born.

Q: As a young poet starting out in the fifties, what did you look forward to? What did you imagine yourself writing in, say, 1975?

JM: I was a perhaps fairly typical mixture of aspiration and diffidence. Certainly I could never see beyond the poem I was at work on. And since weeks or months could go by between poems, I tried to make each one "last" as long as possible, to let its meanings ever so slowly rise to the surface I peered into—enchanted and a touch bored. I looked forward, not without apprehension, to a lifetime of this.

Q: How would you now characterize the author of *The Black Swan*?

JM: This will contradict my last answer about "starting out in the fifties." By then I'd come to see what hard work it was, writing a poem. But *The Black Swan*—those poems written in 1945 and 1946 had simply bubbled up. Each took an afternoon, a day or two at most. Their author had been recently dazzled by all kinds of things whose existence he'd never suspected, poets he'd never read before, like Stevens or Crane; techniques and forms that could be recovered or reinvented from the past without their having to sound old-fashioned, thanks to any number of stylish "modern" touches like slant rhyme or surrealist imagery or some tentative approach to the conversational ("Love, keep your eyes peeled"). There were effects in Stevens, in the "Notes," which I read before anything else—his great ease in combining abstract words with gaudy visual or sound effects: "That alien, point-blank, green and actual Guatemala," or those "angular anonymids" in their blue and yellow stream. You didn't have to be exclusively decorative *or* in deadly earnest. You could be grand *and* playful. The astringent abstract word was always there to bring your little impressionist picture to its senses.

Q: But he—that is, the author of *The Black Swan*—is someone you now see as a kind of happy emulation of literary models?

JM: No, not a bit. It seems to me, reading those poems over—and I've begun to rework a number of them—that the only limitation imposed upon them was my own youth and limited skill; whereas looking back on the poems in *The Country of a Thousand Years of Peace*, it seems to me that each of at least the shorter ones bites off much less than those early lyrics did. They seem the product of a more competent, but in a way smaller, spirit. Returning to those early poems *now*, obviously in the light of the completed trilogy, I've had to marvel a bit at the resemblances. It's as though after a long lapse or, as you put it, displacement of faith, I'd finally, with the trilogy, reentered the church of those original themes. The colors, the elements, the magical emblems: they were the first subjects I'd found again at last.

Q: About the progress of a poem, a typical poem—one, say, you've never written—is it a *problem* that you feel nagging you and try to solve by writing? Are you led on by a subject, or by chance phrases?

JM: Often it's some chance phrases, usually attached but not always—not even always attached to a subject, though if the poem is to go anywhere it has somehow to develop a subject fairly quickly, even if that subject is a blank shape. A poem like "About the Phoenix"—I don't know where any of it came from, but it kept drawing particles of phrases and images to itself.

Q: But by "subject" you mean essentially an event, a person . . .

JM: . . . a scene . . .

Q: . . . a landscape?

JM: A kind of action . . .

Q: . . . that has not necessarily happened to you?

JM: Hmmm. And then I think one problem that has presented itself over and over, usually in the case of a poem of a certain length, is that you've got to end up saying the right thing. A poem like "Scenes of Childhood" made for a terrible impasse because at the point where my "I" is waking up the next morning, after a bad night, I had him say that *dawn was worse*. It took me a couple of weeks to realize that this was something that couldn't be said under nearly any circumstances without being dishonest. Dawn is not worse; the sacred sun rises and things look up. Once I reversed myself, the poem ended easily enough. I had the same problem with "An Urban Convalescence" before writing those concluding quatrains. It broke off at the lowest point: "The heavy volume of the world / Closes again." But then something affirmative had to be made out of it.

Q: You're so self-conscious about *not* striking attitudes that the word "affirmative" makes me wonder. . . .

JM: No, think of music. I mean, you don't *end* pieces with a dissonance.

Q: When you write a poem, do you imagine an immediate audience for it?

JM: Oh, over the years I've collected a little anthology of ideal readers.

Q: Living and dead?

JM: Now, now . . . But *yes*, why not? Living, dead, imaginary. Is this diction crisp enough for Herbert? Is this stanza's tessitura too high for Maggie Teyte? The danger with your close friends is that they're apt to take on faith what you *meant* to do in a poem, not what you've done. But who else has their patience? Three or four friends read the trilogy as it came out, a few pages at a time. I don't see how I could have kept going without their often very detailed responses.

Q: Are these reactions ever of any practical help? Would they lead you to change a line?

JM: That's the point! Ideally you'd think of everything yourself, but in practice. . . . There were two lines in "Ephraim" about a stream reflecting aspen. The word "aspen" ended one sentence, and "Boulders" began the next. Madison Morrison, out in Oklahoma, sent me this little note on that section: "Aspen. Boulders . . . Colorado Springs?" I'd never have seen that by myself. Nine times out of ten, of course, I use those misgivings to confirm what I've done. So-and-so thinks a passage is obscure? *Good*—it stays obscure: that'll teach him! No wonder that the most loyal reader gets lost along the way—feels disappointed by a turn you've taken, and simply gives up.

Q: Yet one of your strengths as a poet is so to disarm your reader, often by including his possible objections.

JM: That might even be the placating gesture of a child who is inevitably going to disappoint his parents before he fulfills the expectations they haven't yet learned to have. I was always very good at seeming to accede to what my father or mother wanted of me—and then going ahead to do as I pleased.

Q: You say in "The Book of Ephraim" that you've read Proust for the last time. Is that true?

JM: I thought so when I said it, but in fact—just before starting to write the party scene which ends the epilogue—I took a quick look at *Le Temps retrouvé*.

Q: In a sense, Proust has been the greatest influence on your career, wouldn't you agree?

JM: I would.

Q: Odd for a poet to have a novelist over his shoulder.

JM: Why? I certainly didn't feel his influence when I was writing novels. My attention span when writing or "observing" is so much shorter than his, that it's only in a poem—in miniature as it were—that something of his flavor might be felt.

Q: Speaking of influences, one could mention Stevens, Auden, Bishop, a few others. What have you sought to learn from other poets, and how in general have you adapted their example to your practice?

JM: Oh, I suppose I've learned things about writing, technical things, from each of them. Auden's penultimate rhyming, Elizabeth's way of contradicting something she's just said, Stevens's odd glamorizing of philosophical terms. Aside from all that, what I think I *really* wanted was some evidence that one didn't have to lead a "literary" life—belong to a ghetto of "creativity." That one could live as one pleased, and not be shamefaced in the glare of renown (if it ever came) at being an insurance man or a woman who'd moved to Brazil and played samba records instead of discussing X's latest volume. It was heartening that the *best* poets had this freedom. Auden did lead a life that looked literary from a distance, though actually I thought it was more a re-creation of school and university days: much instruction, much giggling, much untidiness. Perhaps because my own school years were unhappy for extracurricular reasons, I didn't feel completely at ease with all that. So much was routine—and often wildly entertaining, of course. Once, a long lunchtime discussion with Chester Kallman about whether three nineteen- or twenty-year-old guests who were expected for dinner should be offered *real drinks* culminated that evening in Wystan's removing three tiny, tiny glasses from the big hearts-and-flowers cupboard and asking *me* to "make vodka and tonics for our young friends." (I gave them straight vodka, of course.) The point's not that Wystan was stingy—or if he was, who cares?—but that his conflicting principles (Don't Waste Good Liquor on the Young versus *Gastrecht,* or the Sacred Duty of a Host) arrived at a solution that would have made Da Ponte smile. Soon everyone was having a good time. One of the young Englishmen proposed—this was late in the sixties—that poems should appear in common, everyday places: on books of matches, beer cans, toilet paper. "I sense the need," said Chester, rolling his eyes, "for applied criticism."

It was *du côté de chez* Elizabeth, though, that I saw the daily life that took my fancy even more, with its kind of random, Chekhovian surface, open to trivia and funny surprises, or even painful ones, today a fit of weeping, tomorrow a picnic. I could see how close that life was to her poems, how much the life and the poems gave to one another. I don't mean I've "achieved" anything of the sort in *my* life or poems, only that Elizabeth had more of a talent for life—and for poetry—than anyone else I've known, and this has served me as an ideal.

Q: When you read someone else's poem, what do you read *for?* What kind of pleasure do you take? What kind of hesitations do you have?

JM: Well, I'm always open to what another poet might do with *the line*, or with a stanza. I don't know what particular turn of phrase I look for, but it's always very important, the phrasing of the lines. Elizabeth's elegy for Lowell struck me as such a masterpiece because you read the poem a couple of times and felt you knew it by heart. Every line fell in the most wonderful way, which is perhaps something she learned from Herbert. You find it *there*. I think you find it very often in French poetry.

Q: You're drawn, then, primarily to technical matters?

JM: To the extent that the phrasing leads to the content. I don't really know how to separate those. The poems I most love are so perfectly phrased that they seem to say something extraordinary, whether they do or not.

Q: Increasingly, your work has exhibited a striking range in what would once have been called its poetic diction. Conversational stops and starts alternate with stanza-long sentences bristling with subordinate clauses. Scientific jargon lies down with slang. What guides these choices?

JM: Taste, instinct, temperament . . . Too much poetry sounds like side after side of modern music, the same serial twitterings, the same barnyard grunts. Just as I love multiple meanings, I try for contrasts and disruptions of tone. Am I wrong—in the old days didn't the various meters imply different modes or situations, like madness, love, war? It's too late, in any event, to rely very much on meter—look at those gorgeous but imbecile antistrophes and semichoruses in Swinburne or Shelley or whoever. I'm talking from a reader's point of view, you understand. Poets will rediscover as many techniques as they need in order to help them write better. But for a reader who can hardly be trusted to hear the iambics when he opens "The Rape of the Lock," if anything can fill the void left by these obsolete resources, I'd imagine it would have to be diction or "voice." Voice in its fullest tonal range—not just bel canto or passionate speech. From my own point of view, this range would be utterly unattainable without meter and rhyme and those forms we are talking about.

Of course, they breed echoes. There's always a lurking air of pastiche that, consciously or unconsciously, gets into your diction. That doesn't much bother me, does it you? No voice is as individual as the poet would like to think. In the long run I'd rather have what I write remind people of Pope or Yeats or Byron than of the other students in that year's workshop.

Q: The hallmark of your poetry is its *tone*, the way its concerns are observed and presented. And much of its effect depends on your fondness for paradox. Is that a cultivated habit of mind with you? A deliberate way into, and out of, the world and the poem?

JM: It's hard to know. "Cultivated" certainly in the gardening sense of the word—which doesn't explain the mystery of the seed. I suppose that early on I began to understand the relativity, even the reversibility, of truths. At the same time as I was being given a good education I could feel, not so much from my parents, but from the world they moved in, that kind of easygoing contempt rich people have for art and scholarship—"these things are all right *in their place*, and their place is to ornament a life rather than to nourish or to shape it." Or when it came to sex, I had to face it that the worst iniquity my parents (and many of my friends) could imagine was for me a blessed source of pleasure and security—as well as suffering, to be sure. There was truth on both sides. And maybe having arrived at *that* explained my delight in setting down a phrase like, oh, "the pillow's dense white dark" or "Au fond each summit is a cul-de-sac," but the explanation as such neither delights nor convinces me. I believe the secret lies primarily in the nature of poetry—and of science too, for that matter—and that the ability to see both ways at once isn't merely an idiosyncrasy but corresponds to how the world needs to be seen: cheerful *and* awful, opaque *and* transparent. The plus and minus signs of a vast, evolving formula.

Q: I want to come back to a phrase you just used—"pleasure and security." Would those twinned feelings also account for your affectionate and bracing reliance on traditional forms?

JM: Yes, why not? Now and then one enjoys a little moonwalk, some little departure from tradition. And the forms themselves seem to invite this, in our age of "breakthroughs." Take the villanelle, which didn't really change from "Your eyen two wol slay me sodenly" until, say, 1950. (Of course the Chaucer isn't quite a villanelle, but let's say it is to make my point.) With Empson's famous ones, rigor mortis had set in, for any purposes beyond those of *vers de société*. Still, there were tiny signs. People began repunctuating the key lines so that each time they recurred, the meaning would be slightly different. Was that just an extension of certain cute effects in Austin Dobson? In any case, "sodenly" Elizabeth's ravishing poem "One Art" came along, where the key lines seem merely to approximate themselves, and the form, awakened by a kiss, simply toddles off to a new stage in its life, under the proud eye of Mother, or the Muse. One doesn't, I mean, have to be just a stolid "formalist." The forms, the meters and rhyme-sounds, are far too liberating for that.

Q: Liberating?

JM: From one's own smudged images and anxiety about "having something to say." *Into* the dynamics of—well, the craft itself.

Q: Few words can make contemporary poets cringe more than "great"—I mean, when applied to poems or poets. That's something that certainly doesn't hold for other arts, say, painting. Why do you suppose this is so? Is the whole category outdated?

JM: I hope not. Just because "great" is now a talk-show word meaning competent or agreeable, it doesn't follow that we have to take this lying down. It's really the bombast, the sunless pedantry—waste products of ideas—that make us cringe. They form on a text like mildew. Straining for exaltation, coasting off into complacency . . . Words keep going bankrupt and ringing false, and as you say, this wouldn't be true in painting. A "new" Revlon color doesn't invalidate a Matisse that used it fifty years earlier. Subjects date more quickly; you don't see many weeping Magdalens or meadows full of cows in the galleries nowadays, and I can't think of much celestial machinery in poetry between "The Rape of the Lock" and "Ephraim." But painters still go to museums, don't they? They've *seen* great paintings and even survived the shock. Now surely *some* of our hundred thousand living American poets have read the great poems of the Western world and kept their minds open to the possibilities.

Q: Is "heroism" or "high tone" the word I want to pinpoint what's been missing from American literature these past decades? Or do those terms mean anything to you?

JM: Oh, heroism's possible, all right, and the high tone hasn't deserted some of us. Trouble is, our heroes more and more turn up as artists or invalids or both—the sort that won't be accepted as heroic except by fellow artists (or fellow sufferers). Sir Edmund Hillary will "do" of course, but I don't gasp at his achievement the way I do at Proust's. Must this leave the healthy, uncreative reader at a loss, not being sick or special enough to identify? Does he need to, after all? It's not as though only people in superb physical shape were thrilled by the conquest of Everest. And Proust is subtle enough to persuade us that the real feat has been one not of style but of memory, therefore within even the common man's power to duplicate. It's not the prevailing low tone so much as the imaginative laziness. We don't see life as an adventure. We know that our lives are in our hands; and far from freeing us, this knowledge has become a paralyzing weight.

Q: An adventure without obvious dragons and princesses, composed merely of the flat circumstances of a given life—that's not always apparent to the naked eye.

JM: No. Yet your life, and that means people and places and history along with *la vie intérieure*, does keep growing and blossoming, and is always *there* as potential subject matter. But the blossom needs to be fertilized—you don't just versify your engagement book—and when that bee comes can't ever be predicted or willed.

Q: You'd disagree, then, with Auden, who said he was a poet *only* when actually writing a poem.

JM: Lucky him. What was he the rest of the time?

Q: A citizen, I believe he said.

JM: Oh. Well, that citizen must have heard a lot of funny sounds from the poet pigeonhole next door. I certainly do. Whether you're at your desk or not when a poem's under way, isn't there that constant eddy in your mind? If it's strong enough all sorts of random flotsam gets drawn into it, how selectively it's hopeless to decide at the time. I try to break off, get away from the page, into the kitchen for a spell of mixing and marinating, which gives the words a chance to sort themselves out behind my back. But there's really no escape, except perhaps the third drink. On "ordinary" days, days when you've nothing on the burner, it might be safe to say that you're not a poet at all: more like a doctor at a dinner party, just another guest until his hostess slumps to the floor or his little beeper goes off. Most of those signals are false alarms—only they're not. Language *is* your medium. You can be talking or writing a letter, and out comes an observation, a "sentence-sound" you rather like. It needn't be your own. And it's not going to make a poem, or even fit into one. But the *twinge* it gives you—and it's this, I daresay, that distinguishes you from the "citizen"—reminds you you've got to be careful, that you've a condition that needs watching. . . .

Q: Sounds like that doctor's turning into a patient.

JM: Doesn't it! How about lunch?

An Interview
with Jack Stewart

Q: Your poems are very often very dramatic. Have you been influenced by the theater?

JM: I did a couple of plays. And working with actors—seeing what they could do to your lines, which usually was a happy surprise rather than not—I found it this great liberating thing because up to then I'd only written, you might say, my own voice—writing that I would have to take responsibility for—the attitudes, the perceptions. But in the theater, unless you're writing a one-man show, you can't do that. You have to have a voice that denies what you've just said, or challenges it in one way or another. Of course, you don't have to work in the theater to learn things like that. One of Elizabeth Bishop's loveliest tricks is to say something and then to say, "No, that's not what I mean"—to take it back and to present it differently. She manages simply to interiorize the theory.

Q: In *Scripts for the Pageant,* one of the lines is, "In duality is dimension, tension."

JM: That's what Queen Mother says when they're deciding on Man, after the unicorns and the other previous creatures.

Q: "All the true grandeur wanting in a perfect thing." Is that what you mean by . . . ?

Review, Fall 1982.

JM: No, I'm afraid *she's* probably talking about something, putting it into a far more philosophical context than I'm comfortable with. But perhaps that idea of resistance and duality would go back to the original sense of the theater, just two actors doing the scene together.

Q: You mention philosophy. Has your work gotten more philosophical?

JM: I'm very leery of ideas, and I used to think for a long time that I didn't have any. And I was secretly wanting to emulate that description of Henry James as "having a mind so fine that no idea could violate it." Remember that phrase? And so a friend of mine suggested the role of ideas in the trilogy is really the return of the repressed—that that was a whole side of my mind I never worked consciously to develop, because it seemed to me to make for a great wasteland in precisely the area where you want images and intuitions and much more vivid conditions than those of thought itself, thought by itself.

Q: It seems that in contemporary poetry we have very much set up the imagists versus the more philosophical poets. It seems that philosophy has been left behind.

JM: There are ways of putting it into a poem. I think Stevens is clearly a very philosophical poet, but he seems also to have a great deal of fun while he's at it. He combines the philosophical elements, the philosophical vocabulary, with very gaudy, frivolous words. So if you find the pill of thought is too bitter to swallow, it's sugared with these more amusing effects.

Q: Do you think the poem needs to have effects, different poetic devices?

JM: No, I don't think that's necessary at all. If you're the kind of poet who is not stimulated imaginatively by the need to fulfill a form, then there's no reason why you should think of writing a sonnet or working in rhyme, because it will just paralyze your imagination rather than release it. I'm the other kind. I find it terribly hard to write in what you might call "free verse." Maybe there will be something usable that comes up, but my best ideas are always because I've had to fill out a quatrain, or a rhyme or sonnet.

Q: Does it come from pushing yourself to fulfill that form?

JM: No, I don't think so. It's not a matter of *will*. The account Auden gave of it was that with your conscious mind focused on the technical problem—finding the rhyme or fulfilling the meter—that left your unconscious much freer to come to the surface. That part of your conscious that would have been repressing your deeper feelings was occupied and, therefore, things that you didn't know you had in you to say, came out.

Q: Auden is awfully important in *Scripts*. Was he a close friend of yours?

JM: Not particularly. Not till after he died. I met him a number of times, and his friend and collaborator, Chester Kallman, lived just down the street from us in Athens.

Q: We were talking, or started to talk last night, about the variety of religion, philosophy, poetry in *Scripts*—everything seems to come together in the work. Was that a conscious attempt from the beginning, or did things . . .

JM: Look, none of this was conscious. Let me assure you these experiences happened as I tell it. We were the ones who resisted the material at first and weren't sure we wanted to commit ourselves to that amount of work. But *Scripts* took its own shape, and with *Mirabell*, I had to do a lot of cutting because the transcripts were so voluminous. I cut and condensed.

Q: So you acted more like an editor.

JM: Yes. But in *Scripts*, at least in "The Lessons," those are almost verbatim. Even when they talk in doggerel, it came in doggerel, which I would not have believed possible if I had not seen the Victor Hugo transcripts of his experiences.

Q: You said you've been doing this for about twenty-five years?

JM: We started, I think, around '55.

Q: "Voices from the Other World" is an early poem.

JM: That was written that first summer.

Q: The first time I read *The (Diblos) Notebook*, it occurred to me—this was after I had read "Ephraim"—that it was possibly a natural progression from that to the trilogy.

JM: Oh? Well, that might be so, at least in the sense that there was never any real possibility of writing a prose book after *The (Diblos) Notebook* because prose more or less self-destructs in that book. I'd forgotten that when I tried to treat all this Ouija experience fictionally as a novel.

Q: When did the idea for the trilogy present itself, or was it there from the start?

JM: It was not there from the start. I thought of writing a prose book, either a fiction or a kind of Castaneda pastiche, and kept losing the manuscript. I lost the first in a taxi, as I write in a poem. Then I had the drafts from which that typescript was made, and I left them in a hotel in Frankfurt. Finally, I'd just two pages left, and I was looking at them, and they began to dissolve into verse. With a pencil, I'd make line breaks and fiddle with it a bit, and typed it up as verse, and showed both the prose and the verse to a friend who said, you're mad if you ever write prose again because the poetry's so much better. But I didn't see it as a trilogy. I thought that "The Book of Ephraim" would describe the whole experience adequately, and after I finished it, I went back to writing some shorter poems for five or six months, and then suddenly the *Mirabell* material took over.

Q: You mentioned last night that the setting for *Scripts,* Sandover, is an imaginary place.

JM: It's imaginary, but it took on aspects of the house I describe in "The Broken Home," which was a very grand house, I must say. But actually it is an imagined place, and all of the grounds are much more things out of country life—paddocks and mazes. It's landscaped completely differently from our house on Long Island.

Q: An old, English manor–type house?

JM: Yes.

Q: At the end of the *Notebook* you say that, "The only solution is to be very, very intelligent."

JM: That's something Robert Morse used to say, and I liked it and stuck it in.

Q: Does it have any particular meaning throughout your career?

JM: No, if I were to take a motto, it would be—well, as I then go on to say, after I've used that sentence, that the quintessence of intelligence would be to disguise itself, to take the mask of ignorance or simplicity or whatever. And that's more what I feel. I have a horror of intelligence as it would be used in a literary salon in New York or Paris where people are simply showing off what trends they have espoused, or what books they have read. I think of Isak Dinesen as a very intelligent writer. She doesn't brandish ideas. To her, the most sophisticated ideas can be told in story form. In that way, they really grasp the mind and shape it. I don't know if you've had that experience of being taught how to behave through a story—to try and make something come out right because that's the way it happened in books you liked or stories you liked as a child.

Q: Rather than just a pure philosophical tract, for instance, it's easier to learn from a lifelike situation.

JM: Yes. Otherwise you're acting on some dreary precept, or you're simply obeying a commandment rather than putting yourself through the narrative.

Q: You said last night that your poems are stories—make themselves into stories.

JM: That came to be something that absorbed me, yes. I found that I was reading even the most abstract lyric, often as if there was a narrative that had simply been eliminated from around it—"Go, lovely rose," for example, or any of those songlike seventeenth-century poems. There is implicit a love story, a whole world of behavior. And this then links directly, or indirectly, with the tone of voice which is so important in all poetry because unless there's a story, of what conceivable interest is a tone of voice? That's what alerts you to a potentially narrative or dramatic situation.

Q: It's peculiar to the twentieth century that the autobiographical has crept more and more into the literature, and yet it still seems to matter to the reader—it still comes across.

JM: Maybe it's to the extent that "I" is a very abstract pronoun. How innocently, and how instinctively, one writes early stories in the third person, as if anyone would be fooled into thinking you were not writing about yourself. But later on when you use the "I," the first thing you notice is that it could be anyone, whereas the "he" or the "she" is specific. It means a given person. And yet that's not always true. Look at Kafka.

Q: Along with autobiography, I notice a lot of history in your work—literary history, world history. Has that been a concern of yours, an interest?

JM: Not really. I didn't much care for history in school. I couldn't get it straight and it became almost unbearable "after the Industrial Revolution," as Virginia Woolf says in *Orlando*. I'm interested in it as a form of fiction. I've always had in the back of my head that one could write a much more interesting history if one didn't have to stick to the facts. I also began to feel that the facts were so glaringly unknowable in almost any case, and what we've managed to absorb of modern history is, at least in this country, such a tissue of fraud and deceit and people putting the best possible face on these in the media. Who would give it any credit whatever? It's a pitiful structure compared to fiction.

Q: In *Scripts,* you have the historical characters making new what they said or did.

JM: As I say, let's keep the distinction clear between me—who's talking to you and who wrote the poem—and wherever the material from the poem comes from. Maybe it did come from me, but that comes from somebody who has perhaps a different view of history than I do. When the muse speaks, Clio, she seems to be saying what I am now, that things are unknowable and memory plays you false.

Q: Your work has a certain, what I term, "restlessness" to it. In "The Broken Home," for instance, there are seven sonnets, but they're not divided up, marked, as sections one, two, three, four—and yet they hold together as a single poem or as seven pieces.

JM: Why is that restless?

Q: It tends to want to move toward being together and also toward each being its own set.

JM: I wouldn't call it restless. I think that's part of trying to always be of two minds which has become increasingly my way of looking at things.

Q: The duality we talked about?

JM: There would even be an analogy. Perhaps I might have been thinking of it with that poem. You know those Japanese screens where each panel is a picture in itself, but when you see the whole?—I certainly didn't want to use the old-fashioned numbered sonnet sequence from Shakespeare to Edna Millay. That seemed unnecessary by now. I'm much more pleased, at least formally, with the sonnets that make up the poem called "The Will," where I describe losing the novel, because I get a sonnet within a sonnet there. I start and break off after the sixth or eighth line and interpolate another sonnet and then finish the original. And that was fun to do. But I don't think I would have thought to do something like that if I hadn't had a piece of music in mind—in this case Mozart's Concerto no. 27, I think, where the rondo interrupts about two-thirds through and then you get a minuet somehow encapsulated in the rondo like it's a brilliant thought that keeps you from getting about your business until you've developed it. That's very exciting formally, and to see if you can do something like that in a poem is worthwhile.

Q: Music and some of the other arts seem to be very important to you.

JM: Yes. I find music more of a help in solving formal problems, even problems of tone, where you know vaguely that you want to bring something to a conclusion and you can't imagine how, and if you can suddenly think of a piece of music that has the effect you want, it helps you. The words begin to come, or the rhythms begin to come.

Q: There are the conflicting ideas that, on the one hand, form and content are one, and, on the other, that they are different. How do you feel about that?

JM: Certainly, form for me is a kind of divining rod for content. But I don't think that I simply pick a *form* and decide to see what it dredges up. I think the thing that formally pleased me most in *Scripts* is that poem called "Samos," where already a lot has been said about the numbers five and twelve, and to realize there was a form of five twelve-line stanzas using only five end words in a sestina-like recurring pattern. That poem wrote itself because I knew I wanted a poem in that form at that juncture in the book when the second section began. And I also knew what end words I wanted. I knew they had to be words that were close to the five senses or the four elements.

Q: Earth, air, fire . . .

JM: I used land instead of earth. I picked those words, I picked the form, and I put all this on ice somewhere in my head, and about a year and a half later, I wrote the poem in a couple of days. That's working quickly for me.

Q: So, basically, you wrote around the transcriptions.

JM: Exactly—to try and provide as plausible a narrative context or continuity as I could. And what I really wanted a reader to feel, by all means, what I wanted the reader to believe, was that we'd had the experience. I didn't care what he thought of the experience, whether he thought it was silly or boring, but not to say, "Oh what an interesting device Merrill has hit on," or "How would he have thought to set it up as if it had come over the Ouija board," which people are really dumb enough to do if they've had a certain academic background. But all of the lower case was to try and convince the right kind of reader that it happened the way I said it did.

Q: I also wanted to talk about some of the shorter poems. In "Salome," for instance, you seem to be taking the history and finding the meaning behind it.

JM: You mentioned imagism. I suppose I'm uncomfortable with any event, object—anything I've come into contact with—unless it has a second level of meaning. It doesn't have to be "meaning" in the textbook sense. Maybe it's enough to think of a flower and think of the wonders of nature, and this must be a reaction against the imagists who want simply to present an object. Maybe again, they were much more sophisticated than I'm giving them credit for, and that the "wonders of nature" was the constant, unspoken resonance around these objects they presented—the wonders of human ingenuity in the wheelbarrow. But the same with a historical event: unless an action has resonance it's just another terribly boring fact. And it's this constant worry of mine. . . . Fact, of course, is found dissolved in *Mirabell* when Auden gives that speech which ends, "Fact is fable." And I began to see then that fact, first of all, was inevitably fable because it would become distorted, if it was worth remembering at all, and was sucked by magnetism into the realm of myth.

Q: Earlier you said that histories are often distorted or become lies; a mask is put forth. Is it part of the poet's job to put forth a mask, or to destroy masks?

JM: Poets would disagree about that. I don't think Auden would ever have countenanced the distortion of a fact. But I would like to think that the facts that stay in our minds have the makings of something more than fact—the makings of fable—and that it's partly in the nature of our minds that these transformations occur.

Q: Something like "Days of 1935"?

JM: Yes.

Q: There's a remark by T. S. Eliot on Blake's early work, something to the effect that Blake wasn't a bright young man making grand attempts and just missing, but was making small attempts and doing them flawlessly. Did you have that attitude in your early work?

JM: Yes. Perhaps very clearly. I wanted to write good poems when I was young, but I didn't have very much faith in my reliability as a witness to our times, and the best I thought I could hope for would be to turn out relatively perfect formal poems. I was drawn to the poets that had no virtues except for a kind of perfection, and who had nothing really whatever to say, or so it seemed. People like Elinor Wylie and third-rate French, turn-of-the-century poets. Not Verlaine even, certainly not Baudelaire, but Henri de Régnier, for instance. And, as we were saying much earlier, all of the content, if you want to distinguish, crept up on me without my encouraging it particularly.

Q: Is it partly because it wasn't forced that it came out?

JM: Perhaps so. And you've talked to lots of young writers who have so much to say? But can they get it down on paper? Well, I had nothing whatever to say, and I'm so glad it was that way because, otherwise, when you have something really crucial to say you can't attend to technique unless the technique is by then mastered. This was Rilke's experience. He wrote very minor, very small poems, and they're beautiful, but they don't compare to the elegies or the sonnets. He had his instrument ready when the time came.

Q: Wasn't that Auden's philosophy—to not accept a student who had a lot to say, but one who wanted to fool with words?

JM: Exactly.

AN INTERVIEW
WITH FRED BORNHAUSER

Q: I don't know anything about the origin of the Ouija principle, or its name—except that it is a double affirmative. And yet I notice that you use the YES/NO found at the upper corners of the standard board, along with an interpolated ampersand, as rubrics for the three sections of *Scripts for the Pageant*. How does this figure?

JM: I think what you have on the board are the raw materials of language—of thought itself. The YES and NO came to be especially telling, the more I realized how important it was—not only for the poem but for my own mental balance—to remain of two minds about everything that was happening. One didn't want to be merely skeptical or merely credulous. Either way would have left us in reduced circumstances. It's true that in the glow of some of the later messages, when all the themes began to connect, and every least detail added its touch to the whole, there was no question of *not* assenting to what we were being shown. But the glow fades, as Yeats knew when he compared his system to the stylization of a Wyndham Lewis drawing. What's being conveyed is essentially beyond words, and every artist will have to draw on his own temperament, or way with words, in order to render this.

Q: Did you have any idea when you wrote "Voices from the Other

Contemporary Authors, New Revision Series, vol. 10 (Detroit: Gale Research Company, 1983).

World" that you were on to something that would lead to prophetic poetry on so grand a scale?

JM: No, and thank goodness! For one thing, the prospect of any very demanding piece of work would have sent me into a dither. My ideal poem was less than a page long, with all its connections visible, its overtones audible, and no loose ends. For another thing, I felt it would be "cheating" to use any of the Ouija material—except, as in that poem you mention, in an account of our experience of the board. The prejudice lasted for decades, and probably explains why our own reactions and circumstances loom so large in the finished trilogy.

Q: You spoke somewhere about your surprise at the final length of "From the Cupola"—the Psyche poem and a different kind of poem from what was to follow. Could you generalize about the need for increasing scope and scale in your development as a poet?

JM: I think of it ruefully as a sort of "middle-age spread." Perhaps the general drift is to greater talkativeness, if not garrulity. Ideas, which in youth set out on their quests and find themselves at once in an allegorical wood, in middle life must first cross rivers infested with razor-toothed memories, or be obliged to stop for weeks at a time with a tribe of digressions, naked and giggling . . . I don't know. I still like short poems best, when other people write them!

Q: With the possible exception of Pound's *Cantos,* I can think of no poetic work of the twentieth century longer than your trilogy. Most of us, brought up on Cleanth Brooks and Robert Penn Warren, are used to close meticulous reading of even the simplest lyrics. Clearly, that kind of analysis does not always work. What guidelines or warnings would you give the reader of the long poem?

JM: I, too, teethed on Brooks and Warren. I learned to read, and to write, with as much care as possible. Before them, Keats had spoken of loading every rift with ore. And isn't "God lurks in the details" the motto of the Warburg Institute? The best I could hope for from a reader is that he keep one eye on the ever-emerging (and self-revising) whole, and another on the details. A lot of the talk sounds like badinage, casual if not frivolous, but something serious is usually going on under the surface.

Q: One cannot help noticing that eight years passed between your first and second books of poetry, then three or four years between the appearance of the next four; finally, only two years have elapsed between these most recent really big ones. Given the complexity and importance of your latest work, one would almost expect the length of interims to be reversed. Would you comment on this?

JM: I was writing novels and plays along with some of those early books. But you're right, my early poems took longer to finish. I wanted it that way. Those poems were undertaken, by and large, without my knowing what I wanted them to say. They were occasions for self-discovery, experiments not only in technical matters, rhymes and phrasing and all that, but in attitudes and feelings and beliefs, in the uses of obscurity—everything! Later on, by the time of *Nights and Days*, I knew my mind a touch better than I had at first. Those novels and plays, also, had shown me things I could use, effects of narrative and contrasting voices. Much of the trilogy, of course, was written "for" me, at the board, and what remained to say was in a sense dictated by the need to provide a context for those transcripts. So that it all went like the wind!—at least by comparison with the languorous doodling I'd relied on twenty-odd years earlier.

Q: *The Oxford Dictionary of English Christian Names* gives the meaning of Ephraim as "double fruitfulness," from the Hebrew. Were you conscious of this? The Bible tells us (Jer. 31:20) that Ephraim, the son of Joseph, was called by God His son. Then in *Mirabell*, we find posited the notion that Ephraim was Mirabell's pupil; Mirabell then speaks of "MY TEACHER'S VOICE," one also heard by Dante. Presumably the voice of God? By divine succession, according to DJ, Ephraim could be "a composite/Voice, a formula thought up by [Mirabell]." Clearly you are a student of the Old Testament. How much of the biblical account of Ephraim were you aware of when you first began to establish contact with a spirit of this name? What about the name Mirabell?

JM: Mirabell's name is from Congreve. I don't think his TEACHER'S VOICE is the same as God's. Dante, we learn, received instruction from a mendicant ex-priest who turns out to be one of Mirabell's bat-legions in disguise. *Their* senior officer, as I call him, is a voice identified only as 00, who very much prostrates himself before the angels. Isn't it funny how uncomfortable all these hierarchies make us; yet we read the Table of the Elements with no embarrassment whatever. I'm not at all a Bible person, by the way. I've started the Old Testament again and again, but never get much beyond Abraham and Sarah—though I've peeked, I confess, at some of the later high points. It looks like an utterly fascinating book—if only I knew how to read it. (I have the same problem with *Moby Dick*.) Other people have had to tell me about the biblical Ephraim—there was also apparently a *Saint* Ephraim who wrote poetry—but I never knew what to make of either connection until the poem's epilogue makes it for me, by the revelation that Ephraim and Michael are—how to say it?—aspects of the same power. The ultimate composite voice. Training in wordplay might have alerted me much earlier. Five out of seven letters in those two names are the same. Well, that dictionary says it all: double fruitfulness.

Q: You are bravely mythopoeic in these matter-of-fact days. With a cast including God B[iology], the archangels, Jesus, and Mohammed, do you conceive what you are doing as in any way within the province of Polyhymnia, the Muse of Sacred Poetry?

JM: You'll notice that Polyhymnia doesn't figure among *our* nine muses—that's just one of a long list of revisions the poem puts us through. It's not so much a visionary poem as a revisionary one, I often fear. I don't want to talk—I'm not equipped to talk—about the nonviability of sacred poetry nowadays. Seen at a certain distance, the issue of profane versus divine comes to be that of the self versus the selfless. This isn't something one has any control over; one can't evidently *will* it, much as one might long to get beyond some of those barriers of the self. They're represented, I suppose, by that "hedge" at Sandover, which we overlook from the schoolroom.

Q: Whatever the case, you have not at the same time shied from the looming theories and threats of the atomic age, from the coils and throes of time and history, from the impenetrabilities of psychology. How much learning do you expect from your reader?

JM: Most poetry written today expects none, and I get rather fed up with that diet of nuts and wheat germ. On the other hand I don't—how could I?—expect a reader to have picked up exactly the same odds and ends that have stuck in my mind over the last forty years or so. Ideally a reader might happen to know, let's say, about a third of these things, might have read Proust but not Dante or E. F. Benson—enough to feel partly at home. And he might have on his own shelves books that I've never read, by whose light he might see implications and dimensions undreamed of in *my* corner of the library. I'd especially like this to be the case where science and history are concerned. My "learning" in these fields is paltry, to say the least. Yet this doesn't prevent (it may even have allowed) a broad *view* of science from being set forth in the trilogy. This view might conceivably interest a trained scientist more than it does me—someone who couldn't otherwise see the forest for the trees. Or is that just wishful thinking?

Q: How would you respond to scholarly annotation of your recent work? Or would you laugh this off as unnecessary and inflationary?

JM: No, certainly not. Annotation's probably inevitable. I've made some lists already of things that either needed explaining or the little leaden weight of a reference to keep a passage from seeming merely vapid. I do a certain amount of this in the poem; the classroom format allows for it. Certain other connections get made only much later. *Mirabell* had been published, for instance, when a friend sent me a clipping from that day's paper, with the headline: "Rare Metal Linked to Death of Dinosaurs." Frankly I keep reading the poem, leafing the pages to see what's there, and *where.* Another friend, Robert Polito, is at work right now on an index—a little pamphlet to be published separately—which I expect to find very useful in tracking down a mislaid line or reference.

Q: Are you afraid of ingenious creative criticism? Or are you more like Eliot, who said he was pleased to see, if for the first time, what responsible critical readers might discover in his poems?

JM: Probably more like Eliot. I've always been oddly comforted by the notion that, no matter how well I think I know what I've said in a poem, it might have a whole dimension that's hidden from me—by the very nature of art. The way one can't ever see one's own face, except in a mirror. Naturally one would like the mirror to be both "responsible" and "creative," like the mirror that painters once used to see properly, for the first time, what they'd done.

Q: You give the lie to C. P. Snow's once-famous theory of the two worlds, the conflict and uncommunicativeness between science and the humanities. You do this by the novelistic intensity of your portrayal of the human experience of confronting difficult, elusive, and often abstract concepts. Yet a person like myself is still intimidated by science. What have you assimilated, and what, in order to follow you, must I?

JM: I've assimilated nothing! The tiny bit I learned about science in order to write a few pages of the poem—pages meant to reassure a reader that something *could* be learned and wouldn't be irrelevant to all the "mythology" behind us and ahead of us—came out of books, and sank back into them as soon as I was done. Beginner's books mostly: I relied a lot on Asimov's two-volume *Guide to Science*. So don't imagine that I know. I like your knowing that I imagined. The only lifeline to science, for idiots like ourselves who find the very vocabulary impenetrable, has to be the imagination. Hence the constant drive to *personify* throughout the transcripts—and throughout history. No average person is going to feel comfortable with the idea of solar energy. So a figure slowly takes shape, takes human, or superhuman, form, and is named Apollo or the archangel Michael, and his words, which *we* put into his mouth, become part of the vast system whereby the universe reveals itself to us. What can you and I profitably learn from a neutrino? Yet give it a human mask and it will, as Oscar Wilde said, tell the truth. Read science *this* way.

Q: Have you read Thomas Pynchon's *V* or *Gravity's Rainbow*? Is there anything there that corresponds to your conceptions? Pynchon, of course, was trained at Cornell as a scientist.

JM: Pynchon's enthralling. He's ten times brighter than I am, yet I can recognize, in his centripetal paranoia, a lot of the same energy—the same quality of energy—that shaped the trilogy. We've both made spiderwebs on a rather grand scale. Something fairly sinister is sitting at the heart of his. Is that because he knows things I don't? Or purely a matter of temperament? I'm not sure I want those questions answered.

Q: You report in *Mirabell* that it was "twenty / Years in a cool dark place that Ephraim took / In order to be palatable wine. / This book by contrast, immature, supine, / Still kicks against its archetypal cradle." Are we to take this as ironic, or is there some chance that the book will undergo revision, which is to say that *Mirabell* may retap your word bank?

JM: Oh no, there's to be next to no revision of *Mirabell* or *Scripts*. I've made perhaps a half-dozen very slight changes. One of them involved resurrecting, from the transcript, a distinction between "matter" and "substance." I just couldn't face introducing a new term, then realized that not to do so left a nasty smudge. Throughout those last two volumes, it's true, my nose is very close to the page. I can only hope that what I lost of "aesthetic distance" I gained in "immediacy." In any case, they were too compelling for me to wait till I was seventy to write them.

Q: Are you ever very conscious of your readership—beyond, of course, the critics who write about your work? How much do you think it matters for any writer?

JM: It's madness to think of an audience. It's madness also not to think of one. Who would write on a desert island—beyond making notches for the passing days? With the trilogy, I've begun to get letters—never very many, thank goodness—from people who are, well, let's say, more interested in spiritualism than in literature. Those are usually fun to answer. An intelligent review, whether good or bad, is stimulating. But I like best of all the feeling that *lots* of people are writing, not about me, though they may dimly know that I exist; just as I dimly know that they do. That sense, however dim, of mutual endeavor is the indispensable thing.

Q: It has been said that at the present time there are more really competent, respectable poets, in sheer number, than have ever lived before at any one time. Do you believe it?

JM: Well, poetry has become a fairly loose term, one that often doesn't exceed the epigram, the diary jotting, the scholarly note. You just break these up into a few lines, and there you are. If you include all the people who write *this* stuff, then I'm sure it's true that there are more poets than readers nowadays. They're all "respectable." Poetry, even at that level, is a civilizing force, a kind of compost. There are a very few poets I wish would *stop* writing, and perhaps exactly the same number that I wish would never stop.

Q: Why have almost all nondramatic poets in England and America, from the eighteenth century on, attempted at least one play? Even such disparate and unlikely ones as Hopkins (the fragmentary *St. Winifred's Well*), Longfellow (the book-length *Christus*), and Stevens (*Three Travellers Watch a Sunrise*).

JM: It can't have been in those three instances—though I haven't even heard of the Longfellow play—a wish to try out different voices. Perhaps it's that a play, even a play you read to yourself, appeals to your credulity on a more naive level than a poem does. You begin imagining scenery, gestures for the actors, tones of voice, in a way that you simply don't when you read, oh, Browning or Frost—their narrative or "dramatic" poems, that is. With them, you're still conscious of being in the hands of the artful author. But the dramatic format puts you in the hands of the characters. It's an illusion, but how liberating!

Q: Would it be fair to ask you to comment on your own diction, which has been justly praised as one of your chief virtues? I would have to say I notice in your poetry an absolutely astonishing range—from the arcane and rarefied to the technical, the commonplace, and even the cliché—all of which you manage to endow with a rightness and richness and freshness. And of course a naturalness. Behind the scenes, how hard do you have to struggle for *le mot juste* and the right tone?

JM: The range is nothing I'm aware of striving for. We *have* all these languages—technical terms, clichés, polite circumlocutions, as you say—so why not use them? If you know some French words, use *them*, too. Poets don't write first of all in "English" or "American" so much as each in an idiom peculiar to himself. Naturalness is always becoming. I'm not sure, though, that many poets know what it is. They're haunted by bugaboos like "natural word order," which teaches them to write "See Jane run," when the truly *natural* way of putting it would be something closer to "Where on earth can that child be racing off to? Why, it's little—you know, the neighbor's brat—Jane!" It can take me dozens of drafts to get something right, which often turns out to be a perfect commonplace. What joy when it works—like fighting one's way through cobwebs to an open window. I don't mean that the more work you put into something, the better it turns out. Often you can feel the life ebbing away at the hands of a Mad Embalmer.

Q: Do a dictionary and thesaurus play an active role in the process of your writing?

JM: Indeed they do. So does a rhyming dictionary, though not as regularly. I used to be furious with the *OED* for never taking the etymologies back far enough. But now that I've found the *American Heritage Dictionary* with that splendid appendix of Indo-European roots a serene sort of ménage à trois has been set up. I expect it will go on for years.

Q: Auden, whose poetry could be quite political and topical, said that the poet could never change the world, but that his function was to preserve and purify the language. How do you feel about this?

JM: I don't know. Auden was changed by his reading of poets like Hardy and Eliot, Rilke and Cavafy, and he was part of the world. Writing his or her poems changes a poet, over the years, in ways that perhaps time or society by themselves couldn't. Perhaps he meant that these changes hardly count against the great coarsening drift of things. One doesn't particularly notice that the language *is* being preserved or purified, no matter how busily the poets function. I know one thing: worrying about it helps not at all.

Q: Commentators on your work, especially the late work, quite often mention Dante, Milton, Pope, and Yeats. And I suppose Blake and Goethe (in the second part of *Faust*). The writer I would like to ask about is Hawthorne, who in the introductions to his romances (*not* novels) cumulatively and persistently defines romance as what is familiar by sunlight seen in the transforming moonlight. Would you say that in some sense you are turning both lights, together or successively, on your subject? Can the trilogy be profitably approached as a romance?

JM: A line kept recurring as I wrote my little Greek novel—"the sun and moon together in the sky." I meant that I was drawn to both sides of things: masculine and feminine, rational and fanciful, passionate and ironic. With the trilogy, as I said just now, remaining of two minds seemed the essential thing. I didn't read Julian Jaynes's book on the bicameral mind until I'd finished *Mirabell*, and was all the more struck by how the entire action of that volume took place in two adjacent rooms of the Stonington house: the red dining room where we took down the messages, and the blue parlor where we thought about them afterward. So, yes, both lights were vital to the poem. I'm rather shaky as to genres and modes, but it does seem to be a romance in certain ways—and perhaps a mock-romance in others? Frye says that in a romance "a ghost as a rule is merely one more character." Actually, I suspect that the trilogy touches on a variety of modes, and the one thing that holds it together, if anything does, is that it all truly happened to us, came to us in these various ways.

Q: What about received ideas of "received forms"?

JM: Unfortunately there's a lot of defensiveness on both sides. And self-indulgence—both the formal and the experimental poet too often use their gifts as an easy way out. For myself, I by and large put my faith in forms. The attention they require at once frees and channels the unconscious, as Auden kept reminding us. Even if your poem turns out badly, you've learned something about proportion and concision and selflessness. And at best the form "received" by the next poet to use it will have taken on a new aspect because of what you learned there.

AN INTERVIEW
WITH JORDAN PECILE

Q: Your poems, where do you get your ideas for them?

JM: Ideas, by their nature, are few and everywhere. I usually try to fight them off. ("Poems are made with words, not ideas," said Mallarmé to Degas, who had asked your very question.) The kind of idea that serves a poem well recurs again and again. You may think you're on to something new by writing a poem about your grandmother's old fur coat, till it dawns on you that your real subject is a lament for the passing of time—a subject your poem shares with countless other poems already written in all the languages of our planet. So I usually start from a phrase or an image, and work my way through many indirections to something approaching an idea.

Q: Will you share with us a phrase or an image that led to a particular poem?

JM: Well, let's see. Two winters ago in Key West, we were talking at dinner about memory lapses, a topic increasingly relevant to everyone present. John Brinnin quoted Lady Diana Duff Cooper, who stayed young and beautiful for nearly ninety years. It seems that whenever a fact or a name slipped her mind, she would shrug and say cheerfully, "Oh well—another marble gone!" In a flash the image of the Acropolis in

State of the Arts, Winter 1987.

Athens appeared on my inner screen, and with it the history of Lord Elgin in the early nineteenth century, removing and carrying off to London most of the Parthenon sculptures. I remembered that individual consciousness had virtually begun in Greece; I thought of the periodic angry efforts made by the modern Greek government to get the marbles back from England—and so forth. Having already written poems called "Clearing the Title" and "Stopping the Leak," I suspected that I'd presently find myself embarked upon "Losing the Marbles," and shamelessly said so, then and there. For my birthday a month later one of that evening's guests gave me a little bag of marbles from the supermarket. That present in turn gave *me* the last section of my poem.

Q: Let me ask about the form of a poem—how do you choose it? Or does it choose you?

JM: The line of least resistance, where form is concerned, is to do what you've done before—or what somebody else has done. As far as I know I've invented only one stanza, which I used first when I was nineteen (in "The Black Swan") and again most recently at various key points in *Sandover*. I mean that to let form be determined by "content"—it's awful having to use these rough terms, since form *is* part of your total meaning—is easier said than done. Most of the "open form" poems I've looked at are hard to tell apart. One ends up with something loosely arranged on the page. As John Hollander puts it so amusingly, the "metric" of late-twentieth-century American poetry is a line thirty ems long.

Q: To be more specific: could you maybe comment on the form of one poem?

JM: I have a lyric called "Samos" halfway through *Sandover*, which might stand for a truly fulfilling use of form. It consists of five twelve-line stanzas followed by an envoi of five lines. These sixty-five lines use only five end words, each recurring thirteen times according to a fixed pattern—rather like a sestina, only much more demanding. I decided, before I'd gone very far, to use homophones instead of always repeating the actual word; so we have "fire" and "magnifier," or "light" and "chrysolite." The form isn't my invention but Dante's. A poem called (as many poems of various forms were called in his day) "Canzone" occurs among his collected lyrics. W. H. Auden was, I think, the first poet since Dante to use the form. He has a poem titled "Canzone" which, however, reduces Dante's six-line envoi to five lines. I copied Auden in this tiny, streamlining impulse. "Samos" appears as part of a much longer poem in which Auden is a principal actor and Dante a major influence. The numbers twelve and five, for reasons I can't possibly go into here, are crucial to the doctrines behind the long poem. The end words—*sense, water, light, fire, land*—bring to the mind of a reader who hasn't skipped to the middle of the book a wealth of resonance. Our instructors, for example, in this volume of the poem are four elemental angels, those of earth, water, air and light, and fire. Their refrain, in lesson after lesson, is "make sense of it." Well, to cut these endless matters short, I picked the most constricting form imaginable, yet the poem, which got written in only a day or two, came flowing forth, as if from a part of my mind I'm all too seldom in touch with.

Rilke used to believe in keeping his "instrument" in good working order. This meant writing all kinds of short, not-too-demanding poems in a variety of forms, always humbly waiting for the day when a completely different muse would sit down at the keyboard. When I'd finished "Samos" I understood as never before what Rilke meant.

Q: How do you know when a poem is finished?

JM: Certain operas—like *Falstaff* or *The Rake's Progress*—end with everyone onstage and the houselights coming on before the singing stops. It's like that. There'll be a last hour, or even a couple of afternoons, during which everything connects. Dozens of small, last-minute changes can be made quickly and with confidence in the interest of some finally emerging (and often unexpected) harmony. It's the rapidity of these touches that tells me the performance is ending, and that I'll presently be walking up the aisle with a high heart.

Q: How much time do you spend on a poem? How much revising do you do?

JM: A lot. In the sixties, it was politically correct to revise as little as possible, on the theory that the first words to spill onto the page were the most unguardedly genuine. On the contrary, I thought, they were the most inaccurate and perfunctory. Rules shouldn't be made about this. Some writers are marvels of spontaneity. Look at Byron: now and then he changed a line, always to great advantage, but otherwise it just poured out. It takes me forty drafts or more to sound *that* spontaneous!

Not that it's altogether a matter of tone. Revision is my own way of arriving at my "idea," at what I have to say. (Tone is a vital part of that, of course.) It can be shrouded in murk at the outset. But by the time I'm done the poem will be clear at least to its author. Perhaps not always clear as day. Let's say clear as a fine midnight.

Q: Will you tell us what poets—major or minor—most influenced you—when you were in school, perhaps, or after, just reading on your own?

JM: As an adolescent, I was drawn to minor poets—luckily. The other literati at school were deep into Whitman or Shelley or Eliot. I was reading Elinor Wylie, Humbert Wolfe, José Maria de Heredia. This wasn't wholly reprehensible on my part. I turned to these poets on my own, as models, if you like. The year was 1942 and the major English poets, from Spenser through Browning, were being read in the classroom. The poets I liked were highly accomplished technically, and what they had to say was simple enough to be on a par with my own teenage effusions. Had I tried at that age to write like Whitman or Eliot, the result would have been pitifully mawkish.

At college I read Keats and Pope, Donne and Milton, Proust and Dante. The latter two have remained emblematic, throughout my life, of what a writer can achieve. Before I graduated I'd read—thanks to a teacher, Kimon Friar, who helped me immensely with the poems I was writing—all the modern poetry that, in those days, never appeared in the curriculum: Yeats, Stevens, Dylan Thomas, Pound, as well as lesser figures. My absolute favorite contemporary poet turned out to be Elizabeth Bishop, though I didn't "discover" her until I was teaching, a few years later.

Q: How do you feel about teaching as a way of life for a poet?

JM: Many poets seem to take to it. I might have done so too, if I could have taught subjects like geometry or first-year French. Teaching literature, though, or worse, running a poetry workshop, left me unable to face the English language in any form by the end of the day. So I've done very little teaching. Fortunately, I didn't have to earn a living.

Q: Did you ever have any doubts about devoting your life to poetry?

JM: I seriously doubted, at twenty, if the quality of my work warranted a life devoted to poetry. I had awfully high standards, knew that I could "write," yet saw myself as a narrow, trivial person not much at ease in the world. Who would want to read poems by such a person? Once on the page, however—or better yet, in print—my poems looked almost as authoritative as those by the profound and far-seeing writers I stood in awe of. So I kept postponing the hour of reckoning, and guess what? In about fifteen or twenty years all sense of imposture had completely disappeared. There's a Max Beerbohm story, "The Happy Hypocrite," about how in time the mask *becomes* the face. Look at our statesmen if you doubt this can happen. The psyche is amazingly permissive.

Q: Are there right reasons for becoming a poet—as opposed to the romantic reasons that draw people into writing: ego, fame, freedom, *la vie bohème?*

JM: It's an ongoing education. It allows for a life of self-discovery and self-transcendence, both, in which there is (marvelously) no wasted time. One little warning: if by the age of—twenty? fifteen? ten?—you have never tasted the rapture of writing something down, even the poorest jingle, then maybe the life of poetry is something you'd better not contemplate.

Q: What advice do you have for a serious person who is persuaded he or she has talent and is willing to sacrifice for it?

JM: Learn if possible from reading—and imitating—the poets that enchant you. Don't enter a workshop prematurely. The workshop could be useful, provided you've already developed self-confidence and technique enough to hold your own against the inevitable prejudices of the instructor. Then you can use the experience to test, not your writing, but the quality of your experience and the strength of your character. Travel if you can, cultivate "alienation" if you like. There's no need to wallow in the assumptions of your time and place, since your work will reflect them, whatever you do.

Q: Any hints about publishing?

JM: Publishing? Few national magazines are receptive to work by an unknown. Sad to say, it helps if in your accompanying note to an editor you can drop a name: "So-and-so thought you'd like to see these." (Be sure that's the case!) There's something to be said for waiting. "To be twenty and a poet is to be twenty. To be forty and a poet is to be a poet." Who said that?

Q: What books do you recommend to get a young poet started?

JM: John Hollander's compact manual, *Rhyme's Reason,* is a delight, and tells you everything about form. But anything can get you started on a poem. Science, history, the world outside your window. That's where the images are.

Q: What are the books you keep on your desk wherever you are?

JM: *The American Heritage Dictionary.* They've phased out the wonderful appendix of Indo-European roots, but that edition is still findable if you take the trouble. I keep the complete *Oxford English Dictionary* across the room, both in Connecticut and Florida. The set in Florida used to belong to Auden. His friend Chester Kallman gave it to me after Auden's death. Other dictionaries: French, German, Italian, Greek, and Latin. Brewer's *Dictionary of Fact and Fable.* Smith's *Smaller Classical Dictionary. Whitfield's Rhyming Dictionary* (yes, yes) and *Roget's Thesaurus.* Strunk and White's *The Elements of Style.*

Q: Do you have any strong feelings about poetry in translation?

JM: Translation usually makes a poem sound easier to write than in fact it was. This can be dangerous when there's a vogue for a foreign poet— like Neruda in the sixties or Rilke in the forties—and innocent young Americans start imitating the language of the translations rather than the inevitably more personal (in its complexity and resonance) original. On the other hand, poetry isn't wholly a matter of verbal effects. We can remember images for some poems long after the wording has faded. I suppose I keep an eye on foreign poetry in translation in much the same spirit that I go to a film: to experience something valuable in which language plays a relatively minor part.

Q: Have you been satisfied with the translations of your poems?

JM: I've not been translated very much. I'm not complaining! After all, I usually write in hopes of defying paraphrase. Years ago a short poem, "Mirror," appeared in Italian. It has a line about the grandchildren of the household, grown up by now, sitting at the window "with novels face-down on the sill." The translator did his best—but in his version the grandchildren themselves were facedown on the windowsill, no doubt from reading too much small print.

A few years ago three intrepid women—two Americans and an Italian—wrote to me from Umbria that they'd begun putting *Mirabell* into Italian, and did I mind? Far from it, especially when I saw what they'd done. It wasn't yet a final draft, yet so readable that I was able to forget about "my" original, indeed could often not remember the English wording of a given line. What had come through were things like the story, the pace, the implications—plus the rich new dimension of another language. It was a revelation. Still I'd like to think that the Italian read so well in part because I'd taken such pains with the English. One wants a reward to be for good behavior, not bad.

Q: What may we expect next from your pen?

JM: Last summer I wrote a little play which is being put on for a single performance in December in New York. This year I've been at work on some very short prose pieces. And poems, all along. Oh yes, North Point Press is bringing out a volume of collected prose this fall. Mostly odds and ends. Even interviews like this one!

An Interview
with Thomas Bolt

Q: The traditional question: What are you working on at the moment?

JM: It's hard to say. My *computer* is working on a memoir of the early 1950s, and I'm simply hanging on to its coattails. Prose was becoming increasingly laborious to write—I could spend a week simply working up my courage to start a three-page piece. The computer changed all that. I am Kundry to its Klingsor. I rise from sleep with a shriek to do its bidding.

Q: Why the early 1950s?

JM: It was a turning point. I went to Europe and stayed for two and a half years. Not a particularly happy time, but I must have needed to break with what I knew.

Q: Was something of this period in your life evoked by the mood of Francis Tanning at the start of your novel, *The Seraglio*? What, precisely, were you breaking with, and how? Was it a time of experimentation, sort of an internal *Wanderjahr*? Were you writing at the time?

JM: I wasn't writing, no. Francis Tanning wasn't writing either; that's one reason we were both so unhappy. He seems to represent the person I might have become if I'd had no talent. Not that I was at all sure of *having* talent, back then. The point, in any case, was to break with constrain-

Bomb, Summer 1991.

ing ideas of how I should live. My parents' ideas and my friends', but also my own.

Q: There's more than one way to break: in the middle of *Water Street*, in the middle of the poem "To a Butterfly," the poem's tone, after a "sincere" beginning, is shattered by the word *"Enough."* The sentiment, the metaphors so far developed (and the reader's yes, isn't that so) are called abruptly to account and rejected.

> *Goodness, how tired one grows*
> *Just looking through a prism:*
> *Allegory, symbolism.*
> *I've tried, Lord knows,*
>
> *To keep from seeing double,*
> *Blushed for whenever I did,*
> *Prayed like a boy my cheek be hid*
> *By manly stubble.*

The poem proceeds by encompassing and developing its own critical contradiction. This kind of deflationary reinvigoration, the midstream thought correction so central to *Water Street* and nearly everything you've written since, seems to have become, in your work, a consistent basis for investigation, a way to reconcile hope and fear, a romantic's reality and a realist's disgust with the romantic. When and how did you first develop your technique of abrupt dislocation of tone?

JM: The technique probably came to me from writing dialogue. After my *First Poems* I wrote a novel and a couple of plays. They loosened me up some. Especially the plays. Writing for the stage, you didn't feel obliged to carry an idea to its conclusion, to make the kind of "argument" you try for in the single unbroken flow of a lyric. If things got sticky you called in another voice to interrupt. In a poem the voice would usually be your own, but from another part of yourself.

Q: How important is this tactic (this way of thinking) to your work?

JM: The danger is that the tack becomes a tic, an automatic escape route to the exclusion of all others. At worst it keeps me from facing my true subject or its implications. I try to save it for moments of genuine impatience with my "material"—if that word covers both form and content.

Q: A related question: your poems are continually surprising, in part because of a propensity for self-correction, but that only accounts for part of the inventive unpredictability. How important are surprise, astonishment, an awkward brush with the unknown, to your art?

JM: All that's part of the silver lining. Life's advantage over art is its genius for the unexpected. Just as new wrinkles in the tradition imply something unforeseeable in the life of a particular artist, so dislocations in a text or a painting can take on the look of shorthand for life itself.

Q: Are you *yourself* in poems, a version of your real self, or the famous "I character" of the old New Criticism? If your lyric "I" is James Merrill (apart from JM of *Sandover*), how does the literary James Merrill differ from the one met outside the books?

JM: We shot a film of *Sandover* last summer. I've just spent a couple of weeks in lush Hollywood editing rooms, watching the special effects be added. It's amazing what can be done. Our demonic "bats" now appear in black-and-white negative with a gilt mirror frame—so simple and so weird; in close-up their teeth look black and the dark inside of the mouth reads as a kind of terrible snow-white saliva. But that's not what you asked, is it? I'm one of the actors. I play myself; "JM" rather. When it's over Helen Vendler interviews a me who isn't at all like the character in the film.

Q: How do you account for the difference?

JM: Well . . . Perhaps it's that JM was at no loss for words. The script had been written and he's memorized his lines. *My* lines, if you like. But the person being interviewed has no idea what he's going to say next, so that his face and gestures and tone of voice are all noticeably more ingratiating, more placating—as if begging pardon for all the dumb things he's going to end up saying in a "live" situation where he can't collect himself and work up his answers in solitude.

Q: Like *these* answers.

JM: Exactly. Well, that's just one instance among dozens, or thousands. It doesn't surprise me, does it you?—that we should be different people in our work. Or should I say the same person at different stages of composure? I mean, after all, if art has any advantage over daily life it's that it allows us to get things *right* for a change.

Q: You have a poem, "Santo," in *Late Settings*; and a one-act play in verse, "The Image Maker," in *The Inner Room*, features a Santero. How did you come to be interested in Santería, a major religion in my Lower East Side neighborhood?

JM: It wasn't Santería itself that interested me so much as the idea of repainting and renaming the statuette. This seemed so much like what the artist does—recycling his material, trying it another way if it no longer does the trick. That little poem "Santo" struck me, after writing it, as expressing in miniature the whole self-revising nature of the *Sandover* books where no truth is allowed to rot under a single, final aspect. I mean, in *Sandover* God himself is given a new name and new attributes; you can't get much more antifundamentalist than that.

Q: A remark by Vladimir Nabokov ranking Andrei Bely's *Petersburg* with Proust's *Lost Time* and Joyce's *Ulysses* resulted in an immediate English translation and a new readership, as it was probably calculated to do. Assuming poems are allowed, anymore, to be great (no capital G, but also without quotation marks), what great poems of the twentieth century are we missing out on?

JM: Auden's *The Sea and the Mirror* and/or *For the Time Being*. These two long poems were the first Auden that I read with full appreciation. Along with everything else, they're wonderful showcases for forms and tones. *Artorius* by John Heath-Stubbs. Everything he does has distinction. This is an especially rich and nutty affair based on Arthurian legend. One section is a little Noh play in which a wandering scholar meets Guinevere's ghost. John Hollander's *Visions from the Ramble* and *Aspects of Espionage*—these are marvels of vision and wit. The former's rich, nostalgic frescoes depict the shaping years of a New York poet. The latter shows him irrevocably committed to his codes and fellow agents, working in secret for the mother tongue. *In and Out* and *Academic Festival Overtures* by Daryl Hine. Both autobiographical, both dealing poignantly and hilariously with early sexual stirrings, both triumphant vindications of meter. I should probably mention *The Return* by Frederick Turner; Irving Feldman's *All of Us Here*; Alfred Corn's *Notes from a Child of Paradise*; Gjertrud Schnackenberg's "The Lamplit Answer"; Richard Kenney's "The Hours of the Day" and "Orrery"—where to stop? Shall I embarrass you by including "The Way Out of the Wood" by Thomas Bolt?

Q: I'm beyond embarrassment, but off to the bookstore. What poem of *yours* deserves closer attention, or seems to have fallen through the cracks?

JM: I can tell you one poem I wish *would* fall through the cracks. It's called "Kite Poem," and no anthology for young readers would seem complete without it. So many anthologists do their work by culling from previous anthologies rather than the poets' actual books. When I was a young firebrand of forty I implied as much in a note to a professor somewhere, who'd asked for permission to use "Kite Poem" in his forthcoming textbook. It really touched a nerve. He wrote back a letter beginning, in effect, "Why you little shit . . ." Elizabeth Bishop had the same problem with "The Fish." It was made to seem at times like the only poem she'd ever written. Of course it's a hundred times better than "Kite Poem." One Christmas I received a book all about the zoology of fish. It was inscribed to me from "Elizabeth Fishop."

Q: Very nice. Was Elizabeth Bishop an influence as well as a friend and a colleague?

JM: Oh, goodness, yes. I should have added her to my list of instructors in the art of breaking. Her way of interrupting herself—but much more. Her natural, completely unaffected intelligence. Her love of the trivial: birdcages, paper flowers. The human scale of her work, so refreshing next to the modernist "giants" like Pound, or her friend Robert Lowell. The lucid, intimate tone of voice. She set standards for me as no other contemporary did. I don't always follow them but I can never lose sight of them.

Q: Who, Proust or Cavafy, is the slightly larger inspiration? Why?

JM: Proust more than Cavafy. I love Cavafy. I've learned a lot from him as a poet: his desert-dry tone, his mirage-like technical effects—something one would never guess from his translators. But he hasn't shaped my way of seeing to the degree that Proust has. For one thing, Cavafy is a miniaturist; for another, he writes without metaphor. I mean it! Virtually nowhere in his work will you find metaphor or simile. He's John the Baptist eating locusts in the desert, far from any "Jordan" of metaphor. Whereas in Proust that water table is all but flush with the surface of the page.

Q: Do *you* ever write entirely without metaphor? How important is metaphor to poetry; and what do you think of the flat, photorealist ametaphoric verse that's been popular the past decade or so?

JM: A lot of metaphor must be in the beholder's eye. My kind of mind is so used to "seeing double" that it finds unwelcome subtexts in an instruction manual. To put it too bluntly, I think metaphor *is* poetry; and if I open to a poem without any, I can't help trying to see what's there in a faintly metaphorical or symbolic light. It's the way I'd look at a photograph, if it comes to that. How else could a picture be worth a thousand words? A psychiatrist friend calls the creative temperament Janusian—after Janus, whose nature is to look both ways. I thought everybody was like that but he said no, that for him, the implications of phrases like a "dark white" or a "burning cold"—which are mother's milk to me—left him feeling, you know, seasick.

Q: Speaking of metaphor, my candidate for the greatest American poet of the nineteenth century is Emily Dickinson—what do you think?

JM: Hear, hear! I mean that. She brings off so much of it through puns, rhyme, cadence—things only the ear discovers.

Q: Who is A. H. Clarendon, the authority you cite in the midst of "The Thousand and Second Night"?

JM: A saintly human being and a superb hand at bridge.

Q: Duplicate?

JM: You got it.

Q: Do you feel any kinship with William Blake? Are you on the side of wild prophecy, or careful consideration, or do you moderate between the two?

JM: I'm on the side of careful consideration. I'm suspicious of the wild, the grandiose, the larger-than-life. Taking up all that emotional space. I love the side of Blake that saw eternity in a grain of sand. What an inspired metaphor! So much better than "fear in a handful of red dust." (Wait, though, do you hear, in the Eliot? "Dead rust . . . ?") Even in the prophetic books—not that I've read them—there'll be ravishing details that show Blake's early love of Pope. Of course *Sandover* simply swarms with "wild prophecy," ideas, everything I've tried to avoid in my work, or think myself incapable of. It's the unconscious—personal or collective—taking its revenge.

Q: The word "red" is not in the original. But a poet's mismemory is often revealing. . . . Now, one of your biggest fans I know is a sewer worker who has a band in which he plays electric guitar.

JM: Hmm. . . . Clean him up and bring him to tea?

Q: He's quite clean; he'd be delighted. But transitionally speaking, one wonderful thing about good poetry is the surprising broadness of its appeal. Yet some people appear to want to communicate only in shorthand with a cozy group of folks with shared political or aesthetic assumptions. Is there a kind of discipline that reaches over the obvious problems of disaffection, miscommunication, plain disagreement? What's good and bad about "the tendency toward progressive decentralization in contemporary poetry"? There used to be two or three camps, and now there are, seemingly, hundreds.

JM: To me, what unifies or centralizes all those different camps—and might conceivably discipline them, too, if they gave it a chance—would be the past. The past they derive from whether they know it or not, as well as the past they'll have become in five or ten years. That's all it takes nowadays. Am I wrong?

One gets the sense of tribe after tribe of poets who eat—*read*, rather, only their still-living kinsmen. Even the cannibal who devours his enemy has sounder instincts. I don't mean that you have to have the Grand Tradition of World Poetry at your fingertips; just that there's more to learn from an ancestor like Byron or Herbert than from your buddy in the workshop who reads Neruda in English.

What's good about this situation? It siphons off into harmless backwaters hundreds, perhaps thousands, of young people whom poetry will fulfill and civilize without their really amounting to much. The few of them who do will have had a great deal of provincialism to overcome, a diet of Wonder Bread and Coke. A new regime will make them stronger, more original, more resolute. Like a fat child (I was one) who knows better than ever to let *that* happen again.

Q: Are you saying that awareness of past literature is enough to make what we write more worth reading?

JM: Oh, God, no, is that what I—strike it from the record! I just mean I wish people read more widely and wrote less narrowly.

Q: I think everyone could agree with that—why miss out on anything? You've given us bat-winged angels with glowing eyes, and transmutations to the peacock form; please describe your muse.

JM: You've seen her described at some length in *Sandover*.

Q: Right, wow, yes, all nine muses appear.

JM: No, no, not a bit, that's just vaudeville. The poem's real muse is Maria—"Muse of my off-days," I called her in real life. Mild, self-mocking, worldly; a slow gardener; dressed in black to match her humor;

private, attentive, polylingual. Then we get a more unnerving muse in Nature, who turns out to be a version of Graves's Triple Goddess; her other names are Psyche and Chaos. *She* can appear in any guise she fancies. Her characteristics—the benign ones—are boundless autocratic energy, lack of humor, and uncommon charm. In part to defuse or domesticate her, I pictured her to myself as the actress Ina Claire: bobbed blonde hair, big blue eyes, dressed in white with black ribbons, for a Chekhovian house party.

Q: Speaking of "The Book of a Thousand and One Evenings Spent / With David Jackson at the Ouija Board / In Touch with Ephraim Our Familiar Spirit" . . . in some incidental and some intrinsic ways, *The Changing Light at Sandover* is an apotheosis of homosexuality.

Refreshingly, certainly, compared to the traditional aposiopesis of homosexuality.

JM: My, all these Greek words! Perhaps one or two of our readers are wondering what that second one means.

Q: Aposiopesis means—but I blush to tell. It means leaving an expression of any thought suddenly and resoundingly incomplete, having become flustered, or tripped over the social obstacle of unmentionability. A last minute self-repression, ending in embarrassed silence.

JM: Very nice.

Q: In a well-known passage of the "Mirabell" section, a bat still named (numbered?) 741 proclaims, as he is ("FILLD / WITH IS IT MANNERS?") changing into the peacock Mirabell:

> LOVE OF ONE MAN FOR ANOTHER OR LOVE BETWEEN WOMEN
> IS A NEW DEVELOPMENT OF THE PAST 4000 YEARS
> ENCOURAGING SUCH MIND VALUES AS PRODUCE THE BLOSSOMS
> OF POETRY & MUSIC, THOSE 2 PRINCIPAL LIGHTS OF
> GOD BIOLOGY.
> . . . .
> FOR EVER SINCE THEIR SHAPING OF THE ORIGINAL CLAY
> & THE PLUCKING OF THE APE (OR THE APPLE) FROM ITS TREE
> WE HAVE AN IRRESISTIBLE FORCE TO DEAL WITH: MIND.
> UNTIL THEN ALL HAD BEEN INSTINCTIVE NATURE   A CHAOS
> LIKE FALLEN TREES IN THE EMPTY FOREST   NO ONE TO HEAR,

OR AUTUMN'S UNHATCHED EGG   NO ONE TO REMEMBER & MOURN.
NOW MIND IN ITS PURE FORM IS A NONSEXUAL PASSION
OR A UNISEXUAL ONE PRODUCING ONLY LIGHT.
FEW PAINTERS OR SCULPTORS CAN ENTER THIS LIFE OF THE MIND.
THEY (LIKE ALL SO-CALLD NORMAL LOVERS) MUST PRODUCE AT LAST
BODIES   THEY DO NOT EXIST FOR ANY OTHER PURPOSE

This passage is followed instantly by the disclaimer "Come now, admit that certain very great / Poets and musicians have been straight." But one must feel your double mind is at work. The breeder/reader is perhaps uneasy, but the twentieth century hasn't been particularly easy on readers of any stripe. And of course the real slur here is on painters, though you have written admiringly of Corot. Comments?

JM: I always winced at that put-down of painting. We get a defense of painting in a later volume, but it doesn't amount to much. A kind word for Chardin and Sesshu. . . .

There's a vast amount of questionable dogma in *Sandover*. Remember that the speaker of this passage is demonic. Still, childlessness gets praised by just about all the characters in the poem; yet its high point, for me, is when that baby—Robert Morse's new incarnation—gets born in the "Coda." Nature herself coos and simpers over it. Of course that particular baby has been programmed to become a great musician, which sugars the pill—sorry, wrong metaphor. I wonder, by the way, where they get the idea that homosexuals aren't breeders. I know quite a few who are.

As for any apotheosis of homosexuality, in a cosmos as perpetually self-revising as *Sandover*'s, this or that idea can easily be raised to the highest power, then demoted when it's no longer of use. I'm guardedly grateful for this emphasis within the poem. We have so few texts of really high quality—Shakespeare's sonnets, some Platonic dialogues, some of Gertrude Stein, Oscar Wilde's criticism—for gay readers to find themselves in. Without, I mean, the obligatory pity and terror of, say, *Death in Venice*.

Q: Your poems are included in various anthologies, everything from *The Contemporary American Poets: American Poetry Since 1940* to the more recent *Gay and Lesbian Poetry in Our Time*. Besides satisfying curiosity as to which poets are what and come from where—I never knew that poet was American!—how useful are such categorical breakdowns? In combining the two, I don't mean to infer (though some have) that one's sexuality is a nation-state. But in a time when we who might prefer to read (without hunting in a hundred crannies?) all the good poetry we can, feel absurdly cut off from Australian, Jamaican, Israeli, English, Irish, Scottish, and even Canadian poetry written in this language—not to mention all the many American groups a little or a lot off the meandering mainstream—have anthologies become overspecific?

JM: This goes back to what we were saying about all the different camps. I hate this taxonomic bias. So did Elizabeth Bishop. She wouldn't even allow her work to appear in a women's anthology. Until recently men and women could read and admire each other's work. Now I know a woman poet who doesn't allow men's and women's books in the same room. It's the Salem witch hunt with the genders reversed!

Q: If books rubbing up against each other spawn literary criticism, keeping them apart might not be such a bad idea. But back to categories: what special strengths come to your work as a result of your being an American, or being gay?

JM: The forms I use came originally from Europe. Being American allows me to question them, to adapt them freely and without guilt to my own needs. The attitudes I live by were no doubt first instilled by my parents, but being gay I can turn them inside out, if I like, and having grown up and seen how humanly fallible my parents were I can—well, you see what I'm saying. At sixty-five I'm no longer a national or a sexual being so much as whoever I've become over the years. When I go abroad, or join a dinner party of husbands and wives, I feel like a well-disposed ambassador from the other side; we make one another feel worldly and tolerant. Most of the time, that is. Get me caught in a demonstration and who starts shouting "I'm Canadian!" In six languages.

Q: What kind of anthology would you find most meaningful?

JM: Aside from the multiregional ones you propose, I'd go for the old-fashioned kind, like Untermeyer's or Oscar Williams's. Kimon Friar and John Brinnin did a marvelous one in 1951, full of New Criticism explications, and including passages from *Finnegans Wake* and *Nightwood*. Those were the good old days when literary politics were literary rather than political or sexual. For example, Oscar Williams in person was shall we say rather a creep. Be that as it may, Kimon and John decided to include a couple of his poems; you can be a creep and still write well. But do you know what poor insecure Mr. Williams did? He had his publisher ask for a letter from the anthologists, saying that they weren't including his poems in order to hold them up to ridicule. It breaks the heart.

Q: What's the importance of music to your work? Whose and how?

JM: When I was fourteen or fifteen opera was my *éducation sentimentale*. It gave form to the wildest emotions; I tried them on, one after another, posturing in front of the phonograph. As I grew older I'd find some of my technical problems solved by reference to a Beethoven piano sonata, a Berlioz song. I wrote "variations" on the model of Mozart's A Major Sonata or Beethoven's Opus 34. The very distancing helps, letting your concerns ricochet off another medium. You learn about tempo and tone, the uses of dissonance, modulation into a new key. I'm not sure how this works but it often does.

Q: What's most fun about poetry?

JM: To engage as much of the self as possible . . . and then to forget the self—is that fun? I think so. Innocent fun. I'd like to stress the innocence. Hours go by and nobody's been harmed. The neighbors don't even know you're at home.

An Interview
with Augustin Hedberg

Q: When did it occur to you that writing poetry would be your life's work?

JM: I knew by the time I was fifteen that here was one thing I did well. Still, I didn't presume on my talent being enough to fill a lifetime. Or that poetry would be my métier rather than fiction or playwriting. By the time I was thirty I'd tried my hand at these other disciplines. They helped me a lot. Through them I glimpsed new possibilities for the poems I went on to write. The fiction taught me to be anecdotal; the plays, to use more than a single voice, or tone. So you could say that, yes, by thirty I was committed and even launched.

Q: Can you identify the origins of your interest in poetry? Was it nurtured most by teachers? Family? Peers? Or was it primarily self-motivated?

JM: My grandmother had a school-of-Burne-Jones illustration of Tennyson's "Home they brought her warrior dead," which I pondered very deeply at five or six. My mother wrote charming doggerel to commemorate family events. These "origins" pointed to a notion of poetry as mere entertainment or ornament. Only when I came to Lawrenceville did I find teachers—Thomas Johnson, Charles Raymond—who were so clearly

The Lawrentian, Autumn 1991.

serious about poetry that my ideas changed completely. I should mention a young librarian named Gerrish Thurber, then faculty advisor to the *Lit*, who read everything Freddy Buechner and I wrote. His patience and encouragement meant the world to us—a *grown-up* who read us without condescension! But this brings me to Freddy—the only member of my poetical peer group. I began writing in imitation of him. By the following year we were reading each other's work avidly, lovingly, enviously. Let me quote from a memoir I've been at work on: "Freddy's poems, just by our being friends, and young, quivered with a live magic barely attached to any historical context. I read them the way a spider in Hagia Sophia, oblivious to the great dome, might have scrutinized her neighbor's web." I can't imagine having begun to write without his example.

Q: What were your favorite poems when you were sixteen? What are some of your favorite poems (or poets) today?

JM: I loved the Keats odes. Some Milton, some Tennyson. We were lucky to have been given, in class, quite a thorough overview of the canon, from Spenser through Browning and Emily Dickinson. But on the whole I felt less threatened by second-rate work. Elinor Wylie, or Millay, would be examples. Ideas, let's face it, were hardly their long suit, so that when I imitated them, my own poems didn't come off too badly by comparison. As they did if ever I besottedly tried to write a Miltonic sonnet. (Let me quickly add that the poet whose ideas *are* his long suit—rather than his nimbleness with language and image—is in trouble.)

Today my taste is for slightly less elaborate, slightly more casual work. I love the spontaneity of Byron, the dry, conversational note in Cavafy, the pure, unpretentious working of George Herbert. I came to him through Elizabeth Bishop. She was a major revelation. I read her first at twenty-two. Here, not a moment too soon, was the antidote to those ambitious and daunting "giants" of modernism. Elizabeth (I take the liberty) created, by contrast, an oeuvre on a human scale. Simple enough for a child, subtle enough for a philosopher, sad, amusing, never dull. I needn't go on about her. Since her death (in 1979) her star shines brighter and brighter.

Q: Are there particular poems that you think everyone should read? Poems that should be common intellectual possessions imparted through schools? And what poems would you select for this honor?

JM: This goes back to what we were saying about the need to have a sense of the field. I'm afraid I don't see how you can separate art from a degree of elitism. Even in a primitive society there'll be a drummer or a carver of pictographs who stands out as better than his fellows. Must the tribe's children not be allowed to appreciate this difference? Are we to marvel at Sharon Olds without having read "Lycidas"? Would *she* enjoy that kind of ignorant acclaim? Richard Wilbur told me that he recently gave a talk to the Amherst freshman class not one of whom had read "Lycidas" or knew who wrote it. I wish someone would tell me what particular body of knowledge has shouldered "Lycidas" out of the curriculum.

The list of works vital to a young person's education in our society can't help changing periodically. It doesn't matter if in a given decade Shakespeare is thought more relevant than Dante or Jane Austen, less profound than George Eliot. The point is that Dante and Shakespeare and Austen and Eliot still be on the horizon, and that we keep our sights raised high enough to see them on a clear day. The list in our time would have to be more open and polycultural than it was in, say, Matthew Arnold's. We could do with less Greek and Latin drama, perhaps, and read *The Tale of Genji* instead. But don't get me started here—I'd be at it until Christmas.

Q: Who were the contemporary poets that you read with the most interest when you were a student at Lawrenceville?

JM: In those days it was all but unheard-of to teach a living poet in class. On my own I read Frost, Cummings, Stephen Vincent Benét, Edna St. Vincent Millay. I'd taken a peek at Eliot and Stevens, but my absolute favorite was Elinor Wylie. I still gasp at her technical bravura. Freddy and I also devoured the fin-de-siècle poets on both sides of the Channel. Oscar Wilde and Alice Meynell, Verlaine and Baudelaire. Heredia, Henri de Régnier—anyone so long as they were "decadent."

Q: The teaching of poetry at the secondary school level seems to have changed from an emphasis on reading it toward a greater emphasis on writing it. What's lost? What's gained?

JM: Writing poetry without reading it—or having read a certain amount of it—is a high-risk situation. You could be infected by the poems your roommate writes, supposing she's read nothing but Neruda in a user-friendly translation. It is vital to get some sense of the overall "field." The advantages of being encouraged to write have clearly to do with discovering your feelings and using your own observations instead of stealing Keats's images. I submit nonetheless that reading great poetry teaches us how to feel and how to observe, and that our own fine feelings will interest nobody—even ourselves—until we've mastered the skills needed to articulate them. You don't expect painters or composers to "create" without a good deal of academic discipline. Drawing, orchestration, whatever. Why expect a good poem to be written on instinct alone?

Q: I guess for financial reasons, most poets today are found on university faculties. Has this killed poetry's bohemian tradition and made the typical poet a politically correct teaching professional in designer rags?

JM: Well, clearly the Dark Ages are upon us. If so, the academies, as the monasteries of our day, may be our only hope. They present horrible drawbacks—deadly textual analysis, party-line politics, a dogmatic pluralism almost Stalinist in its rigidity. . . . I keep looking to popular culture for salvation but it doesn't come.

Q: If we were doing an article called "Great Moments in Poetry at Lawrenceville," what anecdotes could you contribute from your years here?

JM: Well, there was a final exam in fifth-form English which asked us to analyze a poem of our own choosing, and Freddy chose a six-line poem he'd written himself, following it with a long tongue-in-cheek exegesis. We imagined consternation rippling through the English department. The poem described a forest pond and began: "To look down into the upness of it all . . ."

Then there was the moment I've already described in a poem:

> In vain old Mr. Raymond's sky-blue stare
> Paled with revulsion when I spoke to him
> About my final paper. "Jim,"
> He quavered, "don't, don't write on Baudelaire."
> ["Days of 1941 and '44"]

Q: Do you have any advice for a young poet?

JM: Don't just read living poets; without a sense of the past, you'll be provincial and expendable. Learn languages. Don't model your work on poetry in translation. Listen hard to good talk. Write on Baudelaire.

An Interview with Roderick Townley

Q: Was there anything to the Williams/Eliot feud? Are there really different breeds of poet?

JM: Of course there are. It's like the Balkans. It's a form of nationalism.

Q: What are the separate nations?

JM: There's the tribe of Pound. That fractions off into Dr. Williams. The racial characteristics would be lines that break off at the word "of" or "the," in order to avoid the appearance of a metrical line. I think this is as much a tribal thing as the practice of circumcision.

Q: But I suppose the difficulty for most poets, regardless of tribal affiliation, is finding the way into poetry, out of the confusion of outer life. How do you do it?

JM: I don't think of it as reaching a sanctum. I like a lot of distraction and interruption within the texture of a poem, so that it does partly imitate the distractions of outer life.

Q: You don't need to hide away?

JM: In the act of writing you are so self-absorbed, you sort of lose yourself, and that is a wonderful stage to reach. But I don't happen to need four unbroken hours in order to do that. I can do it for a bit in ten minutes if necessary. And I don't mind if the telephone rings while I'm working. I love persons from Porlock.

The Keep, Spring 1993.

Q: Who?

JM: Persons from Porlock? Remember the man who interrupted "Kubla Khan"? Coleridge could never finish it after "a person from Porlock" came to call.

Q: He may have saved us from a long bad poem.

JM: That could be.

Q: Most poets dread the Porlockians, because it's so hard to escape them. But you have a number of getaway places.

JM: I'm always on the run, and hiding out. I'm the happiest when most of the people I know don't know exactly how to reach me. I like to stay in a place for a month or two and get away. And the phone will ring and no one will answer.

Q: So you're a fugitive poet?

JM: Yes!

Q: I understand the poetry of exile. Being away from home makes everything bright and new.

JM: Yes. Also I'm prone to sociability, and if I'm where I can be reached for dinner parties, I'll go to them. Then suddenly the fourth evening will be free and I'll just collapse, instead of writing. These things can be very tiring.

Q: Do you assign a time for writing every day?

JM: I usually write in the morning.

Q: About right now.

JM: But these days I'm not counting on getting much work done. I've got this copyedited manuscript to go over and take down to the publisher tomorrow morning. That's the main thing I have to do.

Q: A new book?

JM: It's the memoir I've been working on—or my word processor has been working on.

Q: You've written your memoirs?

JM: Just two and a half years. My first big flight was to Europe at the age of twenty-four, and I stayed for two and a half years. When I got a word processor, since *it* had no memories, it put pressure on me to come up with some of mine. And after about 100,000 words, it flashed on the screen: "Thank you, that will do."

Q: You need a larger memory base.

JM: Perhaps.

Q: So when did you take up computer writing?

JM: About three years ago. I love it!

Q: Does it help with the poetry?

JM: Oh yes. I don't mislay any drafts anymore.

Q: Has it affected the results? Anything a reader would notice?

JM: I think the temptation, certainly in prose, where I'm not very much at home, is to overwrite . . . to make it fancier than it need be.

Q: But it's easier to revise on the computer. Isn't that good?

JM: It's good unless the end product is too ornate.

Q: Oh I see. See, I get ornate at the beginning, then I take *away* the adjectives.

JM: Well, that's what I've learned to do also. Suddenly I can press a button and a whole paragraph goes into oblivion. It's a wonderful absolute power.

Q: Does it go where Auden can read it in the afterlife?

JM: Oh, I think he's reading it as it's written. He may urge me to press that button, who knows?

Q: Do you feel still in contact with the world you wrote about in *The Changing Light at Sandover*?

JM: Not really, no.

Q: You don't do as much with the Ouija board?

JM: Hardly at all. Just a few courtesy calls.

Q: Reading *Sandover*, one might think you were just copying out messages from the Ouija board. At other times one suspects the poem is a work of pure imagination, not transcription at all.

JM: Well, I think it's one of the devices the imagination uses. I'm not embarrassed by the degree of credulity that I felt during the gathering of the material. But as with Yeats, who looked back at a vision and saw his molten excitement cool into the cones and cubes of a Wyndham Lewis drawing, I see more and more, looking back on *Sandover*, that it's an imaginative construct, as the ineffable, unknowable universe is. You have to make some *version* of it.

Q: So it's not reportage.

JM: Certainly we had the experience, we took down the transcripts, but I think whatever the many voices of the poem represent, in our own minds, is something that is geared to our intelligence.

Q: It went through you.

JM: Yes.

Q: And was changed by you.

JM: Exactly. I think I was very close to what the imagination might do. . . . I see myself as having tapped into a kind of collective unconscious. Because some of the imagery, like UFOs and so forth, these are things I wouldn't have deigned to use if it was just me.

Q: It would be too odd.

JM: It would be too adolescent and odd.

Q: Do you feel any kinship with some of the experiences Shirley MacLaine writes about?

JM: Hers is a closed book to me. I suppose I think rather snobbishly that what comes out of the medium has everything to do with the medium's own grasp of language and form. No disrespect to Shirley MacLaine, or the author of the Seth books, but I think if they were more literate and had more of world literature, and *style,* in their minds, from schooldays or from wherever, they would get more interesting messages. And more readable messages.

You either have a honkytonk or a Steinway.

An Interview
with Heather White

Q: Why a memoir, and why now?

JM: It's hard to write about things that aren't in perspective. Forty years have passed away; so have many of those human figures. Also, I acquired a word processor. Otherwise—untidy as I am, always mislaying drafts—I would never have dreamed of undertaking a long piece of work like this.

Q: The surface of your language in the memoir's prose seems even more highly polished than it does in your poetry, where a dissonant emotional tone often underlies its elegance. Is that your impression also?

JM: You're right. And again, it's thanks in part to the computer. I love to revise, but in the old days of retyping, scissors, and tape, I'd often settle for four or five drafts. But with the memoir I could polish—expand or simplify—to my heart's content. The dissonance you speak of in many poems came from my chronic trouble in sustaining a uniform tone. To mask this, I often relied on interruption, change of voice, and so forth.

Q: How does that polish relate to your sense of revealing yourself (or not)?

JM: I never believed that spontaneity was the answer to self-expression. It's too raw, too messy. Loving revision as I do, I have almost a sculptor's

Ploughshares, Winter 1995–96.

feeling for the insight that emerges as the extraneous, the random, is chipped away. Some readers may feel the polish I aim for is a form of concealment; I don't.

Q: What do you think constitutes the "unsayable" in a memoir written in the nineties?

JM: There's not much left that's "unsayable," is there? But the unreadable proliferates. I wonder if they don't often amount to the same thing. Things that are said so ineptly that no one wants to read them.

Q: Were there points in the memoir where you felt you were approaching the unsayable, in a personal or societal sense?

JM: One recurring impulse, given my nature, is to think the worst about myself as a friend or lover, or "intellect." A little self-doubt goes a long way, and most readers gladly do without it.

Q: What are the qualities you value in a memoir?

JM: I haven't read that many memoirs. One that I love is *First Childhood* by Lord Berners. Very casual and entertaining. At the other end of the spectrum I would put Proust: his patience with the reader, his willingness to be long-winded, to explain, his trust in language. What I most value in *any* book, if it comes to that, is style, elegance, pacing, an observer's eye. If you have those, your life can be dull but your book will be enthralling.

Q: Of what value or interest do you imagine *A Different Person* to be to readers of your poetry, in their reading of your work?

JM: That would vary a lot. I can imagine a reader who really doesn't want this kind of clarification (if that's what it is). I myself don't drop everything to read the lives of poets I most admire.

Q: If we could turn to more general poetics, can you account for the emotional effect of words ordered in a particular way on a page?

JM: A very hard question. Let me just say: No, I can't. Or: I know it when I see it.

Q: Is there some essential distinction between poetic language and other kinds of language?

JM: That is the same question I just dodged so gracefully. I'd go on to say that context is everything in these matters. The proportions, the turn of mind. I've seen some shopping lists and lists of checks written in a poem that charmed me. What makes the difference is the writer's sense of form and style.

Q: Why is rhythm so important in a reader's sense of a poem's effectiveness?

JM: Its importance—and I assume by "rhythm" you also mean conventional meters—is twofold. For the poet, it is vital that formal demands be made upon him or her; attending to them leaves the subconscious free to infiltrate the poem. For the reader, there is the increased pleasure these effects bring. And the greater chance of the poem being—literally—memorable.

Q: Can you say to what extent you bring another poem into your own by the act of alluding to it in your poem?

JM: This can take two forms. A direct, conscious allusion is usually ornamental, or one-upmanship, or a friendly nudge to the reader. The allusion of which the poet is unaware is more subtle, more enriching in the long run. That's when you really bring "another poem into your own." Is it what we mean by tradition?

Q: You've written what many readers call a modern epic; what is an epic poem, today?

JM: There may still be poets positively yearning to write an epic. I always found myself shying away from what I saw as megalomania. What perhaps makes *Sandover* most readable is my resistance to the conventions of epic—the grandiloquence, the universal relevance. The models in this field remain what they always were: Homer, Virgil, Dante, Milton. In all of them there are supernatural beings, celestial machinery, and so forth. This definition seems to exclude Pound and *Paterson*—so be it. Lacking a muse to fill their sails, these great modernists have short, splendid passages, but keep running into mudflats from which there's no extricating them.

Q: How does having written an epic inform your sense of direction as a poet (in relation to the poems you write afterward)?

JM: A number of words, which until *Sandover* had figured innocently enough in my work, acquired a new resonance. The names of colors, the senses, sun and moon . . . Right after finishing the poem I had a problem with scale. "Oh good," I thought, "now I can write *short* poems once more." But the first one I wrote reached two hundred lines before it skidded to a stop.

Q: Who is a great poet?

JM: Well, the names I've mentioned to begin with. Whitman, I suppose. Stevens in a certain light. But there are also the great lyric poets, like Sappho or Keats of the odes. The dramatists—Sophocles, Shakespeare, Racine. Even a miniaturist like Bashō or Issa: you can't fully envision the human mind without taking them into account. What do they have in common? You tell me.

Q: Would it please you to be considered a great poet?

JM: Certainly not. Or not since I was fifteen. It must have been around then that my ambition ceased to be cosmic and became a matter of craft and tone. Some Great Ideas were forced upon me by the "epic" convention, though, as I said, and I fought them off as best I could. Besides, "great" is an adjective we more and more reserve for guests on talk shows. It should be applied in earnest, if at all, posthumously.

Q: Is there a sense in which you consider yourself a poet "of your time"?

JM: I don't choose topical themes or subjects for direct confrontation. However, peripheral vision takes in a good deal. I'd like to think that we can "witness" out of the corners of our eyes. Stevens said that in terrible times the poet needs to press back against the pressure of reality. That notion never left me.

An Interview with
Justin Spring

Q: Throughout your memoir, Southampton seems to be the place you identify most closely with your father. Was he very caught up in Southampton life?

JM: My father bought a big white house on Hill Street in his heyday, a year or two before the Crash. He came out from New York every weekend, often with business associates he wanted to charm. The "season"— I'm just guessing—lasted two or three months. Dances and tennis at the Meadow Club, lunches at the Beach Club. You tell *me* if there's been a change.

I suppose society "mattered" to my parents. They themselves were popular from the start, not because they represented the Old Guard but because they were—unlike my letters from Rome—lively and unpretentious. They were southerners, too, which helped to break the ice.

Q: Do you have fond memories of Southampton? Did you spend any extended periods of time here as a child or young man?

JM: Well, every summer. At least one winter I went to the local school. Was I happy? Children don't always know. I had nothing to compare the experience to. Wait—I'd read in the *Book of Knowledge* about how people like us were treated during the French Revolution, and for a week or so I

Southampton Press, December 2, 1993.

cowered on the floor of the Packard when the chauffeur drove me back from the Beach Club, lest the enraged populace drag me forth to the guillotine.

Q: If you were able to decide in what order a reader should read your work, where would you place this memoir? Do you consider it an introduction to your poetry, a concordance, an afterthought . . . or something else altogether?

JM: Isn't that for a reader to decide? That there should be a reader is after all the main thing. Still, one always feels closer to the latest piece of work.

Q: In some ways, it seems that you anticipated your European adventure through Proust: the comedy of the memoir seems based on the repeated collision of Proustian romantic and literary expectations with dumb (but not necessarily uncooperative) reality. Did you have a sense back then that you were experiencing Europe in terms of fiction? Did you embrace the idea? At the time, did you see a parallel between Proust's experience and your own?

JM: Yes, certainly. I didn't—because of World War II—make it to Europe until my formal education was behind me. Some informal education, too: I'd had a number of months as an infantry private. Proust was a wonderful mazy channel I longed to fill with gurgling firsthand experience. Also Henry James: I'd read *The Ambassadors* three times before I ever set foot in Paris. But what is "firsthand" experience? Stendhal says that Madame de Renal would never have fallen in love with Julien if she hadn't been reading novels.

Q: You say your mother edited a "society newspaper." Did it cover goings-on in Southampton?

JM: My mother's paper was edited and published in Jacksonville, Florida, in the years before her marriage. It was called *The Social Silhouette*. It didn't cast a very wide net—mainly local events, though I think she once went to Atlanta to hear Rosa Ponselle.

Q: Proust's response to money and social position seems more closely allied with your mother's views than your own. Did your time in Europe change your feelings about "society," or was all that settled for you well before you went overseas? The question arises because the near presence of royalty seems to have turned a few heads (notably your friend Tony

Harwood's). Moreover, the texture of the writing seems closer to Fortuny than Yankee broadcloth. Would you say there is an inner tension between your appreciation for luxe and your desire to escape it, between American and Continental selves?

JM: As I say, the luxe I trust is that of the art itself. I no longer flee "society," but a little goes a long way. You meet, at best, some very nice people, generous and kind, with lovely manners. Mine is, I suppose, a kind of reverse snobbery, also learned from Proust, who would forgo dinner with a princess if he had a date with a dairymaid. That too wears thin, if I may say so. Your metaphor of fabric—Fortuny versus broadcloth—implies certain attitudes. Art *is* a matter of how the text is woven, not where you go and what you do in your smart new clothes. Perhaps, more than Proust, the name to drop is Baudelaire's. His world of addicts and bohemian dandies was always somehow "above" that of the salons.

Q: Opera and Southampton hardly seem to go together. Yet you date your introduction to opera to a voice recital in your parents' home. Were such things common?

JM: Not a voice recital, just a new family friend playing through a score for me one morning (I was ten or eleven). Our music room was grand enough to handle serious cultural occasions, but I don't remember any offhand.

Q: Does Southampton society still consist of, as you say in your memoir, "narrowminded *nouveaux riches*"?

JM: I really wouldn't know. In my day there were some admirably understated people: Miss Ethel Wickham, who read books, had been to Alaska as a girl, and swam every morning in the club pool wearing a costume that made her look like a great turtle fringed with purple weed. Mr. and Mrs. Goodhue Livingston, whom the younger set spoke of in hushed tones. The Livingstons took to my mother, and at every summer's treasure hunt the side that got *her* was bound to win, because among the objects to find there'd always be one of Mrs. Livingston's shoes, which couldn't be mistaken for anyone else's. She had very long, elegant feet and, liking my mother, was not displeased to play a part, at this decent remove, in the joke.

Q: Which members of your family still reside in Southampton?

JM: My half sister has a house here; so does her youngest son and his family. The "estate"—known in my father's day as the Orchard—passed into other hands: a great burden lifted from him. He'd bought an outsized timber-and-brick beach house, just west of the club, from the estate of his partner Mr. Lynch. Tiny by comparison with the Orchard, it was there that he died in 1956.

Q: You wrote your senior honors thesis at Amherst on the application of the term "impressionist" to Proust. Do you consider this an "impressionist" memoir?

JM: Memoirs tend to be "impressionist" if only by contrast with the chronological imperatives of autobiography. I don't "approve" of autobiography—it is usually fact oriented and quickly replaced, after you die, by a thousand-page Life which sets the record straight. With a memoir, the priorities are altogether different. The impulse is less to tell every scrap of awful truth than to compose a literary text which, whether or not your readers believe it, they will be too charmed and entertained by to put down.

Q: Does the form—regular print followed, at the end of each chapter, by italicized print—derive from a similar strategy in *Sandover*? Where, incidentally, did that strategy come from?

JM: I don't quite see what my italic sections have in common with *Sandover*. Those different typefaces? The postmortems that often follow a given séance? The device, such as it is, came from Mary McCarthy's *Memories of a Catholic Girlhood*.

Q: Has the writing of this memoir made the past more real for you, bringing you closer to the people you knew then; or has the opposite been true—that is, does their presence in writing somehow "fix" them for you, making them less real, more like characters in a novel that can now be closed and placed on a shelf?

JM: More real, I think. Of course any feat of recalling events forty years distant involves a certain artifice. I have very few records at hand. I used to keep carbon copies of my letters, in lieu of a journal. But when I read them over, they were no help to speak of—just about my *feelings*, all unspeakably dull and pompous.

Q: Any plans for another installment of memoirs?

JM: No. Fun's fun.

Q: How is (or was) Stonington (which I believe you describe as "a small town full of semi-famous people") different from Southampton? Are you completely settled into that town, or is your life still peripatetic?

JM: One of the great revelations as we grow older is that one never makes a change. Stonington, it dawned on me belatedly, was a kind of miniature Manhattan, or a Southampton carved on a grain of (Greek Revival) rice. Our life in Athens—which seemed at first so different from anything we knew—became in time indistinguishable from the Stonington arrangements. So, yes, I keep on the move, always hoping for a novel experience, always coming face-to-face with what I've known all my life.

WRITERS

DIVINE POEM

Many readers of these columns will have encountered, as I did, their first Dante in the "Prufrock" epigraph. We learned to smile at the juxtaposition of ineffectual daydreamer and damned soul speaking from the fire. "For this is hell, nor are we out of it," we innocently marveled, peering forth from our own gemlike flames at worktable and bookshelf, sunset and dozing cat. Purgatory and paradise awaited us too, in the guise of the next love affair. In a single elegant stroke Eliot had shown us one way to approach *l'altissimo poeta*: Dante's passionate faith and our intrepid doubts could be reconciled by triangulation with the text itself.

To believe, however, that Dante had in any real sense seen God threatened both the poem and us. Who wanted song to curdle overnight into mere scripture, or himself to be trivialized in the glare of too much truth? Yet we must—or so I begin to think, decades later—allow that something distinct from mere "inspiration" came to Dante. It had come to others; he is not after all our only mystic, just more literary and more fortunate than many. In an age that discouraged the heretic, his vision reached him through the highest, most unexceptionable channels. Its cast included saints, philosophers, emperors, angels, monsters, Adam and Ulysses, Satan and God. To these he added a poet he revered, a woman he

The New Republic, November 29, 1980.

adored, plus a host of friends and enemies whose names we should otherwise never have heard; and garbed them in patterns of breathtakingly symmetrical lights-and-darks woven from a belief everybody shared. Even the pre-Christian souls in hell know pretty much what they are damned for not having known in time. No question ever of an arcane, Blakean anti-mythology. Dante's conceptual innovations—as when he lifts purgatory to the surface of the earth, or reveals his lady as an agent from highest heaven—refigure rather than refute the thought that preceded them. As for his verbal ones, he was in the historical position to consolidate, virtually to invent, for purposes beyond those of the lyric, a living Italian idiom. No poet could ask for more; yet more was given him.

Revelation can take many forms. St. Paul was "caught up into paradise, and heard unspeakable words"—a one-shot trip. Milton, on the other hand, dreamed each night the next day's installment of his poem. Blake kept open house, through much of his life, for spirits with whom he conversed wide awake. Yeats, married to a medium, took down the voices that spoke through her. A lay visionary—where poetry is at issue, someone whose powers of language and allusion aren't up to the demands made upon them—reports a complex, joyous wonder compressed into a few poor human moments and verging dangerously upon the unutterable. Much as it may change his life, the experience defeats his telling of it. Dante imagined this to be his case; it was not.

For he was already a poet. He had completed his apprenticeship in lyrics of high perfection. As for allusion, he had read widely and seriously if, to us, eccentrically. Homer lay beyond his ken, but he knew Paulus Orosius and the *Voyage of St. Brendan*, and may well have come across this sentence from the Sufi Ibn Arabi (found by me heading the chapter on Beatrice in Irma Brandeis's *The Ladder of Vision*): "When she kills with her glances, her speech restores to life as though she, in giving life, were thereby Jesus."

The *Comedy*'s energy and splendor suggest that Dante indeed "saw the light" in a timeless moment. Its prophetic spleen and resonant particulars hint at something not quite the same, that like Milton or Yeats he had mediumistic powers—a sustaining divinatory intelligence which spoke to him, if only (as Julian Jaynes would have it) from that center of the brain's right hemisphere which corresponds to Weinecke's area on the left. This much granted, it would still remain to be amazed in the usual fashion when faced by a masterpiece: How on earth was it brought safely into being and onto the page?

Poets nowadays are praised for performing without a net. "These poems take risks!" gloat the blurbs. Akhmatova saddles Dante with a cold and implacable muse. I wonder. One does not wince *for* him the way one does for Rimbaud. He is spared even the mortification of a system that dates. The electronic marvels of paradise—stars clustering into eagles, and all that—have according to Beatrice been devised to suit the seer: a laser show of supreme illusion projected through Dante's human senses and image banks. (Do hell and purgatory keep being modernized to extract the maximum pain and penance from the new arrival? I suppose they do.) Page after page the powers overwhelm the pilgrim, while treating the poet—the textures of his verse affirm it—with kid gloves.

A reader whose experience of terza rima is limited to Shelley can but faintly imagine its force and variety in the hands of its inventor. At the humblest level it serves as a No Trespassing sign, protecting the text. A copyist's pious interpolation or unthinking lapse would at once set off the alarm. No verse form *moves* so wonderfully. Each tercet's first and third line rhyme with the middle one of the preceding set and enclose the new rhyme-sound of the next, the way a scull outstrips the twin, already dissolving oarstrokes that propel it. As rhymes interlock throughout a canto, so do incidents and images throughout the poem. Thus any given tercet reflects in microcosm the triple structures explored by the whole, and the progress of the verse, which allows for closure only when (and because) a canto ends, becomes a version "without tears" of the pilgrim's own. Rendering here some lightning insight or action, there some laborious downward or upward clambering, the terza rima can as well sweeten the pill of dogmatic longueurs ("This keeps moving, it will therefore end") and frame with aching fleetness those glimpses of earth denied now to the damned and the blest alike.

We feel everywhere Dante's great concision. He has so *much* to tell. Self-limited to these bare hundred cantos averaging a scant 140 lines apiece, he can't afford to pad—he is likelier to break off, pleading no more room—let alone spell out connections for a torpid reader. This *we* must do, helped by centuries of commentary. And what a shock it is, opening the *Comedy*, to leave today's plush avant-garde screening room with its risk-laden images and scrambled soundtrack and use our muscles to actually get somewhere. For Dante's other great virtue is his matter-of-factness. Zodiacal signposts, "humble" similes, glosses from philosophy and myth—there is nothing he won't use to locate and focus his action as sharply as possible.

A random example. Sun is climbing toward noon above the Ganges as we enter a smoke "dark as night" on the slopes of purgatory; meanwhile, these moles that come and go in a passing phrase are kin, surely, to Miss Moore's real toads:

> *Ricorditi, lettor, se mai ne l'alpe*
> *ti colse nebbia per la qual vedesti*
> *non altrimenti che per pelle talpe.*

Singleton renders this: "Recall, reader, if ever in the mountains a mist has caught you, through which you could not see except as moles do through skin." Helpful; but was the mole in Dante's day thought to see through its *skin*? A note explains what is made clear enough in Longfellow's version, where alliteration, moreover, brings a certain music to *"pelle talpe,"* that tiny consonantal lozenge we have paused, I trust, to savor:

> *Remember, Reader, if e'er in the Alps*
> *A mist o'ertook thee, through which thou couldst see*
> *Not otherwise than through its membrane mole.*

It is the merest instance of that matter-of-fact concision I have in mind, and makes a small plea for translation into verse such as this which deftly evokes, as prose or indeed rhymed versions so rarely can, the diction and emphasis of the original. (Why, oh, why is the Longfellow *Comedy* not in print? Comparing it with the latest prose version, by Charles Singleton, and allowing for pains rightly taken by the latter to *sound* like prose, one is struck by how often he has had apparently no choice but to hit on that good gray poet's very phrase. There is also Longfellow's delectable nineteenth-century apparatus, including essays by Ruskin and Lamartine— "Dante a fait la gazette florentine de la postérité"; Boccaccio's account of the dead Dante guiding his son to the missing final cantos of the *Paradiso*; and James Russell Lowell on the poet's monument in Ravenna: "It is a little shrine covered with a dome, not unlike the tomb of a Mohammedan saint. . . . The *valet de place* says that Dante is not buried under it, but beneath the pavement of the street in front of it, where also, he says, he saw my Lord Byron kneel and weep.")

Those moles, to resume, are just one filament in a web whose circumference is everywhere. They presently mesh with an apostrophe to the imagination, which also sees without using its eyes. A case made in passing for divine inspiration ("A light moves you which takes form in heaven, of itself. . . .") gives way to three trancelike visions—Procne, Haman, Amata—appropriate to this level of the mountain Dante climbs. The center of the web is still far off, almost half the poem away, but we may as well glance at it now.

The passage in question, long a commentators' favorite, has lately begun to engage the scientists as well. Mark A. Peterson proposes (*American Journal of Physics*, December 1979) that Dante's universe "is not as simple geometrically as it at first appears, but actually seems to be a so-called 'closed' universe, the 3-sphere, a universe which also emerges as a cosmological solution of Einstein's equations in general relativity theory." Let who can, experience for themselves the full complexity and symmetry of the resulting figure. Roughly, two spheres are joined *at every point* through their "equator," itself a third sphere of sheer connectivity, and the whole suspended within a fourth dimension. The figure has finite volume but no boundary: "every point is interior."

On the threshold of the Empyrean, Dante is given his first glimpse of God, an infinitesimally small, intensely brilliant point reflected, before he turns to gaze at it directly, in Beatrice's eyes. Around it spin concentric rings or halos gaining in brightness and speed in proportion to their closeness to it. These represent the angelic orders, from inmost seraphim to furthest messengers, and compose one of the two interconnected "semi-universes" of Peterson's figure. The other, also composed of nine rings, has at its center the little "threshing-floor" of earth far down at which Dante has just been peering, and extends through the geocentric levels to his present vantage in the Primum Mobile. What he is looking at *now*, explains Beatrice, is the "point" on which "the heavens and all nature are dependent." All nature: the mole and the mountain, the sinner and the sun.

That her words paraphrase Aquinas in a commentary on Aristotle cannot account for the hallucinatory wonder of this little point. We may picture it partly as a model of electrons whirling round the atomic nucleus—in our day, the point on which all nature and its destruction depend; partly as an abstracted solar system—only with the relative planetary speeds reversed, since these Intelligences turn physics inside out. According to Peterson, however, this is exactly what they do *not* do. For the fourth dimension here is speed of rotation, or in Dante's view the dimension of divine precedence. The inmost ring moves fastest, as does the Primum Mobile outermost among the other set, because both are nearest to God. The two universes, heavenly and natural, are alike governed by that tiny point. The vision as reported sets the mind reeling. What must it have been to experience?

Here too we understand, not for the first time, how Dante is helped by Beatrice. Seeing this light through her eyes will enable him to put it into words, to translate into his poem's measures those that depend upon this timeless and dimensionless point, to receive what he may of the mystery and not be struck mad or dumb by it. A further, more profound glimpse will indeed be largely wiped from his mind by the uncanny image of the Argo's shadow passing over amazed Neptune.

Concise and exact, Dante is naturally partial to points. We have come across others before this one: the "point" in the tale at which Paolo and Francesca read no further; the high "point" of the sun's meridian over Jerusalem; the "point" where all times are present, into which Cacciaguida gazes to read Dante's future. A children's book comes to mind—*Adventures of a Hole* or whatever—where the small round "hero" piercing the volume from front to back serves as focus to the picture on every page. It would be in some such fashion that each episode or passing image in Dante connects with absolute Good—or Evil. For there is finally the very terrible point in the last canto of the *Inferno*. At the moral and physical universes' nether pole, it is the other center required by Peterson's scheme.

Here also are angelic spheres, those of the fallen angels. Satan, who as Lucifer belonged to that halo nearest the point of light, now towers waist-deep in ice, "constrained by all the weights of the universe," and at first glance oddly unthreatening. Nine rings narrow downward to this figure of raging entropy. From one to the next we have felt the movement decelerating. Wind-driven souls (Francesca) give way to runners (Brunetto), to the painfully walking hypocrites cloaked in gilded lead, to the frozen, impacted souls of Cocytus. This is "natural" movement; unlike those angels of the Empyrean, it obeys the second law of thermodynamics. W. D. Snodgrass has traced (*In Radical Pursuit*) the pilgrim Dante's regression, as he faces the murderers of parents and children, through the traumatic phases of early childhood, infancy, and birth. Last comes this nadir, this "point" he must pass in order to be reborn. It lies at the exact center of earth, of gravity, of the entire Ptolemaic universe. As the pilgrims skirt it, everything abruptly turns upside down, psychological time once again flows forward, and their ascent begins toward the starlight of earth's further side.

To my knowledge no one appears to have defined this point much beyond the account of it above. "Here all is dark and mysterious," says Singleton. Dante himself, as he clambers down between the deep floor of ice and Satan's shaggy thigh—there "where the thigh curves out to form the haunches"—averts his eyes and language: "Let gross minds conceive my trouble, who cannot see the point I had passed." He means, as we know, earth's center, but he would hardly be Dante to leave it at that. Hell, reads the inscription on its gate, was made by "the divine Power, the supreme Wisdom, and the primal Love"—the trinity in action. In Satan's figure, to which we've been led by a parodied Latin hymn, we see these reversed. Power becomes impotence; wisdom, a matter of mechanical gnawing and flapping; love, a congealing wind. As counterpoise to that radiant, all-engendering point in heaven, we may expect something more graphically awful than a fictive locus. "The sacred number *three* is symbolic of the whole male genitalia," writes Freud in the *Introductory Lectures*; it is the source of endless jokes in Greece today. Satan, as an angel, would lack genitals—a touch appropriate to the nullity Dante wishes to convey. For surely this point in hell is where they would have been and are not: a frozen, ungenerative, nonexistent trinity. And it is hardly from squeamishness or to spare his reader that Dante contrives to "miss the point" in hell. He has come a long way since Virgil's own hands prevented a stolen glance at the Medusa. His wiser reticence here implies a risk to the spirit, which might have vanished at a closer look, as into a black hole.

The point—my point and everyone's by now, not these of Dante—is that the *Comedy* throughout sustains the equilibrium we have been told to look for in a haiku by Bashō. There is no rift, as in conventional allegory, between action and interpretation, physical and moral, "low" and "high." All is of a piece. It is a mystic's view of the world, if you like. It is also a scientist's. And to have it tally with Einstein? For the year 1300, that's seeing the light in spades.

What diction, then, is even faintly suited to divine grace when it illuminates all things great and small? The answer must lie in the entire range, from the courtly metaphysics of the love poems, on which Dante would draw for his highest flights in paradise, to the broad innuendo of those sonnets to Forese. These also served him, as a farting devil in the Malebolge reminds us. Like the Jongleur de Notre-Dame in the pureness of his heart doing *what he can*, Dante will run through his whole bag of tricks, and the performance will be rewarded by an extraordinary universal Smile.

This wealth of diction and detail gave the *Comedy* its long reputation for a grotesque farrago flawed by "the bad taste of the century." The mature Milton asked his muse to help him soar "with no middle flight"— a costly decision. Whatever its glories, the diction of *Paradise Lost* labors under its moral regalia, its relentless pre-Augustan triumphs over precisely this eclectic middle style which allows Dante his touching, first-person particularity, moles and all. It also suggests why he is continually being rediscovered by poets—now by Hugo, now by Pound—and why translations, especially into verse, keep appearing.

Having been asked to write a "general piece" leaves me, I fear, with little space for its occasion—the publication of the *Inferno,* volume I of *The California Dante*: three volumes of text and three of commentary under the editorship of its translator, Allen Mandelbaum.

It is first of all a noble work of typography. The face was designed by the great modern printer Mardersteig and named for our poet. The text is set in spacious forty-two-line pages with, properly for once, the original on the host's, or reader's, right. Touches of red hint that no expense was spared. The book's codesigner, with Czeslaw Jan Grycz, is also its illustrator, Barry Moser. For my taste, used to the groupings and vistas of Blake or Doré, his drawings are too often close-ups; perhaps we may expect a wider lens upon leaving this hell of unleavened selfhood. They are in any case at best fearfully expressive, always beautifully reproduced, and placed so as not to intrude upon a reader who would rather picture things for himself.

The translation, into iambic pentameter with a rich orchestration that includes sporadic rhyme, is lucid and strong. Everyone knows the poem's opening lines in Italian; here they are as done by Mr. Mandelbaum:

> *When I had journeyed half of our life's way,*
> *I found myself within a shadowed forest,*
> *for I had lost the path that does not stray.*
> *Ah, it is hard to speak of what it was,*
> *that savage forest, dense and difficult,*
> *which even in recall renews my fear:*
> *so bitter—death is hardly more severe.*

I should probably have tried—tried and failed, rhymed couplets being a weakness of my own—to avoid them in rendering terza rima. The great success of this passage is, however, its third line. Here at the outset making for luck his ritual gesture toward the original form, Mandelbaum solves *"la diretta via"* in a free, brilliant, utterly Dantesque stroke. Countless more turn up in even a cursory reading—Francesca's "Love that releases no beloved from loving," for instance. "Love that exempts no one beloved from loving," Longfellow has it; but the verb unwizened in our time by the tax collector is surely to be preferred. Mandelbaum is especially good whenever Dante imitates the pains and anxieties that beset him as a pilgrim:

> *Of course I wept, leaning against a rock*
> *along that rugged ridge.*

Some impudent alliteration by Auden comes to mind ("Round the rampant rugged rocks / Rude and ragged rascals run"). Here, though, the device enacts rather than mocks the poet's plight, like a fist struck despondently into a palm as the memory overwhelms him. English, obviously, permits immense variety of diction—whereas a single good French translation of the *Comedy* might suffice for centuries—and Mandelbaum takes full advantage of this. Now and then he gives me pause: at his anti-quated "reboantic fracas" or his hostessy "Do tell me" addressed to some poor souls neck-deep in ice. But such pauses are lost in the overall sweep and felicity. A faint note of self-congratulation in Mandelbaum's elegant, up-to-date introduction is more than justified by what follows. This version will not displace Longfellow's, or Binyon's, or Sinclair's; nor do I imagine it was designed to. Rather it joins a very small company of renderings that stand both on their own as English poetry and to the *Comedy* as disciples round a master grown, thanks to their attention, ever more complex and less obscure.

Unreal Citizen

Mr. Liddell's is the first life in English of the Greek poet Cavafy. A sensitive and informed chronicler, he also quotes generously from Greek sources, Cavafy's diaries and scholia, as well as recollections of people close to him. His treatment of Cavafy's social and sexual life is entirely plausible. Mr. Liddell knows Egypt, too, and guides his reader blindfolded through the Alexandrian genealogical maze, as through the smart or infamous quarters of the city.

Born there (in 1863) into a world of forms and frivolities, Cavafy was to be anchored firmly beyond its shallows, less by impoverishment—for in "le grand cérémonial du tralala" a good family like his would still have a part to play—than by his vocation and his sexuality. He was seven when his father died. There followed years of displacement from one Unreal City to another. His closest ties were to his mother, Haricleia, "one of the most beautiful women in Alexandria" and one of the most idle—"her son affectionately addressed her (in English) as 'Fat One'"; and to his two immediately older brothers, the dependable John who worshipped him, who even translated him, and the unhappy Paul who drank and ran up debts. The latter and Cavafy, both over forty, still shared a flat and "a 'phaeton' in which they drove about. Mention is made of their rings and

New York Review of Books, July 17, 1975.

their ties; one is afraid they may have been rather 'flashy,' trying to prolong youth into middle age." Paul finally went to the Riviera and made ends meet as a kind of Jamesian companion-guide. "To the last he sighed for the great days in Alexandria. . . . Constantine never mentioned him to his younger literary friends."

The prevailing idea of culture cannot have gone much beyond salon music, *vers de société*, and lip service to the illustrious dead. Half Cavafy's life was over before he met, in Athens, any real authors. One of them noted his smart clothes, "slight English accent" in Greek, and how "all his ceremonies and politenesses strike an Athenian used to . . . the shy naïveté and simple awkwardness of our men of letters."

The difficulty of being Cavafy's kind of homosexual in Alexandria in those years must have been staggering: how to choose among a thousand daily opportunities. Cavafy by and large stuck to Greeks, young men of the working class. "We do not know whether his emotions were in any way involved," writes Mr. Liddell, meaning by emotions "genuine affection" rather than the mere desire, compassion, and regret that fill the poems. But he makes the essential observation that

> out of the mess and squalor that occupied part of his life he has created a unique order and beauty. Homosexuality was no doubt a disadvantage to Paul Cavafy, who was *mondain*, and at one time hoped to make a marriage of convenience; but it made Constantine what he was.

As Constantine knew very well:

> *My younger days, my sensual life—*
> *how clearly I see their meaning now.*
> *What needless, futile regret. . . .*
> *In the loose living of my early years*
> *the impulses of my poetry were shaped,*
> *the boundaries of my art were plotted.*

At thirty Cavafy settled down in Alexandria's Ministry of Public Works, as a clerk in the Dantesque "Third Circle of Irrigation." Here he stayed (he was also a broker on the Egyptian stock exchange) until his retirement thirty years later. He would not hit his stride as a poet, in fact, until after the office routine had provided the foil his ever livelier imagination needed. His successor, then a young employee, recalls:

> On very rare occasions he locked himself into his room. [Cavafy was by then a "subdirector."] Sometimes my colleague and I looked through the keyhole. We saw him lift up his hands like an actor, and put on a strange expression as if in ecstasy, then he would bend down to write something. It was the moment of inspiration. Naturally we found it funny and we giggled. How were we to imagine that one day Mr. Cavafy would be famous!

After the Fat One's death and Paul's removal to Europe, Cavafy spent his last twenty-five years alone in a flat on rue Lepsius—"rue Clapsius" as it was known to some, a neighborhood of brothels and shops gradually overtaking some nice old houses. Indoors one found a high concentration of the usual period junk, inlaid tables, carpets, mirrors, shabby divans, fringes of society, photographs, a servant bringing drinks and appetizers cheap or not, depending on who was there; the lighting constantly adjusted—an extra candle lit "if a beautiful face appeared in the room." The company seems to have been predominantly younger men of letters; but one may bear in mind that the guest from a higher or lower world seldom troubles to write memoirs.

Cavafy is that rare poet whose essential quality comes through even in translation. One sees why Auden thought so. By limiting his subject to human deeds and desires, and his mode to statement, Cavafy makes the rest of us seem to be reading ourselves laboriously backward in a cipher of likenesses and generalizations. He writes without metaphor. Of the natural world we see nothing. The Nile?—an agreeable site for a villa. Flowers?—appropriate to grave or banquet table. Not for Cavafy to presume upon his kinship with sunset and octopus. Having once and for all given the lie to the nonhuman picturesque in eight appalling lines ("Morning Sea"), he is free to travel light and fast and far. His reader looks through brilliantly focused vignettes to the tonic ironies beyond.

What ironies? Well, take "The Mirror in the Front Hall." The handsome delivery boy gets that far and no farther into the house, whose rich privacies would in any case be lost on him. Nor is Cavafy about to pretend interest in anything so conventional, so conjectural, as one more young man's inner life. Is there to be no "understanding," then, beyond that which brings him and his boys together in some anonymous room with its bed and its ceiling fixture? Ignorance is bliss, he might answer—or would he? For it is not ignorance so much as a willed narrowing of frame; and it is not bliss but something drier and longer-lasting, which radiates its own accumulated knowledge. Always, in Cavafy, what one poem withholds, another explains. This coldness of his comes through elsewhere as reticence imposed by an encounter with a god,

> *his hair black and perfumed—*
> *the people going by would gaze at him.*
> *and one would ask the other if he knew him.*
> *if he was a Greek from Syria, or a stranger.*
> *But some who looked more carefully*
> *would understand and step aside.*

Indeed, one way to sidestep any real perception of others is to make gods of them. But the ironic wind blows back and forth. The gods appeared to characters in Homer disguised as a mortal friend or stranger. Put in terms acceptable nowadays, that was a stylized handling of those moments familiar to us all when the stranger's idle word or the friend's sudden presence happens to strike deeply into our spirits. Moments at the opposite pole from indifference: though on that single pole Cavafy's world revolves.

The unity of divine and human, or past and present, is as real to him as their disparity. Between the poor, unlettered, present-day young men and the well-to-do, educated ones in his historical poems ("Myris . . . reciting verses / with his perfect feeling for Greek rhythm"), there is an unbroken bond of type and disposition: what Gongora called "centuries of beauty in a few years of age." This bond is at the marrow of Cavafy's feeling. It reflects his situation as a Greek, the dynamics of his language—indeed the whole legacy of Hellenism—and incidentally distinguishes him from,

say, that German baron who spent his adult life in Taormina photographing urchins draped in sheets and wreathed in artificial roses.

The first verb to learn in Ancient Greek was παιδεύω. Pronounced
pie-dew-o, it meant "I teach." In Modern Greek the same verb, spelled as
before, is pronounced *pe-dhe-vo*, and means "I torment." The old word
ἀγαθός (good) has come to mean "simpleminded." These shifts are
revealing, and their slightness reassures. I have heard my host in a remote
farmhouse tell Aesop's fables as if he had made them up; that they had
made *him* up was closer to the truth. I have heard a mother advise her
child to tell its bad dream to the lighted bulb hanging from a kitchen ceiling, and for the same reason that Clytemnestra, in one of the old plays,
tells hers to the sun. For while the ancient glory may have grown dim and
prosaic, many forms of it are still intact. (One feels it less in Italy than in
Greece, where, thanks first to Byzantium and then to the Turks, the
famous Rebirth of Learning had no opportunity to sweep away just this
kind of dusty, half-understood wisdom.)

So, in Cavafy, the Greek—or Hellenized—character shines forth:
scheming, deluded, gifted, noble, weak. The language survives the reversals of faith and empire, and sharpens the dull wits of the barbarian. The
glory dwindles and persists. The overtly historical poems illustrate this
great theme in a manner which certain Plutarchian moments in Shakespeare—Casca's deadpan account of a crown refused—read like early
attempts to get right. Cavafy himself draws on Plutarch, Herodotus, Gibbon, and a host of "Byzantine historians" whom he praised for writing "a
kind of history that had never been written before. They wrote history
dramatically." So did he.

Unexpected strands interconnect these historical pieces. A Syrian "Crafts-
man of Wine Bowls," at work fifteen years after Antiochus in 190 BC, is
overheard while decorating a silver bowl with the remembered figure of a
friend killed in that battle. "The Battle of Magnesia" itself reminds Philip
of Macedonia of his own defeat by the Romans; with scant pity to waste
on Antiochus, he calls for roses, music, lights. We see elsewhere ("To
Antiochos Epiphanis") a grandson of the defeated king greeting with
prudent silence, thirty years later, his favorite's plea for the liberation of
Macedonia—*that* would be worth, to the boy, "the coral Pan . . . the gar-

dens of Tyre / and everything else you've given me." (The issue is still alive in our time.) This very favorite, or another, becomes the ostensible subject of some erotic verses by "Temethos, Antiochian, AD 400"—a flashback from far in the future, the date referring us to poems about the last stages of Hellenism in the Middle East.

In one of these ("Theatre of Sidon") the speaker confesses: "I sometimes write highly audacious verses in Greek / and these I circulate— surreptitiously," much as Cavafy did his own, neither wanting to offend the prevailing Christian morality. Back to Antiochus the Great's lineage, a second grandson ("Of Dimitrios Sotir, 162–50 BC") next occupies the Syrian throne with Roman recognition. This idealistic young king was raised as a hostage in Rome. At last where he belongs, he cannot recognize the Syria of his dreams in exile. It has become "the land of Valas and Herakleidis." Valas is the adventurer who, bribed by a Ptolemy whom Dimitrios Sotir once tried to help ("The Displeasure of Selefkidis"), is presently to overcome Dimitrios. In "The Favor of Alexander Valas," its fatuous object will be found exulting, briefly we may assume, "Antioch is all mine." And the Satrap Herakleidis is none other than he who, years earlier as Antiochus Epiphanis's treasurer, commissions a wine bowl from the melancholy but uncomplaining silversmith.

Thus, fixed to earth at these several points (I have omitted a few), the tent of an entire lost world can be felt to swell and ripple in the air above them. It is not Cavafy's concern to occupy—by spelling out every connection, or cramming with detail—this historical, no, this emotional space. He does something more skillful yet by suggesting it, by manipulating it.

As a reader of Cavafy, Mr. Liddell—while providing helpful glosses and fine insights (he introduces "The God Abandons Antony" as a poem which "seems to take farewell of symbolism")—prefers to let the work speak for itself. But not always. I can't help wishing that he had been able, in a single sweeping period, to express his disagreement with the novelist and critic Stratis Tsirkas—whose continuing studies of Cavafy can at present be appraised only by readers of Greek—instead of paraphrasing his interpretations, nine times out of ten for the sole purpose of disputing them. Thus Tsirkas's reading of the short poem "Thermopylae" (1901) comes off as preposterously topical. Leonidas and the traitor Ephialtes are thinly overlaid upon figures in Alexandria's Greek community in the 1880s—the Persians are the British, etc. Liddell's "ethical" reading raises problems he is the first to admit.

Neither interpretation is particularly absorbing; nor for that matter is the poem itself, except where one feels it come to life through the suggestive interplay of its three proper nouns. Ephialtes (one of those names like Quisling?) happens to mean "nightmare." "Οἱ Μῆδοι"—the Medes—can be heard as a dream-pun allusion to words like μή (no, don't), μηδέν (zero), μηδενιστής (nihilist), etc. At this level "Thermopylae" has little to do with either history or ethics, but implies that a subconscious horror is forever about to betray the self's "warm gates" to a host of negative powers, and that to be truthful or "generous in small ways" is honorable but vain in the face of the recurrent onslaught. Here is Cavafy (under "Table Talk" in Liddell's appendix): "We must study our language since we don't know it. What hidden treasures it contains, what treasures! Our thought ought to be how we are to enrich it, how to bring to light what it has hidden in it."

Liddell and Tsirkas go on to read "the next poem in the canon," "Che Fece . . . il Gran Rifiuto" (1899), according to their lights. The latter has it alluding to the career of an Alexandrian patriarch fifteen years earlier (Dante's phrase, used as title, refers to Pope Celestine V). The former calls it "a generalized reflection with no bearing on any refusal that we know of in Cavafy's own life . . . an unsuccessful work." Uncharacteristic perhaps, in its bald lack of particulars:

> *For some people the day comes*
> *when they have to declare the great Yes*
> *or the great No. It's clear at once who has the Yes*
> *ready within him; and saying it,*
>
> *he goes from honor to honor, strong in his conviction.*
> *He who refuses does not repent. Asked again,*
> *he'd still say no. Yet that no—the right no—*
> *drags him down all his life.*

But surely we know—and know now more vividly than before, thanks to Mr. Liddell—of many refusals in Cavafy's life: the refusal to be a husband and father, an enterprising merchant, a popular poet, or to frequent exclusively the world of "the Salvago balls." This little poem remains a schoolboy exercise unless it is taken personally. (Also, it is an early poem. The quarrel with Tsirkas dies down when Liddell comes to the mature work, whose possible meanings no longer roam freely outside the poem, but are controlled, as it were, from within.)

In fact, as Marguerite Yourcenar says, all the historical poems are intimate, just as all the intimate poems are historical—hence, in the latter, the dwelling upon dates and the exact number of years gone by. We do not know whom any given love poem is for; there is no Agostinelli in Cavafy's life. Nor will most readers know the fuller context of the historical pieces. But we know what happens in history, to ideas and nations. And we know what happens when a loved one is struck down in youth, or disfigured by age, or leaves us for somebody else, or for Australia. To Cavafy's moments of truth are appended consequences so implicit in the nature of things as hardly having to be uttered. One of his notes on Ruskin hints at the turn of mind that made for such far-reaching yet discreet authority:

> When we say "Time" we mean ourselves. Most abstractions are simply our pseudonyms. It is superfluous to say "Time is scytheless and toothless." We know it. We are time.

A reader without Greek will finally, or first of all, respond to the earmark of nearly every Cavafy poem. Like all experienced raconteurs he knows how to repeat himself. Key words—often whole lines—get said over, reiteration serving, since no detail's value can be assured until it "comes to rest in this poetry," to woo it back, fix it more lastingly in the mind. The overall brevity and compression lend relief to these touches, by turns poignant, wry, haunted. Cavafy's economies are lavish. The old gentleman living on a shoestring still tips well for the good services of the telling phrase.

Messrs. Keeley and Sherrard print the Greek *en face* (warning: but not in the paperback edition) and have given it a thoroughly serviceable English version, the best we are likely to see for some time. A few examples may indicate their success and limitations.

CHANDELIER

In a room—empty, small, four walls only,
covered with green cloth—
a beautiful chandelier burns, all fire;
and each of its flames kindles
a sensual fever, a lascivious urge.

In the small room, radiantly lit
by the chandelier's hot fire,
no ordinary light breaks out.
Not for timid bodies
the lust of this heat.

The original (1895) is in two rhymed stanzas. (Notes at the back supply Cavafy's metrical and rhyme schemes whenever relevant. This is most helpful, as far as it goes, though the reader faced with *"ababcdbbef aghbibibjb agklmbbc"* might feel that he is studying nothing so much as the transliteration of an Arabic curse.) "Chandelier," however, is a symbolist poem. In a space scaled to the small room, it presents its glowing image—presents it twice, on the replay spelling out more clearly the erotic message. One cannot greatly mourn the loss of some rather ordinary music. In fact, the translators, by reducing 133 syllables in Greek to 78 in English, actually enhance the poem's dramatic brevity. Many unrhymed, loosely metered poems are equally well served by this approach.

But the mature Cavafy writes a subtle, flexible Greek whose elements—classic, purist, regional, demotic—come together, as Kimon Friar observes, in "an artifice suited to and made integral by his temperament." A comparison to the shifts of manner in a Pound canto would be to the point if, in Cavafy, the unity of temperament weren't everything. Still, this English often reads more dryly and simply than it needs to. The crucial literary note in "Comes to Rest" (1918)—an erotic memory "the vision of which / has crossed twenty-six years and now / comes to rest within this poetry"—is soft-pedaled. The phrase "ἐπύρωνε θεῖος Ἰούλιος μῆνας" requires something on the order of "the fires of divine July were lit" or "divine July had brought us to white heat." Instead we are given "it was a beautiful hot July." This turns Cavafy into a nicer guy, but misses the point he is making about artifice. No great harm done. Cavafy himself prevents any misunderstanding in a poem written later that year, "Melancholy of Jason Kleander, Poet in Kommagini, AD 595":

> The aging of my body and my beauty
> is a wound from a merciless knife.
> I'm not resigned to it at all. . . .
>
> Bring your drugs, Art of Poetry—
> they do relieve the pain at least for a while.

(I should have thought the third line meant: "I do not bear up under it at all." Mavrogordato's version sounds almost chipper: "I have no long-suffering of any sort.")

In other poems, the formal effects, unlike those of "Chandelier," are indispensable to meaning. The famous "Walls," for instance, with its homophonic rhymes. "They," other people, unnoticed by him, have immured the poet—so *he* says. Yet these rhymes, stifling, narcissistic, arrogantly accomplished, tell the inside story—the walls are of his own making—without which the poem is an exercise in self-pity. An effect unrenderable in English? Cavafy's brother John (see a group of his English versions introduced by Keeley, *St. Andrews Review*, Fall-Winter 1974) does nobly by the homophonic rhymes in "For the Shop," but at the cost of clarity and pace.

Formality in the later work appears, so to speak, informally. When it does, it is usually of one fabric with the meaning. Here is the Keeley-Sherrard "Days of 1909, '10, and '11":

> He was the son of a misused, poverty-stricken sailor
> (from an island in the Aegean Sea).
> He worked for an ironmonger: his clothes shabby,
> his workshoes miserably torn,
> his hands filthy with rust and oil.

In the evenings, after the shop closed,
if there was something he longed for especially,
a more or less expensive tie,
a tie for Sunday,
or if he saw and coveted
a beautiful blue shirt in some store window,
he'd sell his body for a half-crown or two.

I ask myself if the great Alexandria
of ancient times could boast of a boy
more exquisite, more perfect—thoroughly neglected though he was:
that is, we don't have a statue or painting of him;
thrust into that poor ironmonger's shop,
overworked, harassed, given to cheap debauchery,
he was soon used up.

By consulting the notes ("Loosely rhymed *abcde fffcfc gfhdhdf*") we notice rum doings in the second stanza. The effect is in fact magical. One foot, then two, are subtracted from the opening's basic seven-foot line. Suddenly, where no rhymes had been come four consecutive ones, each an end-stopped *ee*. (This is now the most common sound in Greek, representable on the page by no fewer than six vowels and diphthongs each of which had its own value in classical times.) Line five moves past another stressed *ee* (the word "saw") to the poem's most passionate verb (λαχταροῦσε, "coveted"), which two lines later will rhyme with "sell." The seven-foot line, as central to Greek prosody as the pentameter to ours, returns, closing this stanza and governing the next. The barrel-organ interlude is over, though two further *ee* rhymes echo it in the final stanza. The Greek attains the ease and freshness of a jingle learned in childhood:

> Τὸ βραδυνό, σὰν ἔκλειε τὸ μαγαζί,
> ἄν ἦταν τίποτε νὰ ἐπιθυμεῖ πολύ,
> καμιὰ κραβάτα κάπως ἀκριβή,
> καμιὰ κραβάτα γιὰ τὴν Κυριακή.

Cavafy's aim here can only have been to imitate, through that poorest, commonest of rhyme-sounds, the quality of pleasure available to the young man with his pitiful needs and by-the-numbers behavior. To meet the same rhyme further on, as Cavafy's "own" voice is winding up the story, sheds light both on his lasting compassion, at its best without pity, and on the means whereby he remade it into poetry.

Of course a rhymed English version is possible:

> *But when the shop closed down at night,*
> *if there was something he'd delight*
> *in having, a necktie somewhat dear,*
> *tie that on Sundays he might wear,*
> *or in some showcase saw and loved on sight*
> *a lovely shirt of deepest blue,*
> *he'd sell his body for a dollar or two.*

Or:

> *As dusk fell, and the shop closed, had there been*
> *something he longed for, something seen—*
> *a Sunday tie, a tie beyond his means,*
> *or shirt of beautiful dark blue*
> *coveted in this or that vitrine—*
> *he'd go and sell his body for a dollar or two.*

These, alas, are barely adequate (the first is Kimon Friar's, the second my own). "This or that vitrine" smacks of fussiness; "delight" and "loved on sight," of gush. Mainly one misses Cavafy's polysyllabic rhyme words, and their expert division among different parts of speech, which keep the passage from sounding like baby talk.

The last poem in the "Days" series, "Days of 1908," begins with twenty-four lines of which nineteen end with assorted masculine rhymes. This time the protagonist is "reasonably educated," feels entitled to better employment than he has yet found. So he gambles, wins, loses, borrows—dressed always in the same wretched "cinnamon-brown suit." The poem ends with an idealized view of him at the beach on summer mornings. The final seven lines, where the boy sheds, along with his clothes, his circumstances and responsibilities, are unrhymed, with fluid, feminine endings. We breathe something of the unconstricted freshness here evoked.

If nothing else, the feminine and masculine endings could have been managed in English without great trouble. A nagging voice in me wants to say that these sound effects—like the more complex ones in "Days of 1909, '10, and '11"—are such a poem's secret power, and that a translation which fails to suggest them is hardly worth making. Having said so, I retract the statement at once. It is too grumpy and too unfair to Messrs. Keeley and Sherrard who, whether or not they have the skill, certainly do not have the time, the lifetime they would need to achieve the—in any case—impossible. On their own terms they have done admirably. Readers who once preferred to existing English versions Marguerite Yourcenar's elegant French prose ones must now admit that these have been surpassed, with respect at least to accuracy and completeness.

Single-handed in our century, Cavafy showed the Greek poets who followed him what could be done with their language. In that quarter, he has had the greatest conceivable influence. Yet these later men, with their often superior lyric or epic gifts, their reverence for earth, their virtuoso talent for metaphor, next to him strike me as loud and provincial (Kazantzakis) or curiously featureless (Seferis and Elytis), through over-long immersion in the new international waters of Eliot, Perse, the surrealists. They have, of course, claimed huge territories for Greek letters; but how gladly, having surveyed those shifting contours, one reenters the relative security of Cavafy's shabby flat with its view of the street and of the ages. I should add that my reading in (and of) Greek is insufficient to justify this kind of pronouncement.

A few years ago, as the Brindisi-Patras ferry was docking, a young Belgian needing a ride to Athens asked if there was room for him in the car. En route he said that he had left Brussels weeks earlier with fifty francs in his pocket, of which nearly half remained. I praised his economy. Ah, he said, he made friends easily; kept up old friendships, too. Would he be staying, then, with friends in Athens? Just so. Night had fallen, we drove on, now silent, now talking a bit. He may have suspected some wraith of education behind my words, for presently he asked if I knew the Greek poet Cavafy. When I said yes, he lit up: "Well, it's with *him* that I shall be staying these next days in Athens."

The lively interest I expressed was rewarded by a description of a man in late middle age, charming, clever, fluent in French, and living on a street quite near to where I stayed. Who knows?—if *I* had been charming and clever I might have played my cards so as to drink coffee later that week with my companion and his host. Instead—it had been a long day—I cut things short by disclosing that the real Cavafy had died of throat cancer on his seventieth birthday, in 1933, having never, aside from brief visits, lived in Greece at all. The Belgian took it badly. He'd seen books, been shown poems done into French, English, Italian, plus hundreds of clippings and critical articles. "At home my friends all know his name. They say: Cavafy, *c'est un monument!*" "How right they are," I agreed sadly; "a monument is all he is, now."

I would have liked to drive my passenger to this Mr. Cavafy's door, but he asked to be dropped downtown, near a telephone. Home at last, tired as I was, I went straight to the directory—where no Cavafy is listed. But it remains a comfort to think that in my very neighborhood a civilized old humbug is still misrepresenting himself to seasonal waves of good-looking if imperfectly educated visitors. Whoever he is, I take off my hat to him, as well as to the marvelous poet he is evidently translating, for once not into some other language, but boldly into life itself.

Object Lessons

"Printanier et merveilleux," René Char called him. Ponge himself can imagine being ranked with Chardin and Rameau. He is seventy-three. The two books under review are selections from his writings, which fill a dozen volumes. While practicing "pure and simple abstention from themes imposed by ideologies of the time," Ponge has been embraced by the existentialists in their time, and by the structuralists in theirs. Only human, and French, he too has devoted his requisite pages to the absurd. Still the bloom does not wear off. This genial lifework will outlast the ideas by which it is judged.

> If ideas disappoint me, give me no pleasure, it is because I offer them my approval too easily, seeing how they solicit it, are only made for that. . . . This offering, this consent, produces no pleasure in me but rather a kind of queasiness, a nausea.

How one agrees.

No thoughts, then, but in things? True enough, so long as the notorious phrase argues not for the suppression of thought but for its oneness with whatever in the world—pine woods, spider, cigarette—gave rise to it. Turn the phrase around, you arrive no less at truth: no things but in

New York Review of Books, November 30, 1972.

thoughts. Was the apricot any more *real* without a mind to consider it, whether this poet's or that starving goat's? We'll never know.

> What is more engaging than blue sky if not a cloud, in docile clarity? This is why I prefer any theory whatever to silence, and even more than a white page some writing that passes as insignificant.

So Ponge, in 1924, restores *l'azur* and *le vide papier que la blancheur défend*, all that rare, magnetic emptiness so prized by Mallarmé and Valéry, to a backdrop for something common, modest, real.

And elsewhere: "It's a question of the object as notion. Of the object in the French language (an item, really, in a French dictionary)."

For a thought is after all a thing of sorts. Its density, color, weight, etc., vary according to the thinker, to the symbols at his command, or at whose command he thinks. One would hardly care so much for language if this were not the case.

One of the ideas that most solicit a poet's approval is that of meter. Ponge naturally distrusts it. His prose arrives now and then at a diffident *mise en page* resembling verse, but only very seldom, as in "The Mimosa," at overt numbers. Unlike Valéry, who could instruct and no doubt surprise himself by recasting his decasyllabic "Cimetière Marin" into alexandrines, Ponge is not absorbed by conventional formal problems. Which of course only helps him again and again, since he is Ponge, to achieve a form, a movement, a kind of poem enchantingly, unmistakably his own.

A tone first of all. Of moss he writes: "Patrols of vegetation once halted on stupefied rocks. Then thousands of tiny velvet rods sat themselves down cross-legged." In a related key Gautier describes the interior of a coach in Spain, and Michaux the actions of a Chinese prostitute. With Ponge, the object being closer to home, the result is more importantly light, more detachedly involved.

THE CRATE

Halfway between *cage* and *cachot* (prison) the French language has *cageot*, a simple openwork case for the transport of those fruits that invariably fall sick over the slightest suffocation.

Put together in such a way that at the end of its use it can be easily wrecked, it does not serve twice. Thus it is even less lasting than the melting or murky produce it encloses.

On all street corners leading to the market, it shines with the modest gleam of whitewood. Still brand new, and somewhat taken aback at being tossed on the trash pile in an awkward pose with no hope of return, this is a most likable object all considered—on whose fate it is perhaps wiser not to dwell too long.

(1932–1934)

The frailty of the crate induces *un faible* in the poet, a weakness for— the weakness of—his subject. Where certain later poems will expose the elaborate nervous system beneath their transparent phrasing, here the form remains suitably minimal, a simple openwork conceit. To read something else into these lines—some lament for untimely death, or statement about form's adaptation to content—would be excessive. Not to read it into them would be no less so. The sacrifice of overtones, whether for the sake of a more concrete image or of a more purified idea, is distasteful to Ponge, unhealthy, inhumane. Thoughts and things need to be the best of friends.

A more explicit poem ("Blackberries," 1934–1937) begins and ends:

On the typographical bushes constituted by the poem, along a road leading neither away from things nor to the mind, certain fruits are formed of an agglomeration of spheres filled by a drop of ink. . . .

. . . With few other qualities—blackberries (*mûres*) made perfectly ripe (*mûres*)—just as this poem was made.

That first sentence, with its provocative sidelong glances (at thoughts, at things) contained by words that stress their place in a black-and-white, two-dimensional composition the more vibrant for not aspiring much beyond design, can stand for what is best in French art old and new and suggest the extent of Ponge's lifelong debt to Braque. Consciousness of his trade saturates the work. The snail exudes a "proud drivel." The dinner plate is manufactured in quantity by "that benevolent juggler who now and then stealthily replaces the somber old man who grudgingly throws us one sun per day." The *y* of "Gymnast" "dresses on the left." The *è* of *"chèvre"* becomes the note of the bleating goat. Meadows "surge up from the page. And furthermore the page should be brown." And man? He too is "one of nature's decisions." He secretes language.

In the closing sentence of "Blackberries" we glimpse a most suspect device, the pun.

A pity about that lowest form of humor. It is suffered, by and large, with groans of aversion, as though one had done an unseemly thing in adult society, like slipping a hand up the hostess's dress. Indeed, the punster has touched, and knows it if only for being so promptly shamed, upon a secret, fecund place in language herself. The pun's objet trouvé aspect cheapens it further—why? A Freudian slip is taken seriously: it betrays its maker's hidden wish. The pun (or the rhyme, for that matter) "merely" betrays the hidden wish of words.

It betrays also a historical dilemma. If World War I snapped, as we hear tell, the thread of civilization except where it continued briefly to baste the memories of men like Valéry and Joyce, the next generation's problem was to create works whose resonance lasted more than a season. A culture without Greek or Latin or Anglo-Saxon goes off the gold standard. How to draw upon the treasure? At once representing and parodying our vital wealth, the lightweight crackle of wordplay would retain no little transactional power in the right hands. But was it—had the gold itself been—moral? Didn't all that smack of ill-gotten gains? Even today, how many poets choose the holy poverty of some secondhand diction, pure dull content in translation from a never-to-be known original. "There is no wing like meaning," said Stevens. Two are needed to get off the ground.

Ponge, to be sure, forfeits no resource of language, natural or unnatural. He positively dines upon the etymological root, seasoning it with fantastic gaiety and invention:

> You will note . . . to what tools, what procedures, what rubrics one should or can appeal. To the dictionary, the encyclopedia, imagination, dreams, telescope, microscope, to both ends of the

lorgnette, bifocals, puns, rhyme, contemplation, forgetfulness, volubility, silence, sleep, etc., etc.

This preamble, complete with disclaimers about the "poetry" that will follow, and reading like the afterthought it may well be, introduces "L'Oeillet" ("The Carnation"), a particularly attractive kind of Ponge poem. The text proper takes off from a glossary, words that may or may not figure later on. He looks up *déchirer, jabot, festons,* connects *dents* with *dentelles. Bouton* (bud) needn't, he observes, be used together with *bout* (end, butt), *bouton* (button), or *déboutonner* (unbutton), since each stems from *bouter* (to push or butt). Scruples like these discourage banality. Ponge makes one fleeting, never repeated, allusion to the boutonnière, and knows better than to spell out even once the second meaning of *oeillet*: eyelet, little eye. With words, then, at his fingertips, the writing can begin. Has begun—already we've been given: "At stem's end, out of an olive . . . comes unbuttoned the marvelous luxury of linen." And: "Inhaling them you experience the pleasure whose reverse would be the sneeze." Now to consolidate the findings of "these first six pieces, night of the 12th and 13th of June 1941, amidst the white carnations in Madame Dugourd's garden."

Ponge may be the first poet ever to expose so openly the machinery of a poem, to present his revisions, blind alleys, critical asides, and accidental felicities as part of a text perfected, as it were, without "finish." (No other serious poet asks less to be reread; this work is done for us by the number of alternate readings left standing. The technique will be put to narrative use by Robbe-Grillet.) One meets a mind desiring and deferring, both, according to the laws of baroque music, solution and resolution, the final breaking of an enchantment that may already have lasted weeks, years.

The next day he begins again:

At stem's end comes unbuttoned from a supple olive of leaves a marvelous frill of cold satin with hollows of virid snow-shadow where a little chlorophyll still resides, and whose perfume excites within the nose a pleasure just on the verge of the sneeze.

Which doesn't wholly satisfy him, not to *be* satisfied being the point. Whereupon he sets about disheveling phrases, breaking up lines:

Deluxe cold satin duster
Deluxe beautifully toothed rag
Frizzed duster of cold satin. . . .
At stem's end bamboo green. . . .
Multiple fragrant sachets
From which the whipped robe spurts

—a quickened pace, a heightened foreplay, reminding us that the sneeze is a minor ejaculation. Some one hundred lines, over the next two days, repeat, vary, modulate, improvise upon these and other motifs (the sneeze presently elicits "trumpets of linen") with the self-reflexive energy of Bach. When this toccata of conceits reaches a crescendo, the subject is sounded again, note by note, letter by letter:

O split into OE
O! Bud of an energetic haulm
split into OEILLET! . . .
ELLE O youthful vigor
with symmetrical apostrophes
O the olive supple and pointed
unfolded in OE, I, two Ls, E, T
Little tongues torn
By the violence of their talk
Wet satin raw satin

—yielding precisely here to an organ point:

Wet satin raw satin
                    etc.
(My carnation should not be too much of a thing; one should be able
to hold it between two fingers.)

Then silence. A silence that lasts more than two years, during which the poem's fate hangs in the balance. Other subjects have come to hand, one of them, "Le Savon," allowing for a far more elaborate treatment. That finished text, the English version by Lane Dunlop, Ponge's best translator, will run to 128 pages. Presented as an (imaginary?) radio broadcast to a

German audience, it is a complex account—hymn, analysis, charade—of the *"toilette intellectuelle,"* the mind's ebullient autocatharsis, typically embodied in the humble cake of soap that, whenever obtainable during the Occupation, was of some ersatz variety that *made no suds* (Ponge's italics). One small passage (July 1943) illustrates, without bearing on "The Carnation," the turn of mind that helped Ponge to resolve the shorter poem:

> *THEME (dry and modest in its saucer) AND VARIATIONS*
> *(voluminous and nacreous) upon*
> *SOAP (followed by a paragraph of rinsing in plain water)*

And indeed, when Ponge returns to "The Carnation" in 1944, his concern is for some rinsing of his hands in a plainer idiom. "Though you should invent," he had written on that distant evening at Mme. Dugourd's, "a pill to dissolve in the vase's water, to make the carnation eternal"— *éternel* with its echo of *éternuer,* to sneeze—"it would still not survive long as a flower." Neither, perhaps, would it have survived long as a poem had Ponge been content to leave it tossing in a high rhetorical fever. But now, to end it, he sets down a few pages describing the carnation's root system:

> . . . horizontally underlining the ground, a long, very stubborn willing of resistance . . . a kind of very resistant string which baffles the extractor, forces him to alter the direction of his effort.

In France of 1944 these were charged words. (Ponge himself had underground contacts during the war.) Yet "resistance" is no more the buried issue here than "faith" is, or "style," or the relation between what one knows deep down and what one utters—all mildly, glancingly apparent through Ponge's own altered effort in these concluding paragraphs. The poem ends with one last, abstracted, decasyllabic blossoming:

> *Let us emerge from earth at this choice spot. . . .*
> *So, here is the tone found, where indifference is attained.*
> *It was indeed the main point. Everything thereafter will*
> *flow from the source . . . another time*
>
> *And I too can rightly be silent.*

The covenant between maker and carnation has been observed.

Words and silence, things and thoughts, excitation and detumescence: no opposites but brought into peaceful coexistence. One remembers those two fingers between which the flower must be held.

Ponge keeps insisting that he does not write poetry. "I need the poetic magma, but only to rid myself of it." He means "demonstrative outbursts," "beauty . . . all dolled up in an illusion of destiny," "gods and heroes." His Athena is a shrimp with "weapons now wilted and transformed into organs of circumspection." His pine woods are "Venus's beauty parlor with Phoebus the bulb inserted into the wall of mirrors." Such imagery, he remarks, would please a poet minor or epic. "But we are something other than a poet and we have something else to say." Whether this other thing ever really gets said, or said so memorably as in the ravishing passages Ponge shrugs off, is for each reader to decide according to his lights. Those who wonder if the "poetic abscess" doesn't leave less of a scar than the programmatic one will have to gauge, from the major and minor triumphs that come through unscathed, how close to life and how essential to art the entire process is.

By major triumphs I mean (to mention only pieces available in the two selections under review) poems too novel and rich to be patronized by any brief account of them—poems such as "The Meadow," "The New Spider," "The Pebble," "The Goat." Mme. Brombert provides for the last of these a helpful context in which "god and heroes" abound, and starry shapes. Among them, not identified as such by her, we can make out that absolute cogitator who in Mallarmé wore "the lucid and lordly aigrette of vertigo on his invisible brow," and in Ponge becomes a characteristically verifiable emblem of himself:

Magnificent knucklehead, this dreamer . . . whose thoughts, formulated as weapons on his head, for motives of high civility curve backward ornamentally.

Well and good; but Ponge remains—it is one of his strengths—open to understanding without apparatus. His words are "conductors of thought, as one says conductors of heat or electricity." One understands, at every blessed turning, why he turned, why he wrote, for what delight, for what beautifully envisionable end. "The poem is an object of *jouissance* [enjoyment, gratification, use] offered to man," he says; and elsewhere, "to nourish the spirit of man by giving him the cosmos to suckle"—item by item, in a lifelong application of sure, brilliant touches (cosmos and cosmetic sharing a single root). And yet again, with simple justice, "I have given pleasure to the human mind."

Ponge, one discovers soon enough, is very hard to translate. Bless him also for that. (And may I not be damned for somewhat tampering with Mme. Brombert's and Mr. Corman's English in my quotations. To refrain, in most cases, would have been to leave well enough alone.) I prefer Mme. Brombert's clear, unobtrusive versions. Mr. Corman, out of long practice, does more with the "line," but his lines, in turn, are more apt to err and omit. (Why does he leave out the phrase about resistance in "The Carnation"?) Or else he will follow the original syntax so doggedly that I had the eerie impression of reading an actual French text, not necessarily Ponge's. Both selections are worth owning. If Mme. Brombert's seems a shade more generous and representative, no one who cares should miss "The Notebook of the Pine Woods," "The Wasp," and "The New Spider" in Mr. Corman's.

ON WALLACE STEVENS'S CENTENARY

I was introduced to Wallace Stevens's work at a time when it had begun to be taken very seriously indeed by people whose opinions mattered. Mine didn't—I was nineteen—but let me tell you how I felt about it anyhow. The first of his books to come my way was not *Harmonium* but the lovely Cummington Press edition of "Notes toward a Supreme Fiction." In it I discovered a vocabulary by turns irresistibly gaudy and irresistibly abstract. Without presuming to guess what the poem or any stanza of it meant, I found myself basking in a climate that Proust might have called one of "involuntary philosophy." A world of painterly particulars—interiors, necklaces, elephants in Ceylon—became, upon little more than a single leafing-through of pages, charged with novel meanings; or potentially charged with them; or alternately charged with thought and (by the enchantment of language) absolved from thought as well. I at once set about writing poems in which colorful scenery gave rise to questions about the nature of reality. Let me read you one of these.

THE GREEN EYE

Come, child, and with your sunbeam gaze assign
Green to the orchard as a metaphor

Recitative: Prose by James Merrill, ed J. D. McClatchy (San Francisco: North Point Press, 1986).

For contemplation, seeking to declare
Whether by green you specify the green
Of orchard sunlight, blossom, bark, or leaf,
Or green of an imaginary life.

A mosaic of all possible greens becomes
A premise in your eye, whereby the limes
Are green as limes faintly by midnight known,
As foliage in a thunderstorm, as dreams
Of fruit in barren countries; claims
The orchard as a metaphor of green.

Aware of change as no barometer
You may determine climates at your will;
Spectrums of feeling are accessible
If orchards in the mind will persevere
On their hillsides original with joy.
Enter the orchard differently today:

When here you bring your earliest tragedy,
Your goldfish, upside-down and rigidly
Floating on weeds in the aquarium,
Green is no panorama for your grief
Whose raindrop smile, dissolving and aloof,
Ordains an unusual brightness as you come:

The brightness of a change outside the eye,
A question on the brim of what may be,
Attended by a new, impersonal green.
The goldfish dead where limes hang yellowing
Is metaphor for more incredible things,
Things you shall live among, things seen, things known.

In Stevens's hands this manner came to seem wonderfully civilized. With the vivid parasol of language to balance the reader, there was less risk of falling, as in Eliot, off any high tightrope of argument. And a greater likelihood than in Pound—or at least in many of the *Cantos*—of being spared the gritty documentary arena for the sake of a grander per-spective. Neither Pound nor Eliot promised very much by way of *people* in their poems. You had on the one hand figures like poor Fräulein von Kulp, frozen forever in a single, telling gesture, and on the other, oh, John Adams wound like a mummy in a thousand ticker-tape statistics. To use people as Frost did was something else again. A young poet could easily have been cowed by the sheer human experience needed in order to render "real life" with even minimal authority. Thanks to the example of Stevens, this pressure could be postponed until the time came. His people were unlike any others. Airily emblematic, yet blessed with idiosyncrasy, they fitted snugly into their poems, like figures in Vuillard. Ideas entered and left their minds easily, words came to their lips, giving point to a passage without overwhelming it or reducing it to mere vignette. They served their poet and departed undetained by him. I kept on trying my hand.

CHARLES ON FIRE

Another evening we sprawled about discussing
Appearances. And it was the consensus
That while uncommon physical good looks
Continued to launch one, as before, in life
(Among its vaporous eddies and false calms),
Still, as one of us said into his beard,
"Without your intellectual and spiritual
Values, man, you are sunk." No one but squared
The shoulders of his own unloveliness.
Long-suffering Charles, having cooked and served the meal,
Now brought out little tumblers finely etched
He filled with amber liquor and then passed.
"Say," said the same young man, "in Paris, France,
They do it this way"—bounding to his feet
And touching a lit match to our host's full glass.
A blue flame, gentle, beautiful, came, went
Above the surface. In a hush that fell
We heard the vessel crack. The contents drained
As who should step down from a crystal coach.

Steward of spirits, Charles's glistening hand
All at once gloved itself in eeriness.
The moment passed. He made two quick sweeps and
Was flesh again. "It couldn't matter less,"
He said, but with a shocked, unconscious glance
Into the mirror. Finding nothing changed,
He filled a fresh glass and sank down among us.

Finally I was struck, even then in 1945, by how naturally Stevens handled his references to art and poetry, the aesthetic performance, the "Theatre / Of Trope." Without embarrassment—without the concomitant cigarettes and whiskeys and women that in those days accompanied any American account of the artist-as-novelist—he seemed to trust his text to hold its own against the world it evoked, as part of that world. And when we read in a little poem that the moon follows the sun across the sky "like a French translation of a Russian poet" we nod in recognition of a creation myth in which both gods and poets conspire. In a word, he pointed and still points higher than anyone in our century. The candle lit by his interior paramour often as not shines *down*, it seems to me, upon Eliot's "culture" and Pound's "history" and even, now and then, upon Frost's common touch. And all this was accomplished affably, without undue intimidation, so that the young practitioner could seek out his own faith, in his own time, and arrive (with any luck) at his own humanity.

On "The Love Song of
J. Alfred Prufrock"

The mere thought of commenting upon T. S. Eliot undoes me. I first read "Prufrock" at the age of sixteen. Back then, in 1942, Mr. Eliot was very much on the scene—in fact he was years younger than I am now—and from his work came a sense of live menace and fascination: you felt that any rash expository impulse might cause it to strike back like a rattlesnake. Some of us old-timers feel that way still.

So let me just say a word about the epigraph to "The Love Song of J. Alfred Prufrock." It comes from Canto 27 of the *Inferno,* and the speaker is Guido da Montefeltro. Here is Longfellow's translation:

> *If I believed that my reply were made*
> *To one who to the world would e'er return,*
> *This flame without more flickering would stand still.*
> *But inasmuch as never from this depth*
> *Did anyone return, if I hear true,*
> *Without the fear of infamy I answer.*

Guido speaks from within a flame, doomed to eternal torment for having given fraudulent advice to a pope. "Promise much," is what he said,

The Yale Review, Winter 1989.

"but fulfill little that you promise." People in high places have been listening to Guido ever since.

Critics are bound to have drawn every possible connection between Guido's narrative and J. Alfred Prufrock's. It could be said that the latter also speaks from within a flame—a Pateresque flame of language kindled by one of its twentieth-century masters. But I think that Eliot is using Dante to make a simpler point. The epigraph "promises much" on behalf of the poem. By its placement we understand that someone with a ridiculous name has strayed like a fly into a vast and inflexible cosmic web. Whatever he now says, we are going to have to take him more seriously than we might otherwise have done. And take his creator more seriously, too? The epigraph, in any case, has been much imitated; I have imitated it myself. It is a highbrow, or theological, version of Mrs. Willy Loman's words: "Attention must finally be paid to such a person." That an Eliot not yet thirty commanded attention by a stroke at once so cool and so incontrovertible is part of what I mean by saying that even now I tremble when I open his books.

On Montale's
"Mottetti VII"

Il saliscendi bianco e nero dei
balestrucci dal palo
del telegrafo al mare
non conforta i tuoi crucci su lo scalo
né ti riporta dove più no sei.

Già profuma il sambuco fitto su
lo sterrato; il piovasco si dilegua.
Se il chiarore è una tregua,
la tua care minaccia la consuma.

•

The black-white swooping
of the martins from telegraph pole to the sea
does not comfort your anguish on the pier,
nor bring you back where you no longer are.

Already the thick wild elderberry
perfumes the air, the drizzle thins.

Field, Fall 1982.

If this clearing is a truce,
your dear threat consumes it.

TRANSLATED BY IRMA BRANDEIS

A beloved already half angel, all somnambulist gloamings and bric-a-brac of the nineties, Montale shakes to alertness in his "Mottetti." Where smoke clears on scattered if not disintegrated sound effects (*"sambuco"* to *"consuma"* is more anagram than assonance), three or four hendecasyllabic columns have been left standing. It's the morning after an earthquake: old vistas sparkle in sun, redeemed by crisis.

FOREWORD TO
NINETEEN POEMS

Robert Morse was born on Christmas Day 1906 in Toledo, Ohio, and grew up in Evanston, Illinois. His maternal grandfather, a Swede, manufactured player pianos. His daughter married one of the craftsmen; they were divorced while Robert was still a child. As a boy he played the piano accompaniment to silent films in the local theater. Going on to Princeton, he received an award for painting, and upon graduation was enabled by a grant to study for two years in Paris. Through his roommate there, he made friends with the son of Joseph Cotton, whose daughter Isabel he was to marry some ten years later. They lived in Manhattan, in Bedford Hills, in Stonington, Connecticut; they traveled to Mexico, to Europe, to Bangkok, to Jamaica. Their son Daniel was born in 1942. Robert died in the summer of his seventieth year.

His accomplishments were just that, in the faintly amateur, nineteenth-century sense of the word. He used them, that is, for his own and his friends' pleasure. At the piano he played Mendelssohn, Bach, Schumann; Mozart (whom he regarded as the Second Coming); four-hand arrangements of the Haydn and Beethoven symphonies, the "Dolly" Suite, and *Pulcinella*. His touch was modest and clean, his technique (as he liked to put it) "almost perfect." In painting he was a gifted, attentive portraitist.

Robert Morse, *Nineteen Poems*, privately published, 1981.

During World War II he visited hospitals, sketching the wounded. There were some who broke months of withdrawal, began to smile and speak again, under his mild, intent scrutiny.

Over the years Robert tried a number of literary forms. He collaborated on a play or two, published some rather creepy short stories. An essay on Dickens appeared in *Partisan Review.* Throughout, he continued to write poetry. *The Two Persephones* was published (Creative Age Press, 1942) through the good offices of Eileen Garrett, the famous witch. These two pieces—the title poem and "Ariadne, a Poem for Ranting," each some hundred pages long—represent the fullest flowering of Robert's early style.

He knew of course that he was living in an age of artistic breakthroughs almost automatic in their regularity, of technology at the expense of technique, and "open-ended" content at the expense of closure; knew it, and went on, a touch perversely, as if the rules had never been changed.

It is upon that special bloom of accomplishment in Robert's early poems—their importance to Our Time is another question—that I should like to linger. Here originality is made to feel at home by little more than a modest turn of mind or phrase. The borrowings are—how to say it?—neighborly: a goblin nutmeg from Miss Rossetti, a bunch of lovage from old Landor up the road. (To watch Robert in the kitchen was itself an education.) The basic elements of verse are a second nature to him. He can put them to use in the same way that Queen Victoria along with thousands of her contemporaries, through having learned young how to wash-in that familiar blue or sepia distance, or scribble the spring foliage of an oak, could produce in one sitting a watercolor landscape both competent and evocative. There exist some translations into English of Cavafy by the poet's brother, not himself a literary man—and indeed the effect is a bit diluted; yet his fluent handling of the meters and rhyme schemes surpass that of any later versions known to me. These were things people once had at their fingertips. "Why do you keep doing it, if it's so much trouble?" one of Robert's sitters asked the artist muttering to himself over the difficulties of getting something on his canvas right— for to be sure none of this was as easy as it looked. Back came the answer in a flash: "Because I *can.*"

A received style discourages quotation. The elegant plotting of "Ariadne," its interwoven voices, its action visible through the brilliant limpidity of the verse, can best be savored in depth. The tone ranges from Oenone's earthy aside during a speech by Pasiphaë

> *We hacked her bridegroom into steaks and chops*
> *many a year gone by, if but she knew*

to the Minotaur's touching soliloquy in the maze he has trustingly watched grow up around him

> *My thigh grew thick and taut beneath its casing,*
> *the varied hide like rough and patchy moonlight,*
> *the black and white discordant pattern, printed*
> *without, and yet more deeply stained within,*
> *so that a slice or section of my soul*
> *would still have shown the same two-colored conflict. . . .*
> *Be animal! my mother's blood cries out,*
> *my father's sperm replies, Assault the angels!*
> *Between these double stones I grind the children,*
> *and for this cause my only wish is death*

to the high concluding speech of a Bacchus straight out of Giovanni Bellini:

> *Whichever goat-foot fingers best the flute,*
> *let him stand forth. Whoever plucks the harp*
> *with most melodious pain, maenad or centaur,*
> *tune his unsullied string. For now to music*
> *she who has slept shall wake, and wake to love,*
> *and love shall crown her with a wreath of stars.*

She who has slept shall wake. . . . Some interpreters of the Ariadne legend have it that, far from being saved by Bacchus in person, the poor grief-stricken princess simply took to drink. *She who has wept shall slake . . . ?* Either way, the unruffled syntax and firm monosyllables ring true. Are we on the verge of a discovery?

Having worked so long at these received patterns, fulfilling them line by line and stitch by stitch, what on earth remained to do with the finished needlepoint: stuff it with kapok? leave it to the children? Robert's inspiration was to reverse it, exposing, then and there, that hilarious and disquieting tangle, the underside of idiom. A certain consonant-transposing slip of the tongue, named for its mortified old victim, produced the Spoonerism. The slip lends itself irresistibly to our Anglo-Saxon—as it does not, say, to French—yet decades went by before anyone thought to try it out as a rhetorical figure. It may well be that Robert was the first. In any case "Winter Eve" impressed Auden enough for him to include it in *A Certain World*.

Although Robert chiefly relied upon the plain, garden-variety Spoonerism (take a shower / shake a tower), his gaudy triple hybrids should as well be admired (gay football fans / fey fatball goons) along with the occasional freak (Super Bowl / superb owl) all but lost in the surrounding abundance, and due less to phonemic cross-pollenization than to a single sideways-flitting Cabbage White space. The fair blossom of a phrase and its dry organic fertilizer (my river's all light / my liver's all right) at every turning "exchange vitalities," as Hugh Kenner said of certain effects in Pound. What, in a word, *isn't* going on in these late poems? With "Fugue," the last and most complex of the four, came a diffident explication:

> *I wonder what you will make of this. . . . I have no*
> *opinion, but then I don't even know my Muse's first name.*
> *The three voices seem to be:*
> *1) A dark swamp with water birds, surrounding*
> *2) an elevated church-crowned town by the sea, at dawn.*
> *3) Burghers and beggars at Carnival time.*
> *The skybirds are a kind of code—the promise of Easter*
> *—all deduced from the bird-steeple-rising-sun. It really*
> *is quite like a fugue in structure, which may be no excuse?*

He also appended a "key" which reads in part:

> *Marsh hen! unlighted still in the gloaming fen,*
> *lift your heads and eye the towers loosed from night.*

Ruff, ree, and sora! hark to the bells,
the old clangor of baying bronᶎe. Rails!
hear out the tolls of shattered bells,
crack-sided gongs, heart-riven gongs.
Grey goose! from the half-light
gander the halls of state, the floating gables.
All Innocence, in fen-bound home (yes, bobolinks
too) wonder at the rich-draped sables
on regal backs, on loving minx and silky punks.

Notice that this version is hardly less bizarre than the original.

When the time came to look again at Robert's "straight" poems (with an eye to making the present modest selection) at least one reader was so on his toes that every phrase could be felt as positively trembling with its imminent subversion. In his own odd way Robert had made his lines command the textual scrutiny we reserve for the masters.

On Elizabeth Bishop

Elizabeth Bishop was born February 8, 1911, in Worcester, Massachusetts, and grew up there and in Nova Scotia. After graduation from Vassar she lived in New York, Key West, then in Brazil for eighteen years, returning to the United States in 1971. She taught for a few years at Harvard, and more recently at MIT. Her books of poems include *North and South*, *A Cold Spring*, *Questions of Travel*, *The Complete Poems*, and *Geography III*, along with many translations from the Portuguese, notably *The Diary of Helena Morley*. She received a Pulitzer Prize in 1956, was a member of the American Academy of Arts and Letters, as well as a chancellor of the Academy of American Poets. She died suddenly on October 6th, of a cerebral aneurism at her apartment facing north across Boston Harbor.

With her death a darkness all but literal falls over our poetic scene; for her intelligence—so all-seeing, original, undidactic—like the very light of day revealed her subjects there in the world where she found them, casting them, for the length of a poem's charm, into effortless and humane relief. This ease, this natural perfection, along with the technical mastery it implied, were not always prized in the workshops. Young people saw by other lights—the lover's candle, the embattled flare, the

Poetry Pilot, December 1979.

bubble-streak of phosphor. Her fellow poets read her, as E. M. Forster said of Jane Austen, "with the mouth open and the mind closed." She, quite casually, went on doing what no one else could: writing poems at once innocent and wise, colloquial and sublime.

ELIZABETH BISHOP
(1911–1979)

She disliked being photographed and usually hated the result. The whitening hair grew thick above a face each year somehow rounder and softer, like a bemused, blue-lidded planet, a touch too large, in any case, for a body that seemed never quite to have reached maturity. In early life the proportions would have been just right. A 1941 snapshot (printed in last winter's *Vassar Bulletin*) shows her at Key West, with bicycle, in black French beach togs, beaming straight at the camera: a living doll.

The bicycle may have been the same one she pedaled to the local electric company with her monthly bill *and* Charles Olson's, who one season rented her house but felt that "a Poet mustn't be asked to do prosaic things like pay bills." The story was told not at the Poet's expense but rather as fingers are crossed for luck—another of her own instinctive, modest, lifelong impersonations of an ordinary woman, someone who during the day did errands, went to the beach, would perhaps that evening jot a phrase or two inside the nightclub matchbook before returning to the dance floor.

Thus the later glimpses of her playing—was it poker?—with Neruda in a Mexican hotel, or Ping-Pong with Octavio Paz in Cambridge, or getting Robert Duncan high on grass—"for the first time!"—in San Fran-

New York Review of Books, December 6, 1979.

cisco, or teaching Frank Bidart the wildflowers in Maine. Why talk *letters* with one's gifted colleagues? They too would want, surely, to put aside work in favor of a new baby to examine, a dinner to shop for and cook, sambas, vignettes: Here's what I heard this afternoon (or saw twenty years ago)—imagine! Poetry was a life both shaped by and distinct from the lived one, like that sleet storm's second tree "of glassy veins" in "Five Flights Up." She was never unwilling to talk about hers, but managed to make it sound agreeably beside the point. As in her "Miracle for Breakfast" she tended to identify not with the magician on his dawn balcony but with the onlookers huddled and skeptical in the breadline below.

This need for relief from what must have been an at times painful singularity was coupled with "the gift to be simple" under whatever circumstances. Once, after days of chilly drizzle in Ouro Prêto, the sun came out and Elizabeth proposed a jaunt to the next town. There would be a handsome church and, better yet, a jail opposite whose murderers and wife beaters wove the prettiest little bracelets and boxes out of empty cigarette packages, which they sold through the grille. [. . .] On our arrival the prisoners had nothing to show us. They were mourning a comrade dead that week—six or eight men in their cavernous half basement a narrow trench of water flowed through. They talked with Elizabeth quietly, like an old friend who would understand. It brought to mind that early prose piece where she imagines, with anything but distaste, being confined for life to a small stone cell. Leaving, she gave them a few coins; she had touched another secret base.

In Ouro Prêto, literary visitors were often a matter of poets from other parts of Brazil—weren't there fifteen thousand in Belem alone? These would arrive, two or three a week during the "season," to present her with their pamphlets, receiving in turn an inscribed *Complete Poems* from a stack on the floor beside her. The transaction, including coffee, took perhaps a quarter of an hour, at whose end we were once more by ourselves. The room was large, irregular in shape, the high beams painted. Instead of a picture or mirror, one white wall framed a neat rectangular excavation: the plaster removed to show timbers lashed together by thongs. This style of construction dated the house before 1740. Across the room burned the cast-iron stove, American, the only one in town. More echoes, this time from "Sestina."

I was her first compatriot to visit in several months. She found it uncanny to be speaking English again. Her other guest, a young Brazilian painter, in town for the summer arts festival and worn out by long teaching hours, merely slept in the house. Late one evening, over old-fashioneds by the stove, a too-recent sorrow had come to the surface; Elizabeth, uninsistent and articulate, was in tears. The young painter, returning, called out, entered—and stopped short on the threshold. His hostess almost blithely made him at home. Switching to Portuguese, "Don't be upset, José Alberto," I understood her to say, "I'm only crying in English."

The next year, before leaving Brazil for good, she went on a two-week excursion up the Rio Negro. One day the rattletrap white river steamer was accosted by a wooden melon-rind barely afloat, containing a man, a child of perhaps six, and a battered but ornate armchair which they were hoping to sell. Nothing doing. However, a "famous eye" among the passengers was caught by the boatman's paddle—a splendidly sanded and varnished affair painted with the flags of Brazil and the United States; it would hang on her wall in Boston. When the riverman understood that the eccentric foreign Senhora was offering, for this implement on which his poor livelihood depended, more money (six dollars, if memory serves) than he could dream of refusing, his perplexity knew no bounds. Then the little boy spoke up: "Sell it Papá, we still have *my* paddle!"— waving one no bigger than a toy. Which in any event, the bargain struck, would slowly, comically, precariously ply them and their unsold throne back across the treacherous water.

Will it serve as momentary emblem of her charm as a woman and her wisdom as a poet? The adult, in charge of the craft, keeping it balanced, richer for a loss; the child coming up with means that, however slow, quirky, humble, would nevertheless—

Nevertheless, with or without emblems, and hard as it is to accept that there will be no more of them, her poems remain. One has to blush, faced with poems some of us feel to be more wryly radiant, more touching, more unaffectedly intelligent than any written in our lifetime, to come up with such few blurred snapshots of their maker. It is not her writings— even to those magically chatty letters—whose loss is my subject here. Those miracles outlast their performer; but for her the sun has set, and for us the balcony is dark.

THE TRANSPARENT EYE

It is a sad pleasure to take up this book. Of all the splendid and curious work belonging to my time, these are the poems (the earliest appeared when I was a year old) that I love best and tire of least. And there will be no others.

Elizabeth Bishop was born in 1911 in Worcester, Massachusetts, and raised largely by her Nova Scotian grandmother and various scattered aunts. Her friends at Vassar included Mary McCarthy and Eleanor Clark. After graduation she lived in New York, Paris, and Key West; then, in 1952, on her way to an Orient blithely renounced, settled for the better part of eighteen years in Brazil. It was there that word of her Pulitzer Prize drew this exuberant response from the local butcher: "All my customers are lucky—just last week Senhora X won the lottery!" Living at such a remove from the literary world brought compensations only a writer can fully appreciate. Still, she came home—"wherever that may be"—to teach for a while at Harvard. She died suddenly in 1979, on the point of leaving her apartment above Boston's harbor for a dinner with friends.

Her original *Complete Poems* (1969) is here expanded to include *Geography III* (1976), a few hitherto uncollected treasures, all her verse

Washington Post Book World, February 20, 1983.

translations, plus some juvenilia and occasional pieces. One could conceivably have lived without certain odds and ends in the latter categories. Yet it is touching to see her at work under influences (like Millay and Hopkins) soon to be outgrown. And after all, in the case of a poet like Bishop, less is *never* more. The book as it stands deserves only grateful praise.

The watercolor on the jacket, a view of a Mexican town done by the poet in 1942, serves nicely as introduction. It's a cheerful scene, in no way traditionally "picturesque." Beyond a balustrade flanked on one side by an absurd ornamental urn (so much for Art?) and on the other by flourishing palm fronds, we see some little, run-down, brilliantly colored houses. Above these, near and far, quite upstaging the few church spires lost among them, perhaps fifty windmills crowd the horizon—so that, like the mysterious flooded dreamscape in "Sunday, 4 A.M.," it appears to be "cross- and wheel-studded / like a tick-tack-toe." The picture illustrates at once Bishop's delight in foreign parts, her gratitude for the givens of a scene, and her typical way with systems. These tend to fade beside her faith in natural powers—here, those jaunty cockades turning in wind to draw water, compared to which the Christian temples, though neatly delineated, look a touch feeble and evanescent.

For systems exhaust themselves; the elements remain numinous. In "Sunday, 4 A.M." the jetsam of a great story—instruments of the Passion, organ music, altar cloth and donor, some unidentifiable "Mary"—litters the waking dreamer's world with useless, cryptic detail. Not until "a bird arranges / two notes at right angles" does life once more make sense. (That bird, we may safely assume, is not a dove.) Or if the Christmas trees in "At the Fishhouses" are, as David Kalstone has remarked, "behind us" in both senses of the phrase, they leave that poem free to conclude with seawater, fire, and stone, together performing a grave alchemical masque:

> *If you should dip your hand in,*
> *your wrist would ache immediately,*
> *your bones would begin to ache and your hand would burn*
> *as if the water were a transmutation of fire*
> *that feeds on stones and burns with a dark gray flame.*
> *If you tasted it, it would first taste bitter,*

then briny, then surely burn your tongue.
It is like what we imagine knowledge to be:
dark, salt, clear, moving, utterly free.

Robert Lowell, among many, praised her "famous," farsighted eye. In her elegy for him, she acknowledges it herself:

I can make out the rigging of a schooner
a mile off; I can count
the new cones on the spruce.

But the marvels that appear on every page are as much acts of imagining as of seeing. Here is fog in Nova Scotia:

Its cold, round crystals
form and slide and settle
in the white hens' feathers,
in gray glazed cabbages,
on the cabbage roses
and lupins like apostles.

And here in New York City at daybreak through a window

Where it has slowly grown
in skies of water-glass

from fused beads of iron and copper crystals,
the little chemical "garden" in a jar
trembles and stands again,
pale blue, blue-green, and brick.

More telling even than her image-making is Bishop's way with tone and overtone. "Arrival at Santos" sounds at moments like a sixth grader's report—rich in pathetic fallacy, trivial detail, and complacent generalization ("Ports are necessities, like postage stamps, or soap"). Technically, and this is part of her strategy, the somewhat amateurish rhymes and meters could be the work of a clever twelve-year-old: the mental and emotional age, after all, of her fellow tourists with their

> *... immodest demands for a different world*
> *and a better life, and complete comprehension*
> *of both at last, and immediately,*
> *after eighteen days of suspension.*

The poem ends, "we are driving to the interior." Precisely. Only a few pages further on comes a poem like "The Riverman" in which her eye, still clear as a child's, penetrates a world unimaginable to the innocents lined up at customs. Here all is primal, animistic—and touchingly matter-of-fact. "It stands to reason," the young witch doctor insists, "that every-thing we need / can be obtained from the river." Yet his world has already been grazed by the cinema and mass production that will destroy it, and so is linked to the earlier poem's tourists in ways Bishop wouldn't dream of spelling out. She shows us that fragile culture. Whatever conclusions we may draw belong outside the poem.

In "12 O'Clock News" she constructs a minithriller whose narrator is both criminal and victim. Thanks to clues in the margin, *we* know that the eerie, war-torn, enemy landscape is no more than the writer's lamplit desk. But here the tone, that of a media analyst pathetically conjecturing under his pretended omniscience, opens up ironies that reach from the Ivory Tower to the Oval Office. As part of a generation that included Lowell, Berryman, and Roethke, she had glimpsed the megalomania lying in wait for the solitary maker—or indeed for anyone "in power"— and her account of it here is all the more unnerving for her superficially playful sleights of scale.

These sleights figure with a difference in "Visits to St. Elizabeths"— the Washington hospital where Ezra Pound, so as not to be tried for trea-son, was detained in the early 1950s. Bishop (then poetry consultant at the Library of Congress) went regularly to see him. As her title hints, how-ever, it was not only the irascible great poet but aspects of herself that she was curious to face. With her own mother in a mental hospital since Bishop's early childhood, she must have known the threat of insanity firsthand. Not that she would ever have been prey to either of those (male?) drives, the one that produced *The Cantos*'s huge unruly text, the other that made its bid to change the map of Europe. More than anything she cared to keep her work and her wits, in the phrase of her beloved George Herbert, "new, tender, quick." To define *and* disarm, then, this figure of Pound—while sympathizing with his predicament if not with his politics—she modeled her St. Elizabeths poem upon "The House That Jack Built." In her hands the painful subject with all its vast overtones (anti-Semitism, the war) takes on a bittersweet, singsong shapeliness, as if a young self were gazing back through time at the formidable, by then half-cracked titan he had become:

> *These are the years and the walls and the door*
> *that shut on a boy that pats the floor*
> *to feel if the world is there and flat.*
> *This is a Jew in a newspaper hat*
> *that dances joyfully down the ward*
> *into the parting seas of board*
> *past the staring sailor*
> *that shakes his watch*
> *that tells the time*
> *of the poet, the man*
> *that lies in the house of Bedlam.*

Last month a young Bishop fan told me that his favorite was "The Shampoo." I wonder if it isn't mine as well. Two of its three short stanzas play with notions of time. On one hand it is cyclical, as unobservably slow as the "gray, concentric shocks" whereby the lichens grow in order "to meet the rings around the moon." On the other hand, time is linear, moves at "precipitate" human speed, is "nothing if not amenable." The phrase is exact: without us to feel it, time would not exist. In stanza three, "shooting" and "flocking" echo those "shocks" at the beginning, which now in the denouement we hear as shocks of hair. Otherwise the language is supremely plain, and the everyday gesture it clothes, supremely tender:

> *The shooting stars in your black hair*
> *in bright formation*

> *are flocking where,*
> *so straight, so soon?*
> *—Come, let me wash it in this big tin basin,*
> *battered and shiny like the moon.*

It is as unexpected and convincing a love poem as I know.

Finally, "The End of March" recounts a walk with friends down the beach on a sunless day of numbing wind. All is "withdrawn as far as possible, / indrawn." The receding tide worries "a thick white snarl, man-size, awash," of string: "A kite string?—But no kite." As they follow "a track of big dog-prints (so big / they were like lion-prints)" a bizarre structure comes into view. In this "crypto-dream-house" Bishop imagines a solitary existence, more like an afterlife, where she too might withdraw and "do *nothing*, / or nothing much, forever, in two bare rooms." Before turning back, she remarks a chimney, infers a stove

> *and electricity, possibly*
> *—at least, at the back another wire*
> *limply leashes the whole affair*
> *to something off behind the dunes.*
> *A light to read by—perfect! But—impossible.*

In short, another system, its attractions recognized and foregone in favor of the elements. (Besides, "of course the house was boarded up.") Turning back brings its own reward, as the sun briefly, marvelously appears:

> *For just a minute, set in their bezels of sand,*
> *the drab, damp, scattered stones*
> *were multi-colored,*
> *and all those high enough threw out long shadows,*
> *individual shadows, then pulled them in again.*
> *They could have been teasing the lion sun,*
>
> *. . . . .*
>
> *who perhaps had batted a kite out of the sky to play with.*

"The ancients said poetry is a staircase to God," wrote Montale. Bishop shows how this can still be so in a world relieved of theological apparatus.

Her conclusion is both playful and lofty. Best of all, the poet does not feel obliged to tell us what the experience did for *her*.

This is characteristic. Most of Bishop's poems are in the first person, singular or plural. Sometimes she speaks as the Riverman, or Robinson Crusoe, more often "simply" as herself. The voice can be idiosyncratic ("Heavens, I recognize the place, I know it!"). Yet because she is to no least degree concerned with making herself any more remarkable than, as the author of these poems, she already is, hers is a purified, transparent "I," which readers may take as their virtual own. Whether this voice says hard and disabused things or humorous and gentle ones, its emotional pitch remains so true, and its intelligence so unaffected, that we hear in it the "touch of nature" which makes the whole world kin. Is this an obsolete way to judge poetry? I cannot envy anyone who thinks so.

624 White Street

Elizabeth Bishop had her own way with houses. A poem might result just from borrowing a friend's place for the weekend. The handsome modern house in Petrópolis, above Rio de Janeiro, spontaneously put forth a wing for the poet to live and work under. Her grandmother's plain white house, still standing in Great Village, Nova Scotia, has evidently been reading Elizabeth's easier poems—like the nifty "Filling Station" where "somebody" arranges the cans of oil to say "ESSO-SO-SO-SO / to high-strung automobiles." For lo and behold, an Esso station has irresistibly risen across the street from it. Elizabeth's last Brazilian house, in Ouro Prêto, which she named Casa Mariana for Marianne Moore, featured not the obvious mirror or painting centered in the living-room wall, but a large gilt-framed excavation revealing the old tea-brown horizontal timbers lashed together by leather thongs, thus firmly dating the house before 1740 when that particular building technique died out. Thanks to this odd, prematurely deconstructionist embellishment the house took on the air of the generic house of a child's drawing, or some ideal Emersonian house built to embody shelter and solidity throughout the ages. By the time I visited it, Casa Mariana had managed to attract a friendly sun overhead and a big bird-infested fruit tree in the garden. Already a beautiful

Printed here for the first time.

young couple had materialized: a gardener named Adam and a cook named Eva. So Elizabeth's magic was as usual in perfect working order. It is working again today by attracting this small but knowledgeable crowd to take note that the plain white easily overlooked house she stopped living in fifty years ago is still in some very poignant sense "hers," and will continue to be as long as it stands.

I've never been inside, but would guess that the interior corresponded both to her faith in preexisting spaces, in established forms like the sonnet or the sestina, which she could then quietly and quirkily make her own, and to her deepest sense of how to live in an ever more competitive and fame-hungry world. [...] But that is not our affair today. Nor is the quality of her achievement; there'll be much to hear about that in the days ahead. No, it is Elizabeth Bishop's human, domestic presence we need to feel this morning. We who loved and revered her miss it keenly still. And now even the stranger passing through Key West may feel pride to find a great poet's residence so lightly yet so decisively commemorated.

Memories of
Elizabeth Bishop

I met Elizabeth at the famous Bard poetry conference in the fall of 1948. I was teaching there just that year, and upstairs from me lived Joe Summers and his wife, U. T. Joe gave me *North & South* to read. U.T. was working at Houghton Mifflin then and was one of the people who'd seen the book through. Elizabeth came to the conference, along with Dr. Williams, Louise Bogan, Kenneth Rexroth, Lowell, Mary McCarthy, and others. I remember meeting Elizabeth there, [but] I have no impressions of her whatever, though Elizabeth told me later that at that weekend she had told Cal Lowell she wouldn't marry him. She was always frightened of mental illness, of course, and she didn't want to involve herself with an unstable person, brilliant as he was and as much as she adored him. She told me—I think it was there—that she and Lizzie Hardwick had had to put Cal to bed, he was so drunk, and as they left the room, Lizzie looked back and said Cal looked just like a Greek god. Elizabeth realized the course things would take from then on.

That winter I still was at Bard. I was just bowled over by "Over 2,000 Illustrations and a Complete Concordance," so I asked Elizabeth to lunch in New York. We went to Giovanni's, where I must have been before and

Gary Fountain and Peter Brazeau, *Remembering Elizabeth Bishop: An Oral Biography* (Amherst: University of Massachusetts Press, 1994).

she turned out to have been quite often. I naively thought I could spend most of the lunch telling her how wonderful I thought the poem was. It only took a couple of minutes, and whatever we talked about from then on, we were on our own. Elizabeth wasn't affected at all. I think she knew how much she had put into her poems. She must have known they were wonderful. Maybe out of a kind of superstition she didn't want to make too much of them in talking about them.

I finally did go to Brazil [in 1970]. That trip turned Elizabeth and me into fairly close friends. I'd gone to Peru with my brother and his wife. They went to the Amazon and I flew to Brazil. Elizabeth met me in Belo Horizonte. We spent the night in that city, because Ouro Prêto was another two or three hours. She was with Linda Nemer at the airport. They had left a child's birthday party and took me back to it. There was a cake shaped like a soccer field, mostly eaten. This sort of thing Elizabeth adored. She said these were the kind of people that Lota would never let her know. All of Lota's friends were polylingual, and there was never a chance to speak Portuguese.

We drove to Ouro Prêto the next day with Linda, who then must have gone back to Belo Horizonte, because Elizabeth and I were alone for a good four or five days. The house was always full of samba music. She adored the music, and she had a lot of records and favorite singers that she played, and either gave me some or had me buy two or three that she especially liked.

Elizabeth's letters had been full of hints about how expensive liquor was in Brazil and how particularly welcome I'd be if I brought some duty-free bourbon with me. I hadn't realized what a problem it was for her, and during our first evening alone we must have killed the better part of a bottle, drinking old-fashioneds by the stove. [...] Elizabeth had gone into the whole story of how she settled in Brazil, how there was a mix-up about her travel plans, then she got sick, and her head swelled up. By the time she was well enough, Lota had invited her to stay, and said she was building a house in Petrópolis and that she could very, very easily add a little studio apartment to it for Elizabeth. That was really what began the tears. Elizabeth said, "Never in my life had anyone made that kind of gesture toward me, and it just meant everything."

Elizabeth did [talk about the death of Lota]. The way I understood the story is that when Lota telephoned from Brazil to say that she was coming, she told Elizabeth that her doctor had said that she was well enough to travel, which was not the case. I didn't get the impression from Elizabeth that there was an overdose. I had the impression that Lota was taking tranquilizers or [some other kind of pills], but she hadn't, to Elizabeth's knowledge, taken more than she usually took. [Elizabeth was] not explicitly [suffering from guilt]. There was every sense of a very, very strong attachment. Part of that evening's conversation was Elizabeth saying how she didn't like being typed as a lesbian. As evidence to the contrary, she talked about the young man with whom she'd had an affair in New York.

I was there about a week altogether. Elizabeth said every two or three days a several-page, single-spaced letter from Suzanne, who was back in America, would come. We took an excursion to a prison town. We looked at churches. We went to a concert one evening in Ouro Prêto. We had an evening, or part of one, with Lilli. There was a party at someone's house.

There was a lot of drinking, aside from our own tête-à-têtes. Elizabeth had invited six or eight people to dinner on perhaps the fifth night, and by then Linda had come back. Elizabeth didn't appear all that day, and I cooked the dinner. I entertained the guests. Elizabeth did not appear. By the time I [left], she was still a bit weak but seemed to be in better shape than she actually was. She had planned to go on to Rio with me and spend a few days there, but that was out of the question.

Before I had left [for Brazil], a strangely shaped package came from a stove works in the state of Washington, and I was about to send it back when a letter came from Elizabeth saying a part of [her] stove needed to be replaced and she had asked them to send it to me. Would I mind bringing it along? It was quite heavy. She goes on a bit in a letter about it and said, "I had better stop or I will end up telling you the first dirty joke I ever heard." When I got there, I said, "What was the dirty joke?" And she said, "Well, simply name three parts of the stove." And the answer is "lifter, leg, and poker." Elizabeth gave me a little tin stove as a going-away present, with little pots with real beans and real rice in the pots, very much her kind of gift, when you think of what the stove means [in "Sestina"].

Elizabeth and I would talk sometimes a little about her students. There was one funny conversation. I called [and] she said, "Oh, you've just caught me as I was taking my grades to the dean." I said, "Did you flunk anybody?" And she said, "As a matter of fact, I did." This was a course she was giving in letter writers. They read Jane Carlyle, Byron, and [a number of others]. She said there was a black man in the course whom she perhaps ought not to have admitted from the start. The students were asked for a paper at the end of the semester. They could write about any other letter writer that hadn't been discussed in the class. She imagined that he perhaps would take George Jackson's letters from prison. But, no, he chose Lady Mary Wortley Montagu. Elizabeth sighed: "When I came to the part in the paper where he said Lady Mary Montagu ought to be cut up in little pieces and burned in cooking oil, I had to flunk him."

AFTERWORD TO
BECOMING A POET

David Kalstone, in a note for his unfinished final chapter, calls *Geography III* Elizabeth Bishop's "last and, in many senses, greatest book." I would like to suggest briefly, without presuming to complete that chapter myself, why my friend thought so. His pages on Bishop in *Five Temperaments* (1977) provide some helpful clues:

> Her "questions of travel" modulate now, almost imperceptibly, into questions of memory and loss. Attentive still to landscapes where one can feel the sweep and violence of encircling and eroding geological powers, poems such as "Crusoe in England" and "The Moose" pose their problems retrospectively. Crusoe lives an exile's life in civilized England, lord in imagination only of his "un-rediscovered, un-renamable island." In "The Moose" we are city-bound, on a bus trip away from Nova Scotia, and the long lean poem reads like a thread the narrator is laying through a maze—to find her way back?

In the chapter David would almost certainly have included readings of those two poems, along with more than a glance at "The End of March,"

David Kalstone, *Becoming a Poet: Elizabeth Bishop with Marianne Moore and Robert Lowell,* ed. Robert Hemenway (New York: Farrar, Straus and Giroux, 1989).

"One Art," the later "Santarém," "North Haven," and the posthumous "Sonnet." There would have been some graceful tying up of loose threads, perhaps a last glimpse of Miss Moore. Nothing is lost by guesswork except the author's own touch.

A further clue surfaces in his working notes to the present book:

> The Real Problem for Bishop: How to turn the descriptive poem into a narrative—while keeping it descriptive in nature. (This is a main thread.)

Whether or not Bishop herself felt the problem hardly matters. Her lifelong devotion to narrative—to Chekhov, to Helena Morley's diary, to aspects of Lowell's own work—was bearing fruit in this late collection. True, some earlier poems had told a story, like the faintly eucharistical "A Miracle for Breakfast" or "The Burglar of Babylon"—though that ballad rides to safety on a raft of pastiche and does not foreshadow the denser narratives in *Geography III*.

Beyond the turning point of the icy promenade in "The End of March" stands a curious green-shingled, boarded-up house—"my crypto-dream-house." Into it Bishop projects a whole lazy self-indulgent life, reading, drinking, talking to herself. "Spring tides"—whose latest victim, a "man-size ... sodden ghost" of string, she has just now encountered on her walk—threaten the house, but it is protected from them by "a palisade / of—are they railroad ties? / (Many things about this place are dubious.)" The parenthesis alerts us to a double meaning. Railroad ties? Well, yes and no.

The poems in *Geography III*, David writes, "revisit her earlier poems as Bishop herself once visited tropical and polar zones, and . . . they refigure her work in wonderful ways." The early poem here revisited is "Chemin de Fer":

> *Alone on the railroad track*
> *I walked with pounding heart.*
> *The ties were too close together*
> *or maybe too far apart.*

Anyone was has walked on a railroad track knows at least this; and to anyone who has known love the merest hint of ties grown unmanageable will suffice. As the narrator advances into the poem's "impoverished" scenery a "dirty hermit" bursts from his cabin and fires his shotgun. A tree shakes, a hen clucks, and

> *"Love should be put into action!"*
> *screamed the old hermit.*
> *Across the pond an echo*
> *tried and tried to confirm it.*

An Elizabethan poet would have quoted the echoing syllable. Bishop leaves it to the mind's ear: action! . . . shun . . . shun . . . shun. For love's sake, the hermit's cracker-barrel version of an Elizabethan dandy has withdrawn into the wilderness. Now, as "The End of March" opens, "withdrawn" is the key word: "Everything was withdrawn as far as possible, / indrawn." Bishop's dream-house fantasy is not, however, "put into action." She imagines it lingeringly, then dismisses it: "perfect! But— impossible." Just as the railroad ties here echo those in "Chemin de Fer," so they combine with the word "impossible" to recall Marvell's "Definition of Love"—"begotten by Despair / Upon Impossibility." Marvell's own proleptic railroad track appears in his two lovers' feelings which, being "so truly parallel, / Though infinite, can never meet." For Bishop, the ties themselves create the impossibility, her own ties to the world, to the friends walking the beach along with her, to all the dubious claims of responsibility and affection. There is accordingly a return to some livable house. The tide also will have turned. The mystery of certain giant paw prints and that corpse of sodden string ("A kite string?—But no kite") is about to be, however provisionally and fancifully, solved:

> *On the way back our faces froze on the other side.*
> *The sun came out for just a minute.*
> *For just a minute, set in their bezels of sand,*
> *the drab, damp, scattered stones*
> *were multi-colored,*
> *and all those high enough threw out long shadows,*

individual shadows, then pulled them in again.
They could have been teasing the lion sun,
except that now he was behind them
—a sun who'd walked the beach the last low tide,
making those big, majestic paw-prints,
who perhaps had batted a kite out of the sky to play with.

Emerging from drabness, cold, apathy, emblems of death, this moment easily outdoes the imagined perfections of the dream-house. The stones, at first withdrawn like the hermit in "Chemin de Fer" or like uncommunicative mental patients coaxed out of themselves, behave as souls in Dante do (the suicides' moaning trees, the talking lights in *Paradiso*) and for something of the same reason: their quickened relation to a generative source. For by now the sun is, both from an earthly viewpoint and in an odd sense of approbation, "behind" the stones, as if the whole scene were somehow *better* thanks to Bishop's turning back. [. . .] That the moment is handled lightly or "teasingly" diminishes its splendor not one bit. David once remarked that both Lowell and Bishop were at heart theological poets. He must have had a passage such as this in mind.

The neatly handled, explicit plot of "The End of March" represents a late achievement for Bishop. Whereas "At the Fishhouses," a poem not dissimilar in length and dramatic apparatus, can be resolved only through an extended alchemical rhapsody, every descriptive touch in the lines just quoted answers to the "inside story" they conclude.

"Crusoe in England" is the longest, funniest, and finally bleakest of these late narratives. Written as from the vantage of her return to New England, using the famous fiction as a mask and a visit to the Galápagos as a field trip, Bishop mythologizes the cheerfulness and awfulness of her own self-imposed years in the tropics. (Or so one might imagine. In fact, the poem must have been written off and on in Brazil. A 1965 letter to Howard Moss says that it needs "a good dusting." And the Galápagos trip came after its publication in 1971.)

New islands, Crusoe tells us without excitement at the start, keep being born; *his* island, however, remains "un-rediscovered, un-renamable." The lavish description of the next hundred or so lines suggests why.

Well, I had fifty-two
miserable, small volcanoes I could climb
with a few slithery strides—
volcanoes dead as ash heaps.

Dead? Presently we read: "The folds of lava, running out to sea, / would hiss." Of course it's the usual rain hissing, or else the giant local turtles sounding like the teakettle Crusoe would have "given years" for. Then smoke appears, on inspection turning out to be the sea up-spiraling within the waterspouts' "glass chimneys." Amid so much elemental confusion it is hard to bear in mind that the volcanoes haven't come back to life—as Crusoe has, warming to his story. The more he tells, the more dreamlike and elusive the island grows. Small wonder no one has found it. It is turning before our eyes to language, having already—its fifty-two volcanoes weeks of the year?—turned to time, time spent, depleted and shrunken like Crusoe's old clothing. Or as Bishop puts it elsewhere ("Poem"): "life and the memory of it so compressed / they've turned into each other."

Defoe's Crusoe, we recall, kept an obsessive calendar, and named his companion for the day they met. Bishop's Crusoe, whose island leaves not a wrack behind, is nonetheless able to *date* the keenest of his losses: "And Friday, my dear Friday, died of measles / seventeen years ago come March." So Geography bows to History.

The sun set in the sea; the same odd sun
rose from the sea,
and there was one of it and one of me.
The island had one kind of everything.

The sun is odd because singular, a solitary like Crusoe, and also because it keeps—playfully? irresolutely?—rising and setting. Instead of being teased, like the sun by the stones in "The End of March," Crusoe's sun appears to be teasing *him*. A certain volcano gets christened either "*Mont d'Espoir* or *Mount Despair* / (I'd time enough to play with names)." The berry juice used to dye a baby goat red merges a few lines later with the blood from a baby goat's slit throat. These details glint cheerful-awful like shot silk. How small are the volcanoes, really?

I'd think that if they were the size
I thought volcanoes should be, then I had
become a giant;
and if I had become a giant,
I couldn't bear to think what size
the goats and turtles were.

Throughout her work Bishop loves juggling relative sizes. In "Jerónimo's House" a chair "for the smallest baby" had "ten big beads." The vast and ominous moonscape in "12 O'Clock News" is a view of the writer's desk. Her dexterity has never been more sinister than here. Crusoe's flute appropriately plays "the weirdest scale on earth."

According to David, "play of curiosity" and "joy" pervade the poem. He acknowledges Crusoe's recurrent nightmare of "being trapped on infinite numbers of islands, each of which he must in painful detail explore. Back in England the nightmare is just the opposite: that such stimulation, imaginative curiosity, and energy will peter out." I would like to suggest (if my friend were still reachable by telephone) that Crusoe's nightmares are waking ones too, and include the maddening blanks and queasy uncertainties that beset all but the last pages of his account. For here those various oscillations come to an abrupt halt.

Just when I thought I couldn't stand it
another minute longer, Friday came.
(Accounts of that have everything all wrong.)
Friday was nice.
Friday was nice, and we were friends.
If only he had been a woman!
I wanted to propagate my kind,
and so did he, I think, poor boy.
He'd pet the baby goats sometimes,
and race with them, or carry one around.
—Pretty to watch; he had a pretty body.

And then one day they came and took us off.

Like stepping ashore from a rocking boat, this language shocks by its flatness: no description, no double takes, no thickening of the plot. Was Friday then neither soulmate nor servant, lover nor cannibal—just another teenager cavorting on the beach at Rio? I once idiotically asked the author, on being shown this poem before publication, if there couldn't be a bit more about Friday? She rolled her eyes and threw up her hands: Oh, there used to be—*lots* more! But then it seemed . . . And wasn't the poem already long enough?

Despite its concluding lines, "Crusoe in England" is an elegy less for Friday than for the young imagination that running wild sustained itself alone. Friday's role is to put an end to the monologue. Until he appears it is chiefly resourcefulness and bravado—reinventing the parasol, making home brew, playing word games, breeding hallucinations—that keep Crusoe going in his solitary realm. Friday confirms the scale of things: a stabilizing figure and a silencing one. The story goes underground. It will remain only for Crusoe to describe the trappings of old age on another island which "doesn't seem like one, but who decides?"

In 1983 David's friend Svetlana Alpers published *The Art of Describing*, a study of seventeenth-century Dutch painting. The book struck him as bearing uncannily upon his own. In particular the polarity between Dutch painters and those of the Italian Renaissance, the latter felt by historians even in our time to be somehow more "important" than the genial naturalists beyond the Alps—couldn't this be fruitfully applied to a view of Bishop and Lowell?

The Dutch manner "will appeal to women"—a slur attributed to Michelangelo. Indeed, Bishop was Dutch in her love of curiosities locatable in time and place (a hen run over, in summer, on West 4th Street); of genre scenes (Faustina and her mistress, the "Filling Station" attendants) or single figures at their daily tasks (the "sad seamstress," the boy Balthazár, the old netmender outside the fishhouses); of microscopic close-ups and lucid distances ("I can make out the rigging of a schooner / a mile off "); of maps, which, as Alpers puts it, show us "not land possessed but land known in certain respects"; and in her general avoidance of allegorical framework as well as of the rhetoric that corresponds, perhaps, to those wonderstruck figures gesturing from the edge of a nativity or a martyrdom, as if the viewer wouldn't otherwise know where to look or what to feel.

Turning from Bishop's open-air naturalism to Lowell can be like entering a hall full of tortured gods, wounded Gauls, patricides, massacres of the innocents. This last subject, Alpers writes, "with its hordes of angry soldiers, dying children, and mourning mothers was the epitome of what [in the Italian tradition] pictorial narration and hence painting should be." As Lowell himself must often have felt: "Always within me is the child who died." Always upon him was the pressure, in David's words, "to make the poem *signify*," the "rhetorical effort to amplify events, to see them as part of the patterns of the past." Hence the revision of *Notebook* into *History*. This urge is central to Lowell's genius; he could never resist it for long. "In truth I seem to have felt mostly the joys of living," he admits in his "Afterthought" to *Notebook*; "in remembering, in recording, thanks to the gift of the Muse, it is the pain." Can it be the same muse who, given the raw materials of Bishop's life, worked so countervailing an alchemy?

"Crusoe in England" is an exception to Bishop's preference for the happy ending, or the ruefully cheerful one. (Marianne Moore made no bones about *her* preference. "Like John Cheever," she confided to the editor of *Writer's Digest*, "'I have an impulse to bring glad tidings.'") So "The Moose" reverts to type, culminating in a wave of joy "we all feel" at the sight of the great, mysterious animal.

The poem has begun with a "Dutch" catalogue of ravishing pictorial details—landscapes, cottages with figures, flower-pieces or vegetable-pieces—glimpsed from an old-fashioned bus traveling from Nova Scotia to Boston (the alpha and omega, virtually, of Bishop's own life). Between this opening passage and the appearance of the moose occurs a haunting slow movement during which—now that night has fallen and the supremely interesting outside world become an "impenetrable wood"—the poet, *faute de mieux*, finds herself attending to History. Voices "back in the bus" begin "Talking the way they talked / in the old featherbed, / peacefully, on and on" until "it's all right now / even to fall asleep / just as on all those nights." David Kalstone suggests that "this discourse and its kinship to her own powers, the storyteller's powers handed down, summon up the strange vision which stops the bus. . . . The moose seems both to crystallize the silence, security, and awe of the world being left behind and to guarantee a nourishing and haunting place for it in memory."

But those voices, however mild and sleep-inducing, have painful—or once painful—tales to tell:

> *deaths, deaths and sicknesses;*
> *the year he remarried;*
> *the year (something) happened.*
> *She died in childbirth.*
> *That was the son lost*
> *when the schooner foundered.*
>
> *He took to drink. Yes.*
> *She went to the bad.*
> *When Amos began to pray*
> *even in the store and*
> *finally the family had*
> *to put him away.*

Death, remarriage, alcoholism, manic spells, the asylum—where have we most recently heard all that? Why, right here, in and between the lines of Robert Lowell's and Elizabeth Bishop's own lives. The themes which in "The Moose" seem so general are in fact achingly particular. Yet Bishop, even as she introduces these "confessional" elements into the poem, consigns them ("not concerning us") to the back of the bus. That is *her* muse's way with Lowell's kind of subject matter. Eloquent at many other levels, "The Moose" can still be read as part of "one of those arguments that goes on throughout eternity"—or so David puts it, looking back on the differences between the two poets.

In that argument there is, mercifully, no last word intended either by him or in this postscript. Instead . . . a handful of memories?

—I saw Miss Moore at the end of her life, accompanied by a nurse, settled in the front row at the Guggenheim Museum. That evening Elizabeth was reading, among other poems, her "Invitation to Miss Marianne

Moore," published decades earlier, in 1948. A year later, its dedicatee had written with characteristic self-belittlement: "We are called poets, Elizabeth, and one of us is." Now here they were, face-to-face, ceremonially, for perhaps the last time.

—Back then in 1948 I was teaching at Bard College when the legendary poetry weekend took place. Cal and Elizabeth (as I wouldn't have dared to call them at the time) were together at one of the parties, delightedly drinking each other in. A colleague—who, lucky man, knew them both—wondered if this intimacy mightn't *lead to something*. A romance? Only now do I realize how young they were. "The Quaker Graveyard" and "Florida" had been written, but not "Skunk Hour" or "The Armadillo." Or "The Moose." Those poems, of course, are what the intimacy led to.

—The phone rings. It is David, in 1984, wanting to talk about "The Moose." I mention the stanza that evokes a household at night, the kitchen where a dog sleeps, tucked in his shawl. "Tucked in *her* shawl," David corrects, the smile audible.

Brief, threadbare impressions at the time. It would take all my friend's sympathy and scholarship to place them in a fuller, truer light. Let me try to do as much for that assertion.

In the famous sonnet already partly quoted Cal is still marveling at Elizabeth's patience:

> *Have you seen an inchworm crawl on a leaf,*
> *cling to the very end, revolve in air,*
> *feeling for something to reach something? Do*
> *you still hang your words in air, ten years*
> *unfinished, glued to your notice board, with gaps*
> *or empties for the unimaginable phrase—*
> *unerring Muse who makes the casual perfect?*

That inchworm is a haunting *trouvaille*. Elizabeth, in her elegy "North Haven"—her only poem addressed to Cal—also finds in nature a poignant and oddly appropriate image, whereby his lifelong recyclings of earlier work come to seem not so much tortured as instinctive, part of a serene Arcadian world:

The Goldfinches are back, or others like them,
and the White-throated Sparrow's five-note song,
pleading and pleading, brings tears to the eyes.
Nature repeats herself, or almost does:
repeat, repeat, repeat; revise, revise, revise.

. . . .

You left North Haven, anchored in its rock,
afloat in mystic blue . . . And now—you've left
for good. You can't derange, or re-arrange,
your poems again. (But the Sparrows can their song.)
The words won't change again. Sad friend, you cannot change.

It should not be surprising that two brilliant, complex, and often self-destructive people late in life chose to depict one another as bent, like those fragile totem creatures, unambiguously upon survival. Amid the human welter what remained constant in the poets was their incapacity not to reach out for words, not to revise their songs. Their feelings, too, of mutual protectiveness. It is what happens when friends persist in seeing each other's best, and it is a note on which to let this book break off. By concentrating on the language used, the clear-eyed readings (or misreadings) of poems sent back and forth, the letters exchanged, and the climate of faith and gratitude that against all odds prevailed in them, our critic has been able to broach at once the mysteries of affinity and those of making.

MEMORIES OF
TRUMAN CAPOTE

One summer he rented a house in Stonington—the top floor of a strange little clapboard box with a lot of glass around it overlooking the harbor. It was the same house that David Jackson and I first rented two years earlier. He was just back from Russia. The refrigerator was full of caviar and he was reading the galleys of *The Muses Are Heard*. Jack Dunphy was with him, though we rarely saw him. They would go out on picnics to the sandbar in the harbor—a crowd of them, picnic hampers, and the terrible dog, lowering all of this into a boat. They had their own friends. Joan McCracken, the dancer who was married to Jack. She came up. David remembers going down to the little beach at the end of the town with her and Truman—Truman so busy talking as he changed out of his pedal pushers that he forgot that he hadn't anything on underneath. Portuguese grandmothers shielding their children's eyes. He got the pants down to mid-thigh, and Joan said, "You're not going to get away with it, T."

He'd put on these shaded glasses and tell these perfectly absurd, exaggerated stories. The lying was beginning even then. I remember one story about somebody who had her nose eaten away on a Greek island by rats.

Truman Capote: In Which Various Friends, Enemies, Acquaintances, and Detractors Recall His Turbulent Career, ed. George Plimpton (New York: Doubleday, 1997).

She and her son had paid a fisherman to take them to this little island. The boatman was coming around to get them the next day. They were going to have a quiet evening with nature—their fishing, their sleeping bags and cans of pâté, and so forth, and at dusk—in the light of their fire— they saw hundreds of little beady eyes around them. The son made it to the sea and stayed in the water all night long. I think the mother finally got in the water with him but not before her nose had been eaten away. You know, she always had to wear a little face veil. He loved stories like that.

MEMORIES OF
MARY McCARTHY

I always have an impression of Lizzie's presence. She's a very vivid presence. I remember the tone of voice and the kind of sweetness that came through at MacDowell. She seemed very pleased to be doing this. I think Lizzie was always rather insecure vis-à-vis Mary. She probably spent a lot of energy trying to cover it up.

Mary gave a very touching reply to Lizzie's presentation, stressing all the things that we loved and sometimes deplored about her. Her reluctance to join the modern world. Her boycotting of mechanical kitchen appliances and electric typewriters and credit cards. She came through as a very crusty survivor, full of charm.

The point of Bard is that the students always have access to you. And the students at Bard were demanding. I was teaching there the year after Mary and I think Mary always had a good deal more sense of responsibility toward her students than I ever did. I would cluster my classes in the middle of the week and then drive down to New York for a four-day weekend. So I escaped.

Frances Kiernan, *Seeing Mary Plain: A Life of Mary McCarthy* (New York: W. W. Norton, 2000).

She wouldn't ever, even as a novelist I guess, begin to envision what it might be like to die. If she killed someone off, it was fast. The end of *A Charmed Life* is a sort of Nabokovian stroke—the lady novelist, advancing on the last page, kills the heroine.

The book that really lost me was *Cannibals and Missionaries*. She interrupted it to do Hannah Arendt's volumes. You can't do that to your own work. In the last years was there much energy left for the writing? Had her domestic life taken over? And all her various projects? I don't know.

There was an evening at Eleanor Perényi's when Eleanor and Mary began talking about that woman who married Gorky and they began a little antiphon of snideness. Jim cleared his throat and said, "I've always liked her myself, and, especially now that she's down on her luck, I don't think she needs to be trampled all over by hot little heels." Mary blushed—a real pink blush by candlelight—and that was that. When I came to know her, I saw that there was a lot of the chameleon in Mary. She took on the aspect— the psychological aspect—of the husband at the time. Bowden encouraged a certain bitchiness in Mary, whereas Jim had no use for it. And Mary cut it right out.

Mary was very nice with Jim's children. Now, Eleanor has always had the feeling that the children—especially Alison—got a bum deal from them. But I didn't see any sign of it that summer. The climax of that summer was a huge picnic. Mary got this old Frenchwoman who lived out in the country to let us use her property. I think there must have been thirty people. Kevin and his family were there. Grace and Eleanor. Harry and Elizabeth Ford were up visiting for the weekend. There were about eight children. Wonderful wines. Rice salad and potato salad. Very elaborate hampers were packed. Those who wanted to could strip down to their suits and hop into a stream with a waterfall. It was just a lovely day. And this was her sense of showing the children something American. We didn't have flags and bunting, but it was a very grand moment.

Stonington is smaller than Castine, and seems rather second-rate after you've seen it. I used to prepare for the Stonington summer by rereading some of the E. F. Benson novels. The Lucia books. But before I went to Castine I reread *Emma*.

·   ·   ·

I just didn't like Hellman's writing. So from that point of view I was entirely on Mary's side. Though it seemed to me a great deal of fuss about nothing. It was stupid of Lillian to claim truth, whereas anybody would know that you rearrange. Your memory does it for you, whether you think you're telling the truth or not.

Indeed there were financial problems. My little foundation gave her an award one year because I understood that she had already spent nearly a hundred thousand dollars on lawyers. One of the last times I saw her—which would have been the fall before she took ill—Mary looked perfectly beautiful but she was inching along. She could hardly move. And she was wearing a kind of Lillian Hellman Blackglama mink coat and I think she said to me, "This is your generous foundation grant."

Introducing
Richard Wilbur

When I first read Proust at the age of eighteen I came in due time to those final pages in which all the characters who haven't died reappear at a huge afternoon party. The narrator having been a recluse for a number of years isn't prepared for the extraordinary change in his friends. They have dressed themselves up in white wigs, drawn wrinkles on their faces, affected a stoop and a cane. Gradually it comes over him that they aren't playacting: they are simply old. This is utterly preposterous, I thought at eighteen. The passage of time is not a coup de théâtre. This whole party scene is a trick of the novelist's, it is what art can do.

It was in those distant years that I first became aware of Richard Wilbur. He had preceded me at Amherst and there was, I fancied, on my favorite teachers' faces a kind of afterglow, a trace of half-bewildered delight: the brilliant youth, whose poems were appearing in magazines and were soon to be collected in a first volume, had only lately sat in their classrooms. To read those early poems, though I hadn't yet met their author, was for me like the first meeting with a lifelong friend. I marveled at their relish for the world, their openness to intimacy, their good humor, and, best of all, their unaffected faith in art—in French art, if it came to that! In a flash I saw a dozen aspects of my own nature—or what was

Envoy, June 1990.

becoming my nature with every page I turned—given form and voice. It was what art could do.

Now years have passed. I have put on a white wig, I lean on a collection of strategic canes, but Dick as you will presently see and hear, does not. Neither does his muse. As I read through his magnificent *Collected Poems* published just a year ago, her glance shining up from them is of the original youthful purity. She has kept her figure too: the longest poem in this book is about 120 lines. No megalomania here, not an ounce of middle-age spread.

As for the book's shortest poem. Last summer I had a sleepless night, tossing and turning with a superactive mind that didn't at first register its invasion by somebody else's words. The words formed phrases, the phrases connected, and before long I understood with delight and wonder that the lines taking shape in my head were ones that I had read weeks before and unconsciously memorized. What's more, they were by Dick himself. Not all bad sleepers are so lucky. I had somehow entered the magical realm of his making and had gained, as it were, inside knowledge of the lavish sensing and shaping of his poems. Try as I might, I could do absolutely nothing to improve it. It was a sobering, exhilarating experience. Here is the poem in its entirety—a haiku:

> *All night this headland*
> *Lunges into the rumpling*
> *Capework of the wind.*

After that I slept like a baby. Checking for accuracy the next morning, I saw that what I'd forgotten was the poem's title: "Sleepless at Crown Point."

Standards of measurement, whether the cubit kept in the tenemos of Demeter at Cnidus or the iridio-platinum kilogram presently at the International Bureau of Weights and Measures in France, have from antiquity been regarded as vital adjuncts to a nation's integrity and well-being. In the old days the names of the various units of measure were topical. In order to be precise one had to speak of the "Babylonian foot" or the "old London mile." In our time the golden cubit of Cummington, Mass., exactly equal in length to the right forearm of our poet, has become the nearest thing we have to a national standard. The measures produced by this means have never cheated us of a single syllable, nor has the thumb of untested feeling ever brazenly tipped the scale. These scruples make also for the triumph of Wilbur's translations. From his *bureau de change* Molière and Racine emerge with their wallets bulging.

It took a mere forty years or so to modify my early views. Reading Proust and Wilbur now, I may still begin by saying, "Yes, yes, this is what art can do"—saying it with measureless gratitude for their devotion to the craft and their faith in the word—but those passing years have taught me a thing or two as well, and leave me with a slightly modified view of the authors I marveled at as an undergraduate. "Yes, yes," I end by saying of them now, "this is the essence of life itself."

In his capacity of our national poet laureate Dick lectured at the Library of Congress upon a subject dear to his heart: riddles. Inspired by his example, I've composed a riddle especially for this evening. Sharpen your wits, here it comes:

> *Myself by now a household word, I write*
> *Such words as fill your household with delight,*
> *Sing Heaven's blues, and dance upon Earth's greens.*
> *I know an English purer than the Queen's.*
> *My tennis game is better than Racine's.*
> *I will go home with each of you tonight.*

Now with a magic gesture into your midst let me see if I can produce an answer to that riddle—you've all guessed it: Richard Wilbur.

HOWARD MOSS

Moss, Howard (1922–1987), American poet of tones ranging from wryly casual ("An underwater haircut by Debussy") to stark and oracular ("Nothing is unwilling to be born"). A city dweller, he evokes nature as fluently from a window box as from a landscape. The constant contentment Moss offers is deep craft met by deep feeling:

> And what the dead have to say today
> Is old, old as the hills, a phrase
> Meaningless until one stares at these
> Great slants of grave sites, reaching up
> Always to the light, which the dead can't do,
> Whose every particular is shelled to bone;
> They say, "Our hearts, too, were full
> Of sunlight once. Joy is in the shade.
> Look at it. Look. It is beautiful."

Moss was born in New York City, January 22, 1922. He graduated from the University of Wisconsin in 1943. In 1948 he joined *The New Yorker*. As the magazine's poetry editor for nearly forty years, he had a profound and tonic effect on American poets.

Collier's Encyclopedia, 1992.

His *New Selected Poems* (1985), which won the Lenore Marshall-National Prize, contains work from his first book, *The Wound and the Weather* (1946), and the ten volumes that followed. Notable among these are *A Winter Come, A Summer Gone* (1960), *Second Nature* (1968), *Buried City* (1975), *Notes from the Castle* (1980), and *Rules of Sleep* (1984). *Selected Poems* (1971) won the National Book Award. By then it was clear that an attractive talent had grown to lucid, bittersweet mastery.

His own masters include Valéry, Elizabeth Bishop, and, equally essential, Chekhov and Proust. Fictional strategies allow almost anything to soliloquize on his behalf, from "The Pruned Tree" ("I am made more beautiful by losses") to "Einstein's Bathrobe":

> *. . . in the dark I waited, knowing*
> *Sooner or later he'd reach for me*
> *And, half asleep, wriggle into my arms.*
> *Then it seemed a moonish, oblique light*
> *Would gradually illuminate the room. . . .*
> *I felt the dawn's black augurs gather force,*
> *As if I knew in the New Jersey night*
> *The downcast sky that was to clamp on Europe,*
> *That Asia had its future in my pocket.*

Moss focuses his intimate themes so as to include peripherally all the terrors of our world. If to screams of protest he prefers an ironic smile, then, as Joseph Brodsky said of him, "one should feel grateful when a merciless mind chooses in favor of humanity."

He is also the author of the unmatchably clear and concise *The Magic Lantern of Marcel Proust* (1962) as well as three collections of critical essays, *Writing Against Time* (1969), *Whatever Is Moving* (1981), and *Minor Monuments* (1986); the parodies on writers, artists, and composers, *Instant Lives* (1974); and *Two Plays: The Palace at 4 A.M.* and *The Folding Green* (1974). Moss died in New York City, September 16, 1987.

On W. S. Merwin

It is a great honor and a great pleasure, for all concerned, to award the Tanning Prize to W. S. Merwin. As my fellow judge J. D. McClatchy put it in nominating him:

> Merwin has not been overwhelmed with grants. He has always kept himself apart from the university and its rewards. He has worked apart, and worked hard all his life to earn a modest living. He has been and remains a prolific poet, and not shied from prose or journalism or translation. His stylistic evolution has been widely influential and nearly charts the course of mainstream American poetry during the past forty years—except that Merwin does it better than most, certainly better than his imitators. He has a political sensibility, but he has never allowed it to bloat or diminish his deeply spiritual imagination.

It is hard to know what to add to that, this evening. Some further acknowledgment, perhaps, of his accomplishments as a crusader for the resources, both natural and cultural, of those islands he calls home. He is not Faust; he cannot *rule* his small corner of the planet; but he has now and then been

Printed here for the first time.

able to outwit the devil—to divert, that is, the influx of unenlightened "development" into wiser forms than the developers could have imagined by themselves, thus doing what even our elected officials seem largely incapable of. As a poet he has also charted a course that we, his first, marveling readers, might never have foreseen. From that early work, with its ravishing detours rich in echo and ornament, he has attained—more and more with every collection—a wonderful streamlined diction that unerringly separates and recombines like quicksilver scattered upon a shifting plane, but which remains as faithful to the warms and cools of the human heart as that same mercury in the panpipe of a thermometer.

The terms of the Tanning Prize stipulate that it be given to a "master." Masters being as always in short supply, we will do well to start thinking, tomorrow morning, about who will next answer to that august term. But meanwhile here before us, and for many years to come, we have in William Merwin an embodied emblem of the best we can hope for, both as artist and citizen of the world. Please join me in congratulating him.

PREFACE TO
BURNING THE KNIFE

"Vissi d'amore, vissi del viaggio" might well be this poet's theme song. He travels in order to love, he loves in order to find himself elsewhere. From deep in this or that interior his reader gets postcards: dissolving views, myth-haunted, radiantly dislocated particulars. Their sender is unlikely to settle anywhere except for a season in the next virgin forest. To be touched, even dazzled, by the results is less a reflex of avuncular complacency than a taste for that precisely *not* familiar self, that revenant stung by rare insects and laid low by feverish embraces, whose poems are here collected for the first time.

Robin Magowan, *Burning the Knife: New and Selected Poems* (Metuchen, New Jersey: Scarecrow Press, 1985).

Robert Bagg:
A Postscript

In dealing with his experiences Mr. Bagg is helped by a sense of form which candidates to graduate schools as well as to the various colleges of hard knocks would do well to cultivate. For instance, the final section of his book is prefaced by Yeats's stanza beginning, "Does the imagination dwell the most / Upon a woman won or a woman lost?" Mr. Bagg's answer is nicely implied by the *kinds* of imagination at work in the two poems that follow. The first and longer, "The Tandem Ride," celebrates a girl who refused the poet. She is an undergraduate at Smith, all airs and poses. Mr. Bagg gallantly rises to her level. Yeats and Keats appear in the first of his thirty-five Spenserian stanzas, Zelda Fitzgerald in the last; between them he drops the names of Blanche DuBois, Belafonte, Emily Dickinson, Donne, Zeus, etc. The poem glimmers with indulgent echoes. The fraternity brothers set out on their "wild swan chase" riding

A phosphorescent Bike of the Baskervilles
Which soon struck bony terror through the Pelham Hills.

The characters see themselves in extravagant mirrors, narcissistically:

Poetry, July 1961.

> *". . . I go on long walks and show off at Proms."*
> *Her look flicked at me from a Hitchcock thriller*
> *Where the stunned eyes of dead nudes photograph their killer.*

The second poem, "The Madonna of the Cello," is by contrast mysteriously open—no tags, no argument, a "free-form" sequence of tender, brimming vistas:

> *Sliding tears drew out of her eyes*
> *The things she saw:*
> *Her mother staring into the whorls*
> *Of the washing machine,*
> *Her father's eyes receding,*
> *Her own body growing beyond her control.*
> . . . .
> *Silence, after music, awakens the child.*
> *Her lover opens his palm*
> *Over her turbulent belly, where the child*
> *Troubles it with his footprints, turning*
> *Against the flesh.*

Clearly, where the woman won is concerned, the poet can unbuckle, discard the entanglements that kept him from getting lost in Yeats's "vast labyrinth." One does not need Yeats, furthermore, to admire the instinctive rightness of conception and execution in these two poems.

The same rightness shows in many another: in the elegy "Ronald Wyn" where the classical scenery and costumes that numb a few slighter pieces truly become the poem, and show the poet what can honestly be made of his friend's death; in the remarkable "Adventures" whose "blank verse" is forever swelling with extra stresses or faltering into decasyllabics, attuned to the young hero's tentative arrogance; in the haunting "Soft Answers." Before reading this one, only twelve lines long, it is wiser not to have decided that the erotic comes through awkwardly in our language, that, for the last three hundred years or so, the French have done these things better. (I am thinking less of Donne's roving hands than of an emotion more passive and fatalistic, as in Baudelaire's "La douceur qui

fascine et le plaisir qui tue," and whose closest English counterpart would
be, conceivably, the "Ode on Melancholy.") Here is how Mr. Bagg's poem
ends:

Lazy as her love is, I have my hands full

With her, letting every beauty she owns
  Slip through my tongue and fingers, still hoping
For the whole of her, soon closing and opening
  Like a giant heart toying with my bones.

What "works" here is an illusion of unpremeditated, languorous movement; one feels that the poet, in his availability to what he is feeling, does
not entirely comprehend it.

He sees to it that *we* comprehend, however. It is their clear hold on the
commonplace, the shared and shareable, that distinguishes the best of
these poems. Mr. Bagg has worn neither handcuffs nor straitjacket. His
"Adventures" are those that may be supposed to have befallen any red-
blooded American boy. Whether through chance or artistry (a good deal
of each, I should think) they present, in exuberant detail, a first person at
once engaging, credible, and oddly larger than life, almost a paradigm of
Youth here and now, with its bewildering privileges, raptures, flaws.
Indeed a young man can easily offend, if seen to go his way accompanied
by no particular view of life, or by a "suburban and collegiate" one,
flashy, gum-chewing, too smart for anyone's good. What is forgotten,
and inevitable, is that the muse matures with her poet. Another few years
may find her lunching on crudités dressed with vinegar—*tout pour la
ligne*—and denying she ever accepted three sundaes in an afternoon from
him. She will teach him some of Mr. Dugan's "dark, harsh humor." But I
should not think he would belittle those early hours of companionship.
The "life" Robert Bagg renders in his first book has been vividly lived.
He has had lighthearted experiences and painful ones, and, what is seldom
enough done, has set these down without bitterness, making one glad that
he has had them.

THE RELIC, PROMISES, AND POEMS

Robert Hillyer's new collection holds no surprises for his readers. There is the usual dependable technique, lifted now and then—as in "Cock of the Wind"—to a truly winning resourcefulness. There is also the dependable sensibility whereby poem after poem evolves at the pace of the *pantoufle* and with the complacency of the peignoir. It is not my wish to run down light, agreeable verse. Mr. Hillyer himself is quite aware that to preserve the lyric impulse during the middle years is no easy matter. In "One Kind of Colloquy" the older poet keeps silent while his young colleague

> *. . . floats through flowers that yesterday*
> *Were treated with manure and spray,*
> *And sees them vaguely as pale gems*
> *Suspended without roots or stems.*

What is hard to swallow here is the falsification, for whatever innocent purpose. I cannot call to mind a single young poet—unless he writes only for Mr. Hillyer's eye—who looks at nature in this fashion. Indeed, it is far more Mr. Hillyer's own view of things that he attributes to the young. In

Voices: A Journal of Poetry, May–August 1958.

his revealing poem "The Bats" (chosen by the Borestone Mountain Poetry Awards as the best poem of 1953) we find bats used as images for

> *our underdreams that keep*
> *Our secrets from ourselves,*
> *The lark becomes half rodent in that dark*
> *Wherein his downward mountain climber delves.*

This is dexterous enough, but the poem ends on a nervous, warning note:

> *Seal all, before.*
> *In ragged panic driven*
> *These nightwings pour to heaven*
> *And seal us from our natural sun.*
> *Of two forbidden trees, there's one*
> *Untampered with till now.*

The subconscious—seal it off! The repulsiveness of Mr. Hillyer's bat image does the work of argument, tells us what horrors to expect from psychiatry and leaves it at that. But are we persuaded? If truth were the poet's concern, mightn't he have cast about for terms that would not taint his subject from the start?—permitting the dark portions of the mind to be seen as, oh, the wings of a stage, the base of an iceberg, even perhaps the manure from which the flower grows. As it is, he ends up less a prophet than a crank.

Among the more likable poems in *The Relic* are "Light, Variable Winds," "The Magicians," "Proteus," and a number of leisurely, discursive pieces, frequently in heroic couplets. Although they lack the vitality, the spleen, and the fun that the form discovers in the hands of Pope (or, to name a living poet, Walker Gibson), these make pleasant reading. Now and then there is a heightened sparkle:

> *The ice puts out, beneath the frosted moon,*
> *A tentative webbed foot on the lagoon,*
> *And mothers, to place débutantes on view,*
> *Sublease a duplex on Park Avenue.*

Something happens here; the icy foot and the insecure matron fuse for an enchanted instant. But "frosted" is weak, the rhymes are undistinguished. . . . Felicities simply do not grow freely on Mr. Hillyer's unforbidden trees.

The more I read Robert Penn Warren's *Promises (Poems 1954–1956)*— which at first glance had seemed a powerful and glittering performance— the more disappointment I feel. The subtitle is all too telling. Mr. Warren, alas, has a virtuosity capable of turning out a volume twice as long in half that time. Most of the poems, good or bad, move at the tonic pace of an ocean breeze.

More specifically: Mr. Warren is master of a long whiplike line that is particularly effective when dealing with guilt and self-realization, as in certain earlier poems ("End of Season," "Pursuit," "Revelation," to name three) where its compulsive elongation has something in common with his heroes' doomed struggle against the poem's truth. It is a line that furthermore adapts itself in this new volume, to a graphic, humorous manner:

> *Their children were broadcast, like millet seed flung in a wind-flare.*
> *Wives died, were dropped like old shirts in some corner of a country.*
> *Said, "Mister," in bed, the child-bride; hadn't known what to find there;*
> *Wept all the next morning for shame; took pleasure in silk; wore the keys to*
> *the pantry.*

It is not, however, a line that lends itself to a transcendent vision. Consider the stanza with which a long poem closes:

> *For fire flames but in the heart of a colder fire.*
> *All voice is but echo caught from a soundless voice.*
> *Height is not deprivation of valley, nor defect of desire,*
> *But defines, for the fortunate, that joy in which all joys should rejoice.*

However simple and beautiful the opening two lines, it appears they will not do, for Mr. Warren sets about obscuring and clotting, adding here an adverbial phrase, there an auxiliary, neither essential, until the perfectly sufficient line

> *But defines that joy in which all joys rejoice*

is lost beneath its trimmings and the rapid, jerky movement of its little feet.

The music of Marvell and Donne, which exercised a certain control over *Selected Poems*, has given way, if my ear serves, to that of Poe's "Bells":

> *His head in the dark air,*
> *Gleams with the absolute and glacial purity of despair.*
> *His head, unbared, moves with the unremitting glory of stars*
> *high in the night heaven there.*
> *He moves in joy past contumely of stars or insolent indifference*
> *of the dark air.*
> *May we all at last enter into the awfulness of joy he has found*
> *there.*

The fault is not entirely with Mr. Warren's ear. "Country Burying (1919)" is a poem of simple, evocative imagery; the final quatrain depicts an empty church, its gloom, varnish, stacked hymnals, "And the insistent buzz of a fly lost in shadow, somewhere." What in God's name, to use a favorite phrase of Mr. Warren's, persuades him to add

> *Why doesn't that fly stop buzzing—stop buzzing up there!*

There is no minimizing the vulgarity of such a stroke, unless the entire poem is meant as a subtle parody. Elsewhere, in the long "Ballad of a Sweet Dream of Peace," a fascinating arrangement of stock Gothic themes for the arch voice of A. A. Milne, the joke is more apparent:

> What makes him go barefoot at night in God's dew?
> *In God's name, you idiot, so would you*
> *If you'd suffered as he had to*
> *When expelled from his club for the horrible hobby that taught him the*
> *nature of law.*
> *They learned that he drowned his crickets in claret.*
> *The club used cologne and so couldn't bear it.*
> But they drown them in claret in Buckingham Palace!

> *Fool, law is inscrutable, so*
> *Barefoot in dusk and dew he must go.*

But at whose expense is the joke planned? The vulgarity is not that of a single ill-advised line, but of overall proportion. The reader fidgets as the poem repeats itself again and again, harrowing irony upon mellifluous sadism, with no real heightening of effect. The game just isn't worth the candle.

The most impressive poems in the book are several composed in modest five-line stanzas, with lines kept relatively short. An easy, clear voice is heard making a number of things quite brilliantly vivid:

> *The springs of the bed creak now, and settle.*
> *The overalls hang on the back of a chair*
> *To stiffen, slow, as the sweat gets drier.*
> *Far, under a cedar, the tractor's metal*
> *Surrenders last heat to the night air.*
>
> *In the cedar dark a white moth drifts.*
> *The mule's head, at the barn-lot bar,*
> *Droops sad and saurian under night's splendor.*
> *In the star-pale field, the propped pitchfork lifts*
> *Its burden, hung black, to the white star.*

But as fine a poem as "Summer Storm (Circa 1916), and God's Grace" falls prey to Mr. Warren's formula; to end it he must pull out all the stops and turn on the houselights:

> *Oh, send then summer, one summer just right,*
> *With rain well spaced, no wind or hail,*
> *Let cutworm tooth falter, locust jaw fail,*
> *And if man wake at roof-roar at night,*
> *Let that roar be the roar of God's awful Grace, and not of His flail.*

It is a pity to see Mr. Warren giving way to mannerism of language and feeling alike. Conceivably he has counted on the rapid composition of these poems to keep them alive, as indeed they are, on the page and on the tongue. His *Promises* are genuinely exciting, but they remain promises. May Mr. Warren bring more judgment and patience to the next ones he makes.

The new books by William Jay Smith and William Meredith have been ten years in the making. Mr. Smith gives us a selection from his two earlier books, as well as new poems, light verse, and translations. Mr. Meredith's third volume contains forty-six poems hitherto uncollected. Both are highly artful poets in different ways. If Mr. Meredith's work has the careful depths and lights of a master of etching, Mr. Smith's shows the aplomb of a first-rate watercolorist, that air of vivid temperament, blotched arbitrarily, always very light in atmosphere and execution.

Among his choicest poems are some whose wells are ever so slightly tainted by the thirst of a gorgeous savage. Witness "American Primitive" with its mirthless refrain:

> *Only my Daddy could look like that,*
> *And I love my Daddy like he loves his Dollar.*

Or "The Ten," which begins: "Mme. Bonnet is one of the best-dressed ten: / But what of the slovenly six, the hungry five . . ." and ends evoking "the weird, monotonous one . . ."

> *who grasps your pen*
> *And lets the ink run slowly down your page,*
> *Throws back her head and laughs as from a cage:*
> *"Mme. Bonnet is one, you say? . . . And then?"*

There are several debts to France in Mr. Smith's poems. "The weird, monotonous one" is surely kin to the muse of Baudelaire or Gérard de Nerval. Also, lesser Frenchmen have taught Mr. Smith the value of having, time and again, no motive other than to make a small, perfect poem— whose subject matter may even be calculated not to engage a reader overmuch; something leanly modeled, its elements composed and juxtaposed to give a sense of much ground covered in mysterious ways. For instance, from "Interior":

> Past and future, two lean panthers
> Black as coal,
> Paced out the limits of his brain,
> His life's veined ore;
> And he could see
> Gates opening before him quietly
> Upon a rose-banked carriage waiting in the rain.

A movement of terror into gentleness is achieved with an authority the more impressive for the conscious slenderness of materials. The interested reader may turn to an earlier poem, "Elegy," whose analogous theme has been enlivened and purified in the passage above.

Now and then I feel that Mr. Smith has not prepared a proper canvas; the physical or psychological donnée is too flimsy to bear the meaning he wants to draw from it. This is perhaps the price one pays for working largely in miniature: the eye tends to wander, the fancy to quicken, the ear to prompt the next line instead of the mind. Mr. Smith is at his best, accordingly, when he has either a dramatic situation so strong and simple that it needs—one fancies—only to be set down ("Light," "Death of a Jazz Musician," "Cupidon") or else a wealth of sense-impressions to be informed by moods ranging from the spare felicity of

> Waking below the level of the sea,
> You wake in peace; the gardens look
> Like roofs of palaces beneath the water,
> And into the sea the land hooks,

to the opulence, on the facing page, of "Persian Miniature":

> . . . Higher still the laden camels thread
> Their way beyond the mountains, and the clouds
> Are whiter than the ivory they bear
> For Death's black eunuchs. Gold, silk, furs
> Cut the blood-red morning. All is vain.
> I have watched the caravans through the needle's eye

> *As they turn, on the threshing floor, the bones of the dead,*
> *And green as a grasshopper's leg is the evening sky.*

Mr. Meredith, handily enough, has a "Miniature" from Persia. In it he becomes involved in a little tale of Eastern courtesy toward the shy:

> *. . . I have not been to Persia but they tell*
> *How nothing is too much trouble all at once*
> *For irritable beaters when a shy man hunts.*
> *A forest bird was heard to trill for two,*
> *Awkward in one another's presence still—*
> *Two ornithologists—over and over until*
> *They had noted down its call in turquoise curls*
> *On the scrolls they paint with pictures of the fowl.*
> *In the spiced equivalents of cafés there*
> *Waiters grow civil to the ill-matched pair,*
> *The bald and raven-haired, the strong and halt;*
> *And indeed everyone is delicate*
> *Of their delays.*

Suddenly it is as though one were reading fiction; the subject is a human relationship, a scene changing with the passage of time. Mr. Meredith makes his concessions to the picturesque; he throws off "turquoise curls," he lapses wryly into a rhymed couplet or two, like a background of intermittent mandolins. The sensuous, in short, is put in its place, which is not far from where Mr. Smith himself arrives, by such a colorful route, in his own poem: "Gold, silk, furs," and finally—for, to the vision sated with these, the ultimate luxury would be that of abstract utterance—the pill beneath the sugar: "All is vain."

Their difference as poets is essentially temperamental. If Mr. Meredith is, as I feel he is, the more rewarding of the two, it may be because he adopts the more humane stance toward experiences more varied and complex, yet which—because of the dramatic sense, the restraint and compassion he brings to them—permit a very deep response from his reader. To go even a step further: Mr. Meredith's feeling for his subjects is, I suspect, directly linked with the unusual variety and resourcefulness of technique that distinguish his work. As he writes in "To a Western Bard":

> *Cupped with the hands of skill*
> *How loud their voices ring,*
> *Containing passion still*
> *Who cared enough to sing.*

There are many beautiful poems in *The Open Sea*, poems that are elevated without arrogance or sacrifice to the sound of speech, and delicate without fussiness. The tone is intimate and urbane; frequently, the rhythms of a passage, though under full control, present some pleasurable resistance to the ear, suggesting the mint condition of a book with uncut pages. In a poem as bland as "The Chinese Banyan" the following lines may be felt as a flaw:

> *Teacher and bachelor,*
> *Hard forces both to measure.*
> *With Sammy, a small white cur,*
> *Who would dance and yap for pleasure.*

The movement here seems too creaking, and one of the rhymes too emphatic, not to blemish the grisaille of the rest of the poem. But that one should be reduced to this delicate dispute points of itself to Mr. Meredith's excellence.

My own preference is for "Starlight," "A View of the Brooklyn Bridge," a half-dozen very engaging sonnets, and the amazing "On Falling Asleep by Firelight"—a poem that, with its images of heat and slumber, the poet's voice raised from within a dream, gives a sense of eerie deceleration, stanza by stanza. It is a poem that should be read entire, and I have, alas, no space in which to quote it.

THE YALE
YOUNGER POETS

FOREWORD TO *THE EVOLUTION OF THE FLIGHTLESS BIRD*

Why is our poetry so wary of things "the reader" might not know? Surely such delicacy is an earmark of discourse between strangers. Among intimates—as reader and poet, however reluctantly, are—the opaque allusion is forgivable and besides, can always be looked up sooner or later. Of course we cringe when yesterday's household word needs a footnote. (The Esso cans in Elizabeth Bishop's "Filling Station" would be a case in point.) But does it solve the problem to forgo, just because they fade, those goblin gifts of circumstance, and sing purely of tree and stone, body and breath? For in so doing we reduce the self's prodigious cross-index to at best a heartfelt small talk, a poetry of objects, behavior, syntax, all chastened in the service of this or that mood or mania, some inside story translatable more readily into Spanish than into even a close friend's fullest experience.

It is precisely to those outer, shaping circumstances, the world's great givens, that Richard Kenney does full and unusual justice—a justice that includes, to be sure, whatever chords the process strikes in him. He is not out to disguise the liveliness of his mind or the breadth of his leaning. He has read science and history and philosophy as well as Hopkins and

Richard Kenney, *The Evolution of the Flightless Bird* (New Haven: Yale University Press, 1984).

Browning, Crane and Frost; what remains unheard is the drone of last year's workshop. With its agreeable eddies of temperament, reflections that braid and shatter only to recompose downstream, this book moves like a river in a country of ponds.

The opening poem, "The Hours of the Day," can be read as a high romantic fantasia on certain inescapable doublings: self and world, past and present, loss and recovery. Its occasion is an injury to which, in the course of healing, images by the dozen centripetally minister. A turn of the kaleidoscope and the poet's fractured neck and threatened nervous system become a ship's mast with "shrouds / and ratlines loose"; a May-pole with "one ribbon torn"; a web of planetary "disconnections / strung so through a spider's eye." Having acknowledged frayings and severings, the "thoughts that tear / the very fabric of their weaving," he at last gives thanks to whatever brought him through his trials intact:

> *I test my spars,*
> *my riggings; I stand my watch. I grope like the leadsman*
> *sounding deep night, reckoning by no fixed stars'*
> *reflection there— But oh, how a whole net bled*
> *with dewdrops in the dawn! What darkness I've been spared!*

It is through an injury that his stormlit connections are glimpsed, and Kenney is not the first poet to equate pains with panes. His are, however, characteristically particular panes, of early American crown glass with, at the center of each, a swirl or bubble, "A glazier's long-held breath and spy- /glass pharynx, old airs crimped inside the pipe . . ." Rain or hail sets the panes ringing "like banjos," but they stay whole. Meanwhile the double image of their rectangular "framed pools" sows the entire poem with circles and oblongs: collar box and Byzantine icon, moonlike pewter plate and rug weaver's loom frame, section of spinal column and "intelligence . . . latticed like a quartz"—these and many more held in the

> *various spun*
> *and pressed and blown glasses of old windows,*
> *of which these poems have become the square panes.*

Looking back, we discover that "The Hours of the Day" is a sequence of twenty-four fourteen-line stanzas nicely separated by titles serving now as catchwords, now as part of the text. The form governs, in one way or another, the entire book. It soon becomes apparent that Kenney's "sonnets" are not well-wrought urns so much as complex molecules programmed to coalesce into larger structures. Rhyme grows visual or blurs into assonance. Meter, often headlong and approximate, sways us down the corridor of some hurtling train—of thought? of mere syntax? The risk here is that the poetic wheels just spin and spin, getting nowhere fast. But Kenney—it's what one likes best about him—nearly always has an end in view, a story to tell.

He is partial to heroes and grand deeds; he and a friend actually swim the Hellespont. Bravado is kept to a minimum, and so is the other side of that coin, a self-belittling irony. The story of "The Battle of Valcour Island" involves Benedict Arnold. It is curiously refreshing to see these easel-painting "subjects" coming back into their own. Had this particular canvas dated from fifteen years ago, during one of the muse's recurrent honeymoons with politics, the point would have been to highlight an anti-hero whose sly evasion of the enemy foreshadows his eventual, crowning defection to them. Kenney's speaker, instead, is a young Englishman; his focus, a fellow officer's "extraordinary act of courage," offset but not dimmed by the stupidity of their captain. The setting (a "freshwater wilderness farther and farther / from a decent sea. I felt—lost there") barely hints at a poem in which some homophonic "decency" might be the explicit issue. For the narrative sweep, with its gusts of fact and bursts of flame, at once magnetizes and minimizes such overtones:

> *Slowly the black*
> *schooner swung round, until she lay still before*
> *the crescent enemy line: like a focused mirror*
> *throwing gunlight on a single point, the surface*
> *of the water buzzing like bees, and fire from the* Congress.

(*Gunlight!* A hole-in-one at word golf.) The passage itself blazes with disparate, converging clues: the gender of ships, the peril in a flashing glance, Chaucer's villanelle or Bachelard's "whatever shines, sees," Graves's Goddess as the queen bee who kills her consort; and the result gives us *in passing* all the famous honey and havoc of battle.

What on earth follows such exhilaration? Will life reconcile the young hero to his distance from that "decent sea" he began by missing? A debonair click of heels raises the question even as it brings the poem to its perfect close:

> *What came of that was Edward Pellew, Lieutenant*
> *Dacres and I smelled no salt water all winter,*
> *and kissed a number of ladies in Montreal.*

By now I trust "the reader" will be impatient to embark. One last brief glimpse of things to come. Here (from "Notes from Greece") is Easter, a midday lunar feast, in a village below Parnassos. It is yet another instance of Kenney's way of rendering a given scene in sound so artful and imagery so burnished by myth that words appear to have found their poet, rather than the usual way around:

> *In that glare pastures draped*
> *down like cheesecloth liquid with bees and poppies*
> *that sheeted and tided the distance as if the moon*
> *sucked at them each bloom a turgid droplet*
> *a blood-drop. Bouzoukis blinked two ropeveined men*
> *circled the music slowly slowly a sweaty handkerchief*
> *twisted like the limestone valley between their hands.*

Foreword to *Navigable Waterways*

A series of white squares, each
an hour's flying time, each with instructions
in pencil: the organized adventure.

Pamela Alexander's book begins with a map, one whose arbitrary divisions recall pages of manuscript. The poem is dedicated to Amelia Earhart; its subject and way with scale may well be courtesy of Elizabeth Bishop. Poet and pilot are both given to flights. And while never saved by a stanza as provably as by a well-drawn chart, we readers feel at home with the analogy and come to see in those white squares the very building blocks of experience: units of space, time, energy, information. "Like quickened days," Alexander presently tells us, they "take turns showing her senses / what to do." (Another poem will speak of "the glass doors between my days.") Such chambers, forever varying in substance and dimension, are vital to her world.

The poet-pilot "renews / herself, like the engine, for / one thing. Flight. . . ." During a brief earth-walk she joins

Pamela Alexander, *Navigable Waterways* (New Haven: Yale University Press, 1985).

> *a crowd of Javanese walking up a volcanic mountain.*
> *They laugh and talk, they carry baskets*
> *and various loads on poles.*

Random detail? Not really, with its overtone of spiritual quest and the resonance of "poles" whereby the weave of those baskets mimics that of longitude and latitude, as in primitive models of the globe. That people carry their worlds uphill with them she *doesn't* say, doesn't need to—continuing instead to trust her imagery. The map which underlies this whole poem now brings it to an end, along with Earhart's life, as

> *The plane staggers with the weight of fuel,*
> *becomes lighter and then*
> *light. The last square has*
> *an island in it, but cannot*
> *lead her there.*

A rhymed, concluding couplet lies in wait for us here. So does a sense of flight from which legerdemain has abstracted the initial *f* (present also, from the start, on the fuel gauge). Any child learning how to spell can play this sort of Scrabble. To quicken a poem with it, however, ear cocked for the hidden thoughts of language, calls for temperament and skill in no way childish. As the Warburg Institute's motto puts it, God Lurks in the Details.

> *Under a microscope there are lights in a leaf*
> *that flicker and go out, as the leaf dies.*

The least chamber in her poems is found to contain and emit energy. Present now as the star in a bedside carafe, or "nightjar," now as that bird itself with "wingbars like lights shot / from a wave," this innermost quantum fuels the self, renews it; also, in ways a mystic would understand, effaces it:

> *She wonders what holds her life together.*
> *Not herself; she too is held.*

> *Something does it like daylight through*
> *a glass of water.*

Given such diffidence, or such faith, no wonder that only midway through the book's fifth poem does Alexander take on the first-person singular, stepping from the wings with characteristic droll precision into "the middle of chart 13260, / east of Maine." She is discovered standing in a sailboat cabin a bird has just flown in and out of.

This poet works elegantly, unpredictably, without teasing. Her voice can be wholly direct ("Hey you,"); her subjects—heat, air, sex, trees, the peerless dog Pfoxer—impeccably democratic. Yet she is most at home in distance, and the more she offers herself for inspection, the more cryptic the result is. "Talking to Myself at 27" constructs in paradoxical detail a psychic shadow box in which personality is upstaged by cyclical, genetic events. A "line of little girls" lengthens in the opposed mirrors she studied as a child. Here

> *Trying to get my head out of the way*
> *without moving my eyes*
> *was an occupation that gave me numerous headaches*
> *and glasses before I was five. Older philosophers*
> *have gotten worse results*
> *from similar exercises.*

Whereupon the poem all but shudders into prose, as if at the tread of the "large old lady" whom her own grandmother's "ungainly silhouette" shows Alexander she will become. Then her voice lifts in wry urgency:

> *One thing the mothers and sisters and teachers*
> *were careful not to mention*
> *but that grandmothers boldly engaged in*
> *as if it didn't matter what anybody said,*

> *was dying, walking into*
> *the empty mirror just out of sight,*

> *darkening to a silhouette in which someone else*
> *appears, someone familiar—*

It's anything but dull, this minimal view. What we share with one another, the solo, spotlit rehearsal of human concerns, is dimmed in favor of structural excitements shared with all creation. The little girl notices "the grain in desktops," sees in the desk an "iron-legged comrade, confidante, mentor." The trees in "Scherzo" become great floating nightclubs where "green flares go off, and smallish gongs" and "waiters circulate / with drinks, and wiry insects perform / skating tricks." Slung between them, a hammock lines its occupant's back "with longitude / and latitude, tropical waist / to temperate brain." Some cells "tend the elevators / of respiration; others drive sports cars wildly / through the tumbling blue traffic / of the blood"—the adventure, by now less "organized" than positively organic, depicting the grain of one's precious individuality as

> *an imitation grain,*
> *small strokes and walnut swirls,*
> *intricate as weather patterns*
> *in a satellite's eye*

or, even more openly, unmasking it as

> *the imagined person, the one*
> *made with small strokes*
> *on this paper*
> *that used to be trees.*

The small strokes now and then involve more wordplay than usual in a serious poet's work. Surely "Libretti," the book's last section, owes not just its title to Gertrude Stein's *Operas and Plays*:

> *IV.*
> *Ivy that is.*
> *Had you forgotten.*
> *X.*

Spelt out, the roman numeral becomes a vine; romanized, the past participle's final syllable imitates two crossing vines, an unknown quantity, a graphic kiss. Small strokes indeed, but done by a master illuminator. Again: when is a door not a door? Alexander answers the old joke with fairy-tale logic: instead of "ajar," a finished piece of crockery. Notice how "-ful" and "empty" complete and cancel each other, the way a dark shape prints a radiant afterimage:

A stone jar smoothes with us. Useful.
An open door is empty.

Such effects are dictated by "historical necessity." If World War I caused, as we hear tell, the total cave-in of civilization except where it glinted on in the minds of writers like Valéry and Joyce, the problem for later generations has been to create works whose resonance would last for more than a season. A culture without Greek or Latin or Anglo-Saxon goes off the gold standard. How, then, to draw upon the treasure? At once representing and parodying our orphic wealth, the lightweight crackle of wordplay retains no little transactional power in the right hands. Of course, it raises—as for that matter did the gold itself—the question of ill-gotten gains. Even today, how many poets and readers choose the holy poverty of some secondhand diction, pure dull "message" in translation from a never-to-be-known original. "There is no wing like meaning," said Stevens. Two are needed to get off the ground.

Certain poems, like "The Vanishing Point," to the degree that they seem constructed upon purely playful impulses, run the risk of reducing the unsympathetic reader to fury, or the receptive one to trance. Somewhere along the line Alexander's point *does* vanish, into the kaleidoscopic symmetries and elisions of the text.

And yet not so. Her scene is a monastery. Her characters include donkeys, doves, monks, and their guests:

They raise honey bees as well in the alcove,
the oldest part of the wall.
Their will is very old. They and we
arrange straw for the bees in niches some of which are

> *occupied also by stone saints.*
> *The bees are particular since*
> *the straw creates their cloisters.*

Here still are chambers, lodgings of energy: the dovecote, the hive. As the last hypnotic bells (well/wall/will) fade away, a flat, unmusical sentence concludes the book:

> *Finally we forget what we are carrying and do not*
> *make mistakes.*

Rest in action? Faust's solution, or the saint's. But a specific echo, too. It would have us turn again to the opening poem, where holiday-makers were carrying baskets on poles up a mountain, and where a navigational "mistake" sent the pilot to her death. The poet, surviving, casts this backward look, austerely nonchalant, which puts the world in its place: for her purposes, the printed page.

FOREWORD TO
TERMS TO BE MET

In the air, at thirty thousand feet or so, we keep to ourselves: make notes, watch a film, prefer the company of clouds. "Inwardness hangs aloft," as John Hollander put it. To the good old days of railroad travel belong the compulsive talkers with their family stories and snapshots: Here's Velma before she and Fred broke up; here we are with our youngest at the Petrified Forest. Now that trains are being phased out, what's become of those self-delighting chatterers? Are they being phased out, too? Not on your life. They are writing poetry.

George Bradley takes a firm stand against all this. As if we opened a book in order to meet the people next door! Love poems? Not really; the *you* he presents is, more often than not, a modest surrogate *I* who forestalls voyeurism by inviting the reader into his thought. Personal history, what it means to numberless poets harvesting it even as I draft this sentence, is simply put on hold. "Leaving Kansas City," whether or not its author began there, he strikes out, with his back turned also upon the prevailing poetic manners of the heartland, for Bruges and Byzantium, for lofty places and long views, Colorado, the Himalayas, "M31 in Andromeda." Yet it will not do to complain that his poems lack human interest. It

George Bradley, *Terms to Be Met* (New Haven: Yale University Press, 1986).

297

is with the human interest precisely of inwardness that they quiver—the ongoing adventure, the world as meditation.

Emblems punctuate the book: a globe and an hourglass, shapes which accord well with Bradley's travels in space and time. The opening poem may not be *shaped* like a bridge, but its form—through end words which attain the middle line's "summit" only to repeat themselves in reverse or descending order—enacts the little triumph of engineering, as one might call any span's metaphorical dimension:

> *The structure of our adventure, the road*
> *We went by, protected us from the view*
> *Beneath us,*

until, on the river's far side, setting us

> *down out of the sky*
> *According to the prescriptions of our beginning*
> *Into a difficult place, though we weren't particular.*

"Prescriptions" as of a destiny written, say genetically, *before* it is lived; "protected" as one must be if the quest is to succeed; "the view / Beneath us" in both senses of the phrase. Finally, "though we weren't particular" conveys at once self-effacement, indifference—the road is everything, where it leads hardly matters—and some trace element of necessity: even though we've traveled light, left behind the particular in favor of the essential, observed, in short, the poetics of *this* adventure, the end remains "a difficult place," the last act is always bloody. Touch by touch, Bradley's language, at first glance plain as the Kansas his next poem will be driving us through, begins to shimmer like a mirage. Midway through his book, or nearly, and at the heart of his "globe," where Dante placed Satan, Bradley plants a colon: the tiny doubled point standing for the wobble inherent in our most lucid views, or the dazzle that besets our least abandoned diction.

"Leaving Kansas City" goes beyond the dry humor of

> *On the only radio station, a voice explains,*
> *In an accent you wouldn't have thought possible,*

The most practical way of doing something
It would never have occurred to you to do,

past these notes artlessly wistful as a cowboy's guitar:

You move on because somewhere up ahead,
If you remember right, if you're going the right way,
If everything they told you was true . . .
There is a place called Colorado

and concludes with a passage that links—another bridge—the westward impulse of our forebears to the no less instinctive one which (like the conquistadors' El Dorado, Cavafy's Ithaka, and Proust's Venice) locates in our own imaginations the places we yearn for.

Bradley is perhaps too much at home in a secondary world, but who makes the rules? In attempting to fathom the primary one, we need all the help we can get. Old painters and architects stand guard over this book, as do Marianne Moore and Wallace Stevens. Cavafy comes through as an example more fruitful yet, with his singularly unmetaphorical language and deft explorations of creative strategy. Now can be glimpsed the human figures we might have missed elsewhere: Fayoum casket portraits, Socrates, Galileo, Brunelleschi, even "the old poet" himself "at our café" in an Alexandria established by his latest disciple as properly fictive from the start. Glimpses only, trick perspectives—what trouble with the here and now makes a poet cling to such devices?

For one thing, they reinforce the mind forever haunted by collapse and erosion, like the dome of Hagia Sophia or the rock formations in Monument Valley. Descent from the "summit" of any mental span is inescapable. So is art's patchwork aspect, which, says Bradley with lovely forbearance (note the play on "content"),

arises out of a chance accumulation,
Out of a mind that perhaps achieved optimum content
Months or even years ago, say one morning in winter
When the sky was so blue and steam rose off the ocean
Into the other element of air.

Then too, a thoughtful poet will want to check the rush of sensation. "Feelings and images," wrote Camus, "multiply a philosophy by ten." All the more reason to use them sparingly. At times the very realities that most interest Bradley require "the mirror images of scientific equipment." The naked eye, or indeed its naked homophone, can make nothing of "M31 in Andromeda." But give a man a telescope, this poem seems to say, and he will tell you the truth about his inmost psyche:

> *Stellar Body M31 was long remarked for an odd imbalance,*
> *Revolving in mysterious concert with its own dark motives.*
> *The hidden motivation turns out to be ourselves, our Milky Way,*
>
> . . . .
>
> *The great gathering of light spins majestically in space,*
> *Centrifugal force and the force of gravity conspiring*
> *To yield configuration, an elegant ellipse, though why*
> *To turn in emptiness, in absence of light or any warmth,*
> *Should form anything is not easy to imagine, any more than why*
> *Our own thoughts and dreams should take shape out of darkness.*

The message, familiar since Greek tragedy, is plain: man is himself both marvel and monster. As the poem concludes, the relevant myth surfaces:

> *it seems Andromeda*
> *Was a woman so beautiful she was set out on a rock, bound*
> *Beside the sea and with a sea of stars over her head,*
> *There to satisfy something terrible, something that no one,*
> *Not her father, who was king, nor her father's priests,*
> *Nor we who read the tale, had any real hope of averting*
> *Or could think to comprehend.*

This must be the only version of the Andromeda story in which her savior Perseus fails to materialize—except that he has already done so, as the artist-scientist turning his mirror shield upon the mystery. By these last lines the "extraordinarily beautiful" galaxy has merged with the doomed princess. So has that "something terrible" with "ourselves, our Milky Way." ("Our Milky Way"—doesn't the phrase give out some glimmering of our performance as mammals?) The connections are drawn gravely yet companionably. It is all worth hearing, and Bradley doesn't patronize us with gimmicks or grimaces in the telling.

We have grown used, in all the arts, to a spasmodic, Dionysian approach to experience, with points for a hot vocabulary, "involvement" and "witness"—the red shoes of the actual, twitching by themselves, to no music worth the name. In such a context Apollonian measures are welcome, especially at the hands of a poet able first of all to hear the interval between cosmos and psyche, then skillful enough to strike pianissimo that vital octave:

> *If you listen closely some morning, when the sun swells*
> *Over the horizon and the world is still and still asleep,*
> *You might hear it, a faint noise so far inside your mind*
> *That it must come from somewhere, from light rushing to darkness,*
> *Energy burning towards entropy, towards a peaceful solution,*
> *Burning brilliantly, spontaneously, in the middle of nowhere,*
> *And you, too, must make a sound that is somewhat like it,*
> *Though that, of course, you have no way of hearing at all.*

What impresses is the wide, sure orbit by which such conclusions are reached. That Bradley's so often appear foregone means in part his sensible reluctance to break new ground indiscriminately, in part that he has attained that rightness of wording which is a poet's best chance of being remembered.

FOREWORD TO
ABOVE THE LAND

"So much sensation is unknown," writes Julie Agoos, and proceeds to challenge the sorry state of affairs:

> *On the banks of that river that parts the city*
> *of Florence, should you straddle the wall,*
> *your pink legs will glow in twilight,*
> *her fan up against the iron lampposts.*

It's a "you" we recognize at once—the updated Henry James heroine savoring her Italy from an uncommitted vantage not thinkable to the local adult population.

Poets needn't travel. Look at Emily Dickinson. Look at Marianne Moore, who got more from a single issue of the *London Illustrated News* than Mother did from her entire junior year abroad. And yet, if travel is in the cards, Italy may still be its most reliable object. To see why, we should first ask, as Henry James never stopped doing, what claim the forms of art can possibly exert upon a writer with the usual blurred American perception of the forms of life. What have the look and speech and manners of our hometowns—settled only a few centuries ago by a

Julie Agoos, *Above the Land* (New Haven: Yale University Press, 1987).

fanatic sect or a shipload of criminals—in common with Parma's or Fiesole's age-old ways of doing and saying, just as effective in the pruning of trees as they are about to be in the seduction of that Lit major reading her guidebook at the café table? (Where better than Italy, for that matter, do we find writ large the offenses that comprise so much of the small print of American politics?) Until the forms of life are clearly felt, the forms of art will mean little. At best those we call "organic"—like fertilizer—may blaze in a master's hands. But Italy *teaches*. Here are the proportions that ease the heart, the images agleam with use, the spoken phrases of a fluency so natural that we forget how we distrusted it back home, where to grope for words proved our utter sincerity. In short, the poet straddling the wall may return to America thinking:

> *It will have been worth something to have*
> *connected that life to your own existence.*

Agoos makes her connections, and uses those foreign ways, as directly or obliquely as she pleases. "Porto Venere" is a distillation of impressions not unlike Browning's "Englishman in Italy," but with the feelings volatized out of sight. A more complex and ambitious piece, "An Afternoon's Activity," has two middle-aged women arriving exhausted in an Italian town—Florence? After lunch they part for a few hours. Diana, unwell, takes to bed with her dictionary, bent on learning and whenever possible using the numerous words prefixed by *porta-* (denoting what bears or contains, as in porter or portfolio, but also by itself the noun for door). Her friend goes for a walk, idly planning a card or letter to Diana's son at home. By the poem's end the Italian words are everywhere, the mother is even addressing her son *in* Italian. Doors, too, have proliferated—after all, in the beginning was the word for them. "Are these the doors to Paradise?" wonders Diana, early on. No, to a restaurant. But the question has been asked. Presently above certain doors appear terra-cotta plaques of the Madonna and Child, as do, in the appropriately italic inner monologues which edge the poem's action, some discreet sacramental images—oil, linen, wine. Thanks to a happy homophone, the absent son is balanced by "The sun in my lap as I try writing this postcard," and the card, whether written or not, merges with Diana's invocation to him as the doorkeeper to her very life:

> *Ma spero che stia*
> *in ogni caso*
> *alle porte*
> *quando arrivano*
> *queste lettere,*
> *quando arriverò,*
> *e quando vado via.*

Risky, that shift into Italian. Not all readers have a second language. Those who do, however, will recall times when they resorted to it for complicity ("Pas devant les enfants") as well as respite from the ready dramatics of the mother tongue. Both motives are at work here, for the poem's mother needs to spare her son—and herself—depths that might otherwise be too bluntly sounded. A similar tact informs the poem's "Christianity," which lacks the dead dogmatic weight of an idea put forth in earnest. Rather, it comes through as a construct the poet has found to her liking, already implicit in the sounds and sights themselves of Italy, "this place where all the pretty roots of words are."

The real test is getting the culture home, like yogurt kept warm in an immigrant's bodice during the long crossing. Agoos slips gracefully through customs. Rhythms to the speech, logic to the television tower, farm scenes, town meetings, the haunting "Lunar Eclipse at a New England Funeral"—forms present from the start are now easier to perceive. The four cardinal points, the four seasons? Without a single baroque painter to personify them, haven't we known by instinct how vital, how useful, such notions are? Here is the way Agoos develops one of these motifs in her book:

> *No one has unlocked*
> *the incidental farmhouse*
> *from its four views,*

she writes in the first poem, "Living Here." And later, in a poem wonderfully evoking Weather as an old laborer in the fields:

> *Where is beauty, except*
> *in the ground, like this idea*

> *of a crossroads in a field? Does continuity*
> *count for nothing? At winter's end*
> *the fields are wide open,*
>
> *and it would be easy for the weatherman,*
> *or me, ignoring the four*
> *seasons, to lie down in them.*

Finally, these crossings and quarterings having become second nature, like the steps of a folk dance, she is given a startling glimpse: living quarters, herself centered there, rising from her lover's bed, snowlit and on the move:

> *Covering myself,*
> *your four mirrors struck me: gazing at*
> *myself in a fine state, I saw, four times,*
> *a quick stirring sweep you, like a last*
> *dream, beneath the sheets . . .*
>
> *And I went, thinking:*
> *Hurry. Already the sea is wet and*
> *the waves unhesitating . . .*

This moment of truth, too fleet to count as self-knowledge, holds nonetheless in a flash the figure of a young artist fully occupying a space until now impersonal or traditional. What would the insight augur in practice? Perhaps "The Search" gives a clue. Agoos dedicates it to her sister, from whom as a child she learned the Latin names of trees and shrubs. The poem reads like an elegy—if not for a person, then arguably for the sentimental pedant its author didn't grow up to be. It begins:

> *Recalling terms you threw to me on walks,*
> *I asked for you among the trees*

and ends:

> *Whom were you reassuring with Latin names?*
> *What love made you believe the earth was stirred*

> *to take you in? Though often enough I've caught*
> *your track in snow, stark, and cavernous as scars*
> *that last forever on the Fagus, even the Betulae,*
> *like cliques of graceful women, scorn you now,*
> *white with pity, graceful and paperthin.*
> *I cannot blame them, nor the blushing Acer*
> *who fades unmoved by your particular step.*
> *That bark is not your skin, and roots long sunk*
> *in moss do not drink rain for you, or carry*
> *your memory to be dug at like a scent.*

The dryads of this passage cannot distract a reader from the point. Indeed they enforce it: things sooner or later shrug off the glamour of even their finest names, and ask to be clothed in fresh language. The sister's Latin no longer becomes the trees. It will be *her* sister—Julie Agoos—whose words may one day do that.

Foreword to *To the Place of Trumpets*

"Man is only man superficially," wrote Valéry. "Remove his skin, dissect, and at once you come to machinery." True enough; and cutting through the surface of personal experience, you arrive at a realm of myth, archetype, fable, and metaphor—machinery of the sort in which a god descends. Here, oddly enough, we are more often at home than in the world of fact. Only a specialist, a pilot for instance, or an engineer, lives by his knowledge that the earth is round. The rest of us daily make do with an old wives' tale.

But "make do" hardly describes Brigit Pegeen Kelly's exuberant ways with words. At the simplest level she retains the wild, transforming eye of childhood. "Sundays" evokes that stage when names are just beginning to stick to their referents, and "Mr. Fudd" is as delicious to utter as "red" or "rabbit." When Anna's husband, in his churchgoing best, smiles

> *his head comes forward*
> *and his teeth come forward*
> *as if he brought his fence out farther*

Brigit Pegeen Kelly, *To the Place of Trumpets* (New Haven: Yale University Press, 1988).

> *to make the yard larger*
> *to let more people in.*

To *take* more people in, the grown-up poet might say, but slyness is out of place in this child's drawing. The same poem gives us "red trees, ruby grass, crimson sun," like some primal orgy with a box of crayons. Such effects grow subtler as her personae mature, but Kelly never abandons color as a virtual myth in itself, the way it is in Stevens or Chagall.

Many poems reflect her Catholic background. A lapsed Episcopalian, I can both marvel at my narrow escape and catch myself sighing in retrospect for the deeper dyes and more forceful early imprint of Rome. We tend to think that any religious education has its drawbacks—a warped view of history, say, or of science—yet here in Protestant America, whose children are raised believing that nothing is truly intricate or miraculous, and no longer know even the stories of Aesop and Grimm, let alone Bulfinch and the Bible, to have been partly educated by nuns or rabbis or the imam at the mosque downtown is a distinct advantage. You enter college, as it were, on a scholarship of which your smiling WASP classmates have been pitifully deprived.

In Kelly's work the Catholic heritage will be transmuted beyond any taint of dogma. First, though, she must escape. One angry poem has a little girl focusing her rebellion through figures in the stained-glass church windows:

> *When the sun comes up behind the angels*
> *then even in their dun robes they are beautiful,*
> *with their girlish hair and their mean lit faces,*
> *but they do not love the light. As I*
> *do not love it when I am made clean*
> *for the ladies who bring my family money.*

The angels are "sick of Jesus, / who never stops dying," thinks the child, and "One night they will get out of here . . ."

> *together, as in a wedding march,*
> *their pockets full of money from the boxes*

for the sick poor, they will walk down the aisle,
imagining their own hymns.

Rebel angels—like the child, sick of the sweetness and light she is made to embody. Those last four words give this poem its title, and reading further we understand that to imagine her own hymns after leaving church is the project (again Stevens comes to mind) for all of Kelly's poetry to date. Most ominous here is the falsification inflicted upon the child for appearances' sake. In "Queen Elizabeth and the Blind Girl," so as not to forgo the gift brought by its royal godmother, a dead infant is rouged into the semblance of sleep. The deception sets off a toccata for a deaf bell-ringer and a shopful of talking birds. Fairy-tale touches like these repeatedly work their counterspell. Through them—linked as they are with necessities ("money . . . for the sick poor")—Kelly does considerable justice to the Church's hold upon her young life, and to the cost at which she struggles free of it.

Free of the shaping past? Isn't the most we can do, to be free *with* it, submit it to some shaping of our own? This freedom, in any case, I find especially heartening in Kelly's poems. Far from leading to negation or bitterness, her lost faith becomes the stuff of vision. She fabulizes, she distances. The "Mount Angel" poems depict a community grown simpleminded, even bucolic. The priest's sermon "was nothing to me,"

so sure was I of the crown
of rain falling over the flowers, the stone
benches, the fields far below where the Old
Believers, haloed with strawberry moths, bent
and picked fruit . . .

Here the language of transcendence is deflected onto the landscape surrounding the monastery, and given the lightest possible coup de grâce by those haloes of moths. In a landscape more idyllic yet flow streams "over whose waters / the sun passes like a silver hand carrying a cup of wine," an image as ecstatic as any in the Song of Songs. Elsewhere a bull named Moses "all improbably" *eats* a burning bush. Or (in "Garden Among Tombs") a soldier who sleeps through the Resurrection tells on waking not that Judas's palm but that his, the sleeper's, own legs have been "crossed . . . with silver" by the passage of nocturnal snails. Kelly's imagination breeds heresies as innocent and plentiful as mayflies. Thanks to it we can feel this Christian story—which has weighed so painfully upon the world for centuries—at last breaking down, granite to schist, leaving only the odd recalcitrance of a phrase or the fractured mica-flash of an ancient image.

Thus delivered, Kelly writes some of her best poems. One of them ("Those Who Wrestle with the Angel for Us") tells how her brother, now an aviator, as a little boy

> *dragged a stick along the fence rails, and listened*
> *To the slatted rattle of the railroad cars, and knew by*
>
> *Instinct how railroad lines look from the air, like ladders*
> *Running northward to the stars, to the great constellations.*
> *And he began then tracking his way through the names*
> *Of all our fears, Cassiopeia, Andromeda, the shining Ram,*
>
> *Tracking the miles and years he logs now.*

We hear the stick echo the railroad cars, see rails and cross-ties form the upraised ladder, feel cars merging with stars, and tracks with the young stargazer's tracking eye. These are lines finely conceived and written. For all its plainer language, "The House on Main Street" ends upon a note no less exalted—which suggests, too, where some of those renegade angels may presently be glimpsed. The poet and her daughter, collecting feathers in the cemetery they've been using as a playground, imagine themselves

> *connected with flight, not with the stone angels*
> *shadowing the frozen*
> *ground, but with a body*
> *that has truly flown, with a mind*
> *that makes the sky*
> *its home.*

With this poem Brigit Pegeen Kelly casts a wide descriptive net, in the manner of Marianne Moore's "The Steeple-Jack," over a townscape with figures. The occasion, "a funeral to which I was not / invited," gives her lavish access to the world of fact: the full church with "the whole town . . . singing / inside"; a recent case of arson; hydrangeas withered (by their abuse in a previous poem?); a bag of clothespins "like a wasps' nest"; a murdered girl. The scene comes to life through the eyes of the poet, who—nostalgic for a home left far behind, but easy in her present, somewhat "Aquarian" way of life—includes herself among the local oddballs. No, not quite: she has settled on a nearby hill, reluctantly but significantly above them all.

FOREWORD TO
OUT OF THE WOODS

As we know from galleries hung with studies of the same apple-strewn tablecloth, the painter who mines a single vein is felt to have looked profoundly into both his subject and himself. But for a poet to dwell, page after page, upon the same small family of images may argue a certain limitation. Language is after all an Ariel free, unlike the Calibans of brush and pigment, to embody every nameable bit of the universe. Here, though, is Thomas Bolt, whose grimy, late-twentieth-century pastoral fills up a whole book. Has motif given way to obsession? The corner Bolt paints himself into commands too wide and too sobering a view for us to think so.

The scene could be almost anywhere in the original thirteen colonies. It is largely unpeopled, but not idyllically so. Humankind is very much present in the things it has used and discarded. We recognize all too well those wrecked cars, rusted appliances, empty Clorox bottles. Like the soil itself they represent our common heritage, having merged by now with the abandoned orchard and picturesquely decaying homestead that horrify the visitor from abroad. Good land neglected—what madness! No wonder America produces children it then ignores, who will grow up to be killers. No wonder its principal exports in 1986 were scrap metal and

Thomas Bolt, *Out of the Woods* (New Haven: Yale University Press, 1989).

wastepaper. Such facts positively quiver to fuel a fire-and-brimstone sermon. Bolt, however, remains cool, sharply focused; a steady hand crops his lines. Not to worry, he might be telling us: the worst is over. Apocalypse has already taken place, long ago, at some remote juncture in our lives. The evidence lies all around us.

Fortunately there are overtones that sweeten the pill. Just as the famous red wheelbarrow surrounded by chickens merges—in the mind of a reader given to association—with Aphrodite's sparrow-drawn chariot, so the woods in which Bolt keeps losing and finding himself tend to be more than mere doomed sylvan interstices in our urban sprawl. They come to him by way of Dante and Auden, Augustine and Thoreau. Centuries ago he might have written:

> *Already my slow steps had carried me*
> *Into the ancient wood so far, that I*
> *Could not perceive where I had entered it.*
> *And lo! my further course a stream cut off.*
> (Purgatorio *XXVIII, trans. Longfellow*)

Instead:

> *I shook from my own shudder of surfaces*
> *And heard the sound*
> *Of the narrow water, moving as before*
> *Between where I was*
> *And had to go; I balanced at the edge,*
> *And crossed the creek.*

Writing a poem, or reading one, is always to some degree a spiritual exercise. A reader who, understandably nowadays, wants to skip the allegory, still responds to Dante's urgent topography, and it is a kindred energy in Bolt that keeps us on his track. Whatever his woods once "stood for"—sin, unredeemed human nature, the animistic emperies of Pan—he can't be much bothered to recall. Oh, here and there an old Pontiac suggests "truth /...up on cinderblocks," and a "barren ditch" turns into "the ditch of belief." Yet considering how prodigally another poet might have strewn his way out of the woods with italicized Hindu or

Christian terminology, we can overlook a few youthful indulgences. More to the point, by sidestepping the overtly personal, Bolt shows not alienation but good sense. As in that parlor game beloved by amateur psychologists, the subject who describes the elements of a made-up landscape—the key underfoot, the body of water, the old wall—has already revealed himself with respect to religion, Eros, and death. Here the entire metaphorical field is so rich that the plainest words—path, tie, lot, dark, flow—vibrate from the start with human overtones.

Bolt's fullest investigation of his dark wood takes up the last half of his book—a single poem. Partly followed, partly improvised, its path is too arduous for the imagination to stray very far. Here are no "flights," just the syntactical coping with a terrain brought line by line onto the page. The one backward look in time (late in section I) is rendered in images of the here and now. Accordingly the reader must bear some of the protagonist's frustrations. But the adventure is so vivid, so psychologically engaging—as it moves from thicket to railroad track, from swamp to "good, cold creek cleaning its bed / Of mattress-springs," from fields strewn with "great annihilated iron things" to a vast junkyard where Dante, as it were, meets Henry Ford and which Bolt's exertions earn him the momentary right to claim as "The secret center of America"—that we too are left with second wind and want nothing more than to read the poem all over again.

On so doing, many lovely progressions and adjustments will come to light. A single illustration. In section II "tall sycamores / Still hung with burrs" appear. In III the sky, seen through "skin and bones of tattered sycamores," is "Nailed to naked branches overhead / With iron burrs." Later (VI) come "decorated sycamores, / Bone white, / Hung with round burrs / Like ornaments." And finally, "starry points of sycamore burrs /. . . buried / In the smoke of the cold sky darkening." These variations have a concise logic. The burrs, first nail heads as of a crucifixion, then ornaments as on a Christmas tree, sparkle forth from murk at the close, a humble *cielo stellato* to welcome the fulfilled pilgrim.

In "Temporary Structure" Bolt returns to an earlier image: a bucket slowly disintegrating in the creek where "it is beaten back and forth." It is the form given by thought and language to a present continually improvised,

> *New, a booming shape*
> *Banged and battered,*
> *Its drum curve*
> *Beaten by water,*
> *Its flattened crystals blazing*
> *Jammed between rocks,*
> *One side in silver shadow.*
> . . . .
> *Turned and overturned,*
> *Bright zinc will wear off,*
>
> *The bottom pock with rust,*
> *Each pock*
> *Enlarge with ruin, and,*
> *Worn to a wafer,*
> *The whole, punctured crust*
> *Finally crumple under a loop*
> *Of new water into a whorl of flakes.*

Now charged by electrical alliterations, now at rest in a random pentameter, the language lightly thuds and dances; the *k* and *b* sounds of "bucket" ricochet, dispersing within the description like bits of the thing itself. If, presently, we pause to notice how "whole" relates to "punctured," or "wafer" to "crust," or if Bolt himself pauses long enough to reflect that

> *This living framework,*
> *Scaffold for a life,*
> *Will plunge into a cold scattering*
> . . . .
> *The scaffolding of my language taken down*
> *Leave an emptiness of objects,*

it may seem that simple justice has been done to incoherent nature's way with words.

FOREWORD TO
HERMIT WITH LANDSCAPE

If Memory is the mother of the Muses, concision is their mentor. Faced even with the vast canvases of Dante and Proust, we appreciate how much is foreshortened or left out. Who has not heard from his literature teacher that "the whole story is there on the opening page," and wondered why the author bothered to go on. I'm making no case for bonsai forms. (Too many haiku at one sitting, warns Richard Howard, and you feel you've been nibbled to death by goldfish. "Excellent," said Chamfort on being shown a friend's latest couplet, "except for the dull stretches.") But the short poem, at most forty lines long, a legacy of symbolism if not of the Greeks, remains an ideal, and it is in this compact arena that Daniel Hall is largely at home.

Consciously at home, too. Enclosure beckons to him like an open road:

> *No sound of the sea in this inland town.*
> *There ought to be: the stillness around us*
> *cries out to be filled with something vast,*
> *something that stirs and soothes at once.*
> *And the moon by day, pale but plausible,*

Daniel Hall, *Hermit with Landscape* (New Haven: Yale University Press, 1990).

> *could be working greater wonders here.*
> *But this will do*

—"this" being a curtained room, nondescript, which nevertheless at a gust of air "rises up in a flurry / of its own detail." That the space is occupied appears from little more than "a scrim of smoke." But presently, inside the room with its ghostly occupant, another, even smaller space comes to light, with its own, even ghostlier occupant to take over the poem's self-consuming drama:

> *Only the carp*
> *hangs unperturbed in his cloudy cubic meter,*
> *dead but for the fanning of his fins.*
> *He might be listening, but we can hear*
> *no sound of the sea in this inland town.*

The first and last lines of one stanza (*room* in Italian, after all) become the last and first of the other, an easy mirror trick that works here to surprising effect.

Hall's title poem handles its spaces more tellingly yet. The hermit-protagonist, on leaving "the city of gold," has had pressed upon him a

> *snuffbox, rosewood, worked*
> *by knowing hands and packed*
> *with a troy ounce of the glistering stuff—*
> *worth nothing here, but enough*
> *for a year's indulgence there.*

"Here" is a cell of "whitewashed stone whose eight / corners gaze inward . . ." (How about those eight corners? They've changed forever my sense of a room.) Nor do the enclosings stop here; finally, a "sunny, bird-woven" outside world contains the whitewashed cell, even as the cell contains the snuffbox full of gold. Such nestings of one figure within the next belong to what Bachelard called the poetics of space, and the vibrations they set up are not those of language, much as language (note the light couplets in which all this is cast) engages and prolongs them. For there are meanings, too, nested within meanings: the gold both worthless and precious; "indulgence" conveying at once dissipation and leniency; the overtones of "purchase" and "credit" which add a kind of humming weight to the final lines. By such degrees Hall approaches the magnetic field of Herbert's "Redemption"—that carefully worked out, sonnet-long miracle play—only with an Escher-like spatial dynamics in lieu of personification.

Having done time also in the great outdoors, Hall gallantly holds his own against it. He counters the western landscape's "stare of such absolute / lifelessness" with a burst of Satie over the car radio, or answers an enormous vista of glacier and logjam with something between a sniff and a sneeze: "sphnx"! (Inserting the *I* of the sneezer, we can glimpse the framer of a famous riddle, and its solution.) So high a hand with awesome nature won't be to every taste, yet on fine days it must be granted, as at the close of "A Sneeze on High," when the poet is still seeing stars after his convulsion—

> *I linger a moment*
> *longer, haloed*
> *in a fume of bright*
> *synaptic mayflies*

—that he has made the best of both worlds.

Our poetry, like our planet, suffers from overpopulation. After reading a thousand poems about relationships (grandparent, lover, child)— and writing the odd one myself, being only human—I positively ache for an anthill, a cloudscape, a blank mirror, *anything* but these enthusiastic home movies, which offer no surprises in the darkroom. Hall's human subjects are few, and obliquely presented; one direct encounter ("13th & Aloha") is a near fatality. Yet his very reserve brings to mysterious life those others he focuses upon.

An etcher is at work in "Andrew's Jewelweed." No doubt it behooves the artist to suffer, and Andrew is no exception. Instead of juicy details, however, we have only a little lexicon of hurt to go by: *bruising, spurs, pains, aching, sharp, bittersweet.* The words allude to more than they dream of telling. In "The People's Hotel," what seems at first a Cavafyesque brief encounter takes an unconventional turn. Money, a handful of change on the point of changing hands, is itself changed through being quietly, intently sketched by the guest, so that an afterglow of wonder lights up the vignette. Readers of Cavafy are used to the artistry in such transactions being entirely on the poet's side. It's nice now and then to see the tables turned.

Out of Cavafy, too, could have stepped the young hero of "X." The title suggests the speaker's namelessness, his unknown quantity in whatever equation, as well as the rating of those films that beam forth from his lonely projection booth. A proper name and the haunting term for cinema in one of his languages help to define him as the son or grandson of a transplanted Chinese family, working nights to complete the sad process of Americanization. Well and good; yet "X" is so conceived and worded that the patrons of its seedy theater have been led before they know it into Plato's cave, with the controller of those "electric shadows" emerging as something of a god in his own right. Whereupon Cavafy again comes to mind, for whom the unity of divine and human is as real as their disparity. Hall's language, plain, even unremarkable on one level, grows strikingly resonant on the next:

> *It's all*
>
> *I can do to keep my mind*
> *on tomorrow morning's test*
> *in Physics 101 . . .*
> *Another steps in, blinded*
> *by the dark. Who thinks of me*
> *alone up here? No one.*

The reader who cannot think of the Prime Mover as being continually tested in physics—indeed, challenged in all the sciences and humanities—had better pay closer attention to current events. In my weakness for effects of this sort, I catch myself seeing "Physics 101" as a numerical stab at the biblical tautology "I am that I am." Be that as it may, the poem, as vitally compact and unassuming as an Asian face, is a model of concision, allowing for the kind of active, boundless revery to which concision alone gives rise. This paradox—if it is one—opens onto illustrative peaks and flights over deep water, but inspired by Daniel Hall's example I shall say no more.

OCCASIONS

THE BEATEN PATH

Japan

Here in Kyoto where the amenities reach fever pitch we have been grateful for A. who, while practicing them on all eight cylinders, remains amusing and articulate. "That brazier? It's nothing at all, perhaps sixty years old. That is to say, it's the poorest of all *possible* braziers; there are others that frankly couldn't be displayed. I don't mean that this one didn't cost, oh, $200, but a *good* one will bring $10,000 at auction, even $50,000 now and then. As an American I take shocking liberties. I do a tea ceremony, for instance, serving Campbell's cream of mushroom soup instead of the *correct* soup, which takes three days to prepare. Getting back to my brazier, it formerly belonged to . . ." Every so often A. interrupts himself to call out, in petulant Japanese two octaves higher than his ordinary speech, queries or instructions to his secretary, Rev. H. This poor sweet man is struggling to complete his doctor's thesis by February. Nobody believes that he will. "When the time comes," A. chuckles, "we'll arrange for an extension; perhaps we can manage to get him sick."

David and I exchanged a glance. Each time we have seen H. he is on the run: bicycling off to purchase a "possible teabowl" from a widow; darting back to photograph an old man changing his trousers in public;

Semi-Colon, 1957.

there is A.'s wheelchair to push, of course, and A. himself, who looks heavy, to lift, often single-handed. The other day, watching jugglers at Nijo Castle, David ran out of cigarettes. Before either of us had realized it, H. was heading at a trot for the nearest shop, a good half mile away. While he was gone A. had a brainstorm. "Now tonight, what might *really* interest you," dismissing the jugglers with a shrug, "is to go with H. to his acupuncture. Yes, he hurt his back rather badly last year, jumping off a wall, but these treatments . . ."

We went, naturally. Rev. H. led us through dark reeking streets to the clinic, a poorly lit house, inspiring no confidence. Upstairs, cushions were brought for us, the doctor took out a small metal case, H. stripped to his underdrawers and placed himself meekly facedown on the mat. Out came the needles; they are two inches long, and flexible. Each is dropped through a thin metal tube, softly, enough to penetrate the skin, then the tube is put aside and the needle guided in by hand, in, in, in, until it strikes the nerve. "But it must hurt!" exclaimed David. No, no, the patient smiled, a faint electric shock, nothing more, perhaps some trifling soreness the next day. We watched two dozen needles go in and out of the scant flesh along Rev. H.'s spine. He gave the oddest impression of basking in his treatment, there under the weak lightbulb. According to A., one can turn into an acupuncture addict; there are those who crave it once or twice a week. Could it be that Rev. H. . . . ? But no, it is bound to be the pleasure of just lying down for a bit, needled but at rest.

We took shelter from the rain with guess who on the last lap of a trip round the world. He has carried along mescaline capsules to be swallowed at key points: one at the Prado, one at Angkor Wat, etc., and is vexed to find no occasion for the one he saved to use in Japan.

We exchanged another glance, and yet— It *is* very lonely here, with no way of sharing in anything. The language barrier is severe; that of manners, monstrous. One can endure just so long the hours spent drinking tea, or trying to get a straight answer, or holding some inscrutable ornament to the light in one's great clumsy fingers. Conceivably it is a strain upon the Japanese as well. I doubt it. They sink back into their splendidly contrived formulas as into those scalding baths, while the Westerner, in either instance, simply shrieks with pain or, if at all lucky, faints dead away.

Take their sweets. The papers are full of shocked letters about certain inferior Japanese products sold at a recent manufacturers' fair in Peking. Hollow fountain pens, watches packed with sand, *candies without flavor.* An unfair charge, I thought, seeing that no Japanese confection has any taste whatever. They are for the eye alone, and take the shape of masks, ships, autumn leaves. Here, try this specially ingenious one; it is a clam, you see, with cookie shell ajar to reveal some chocolate-colored treat within. Ah, but bite into it!—a taste of long ago, of letters in an attic trunk; the bean-paste center is torpid, dazed, as if having crept in for a midday snooze. . . . Never again!

A chronic ethereality. Given any choice in the matter, these people would not exist physically. Neither would their rooms, their clothes, their verses. It is the *idea* of the room (or kimono or haiku), more than any embodiment of it, that has become their triumph. And it *is* a triumph, oh dear me, yes. Think of the Western writer or even the Western couturier—doesn't everything he turns out imply some bold stand taken against chaos, conformity, tastelessness, the sluggish drift of a public whose ideas, if any, are at odds with his own and one another's? But the Japanese have laid up treasures in heaven, safe from fever, earthquakes, decay.

And yet, where else does the physical world appeal so irresistibly to the eye?

Over and over the point is reached where Art and Nature cannot be told apart. The persimmon trees, with so few leaves and so much fruit; perhaps a crow, yellow rice-fields beyond. This afternoon I saw a garden paved with fifty varieties of moss, blue-green, gold-green, rust-green, thick as plush, one or two sallow leaves floated down onto it. It had been designed to resemble somebody's description of paradise. One gets there through a grove of bamboo, innumerable hollow green tones, soaring, intersecting, like gamelan music for the eye. . . .

Why not carry it a step further? Paradise is *here,* in these rocks, in that white sand! Why not say so?

No answer to such a question.

Hiroshima

Helen was right; it is one of the most painful experiences imaginable. Oh, some of it is rebuilt, a big restless shopping section, a couple of buildings that either stood up under the Bomb or were deliberately built in the style of 1910 to look as if they had. But the rest—! Mud streets, dull empty vistas of rubble and strange, stunted trees, trunks like toothpicks. In the middle of the wilderness stand three concrete modern buildings: the New Hiroshima Hotel, the Peace Museum, and a second museum (empty as far as we could tell) with an unwisely named "Grill Room" upstairs. The Peace Museum is given over to displays relating to the Bomb, from scientific charts and diagrams all the way to the end of a child's thumb, with nail, brown, dry, cooked, which dropped off during the five days before the little boy finally died. This is displayed, bedded in cotton, along with a photograph of him in school uniform. A sickly delicate face, great big eyes, even the picture somewhat faded. Elsewhere, melted rock, flattened bottles, scorched clothing on charred mannequins, photographs of scar tissue, a shot of Truman at the telephone—and beyond the plate glass, the filthy flat field with a man on crutches picking through a trash can. It is a favorite tourist spot. Busloads of Japanese come, gape, and, as the brochures say, "realize the mistake of their militarism." There is an Atomic Souvenir Shop where you can buy don't ask me what. . . .

A Vision of Greatness

Arnold Toynbee is visiting Japan. Of his arrival a reporter wrote: "His magnanimity was apparent to all who met him. Never once did he reveal his true feelings."

Tantalizing words, almost delphic. After pondering them for a full week, we had our reward at Koyasan.

Few places can match that mile-long avenue of evergreens, towering bluish above mossy tombs where sunlight turns to marble the clouds of incense and lingers upon cloths, rain-washed reds or limes, in which pilgrims have dressed certain stone dolls.

An abrupt rustling. The first snake we have seen out-of-doors in Japan (there are shops full of them; you grind them up and take them for sexual disorders), a big striped one, abulge with eggs, hurried past us, shooting cold forked looks. We quickened our pace somewhat, and so witnessed, in the holiest spot of all, the materialization of the great historian. Tall, silver and white, an angelic smile on his large sculptural mouth, he moved noiselessly in a throng of sages, black-and-white-robed, some with beards like winter waterfalls. "Maybe noble interpleters," K. whispered, "and noble pliests." We gazed and gazed.

KYOTO. AT THE DETACHED PALACE

Struck by the soft look
Of stone in rain, wet lake,
By a single evergreen
Wavering deep therein,
Reluctantly I sense
All that the garden wants
To have occur.
Part of me smiles, aware
That the stone is smiling
Through its tears, while
Touched by early frost
Another part turns rust-
Red, brittle, soon
To be ferried down
Past where paths end
And the unraked sand
Long after fall of night
Retains a twilight.

The Sexes

A girl's voice is recorded at 33⅓ RPM, then played back at 45. She becomes the mother of that strutting male child to whom, on streetcars, the aged offer their seats. She retains until death the knack of collapsing like a fan into three folds, forehead touching the floor.

The hotel maid is jolly and clean-minded, always helping you undress or feeding you like a baby. The red-light district in Tokyo could be a little stage set. A hundred pretty girls in a hundred artful doorways.

(That first night in the café named Starlit Chrysanthemum Water, a drunk broke a glass. He had been sitting alone at the counter, his refreshment already before him. A few soft words. The waitress at once began to remove, one by one, the dishes she had set down, each different and delicate. He didn't try to stop her. Back went the tiny brochette, the bowl of five dead minnows, silver, staring; back went the saké bottle, the cup. He lifted a stool once, menacingly. A girl took it from his hand.)

Woman, in short, does not matter much. She has less face to lose and proportionately more "personality" than her refined husband. *He* knows that he invented her, that she is part of the Dream, and his only smile is a downward baring of gritted teeth.

K., a Buddhist novice studying Plato, explained it thus: woman has exclusively *personal* feelings and desires; you must never discuss anything serious with her, lest she corrupt you.

(For nearly a century Buddhist priests have been permitted to marry. Permitted? Such pressure is brought to bear upon them, if anti-Shinto circles are to be believed, that in all five hundred temples at Koyasan there is but one priest strong enough to resist the trend. Formerly barred to women, the holy mountain crawls with waitresses, shop girls, wives of abbots, daughters, granddaughters of abbots. One fancies the regime rubbing its hands. "Those Buddhists, ha! soon they'll be good for nothing. . . .")

In Kabuki, to be sure, no women are allowed.

We saw Utaemon, who is probably sixty, play a virgin priestess tricked into drinking aphrodisiac wine. The hoax uncovered (a lizard is found pickled in the empty flagon), she stabs herself with a sacred arrow. An "invisible" stage attendant fixes it to her costume, at the same time deftly revealing a blood-red undergarment. She is then free to die for ten minutes of quavering speech and rapid subsidings, with hands aflutter into exquisite disarrayed postures, while three other characters, including her partner in shame, sit on their heels and study the floor.

At one time the actor of women's roles learned many a trick from geisha. But I think there must always have been geisha in the audience, white-faced, attentive, getting pointers on how to be themselves.

In the end, perhaps, even man falls short of the Dream.

The Osaka puppets fume and float, each lifted at once to a realm of pure disposition, by two or three manipulators. These wear black, with black face-veils, all but the master manipulators who have learned to veil their faces without concealing them. Like embodied passions they cluster

about their creature; its eyebrows rise, its fan slams shut; it mounts a puppet horse and lurches off, howling promises, sleeves flying in no wind. It
is strangely dull. To begin with, I felt weak that day, our last day in Japan.
A very grown-up audience was following the text. . . . What does it really
mean—*to be moved*?

What They Are Saying

1. At a party in San Francisco a poet accosted the decent German
maidservant: "I sympathize with you." "Oh my Gott," the maid gasped,
"you don't need to do that!" "Well I will," said the poet, "whether you
want me to or not."

2. The *President Cleveland* has sailed; in its wake dwindles the Golden
Gate. One little girl warns another to take her "last look at civilization."

3. In Yokohama harbor—Asia at last! Dr. F., an eighty-two-year-
young dentist from Oak Park, put his lips conspiratorially to my ear. "So
many folks on this ship," he whispered, "wear artificial upper dentures. It
spoils the whole shape of the mouth."

4. One sees Hong Kong reflected in a tailor's mirror. Everywhere,
things are being fitted to the taste of somebody. But not everybody is
pleased. At lunch a longtime resident brought her fist down onto the
table. "The young people they send out to us nowadays!" she ranted.
"Most frightfully disappointing! No conception of empire-building!"

Bangkok

Gold leaf floats through the air. You buy it by the square inch and affix
it to your favorite Buddha. The most popular are quite furry with gold; it
flutters about their lips like traces of a recent meal.

The sacred buildings imitate fabulous paper lanterns not altogether
unfolded. From under a roof another roof emerges. With every flight the
steps grow steeper. Our climb began pleasantly enough, like the opening
chapters of a society novel. By the time we had reached the top we were
in the heart of a quatrain by Mallarmé.

The opium, a black bead, bubbles far, far off, along the bamboo-and-
silver pipe. How to get at it? I tried too hard and was sick, but David had
visions all night long of unknown charmers and moonlight on leaves.
These temples were first glimpsed in such a vision.

From afar they are seen to be constructed of mauve-and-pink or green-and-yellow ceramic tiles, or of gold, sometimes purple, mosaic. Think of Istanbul, Hagia Sophia and the mosques, turned completely inside out by a miracle, festooned with the "quaint enameled eyes" of Milton's flowers, and shining in the sun! Seen close, of course, it is only too clear that they have been put together out of chewing gum, sequins, whitewash, and broken willowware. If you still care for them after this discovery, nothing is easier than to break off a piece and carry it home.

They are akin to the works of Congreve, of Couperin, to the buildings of Borromini and Gaudí, through that air of being a trifle too chic and therefore, out of somebody's sheer ennui, wrought in dangerous, perishable mediums, ornament which the underlying structure may or may not support—mightn't the fun lie in the uncertainty?

Some Buddhas wear the smiles of brilliant hostesses, lips curled into a V, with a single beauty patch of gold. On the huge gilt toenail of the Standing Buddha a modest community subsists, day and night, made up of houses two inches high, people and animals, all of whitewashed clay, sparsely painted and half hidden anyhow by a couple of wilting lotuses. I think you can climb up into the Buddha's head and look down onto them through his very eyes. The stair was closed today.

The Buddha's smiles are repeated on every human face. Consider that the priests here (in robes of gamboge, a color that means *Cambodia*) must renew their vows only for the month ahead. They may go back into the world whenever and as often as they please. This may account for some of the smiles, that there is nobody who hasn't gone back into the world, as we all should, over and over and over again.

A ferry navigates the tide, rapid, topaz-colored boulevard. In the long ripple of its wake the melon rinds and almond shells manned by old ladies, infants, priests, vanish and reappear, hardly bobbing. The seller of charcoal plies an ash-gray craft, she herself wears black and a lampshade hat. The butcher's boat is scarlet, freshly painted. Along the banks, stairs lead down into the water; the open rooms are alive with waterlight. There is nothing for a dog to do here, beyond watching somebody scrub himself in the river.

From the landing a maze of boardwalk takes us to Chew's house.

It is larger than many. Half of one whole room is occupied by the shrine—twenty Buddhas on bleachers, surrounded by flowers, photographs, extinct incense. "That fat lady is my mother," Chew says of a retreating form. Near a hole in the roof a beehive simmers.

We are seated in the parlor. It is entirely of dark wood with pale pink plastic curtains. Photographs are pointed out: Chew (aged seven) as a priest; Chew as a scout; Chew as he is now (many poses) peering up through the glass tabletop in happy consort with Elizabeth Taylor (wearing white fox), Rory Calhoun (stripped to the waist and driving a nail into something), and, inevitably, James Dean. Chew, you might say, *is* James Dean. That name at least appears on every shirttail a younger sister is ironing in the next room. When five years are up, although his teeth, his dancing, and his English are not good, Chew will go to Hollywood and be discovered.

His mother brings lunch. Ice has been procured for the visitors. We are thankful for it because there is chili in the rice.

Afterward we each put on a sarong and take a dip in the klong with Chew and his friend Suripong.

Chew gives us his photograph, inscribed "To my best American friends. I hope you will not remember me."

Then back along the boardwalk. No wonder the Siamese are graceful! What it must be like to be always stepping on planks of varying flexibility, interminable xylophone, under banana trees, past gingerbread porches; to be always setting forth in a barque so flimsy you can feel a fish nuzzle it. . . .

I rode in one, finally, down a country klong, doubled up against the knees of an American girl called Ann. The prince paddled, confessing that he had all but forgotten how. Even so, the high overgrown ruin we had gone to see slipped behind trees and the sun beat down. Slowly, very slowly, the tiny boat filled with seepage. At the landing I turned my head. The movement sufficed. I saw the prince's eyes narrow. These Americans, he might have cried, must they *force* their easy manners upon us? But by then we were all three waist-deep in the warm exhilarating water.

GARLIC SOUP

Having parted for the night over the story of the society woman who persuaded a friend's cook to tell how on earth she made that inspired soufflé—only to learn that to the mixture of butter, flour, cream, Camembert, and egg yolks must be added "about a mouthful of water"—we found, the next noon, our host and hostess still thinking it over in the kitchen. Robert made a slight apologetic gesture toward some onions cooking in olive oil. "I had to use oil," he said, "because butter wouldn't melt in my mouth. This is going to be a Spanish soup, a very *poor* person's soup," he went on, brightening. "It can also be made with garlic instead of onion," said Isabel.

Back home, the following, weeks later, had evolved:

Cook lightly in about a mouthful of olive oil *at least* one large, thinly sliced clove of garlic for each person. Add a cup of stock (equal parts chicken, veal, and fish, or any two of these) per person, bring to a boil, and simmer for thirty minutes. Now should be added whatever comes to mind; for instance, again per person, a small cabbage leaf, a pinch of minced fresh ginger or grated orange rind, and some slivers of turnip; then, when these are not quite tender, two or three raw, shelled shrimp, split lengthwise. Cook seven minutes more. Season to taste. Before serving, one egg yolk for every two portions may be beaten with a teaspoon

Contact, May 1961.

of vinegar and the hot soup slowly stirred in. It's rather good. People with whom garlic disagrees have been known to eat it a second time.

Olive oil (about a mouthful)
1 large thinly sliced clove of garlic per person
1 cup of stock (equal parts chicken, veal, and fish, or any two of these) per person
Small cabbage leaf per person
Pinch of minced fresh ginger or grated orange rind per person
Turnip slivers
2 or 3 raw shelled shrimp split lengthwise
1 egg yolk (for every two portions)
1 teaspoon vinegar

Notes on Corot

The writer will always envy the painter. Even those who write well about painting, he will envy for having learned to pay close attention to appearances. And not the writer alone; it is the rare person who can look at anything for more than a few seconds without turning to language for support, so little does he believe his eyes.

Daily the painter masters new facts about the world. But years pass, and the writer is still studying his face in the mirror, wondering at what strange tendencies lie hidden beneath a familiar surface. "Pleasant enough, but what does it *mean?* " That traditional response of the layman is one he will never contrive to repress. Making it to the oeuvre of Corot, he will feel the least bit foolish. What does *it* mean? What does *he* mean? Here are the landscapes—ruins, trees, water, cows; here are the models, both with and without clothes. What can it possibly add up to but Art? The retort, by endowing the pictures with unquestionable value, gracefully waives the little matter of their significance.

He stands before a painting by Corot. As he is not himself a painter, or even if he is—painters are forever talking nowadays—he will suffer a brief, defensive spell of verbal dizziness. Phrases to be distinguished by

Corot 1796–1875, Art Institute of Chicago, 1960.

their incoherence—linear values, tonal purity, classical heritage—will explode between himself and the canvas. When the first smoke clears, he may look more attentively; he has routed the babbling imp. And though he will end by using the dreadful phrases, seeing at last their truth if not their beauty, an observer who is by nature oriented toward language, who in the deepest sense of the cliché requires that a picture *tell a story*, must meanwhile listen for its opening words.

"Once upon a time, in a far country . . ."

The small Italian sketches are praised by those who prefer the natural to the invented, Rousseau to Chateaubriand, the early Corot to the late. They are indeed very beautiful, as well as revolutionary, with their simplifications, their early morning, open-air clarity. Let it be added, however, that they respond to a revery of the idyllic instilled in Corot by Claude and Poussin, and that, when we are moved, it is not only by their naturalism but by a revery of our own.

His rapidly brushed Rome, the Rome he transported back to France for prudent investment, is the city of our dreams: physical, somnolent, un-imperially casual and even-tempered. Its domes rise from dusky washes into the sun, or by magic from the brimming, shaded fountain on the Pincio. A pane flashes. The island of S. Bartolomeo suspends its structural Gordian knot between sky and stream. The wonderful trees are everywhere, dwarfing the monuments they frame, taking the rich light upon their bulk, like placid thunderheads. Umber shadows flood the pavements of Venice, Genoa, Florence, Naples: the eye is drawn over a balustrade and down into the radiant depths of the scene, with the same sinking delight felt on the verge of sleep. All is joyously, economically accomplished, and it is an unfortunate visitor to Italy who has not, even in this day and age, enjoyed some such delusion. Over the shoulder of an old country man sitting on a trunk, beyond a crooked window frame, the sky, of a soft, blank brightness hard to mistake for any other, is enough to send one headlong down the stairs and out into that still barely retrievable world of awnings and ochres, sunstruck ruins, umbrella pines.

Italy—like youth, a simple word for a complicated, often idealized experience. No one would resist its appeal, as rendered in these little paintings. But each of us knows, in his way, what happens when it is over. Corot knew too. *A View near Volterra* (in the Chester Dale Collection) shows it happening in a scene so ravishing that it emerges unscathed from the jaws of allegory: the artist-prince, in peasant dress, heads his white horse (!) straight into the trees. Slowly it dawns on us what awaits him there, when he dismounts and sets up his easel. A change of light, a corresponding change of sensibility; in short, the paintings of Corot's maturity.

More than ever, as we look back on them, these Italian scenes take on a quality of legend. No need to people the glades with nymphs, or top the hill with crosses. The world itself is a marvelous tale. And as in all legend is found—what distinguishes it from myth—traces of the provincial, of genre, it is a happy accident, or no accident at all, that led the young painter to that already much-painted landscape where the peasant's cottage stands in relation to the aqueducts and arenas of the Giant. Taste, far more than credulity, is strained by the costumes of Corot's women. They belong to a world of story; it is well that they are a bit fussy and quaint.

"... there lived a woman ..."

One woman or hundreds of women, it makes no difference. A single impulse turned a Roman girl into a sybil and a French girl into a Vermeer. What is strange is how we believe in them, for all their artifice of posture and ornament.

Who *are* they? The last of the Lamias? The first patients of Freud? From the start, they fascinate and appall us by their listlessness, their fatalism, combined with an oddly bourgeois presence. Standing by a fountain, trusting vainly to participate in all that freshness; balancing an unplucked instrument in their laps; musing without comprehension upon book or letter, upon the enigma of a nudity or a costume they would never have chosen, their faces drain of animation, a mortal tedium falls, glimmering downward from a gray sun that does its best to shine and to cheer. But alas, their painter is older now, probably indoors as well, and he will not fake a happy light either in the world or in his own eye. Thus the reader of the Metropolitan Museum's *The Letter* sits in a shuttered space at the bottom of a well. No other interpretation will do for the light that barely exposes the musty furnishings and our heroine's unlovely, heavy-skinned features. What has happened to interiors—of rooms and of people alike? One has the feeling of Venice and Delft being recreated at nightfall, on a rehearsal stage. The solitude of any Renaissance woman never bothered us; she sat at her ease on an invisible throne of philosophy and manners. In the Lowlands, there was always a music lesson, or some household matter to be dealt with, and we enjoyed looking through a door at mistress and maid, off and on during the day. The pomp and pride of one tradition, and the charming resourcefulness of the other, are lacking in Corot's women. The most they can do is *look* as if they were reading or able to pick out a tune; their minds are elsewhere, we feel anxious for them. Another *Reader* (also at the Metropolitan) has elected to sit out-of-doors in her cumbersome contadina dress; the sun beats down muggily from a mournful zenith; one guesses the strain she is under, the trickle of sweat forming beneath the silken sleeve. Behind her, a tiny figure we shall see again tries and tries to steer his boat out of the rushes.

These ladies could not say, any more than Corot, what ails them. The *maladie du temps,* to be sure. But, specifically, do they not chronically suffer from their legacy (both classical and Dutch) as surely as from a "delicate constitution"? They are the last figures that a serious painter will ever render with that particular sober "studio" look—a result of training and procedure that infect his treatment of flesh and bone in much the same way as the inbred values of an Arcadian education might have done any young person in the nineteenth century. Their postures show what art has taught them to expect of life; their faces, what life has taught them to suspect of art. And yet they cleave to it—they are timid. They have *heard* of their shameless sister, with her parrot or her paramour, but in their eyes she is worse than any chattering bird. Better to waste away, unloved, than to break faith with their creator. In the mercy of his brush salvation lies.

Arkel to Mélisande: "I have been watching you: you were there, unconcerned perhaps, but with the strange, distraught air of someone forever expecting a great misfortune, in sunlight, in a beautiful garden."

Humble, not visionary, a virgin without child, the *Reader* resists knowing herself. She would deny that the hand on which her cheek just fails to lean is constituted differently from its Raphaelesque prototype; more loosely brushed, it is nevertheless doomed to obsolescence (hence her repressive calm) by new or imminent techniques and tastes. One wants to take that hand, open those somber eyes. Triumphs lie ahead. *She* will vanish, yes, but in her place we shall see the molecules of Pissarro, the brilliant glazes of a later reader—*L'Arlesienne*. Her nieces—she has no direct descendents—her nieces, clothed in colors as light and strokes as rapid as air, will dance all day at Bougival with bearded, floppy-hatted men. They will eat oysters! Or they will once again do *useful* things, such as bathing themselves or setting the table. If they are melancholy, it will be at their milliner's or in their music halls. (The provincial branch of the family will evidently stay on at Barbizon, ever more numerous, rich, and insufferable.)

Ah, and yet—

Lost in so much female activity will be precisely the solitary romance, the sense, however obscure, that our moments of uncomprehending loneliness are the most true; their profound dark spotlight reveals more about the human condition than any number of hours spent in dramatic relation to this or that figure or set of objects. To convey this truth, in all its narrowness, the artist may have no recourse to drama. Once seen to inhabit a setting—the saint in his cell, the siren in her loge—the supreme solitude can be shrugged off as a matter of individual preference, when it is really, as for Corot's women, a destiny, a state of soul. Some, like the *Sybil*, are strong, requiring almost a violence of execution; others make subtler claims—consider the air of baleful French tenacity that envelops the *Young Woman* in the Hirschland Collection, all her weakness concentrated into a force; others yet are merely beautiful. But even these, at their most memorable, remain at the heart of life, which is to say, beyond any of its resources, beyond even the methodical debauchery that sheds so cold a light upon Lautrec's unhappy women. We must wait for Picasso to renew the glamour of pure identity.

Seeing this far, we should not be astonished by the *Girl with a Pink Shawl* in Boston. Flattened, simplified, positively postimpressionist in feeling, she sits against three large, quickly done jigsaw pieces, two light, one dark. Somehow this background escapes transformation into furniture, foliage, or sky. Somehow her loose white smock escapes being fitted or embroidered. A thin wash of mauve covers portions of her otherwise pale strawberry-and-cream face. One hesitates to admire her, suspecting that, if one does so, it is thanks rather to a later master than to Corot. Yet she is his—awkward, virginal, unsmiling. The painting may be unfinished; her being is intact. Indeed, the rapid execution makes the difference. It suggests that she does not weigh too heavily on the artist's conscience; he has not shouldered her with *his* inheritance and *his* destiny.

We are led to reflect on the degree to which these were embodied by so many of his other women.

At times Corot's mysterious heroine is literally garbed as a muse, with wreath and scroll; or lies nude, a gross-featured bacchante looking up, deadpan, at the tame leopard advancing, a child astride it, to sniff politely the lifeless bird she dangles. We may hope that such a composition is lighthearted, a spoof on certain big moments out of Titian or Poussin. But is it? She has appeared too often in pensive, humorless guises for us to be sure.

In one of the most suggestive—the Widener Collection's *Artist's Studio*—she sits with hound and mandolin, in Italianate finery, facing away from us and into a small "typical" Corot landscape. Dreamily she fingers her instrument; the dog paws her skirt in vain. She might as well be looking into a mirror, so enraptured is she by the painter's expression of her feelings.

Though we no longer readily translate scenery into emotion, the landscape that resembled oneself or one's mistress was a widely spoken Romantic language ("the rocky horizon seen while approaching Arbois on the main road from Dôle, was for me a clear, live image of Métilde's inner self."—Stendhal, *The Life of Henri Brulard*). Faced with Corot's most celebrated pictures—the post-Italian landscapes—to make sense of, we must not despair. Many of them, it is true, appear to have issued, like himself, from the milieu of a small tradesman who has learned the rules of mass production. But, having identified the type of scene with his muse, we must recognize it as one that deeply stirred Corot. He returned to it, after all, again and again, often dully, always humbly and unquestioningly.

The elements of the scene are quickly named: the little glades, pockets of poetic rurality, farmhouse, stream, a far-off figure bending over the earth not so much, one feels, to gather anything, as just vaguely to keep in touch; a white-masked cow stands by like an anesthetist. These small human or animal figures at first greatly control our responses—the nostalgia of one long pent in his hectic, Balzacian metropolis, as well as the country cynic's impatience with the too-easy idyll. As we go from picture to picture, we find that we can dispense with these little guides; we are learning to "read" Corot. The Boston Museum's *Beech Tree*, in which neither man nor beast appears, nevertheless vividly suggests a human, perhaps a superhuman, presence. Attended by quiveringly erect younger trees, the strong, whitened trunk stands out against their familiar cloudy greens; this background is thinly painted and sets off a cluster of leaves, belonging to the subject, that might almost have been dribbled onto the canvas. At the foot of the tree a torn-off limb reinforces our impression of veiled narrative—we could be looking at a metamorphosed king.

The story grows more subjective.

The Ville d'Avray scenes, for example, place the sunlit building Corot had loved and learned to paint in Italy, deeper and deeper within the picture, frequently on the far side of still water. Young, white-trunked trees now grow in the foreground; they are seen less often massed from a vantage, than from a point in their midst. Even when fully grown, they rarely command the space; they filter, they intuit. Corot recreates for the eye, in two dimensions, something of the pleasurable hindrances of a winding progress through woods. We are left purer and warmer for the experience. At the last moment a few touches of bright color are added; earlier, they would have threatened the tone of an essentially spiritual exercise. In one picture (*Ville d'Avray* at the Metropolitan) a foliage diffuse and atmospheric overlays the entire canvas, a coarsely woven veil of branches at once dark and shining. It is a perilous moment. The artist is intoxicated by the degree to which his own powers can enter the trees, can alter, withhold, make precious the clear view beyond, which they are in danger of shutting off forever.

To the trees, then, we turn, to the water and the light, for clues to the meaning of these pictures. As with the Italian sketches and the female portraits, we feel the pull of tradition. But by now, the tiny rustics and the diaphanous vegetation bring to mind Hubert Robert more than Poussin. The mood remains Corot's—passive, trustful, melancholy; let others call it unhealthy. Those stretches of water! They sustain and extend the sky; their calm shimmer overwhelms a field. Slowly, as they accumulate in scene after scene, they begin to speak of relinquishment, of escape, of an *Embarquement pour Cythère*, only ascetic, lacking the exuberant iridescence of Watteau's.

One motif recurs and recurs: the single boatman leaning over the side of his boat in what might be an effort to free it from certain reeds or bushes at the water's edge. This accomplished, he has only to cast off and glide forth across the breathless mirror. He is kept from doing so precisely by the rest of the composition, with its sum of allusions to an ideal world. The farm, the cattle, the woman and child, even the harmonious intricacy of boughs—would these not be missed, once one had given oneself up to sheer reflectiveness? Would it not, on the other hand, be braver to strike out, to dream one's own dreams for a change? Elsewhere, as before, the boatman does not need to be in sight for us to experience the delicate and crucial conflict.

The setting in motion of such insights hardly adds up to Meaning or Subject Matter (as found in, say, Millet's peasant scenes). And yet Corot's principal dilemma—loyalty to the senses or to the imagination?—does get expressed, all the more movingly for its understatement, its perverse tenuousness. There come to mind Rilke's lines:

> *Were you not astonished, on Attic steles, by*
> *the circumspection of human gesture? were not love and farewell*
> *so lightly laid upon shoulders, they might have been made*
> *out of some other material than ourselves?*

If anything can stir us in this Romantic version of classic pastoral, Corot has divined it.

His development is very subtle, hardly a development at all. We can see him applying to one period lessons learned from another: something of the convincing, pure repose of the early Italian scenes, recurs in the quite late *Venus Bathing*, and of their architectural angularity in the *Interrupted Reading* here in Chicago. But, throughout his work, his main concern was to invest places and people with the nuance of a golden or a silver age. The increasing subjectivity of his later mood can be attributed to the tarnishing of that silver in the atmosphere of his day. He was too much of an artist not to breathe it. While able, as how few dedicated painters since, to give a large contemporary public what it wanted, at the same time he could not help but reveal, particularly in his figure paintings, the inner unease of that public caught between its own sense of a way of life lost, and its imminent place at the dreamless center of the stage.

Ten More

I.   Thou shalt do no manner of work, thou and thy son and daughter, thy cattle, and the stranger that is within thy gates. Thou shalt keep holy the Sabbath every day.

II. Thou shalt compose upon the typewriter. Glory be to the curious symbols thereof.

III. Take care that thou fall not into known meters; lest thy songs be remembered.

IV. Thou shalt whenever possible drop the names of poets, philosophers, starlets, and jazz musicians, quick or dead, whether thou truly knowest them or not; that these names may magnify thine own.

V.   Thou shalt not write short songs.

VI. Thou shalt not revise.

VII. Thou shalt take drugs; that they may inspire thee. Thou shalt suffer arrest; that thine antics may land thee on the front page.

VIII. Thou shalt retain the innocence of a little child. For the LORD knoweth, thou art worldly; yea, that thou reapest the fruits of the earth. Yet go thou forth in filthy raiment; that no man may accuse thee.

Intransit, 1968.

IX. Thou shalt intimidate thy neighbor with scorn, and drink his liquor with good cheer. Thou shalt not covet his house, nor his wife, nor his best lines, nor anything that is his. For lo! all are thine for the taking.

X. Thou shalt dig thine own grave.

YANNIS TSAROUCHIS

A guidebook I took to Greece in the fifties featured, along with information and phrases, a "reply" to Henry Miller. His *Colossus of Maroussi,* that famous prewar rhapsody on demotic themes, bore an innuendo the editor wished to challenge. Was Mr. Miller so naive, she wondered, as to fancy that those qualities he loved in the Greek character—generosity, inventiveness, fatalism, pride—risked being diminished by a rise in the standard of living?

The question might still be worth asking—not of Tsarouchis, who is never naive, but of his early sitters. Athens in their day, as in Henry Miller's, was at best a provincial town. Only steps from "smart" Constitution Square where Tsarouchis kept his studio, cafés and taverns innocent of decor, depending on the hour, dined or drowsed. His subjects would have felt tentatively at home in them: sober, straight-browed bumpkins in uniform or their one pathetic pin-striped *kostoúmi,* companioned by a glass of water and an empty chair. How have *they* fared, one would like to know, in that quarter century since he painted them? Did they, too, prosper when tourism and industry caused the per capita income to soar? That their answer—the shrug, the downward smile—can so readily be imagined is one measure of Tsarouchis's craft. It dawns on us that we are being shown not just how these young men patiently sit but how they will presently rise,

Printed here for the first time.

talk, gesticulate. A votive scene like *The Sacrifice of Iphigenia*, artless at first glance, manages even to depict what they imperfectly remember from church or school. We are faced, in short, with psychic musculatures every bit as explicit as any of flesh and blood. They are poor, these young men. Back in the village their sisters are unmarried. Their uncles write less often from Australia. Germany—the Occupation fading in the subsequent horrors of civil war—has not yet opened her mills to the *Gastarbeiter*. Mere touches in some total picture, such facts come to assume, like bandaged thumb or vase of paper flowers, an emblematic gravity. Or lightness: already certain models have sprouted wings.

So that one hardly needs to graph the economy or the statistics of urban growth. What happened between, say, 1950 and today is one of countless messages decoded by Tsarouchis. The surfaces of his pictures, like those of life itself grown over those years more prosperous, less joyfully improvised than before, reflect changes the perennial visitor must acknowledge with a pang. The broad brown peasant hand sports a manicure. In the jeweler's showcase appear worry beads of lapis lazuli. The tavern with its dirt floor and unshaded bulbs, its ill-carpentered table revolving, plates and all, in a dancer's strong teeth, has been supplanted by some "instant" folklore of whitewash and candlelight, woven hangings, and music to which no one moves except the maître d'hôtel, advancing with a bilingual menu. Small wonder that in the later work an air of nostalgic artifice prevails. Gone are the first brash frontal icons. Light by now sidelong, Caravaggesque, conjures up a theater of memory in which the odd urn or bust punctuates ambiguous groupings, figures divorced from their darkening backgrounds, stunned into awareness—as if the eye more luminously brushed actually saw farther than it did in simpler days. The artist himself has entered the studio, sits with back turned. Never a satirist, Tsarouchis avoids painting the bourgeoisie. Today's model is still young, still poor. The unmarried sister and far-flung uncle are still, no doubt, part of his case, though they no longer noticeably preoccupy him. He stands with fruit and wine. "Autumn" is here: a knowingly makeshift impersonation. For this boy in his tie-dyed singlet, with his rebellious hair and face of a streetwise dropout, remains mythproof, individual. Less individual perhaps than he supposes, some least atom of contemporary life—yet rendered glowingly enough to ripen the timeless peach in his hand.

Acceptance Speech, National Book Awards, 1967

Mr. Vice President, Mr. Minow, Ladies and Gentlemen:

I feel altogether innocent of what—apart from accepting the award, which I now promptly do, and with delight—is further expected of me at this moment. My publisher and friend, Harry Ford, who so far as I know has never lied to me in either capacity, telephoned Athens nine days ago with the news, and here I am. Now that I see the size of this audience and this auditorium, it is not easy to resist—though I shall—expanding my remarks at least to the point where they touch upon the artistic and the political conscience. As for the moon, I shall do no more than name it.

One reason I stay in Greece months at a time is that there, discounting the occasional gossip with American friends, the occasional reassuring letter home, and the English one speaks to those whose mother tongue it is not, my main contact with our language can be through reading and writing. It is a curious, possibly a dangerous, luxury, but it has borne fruit of a sort. The Greek I mostly speak is at once fluent to the ear and infinitely primitive: no question, even in my own mind, of overtone, allusion, irony, wordplay. Only the happiest accident allows me to say anything I don't mean, and I can't begin to tell you how refreshing that is. Of course I haven't reached the same level in English, and certainly not

Printed here for the first time.

for the purposes of any public intercourse with the mother tongue, but I'd like to think I was getting there slowly. Be that as it may, the phone rang and here I am—as I said, and meaning it, delighted.

I'm delighted especially to have been chosen from among such distinguished company as the other nominees. Mr. Ashbery, Miss Howes, Miss Rich, and Mr. Smith are poets whose work I have known and treasured for years. Any one of them would have done particular honor to this award. Marianne Moore is another matter. Not even in Greek could I find words to accept a prize won in competition with her if it were not plain as day that her magical supremacy has, this one time, simply been taken for granted by absolutely everybody involved, including all of us here this evening.

I am sorry that under the circumstances, I cannot very well praise the excellent taste of Mr. Auden, Mr. Nemerov, and Mr. Dickey. The most I can say is that I would be hard put to name three other poets whose critical intelligence I have admired more on previous occasions. Their faith in my work comes as a most pleasurable shock. Of the three, I believe only Mr. Dickey has written anything about me—a stern and tonic paragraph still vivid after seven years. It did me a world of good.

In closing, I want to thank them, the judges, for the distinction they have conferred; the donors of the award for their generosity; my publishers and Mr. Ford in particular for their constant faith; relatives and friends, both living and dead, whom I daren't begin to name, for their encouragement; and all of you for what looks remarkably like patience and goodwill.

Acceptance Speech,
National Book Awards, 1979

Hesitation comes over me even as I put this safely in my pocket. The NBA is after all an award I've received before. Oughtn't it therefore to go to someone else? To the vision and craft of Robert Hayden, or to the wise magic of May Swenson . . . ? My own vote would have gone to a book of work (both new and selected over the past twenty years) by a poet who— if we recall Marianne Moore's famous definition, and if we agree that the poetry of those twenty years has all too often been a festival, a very Woodstock, of real toads—a poet whose concern from the start was to cultivate the imaginary garden; to provide, that is, a distanced and meditated context for all the homely, leaping life which, without it, perishes so quickly. I mean John Hollander and his book called *Spectral Emanations*. If this year's award had gone to someone else, my first wish was that it be given to him.

It then struck me—and those of you who may have turned the pages of *Mirabell* will know what I mean—that in fact the award *was* going to someone else. The self who over the years wrote poems and was praised (or not) for them had been elbowed aside by an author unknown to me. His identity remains debatable even now. I've heard of a bookstore, right in Connecticut, whose owner isn't reordering *Mirabell* on grounds that

Printed here for the first time.

the devil wrote it. In these matters of course one sides with Shaw. Asked if he believed the Gospel according to St. John was written by the Holy Ghost, Shaw said that any book worth reading was written by the Holy Ghost. Whoever the author may be in my case, I accept this award on his behalf, with all of the pleasure and none of the responsibility that such honors generally entail. Thank you.

A Class Day Talk

Years ago in Paris a friend of mine was taken by her husband to have a
pair of evening slippers made by the great shoemaker Roger Vivier. The
gift entailed many weeks of conferences and fittings in whose course the
kind of intimacy that develops between client and artist allowed my
friend to ask a personal question of M. Vivier. Had making shoes, she
wondered, been his only drama, his only dream? Was there perhaps
something else he had ever once thought of doing with his life?

"Ah *yes*," he replied. "I could have done anything! I could have made
dresses, I could have made hats—!"

Very frivolous, very French. But suppose we place his remark under
an X-ray beam and watch it come to mean something like this:

"True, dear lady, I may appear to give myself wholly, to take my stand
if you like, upon pedestrian matters. But within my imaginative grasp is
also a living body of knowledge, free and passionate and brilliantly dis-
guisable. While above that we have the whole vast sphere of the human
head and the question of how its changing contents are to be both protected and dramatized by the intellectual milliner at work within it."

So: what goes onto expresses what comes out of the head. "If they
tried rhomboids, / Cones, waving lines, ellipses—/ As, for example, the
ellipse of the half moon—/ Rationalists would wear sombreros." That's

Recitative, ed. J. D. McClatchy (San Francisco: North Point Press, 1986).

Wallace Stevens. Another Frenchman, Mallarmé, inferred an "aigrette of vertigo" rising from the thinker's forehead. And a final example, closer to home:

Our late President Cole, introducing a reading by Robert Frost, said what we all felt—even as he illustrated a principle the canniest among us wouldn't grasp until much later in life, namely that the limitations of an instrument can make for its most memorable effects. "The winkles," said Dr. Cole, "the winkles that you see on Mr. Fwost's bwow do not come from old age or wowwy, but the weight of the weath."

Sorry—one gets so caught up in quotation—many hands make light work. Before going any further, let me thank my sponsors for the wreath of today's occasion.

In my invitation to speak, something was made of this Class of 1980 being the first in Amherst history whose graduating women were completing the full four-year course. It left me wondering what could be said about the sexes, if only with regard to the poets, the men and women of this century, whose work means most to us. When we look at the men we notice a drift toward the more or less monumental. Sometimes a highly compressed monument, a sketch for a monument—I'm thinking of *The Waste Land* or "Notes toward a Supreme Fiction"; sometimes, as with Pound or Lowell or Dr. Williams, a huge, unruly text that grapples ravenously with everything under the sun. Now these men began by writing small, controllable, we might say from our present vantage "unisex" poems. As time went on, though, through their ambitious reading, their thinking, their critical pronouncements, a kind of vacuum charged with expectation, if not with dread, took shape around them, asking to be filled with grander stuff. As when the bronze is poured in the lost-wax process of casting, what had been human and impressionable in them was becoming its own monument. I speak, alas, from experience, having felt a similar pressure at work in my own case, and seen also, though fighting it every step of the way, how little choice I had in the matter. And wistfully thought how while men have built monuments to themselves—as well as to women: look at the Taj Mahal—no woman has ever gone on record as wanting one. But that's too neat. Look at poor Anne Sexton who, submitting a poem to an editor, wrote: "I realize it's very long, but I believe it is major."

Another true story. In the early 1950s a Professor degli Alberti was conducting his last class of the year at a finishing school in Florence. He reminded his young ladies—as they were called in those days—that they'd learned a lot of history and seen a lot of art, churches, museums, and whatnot. Here now was their chance to clear up any remaining questions. Silence; all had been understood. No—a shy hand went up: "Professor, we've looked at these hundreds of statues and paintings of the Madonna and the Child, but the child in her lap always seems to be a little boy—why's it never a little girl?" It would take only twenty years, until the publication of Mary Daly's *Beyond God the Father*, for that exact question to turn from an ignorant into a profound one.

I've been too regularly bullied by women to believe in a male mafia. Yet when I come across language I dislike, it'll usually be a man's. We hear the *man* in *manifesto*. We see, as I've said elsewhere, in such common expressions as "to erect a theory" or "a seminal idea," the worst kind of Don Juanism. Men write more universally than women, perhaps; but they also—at least up until these years of the raised consciousness—take the cake for ponderousness and complacency.

One exception would be Mr. Frost. He dealt with monumentality now by smiling (or wincing) at how his mind worked, now by taking directly into public life those attitudes he knew better than to inflict upon his poems. Thus the friendships with presidents, the grand illusion that he and Khrushchev face-to-face could settle the differences between their two nations.

Then there's Elizabeth Bishop. There was, rather—she died last October: the last and, I think, finest of a generation that included John Berryman, Robert Lowell, Randall Jarrell, and Theodore Roethke. Lowell called her one of the four best women poets ever—a wreath that can hardly have pleased Miss Bishop, who kept her work from appearing in the many recent "women's anthologies." Better, from her point of view, to be one of the forty, one of the forty thousand best *poets*, and have done with it. If I raise the issue at all, it's to dissociate her from these shopworn polarities.

"I don't much care for grand, all-out efforts," she wrote to Anne Stevenson. "This is snobbery, but . . . in fact I think snobbery governs a good deal of my taste. I've been very lucky in having had some witty friends—and I mean real wit, quickness, wild fancies, remarks that make one cry with laughing. . . ." And from another letter to the same person:

"I think we are still barbarians, barbarians who commit a hundred inde-
cencies and cruelties every day of our lives, as just possibly future ages
may be able to see. But I think we should be gay in spite of it, sometimes
even giddy—to make life endurable and to keep ourselves 'new, tender,
quick.'"

Not a manifesto—yet what honesty, what simple nerve it takes to put
such thoughts into words.

The threat of human indecency and cruelty can be felt always between
her lines. Her most popular (though surely not her best) poem is a first-
person account of catching "an enormous fish." As it hangs by the boat,
half in water, Bishop examines it, imagines it so closely—the skin like
peeling wallpaper, and underneath, "the coarse white flesh packed in like
feathers"—that the written conclusion could not be otherwise:

> *I stared and stared*
> *and victory filled up*
> *the little rented boat,*
> *from the pool of bilge*
> *where oil had spread a rainbow*
> *around the rusted engine*
> *to the bailer rusted orange,*
> *the sun-cracked thwarts,*
> *the oarlocks on their strings,*
> *the gunnels—until everything*
> *was rainbow, rainbow, rainbow!*
> *And I let the fish go.*

"Rainbow, rainbow, rainbow! / And I let the fish go." Two free associations here. The first: a friend of Elizabeth's gave the book in which this
poem appeared to her husband, himself something of a fisherman. He
singled out "The Fish" for special praise, saying "I wish I knew as much
about it as she does." Four years later this man published a novella, a fishing story some of us will remember as ending quite differently from the
poem. He called it *The Old Man and the Sea*. Now what are the facts
behind such fictions? It would surprise nobody to learn that, in his long
career as a sportsman, Ernest Hemingway let go far more fish than Elizabeth Bishop ever hooked. Besides, *her* fish wasn't let go at all, not in real

life; she told in an interview about bringing it proudly back to the dock—intact. But both she and Hemingway, whatever their private strengths or weaknesses, were concerned in their work with attitudes, "emblems of conduct"—or shall we say, some form of moral headgear—for the reader who wanders out unprotected into the elements. Thus, both fish are invested with grandeur and wisdom, and the respective fishermen behave nobly, even reverently, according to their lights. That remark about her poem, Elizabeth told the interviewer, "meant more to me than any praise in the quarterlies. I knew that underneath Mr. H. and I were really a lot alike."

Rainbow, rainbow, rainbow . . .

My second association is a memory. After a solid week of rain in Brazil, ten years ago, out came the sun and Elizabeth proposed we visit a pretty town nearby. Presently a taxi was jouncing through sparkling red-and-green country, downhill, uphill, then all at once *under* a rainbow—like a halo on the hill's brow, almost touchable. She said some words in Portuguese; the driver began to shake with laughter. "In the north of Brazil," Elizabeth explained, "they have this superstition—if you pass underneath a rainbow you change sex."

And this memory in turn brings to mind one of her early, never-collected poems—written perhaps in the very hour when the young lady in Florence was asking her haunting question. Let me read it to you now.

EXCHANGING HATS

Unfunny uncles who insist
in trying on a lady's hat,
—oh, even if the joke falls flat,
we share your slight transvestite twist

in spite of our embarrassment.
Costume and custom are complex.
The headgear of the other sex
inspires us to experiment.

Anandrous aunts, who, at the beach

"Anandrous"—in Greek "without a man"—doubles as a botanical term meaning "having no stamen."

> *Anandrous aunts, who, at the beach*
> *with paper plates upon your laps,*
> *keep putting on the yachtsmen's caps*
> *with exhibitionistic screech,*
>
> *the visors hanging o'er the ear*
> *so that the golden anchors drag,*
> *—the tides of fashion never lag.*
> *Such caps may not be worn next year.*
>
> *Or you who don the paper plate*
> *itself, and put some grapes upon it,*
> *or sport the Indian's feather bonnet,*
> *—perversities may aggravate*
>
> *the natural madness of the hatter.*
> *And if the opera hats collapse*
> *and crowns grow draughty, then, perhaps,*
> *he thinks what might a miter matter?*

Here now come the poem's last two stanzas, where what's happening almost gets upstaged by the verbal bravura. A single past tense in their opening line; the unexpected adjective "avernal"—and it dawns on us that a certain uncle and aunt are no longer among the living, are rather shades in a classic underworld. The meter too has changed, iambic to trochaic. Most telling of all, each figure now wears forever the hat appropriate to his or her gender, a lone identifying attribute, limiting and melancholy, like the headstone on a grave.

> *Unfunny uncle, you who wore a*
> *hat too big, or one too many,*
> *tell us, can't you, are there any*
> *stars inside your black fedora?*

Aunt exemplary and slim,
with avernal eyes, we wonder
what slow changes they see under
their vast, shady, turned-down brim.

Before leaving that graveyard, here is its poet dressed for an occasion we shall all, by tomorrow, have participated in. "I bought a simple B.A. gown at the Coop yesterday," she wrote when she had to read the Phi Beta Kappa poem at Harvard in1972. "It is so cheap and flimsy—it looks exactly like a child's witch costume for Halloween. But when I received my one honorary degree my hat was too big and the gown reached to the floor and covered my hands. Another recipient, an actress, had had the forethought to get a really mini-gown, above the knees, and she got the biggest hand and the rest of us felt jealous—so I thought I'd take one that more or less fits this time." Afterward she described the tassel on her hat swinging back and forth across her line of vision "just like a wind-shield wiper."

So there we are, back at what goes onto and into the head, plus a characteristically functional image, the windshield wiper—merely a tassel perhaps, if not the whole academic experience: that series of rapid, brief, ongoing clarifications which allow us to face, through glass no doubt, but on our worst days, the inrush of emotion and event. It's an image we might want to recall tomorrow—the rest of us mostly bareheaded, in our natural (or unredeemed) state—when the Class of 1980's young men and women go forth under their identical mortarboards. These of course will be too square, too colorless, too obviously exchangeable. But one has to start somewhere.

Foreword to
Le Sorelle Brontë

This remarkable work, a libretto set to popular tunes of variable vintage and familiarity, will be known to few readers. Although over ten years old, it has never been performed for more than a handful of its Alexandria-born poet's friends. As editor I venture to hope that its beauties will attract a larger public.

It is designed for that small red theater in the soul where alone the games of childhood are still applauded. The obsessive role of music in these games is well known. It gave them form, permanence, and power. Whoever first set the sentence beginning "Passengers will please refrain . . ." to Dvořák's "Humoreske" made one of those tiny, vital discoveries for which thousands have been grateful ever since. Once made, such a discovery cannot be ignored. The music imperiously calls up the words, and vice versa.

Bernard de Zogheb has given us what may be the first extended works in this genre. A real difference lies between the conventional "ballad opera" and *Le Sorelle Brontë*. Here there is no dialogue; nothing is left to chance. Neither is there a musical accompaniment; the melodies begin and end in the reader's ear or the performer's voice. Experiments with a piano have convinced me of the wisdom behind such austerity.

Dramatically, these are works of high quality. On every page some-

Bernard de Zogheb, *Le Sorelle Brontë* (New York: Tibor de Nagy Editions, 1963).

357

thing is made clear about the tenacious inanity of human emotion. As we had gathered from Verdi, it can be set to any tune. We laugh and weep along with M. de Zogheb's characters; they work like puppets upon us, being at once so much smaller and so much larger than ourselves. Actions are simplified and debased, as befits a "popular" retelling of famous lives. The idiom—no less popular, no less debased—in which they are composed is therefore of the essence. One would not want a syllable changed; I have altered only a few ambiguous spellings.

Le Sorelle Brontë, the earliest of these libretti, is in many respects the most genial. *Byrone* may be more massive, more epic; *Vaccanze a Parigi*, more consciously sparkling. But it is to *Le Sorelle* that one has turned time and again. The reader will search in vain for the gloomy, introspective Brontës of his literature class. In their place, three wild extroverts ride the familiar Mediterranean pendulum between the most lavish endearments and the coarsest recriminations. They are concerned with money, food, sex, and renown. It is what one had always suspected of great writers, and it is but a single strand in the web of truths that M. de Zogheb has woven.

Concerning the language:

From 1880 until just recently, nearly every house in Alexandria had an Italian servant—a Triestine maid, a Genoese chauffeur. It seems to have been the smart thing to do. Dutifully the native servants added the new tongue to their attainments. Count A——'s Osman, impressive in silk robes and white handlebars, spoke it excellently well, if with a Sudanese accent, while his master fancifully continued to address him as an imbecile or a foreign child: "Osman, caro, mi prendere bagno. Tu aprire la kanafia ['tap' in Arabic] adesso? Merci, caro." Thus, the idiom of *Le Sorelle Brontë*—so richly macaronic, so poorly construed and spelled—represents both the bad Italian cultivated by the upper class and a kind of lingua franca used by their domestics.

Overpliant as mistletoe, it is upheld by the stout tree of song. Like the feeble remora glued to the shark's back, it pilots those powerfully shaped, dull-witted tunes—those scavengers of music—toward our hearts' inmost haven, which they had never before attained.

Sometimes the words must shift for themselves. One can go weeks at a stretch without meeting anybody who knows "La Fille du Bédouin." Copyright laws, moreover, would discourage an index of tunes in the present volume. But even where the melody is unknown, the song's title may provide a suggestive rubric. "Civilization" marks the excited decision to visit Brussels; another decision, Anna's to enter a convent, is more cynically labeled "Fools Rush In." Wherever possible, of course, the reader is urged to fit the tune to the text. It will take patience and imagination. The first lines of the libretto, for instance, falling into the following pattern

Che tris-   tes-sa   mor-to^il pa-   dro-ne

are easily scanned. The third and fourth lines, rhythmically no different, oblige us to wrench the accents:

> *Non ha lácciató nella casa*
> *Némenó le venti pará.*

(What is *venti pará*? the Italian student will ask. It is in fact an old Turkish coin. Lacking such information, the Italian student could do worse than to think first of the French—in this case, *paravents*—so that later he will be able to fathom Carlotta's *falsa cuccia* and Dickens's *libro di chevetto.*) Displacement of accent occurs relentlessly throughout the opera. Let us remember Stravinsky's setting of English and neither scorn nor wince at M. de Zogheb's methods.

Ravel's Mother Goose

---

1. A terrible evil, predicted from her birth, has befallen the lovely young Princess Floriana. A prick from her old nurse's spindle leaves her in a deep swoon from which no one can rouse her. In this death-like slumber she will dream fragments of three stories as haunting and perilous as her own. But first, under the supervision of a Good Fairy, courtiers and ladies-in-waiting dance a melancholy pavane round their Sleeping Beauty, laid out on a couch in her garden.

2. Deeper and deeper into the forest where an ogre waits to devour them, Thumbkin and his brothers advance. The brave boy imagines he can easily retrace his steps thanks to the breadcrumbs he has been careful to scatter along the way. But when the time comes he cannot find a single one: the birds have flown down and eaten them all up.

3. Poor little Princess Hideola arrives with her dragon lover at the Land of the Pagodas. Here they will both turn beautiful again. To that end she undresses and enters her bath. At once her tiny emerald and porcelain attendants begin to sing and play instruments in proportion to their size—walnut-shell lutes and almond-shell fiddles. A magical concert—listen!

Printed here for the first time.

4. Our sleeping princess hears in her dream snatches of a famous, on-going dialogue:

> "When I think of your kind heart you don't seem so ugly, after all."
>
> "I may have a kind heart, but I'm a Beast nonetheless."
>
> "There's many a man more beastly than you."
>
> "If I were witty I'd find fair words to thank you, but I am only a Beast."
>
> "Beauty, will you be my wife?"
>
> "Ah, Beast, not that!"
>
> "I can die happy now, I have seen you once again."
>
> "No, my dearest Beast, you shall not die. You shall live to be my husband!"

And in his place, at her feet, kneels a prince more beautiful than Love himself.

5. Her last dream fading, Princess Floriana sleeps on in her supernatural garden. But now a prince of her very own appears, and awakens her with a kiss. All the various characters in her dream gather round, as the Good Fairy descends and blesses the young lovers.

Barbara Kassel

Another room full of landscapes? Look again. Along with them on the wall hang paintings of walls—the interior walls of a house—on which an itinerant artist has painted landscapes. He or she is long gone. Some of the work has already begun to crack and peel.

One question raised is metaphysical. The painting *on* a flat surface periodically loses face before the painting *of* one. It surprises nobody that Bergotte, in Proust, dies believing that his whole life and work have been outweighed by a patch of yellow wall as rendered by Vermeer.

A question also of ecology—literally "science of the House." In abeyance now is the faithful old plein-air exaltation that once bound together painter and scene. A beholder wants first of all to make sure these scenes will last. The phantom impulse to preserve them—as if their preservation depended not upon the artist but on you and me—goes to prove how powerfully the artifice has worked upon us, made us take it like silk between thumb and forefinger to test its fineness and durability.

As for that mysterious House whose walls the natural world decorates, it varies with the temper of its occupant. Certain schools of therapy ask us to design our own, purely psychic dwellings. Here, too, we find ourselves surrounded by alcoves answering to every need—love, sleep,

Barbara Kassel, *New Paintings* (New York: Maxwell Davidson Gallery, 1987).

speculation, prayer—placed snugly within this or that illusion of twilit vastness. Such arrangements, no matter how humble or démodé in their particulars, nevertheless offer luxury and repose to the spirit. The author of *Invisible Cities* would have understood. So would Valéry, for whom a burst-open pomegranate "sets one of my former selves to dreaming of its secret architecture."

Thirty years ago it seemed that violent, vivid abstractions alone did justice to that psychic life. We had forgotten, for a while, that landscapes were already interiors, that the world was less than nothing until it had entered us, bringing images whereby the incoherence at heart might be clothed and sheltered. This truth, which took Proust all his skill to drive home in words, Barbara Kassel sets before us—deftly, teasingly, hauntingly—in painting after painting.

MEMORIAL TRIBUTE TO
DAVID KALSTONE

David was given no formal funeral. Hard as it is to let go the image of his trustful, inquisitive, nearsighted face, or the sound of his laughter we all went to such lengths to hear, I can imagine many of his friends wanting to know what became of him after the cremation. His own wish was to end up in Venice, to be scattered near his beloved Palazzo Barbaro. There was, however, the foreseeable difficulty of arranging anything of the sort through "channels," or (worse) the real possibility of being caught smuggling into Italy what had turned out to be a somewhat bulky package.

Reluctantly but with relief, a few of us agreed to let the part stand for the whole. Early in the summer a small vial was carried through customs by Maxine Groffsky and Win Knowlton. Before long these two, and George Smith, were having dinner *da Ivo*—a restaurant many of us will have spent festive evenings in, with David. Afterward the little party went in a gondola to the palazzo, and had it pause just below David's windows. Here Maxine took from her purse what she had brought, and emptied it into the black, starlit water of the Grand Canal.

I had offered to take care of the rest. One morning I wrote a few lines to David, then burned them in a saucer and added their ashes to his. We have no gondolas in Stonington, but Peter Hooten and I took a dinghy

A Memorial Tribute to David Kalstone, privately printed, 1986.

out into the tidal river just east of the village. It was a calm, brilliant day. Peter held on to a mooring, while I emptied the box underwater. In the sunlit current the white gravel of our friend fanned out, revolving once as if part of a dance, and was gone. So, for the time being, were the dread and sorrow with which that day had begun.

A last teaspoonful had been saved to mix with earth. A week later David Jackson and I scattered it among the lilies-of-the-valley under an old apple tree in Eleanor Perenyi's garden. On this occasion we read two poems from David's edition of Sidney. One was the sonnet "Leave me, O Love which reachest but to dust." The other was Sidney's translation of the Twenty-third Psalm:

> *The lord the lord my shepheard is,*
> *And so can never I*
> *Tast misery.*
> *He rests me in green pasture his.*
> *By waters still and sweet*
> *He guides my feet.*
>
> *He me revives, leads me the way*
> *Which righteousness doth take,*
> *For his name's sake.*
> *Yea tho I should thro vallys stray*
> *Of death's dark shade I will*
> *No whit feare ill.*
>
> *For thou Deare lord Thou me besetst,*
> *Thy rodd and Thy staffe be*
> *To comfort me.*
> *Before me Thou a table setst,*
> *Ev'en when foe's envious ey*
> *Doth it espy.*
>
> *With oyle Thou dost anoynt my head,*
> *And so my cup dost fill*
> *That it dost spill.*

> *Thus thus shall all my days be fede,*
> *This mercy is so sure*
> *It shall endure,*
> *And long yea long abide I shall,*
> *There where the Lord of all*
> *Doth hold his hall.*

Missing on all these occasions was music. We're making up for that today, thanks to these gifted friends, who will now end our little program with the Mahler song. But I wanted David to have the last unsung word of the afternoon. Let that be an entry from his Venetian journal, dated July 28, 1984:

Tonight, standing in the Barbaro window, I think must be the most beautiful night in the world. Cool. Soft vanishing sunlight and slow shadows on the Grand Canal. One deep sun spot. Being alone. Oh, to open my heart as I have not for years—Venice, my beautiful Venice. The heart aches as the light passes. The town is full of beacons, each with its own hour—I have never known it so beguiling as this summer—the lightning and hail of the other evening . . . Oh never *not* to return!

MEMORIAL TRIBUTE TO
JOHN BERNARD MYERS

In 1945 John was living in the East Thirties, having moved some years earlier from Buffalo in order to cast his lot with the likes of us—the New York poets and painters. He seemed to know them all. At least I reasoned that if he knew me, unpublished at nineteen, he must indeed have known everybody. By that year, I think, he had phased out his career as a night-club puppet-master, but throughout the fifties and early sixties he could still be persuaded to do some of his routines in a living room. Can anyone who heard them forget "The Oratorio" or "The Address to the Buffalo Cinema League"? At such moments one felt that John could act absolutely anything except his age.

A large and grander audience than usual saw him play the master of ceremonies in a masque written by Alan Ansen and staged in Peggy Guggenheim's Venetian garden. John was given the last words, bidding the guests to table. The table in question—Peggy's—never exactly groaned with delicacies; John's always did. Ansen understood this, and wrote a poem for John, called "Mine Host," which began, "I'd rather have the world at my own table / Than sit at its." There was John's view of parties in a nutshell. He and Herbert Machiz gave the best ones I ever went to, but even other people's parties somehow became better once John had finished advising them about the guest list and the refreshments.

A Memorial Service for John Bernard Myers (New York: Sea Cliff Press, 1988).

This company hardly needs to hear from *me* about John's taste in painting and poetry. In those first seasons when he was publishing the legendary Tibor de Nagy editions—Ashbery, O'Hara, Schuyler—David Jackson showed him a little sheaf of verses by his mother: old-fashioned, sentimental, not really very good, as we all perfectly well knew. John offered to publish them out of pure kindness, and what's more sold a few copies to his faithful collectors. It made Mary Jackson proud and happy for the rest of her days.

John never lost his old liberal starry-eyed sense that things could be *done*. Spanish War refugees could be helped; so could a painter down on his luck. If commercial middlemen weren't interested, so much the worse for them. Books could be issued under his own imprint. Plays could be commissioned and staged. Critics could be shamed into taking note. Poets were told what to write about, painters what subjects to paint. He was a lifelong, passionate impresario and he will never be replaced—not by anyone with his vivid, crusader standards, his gadfly enthusiasms, and that irresistible combination of a warm heart and a sharp tongue.

To the end he adored being contradicted. It assured him that he was still an *enfant terrible*. Most of us, I think, obliged him whenever we could: "John, that's ridiculous! John, you don't know what you're saying!" Then we'd get to see him toss his head and sniff, rising majestically above it. And of course, more often than not, time has proved him right. But one day last July he committed the greatest of follies, and by now it has dawned on us all that he will never live it down.

MEMORIAL TRIBUTE TO IRMA BRANDEIS

When I was in Greece some twenty years ago a letter came from Irma telling what a frightful winter she'd been through. Her back was giving out, every movement, every moment meant pain. I was going through a bad season myself—the pain less physical than emotional, even self-indulgent—and her letter somehow made me feel that we were fellow sufferers. I pictured the round of her days, the objects in her New York apartment, the flute she played less and less, the portrait of her in her twenties, that pale, ironic, challenging face summing up everything I knew about her life, as well as everything I didn't know; and found myself writing, instead of an answer to her letter, a poem about what was "happening" to us, and how we were being—for that season at least—transformed by our respective trials. The poem, which turned out to be windy and rambling, ended

> *You with me here where I do not belong,*
> *I with you there, where all is real and wrong.*

I sent it to Irma, imagining no doubt that it would please her, but the letter that now reached me might have been written by one of those ladies

Published here for the first time.

in Dante, lofty in bearing and principles, divided by a river—or in this case the Atlantic Ocean—from the pilgrim with his pitiful human failings. Those ladies bore garlands or a musical instrument. They were quick to chastise the unvirtuous, though gentle in heart and speech as they were stern in spirit and intellect. There was no need to marvel at how gracefully Irma moved in their midst. I already knew those poems by Montale, perhaps the greatest Italian poems of our century, which evoke this aspect of our friend. But friendship like a sestina had its rules, and her letter made me feel that I had strained them by writing a poem so intimate, so free with her own past and present. A few weeks later, when I'd recovered from the rebuke, I reworked my lines, cutting away its perishable tissue of narrative, and leaving only a skeletal trellis of images and feelings. Thinking of Irma's flute, and of the nymph who turned into the reeds from which Pan made his pipes, I called it "Syrinx," and Irma's next letter gave out the fragrant balm of her full approval. That is what it is like to have a muse in one's life.

I'll close with a lyric from *The Changing Light at Sandover*. Irma took with a large grain of salt—as I myself did—the Ouija board communications on which this very long poem is based. I couldn't, of course, resist getting in touch with Irma after her death, and I hope no one will be offended if I share with you her first brief impression of the other world. The pain had faded into sleep, the trancelike passage was complete, and our dear one came to herself, she said, with the vitality of a girl skipping rope—a rope whose ends were held, in a manner of speaking, by Montale and Eleanora Duse.

A Tribute to
Marie Bullock

In the handsome new postmodern offices of the Academy of American Poets hangs what at first glance looks like a recruiter poster for World War I. A beautiful starry-eyed woman bearing emblems of glory to the dazzled young person who might want to enlist. On closer inspection we see that she is offering not a flag and a martyr's crown but a lyre and a laurel wreath: we are being greeted by the muse. The sketch (dated 1935) is by Howard Chandler Christy, the well-known illustrator, and it is titled "To the Poets of America." The people in the office believe that it's a portrait of Marie Bullock, that just as Sir Joshua Reynolds, or whoever, painted Mrs. Siddons as the Tragic Muse, Mrs. Bullock is here depicted with the attributes and shining eyes of Erato herself; and I'm happy to go along with the notion. But I also stick to my first impression. For haven't we all—every one of us who writes or reads or listens to poetry in America—found ourselves in the ranks of that charming, imaginative, generous, and self-effacing patroness. The faces in this hall tonight testify to her success as a recruiting officer; and so do the pride and pleasure we are more and more able to take in being part of poetry in America today.

Poetry Pilot, November-December 1992.

M. F. K. FISHER
(1 9 0 8 – 1 9 9 2)

Mary Frances Kennedy Fisher was born in Michigan in 1908, and moved at the age of four, with her parents and younger sister, to Whittier, California. She went to France very young, newly married to Alfred Fisher, and stayed for three years. The pattern of displacement and return—not to mention that of marriage—continued for the next couple of decades. Separated from her third husband, she was now one of our most distinguished single mothers, with daughters to raise and a series of charming and original books to go on writing. The first of these appeared through the good offices of the well-known novelist Anne Parrish, sister of the man who would become her second and best-loved husband, Dillwyn Parrish. Her next two or three books, which should bring her complete works to at least twenty volumes, will no doubt be posthumous, for she rarely stopped writing—or entertaining—until her death early last year in her beloved California.

Asked why she wrote so much about food instead of "the really important subjects, like the struggle for power and security," she replied: "It seems to me that our three basic needs, for food and security and love, are so mixed and mingled and entwined that we cannot straightly think of one without the others. So it happens that when I write of hunger, I am

Proceedings of The American Academy of Arts and Letters, 1992.

really writing about love and the hunger for it . . . and it is all one." Her principal excursion into fiction—starring an irresistible anti-self, heartless and freedom-loving as Carmen, who coolly walks away from the lives she has fed on and ruined—illustrates, for all its verve, the good sense behind Mrs. Fisher's oblique approach.

W. H. Auden, who loved to surprise people with his opinions, wrote that "in a properly run culture, [she] would be recognized as one of the great writers this country has produced in this century." Be that as it may, she is perhaps the closest we'll ever come, in America, to that archetypal European literary woman—one thinks of Colette or Karen Blixen—in whom the aristocratic pleasures of travel and the table, of conversation and memory and love, are balanced by a store of peasant wisdom. She translated *The Physiology of Taste* by Brillat-Savarin, but also published a book of folk remedies, and knew the workings of a French town as if she had been born and raised there. She wrote a screenplay, children's books, travelogues. It is this wide human perspective that sets her apart, even as a writer about food. The first dish we hear of her preparing, at age ten, are "Hindu eggs" so full of curry (for surely one couldn't have too much of a good thing) that she and her little sister are found sitting on the edge of the bathtub, feet in cool water, their blistered mouths full of mineral oil. In later life she will describe dining with a recent widower who, in his bereavement, has taught himself how to cook. It is a meal of terminal ghastliness—meat from a tin, muscatel mixed with lemon soda and served in jelly glasses—but her host is so proud of his achievement that our heroine, too, manages to enjoy every mouthful, and calls it one of the best dinners she's ever eaten. Auden would have approved.

In between these extremes of self-indulgence and self-sacrifice will have come hours—hundreds of thousands of hours—whose delights a reader can share without heartburn or apoplexy. Let M. F. K. Fisher have the last word: "But gradually, over the measured progress of the courses and the impressive changing beauty of the wines, snobberies and even politics dwindled in our hearts, and the wit and the laughing awareness that is France made all of us alive."

MEMORIAL TRIBUTE
TO JOHN HERSEY

John's gentle manners. His modesty, his probity. Gentlemen are mannerly, no doubt, and their word is, by and large, to be trusted; but how often beneath the surface stretch terrible wastes of dullness and false bonhomie, where cameo appearances are made by the Seven Deadly Sins. It was John who most embodied, for me at least, that "parfit gentil knight" in Spenser, or the Christian gentleman whom Hopkins considered nature's highest achievement. Not that John, for all his sweet Charity, had retained any overt Christian bias; his were largely the older, Platonic virtues—Prudence, Temperance, Justice—and, if I may say so, no less welcome for that.

John as a literary man. Writers are fragile vessels: rivalries, breakdowns, messy love affairs. Their often uncommon intelligence brings poignancy to the harm they do to themselves and those who love them. Fragile along with the rest of us (or do I mean the best of us?), John and Barbara together made a life neither storm-tossed nor reclusive. Theirs was a compassionate merry serenity rarely seen in a respectable writer's household. By the time I knew him, John had distanced himself from the great spheres of witness, influence, and publicity. He didn't seem to miss them one bit, just went on making fictions for his own pleasure.

John Hersey, privately printed, 1993.

Meeting John late in his life and ours, David Jackson and I would try to imagine him in his youth. In a sense, though, John never left his youth behind. It simply became part of his outlook, his eager, flexible, attentive mind. If long lives can be deduced from the clutter they've accumulated, John struck us as having attained—perhaps it was there from the start—a wonderful spareness. No extra pounds, no unwanted possessions. A computer, yes, and books, and a classy car. Still, we felt the pride he took in his spareness, and I believe it is what he's writing about—with metaphorical license—in these sentences from *My Petition for More Space*:

> Each person tries to give his space a private style. I have adopted a quite common practice of bunking like a seaman on top of a long chest of drawers. The distinction of my space is that, apart from this chest-bed, it is bare. It is empty. Nothing but uncovered pine boards. No desk, no chair, no rug, no lamps, no TV, no books. Nothing. I have achieved a highly personal style by reducing my property—and my needs—to an absolute minimum. People think I am either pathetically poor or barren in imagination, but I have noticed that whenever I have guests, they get very high in my space, just from being in it. That is because so much of it *is* space. In a sense I have the largest home in New Haven.

Dear John, we all know what it was like to get high in your space.

PATMOS

High seas and overcrowded boat make for panic: D. will "do anything" if only I agree to get off at the next island. Patmos too is overcrowded, a holy place on 15 August. We end up sharing a straw mattress in a hot airless cubicle of the Tourist Policeman's house. The household, however, has a beautiful daughter. Next morning as I return, toothbrush in hand and towel round neck, from a remote washroom, she and an older sister ask the usual questions. Who art thou, Stranger, and what brings thee hither? Telling them I'm a teacher on holiday, I stumble through this "maiden" conversation in Greek, with no phrase book for support. Presently the beautiful girl looks deep into my eyes: "Eisai kalos" ("You're nice"—or even "good"). It takes me a while to bring out my reply: "Likewise"—and move on. Both of us are now blushing, pleased with ourselves and each other. Over coffee on the jammed waterfront David meets the legendary Daisy de Belleville ("encore fort baisable" as a Paris hustler described her) who flirts with *him*. She will be on tomorrow's boat to Athens. Paying our bill I want to say good-bye to the lovely girl, and am told that she's been shipped to her grandmother in the countryside, out of harm's way.

David Jackson and James Merrill, *David Jackson: Scenes from His Life* (New York: Nadja Press, 1994).

STORIES

ROSE

After his second glass of wine he sat at the piano and became an insect. The children applauded his transformation—he had arrived for dinner looking much like any other young man. But as the visitor sat talking with their parents, they perceived suddenly that he had begun to resemble nothing as much as a rabbit, a brown rabbit with erratic eyes and an improbable nose. Robbie saw it first and whispered it to Rose who, because she was an albino and therefore something of a rabbit herself, a white rabbit with crimson eyes, refused to look in his direction until they entered the dining room where she was told to sit opposite him.

By this time, however, no longer a rabbit, he was alternately a frog, a groundhog, a bird, a goldfish. The children watched each evolution with delight, trying, as the meal progressed, to catch him in the act of change, at the moment when the bland greed of the groundhog should become the bland precocity of the bird, or when, turning from his salad to his sliced oranges, the goldfish eyes were lidded and the whole face grew round and composed and unobtrusive like a fruit. And after dinner he took his wineglass to the piano and became an insect. The music, too, was insect-music, as though the very notes on the page were eggs to be hatched. The light was faint, because of Rose's weak eyes, but the chil-

Glass Hill, October 1949.

dren could see him smiling and his eyes, which were now enormous, darted against them decorously, as moths beat on a windowpane.

It was their bedtime. "Good night," said Rose to the visitor. "Good night, Rhoda," he replied, resting his hands for a moment on the keys. He doesn't even know my name, thought Rose, all the way up the stairs. But as she stood at her bedroom window, waiting to see him leave, it occurred to her that, by his calling her Rhoda, he had in some way endowed her with a new identity, just as he had changed from one creature to another throughout the evening. She was pleased, and braided her white hair until she heard the door shut below, and saw him, faintly luminous, received into the night air. It was the last she ever saw of him or, if she did see him again, she never recognized him.

The next morning Rhoda woke early. When she finished breakfast she told her mother she was going to play at a friend's house; then, wearing her dark glasses to protect her eyes, she ran into the street and began walking toward the center of town. Through the deep green of her glasses Rhoda could guess the extreme brilliance of the day, and she found herself tempted to snatch brief glimpses of the dazzling street out of the sides of her glasses, with her bare eyes. It was cruelly bright; a white wall was brighter than she had ever seen the sun; the sun, flashing on a windowpane, cut into her eye as if it had been a blob of jelly. The sidewalk was strewn with bits of mica; she walked on knives. Her eyes watered from this first blink and she shut them in terror, yet at the same time laughing at the shy ghost of Rose, who had never risked such an injury: shy Rose, laughing, deceitful, wicked Rhoda. Passing a fountain, she looked over the rim of her glasses at the sun striking the jet of water; it was less painful than the time before. When she reached the center of town, she paused before a mirror in a shop window. Carefully she removed her glasses, stared for a moment at her red eyes, her white hair and lashes, her almost translucent skin, then turned deliberately and gazed for five seconds directly into the sun.

She remembered screaming from the pain, which somehow did not reach her until she had covered her eyes with her arm. She was sitting on a bench in a dark hallway, and the first thought that came to her was that she was no longer herself. A man stood beside her, his hand on her forehead. "What's the matter? Are you all right?" he asked softly. "I looked into the sun with my eyes," she whispered. "She's an albino, poor dear," said another voice, a woman's. "Light affects them dreadfully." "Tell me your name," said the soft voice.

She turned her face in the direction of the voice, her arm still across her eyes. "Rosalind," she said.

"Your last name?"

She paused. The question was repeated. "Rabbit," she said very quietly. There was a long silence full, no doubt, of expressive glances. Then someone lifted her arm from her eyes.

"Open your eyes," said the man with the soft voice. "Can you see my hand?" He stroked the air in front of her face; she could see his hand. "Yes," she replied.

"She'll be all right," the man said. He smiled at her—she could see him smile—and told her to stay there for a little while, and that if she wanted he would take her home. "No thank you," said Rosalind. "I'll be all right." They left her alone on the bench in the dark hallway.

In a few minutes she put on her glasses and returned to the street. She bought a bunch of violets at the corner. Rhoda had hated flowers. On all sides, Rosalind saw the streets, the fountain, caught up in a killing light. Surely somewhere a darkness was implied.

The museum was cool and dim. She stopped before each painting and entered it, sat under the trees by the river, fingered the tablecloth sprawling with apples, combed the hair of the naked lady in front of the mirror. In one picture a child lay asleep in the desert; above her an angel flew, holding close to the child's ear a large silvery snail, the graceful animal protruding from its shell like a talisman in some private ritual. The angel had eyes like last night's visitor as he played the piano, and her love for him grew very deep in the minutes that she looked at the painting. She became the child asleep.

A hand touched her shoulder. Turning, she faced a woman in green who gazed at her a long time before speaking.

"Are you prepared for death?" the woman chanted. Rosalind lowered her eyes. "Can you look into your heart and say: I am prepared for death? You are a child and a freak, and therefore the choicest of Christ's innocents, but even a child, even a freak, must be prepared for death which comes to all creatures." The woman moved away, smiling. Rosalind walked out into the sunlight, her violets gripped so tightly in her hand that her palm grew moist and stained by the green leaves. Her eyes still ached a little, as from an excess of sun.

Walking home, she repeated to herself the names she had assumed during the day: Rose, Rhoda, Rosalind. They were all wrong, now that she thought about them, just as it had been wrong to think of the magical visitor as any one of his multiple disguises. He had not been a rabbit, a goldfish, an insect, but something common to them all. And then she said aloud, "Death. Death."

When she reached her house she went swiftly upstairs to her room, and with her fingertip, in the dust upon the windowsill, she wrote her new name.

DRIVER

A single lesson converted me. I heard the call and would obey it happily ever after. This was in the summer of 1919. My father, back from France, gave me thirty minutes of instruction, after which I was on my own, learning by experience over a network of frail dirt roads flung outward from our village into the surrounding farms. I should be able to describe those roads, those farms. People we knew lived on them. Without question I must have stopped to talk, enjoy a piece of cake or, the following year, a cigarette, to stroke the long face of a stalled animal before, my own face brightening, I leapt back into the sputtering Ford. But I have no such memories. That summer of being fifteen, conjured up today, might have passed exclusively within the moving car. My teeth would clack together over ruts. Off to my right a discoloration of the windshield made for the constant rising of a greenish cloud. I inhaled a warm drug compounded of fuel and field. My feet, bare or sneakered, burned, grew brown, grew calloused. One day at summer's end I noticed in the rear-view mirror a tiny claw of white wrinkles at the corner of each eye.

In those days to my embarrassment, as later to my pride, I was not mechanically minded. Other boys my age preferred the languorous exploration of parts to the act itself. I took as much interest in what lay beneath the hood as I did in visualizing my entrails; that is to say, none.

Partisan Review, Fall 1962.

Quite simply, I adored to drive. Enlarged to the dimensions of my vehicle, I took on its blazing eyes, its metallic grimace, its beastlike crouch. Or am I ahead of myself? Were not, at first, humbler qualities instilled by those early models? They rattled but stood upright in sober garb. Fallible, they departed like Pilgrims out of faith, theirs and mine. But now I suspect I am *behind* myself: I have no real memory of that Eden of the Model T, in which the car was yet one more patient beast for man to name and rule. Temptations of Power, Speed, and Style were already whistling loud in my young ears. A windshield clearing, I gazed through the forehead of my genie. Other drivers, rare enough still, I hailed silently as having drunk from the same fountain. At night each learned how to lower his gaze, conscious of what blinding foresights were to be read in the oncoming other's. A needle registered the intensity of the whole experience. When I saw my first wreck, complete with police and bodies under sheets, I found in my heart a comprehension, an acceptance of death that has never—or only lately—deserted me.

My parents were amused, if alarmed. "We gave you the wrong name, boy," my father would laugh (I am called Walker after *his* father), but he soon learned to make notes of mileage and to deduct the fuel I was using from my allowance. "Walker, if you're going driving at this hour of the night," my mother would begin. "Your mother's right," my father would add as I rose yawning from the dark oval table where we ate, brushing to the floor, like any destiny they might have arranged for me, a constellation of crumbs. For by then I had ceased to take seriously, or indeed to recall, anything that occurred while I was off the road. The abrupt standstill left me groggy and slow on my feet, as in dreams or on the ocean floor. My parents gesticulated, their lips moved. I cannot explain their helplessness. I was a boy, perhaps in my first year of college: I did not even—but yes! By that time I did have a car of my own.

Once more I have paused to see if I can remember how it came about; I cannot. I can shut my eyes and imagine odd jobs, see my hand, wrist bare and brown beneath a rolled-up cuff, pressing a plunger marked VANILLA—a shiny brownish stream braids downward into the glass; or holding a brush and rhythmically, as if to obliterate any detail that might distinguish such a moment from a million others like it, covering a clapboard wall with ivory paint. I can invent, if not truly recall, the death of a grandparent, a legacy in which I must have shared to the extent of a yellow diamond or dented gold watch immediately pawned. Anyhow, I drove to college in my first car, old-fashioned but sufficient, and finished my education with honors, having been promised a new car if I did.

What is strange is that my teachers complimented me upon my excellent mind. If only I could think of a single occasion on which I used it!

Toward the end of the summer following my graduation the question of what I was to do with my life must at last have arisen with some intensity. Evenings come back, of straight roads traveled in fury, the dog on the seat next to me listening while I rehearsed manifestos aloud. "No," I told him. "You may be my father but I refuse to work in the business you have built up. I want to travel, get to know my country. Besides, I scorn both your methods and your product. What are these prosperous times for, if not to . . ." It may be that I ended by delivering this speech to the right audience. More likely it sank without a ripple into those trustful brown eyes fixed upon me through the warm and whizzing night.

I became, in short—but it does not matter what I became. If I am to set down the truth about my life it will not be found in dates and labels but in this brief memoir of my supreme pastime and of those who now and then shared it with me.

My first passenger was the dog I have mentioned. He was brown, shorthaired, virtually nameless—we called him Pal. He and I had loved each other for many years. By the time he began to drive with me, habit and trust had taken the place of passionate contact, kisses, exclamations. Neither now had any particular need of attention. Pal's head would be thrust, tongue flapping gladly, into a torrent of sunlit odors. If I reached to stroke him absently he would look round, not displeased but puzzled, then turn with one token thump of his tail back to the window. When I talked, he would, as I have said, listen, especially at night. His face, no longer transfigured by adoration, had grown serious, almost ascetic. I felt he wanted me now merely to illustrate certain still baffling but minor aspects of human behavior, against the day when his own turn came.

A truck hit him, one morning early, in front of our house. The cook kept marveling over how the driver, "crying like a baby," had carried him right into the kitchen. I found him there on newspapers when I came down for breakfast.

I am glad to say that in all my years of driving I have never been responsible for the death of an animal. Nothing pains me more than those little corpses that accumulate on our highways. The first one appears just after sunrise—a rabbit, or cat, glittering with fresh dark blood—but as the day wears on they become uncountable and unrecognizable, a string of faded compresses dried out by fevers they had merely intensified. All night they are mourned by shining green or amber eyes. And by dawn they have become part of the road itself.

Not long after the death of Pal I left home.

I still preferred to drive by myself. At college, the car had made me popular. Every weekend filled it with classmates, girls, banners, flasks. I drank from the flasks, I waved the banners, I kissed the girls. And yet it was all beside the point. Their emphasis was forever upon *destinations*— the conventional site of waterfall and moon and mandolin; or else of the shabby "club" where liquor could be bought and consumed, where one danced to a phonograph in the red dark. Hours would pass this way, pleasurably no doubt. But I think there were few in which I did not once ask myself: How long will it last? When can we go back to the car?

This is something that happened not long after I left home:

One lovely autumn day I found myself on a road that dipped and rose through golden shrubbery and tall, whitened trunks, when out of nowhere, on a steep curve, two figures appeared. They were all but under my wheels before I could stop: an old country couple patiently signaling for a ride. I let them in the back door. They were brown and wrinkled, dressed in patched blacks and raveling grays. The woman wore knitted stockings. In both hands she held a coffee can planted with herbs. As we drove I would catch sight of her in the mirror, watching them, lips moving, giving them courage. The old man carried on his lap a basket of apples, pocked, mis- shapen ones that nevertheless had been beautifully polished. Perhaps he had not been in a car before; he kept looking about and moistening his lips. I asked how far they were going. When neither answered I asked again, this time turning to look square in their faces. They looked back. The old man rested his fingertip against the window glass, appreciatively. I understood his pleasure and was pleased myself to have brought it about. We drove in silence for a number of miles.

Then the old man began to utter noises of unrest. Seeing no house or road, I drove on. His dismay increased. "Master," said the woman eventually; and when I had stopped the car, "there was a road," she said, and waited. I realized that they had wanted to get out, and, rather than cause them an extra inconvenience, I backed some hundred yards to where, indeed, a narrow dirt road forked off.

I followed it without hesitation. An emerald green ribbon grew between its ruts. Overhead, branches met. I felt a foolish smile cross my face. The road itself soon petered out. We came to a halt in the middle of a cluttered barnyard. Dogs, pigs, doves, and a few small, soiled children moved in and out of larger, motionless shapes, a rusty tractor, a cow. One lone peacock trailed his feathers in the hard dirt. To greet us, four young people rounded different far corners and stared taciturn and crimson-eared at the car. Were they all descended from my old couple? I could imagine that, instead of expelling anyone from the garden, God and the angels had found it handsomer to pack up and go themselves, for all that could be done without *their* guidance and example.

My passengers had alighted and were making signs of hospitality. Too young to be gracious, I could only blush and stammer a protest. The poetry of the invitation depended upon its refusal. Each of us, in fact, must have felt as much. In a single gentle movement the old woman set down her herbs, took an apple from her husband's basket, and handed it to me. As I circled the yard they stood waving. A dove fluttered out of my path.

I got back to my original road. The sun, pale and lowering, was waiting for me beyond the first crest. The apple tasted bitter, hard; it could not have been an eating apple. I tossed it away with a shudder. Night fell before I came to a town.

From now on I would offer rides to people. Absently at first, discouraging talk, moved chiefly by the missionary's fervor to acquaint others with Revelation. I drove well—too well, perhaps. As I rounded curves with a graceful one-handed gesture, certain passengers would look admiringly at me instead of at the road. I was young, husky, I had a pleasant face; people told me their stories. Having little to say myself, I became, depending on the occasion, grandson, son, big brother, kid brother, and would do my best not to destroy the illusion while striving to deflect attention back to the main points, those Olympian secrets of Fuel and of the Wheel. Until one day, inevitably, I added to these a role that by its nature and at my age was less easily given up than the rest: the role of lover.

She sat beside me at a counter one early evening, blonde, full-blown, and looking heartbroken. She had to go to another town, not far, but had missed the last bus and was I headed that way? Well, she paid for my coffee and I drove her off. Soon she was chatting and patting her hair. "I thought you'd be gone when I came back with my grip. Sure are a nice boy to do this. Shouldn't call you a boy, though. Bet you know more than I do!"

I can smile now at my innocence. She guided me past her town, past the next. Night was falling, I wanted to stop. Even when I understood and drove without protest, indeed with my heart thumping, down the dark dirt road, her hand reaching across me to turn off the lights—even then I had a surprise in store for me. Opening my door, I started out. "Where you off to?" said my friend coyly. I stood frozen with stupefaction. It was going to happen in the *car*! I forced a casual reply and turned from her to the underbrush, lifting my face to the stars, letting her imagine what she liked, while I tried to make sense of my feelings.

I knew that love was made in cars. Mine, though, *my* car—could I put it to these uses? And were the uses high or low? As for love, I can use the word today, but a molten gulf separated its earlier meanings (a girl to be kissed between drinks, an imitative couple in the backseat) from *this* experience, wringing and intense, that within an hour had left the dry track of a tear on either cheek as I drove deeper and deeper into some dark western state. The woman nodded at my side. I did not know whether I had degraded or fantastically enlarged the road ahead.

That first love rose and set, establishing a pattern others were to follow. First came days, or weeks, during which the fact that we desired, but did not know, one another, kept us both good-humored. Then, gradually, at the woman's insistence, our passion overflowed into rooming houses and hotels, although with luck I was still able to confine it to the car, reserving our shared bed for sleep. Mornings, we drove on; the woman would not mind, not at first, waiting in the car while I transacted my business. Thinking it over, I shall not emphasize my profession by concealing it. I was a salesman, of countless different things, encyclopedias, garden supplies, trusses, religious texts, all or none of these. I would reach into the backseat for my case. The car door shutting behind me threw a switch. Two minutes or two hours later I would be back, whatever had passed between me and "the lady of the house" forgotten now unless translated into clues: money in my wallet, a thumbnail blackened by a slammed door, more than once liquor on my breath and lipstick on my ear. The patience of the woman in the car came to be tried. We would drive on doggedly, a capsule of discord, she questioning, pleading; myself silent, not guilty, amazed by the recurrence, from one to the next, of the same demands, the same voice first injured then sarcastic before its final sickening fall into a nastiness without nuance or remedy.

I would want only to be rid of her.

I soon learned to avoid these climaxes. At the first sign of strain—when the woman, say, was no longer content to do her nails in the car, but sat making lists of food to buy or friends to surprise with postcards—I would persuade her that I meant to stop several days in a certain town. On being shown to our hotel room, I would make impetuous love to her before going down to "see about the car" (in which I would happen to have left my things) and driving off into the night alone. Those were hours of resolution, of pride in my lonely calling. The renounced woman roared in the motor and wailed in the fleeing dark.

Somewhere I have read that driving is a substitute for sexual intercourse. I am as good an authority as the next man on both subjects, and can affirm without hesitation that for thrills, entertainment, and hygiene the woman is no match for the automobile. There is furthermore the efficient, even temper of the latter, and the fact that you may obtain a younger and more beautiful one as often as you like.

There were bad moments, though. I had no ties. My parents were dead. I was thirty-five years old, one moving body inside another. What does anyone do in my position? I got married.

Muriel.

This poor, foolish, virgin librarian had staked her job, her room, perhaps her entire future, on a summer's trip west. Up to then she had spent her best moments scanning the heavens above Iowa, filling her little heart with the play of clouds and tints, and her little head with the certainty that if once those skies were seen reflected in some vast expanse of water—the Pacific Ocean for instance—all would be changed, life would no longer pass her by, she herself would turn lovable overnight.

Again, that curious faith in destinations.

She never saw the Pacific, she may or may not have become lovable, but life definitely did not pass her by—*I* stopped for her. She had been resting on her suitcase at a crossroads; a placard round her neck read "California or Bust." She saw the car stop, saw that it was powerful enough to take her where she wanted to go. She was too tired, hungry, and sunburned to wonder about its driver. That came later, offshoot of the basic physical infatuation with the machine.

We *headed* west—my intentions were honorable. We might have gone all the way but for that billboard somewhere in Nebraska advertising a "Motorists' Chapel. Worship in Your Car." My weakness for novel experience within the traditional framework, or chassis, together with Muriel's empty, peeling face, caused me to stop, propose to her, and, once accepted, make inquiries that led to the first marriage ceremony ever performed in an automobile. A national magazine paid all expenses. For weeks people recognized us wherever we went. Many wished they had thought of doing the same thing.

My marriage was not unhappy, it was unreal. Legally each other's dearest belonging, we spent, as I might have foreseen, more and more time in rooms, eating places, shops, or under trees with sandwiches and books of verse. "And if thy mistress," read Muriel aloud, "some rich anger shows, "Emprison her soft hand and let her rave, / And feed deep, deep upon her peerless eyes." Parked up a hill, the car shimmered in waves of heat, gazed wrathfully, peerlessly out over our heads.

Muriel's underclothes hung drying on a cord rigged across the backseat. She wanted to settle down. I tried to dissuade her from this step, the one of all that would lose me to her. Had she forgotten California? Ah, she didn't *need* California now! The denouement can be imagined. One cool blue morning that fall, or the next, I left our secluded cottage—a last rose blooming by the gate, a letter of farewell written and ready to mail when I stopped, if I ever stopped. I got into the car for the first time in three days. A miniature Muriel waved from the house into my rearview mirror, then staggered abruptly and lurched with a whine out of sight. I was off, life lay ahead once more! In the nearest town faces stopped me. It was the morning after Pearl Harbor.

A voice on the radio was already predicting the rationing of fuel.

I quickly appraised the situation. Six months too old for the draft, I could settle down where I was, with Muriel, in the middle of our continent. This life at best would permit me the daily drive of a few miles to and from some nearby parachute or food-packaging plant. I decided on the spot to enlist in the Ambulance Corps. Weeping over the telephone, Muriel promised to wait. Laughing, I promised to send money. A year later I was driving in North Africa.

I think of landscapes, of roads erased by sand forever rippling under washes of light. A grove of palms, women in veils, the tank burning on the horizon. Above all, a vastness in which hovered black birds of indeterminate size. Whatever the scale, it was not human. This comforted us; we permitted ourselves colorful, passionate acts, at once proving and outweighing our tiny statures.

Made up of volunteers, our company had an odd, aristocratic flavor. Books were passed around—Tolstoy, *Les Liaisons dangereuses*, collections of fairy tales. These showed me how far I had gone along certain roads never noticed while concentrating upon their macadam counterparts. I found in myself traces of the sage, the pervert, and the child.

Nothing bored me, nothing frightened me. Up from a half hour's sleep in the shade of a wall, I would face into a warm wind blowing at the exact speed of my life. The laugh and the wound, the word of the wise man and the bullet's sunburst through glass, converged and drove me onward, light as a feather. It became all but superfluous to take the wheel again in search of casualties.

I see now that I did not belong. My heroics were prompted by exuberance, not humanity. My passengers suffered and prayed and died like the natives of a country I was content merely to visit. I had myself photographed smiling in front of grand Roman arches preserved for centuries in that climate. And then I went home. Sand covered them quickly. The war was won and lost, both.

Ours was now the oldest in a cluster of similar bungalows, each occupied by an older couple or single woman waiting, like Muriel, for her hero to return. This colony, having taken my wife to its heart—"you clever, darling child," I heard her addressed with my own ears—welcomed me avidly. Neighbors came to the door bearing covered dishes. Muriel kissed them, led them to where I squirmed. Poor, popular, outgoing Muriel. I was outgoing, too, in a sense. "Sorry," I would say, leaping up. "You caught me on my way to work."

My restlessness neither fazed nor puzzled them. It did me. Often I turned back after an hour on the road. People were buying anything, I could have sold rocks. And yet—

One day I drove home to witness the following scene. A car had stopped, motor running. My wife stood leaning across the gate, talking to the driver. A bleak wind lifted her hair and skirt, she was having to raise her voice. I heard nothing. As her eyes darted my way the car moved on. Its driver had got lost, Muriel said; she had given him directions. I shrugged. We did live off the main road.

Two nights later I heard the truth. We were returning from a drive-in movie. We had sat, not touching, in the car and watched a couple of starlets barely out of grammar school learn "the hard way" (burned biscuits, Mme. de Merteuil for a neighbor, a miscarriage leading to a reconciliation under moonlit palms) that it took two to make a marriage. A mile from home Muriel spoke. "Walker, let's stop here." She had to touch my arm. "Can't we stop."

"If that's how you feel."

"I mean the *car*."

"Of course you do." I pulled uneasily to the side of the road.

"Now let's get out."

"What's got into you? We could be home now."

"Just for five minutes. I want to talk to you."

"All right, talk to me."

"Not in the car. *Please*. I can't think in the car."

"You said you wanted to talk. Make up your mind."

Muriel started to weep.

With my feet on earth, my head emptied automatically. The night stung and shone. Something of that cold clarity may have prompted her words; of those distances, too, without a sense of which the starry sky would be just another town on a hillside, soon to be entered and left behind. I tried to take her hand. These were things she did not need to tell me. At one point a silence fell, long enough for a small oblivious animal to amble past us on the icy road. I looked wistfully after it.

At last we were heading home. "You can keep the house," I said.

"You haven't understood, Walker," said Muriel in a higher, sadder voice than usual. "I don't want you to go. I don't love him—yet. But you're driving me to it."

"Driving you?" I stepped on the accelerator, wanting to turn it into a joke. "You mean like this?"

The car jolted forward.

"Yes!" Muriel screamed. "Exactly like this!"

Then, in our lights, two amber-green eyes were glowing. I pulled out of the creature's way. We turned over.

Muriel was not killed—I have never killed a living thing. But there was no further question of staying together. And early the following summer she and her new husband were drowned in a storm on Lake Tahoe.

Toward my next car, as toward the next and the next and the next, I felt a kind of disabused tolerance. Each could have been my heavy, middle-aged person—not yet a source of suffering, no longer a source of delight.

In fact I have nothing more to relate except the incident which decided me, some weeks ago, to write these pages. Today I wonder if what I have set down leads anywhere, let alone to that warm, bright morning.

I had bought a convertible—not that it promised to change anything—and had thrown back the top before setting out. It was late June in the South. My road led without warning to a group of old-fashioned buildings, shaggy with ivy and vacant behind pale buff window shades. A black-and-gold sign in their midst read State Teachers' College. I had slowed down for no reason—the place was clearly deserted—when a young man stepped from under a lintel that bore in large block-lettered relief the word POULTRY. He raised a careless hand, as if saying, "There you are!" to a friend.

Although I take no riders nowadays I stopped for him. He was dressed with an undergraduate's nattiness: white shoes and seersucker. In my day he would have carried a mandolin. After we began to move he named a town some fifty miles distant—some fifty miles out of my way, too, if a "way" was what I had—then closed his blue eyes, enjoying the ride, I supposed.

He opened them soon enough and, turning to me, made, in the pleasantest of voices, a series of wholly uncalled-for remarks. Cars had grown (he began) too ugly for words. So pompous, so unwieldy. He only rode in them when absolutely essential. The seats were no longer covered in cloth or leather, but some hideous synthetic material. The dashboards were cushioned. As for the color schemes—well, why not put a bedroom on wheels and get it over with? I decided he was a fairy. I suppose *you* fly, I nearly said.

As if he had read my mind he burst into laughter. His name was Sandy, he continued. He had known I was coming. Hadn't *I* felt, too, that something unusual lay ahead that morning? "Look," I said firmly, but he went right on. I could expect something far more unusual than him. A woman, a Princess, was waiting for him—for us. Already I was part of their mission, his and hers. I felt him watching me closely. The Princess was a medium. I knew what that meant? Good. They had been for many months in communion with a guide—did I understand?—a guide who at last had judged them ready to receive and carry out a set of elaborate instructions. They were to fly that very afternoon to the West Coast, thence to an island in the South Pacific. They had been given quite a timetable of duties, contacts with strangers minutely described by this guide as to both appearance and spiritual pedigree—one of the most useful was to be a thirteen-year-old fisherboy who in a previous life had been Sandy's grandfather. Just what they hoped to accomplish he was forbidden to say. But the general aim, I might as well know, was to save mankind from annihilation.

I shot him a startled look; he was smiling. Beneath his tanned cheeks the young color danced.

"You've seen the newspapers," said Sandy. "The end gets nearer and nearer. Nobody else is really trying to stop it."

Casting about for a badly needed plausible touch at this point, it occurs to me to mention his "hypnotic voice." It was nothing of the sort, rather a boyish, matter-of-fact voice, yet I hesitate to put forth any *serious* explanation for what was happening. My early impression of him had vanished. In a strange apprehensive sleepiness I found myself hanging upon his words. I thought of the "missions" of my own youth, the awakenings I dreamed of bringing to my fellow man. Rooted behind my steering wheel of white, sun-warmed plastic, I had a glimmering of how those others would have reacted, as I did now, half with the drowsy numbness of Muriel's favorite poet, half with a heart shocked by its sudden pounding.

He talked the entire hour. Of that crazy quilt only scraps come back today. Good and Evil existed, pitted against one another. He, Sandy, had seen an angel routed by Lucifer in the New York subway. The beautiful white yarn of vapor trails was being used to entangle us all by statesmen, adult impersonators, lurching from one trouble spot to the next. Their explosions in the press and on TV caused a kind of horrible psychic fallout in people's living rooms. Forces in the next world were fighting to reach us with messages rarely heard, almost never heeded. The resurrection of the body was at hand; we were no longer to be slaves of—personality? nationality? His exact word escapes me; no matter. We had reached the town. The Princess might or might not see fit to tell me more. Sandy had already implied—with a touch of condescension which, in my increasingly pliable state, turned my very bones to wax—that I had been chosen from among thousands to help them through this stage of their mission.

"A lot depends on what she thinks of you," he said earnestly.

We parked in front of a willow-shaded Tourist Home. From the car I watched Sandy leap up the steps to the porch and into the house without knocking. A fly lit on my face. I could not have driven away.

He held open the screen door for a girl in a black, armless dress. She was using a cane and watching her feet, in sandals, descend the porch steps. At the car door she hesitated, then turned upon me the face of a middle-aged woman, sick-eyed and freckled, but not by this year's sun. I got out to help her. She motioned Sandy into the rear seat and settled herself awkwardly up front.

I looked back at the house.

"No baggages," said the Princess. "This." She patted a bulging leather purse. It sprang open. She took out a scarf of milky chiffon to keep her hair in place. "Everything gets done for us, so we travel light. You are very kind," she added in the same breath, ridding herself as neatly of the obligation as of the unwanted suitcases. "We—I can say?—*anticipate* kindness."

"I think she means," Sandy began.

"He know what I mean," said the Princess grandly. "He understand my English." She gave a formal signal to depart.

Idiotically, I relished my place in their little aristocracy. It was all so effortless! Poor clods (I thought) who had still to rely on telephones and timetables. I drove with my whole heart, bent on getting my passengers to their destination.

The airport was thirty miles farther on. Noon had struck; the plane would leave at half past one. Leaning forward to make himself heard, Sandy pointed out turns. Once on the straight road he announced as if casually, "This isn't a scheduled flight. A DC-4 picks us up at this field and takes us to New Orleans where a connecting jet to San Diego will be waiting."

I nodded too quickly. We were driving through broad fields.

"Oh, not waiting for *us*. We mean nothing to them. Any delay will be dismissed in the usual way—a motor check, a confused weather report. Don't you know what goes *on* at airports? Let me tell you, it's a scandal. They're debasing something pure and rare. I have to say this in spite of times like now, when their obtuseness works to our advantage."

Here Sandy digressed at length on the subject of flying. I was too much a part of the adventure, by now, to feel the annoyance his earlier speech about automobiles had provoked. Instead, I listened humbly, as ready as not to accept the judgment implicit in his words. I shall not try to reproduce them. The impression he gave was of intense, disquieting enthusiasm for aircraft, for certain models over others, for the view one came, as a pilot, to take of things. In the islands, he remarked, they would be flying their own plane.

My self-respect spoke up: "But you don't even drive a car!"

I never felt it took great perception to tell the drivers from the rest. All the same, Sandy shouted with delight. "You knew that! What a beginning! Did you hear him, Anya? He's one of us!"

At my side the Princess started—had she been asleep?—and spoke in a new gruff voice whose accents were not hers. "The road first traveled is the longest road," said this voice.

Sandy touched my shoulder. "It's Uncle Sam."

"Who?"

"Our guide. We call him that. She's in a trance."

I looked at her in alarm. Beyond the whipping scarf her jaw hung open.

"Don't worry," said Sandy.

"It is a long and painful road," intoned the Princess. "It will seem shorter and easier a second time."

"Is this message for us, Uncle Sam?" Sandy inquired.

"For your friend. Wait."

"He's such a darling," said Sandy. "He followed the Princess to America last year and *loves* it. He wants to be the fifty-first state."

Suddenly from the Princess came a high, plaintive, uncertain voice: "Walker, have you learned to walk yet?"

I gripped the wheel for dear life.

"I couldn't teach you. Learn to walk, Walker. Learn."

"All right," I said stupidly. "Where are you, Muriel?"

"Here beside you. There's someone else."

"That's the Princess, Muriel."

"Not *her*," the voice giggled. "Someone *here*. Someone who loves you."

I could barely whisper, "Who?"

The Princess whimpered excitedly through her nose.

"It's Pal," said Muriel's voice. "Your little dog."

My throat filled with tears. My hands fell from the wheel. Sandy must have kept us from driving off the road.

We sat there. The Princess was inspecting me with vague, puffy eyes. She gave me a Kleenex from her purse, and shifted her attention to her own appearance where deeper ravages had been sustained. Into a large oval mirror she peered, touching a fingertip to her various features, testing their firmness. Soon she was intently painting her mouth.

Without a word I pressed the starter. They were watching, waiting to bind me closer and closer to them, but I kept gazing straight ahead, mile after mile. I had borne all I could. I already believed.

I believed, too, at the deserted rural airport where I deposited my passengers and waited with them. I believed well after they had exchanged that single faintest of frowns with which one tries to shake a stopped watch into running. When I left at their insistence—as if my presence had thrown the wrench into the works!—I drove away still believing.

The road climbed. At one turning I was able to look back and distinguish, in a dream's deepening light, the two figures motionless outside the locked hangar.

Something glittered on the front seat; the Princess had left her mirror.

I peered at myself in it—I am nearly sixty—and threw it down. Phony, hysterical pair! There was no more to be learned from them than from those fat "psychical" studies of the last century, with titles like *Footsteps behind the Veil of Life* and *The Nine Stages: Dante's Vision Corroborated*. Though I had never opened one, I have only to think of their Victorian embonpoint, their black or purple bombazines, to invest that whole day with the worst kind of dowdy ineffectuality. Uncle Sam indeed! Would the American Way of Life save mankind from annihilation? Was *that* the level of arcane innuendo from beyond the grave? One thing I knew, though no prophet: their plane would be a long while coming. They might have gone farther by horse and buggy.

If I am angry now it is because I still believe, but not in them.

Driving, I kept glancing skyward, prepared, in spite of everything, for the glint of wings. Cross with myself, miles from my road, how gladly I would have hailed an order of machine superior to mine. To this day I cannot see a plane without stopping to wonder, to reenter those last lonely hours in the car—the mirror, face up beside me, shooting provocative flashes into the bare heavens.

Peru: The Landscape Game

Our cub plane growls and quivers for the pounce. K has fallen asleep, out of simple nervous tension. It is still dark. Lima twinkles under its habitual dense ceiling.

The luggage label of the Hotel Périchole is a much reduced page from the Offenbach score.

There. We're off.

Last night after dinner a white-haired lady from Zurich had us play that psychological game in which each person describes a house he then leaves in order to take an imaginary walk. One by one he discovers a key, a bowl, a body of water, a wild creature, and finally a wall. Free association is invited at any stage, and nothing explained until the last player has spoken.

The house is your own life, your notion of it. Trees roundabout stand for Other People.

The key is Religion. The bowl, Art. The water, Sex.

The wild thing is Yourself—the unconscious.

The wall is Death.

Our companion, K decided, was really Jung's widow. She noted our replies on a paper napkin:

Prose, Spring 1971.

K—apartment whose vine-covered terrace overlooks a piazza with
    fountains;
small gold key, to a lost diary?
goblet of iridescent glass, quite undamaged, which he kneels to
    fill at
a clear deep river;
a polar bear—K runs away;
high brick wall complete with electrified alarm system, enclos-
    ing the estate of an industrial magnate.
J— Victorian house, many rooms, gingerbread, topiary garden;
key to grandfather clock;
mixing bowl, cracked—fearing botulism, I kick it out of my path;
a pond stagnant in appearance but full of activity: lily pads, tad-
    poles, buzzing dragonflies;
a raccoon, masked, washing its little black hands on the far
    side—*it* runs away;
stone wall exactly my height, over which appear eaves and
    chimneys of a house much like the one I started out from.

"Are you sure you haven't played this game before?" asked the Frau
Doktor, not unreasonably. Yet she interpreted our answers at length,
scanning our faces for the intelligence we were too far gone to muster.

"What was it your bowl meant?" K yawned, up in the room.

"I'm a good mixer. But liable to go to pieces."

Sunrise. The foothills of the Andes—crumpled brown paper everywhere
mended with lighter or darker oblongs of the same, and riddled by a
canyon's bookworm course.

At once and stupidly, we succumb to the altitude. K's nose is bleeding,
I cannot breathe. Small unreal men emerge from the hotel. Are they
porters, these meerschaum apparitions in espadrilles and ponchos striped
pink and rust, who lift our bags onto their heads and trot off in what can't
be the right direction? Two others in black alpaca cutaways advance like
penguins—*¿permiso?*—and taking our elbows guide us, with frequent
pauses, up a flight of steps. It must be early still. Tiny gold crumbs adorn

my Samaritan's white piqué waistcoat. The steps, of stone like our legs, are seven in number and sparkle with frost.

Opening the register at random I see a familiar name: Mary Klohr, August 1938. A window behind the desk frames scenery for which words will be found another time. Our room is ready. K is handed a profusely tasseled iron KEY.

We give onto a courtyard. Ice films the dung-spattered water trough. Next to an "unhinged but brilliant" green door hangs an armadillo—quite incurable, K suspects as he unpacks vial after vial of pills. His nose bleeds on. The maid, impervious to our pantomime, leaves a star drowned in the thick glass decanter on the chest of drawers. She has no "soul" in *our* sense, of individual resonance to this or that. But she knows how to live twelve thousand feet above the sea. We shoo her away and lie down, overcome.

The Cuzco market is a grass-and-cobble arena outspread among baroque, whitewashed ramparts. Smelling of the tinsmith, the tanner. From under their awnings Indian women whistle and coo to attract us. No young one without a baby. Wherever you look blouses have been unfastened to expose a single breast, full, soft, and of the pearliest gray.

This booth sells only skeins of string dyed burnt orange. Instead of letters the Incas used knotted cords. The "yarn" as history. No older woman without a bobbin in her hands.

Poverty, death—the great shears everywhere poised and parted.

Mirrors. Papayas. Ponchos. Nescafé.

Woven stuffs by the bolt. The Incas lived in communes. Ornament was forbidden in their houses, mothers were forbidden to dandle their own children. Lives crisscrossed, warp and woof, with *relevance*—coarse dense fabric of the state.

A witchcraft booth. Herbs. Candy hearts. A bin of dried-up doll dinosaurs. The llama fetus has powerful juju.

On backstreets you will see unlit, dirt-paved shops which contain a single sewing machine, nothing else. Or a tall glass cupboard piled full of unleavened loaves. Silence. Or the click of billiards behind closed doors.

A booth where newts and lizards of all sizes hang in festoons, their baby limbs twitching. An Indian delicacy? Necklaces for the ogress?

Shiny purple-black beans in piles. Piles of white maize. Great petrified tubers splattered with grayish mold.

I walk and walk, buying none of it. Entirely cut off, entirely at one.

Mangled portions of meat. Skins stiff with blood.

Saddlebags. Ponchos. Oranges.

The silver ornaments smell of cardamon. K buys a bracelet for L. Farther on, I pick out a shallow unglazed BOWL for DMc. It has one vaguely genital lip, for pouring, and a stern, long-suffering face worked into the opposite rim. The handles are two arms akimbo.

Four exquisite young llamas eye the crowd as in a ballroom. Four Natashas.

A sentence from Prescott:

> The animals were no less above their comprehension; and when the cock crew, the simple people clapped their hands and inquired what he was saying.

The train, after doggedly trailing for hours the rapids of the Urubamba, gives up with a sigh. We get out.

(Far, far north, this capricious water, swollen beyond recognition, scummed with topaz and hostess to ten million razor mouths, becomes unalterable law. The river steamer blisters and moans. The banks suck their gums endlessly as it shudders upstream.)

"Good day," says a small man in whose amber features we discern the fossil slave. "I am your guide, Porfirio."

The site of Machu Picchu would make a blind man's heart pound.

You must imagine an unscalably huge system of interlocking pyramids and cones, clawed, raddled, packed in dry ice all smoking and swirling in the high damp green. Where you stand their upper twentieth has been battered almost level to form this rock garden of touching gravity.

Bamboo. Thatch. Cloud. A primitive Japan. Le Douanier Sesshu.

Monoliths made to fit like a puzzle. The Katsura palace built by trolls.*

Innumerable terraces rake Huayna Picchu's vertical jungle like any

---

*By hobbits, say the Swedes we meet in La Paz. Each to his own, says K.

temple garden. This paradox of steaming nature at the most rarefied level is something we have all had to contend with in our day. As in the person of an epileptic monk serene amid utter instability—for earthquakes take lives by the thousand in these young, visionary mountains—danger and prayer assume a single face.

Which comes and goes in mist—a floating world. Suddenly you are left alone with the Inca-Kola bottle cap underfoot.

Then, the great eye focusing as through a burning glass, you plunge on, goaded.

K says, "I don't see any of that. Why complicate things? This place is simply heaven. I mean, you go up through clouds to get there, and what do you find but all these good old friends—begonias, hydrangeas, gladiolas, Spanish moss. I'm serious. That's a red gladiola right over there. It's our own fault if we thought they were tacky in the world below."

Meanwhile Porfirio keeps emphasizing History—heads on pikes, imperial flatulence, drinking parties, disease—until what's to choose between past and present. We know these stories, we would hardly be here if we didn't. To make him stop, we inquire about his own life, and he obliges with a smiling tale of hardship, obedience, decency, such as one tells to any stranger *just in case*. Only now do we notice how far off the path he has led us. He gestures for us to wait outside a tin-roofed shack. "Here," says K, "is where Porfirio kills yet two more Yanquis." But from the stifling dark interior the little man emerges with a BABY in his arms— "mi niña." She is complete with eyelashes and earrings. Her complexion is some magic chocolate made out of pink rose petals.

While lunching on seven kinds of tuber and a sweet bean tart, K and I play the landscape game with the genius loci:

His house is Sagittarius. "Mutable, fiery, and masculine," according to K's horoscope paperback. "Travel, self-projection to new horizons," are indicated.

His key. Here we disagree. I want C-sharp minor (the three Urubamba maidens lamenting the theft of their gold by international museum directors), but K would settle for a key to the puzzle of the stones.

His bowl: golden.

His body of water: a drop of eau de cologne; he bathes in it.

His wild creature: the condor (K); Porfirio's baby (J).

His wall: cloud masonry he ascends and paces, gleaming fitfully down upon all our houses.

Indeed, Huayna Picchu is now altogether lost behind a WALL of mist. K slings his binoculars and strides off in its direction.

J: You're not thinking of climbing it! Whatever for?

K (already indistinct): Because it isn't there. . . .

Midafternoon. I found in a pocket certain leaves Porfirio had given me when I asked what he was chewing. Leaves the shape and green of bay, only more pliable; bitter to the taste. From a westerly terrace this steep trail led downward, dizzily, never looking back. Steps cut into rock, matchstick railings, slick ledges curling like smoke above the chasm. I chewed my leaves, assurance flowed through me, and I sent grateful thoughts back to Porfirio as down and down I zigzagged, all but dancing.

I see now that this place is a vast theater turned inside out, its lichened granite and green plush parterres, balconies, and smoking rooms thrown open to the elements. Not far from a chandelier forever dimming and brightening I am seated among ferns in an acoustically perfect loge. A gala by Berlioz is under way. Having whipped the pit to a shimmering spate, he now introduces daring new effects (tropical birds, chug of that toy locomotive) among the strings and reeds, the gongs and cymbals—

And something nearer? The pounding in my ears is after all / Not so much terror as a WATERFALL / Shaking and shimmering till the blond / Air has been atomized to diamond—

An icy mountain stream. Voice of mercury. Elvire Cascadin singing the *Nuits d'été*—

> *Tu me pris encore emperlée*
> *Des pleurs d'argent de l'arrosoir,*
> *Et parmi la fête étoilée*
> *Tu me promenas tout le soir*

—and I think of you whom I am too old to love, yet love so intensely. No. From *within* intensity: a dry place, a niche behind the waterfall, yes.

Stream forever at the end of its rope. Frayed. Unafraid. The nudged pebble touching earth once or twice only in the course of its long, slow-spinning—

Ah!

Broken out through spray, this fantastic thing, green fire in a soap bubble, wings slowly beating, in spirals up up up—

Utters in Quechua a single cry:

"I am the QUETZAL. I will never die."

In this virgin hemisphere the bath drains counterclockwise and a man facing the pole will see daybreak on his left hand. Does the fingerprint's whorl flow backward, too? Does the very hair grow otherwise on the scalp? Those new stars rising in their new way all night long—can't you feel an illusion risen with them, my dear one, of fatal processes reversed?

Of springs great and small being unwound? Slowly but surely. Until the anaconda and the music box lie down together.

K joins me at this point, his binocular case full of wild strawberries.

How to find the right words for a new world?

One way would be to begin, before ever leaving home, with some anticipatory jottings such as these. Then, even if the quetzal turns out to be extinct, if surefooted grandmothers from Tulsa overrun the ruins, and Porfirio's baby has a harelip and there are cucarachas in the Hotel Périchole, the visitor may rest easy. Nothing can dim his first, radiant impressions.

Back in New York, K and L will have finished dinner. They hold hands, they giggle. Perhaps they have been playing the landscape game.

My jet veers sickeningly into the "habitual dense ceiling" above Lima. So far, so good. Now the capital's slums, squares, and fountains twinkle beneath me. This is Peru—a déjà vu to be revised henceforth like galleys from the printer, in solitary pleasure and exasperation.

TRANSLATIONS

SELECTIONS FROM CHAMFORT

1. Weakness of character, paucity of ideas—in a word, whatever prevents us from living with ourselves—have saved many a man from misanthropy.

2. M. de Barbançon, who had once been extremely handsome, owned a beautiful garden which Mme. de La Vallière one day went to look at. The proprietor, then a gouty old man, confessed that he had been madly in love with her, long ago. "Alas!" she exclaimed, "but good heavens, why did you never speak? You would have had me like all the others!"

3. Louis XIV was sending to Spain a portrait of the Duke of Burgundy, by Coypel; but, wishing to keep a copy for himself, he ordered Coypel to have one made. Both paintings were exhibited side by side in the gallery—it was impossible to tell them apart. The monarch, foreseeing an awkwardness, took Coypel aside. "It wouldn't be right," he said, "for me to make a mistake, so tell me: which is the original painting?" Coypel pointed it out, and Louis, strolling past, remarked, "The copy and the original are so much alike that one might easily confuse them; however, by looking closely, one can tell that *this* is the original."

Semi-Colon, 1955.

4. "Death has forgotten us," said a ninety-year-old woman to Fontenelle, himself aged ninety-five. "Hush!" he replied, putting his finger to his lips.

5. False modesty is the most decent of all untruths.

6. It's unbelievable how alert one must be in order never to appear ridiculous.

7. A man disorients his soul, his conscience, his mind, as easily as he ruins his stomach.

8. M. de Lassay, a very gentle person who knew, however, a lot about society, used to say that one would have to begin by swallowing a toad, if one wished to find nothing else disgusting during the rest of any day spent among one's fellows.

9. X asked a certain bishop to give him a country house, where he never went. The latter replied, "Don't you know that a man must always have a place to which he never goes, yet where he believes he would find happiness, if he *did* go?" "You're so right," said X, after a pause, "and isn't that the splendid thing about heaven?"

10. Most anthologists of verses, epigrams, etc., resemble those who, eating cherries or oysters, first choose the best, but finish by cleaning the plate.

C. P. CAVAFY,
"IN BROAD DAYLIGHT"

I was sitting one evening after dinner at the San Stefano Casino at Ramleh. My friend Alexander A., who lived in the casino, had invited me and another young man, a close friend of us both, to dine with him. As it was not an evening with music, very few people had come, and we three had the place to ourselves.

We talked of various things. Since none of us was very rich, the conversation turned naturally enough to money, to the independence and consequent pleasures it brings.

Our young friend said he would like to have three million francs and began to describe what he would do, and above all what he would stop doing, once in possession of this large sum.

I calculated, more modestly, that I could get along with twenty thousand francs a year.

Alexander A. said: "Had I wished, I should today be who knows how many times a millionaire—but I didn't dare."

These were strange words, we thought. We knew our friend A.'s life thoroughly, and could not recall his ever being presented with an opportunity to become many times a millionaire. We supposed therefore that he had spoken lightly, that some joke would follow. But our friend's face was grave, and we asked him to explain his enigmatic remark.

Grand Street, Spring 1983.

He hesitated a moment—then said: "In other company—for example among people who call themselves 'evolved'—I would not explain myself, because they'd laugh at me. We, though, consider ourselves a bit above these so-called 'evolved' people. That is, our perfect spiritual development has brought us round to simplicity again, but to a simplicity without ignorance. We've made full circle. So naturally we've returned to our point of departure. The others are only halfway. They can't know or imagine where the road ends."

These words startled us not at all. Each of us had the highest regard for himself and the other two.

"Yes," Alexander repeated, "had I dared, I should be a multimillionaire—but I was afraid.

"The story goes back ten years. I hadn't much money—then as now—or rather I had no money whatever; yet in one way or another I was getting ahead and living, on the whole, well enough. I was living in rue Chérif Pacha. The house belonged to an Italian widow. I had three nicely furnished rooms and my own servant, not counting the landlady who would have done anything for my comfort.

"One evening I had gone to Rossini's. Having heard nonsense enough, I decided to break off and go home to sleep. I had to rise early the next morning, since I'd been invited on an excursion to Aboukir.

"Once in my room, I began as usual pacing about, thinking over the events of the day. But they were of no interest, drowsiness overtook me, and I lay down to sleep.

"I must have slept one and a half or two hours without dreaming, for I recall being awakened perhaps an hour after midnight by a noise in the street, and can remember no dream. I'd fallen asleep again at about one-thirty, and it then seemed to me that a man had entered my room—of medium height, fortyish. He was wearing rather old black clothes and a straw hat. On his left hand he wore a ring set with a very large emerald. This struck me as out of key with the rest of his attire. He had a black, white-streaked beard, and something peculiar in his glance, a look at once mocking and melancholy. All in all, though, a fairly ordinary type. The kind of man one sees over and over. I asked what he wanted of me. He didn't answer straightway, but studied me a long minute as if suspiciously, or to make sure he'd not been mistaken. Then he spoke—in a humble, servile tone of voice:

"'You're poor, I know that. I've come to tell you a way to get rich. Near Pompey's Pillar I know a spot where a great treasure lies buried. I want no part of this treasure myself—I'll take only a little iron box, to be found at the very bottom. The rest, all of it, will be yours.'

"'And of what does this great treasure consist?' I asked.

"'Of gold coin,' he said, 'but above all of precious stones. There are ten or twelve gold coffers filled with diamonds, with pearls, and I think'—as if trying to remember—'with sapphires.'

"I wondered why he didn't go alone to take what he wanted, and why he needed me. Before I could ask he answered: 'I can read your thought. Why, you wonder, don't I go to take what I want by myself? There is a reason, which I cannot tell you, and which prevents me. Some things even I cannot as yet perform.' On the words 'even I' a kind of brilliance shone from his gaze, and for a second an awful grandeur transformed him. But at once he recovered his humble manner. 'Thus you would do me a great favor by coming with me. I absolutely need somebody, and choose you because I wish you well. Meet me tomorrow. I shall wait for you from midday until four in the afternoon, in the Petite Place, at the café over by the blacksmiths' shops.'

"With these words he vanished.

"The next morning when I woke, the dream had slipped completely out of my mind. But after I'd washed and sat down to breakfast, it returned, and seemed quite strange to me. 'If only it had been real,' I said to myself, then again forgot it.

"I joined the excursion to the countryside and had a very good time. We were a large party—some thirty men and women, all in unusually high spirits. I shan't give you details, for they don't bear on our subject."

Here my friend D. remarked: "And aren't needed. Because I at least already know them. Unless I'm mistaken, I took part in that excursion."

"You did? I don't recall your being along."

"Wasn't that the excursion Markos G. arranged, just before he went to England for good?"

"Yes, that was it. Then you remember what fun we had. A marvelous time. Or rather, a time long vanished. It's the same thing. But back to my story—I returned from our outing quite tired and quite late. I had scarcely time to change clothes and dine, before going off to some friends' where a sort of family evening of cards was in progress, and where I stayed on, playing until half past two. I won a hundred and fifty francs and went home, more than pleased. I lay down with a light heart and instantly fell asleep, exhausted by the long day.

"But no sooner was I asleep than a strange thing occurred. I saw a light in the room, and was wondering why I'd not put it out before going to bed, when I saw emerging from the depths where the door was—my room was quite large—a man whom I recognized at once. He was wearing the same black clothes, the same old straw hat. He looked displeased, though, and said to me: 'I waited for you from noon until four o'clock at the café. Why didn't you come? I offer to make your fortune, and you don't jump at it? I'll expect you again at the café this afternoon, from noon to four. Be there without fail.' Whereupon, as on the previous night, he disappeared.

"But this time I woke up in terror. The room was dark. I lit the lamp. The dream had been so real, so vivid, that it left me stunned, appalled. I couldn't resist getting up to see if the door was locked. It was, as always. I looked at the clock; it said half past three. I had gone to bed at three.

"I will not conceal from you, nor am I in the least ashamed to admit, that I was very frightened. I feared to close my eyes lest, falling asleep, I see again my fantastic visitor. I sat up in a chair, all nerves. Around five, day began to break. I opened the window and watched the street gradually waking up. A few doors had opened, the first few milkmen were passing, and the first bakers' carts. The light somehow calmed me, and I lay down once more, to sleep until nine.

"Waking then, and recalling my anxieties of the night, their impression began to lose much of its force. Indeed, I marveled at having worked myself into such a state. Everyone has nightmares—I'd had many in my life. Besides, this was hardly a nightmare at all. True, I'd had the same dream twice. Which proved what? To begin with, did I in fact dream it twice? Mightn't I have dreamed once of seeing the same man a second time? After examining my memory carefully, I dismissed this notion. I'd undoubtedly had the dream two nights earlier. Even so, why call that strange? The first dream would seem to have been a most vivid one, impressing me so strongly that I dreamed it again. Here, however, my logic was faltering a bit. For I did not recall that first dream having impressed me so. All through the following day I'd not for an instant thought of it. On the excursion, at the party that evening, everything conceivable passed through my mind, except the dream. Again, proving what? Don't we often dream of persons neither seen nor thought of for many years? It appears that their image remains engraved somewhere within the spirit, to reemerge abruptly in a dream. What then was strange about my dreaming the same dream in the space of twenty-four hours, even if I hadn't recalled it during the day? I further told myself that I'd perhaps read somewhere about a hidden treasure, which had worked upon my memory; but no amount of cogitation brought such a text to light.

"Finally, tired of thinking, I began to dress. I had to attend a wedding, and my haste and the question of what to wear soon drove the dream wholly from my mind. I then sat down to breakfast and, to pass the hour, read a periodical published in Germany—*Hesperus*, I believe.

"I went to the wedding, where all the best society of the town had gathered. In those days I had many connections, and so was obliged, after the ceremony, to repeat innumerable times that the bride was lovely, if a touch pale, that the groom was a fine young man, as well as rich, and so on and so forth. Around eleven-thirty the affair was over, and I went off to Bulkeley Station to see a house I'd been told about, for possible rental to a German family from Cairo, who planned to summer in Alexandria. The house was indeed airy and well arranged, but smaller than reported. Nonetheless I promised the owner to describe it as suitable. Thanking me profusely, and in order to touch my heart, this lady began relating all her misfortunes, how and when her blessed husband had died, how she had even been to Europe, how she was not the sort of woman who rents her house, how her father had been the doctor of I can't now think which pasha, et cetera. This duty done, I returned to town. I reached my flat around one o'clock and ate a hearty lunch. After coffee, I went out to see a friend whose hotel was near the Café Paradiso, to arrange something for the afternoon. The month was August, and the sun blazing hot. I descended rue Chérif Pacha slowly to keep from perspiring. The street, as always at this hour, was deserted. I encountered only a lawyer, whom I'd asked to draw up the papers relating to the sale of a small lot at Moharrem Bey. It was the last piece of a fairly large property which I'd been selling bit by bit to cover some of my expenses. The lawyer, an honest man—that's why I chose him—was also a great chatterbox. Much better to have been cheated a bit than bored witless by his nonsense. The slightest pretext launched him upon an interminable discourse—he talked commercial law, Roman law, dragged in Justinian, cited the ancient cases he'd pled in Smyrna, praised himself, unraveled a thousand irrelevancies, and even took hold of my lapel, something I can't abide. I put up with this fool's babble because every so often, when his verbal powers failed, I could ask a question about that sale which so vitally concerned me. These efforts took me out of my way, but I stuck by him. Following the sidewalk of the Stock Exchange on the place des Consuls, we turned into the little street which joins with the Petite Place, on at last reaching whose center I had obtained all the information I needed, and the lawyer, recalling a nearby client to be visited, took his leave. I stood a moment watching him retreat, and cursed his blathering which in so much heat and sun had led my steps astray.

"I was about to retrace them in the direction of the Café Paradiso when all at once it struck me as odd that I should be here in the Petite Place. I asked myself why, then remembered my dream. 'It's here that the famous master of the treasure made our appointment,' I thought, and smiled, and mechanically turned my head toward that side where the blacksmiths' shops were.

"Horrors! There indeed was a little coffeehouse, and there indeed he sat. My first reaction was a kind of vertigo, I felt on the point of falling. I leaned against a merchant's booth, and looked again. The same black clothes, the same straw hat, the same features, the same glance. And he, unblinking, was observing me. My nerves tensed as from a transfusion of liquid iron. The idea that it was high noon—that people kept passing by unconcerned, as if nothing remarkable were happening, while I, I alone, knew that the most horrible thing *was*: that over there sat a specter endowed with who knew what powers and risen from what unknown sphere, what Inferno, what Erebos—paralyzed me. I started to tremble. The specter's gaze never flickered from me. Now terror overcame me lest he rise and approach—speak to me—take me with him! If it came to that, what help would any human force have been? I flung myself into a carriage, giving the driver some remote address I can't remember.

"When I'd somewhat collected myself I saw that we'd nearly arrived at Sidi Gaber. Cooler now, I set about examining the matter. I ordered the coachman back to town. 'I'm mad,' I was thinking, 'clearly I've deceived myself. It will have been somebody resembling the man in my dream. I must return to make sure. In all probability he'll have left, which will prove that it wasn't the same man—because *he* had promised to wait until four.'

"With these reflections I reached the Zizinia Theater; and here, summoning all my courage, told the driver to take me to the Petite Place. My heart was beating, was at breaking point I thought, as we approached the café. At a short distance from it, I had the driver stop, seizing his arm so violently that he nearly fell from his seat, for we were drawing very near—too near—the café; and because there, there sat the phantom still.

"I now made myself examine him attentively, hoping for some discrepancy between him and the man in my dream, as if who he was needed any further proof beyond the fact of my sitting in a carriage and staring at him with a gaze so penetrating that anyone else would have found it peculiar and demanded an explanation. Far from it: he returned my gaze with one equally penetrating, his expression full of concern for the choice facing me. It seemed that he was reading my thoughts, as he had read them in my dream, and to relieve me of any last doubt as to his identity, he shifted his left hand toward me, displaying—so markedly, I feared the driver would take note—the emerald ring that had struck me in my first dream.

"I cried out in terror and told the driver, who was by then concerned for his customer's health, to take me to Ramleh Boulevard. My one aim was to get far away. At Ramleh Boulevard I told him to head for San Stefano, but when I saw the driver hesitating and mumbling to himself I got out and paid. I stopped another carriage and had it drive me to San Stefano.

"I arrived in a dreadful state. Entering the main room of the casino, my face in the mirror appalled me—pale as a corpse. Fortunately the room was empty. I fell onto a divan and tried to consider my next move. To return home was impossible. To reenter that room through which had glided, by night, like a supernatural shadow, the One I had just now seen sitting at an ordinary café under the guise of an ordinary human being, was out of the question. Bad logic on my part, for of course he had the power to track me down anywhere on earth. But for some time now I'd been thinking disconnectedly.

"At length I resolved to seek out my friend G.V. in Moharrem Bey."

"Which G.V.?" I asked. "The eccentric one, who used to spend his time studying magic?"

"The same—and this played a part in my choice. How I took the train, how I arrived at Moharrem Bey, staring right and left like a madman in dread lest the specter rise up again at my side, how I reached G.V.'s room, I can recall in a vague, jumbled way. My one clear memory is that, finding myself with him at last, I began weeping hysterically, trembling from head to foot, as I related my horrible experience. G.V. quieted me and, half serious, half joking, told me not to fear; that the specter would never dare to enter his house, and that if it did he would cast it out at once. He knew very well, he said, this type of supernatural apparition, and knew also the way to exorcize it. He further implored me to believe that I no longer had any reason to be afraid, because the specter had come to me for a particular purpose, to obtain the 'little iron box' which, apparently, it was unable to do without the presence and help of a mortal. This plan had failed; the specter would already have understood, from my terror, that it had no further hope of success. It would no doubt go on to persuade somebody else. G.V. regretted only that I hadn't contacted him in time for him to go and see the specter, and speak with it, because, he explained, in the History of Specters the presence of these spirits or demons in broad daylight is most uncommon. All this failed to soothe me. I spent a very restless night and woke the next morning with a fever. The doctor's ignorance and the excitation of my nervous system brought about a cerebral fever, from which I barely escaped dying. When somewhat recovered, I asked what day it was. I had fallen ill on August third, and fancied it would be the seventh or eighth. It was the second of September.

"A short trip to an island in the Aegean hastened and completed my convalescence. I spent the whole length of my illness at G.V.'s, who tended me with that kindheartedness you both know. He was vexed with himself for not having had character enough to dismiss the doctor, and to treat me through magic alone, which I believe would have cured me, in this case at least, every bit as quickly as the doctor did.

"There you are, my friends: my opportunity to have millions—only I didn't dare. I didn't dare and I don't regret it."

Here Alexander fell silent. The utter conviction and simplicity of his narrative precluded any comment we might have made. Besides, it was now twenty-seven minutes past midnight. And since the last train for town left at twelve-thirty, we were obliged to say good night and be off in a great rush.

Vassílis Vassilikos, "The Three T's"

He entered like a man in search of the toilet: standing on the topmost stair, head craning right and left in search of a sign, one quick glance at the waiter for guidance.

The only waiter was occupied just then with a customer who had called for soda in his drink. The newcomer, tall as a stork, took in the come-and-go of this upper room, but its neutral layout gave no clue. A toilet could be located either to the right or to the left of where he stood. So that, flipping a coin within himself, a modern Hercules at the crossroads of Good and Evil—reluctant also to confess his need by asking me—off he went decisively to the right.

I smiled. I came regularly to this bar from five to seven, took the same table, and watched with relish the pantomime of human suffering. The toilet which the Stork had gone to look for lay in the other direction. Most people made that first mistake. Presently he would reappear, doubly at a loss, his patience dissolving in proportion to the severity of his need.

I summoned the waiter, once he had spurted the soda into his customer's glass. The point was to keep him occupied.

Now the Stork emerged from the suggestively lit alcove. He stumbled against two roosting lovers, begged a gauche pardon, and regained his

Shenandoah, Fall 1978.

starting point at the top of the stairs. He was wondering where he had gone wrong.

On purpose I kept the waiter busy, while watching the stranger out of the corner of my eye. Instead of heading left now, he was standing still in painful cogitation. I gave him low marks for ingenuity.

Like all who seek to relieve themselves, he was suffering from a faint sense of guilt. He was ashamed. Not of eating and drinking—the intake, so to speak, troubled him not a bit. But the output! Like those toll roads entering which you unthinkably accept a ticket, only to find that on emerging you must pay. . . .

In fact the Stork now went downstairs to ask the cashier for directions. Then, like Christ, he mounted to his Golgotha once again. This time he did not hesitate, but promptly lunged down a little corridor to the left which led to the two "rest rooms." Here, however, he had to wait. Two or three pretenders were already in line for the marble throne.

I preferred this café to the others in the neighborhood. The toilets were upstairs rather than at street level, and from a window table I could have looked my fill at the passers-by, their cheerful faces—hypocrites and liars all of them. But the parade of self-protective, walled-in waste had begun to sicken me. The minks and foxes, the costly high-heeled pumps, the skirts and stoles of astrakan—as if the pages of *Elle* had come undone, letting loose their animated mannequins like heroines in a novelist's brain. Seriously: much was beautiful, much was intolerable. Just as garbage was removed to special dumps outside the city, so had this arrogant, provocative urban luxury found its showcase—where it could display, where it could *be* itself, though for closed-circuit viewing exclusively.

Not that I disliked seeing pretty women and smartly dressed men go by, but the unrelieved luxury grew stale. So I chose this corner where the café forked, on the upper level, next to the telephone, and force-fed my fictions with idle chatter, while filling the void of my inner room with a tiny television screen on which came and went, "live," whatever figures reached the top of the stairs and paused wondering where the toilet was.

Certain beautiful women who set the streetdecks creaking, who in their passage displace as much air as a supercruiser does water, "sex-bombs" they used to call them, today slender as planks in the hairy thrill of their furs, with smiles frozen by fixative, happening in from the street and reaching the head of the stairs, would seem not to have to "go" at all, would never for a moment acknowledge their merciless stripping by my glance, while on reappearing they would assume that "nothing happened" look with which one leaves church after lighting a candle to the Virgin, as if at no point had they pulled their furs up and their panties (if they wore them) down, then wiped themselves dry with the pink "facial quality" paper that fluttered into the bowl like a moth singed by the lampfire. How I despised those women!

On the other hand I was immensely stirred by some Japanese tourists, two by two in dovelike innocence, petite, modest, forever on the brink of tears, who with lowered eyes entered the toilet and emerged lowering their eyes, heads bent, double-jointed geishas.

With mothers I was helpful. Seeing them burdened with their broods, I eagerly pointed out—down the corridor to the booths—where one goes to vote.

And I timed all these women. They stayed twice as long as men. None emerged looking quite as she did on entering. The inexorable mirror required of each some freshening, some combing and brushwork, a restoration of the personal icon.

But over fifteen minutes had passed, with no sign of the Stork. The waiter shrugged when I mentioned it. Many addicts, he said, used the toilet for their fix. However the Stork hadn't struck me as one of those—an English tourist, rather, in the tracks of Byron or Keats. At last even the waiter grew anxious. Together we entered the rest room. From under the door of a booth his shoes' worn soles grinned broadly at me. Was he laid out flat? I climbed onto the hopper in the neighboring booth and looked down. Luckily he was absorbed in reading, there on his marble throne, feet outstretched, at ease. I reached across and pulled the chain. At the splash of waters he quickly rose and fled.

How else, I ask, how else am I to fill this fearful void caused by her leaving me, running away with my best friend? The faithless slut. It's all over. Together they caught a train—destination unknown. It's happened as I knew it would, sooner or later, inevitably. Things pile up in time and force a solution. He seduced her, stole her from me—I who was patiently helping her to grow, to unfold, to become (in a word) my own creation. Enter then the devil in angel guise, the gooseflesh spy arrayed in magical tints. What was I to do? Throw myself into the river? To what end? To the sound of what rejoicing from on high? Instead, I chose immersion in this therapeutic public bath. Crowds heal the wounds you thought incurable. Face it, you too are an animal, with more or less the same problems as the rest of the species.

I understood as much from the telephone located next to my table. It is reserved for long-distance calls—local ones can be made on the ground floor—and bears a striking resemblance to an upright pinball machine: signs, numbers, blinking lights, all that fantastic oddity electrified by a coin. First you feed it with a deposit of small change, the amount depending on where you are calling, which then, if the call is completed, you must keep supplementing at short, regular intervals. Like an hourglass, each grain of sand a coin.

I became an unwilling witness to some genuine tragedies. One afternoon a young woman was explaining to someone that the "other man" he had surprised her with was in fact only a childhood friend (ah, these women, they're liars, all of them) and with such fluent sweetness that Someone was surely on the point of believing it (she must be good in bed, I thought, how else could he swallow such crap from a slut like that) when suddenly her coins ran out, a warning bell jangled angrily for more—but where to get them? The line went dead. She ran downstairs to the cashier, returned with a fistful, fed the machine, dialed the number. The fuse, however, had fizzled out. In his other town, his other country, his other world, Someone wasn't answering. That was that. The spell had snapped. A few more coins and she might have unbound from his brow that crown of horns she herself had set there. At last she replaced the receiver, and her original deposit poured forth in a glad jingle.

Tears in her eyes, she now came to return the single coin I had loaned her, slumping against me as she did, so that I positively sensed within her loose furs the warm, full breasts athrob with milk. She was weeping now against my shoulder, the shoulder of a stranger who had briefly helped, while I stroked her hair. At heart I was delighted by her anguish—all women being, to my absolute certainty, at least potential whores. Someone had first done to her what she hadn't quite had time to do to him. The question was merely technical.

I offered her a drink, and before she could reply ordered a double cognac from my friend the waiter.

"I don't . . . I don't drink," she half sobbed.

"You need it. It will do you good."

She looked at me now for the first time, as if she had never seen me before.

"There is some kindness in the world," she murmured more to herself than to me.

"Ah, we screen people, you know . . ." I took care to leave my meaning ambiguous.

She blotted a tear which threatened to ravage her beautifully painted face.

"Down the hall to the left," I suggested, happy to have at last established a link between the two: telephone and toilet.

Without embarrassment she rose and left. Hard as I tried, I failed to avoid dishonorable thoughts. Insistently my mind spun with *her* phrases, phrases uttered before she left me: woman biologically superior—three holes instead of two—ducts of excretion separate from that of pleasure—man on the other hand—both sperm and urine passed through the same hole—obvious inferiority of male sex, etc.

The lovely stranger returned, stranger than ever: painted, dry-eyed, coolly wondering, "Should I try that number again?" (and what was I meant to answer?) as sip by sip the cognac turned into a launching pad for her morale.

I led her finally to the inner lounge which has a television set. A Western was playing. A number of young, embracing couples were watching the film. Again, the magic of togetherness, the therapy of crowds! Common images were creating common dreams, common ideas. Every morning at the supermarket I hear the previous evening's programs being discussed. So there I was, the 3-T man. Toilet, telephone, television. And nuzzling her soft furs I was almost comforted.

JUVENILIA

MADONNA

The sun was a disc of amber in the sky when Mlle. Plessis arrived at the Baldwin home. She was not an old woman, but gave the appearance of having seen happier days; she looked so frail to the butler when he opened the door for her that he half expected her to be blown across the threshold, but she only smiled and said she was the new governess and that she hoped she wasn't late. The man nodded mysteriously, as if to confirm her suspicion of tardiness, lifted her two suitcases with an air of extreme martyrdom, and requested her to follow him up the staircase. The upstairs hall was narrow and somber, paneled in knotty pine; it was hung with several dull etchings, including a drawing of Wordsworth's tomb and a view of the Magellan Straits. At the end of the corridor, the butler paused, then opened a white door, adorned with a knocker in the shape of a griffon grimacing in green bronze.

"Mrs. Baldwin would like to see you whenever it's convenient," he said in a tone which implied that it was convenient as soon as possible. "She's in the room at the head of the stairs."

Mlle. Plessis bobbed her head. "Thank you very much," she smiled.

The room, surprisingly enough, was airy and delightful. Two large windows, curtained in yellow chintz, presented a view of the lawn and the

Lawrenceville Literary Magazine, February 1942.

apple orchard. Unconsciously she straightened a small picture on the wall and surveyed her work with the care of an artist. But, she thought, I mustn't keep Mrs. Baldwin waiting. She started for the door, then stopped. She would unpack just one thing. With infinite caution she opened her smaller suitcase and removed with loving fingers an object wrapped in tissue paper, unwrapped it slowly, and folded the paper again. It was a slim Madonna made of age-yellowed ivory and mother-of-pearl. Tenderly she set it upon the bureau and remarked to herself how well it looked standing there, and how modest and becoming a blush the setting sun had painted upon the smooth cheeks of the statuette.

Mlle. Plessis was humming one of her favorite tunes—the air of the Happy Shade from *Orfeo,* to be exact—as she went back down the hall. She knocked on Mrs. Baldwin's door, and obeyed the bright "Come in."

Kitty Baldwin was trying to look very occupied at a delicate mahogany desk. She glanced upward at Mlle. Plessis with that fine expression of questioning mingled with polite surprise which she had perfected during twelve years as a wife.

"Mlle. Plessis?" she smiled. "Do sit down."

The older woman drew up a chair and fingered the hem of her dress.

"These references are quite excellent," said Mrs. Baldwin, turning over two or three letters, each with the familiar salutation, "To whom it may concern." "I've checked them all, of course, and they were confirmed most heartily."

Mlle. Plessis almost allowed a smile to cross her face.

"There's just one thing, however," said Mrs. Baldwin with a pout, "that I hadn't thought of before. You are, I believe, of the Catholic faith?"

The governess nodded.

"Well, I'm afraid—" said Mrs. Baldwin with a tactful smile. "You see, our children have always been strict Protestants and—" (the smile developed a shadow of falseness) "although my husband and I have nothing whatsoever against the Catholic religion—I really don't know, unless—" Her eyebrows arched in thin crescents.

"Naturally, Madame," said Mlle. Plessis, talking and thinking very rapidly, "I shall do nothing to influence the children in any way. I shall take pains to raise them according to the requirements of their own faith.

I have met with this problem before, Madame, and you may be assured that I will not fail you." And with her eyes she said: "Let me stay! Let me stay!"

"Well—" mused Mrs. Baldwin.

"Madame, I assure you," echoed Mlle. Plessis.

"All right, we'll give it a try," said Mrs. Baldwin with no great optimism, "but only because of your references. If I should find that it doesn't work out, then I'm afraid nothing can be done."

"Of course, Madame," Mlle. Plessis said happily. "I understand perfectly."

Then Mrs. Baldwin swallowed a yawn, lowered her eyes to the vermilion lacquer of her fingernails, and said that since the children would spend quite a bit of time in the governess's room, she did not think it wise to have any "Catholic ornaments" about as they would only "intensify the religious differences."

Mlle. Plessis said that was understood, of course.

But when she was outside the room, she gasped with the pang of realization. Her Madonna! Her beautiful Madonna! She almost ran down the hall to her room. Sadly, tenderly, with fingers of cold glass, she lifted the statuette from her bureau and placed it with a sigh, face-downward in the top drawer.

There were two children, Isobel, who was eleven, and the seven-year-old Michael. Both were plump and good-natured, and they instantaneously adored Mlle. Plessis and compared her most favorably with their departed Nannie and her reign of tyranny. The new governess had more than her share of free time, for almost each afternoon Mrs. Baldwin would take Isobel and Michael horseback riding, a sport of which they were excessively fond. And at that time, Mlle. Plessis would open her bureau drawer and remove from its depths the Madonna made from mother-of-pearl and old ivory.

It had been given her one day by the kindly old abbé of her village, which was situated a few miles distant from Marseilles, within view of the sea; it was redeemed from the completely commonplace by its church, which was one of those exquisite examples of pure Gothic architecture. The village was inordinately proud of its "cathedral," as the villagers chose to call it, and it caused a sizeable tourist trade which even more endeared it to them. It was indeed a magnificent structure with splendidly dignified lines and antique carvings of great beauty. The abbé loved his cathedral as one might love a human being; Mlle. Plessis could recall his saying that it had more personality than any man or woman he had ever known. The villagers were extremely fond of their abbé, and would attend all his services if for no other reason than to enjoy his pleasant smile of welcome.

Then there had come a very beautiful day—beautiful in its anguish as well as in its joy. Mlle. Plessis had gone to the cathedral to pray for her younger sister who was dying from rheumatic fever. It was difficult to pray; she was tormented with memories of those cruelties which children unwittingly inflict upon one another. One day she had twisted the little girl's arm until the child wept with pain; once she had purposely broken the china head of a well-loved doll. Hot tears of remorse ran down her cheeks until she felt the cool, strong hand of the abbé upon her head. Mlle. Plessis has long forgotten his words; she now only remembers that he spoke to her in his low, mellifluous voice and that when she was quite calm again, he gave her an image of the Madonna, and told her to have courage.

When the events of that memorable afternoon had been recalled to her—made even more poignant by the bitterness of time—then Mlle. Plessis would laugh softly to herself, or perhaps she might even cry a bit. She would gaze for long moments into the passionless, medieval features of her Madonna, with the curiously sorrowful expression about the eyes, which made the whole face look like an ancient mask, with just a glimpse of the real self showing through. She would caress with her fingertips the cool, dry ivory which formed the face and gown, and the polished hardness of the mother-of-pearl cloak. Perhaps she might think of her home and of what she left behind—her furniture and her books. Of all her possessions only the Madonna remained, and through the years it had become somewhat of a symbol of what she had owned and of what she had been. And now it had to be concealed in a drawer, hidden from sight, very much like her own past.

With a start, Mlle. Plessis would wake from her dream, just in time to put the Madonna back in the drawer and to pat her hair into place, before the children burst into her room to tell her how they had cantered for over two miles, and how Michael almost fell off.

And Mlle. Plessis, a governess once again, would say: "Now hurry and take your baths before you catch cold!"

But there was one afternoon in July when Isobel and Michael were too exhausted from their ride to come racing down the hall. They walked with short steps, breathing heavily. Michael opened Mlle. Plessis's door, and Isobel was about to say "We're back," when they saw their governess. She had fallen asleep in her chair by the open window, her lips parted in a serene smile.

Isobel giggled: "Sh! She's asleep!"

"What's that in her hand?" asked Michael.

"Why it must be a doll!" cried Isobel with a shrill burst of laughter, and Mlle. Plessis awoke.

"Oh!" she exclaimed, sitting up quickly, "I didn't expect you this early."

"Early?" said Isobel. "It's six o'clock."

"What's that in your hand, Mamzelle?" asked Michael.

"Yes, show it to us!"

"No, Isobel," said Mlle. Plessis, holding the statuette behind her back. "It would not interest you at all. Now hurry and take your bath, or you'll catch your death of cold."

But Michael had sneaked behind her and with a shout of triumph had seized the Madonna from her hands. "I've got it!"

"Michael!"

"Look, Isobel! It's a statue."

"Michael!" gasped Mlle. Plessis in terror. "Give it back to me!"

"Give it to me, Michael," said Isobel, reaching for the statue. "It's so pretty."

"No!" shouted Michael in a frenzy of excitement. "It's mine!" And he began to leap around the room, screaming and laughing hilariously. But suddenly he tripped on the lamp cord, and he fell, losing grasp of the Madonna as he did so. It shattered on the floor.

"Michael!" Mlle. Plessis's voice rose in agony.

"Look, Michael," said Isobel, "what you've done! You should be ashamed of yourself, breaking Mamzelle's statue." She ran to put her arms around the governess's neck. Mlle. Plessis knelt by the fragments of her Madonna, and tried ineffectually to pick them up and to keep from weeping at the same time.

Neither child had ever seen a grown-up cry. They regarded adults as almost magical creatures, subject to no emotion except occasional anger or joy, and the sight of an elderly woman sobbing her heart out was a revealing and strangely pathetic vision.

"You've made her cry," whispered Isobel staring at Mlle. Plessis. Then after a moment she said with determination: "Michael Baldwin. I'm going to take you to Mother this minute, and you're going to have to buy Mamzelle another out of your allowance!"

Somehow Mlle. Plessis managed to get to her feet and stop the little girl before she left. She could almost hear Mrs. Baldwin's distinct voice lifted in surprise. "A statue of the Madonna, Mlle. Plessis?" And then she would add, because she never forgot anything, "But I thought it was all settled about your religious ornaments."

So the governess smiled. "Don't bother, my dear Isobel. And you, too, Michael. We'll just forget all about it. And I don't really care about the statue. It—had no value."

And the children stood on tiptoe and kissed her where the tears had been.

ANGEL OR EARTHLY CREATURE

Supreme in the realm of gems is the diamond whose fire is alternately blue and white, and whose glitter proclaims the mastery of the cutter's work. So precious a jewel is revolved between thumb and forefinger with awe and pleasant surprise, for at every angle, the stone catches the light with equal brilliance. Such a diamond is, in the respective world of literature, Elinor Wylie. Her poetry may be divided into headings and subheadings that parallel the intricacies of her own mind. Her verses have been "carven to cut and faceted to shine,"* and may be viewed from any point with the same wonder and pleasure. Beginning early in her childhood with the spiritual devotion to Shelley which influenced a great part of her life, through the private publication of her first slim *Incidental Numbers,* and culminating in the last supreme proof of her talent, *Angels and Earthly Creatures,* her skill as a poet developed into positive genius. Her writings are the best testaments to her success; she is never artificial in her verse, but this sincerity of form and content is perhaps the only quality that can be said to be representative of all her poems. She was in real life a creature of moods, as she confessed in the profile written by her for *The New Yorker:*

Lawrenceville Literary Magazine, October 1942.
* Sonnet: "Nancy."

> *Sometimes she gives her heart, sometimes instead*
> *Her tongue's sharp side. Her will is quick to soften.*
> *She has no strength of purpose in her head*
> *And she gives up entirely too often;*
> *Her manners mingle in disastrous ways*
> *"The Lower Depths" and the Court of Louis Seize.*

This changeable personality produced poems that are quite as varied in mood and subject matter. Some are tinged with quick humor; some are lyrics of great beauty; there is an intellectual side to her writings, while much of her verse has a distinct strain of romantic medievalism and mysticism.

Of all these, I feel that the most interesting are the two which were in great part a result of the influence of two poets—John Donne and, of course, her beloved Shelley. Although Elinor Wylie's love for the latter individual was present throughout her life, I think that by the time *Angels and Earthly Creatures* was printed, she was more under the spell of Donne. Up to this point, she believed that she actually *was* Shelley, and that by some strange act of destiny, his soul was transferred to her own. At other times, she fancied herself to be his closest friend, but always she had felt that he was present at her side to inspire and protect her. She voices this feeling in the incomparable ninth sonnet of "One Person":

> *A subtle spirit has my path attended,*
> *In likeness not a lion but a pard;*
> *And when the arrows flew like hail, and hard,*
> *He licked my wounds, and all my wounds were mended;*
> *And happy I, who walked so well-defended,*
> *With that translucid presence for a guard,*
> *Under a sky reversed and evil-starred;*
> *A woman by an archangel befriended.*

Surely this is proof of the mystical association of the two. She had a love for his spirit that was a chaste and burning worship; she preferred his company rather than the lowering of herself to human affections. But in the same sonnet, she renounces him completely:

Now must I end the knightly servitude
Which made him my preserver, and renounce
That heavenly aid forever and at once.

It is strange, to say the least, that so amazing and beautiful a connection should be severed voluntarily. But there is an extremely personal reason for it. Carl Van Doren, in his autobiography,* tells us that, while in England, Elinor Wylie met a man whom she instantaneously adored; they were together no more than four times, then parted forever. From that experience came the sonnet sequence which ranks with the world's great love poems. It was written in a mingling of intense pain—for the poet had suffered a fractured vertebra—and the passionate result of her affair. So compelling was her emotion that she did not even realize that she had omitted a line from the octave of the seventh sonnet. But the important fact is that under the sway of her human love, Elinor Wylie gave up the celestial guide which had led her up to that time, for Shelley could no longer help her.

The inspiration she received from Shelley, before she met her mortal idol, was more a result of her love for his spirit than of any of his poetry. She was influenced by Shelley, the man, not the writer, and wrote far more *about* him than with his work as a model. Such writings included two novels, *The Orphan Angel* in which she supposes that he was not drowned, but picked up by an American vessel and taken to the United States, and *Mr. Hodge and Mr. Hazard* which is less directly concerned with Shelley—although his influence is seen in the character of Mr. Hazard along with a potpourri of the other later English Romantics. She wrote essays and stories about him; some of her loveliest and sincerest poetry is to be found in the short sequence, "A Red Carpet for Shelley," in which she offers to

unroll the rounded moon and sun
And knit them up for you to walk upon

and stain this celestial carpet scarlet with her own blood. Her most treasured possessions were some letters, written in his sacred hand, on the

---

* Van Doren, *Three Worlds* (Harper & Brothers, 1936).

paper which had been immortalized by his touch, while perhaps one of her most enchanting experiences was her meeting with Shelley's grandson, by that time an old man.

One element which sprang from her association with Shelley is that of mysticism, which influences a great deal of her verse. I believe that quality developed from her idea that she was the reincarnation of the poet. She felt that, in some way, she was psychic, and in various phases of her life, was known to have premonitions of accident or death. She attempts to account for this supernatural knowledge in such poems as "Atavism," while "A Red Carpet for Shelley," "Cold-Blooded Creatures," and "A Strange Story"— in which she dies five times before her final death—support her mystic beliefs of reincarnation and divinity. There is also the element of magic in Elinor Wylie's poems, which call to mind parts of Shelley's "Queen Mab" or "The Witch of Atlas," as well as some of Donne's verse, such as the "Song" beginning "Go and catch a falling star." Magic and witchcraft abound in her poetry; she had always wished to write a novel about the Salem witches, one of whom was an ancestor, but this inclination developed instead into *The Venetian Glass Nephew*, which, although not her original intention, is a masterpiece of delicate irony with much of the supernatural mixed in. In her sonnet, "Unfinished Portrait," Elinor Wylie writes:

> *I have been accused*
> *Of gold and silver trickery, infused*
> *With blood of meteors, and moonstones which*
> *Are cold as eyeballs in a flooded ditch.*

This accusation might easily have been a true one. Poems such as "Fairy Goldsmith," "Lilliputian," or "The Madwoman's Miracle" are all steeped in unearthliness. Her style, too, completely apart from her subject, is austere and almost stilted; her words and phrasings are those of another age. Such phrases, plucked at random from her poems, as "archangelic levity," * "sarcastic sigil," † "prismatic plain,"‡ and "force centrifu-

---

* "To a Book."
† Sonnet: "Self-Portrait."
‡ "A Red Carpet for Shelley."

gal,"* sound more as if they had been taken from Donne's work, rather than written by a twentieth-century poet. She is wont to employ such archaic forms of words as "addressèd"† or "disgracèd,"‡ while in some of her verse she used "imagination"§ in six syllables, or "contagion"‖ in four. Such forms as these were in common use during the Elizabethan era, and still existed to quite a large extent in the days of Shelley.

There are several less obvious bonds between the two poets. Each appeared to have been preoccupied with the mutability of life and nature. They realized that nothing, however great, could possibly last. Shelley voices this in the often-quoted "Ozymandias." There was also somewhat of a pagan touch to this conception, since both urge us to be joyful while still we can. Elinor Wylie's

> *It is sad to remember and sorrowful to pray:*
> *Let us laugh and be merry, who have seen today*
> *The last of the cherry and the first of the may;*
> *And neither one will stay*#

appears to echo Shelley as he wrote:

> *The flower that smiles to-day*
> *To-morrow dies;*
> *All that we wish to stay*
> *Tempts and then flies.* **

In a later stanza, the poet advises us to "make glad the day"†† before it is too late.

---

* "To a Book."
† "A Tear for Cressid."
‡ "A Tear for Cressid."
§ "The Falcon."
‖ "Birthday Sonnet."
"Fair Annet's Song."
** "Mutability."
†† "Mutability."

Both had a keen feeling for nature; almost two-thirds of Shelley's poetry has to do with the outside world which he loved so well. Some of his loveliest verse was inspired by the elements of nature. Elinor Wylie wrote less along these lines, but there are enchanting bits of description in "Miranda's Supper" or "As I Went Down by Havre de Grace . . ." More reminiscent of the romantics is the richness and opulence of "Wild Peaches"; in this sequence she states her preference for "landscapes drawn in pearly monotones" and "cold silver on a sky of slate" as opposed to the brilliant abundancy of the "milk and honey" land near Baltimore. Shelley, also, seemed to appreciate the blue-and-silver side of nature, and is more likely to speak of "winter robing with pure snow and crowns of starry ice"* than "springs voluptuous pantings."†

The two were alike in many ways. Beginning with the frank adoration of Shelley, the man, Elinor Wylie gave proof of her worship in innumerable pieces of prose and poetry. In many respects, she patterned her existence on his own, becoming so entranced with their spiritual connection, that she thought as he might have, acted as she felt he would, and—though perhaps unconsciously—spoke in his characteristic high-pitched voice.

But Shelley only accounted for one side of her nature. Just as he was her inspiration for many of her superb lyrical works, another man's influence is seen in her intellectual poetry. John Donne, whose poetic enigmas and philosophical monologues Elinor Wylie admired intensely, was quite as important a factor in her writings. There was nothing she liked better than to "enjoy with Donne a metaphysical frolic," as she admitted in her *New Yorker* profile. It afforded her mental relaxation to concentrate over his letters in verse or the "Elegies" which delve deep into the mind and the heart.

The Donne influence had always been present, and even in Elinor Wylie's earlier works, was recognizable in poems of a metaphysical tone such as "Full Moon" and "A Crowded Trolley Car." In works like these, the poet echoes the Elizabethan philosophers' preoccupation concerning the respective values of the mind and the flesh. This was a matter of great interest in the days of Donne, and Elinor Wylie revives it, bringing

* "Alastor."
† "Alastor."

import and distinction to its challenge. The instances of this struggle to be found among Donne's poetry are too numerous to list; notable are "The Progress of the Soul," "An Anatomy of the World," and "The Ecstasy." His attitude toward the spirit is that it surpasses in importance anything else to do with the body or the mind. He does not speak of "man," but "the soul," letting it stand for the entire person whose body contains it. Elinor Wylie does not disregard the flesh; there is an eternal fight raging inside her—her intellectual, thinking self opposed to the desires and impulses of her body. Her "jewelled brain"* was always set against her physical person, and it was not for many years that she found her own solution. The ways in which she treats this contest are varied and interesting to examine. Either she will cry, "My body is weary to death of my mischievous brain,"† or she will see through her "carnal mesh"‡ and hear her bones weeping to be "bare ivory in the silver air."§ Elinor Wylie was no fool; she comprehended the excellence and precision of her mind, but she also knew what she wanted physically and emotionally. The struggle widened in scope just as her intellect did; as her experience progressed, she discussed this metaphysical problem more deeply. This line of poems culminated in "This Corruptible," a dialogue among the Mind, the Heart, and the Spirit, concerning the Body. The Mind accuses the flesh of being "grosser stuff," the Heart considers it a "fustian cloak," while the Spirit, who is wiser and kinder, appeals to the Body as the "grain of God in power." Here, the poet hints at a reconciliation between the body and the soul, but she clearly states her belief that the spirit is the supreme element, thereby bearing out Donne's doctrines. However, it is not until in the "Birthday Sonnet," when she prays to God to "marry her mind neither to man's nor ghost's" in order that "no drop of the pure spirit fall into the dust," that Elinor Wylie has realized the true solution to the struggle: The soul must be triumphant.

A different instance of Donne's influence and one that speaks for itself, are Elinor Wylie's "Elegies and Epistles"—by which name is titled the fourth part of *Angels and Earthly Creatures*. The poems which make up

---

* "Song" ("It is my thoughts that colour").
† "Nebuchadnezzar."
‡ "Full Moon."
§ "Full Moon."

this section are five in number and in my opinion contain the most interesting and brilliant poetry in all Elinor Wylie's work. They are, for the most part, written in the same form as Donne's own elegies, and if they were deprived of their references to modern matters, might almost without notice be included among his own poetry. They are strange minglings of intellectualism and lyricism; the poet has explored quite thoroughly her own emotions, analyzing them and demonstrating the influence of certain events upon her temperament, but, apart from this reflective attitude, there is such a strength of feeling, such truly intense sincerity that the reader cannot bear not to understand and pity her for her unfeigned emotion.

"The Broken Man," the longest of these, is the story of the poet's childhood devotion to a china figure, which was to her, child, father, and lover. It was broken, and mended with a steel rivet, which metal gradually entered its very soul. In theme and construction, it is not unlike Donne's short elegy, "His Picture." In "The Broken Man," however, the love element is still an important factor; it was not written at such white heat as were the love sonnets, but in a more pensive, philosophical mood. The presence of the beloved man is quite clearly indicated; Elinor Wylie is supposedly writing it to him, recounting how, transformed into the figurine, he broke her heart. The love is less passionate; "The Broken Man" was undoubtedly written after "One Person"—when the first impact of meeting and adoration was over and the time for consideration was at hand. The sonnets were composed in a period of transition; Shelley had been renounced, and her inspiration came solely from her consuming love. But Elinor Wylie was "a creature so clearly lunar"* that she could not bear mortal rapture alone. Her heart and spirit cried out for something more and in this state of mental as well as emotional yearnings, she turned to John Donne as a natural choice to relieve her tension. Two more of these *Elegies and Epistles* are directly comparable to Donne's poetry. These are "The Loving Cup," in which the poet condemns her lover because he has been unfaithful to her, and "The Lie," which is a dissertation upon the subtleties of the various types of lies. In both of these there is the same reflective quality as in "The Broken Man," and the

---

*"Speed the Parting."

object of her affections is also present. In each epistle, Elinor Wylie begins by chiding him. It becomes evident that her love is not quite as strong as it was in the bright days of the sonnets; she is becoming impatient once more for the days when she wore "the hard heart of a child."* So she gradually veered away from her human passion and, guided by Donne, followed—or started to follow until she was cut short by her untimely death—a new twist which heretofore she had never stressed. In my opinion, if she had lived longer, Elinor Wylie would have become one of the great devotional poets of our time.

This side of her poetry remained undeveloped for a long time; among her early works are found a few poems with religious significance, among which are "The Crooked Stick," "The Lion and the Lamb," and "Peter and John." When she began to concentrate upon Donne instead of Shelley, she became interested in his religious ideas and experimented along these lines herself. Though she did not write more than three or four truly holy poems, yet as she approached her death, all of her works seemed to take on a more ecclesiastical tone. She was a fervent believer, as was Donne, in the immortality of the spirit—that God who made man would surely not destroy him completely at his death. Donne wrote in one of his "Holy Sonnets":

Thou hast made me, and shall thy work decay?

while Elinor Wylie voices the same thought in the "Letter to V——":

I can't believe the hand that made me
Shall so unmake me in the end.

Her belief in man's divinity appears constantly throughout such poems as "A Crowded Trolley Car" and "Farewell, Sweet Dust," and it is repeatedly stated in Donne's holy poems.

An outgrowth of this belief is the idea expressed in perhaps the most beautifully restrained piece of poetry that Elinor Wylie ever composed. In the "Birthday Sonnet," she wishes to be attached to neither a human

---

*"Beauty."

nor purely spiritual devotion. She will be preserved by her Maker apart from all others, in order to be prepared for the day when she will be lifted to His side. It is interesting to note that Donne expresses the same desire in "The Litany":

> *From this red earth, O Father, purge away*
> *All vicious tinctures, that new fashioned*
> *I may rise up from death, before I'm dead.*

I cannot deny myself the pleasure of quoting this "Birthday Sonnet," for in it is revealed the solution to the poet's emotional struggle. She realizes that she is not made for mortal love alone, and also that the mystical connection she held with Shelley was based too much on make-believe to satisfy her completely. The entire contest between her two loves resolves quietly and naturally into her one true worship of God. It takes this final realization of her heart's desire to bring Elinor Wylie to the peak of her genius as one of the truly sensitive and inspired poets of our time.

> *Take home Thy prodigal child, O Lord of Hosts!*
> *Protect the sacred from the secular danger;*
> *Advise her, that Thou never needst avenge her;*
> *Marry her mind neither to man's nor ghost's*
> *Nor holier domination, if the costs*
> *Of such commingling should transport or change her;*
> *Defend her from familiar and stranger*
> *And earth's and air's contagions and rusts.*
>
> *Instruct her strictly to preserve Thy gift*
> *And alter not its grain in atom sort;*
> *Angels may wed her to their ultimate hurt*
> *And men embrace a spectre in a shift*
> *So that no drop of the pure spirit fall*
> *Into the dust: defend Thy prodigal.*

•

This has been the story of Elinor Wylie and her Shelley and her Donne. I do not know how much of it is true; what I have written is based upon actual fact and my own interpretation of the poetry involved. As an introduction to "One Person," she wrote:

> *Although these words are false, none shall prevail*
> *To prove them in translation less than true.*

I hope I may use these lines as an apology for this essay, which I have intended to be a tribute to a great writer and a great personality.

Undergraduate Comment

Winter being necessarily the season of intellectuality, we have occasionally caught ourselves (before an open fire with the cold night eyeing us somewhat ominously through thin oblongs of glass) meditating upon the profounder aspects of Life and Time. It might have come about—as it did in my particular case—at a rather out-of-the-ordinary beer party, designed as a formal welcome to the four-and-twenty new freshmen with emphasis laid upon the recapturing of those proverbial college days which have somehow eluded us for the past year or so. The evening began, reasonably enough, with the faithful drinking beer, the pure in heart drinking cider, and everybody consuming enormous quantities of potato chips—when suddenly a blackout was announced and within a few minutes College Hall was properly quite black. Then occurred a fantastic transformation: as a silhouette is often more striking than a colored painting, the entire unspectacular gathering underwent a change into a definitely Mephistophelian bacchanal in black and red, the red supplied by innumerable cigarettes which like confident fireflies moved and brightened and vanished. A match would strike, and for a moment shadows towered on the walls. Most of the revellers were at the piano, singing loudly and gaily. It was in a way magnificent, but even more so from a distance, the

Amherst Graduates' Quarterly, February 1944.

laws of perspective being observed, when the noise and movement seemed less real but more complete. A misty moon, silent and immobile, clung to the skies. There was a question asked, one might have thought, but it could not be answered; there was a vision set forth, but it could not be translated. It might have been blind frivolity—or courage equally blind. Mostly, perhaps, it was the ability to forget—an art confined to those who have nothing terrible or splendid to remember—which made the experience unforgettable. It was unforgettable because it was something that had not changed, change being all that we have to fear and to cherish. We do not want a world where change does not exist; we want a world of change; but it is gentle and consoling to recognize traces of what is intrinsically changeless, as we did that night.

It is tiresome after a while, though, to probe surfaces, as I have done in order to find a truth which in all probability is not remotely true. Words as such are notoriously inadequate to describe what is not meant to be described, and surfaces are often better and more rewarding. The most evident surface of the autumn season has been the brief blossoming of "pea-greens," momentarily discarded but now revived and worn with mingled emotions by all freshmen. The caps were unfortunately not a vegetable green in color, rather a venomous emerald to the purist's eye, but this detail has been charitably overlooked by all concerned. With these appeared, "to avoid embarrassment," a rather painless set of rules, foolproof instructions as to wearing and use. They were to be worn all week but for the Sabbath, tipped to professors, and so on. One particular faculty member (who shall be nameless) mentioned his surprise to notice the caps and the phenomenal courtesy of their bearers. I told him we were obliged to salute all masters in that fashion; he was disappointed.

"I thought it was a spontaneous act of respect," he said.

Our sense of humor—laughter being germane to all seasons—is still with us. We still smile as we curse the army and navy for having taken over the college with fiendish thoroughness, and our delight is tempered with incredulity when we actually meet a fellow student upon the campus. A further novelty for freshmen is Public Speaking; we stand in front of a room full of evil eyes and with dreadful seriousness make discourse upon secret weapons or politics. The movies still attract us but do not improve. Occasionally we will ask ourselves what is lacking, why we seem obscurely estranged from what we had always fancied life to be. Unreal is stronger than real. We are suddenly cold. Setting aside our imaginings, we put on our coat and pea-green, shuddering at the color, our hearts set on nothing more amazing than a hot chocolate at Valentine. Almost as green as our cap, though mid-November, is the grass outside; a mild winter . . . ? But opening the door, we see that it is snowing very softly and whitely. The sky is altogether plumed with flakes, a faintly absurd but lovely miracle.

THE TRANSFORMATION OF RILKE

It is perhaps not remarkable that the two leading poets of modern Germany should be so far apart in nature and aspirations. Out of the great confusion attendant upon the development of German Romanticism, several courses of individual action or reaction could conceivably have been adopted. George chose the impersonality of certain Greek temples—polished, white, aloof, the refined elegance of contemplation and execution implied by them; the empty marble eyes that conceal what might have been unique in the model have the same quality found in his poems. Rilke, on the other hand, with his passion for endowing everything with life, finds in a headless stone torso of Apollo more meaning and individuality than George discovers when he is treating a human being: "Du schlank und rein wie eine flamme . . ." It is safer, certainly, to speak of the most intimate things in securely generalized terms, but what we look for in poetry beyond pleasing language is a quickening of knowledge, an intensification of what happens to *us*, which can only be found in a poet like Goethe or Rilke who has plunged into the flow of experience and found his wisdom there. And we must make this concession to the poet: we must take him at his word, accept or at least see the truth he is

Yale Poetry Review, Spring 1946.

making clear, and acknowledge that it is in one sense true if for no other reason than that it has appeared so to him.

It is not a question of the authenticity of George's vision. It is simply that, compared with Rilke, he exhibits a baffling lack of vision in, paradoxically, a highly unprosaic manner. His lines have the fascinating secrecy of a shell from which all that was alive and warm has vanished. Whereas the obscurity of Mallarmé is the result of a highly complex philosophy and an equally difficult verbal facade, George's is less easily defined; he is investigating, except in a few of his landscapes, something that has meaning only in his most private experience. Even when he supposes we have understood him, our interpretation will be refuted by one of his intimates who alone know what he wished to say. Interest in his work, if it is to be sustained for any length of time, becomes by necessity a process of increasingly microscopic analysis, involving finer and finer points to be settled. Rilke's poetry, however, more and more expands the physical and spiritual landscape, like the very roses he depicts in so "bewilderingly beautiful" a manner, an "endless moving out, / space-consuming, with no space for that space / to take, for things nearby diminish. . . ." Wherever his eye falls, his vision is so filled with reverberation and suggestion that what he has failed to see becomes unimportant by comparison.

What many do not realize in respect to the attitude of the artist is that the "detached" or "objective" aesthetic viewpoint can nevertheless be a highly individual and human one, one that can be appreciated by a larger audience than the emotional, obscure, subjective approach. The keenest understanding comes only when the eye and the emotions are both unclouded. Rilke's detachment does not imply an absence of sympathy, but the creation of a symbol out of the single thing or person involved. This is not, of course, an original technique in poetry. George created his symbols also, but more brutally, more egocentrically, one feels, than Rilke; and, more important, George's self is seldom in the background, even in what are considered his most perfect lyrics:

> *Du bist mein wunsch und mein gedanke*
> *Ich atme dich mit jeder luft*
> *Ich schlürfe dich mit jedem tranke*
> *Ich küsse dich mit jedem duft*

This stanza, in which every line contains a reference to himself, illustrates how thoroughly on the simplest level the symbol operates for the poet and for none other. Rilke is invariably more tender, more modest. He turns outward, inviting us to share in his experience, as who should say, "See, it has meaning for you also."

A further point may be made. George's symbolism is to a large extent synthetic; he is more apt to suit his poem to the symbol rather than let his meaning predominate, the symbol serving only to heighten it. His parks and gardens are very conventional settings, and there is a certain glamour in the mixture of nature and civilization found in them—but he is not concerned with this. It is interesting to notice the difference in Rilke's treatment:

> . . . *die Strassen sprühn und klingen,*
> *und auf die Plätzen die Fontänen springen,*
> *und in den Gärten wird die Welt so weit.—*
> *Und durch das alles gehn im kleinem Kleid,*
> *ganz anders als die andern gehn und gingen—:*
> *O wunderliche Zeit, o Zeitverbringen,*
> *o Einsamkeit.*

The park, fountains, streets, all things seen through the child's eyes are alive and full of significance. George's "totgesagten park" (the adjective is again synthetic) is actually dead; neither it nor the beloved wandering through it is sufficiently vivid to arouse or sustain our belief in his vision. "Der Schwan" contains an excellent use of metaphor. Clearly Rilke has used the swan as a channel of communication for his feelings about the nature of death; he could not have first taken the bird and fitted his theme around it. The result is what is achieved by all understanding use of metaphor—the theme is made more explicit and the image more significant by its association with the theme. George does little explaining; he takes pains to avoid the humble image, except in rare cases when he speaks of a blue, the color of indigo used by washerwomen. Even this, however, is the naïveté of the ingénue who is nevertheless an accomplished actress. Rilke's sophistication is so natural to him that it retains a great deal of the childishness in which it first developed; he consequently is never obliged to play at being innocent.

Rilke's gradual spiritual maturity may be traced in several ways—through his awareness of the supernatural, his concept of death, his treatment of "things." This last is perhaps Rilke's most unique achievement. The first phase of his relations with the world is concerned with an unusually sensitive glorification of it. In his earliest poems the pleasure motif predominates—"Ich liebe vergessene Flurmadonnen." This develops with gathering complexity into such remarkable poems as "Der Sänger singt vor einen Fürstenkind," which as poetic language, from the standpoint of pure tonal sumptuousness, richly surpasses anything of George's. Here we discover that "things" come together to form the very personality of an individual; jewels, daggers, brocades, faces, murder, passions—all make up "der Sinn von allem, was einst war."

> *Vergangenheiten sind dir eingepflanzt,*
> *um sich aus dir, wie Gärten, zu erheben . . .*
> *Im dunkeln Dichter wiederholt sich still*
> *ein jedes Ding: ein Stern, ein Haus, ein Wald.*

This poem represents more than pleasure-praise; the subject is too complex for so simple a treatment. The sense is conveyed (for the first time here, and to an increasingly larger extent throughout his work) that the things are really not valuable to the poet except by their power to arouse reverberations within him. The things breathe out, as it were, an essence rich in a certain quality of meaning, under the influence of which their physical natures evaporate, leaving only this sense of some true being in another realm which is the true country of the poet. In "Rosenschale," a further development, the roses themselves are so outweighed by the wealth of significant conjecture set upon them by the poet (which we realize, from the first stanza, amounts to a moral lesson) that we have no sense of the simple thing we had previously considered a rose to be; instead we begin to understand just what a rose *could* be. Taken out of the context of Rilke's development, this poem would not be successful, and perhaps it is not; he may have made too much of it. Apart from any consideration of verisimilitude, of our own ideas of reality, it nevertheless serves to enlarge our aesthetic vision and is therefore worthy of our attention, if not our praise.

A parallel technique in dealing with "things" is more commonly comprehensible and equally admirable. The method that produced "Der Panther" and "Spanische Tänzerin," though far simpler than the one discussed above, is basically the same, except that the poems are results of less extended contemplation. At this time in his life, Rilke was greatly impressed by Cézanne's works and aesthetic theories. The artistic vision that perceives only what *is*, would be—we can see—quite appealing to Rilke, whose life was spent effacing himself. These two poems and the others similar to them are notable for the control behind them, a quality (not to be confused with restraint) occasionally lacking in the poet. A surer balance between words and meaning is achieved; it is possible for us to see the panther and dancer, not merely what they represent.

As he grew older, and the "things" more elusive, he held on to them as though by some sad necessity. With the appearance of the *Duino Elegies* and *Sonnets to Orpheus,* a crisis seems to have been reached—for example, this statement from the Seventh Elegy:

> *Nirgends, Geliebte, wird Welt sein, als innen. Unser*
> *Leben geht hin mit Vervandlung. Und immer geringer*
> *schwindet das Aussen.*

His metaphors, too, were becoming more and more ethereal: mirrors, music that was the "breathing of statues," unicorns, angels. A transformation for every thing was the only way he could find meaning for it. A few quotations from the *Sonnets* will illustrate:

> *Singe die Gärten, mein Herz, die du nicht kennst; wie in Glas*
> *eingegossene Gärten, klar, unerreichbar.*

> *Wehe, wo sind wir? Immer noch freier,*
> *wie die losgerissenen Drachen*
> *jagen wir halbhoch, mit Randern von lachen,*
> *windig zerfesten . . .*

> *Wie viele von diesen Stellen der Räume waren schon*
> *innen in mir. Manche Winde*
> *sind wie mein Sohn.*

> *Tanzt die Orange. Wer kann sie vergessen,*
> *wie sie, ertrinkend in sich, sich wehrt*
> *wider ihr Süssein. Ihr habt sie besessen.*
> *Sie hat sich köstlich zu euch bekehrt.*

This belief in transformation, as Mr. C. M. Bowra in his essay on Rilke points out, amounts to a philosophy of life, but it is perhaps more workable as a philosophy of art. Only by the metamorphosis of the objects he has loved can the poet hold on to them. They rise again within him, are stenciled permanently there. And yet, up to this point, Rilke had never the courage to renounce them utterly. This would require a new poetic language.

He found this in the French tongue. He needed words of a precision and subtlety that could not exist in his German idiom, rich as almond paste. There was an airiness in French that pleased him, and his *Poèmes Français,* although obviously written with little confidence, form an appropriate conclusion to his treatment of "things." They have wholly disappeared, the animals, landscapes, temples, roses, leaving only the smallest trace:

> *Petit flacon renversé,*
> *qui t'a donné cette mince base?*
> *De ton flottant malheur bercé,*
> *l'air est en extase.*

The fate of his roses is clearest of all. Miss Butler speaks of it as "a deathbed repentance for his lifelong treatment of roses which he had plucked so often and caressed so much, as children maul the animals they love; and he had deflowered them too by using them as symbols for death." Undoubtedly he had overburdened them, but now he set them free again: "Est-ce de toutes ses pétales que la rose s'éloigne de nous? Veut-elle être rose-seule, rien-que-rose? Sommeil de personne sous tant de paupières?" This last phrase, in German, was Rilke's epitaph.

We cannot question the artistic morality of this action if the art we admire is that which combines inner and outer vision so that neither one dominates too forcefully. Although Rilke does not succeed in this combination, his awareness of "things" and all experience is so acute that in spite of the transformation they have undergone they remain more vivid than the gods and glories George employs. Rilke is left, ultimately, with what one supposes he always desired—pure space, a space filled with these "spiritual essences of things," filled with angels, constituting a kind of permanent truth.

Rilke developed to the utmost a view of experience that eventually had to be developed in poetry. To develop such an idea meant in his case that he had to give his life for it, "costing not less than everything," to use Eliot's phrase. He reached the point, in his relations with the inner vision, where a further step would be madness or silence. All things, including language and sound, would then become intangible and inarticulate. Hölderlin discovered this and went mad. Rimbaud discovered it and dared write no longer. Rilke was not driven to either of these ends—he died accidentally. But there is a logical progression from his first poems of praising everything to his last in which he praises nothing, literally nothing. The fact that he was able to do this is nearly of more interest to us than the fact that he did it. The paradox in his poetry is that he has made things infinitely real to us at the same moment that he proclaims them insubstantial. Apart from any consideration of his poetic language, unique religious faith, or skill as a writer, this alone should mark his poetry as being of the greatest importance as a heightening of human experience.

A Different Person: A Memoir

(1993)

For J. D. McClatchy

I

Decision to Go Abroad.
My Dearest Friend and My Latest Love.
A Proustian Party.
A Night in Vermont.

Meaning to stay as long as possible, I sailed for Europe. It was March 1950. New York and most of the people I knew had begun to close in. Or to put it differently, I felt that I alone in this or that circle of friends could see no way into the next phase. Indeed, few of my friends would have noticed if the next phase had never begun; they would have gone on meeting for gossipy lunches or drinking together at the San Remo on MacDougal Street, protected from encounters they perhaps desired with other customers by the glittering moat, inches deep, of their allusive chatter. I loved this unliterary company; it allowed me to feel more serious than I was. Other friends, by getting jobs or entering graduate schools, left me feeling distinctly less so. On the bright side, I had taught for a year at Bard College, two hours by car from MacDougal Street. My first book of poems had been accepted by the first publisher I sent it to. And I had recently met the love of my life (or so I thought), who promised to join me in Europe in the early summer, by which time we should both have disentangled ourselves from our past and present worlds. Was I ever coming back? Yes, yes, one of these days. But of course I would be a different person then.

It took a fair amount of perversity to want to distance myself from my friends, for with them only—never in solitude or with my family—did I feel at ease. After a day that typically included lunch uptown at my mother's bedside, followed by an hour or two of "work" in order to deserve the evening's fun, I plunged giddily into their midst, drinking and laughing and "being myself" until my face ached and it was time to return, alone, to my apartment in the East Thirties. Following me out of the subway, my shadow wavered past a shop I'd never found open, its dark window dingily lettered in gold: LUST'S BAKERY. I slept late. By noon the evening's goblin pleasures left no trace, beyond a dim cranial throbbing, upon the ornate stanza under way about loneliness and pain. So there was a side to the story that my friends didn't know. And just as well, I told myself; the way they saw me—the way I had invited them to see me—was already straitjacket enough. How glad I would be to get away from them.

I was glad also to be putting an ocean between me and my parents. My mother was ill that year with a gastric ulcer, and I knew why. Four years earlier, she and I had each done things the other could not forgive. Since then, despite the rare hour when the old unconditional intimacy shone forth, each had felt a once adored and all-comforting presence slipping gradually, helplessly away. For good? Who could be sure? Our dear ones' behavior is seldom hard to justify; whether it can be tolerated is the issue. With hurt aplenty on either side and no quick or painless remedy forthcoming, it had begun to seem like mere human kindness on my part to speed up the process and distance myself from her. Keeping out of range of my father, on the other hand, might well have defeated me had he not himself, twelve years earlier, taken the first step by leaving my mother and persuading her to divorce him. (It "looked better" that way; and given this latest and most stubborn of his infidelities, what else could she do?) In time a series of heart attacks left him progressively more self-absorbed, less in control. Even so, he was talking of joining me in Italy for the month of May. Not exactly what I'd had in mind, but my father had more irons in his fire than my mother did—two older children, *their* children, business interests, the third wife—and this spell of unprecedented closeness abroad would do for both of us for a long time to come.

As it happened, my father had taken a much earlier step to ensure his children's independence, by creating an unbreakable trust in each of our names. Thus at five years old I was rich, and would hold my own purse-strings when I came of age, whether I liked it or not. I wasn't sure I did like it. The best-intentioned people, knowing whose son I was and powerless against their own snobbery, could set me writhing under attentions I had done nothing to merit. So I looked forward to distancing myself from all that as well, in places where the family name cut no ice, the Firm had no branch office, and I might if need be, like the Duke of Mantua in *Rigoletto*, pass myself off as a poor student.

Friends, family, money . . . wasn't there something else? From the mirror stares inquiringly a slim person neither tall nor short, in a made-to-order suit of sandy covert cloth and a bow tie. My bespectacled face is so young and unstretched that only by concentration do the lips close over two glinting chipmunk teeth. My hair, dark with fair highlights, is close-cropped. I have brown eyes, an unexceptional nose, a good jaw. My brow wrinkles when I am sad or worried, as now. Not that what I see dismays me. Until recently I've been an overweight, untidy adolescent; now my image in the glass is the best I can hope for. Something, however, tells me that time will do little to improve it. The outward bloom of youth upon my features will fade long before the budlike spirit behind them opens—if ever it does. It is inside that I need to change. To this end I hope very diffidently to get away from the kind of poetry I've been writing.

That same March, not long before sailing, I accepted an invitation to read with Richard Wilbur at Amherst College, our alma mater. Poetry readings, in those days before Dylan Thomas and the Beats, had yet to become the rage. Still, the room was filled with faces, and I was proud enough of a few recent poems to fancy they could hold their own in such company. But the mere act of reading them aloud—something I was doing for virtually the first time—quickly disabused me. Despite all I had learned about "tone" from my teachers (many of them right there, nodding encouragement), despite the presence on campus, twice yearly, of Mr. Frost and *his* campaign for the sound of sense, my poems remained verbal artifacts, metered and rhymed to be sure, shaped and polished and begemmed, but set on the page with never a thought of their being uttered by a living voice. As I read, part of me listened to how I sounded, nasal, educated, world-weary as only those without experience of the world can be, and thought how much I would like this sound to change; or failing that, what a relief it would be to live among Frenchmen or Italians, who wouldn't automatically "place" me each time I opened my mouth. At the reception everyone was very kind. Dick Wilbur—his own performance a master class in resonance and poise—asked for a copy of the poem I had closed with. But I returned to New York depressed, with a vision of my inner self as a lone teardrop glittering deep in tissues of shyness and plain incuriosity.

According to Rilke, a young poet can't have enough solitude. I pondered the dictum ruefully. Being alone was not my long suit. Aside from activities that might loosely figure as aesthetic—going to the opera or a museum, reading, writing a term paper or a poem—I was not in the habit of doing things by myself. I was eleven when my parents separated, old enough to be allowed some liberty. Instead I have the impression of proliferating guardians: no longer nurses and maids, perhaps, but schoolmasters, camp counselors, army sergeants. Grown up at last, I was free to board a train to a strange city, but to do so without a companion, or without the promise of meeting an old friend on my arrival, would by then have seemed a great oddity, doomed to failure. Like those children who, undetected until it is too late, lose the use of one eye by favoring the other, I functioned blankly, imperfectly, without a confirming viewpoint. The unexamined life wasn't worth living? Even so; only in my case the phrase meant a life not examined by someone else. This is where a lover came in. For could I truly have contemplated stripping and plunging into the unknown without Claude's life-preserving arms about me?

We had caught sight of each other in January at a party for the publication of Frederick Buechner's first novel. Freddy had been my dearest friend since boarding school. But for him I might have left adolescence behind without ever knowing the perfect admiration, the boundless trust one can, at fifteen, both feel and inspire. Each worried about the other, took to heart his triumphs and setbacks, loved his mother and his jokes.

Freddy and I shared—had indeed mutually cultivated—a quasi-ideological passion for the "literary." The novel in question, finished two summers earlier in a house we rented on the coast of Maine, was called *A Long Day's Dying*, and its ecstatic reception would make him the wonder of that winter of 1950. More New York nonsense to be shrugged off? If so, it would take some doing—wasn't that Leonard Bernstein sitting at the young author's feet? It was then that I met Claude's eyes and remembered him as one of the little group who, four years earlier, saw Kimon Friar off to Greece. Because Kimon was my first lover and Freddy my best friend, I could pretend—by triangulation, as it were—that Claude was perfectly at home in my life, and I greeted him with a warmth that must have taken him aback. He had been brought to the party by Carl Van Vechten. That connoisseur of celebrities was already making plans to photograph Freddy in profile against the backcloth of unironed satin that was his trademark.

Claude Fredericks had a round, fair-skinned face, by turns elfin and exalted, under thinning brown-gold hair. He was a printer, living in Vermont with another man. Thanks to Van Vechten, who was Gertrude Stein's literary executor, they were about to undertake the first edition of an early novella, too scandalous for its day and too forthright ever to fit easily into the Stein canon. He was spending the midwinter months in a hotel on Union Square; his partner had gone farther south. It seemed that the Vermont house had no furnace. By choice? I wondered, as much of the friend's absence as of the furnace's. Yes, said Claude, presumably meaning the latter—he believed in living according to classic patterns. I gave him my telephone number, and he invited me to an Elisabeth Schumann recital a few days later. We both had full engagement books—he because he was so rarely in New York, I out of my dread of solitude—but stole what hours we could together, meeting at midnight on a street corner near where one of us was dining, or walking back and forth between his hotel and my apartment until the sun rose. I wanted to show him off to everyone I knew, as if his discreet person and unfrivolous conversation would explain how little I'd be seeing of them for the rest of my life. Claude, two years my senior, took care that his friends and I didn't meet. By the third week we were both intensely committed, though we had yet to become lovers, and the plan of joining up in the south of France (as soon as the

Stein book was finished and my father's visit over with) took shape. And then? Why, anywhere we pleased. A summer in the mountains, a winter by the sea. We could go to Persia, we could go to Portugal—

"Portugal!" echoed Claude, and the name from then on encoded every delirious possibility of love.

So it was all at once the easiest and most exhilarating thing in the world—this embarking upon a *vita nuova*, as we each trusted it would be. Claude had raised a few questions I found hard to answer. What, for instance, was *Wayne* still doing on the scene? If I no longer loved him or he me, why hadn't I taken back his key to my apartment? Who were all these silly *girls* who greeted me with shrieks and kisses? What did my drinking champagne from a slipper kicked off by one of them mean? This wasn't Claude's world. He had grown up in a small town in Missouri, where nobody had heard of Euripides or Joyce. At fourteen, wearing, despite his mother's upbraidings, a kirtle out of Theocritus and a scowl out of Thoreau, he had raised "Greek vegetables"—beans and turnips and cucumbers—in their front yard. (The people I cared for most didn't, by and large, have fathers. Claude's had faded from view, keeping only minimally in touch after the divorce. Freddy's had killed himself. The trauma seemed in every case to have quickened the child's imagination.) With a dowser's blind instinct, Claude had found and devoured the *Symposium*, the sonnets of Shakespeare and Michelangelo, also a shelf of illustrated medical texts in a neighbor's house, and seen his path shining before him like the rising sun's over a rough sea. To a degree I'd have found inconceivable without his example, he had made—remade—a fussed-over only child into a proud, uncompromising young man. Not that I myself was innocent; I'd read every word in print about Oscar Wilde and knew by avid, pounding heart the juiciest of Havelock Ellis's case histories. But I was immature. My nature, like the slipper dripping champagne, sparkled messily, next to Claude's. I asked nothing better than that it, too, be remade according to his guidelines.

My second-best friend from boarding school, Tony Harwood, had arranged to sail with me. Tony lived abroad but had spent the past ten months in New York. Back when this was an uncommon thing to do, he rented and made livable an enormous loft in Chelsea. His next step was more conventional: he joined the dozens already fluttering mothlike round a young man named Bill Cannastra, whose incandescence I found cheap, perfunctory as neon. Why Tony felt ready, at winter's end, to put Bill and New York behind him I can well imagine but not recall. The unimaginable thing was to leave without a party. After all, a chapter was ending for both of us. How better to signal closure than by some large emblematic gathering to glide knowingly through, like Proust at the end of his book?

Upon Tony's candlelit space over a hundred people in evening or fancy dress converged for pastries and champagne. (It was on this evening, I'm afraid, that I drank from a Miss Morrison's slipper and Claude's patience with my social instincts snapped.) There was a rented piano on which somebody played the kind of music one is meant to sit down and listen to. A soprano sang settings of T. S. Eliot's "Preludes." Tony's guests included quite a few patrons and practitioners of the arts. As I had agreed to pay for the champagne, I was allowed to invite whom I pleased, so Freddy and his mother were there; *my* mother as well, risen from her sickbed—and Claude, whom I now with studied casualness introduced to her. When I wondered the next day what she'd thought of him, she said mildly that she hadn't been impressed. It only strengthened my resolve.

Freddy, aware of my feelings for Claude, came over to greet him. My dearest friend was tall and well made. His large sea-green eyes shone from a face striking for its air of serenity—inviolable, masklike, benign— which somehow dignified whatever issued from it, whether a dirty joke or, as now, a bouquet of charming small talk. Claude looked puzzled—he had other ideas of discourse, even at a party—and presently moved away. It was one more sign of how different my life was going to be, with him. Freddy's Princeton of suntanned girls, gin drinks, and laughter in the primrose glow of late spring afternoons—setting and figures lifted straight out of F. Scott Fitzgerald—already promised little where I was concerned. With equal force I felt both the enchantment and my insusceptibility to it. Our sexual selves, so long untried except in wish, were bearing us off in contrary directions. Now, after putting our mothers into the same uptown taxi, we stood at Tony's, as we made a point of doing at the height of any good party we'd ever attended, in make-believe gazing back upon it from the far side of decades to come. We shook our heads sadly and tenderly over that dear droll distant hour whose participants knew no better than to have the time of their lives. "I still worry about you, old friend," said Freddy softly, almost to himself. He meant that he worried about *us*. Although nothing would change our loyalty to each other, and although he'd just finished promising to visit me in Europe without fail before the year was out, Freddy and I would meet less often from now on and have less to tell when we did. The candles had burned low in Tony's loft; even the younger guests were beginning to leave. We filled our glasses with champagne, and Freddy gave his favorite toast: "*La vie, la vie*—we'd be dead without it!"

Before sailing I went to Vermont with Claude. The handsome white Federal house stood on a hillside far from the main road and any neighbor. Claude had bought it during the war, along with a hundred acres of field and woodland, for next to nothing. Indoors it was very cold; the pipes had been drained since Christmas. Once both downstairs hearths were blazing and my teeth had stopped chattering, I was shown through a number of minimally furnished rooms: here a round table with four chairs, there a lamp. A mattress made up into a neat bed. A wall of books. These, consistent with Claude's decision after a year at Harvard that he would do better to educate himself, were of a breathtaking high-mindedness: Greek philosophers and Latin poets in scholarly editions, Aquinas and Dante, Gibbon and Donne, scores of the Bach Passions and the Beethoven quartets. Twentieth-century authors were strictly limited to "classics" like Frazer and Freud, Pound and Eliot, Joyce and Mann. I couldn't imagine any work of mine ever being admitted to this august senate. It was here, in the library-pressroom, that Claude and his friend, whose life together was now ending, set and printed the exquisite editions they published. The old press, painted dark red and worked by the rotation of one shieldlike wheel at its flank, stood five feet high, a presence challenging and inscrutable as any samurai in full armor. Late in the tour I was glad to see a fully modern bathroom and kitchen. Supper was under way; we would presently eat cross-legged by the fire.

"Who are your friends here?" I asked.

Claude hesitated, laughed, named a literary couple forty miles away. Oh yes, and the farmer's wife (down the hill, across the road) dropped in for tea every couple of weeks. I kept looking at him expectantly. "Friends from New York like to visit in the summer," he finished, looking shy and proud. Outside the glittering panes, night and cold stretched for miles. Was it here that I would live, in this disciplined isolation, if and when we ever came back from Europe?

The fire we slept by died during the night. All too soon day broke through uncurtained windows, a day so cold it sent us howling and dancing into our clothes. I thought of my New York bedroom with its carpeted floor and heavy curtains, which kept out every ray of light, while the steam heat rustled like a housekeeper through the pipes. I thought of my sitting room's dark tobacco-brown walls and black, flowered carpet, where even at noon you needed lamplight. I had a piano and the Mozart sonatas, along with every piece I'd ever learned as a child. And yet it didn't do, at any age, to put one's faith in arrangements. Wouldn't I live a wiser, freer life without twice my weight in scratchy opera recordings, and shelves overloaded with books very few of which were enduring classics? Alas, I had never thrown anything out. In its three small rooms this first apartment held all the accumulated "signifiers" of my twenty-four years—or am I misusing a fashionable term? These were the obvious things to strip myself of, or to turn the key on for an indefinite period, if I was to become a different person. To that worthy end the cold bare light of Claude's house, and the fun and fluency of breakfasting with him by a new fire, felt like a suit of magical properties laid out for me by elves. Let yesterday's tatters be consigned to the flames.

•

A different typeface for that person I became? He will break in at chapter's end with glimpses beyond my time frame. Who needs the full story of any life? Biologists are learning how to reconstruct the complete organism from a cluster of cells; the part implies the whole. Here, too, is a likely spot for the reveries suitable to a pillow book, for gossip, for shoptalk.

I began writing poetry in my second year at Lawrenceville, soon after meeting Freddy. He had shown the way by publishing in the school literary magazine eighteen lines (they gave it a whole page) in a delectable pre-WWI mode. Cathedral imagery prevailed; "my soul" was the protagonist, "pale" and "dim" the most telling epithets. It was like a sibylline, aesthetic maiden aunt of those red-blooded lyrics by Housman or Rupert Brooke—the masters at St. Bernards had to blow their noses after reading them aloud—and I hailed it at fourteen as the real thing. I set about modeling my writing—not just poems, my very handwriting—on Freddy's. Oddly, those period pieces took little work to imitate. The school magazine soon devoted a page to my "Sonnet" apostrophizing a "maid of Nippon," ivory-pale and passionless on her painted screen. Now that Freddy and I were both in print, we had our mothers buy for us DePinna's identical overcoats whose contrasting lapels, formed by the lining of artificial, cocoa-brown fleece, suggested, to none but ourselves, something Oscar Wilde had been photographed in. We wore them all through college.

Our teachers meanwhile were busily exposing us to the whole of English poetry from Wyatt to Browning. On our own we pored over the Pre-Raphaelites, Baudelaire, and Verlaine, even the ground-breaking new names in Louis Untermeyer's anthology. Our schoolboy stories and poems gave off a dewy, fresh-faced unhealthiness, a Yellow Book *fever from which Freddy recovered more quickly than I did—though to tell the truth, neither of us evolved very much during those years at Lawrenceville. A precocious adolescent makes do with whatever odd conglomerate of wave-worn diction the world washes up at his feet. Language at this stage uses him; years must pass before the tables turn, if they ever do. Our early efforts nevertheless filled us with wonder. Freddy's poems, just by our being friends, and young, quivered with a live magic barely attached to any historical context. I read them the way a spider in Hagia Sophia, oblivious to the great dome, might have scrutinized her neighbor's web.*

> *My long sealed memory recalls*
> *The perfect shadows we once made on walls.*

Lines such as these, which he wrote at eighteen, embodied for me everything— chaste, cryptic, melodious, infinitely sad—a poet could ever dream of achieving. But Freddy had other strings to his bow, wit and semicomic human presences, like a certain Madame Fogg, who loved her suitor "none the less / When he proposed to her as less the nun / And more the lass"; images, too, that when I got round to him, seemed almost to prefigure Wallace Stevens—"Superfluous as angels in a dogwood tree." I wrote Freddy from Amherst to drop everything and read "Notes toward a Supreme Fiction," saying that it reminded me of him. A tactless move, I fear. Freddy, who at Fitzgerald's Princeton had been gravitating toward prose, now more and more consigned his own poems to a bottom drawer, refused to read a single tercet by that insurance-mongering humbug I claimed to admire, and with no further visible ado became a novelist.

In my second semester at Amherst one of my teachers arranged a tête-à-tête with Robert Frost, suggesting that I bring along two or three short poems. Sure enough we were presently left alone, I and the famous old man bent over my stanzas. When he looked up it was to say kind things; there were turns of phrase he liked, and touches of "seeing" he found original, whereas I knew secretly how much they owed, that year, to Rilke and Yeats. So no doubt did Mr. Frost; only, gentler with students than with their teachers, he hadn't wanted to dampen me by saying so. What he didn't know was how much these juvenilia owed to my gifted schoolmate. I felt obscurely to blame for Freddy's defection from poetry, and lonely in the vast chamber full of voices. But relief was at hand.

II

Tony Puts One Over on the French.
Visit to Kimon in Greece.
Illness and Recovery.

Here I was, off to Europe. My weeks in Paris during a winter break at Bard hardly counted. This time, long unbroken months—years if need be—lay ahead. Claude did not come to the sailing; it would be intolerable, he wrote, to say good-bye in a cabin full of my chattering friends. When I saw the space in question, big as a closet, with double-decker bunks and no porthole, I wondered if I shouldn't have stayed in Vermont with him. (*"Amants, heureux amants, voulez-vous voyager?"* asks La Fontaine in a passage I can recite to this day but have never sufficiently acted upon.) Tony, who had made the arrangements himself at the French Line's office on Fifth Avenue, was already at the purser's desk, two decks up, complaining. Wasted breath: the cabin was ours for the next nine days. So much for my old friend's savoir faire.

Tony had lately spent a season or two in London and Paris, and let it be felt that he knew the ropes. Even at fourteen he had been dazzlingly urbane. Tall and olive-skinned, with the features of, if not a Greek god, perhaps a Sicilian one; all willowy visibility in foxglove-colored tweeds and scarves that trailed the ground; in hushed accents holding forth upon French porcelain, English furniture, and the genealogies of "old New York," he was from the start the most insufferable boy in school, or would have been had he not so roguishly endorsed the consensus. To be insufferable was the role of a lifetime, and he played it with style and nerve. His snobbery exasperated, his frankness disarmed. Tony's was also the biggest "tool" among us—a mixed blessing but one imprinted willy-nilly upon his fans and his detractors alike. The other boys never baited or tortured him as they did me, who, small and bespectacled, lived in provocative terror of them. From Lawrenceville he had gone on to Harvard. Tea-pouring women took him up; he attended meetings of the Vedanta Society. Soon he was referring to Those Who Know and calling what he wrote Poyetry. Behind his back I mocked his literary efforts; to my face he patronized my own. Our friendship, while allowing for flashes of uncommon intimacy, remained faintly unreal, tinged with irony and sapped by worldly claims. Once in Paris, for instance, Tony would be moving on. Friends were expecting him in Madrid.

We had ordered a small Citroën, to use alternately. Tony would drive it to Spain, I would take it over the summer. The car needed only to be picked up; its co-owner, however, bored by the driving lessons he'd begun taking in New York, had neglected to get a license. I secured my own international permit without fuss, but at the same Parisian window Tony's blandishments were met with firm headshakes. Easter weekend was upon us. A driver's test before next week? Unthinkable. At length pure luck saved the day. A harried official at some remote, complacently francophone desk, mistaking an expired learner's permit for the real thing, issued the vital papers. Tony was off. So was I. As I hardly knew how to spend an hour by myself, and a whole month yawned before the rendezvous with my father, I had arranged to visit Kimon Friar in Greece.

My subsequent years in that country and the mix of memory and invention in a novel I wrote about those long-ago weeks make evoking them today problematic. Despite the rapturous letters Kimon had written me during his two previous stays there, I'd formed few expectations. Unlike Paris, where the most banal sidewalk set me quivering because Debussy or Wilde or Cocteau might have set foot on it, Greece and all its splendors would have to work long and hard, like Greek immigrants in the slums of New York, to earn their keep in my blocked imagination. My plane arrived at twilight; Kimon was waiting; the Athens we entered was dark, cheaply lighted, full of language. Having taken some ancient Greek at college, I could transliterate the billboards and street signs. But the great, the single luxury now freely available in this society shattered not only by the German and Italian occupations but by the civil war that in 1950 still smoldered in craggy provinces was talk, and this I could not share. Everybody else, from teenage surrealist to white-haired bootblack, was engaged in dialogue, in fluent speech and vehement gesture. New ideas glowed with the lighting of a fresh cigarette. It hardly mattered that these "ideas," far from originating with the speaker, were often little more than conventional responses picked up in a café or from an editorial. A conventional response so deftly internalized as to set eyes flashing and smoke pouring from lips wasn't to be scorned; indeed, it answered to the kind of poem I hoped to write.

Kimon took me to a large popular restaurant in Omonia Square. I sampled politely a number of specialties I had no taste for. He was, I could tell, equally touched that I had come to see him and saddened by the sight of me. Our story was fresh in both our minds. Early in 1945, when I returned to Amherst as a veteran of nineteen, Kimon was teaching world literature to the would-be army officers still on campus. This slight, graceful man, whose waxen brow and bespectacled austerity radiated self-knowledge—at once the ideal of his Greek ancestors and the fruit of his psychoanalysis—resembled no one I knew. Then in his early thirties, Kimon fraternized easily with the as yet small group of civilian undergraduates; some of us began to meet at "his" table in the college dining hall. Soon he was regularly criticizing my poems and I was attending his weekly workshop and lectures at the YMHA in New York, for he had a career quite apart from his duties at college. As a lecturer he performed eloquently. His topics included Euripides and Djuna Barnes, the myth of the Medusa and the symphonies of Beethoven. After the lecture we would stop by the Gotham Book Mart and stock up on poets I'd never heard of. Then? Why not tea with Anaïs Nin, a drink with W. H. Auden, a late party at Maya Deren's? Anything was possible. In a matter of months my existing sense of how to write, whom to take seriously, what to feel, and where to go from there had undergone lightning revisions. Not all of it stuck, but when the smoke cleared, the schoolboy imitator of Elinor Wylie had turned into this new person who read Hart Crane and Robert Lowell with an air of total comprehension and whose own poems— designed, after Stevens's dictum, to "resist the intelligence / Almost successfully"—now began appearing in magazines. By then, too, Kimon and I were lovers. The double goal of numberless adolescent daydreams was being realized.

And yet this first love, so largely the intoxication of *being* loved by such a man, failed to surmount the three obstacles in its path: my own callowness, my mother's horrified opposition, and a year away from each other. On his return from that year, in 1947—I was twenty-one then, able to do as I pleased—I nonetheless told Kimon that I couldn't cope; the break left both of us numb, confused, guilty. He went back to Greece the following spring. Our reunion this evening in Athens bore only the sorriest resemblance to the one we'd imagined together before Kimon's original sailing, when I, a snow sculpture of constancy, had vowed to follow him as soon as I finished college.

Back in our hotel room after dinner, I was still too callow and, yes, too unthinkingly lustful not to take him in my arms. He might have been wiser to rebuff me without a word; instead he explained wryly that his Greek lover had left Athens only hours before my arrival, after a passionate couple of days designed to drain Kimon of every last erotic impulse by the time he met my plane. Had he so dreaded the sight of me? The thought left me morose but flattered. In return for his confidence I could now talk openly to him about Claude, whom he remembered with pleasure, having commissioned him to print a little anthology by the YMHA poetry class. (Claude's having set lines of mine by hand thrilled me like a kiss.) On this new, different footing with Kimon, I might even take in something of the world he now called home.

The next morning—it was early April, warm and blindingly bright— we walked downtown for my sojourn permit. The Tourist Police office, littered with ashtrays and tiny white coffee cups drained to the black silt-like dregs, was lined with dossiers old and dog-eared enough to have been carved in time-browned ivory by a Chinese master. We then went to call upon a friend of Kimon's, the not-yet-famous painter Yannis Tsarouchis, in a vast and squalid bedroom-studio only a step or two from Athens's smartest hotel. It stank of more than cats; a couple of barnacled amphorae served his models as chamber pots. Tsarouchis was youngish, slightly built, blotched and balding. He greeted me in a casual, amusing French I wasn't equal to. At Kimon's insistence he showed a number of small oils, freely and vividly brushed, of swarthy young men in and out of uniform, gazing without emotion at one another from unmade beds or barracks bunks, their bodies virtual cartoons of slim-hipped, lantern-jawed sexiness. The paintings cost little enough; why didn't I buy one? whispered Kimon when our host went to make coffee. What, and hang it in the back of my closet? I blushed, scandalized. Besides, who was the artist? Merely a living Greek, not Monet or Vuillard. . . .

Time for lunch. After changing a traveler's check—twenty dollars stuffs your every pocket with ragged thousand-drachma notes—we enter one of the little vine-roofed taverns oblivious to their imminent replacement, here at the heart of town, by tall glass banks and world-class jewelers. The clientele includes, or so it seems, many of Tsarouchis's models—sailors, policemen, evzones. The latter, allowed in those innocent days to wear off-duty their short, petticoated *foustanellas*, sit with legs spread like resting dancers by Degas. When a phonograph strikes up the bleat and twang of a popular song, one or two of the sailors rise as if hesitantly setting out for a far place. A little cement floor serves their purpose. The dance, grave and slow and in no sense a performance, is never quite so introverted as to exclude the abrupt leap and glad slap of palm on shoe leather and tends to leave the dancer with both his empty glass and his self-esteem replenished. Even the brown marble faces out of Tsarouchis come to life when Kimon addresses them, shares a joke, or asks a riddle, then with a conjuror's flourish presents me as an "American poet who is visiting your country." Does he speak Greek? Not yet? Too bad. . . . But knowing the alphabet, I am able to amaze them by writing their names in Greek letters. The scrap of paper is then reverently pocketed, like a poet's work sheet by a Texas librarian.

The museums were still closed for reorganization in the aftermath of the war. We visited the Acropolis by moonlight and (through a curator Kimon knew) paid our respects to the great bronze Poseidon in his dressing room. But Kimon was eager to take me to his island. Another day, and we had sailed for Poros. Approaching the harbor, our white steamboat passed the headland where I would spend the next two weeks. For over a year now Kimon had been the guest of a Mrs. Diamantopoulos—or Mina, as I was told I must call her. She and I knew more about each other than most people do on the verge of a first meeting.

We were met on the quai, however, by Mitso, Mina's gardener and Kimon's lover. He loaded us and my baggage into a little rowboat over which a fringed canvas awning had been stretched, then, facing us, rowed across the kilometer of pale silken water to Mina's dock. Kimon and he chatted in Greek translated at intervals for my benefit. "He says you have a sincere expression," I was told at one point. So did Mitso. Unshaven, with curly blondish hair and a vulnerable smile, he resembled the models of Tsarouchis not at all. He and his wife and baby lived in one of the cottages on Mina's property. Because of the voracious local gossips, his trysts with Kimon called for the greatest discretion, usually a night in Athens on one pretext or another. Mitso's wife could then rest easy: the abstemious professor would keep her young husband from the fleshpots.

Mina came down to the landing to greet us. She was in her early sixties, with dramatic Byzantine eyes, silvering hair in a bun, and a manner of perfected naturalness. Just as Kimon and I, to the degree that poetry filled our lives, shared a dozen interests and assumptions, so Mina and I, when we met, recognized the upbringing that marked us as deeply as any tribal scarification. Years before Kimon grew up in the linguistic no-man's-land of a Chicago slum, Mina had learned from her tutor in St. Petersburg, where her father was ambassador to the czar, the same manners, the same French and German courtesies, that my beloved Mademoiselle would try (with less success) to teach me in her day. Comfort and privilege, ours from birth, had left us with a lightness of tone that worked like a charm in the right company but could swiftly frustrate whoever wanted, as Kimon often did, to get to the bottom of things. His was the tragic view of life; the affirmation added inches to his slight frame. Mina's view and mine, however we might rail at the given moment, counted on its being seemlier to shrug and smile.

Above the door into the Medusa, as Kimon had named the cottage where I would be staying with him, hung an ominous assemblage, a large grinning head made of hardware and jetsam. Thus Kimon, bent over work under her petrifying eye, could see himself as a latter-day Perseus, saved by the mirror shield of Art. Amused by his own snobbery, he added that Ghika, the maker of the gorgon mask, was not only a renowned artist but a prince. At once my personal snobbery set about ranking him beneath Tsarouchis, as if the misfortune of being wellborn would automatically prevent him from doing serious work. Kimon took me inside. I already knew, from letters and photographs, the two rooms, beds and windows, table and tiled floor. Here, too, I felt at home. Within hours my place, along with the baby's and the dog's, had been secured. I would play the young foreign guest in the ongoing *piccolo teatro* of Mina's domain.

The main house had been designed by Mina's late husband. Tall windows in the dark, paneled library framed views of the bay and the sunny lemon groves on the mainland opposite. This room I also knew from letters as the scene of anguished talks throughout the previous winter, when Mina and Kimon, drawing upon all the experience, irony, and compassion at their command, wrestled with her demon: she'd fallen in love with him. That drama lay safely in the past, Kimon assured me as we sailed towards Poros; they were at last the dear good friends life meant them to be. Sitting down to supper with these grown-ups in the afterglow of their recent ordeal, I kept glancing uneasily at them, like a child who has just discovered what his parents *did* in order for him to be born. By the meal's end, however, I had grown passive, suggestible, at peace. I'd landed in a benign revision of my own family romance: a father who read Yeats, a mother without prejudice—parents whose primary interests were cultural and whose mutual attraction, bewildering to a youngster, had burned off like fog in morning sunlight.

Beneath the gorgon's ghastly smile I wrote my letters to Claude, reassuring him of my love and conveying Kimon's hope that we would return together for a long stay in Greece before the year was out. The small patio in front of the cottage was never quiet for long. Mitso's wife came with a question from Mina—did we want chicken for dinner? The baby was brought to be watched. The dog needed patting. Mina's grandson—a beautiful child of six, crowned with water lilies—ran up to ask the population of New York. Alone for an hour, Kimon turned gratefully to a mountain of books and manuscript on his desk. He was translating the modern Greek poets—and how many of them there were!—into English.

One evening Kimon and I went by ourselves on foot to a tavern on the port; he needed periodically to assert his independence from Mina's household. The food and wine here were terrible—it seemed to be the price one paid for eating where the sailors did—and I wasn't myself the next day or the next. Another afternoon we boated across to the mainland for a festival among the lemon groves: roasting meat, musicians, retsina. Arms draped over each other's shoulders, dipping and gliding in unison, Kimon and Mitso—or was I feverish?—danced the witty "butchers' dance" together. We returned after dark, and I spent the next day between toilet and bed, with boiled rice and tea for nourishment. A doctor came from the village; a white emulsion was prescribed. It helped but not for long. Was it too late for ordinary cures? Weak as a flower, I continued to waste away.

We canceled an excursion to Epidauros. I sat out the mild afternoons in a reclining chair under pines. Mina took to joining me for a half hour at a time. Did I see that mountain across the water? She and her brother climbed all the way to the top of it when they were twelve and fourteen. Yes, and their guide was a notorious bandit, feared throughout the region, but a man of honor too, as bandits were in 1900. He asked no more than the Christmas gold piece they had agreed upon before setting out. How angry her father had been, and how secretly proud, when— Here, with a worried glance at me, Mina rises. What can she get me? Do I need anything? I might have thought, or she might, to have the local doctor's prescription refilled. But such are the risks we run when seeking far from home the loving care we can no longer accept from our parents. Mina's concern for my comfort is that of a hostess, not a mother, and I haven't yet learned how to look after myself. Her serene, candid presence charms me nonetheless. Listening to her talk about Kimon, in my eyes a middle-aged victim of his own habits and attitudes, I begin as never before to see the young man he still is, all fiery daring, resilience, ideals. She loves him as he (or anyone) needs to be loved, for "himself" and not, as I had done, for his greater experience, his faith in me, which I treated so cavalierly. In Mina's company I feel my own youth forgiven, along with my unmasculine tastes. "Here," she says one day. "I've had this ever since I was a child. Would you like it?"—handing me a tiny Russian needle case of green and blue enamel.

A caïque full of young people connected with the British Council arrives from Athens on my second weekend, anchoring in the cove below

Mina's house. The twilight rings with merriment. But they also have the Anglo-Saxon's healthy concern for his bowels—or in this case mine—and the extremists among them want to see me hospitalized. On Sunday evening, with the owners' cabin surrendered to Kimon and his glassy-eyed American poet, we sail for Athens. Half dreaming, I pluck from the shelf above my creaking bunk a memoir by an English traveler. The weather-stained book opens to his account of being received by Mina, before the war, in the house I've just left. My fortnight there recedes (as I blow out the lamp) to the dimensions of a paragraph.

At the hospital I had a room to myself. The nurses were nuns—Orthodox? Catholic? Nobody spoke English. I was given white pills and a painful injection every six hours. By the second day my diarrhea stopped. But I had been so strictly trained in childhood to perform "number two" each day or face the consequences (enemas, laxatives) that I dragged myself each morning to the toilet across the hall, where Herculean labors produced a few blood-smeared votive pellets. When the doctor arrived and asked his one question (*"Avez-vous fait quelque chose ce matin?"*) I was able to answer with a feeble but proud *"Oui."* Whereupon he ordered—like Scarpia's gruesome *"Insistiamo!"*—further pills and injections. After a week I gave up, confessed to failure, and was discharged from the hospital, cured.

Kimon and I flew to Rhodes for some last days together. No Colossus bestrode the entrance to the harbor, but in grassy yards behind the municipal buildings lay monumental heads and arms, fragments of Mussolini's dream. Kimon gleefully set about posing me with the broken statuary; his photographs looked like stills from an unsuccessful screen test for a Cocteau film. We spent an hour in the town's one nightclub. Too refined for Greek music, the band played tangos, to which the beau monde of Rhodes performed a mechanical two-step without variation, like so many windup mice. At the British Council on my last evening in Athens we saw Louis MacNeice, of all people, act the bumpkin suitor in *The Playboy of the Western World.* After that, just as on those evenings in New York after Kimon's lectures, anything was possible. As we drank our cognacs at the Café Byzantion in Kolonaki Square, all the figures who would mean most to me fifteen years hence strolled past our table—or might have been made to do so by only the slightest warping of my time frame: Maria in her perpetual black with movie-star dark glasses, en route to a polyglot dinner party; Tonáki (our darling Alexandrian Tony, not to be confused with my high-handed classmate) on leave from his navy clerk's office in Patras; Strato at nine or ten, the age when Greek males are at their cleverest, his joyous green eyes missing nothing. Save for a screen of undistinguished architecture, I might have seen, gazing vaguely into the purple dusk, the house halfway up the slopes of Lycabettos, where David Jackson and I would spend so much of our long life together. But who in his right mind wants to know what lies ahead?

•

My friendship with Kimon, however smoothed over by these reunions, kept deteriorating. David, for instance, thought him stupefyingly pompous. The day came when we agreed not to see each other or communicate for a while, and twenty-five years passed. Out of sight wasn't, however, out of mind.

Kimon believed that myth was indispensable to poetry. In times like ours, when religion played no vital imaginative role and the political myths were turning to radioactive ash in the hands of the superpowers, the poet had no choice but to live by some personal mythology of his own construction. One day, when the time was ripe, Kimon planned to write a long poem based on Yeats's system: spiritualism, the phases of the moon, the gyres of history. A long poem was the test of any poet's powers. He cited Dante, Milton, Rilke, Pound. What would their shorter works amount to without the great achievements that crowned them? The notion struck me at twenty—at forty, too, for that matter—as a dangerous form of megalomania, and I wasn't buying any of it. But at fifty? Longer than Dante, dottier than Pound, and full of spirits more talkative than Yeats himself might have wished, the Sandover *project held me captive. It was Kimon's dream, only I was realizing it in his stead. In his copy of the poem I wrote: "Dear Kimon, who'd have thought? You would!"*

Then there were Kimon's translations. They began as a grateful gesture toward his heritage—after which he would be free to resume his "real" work, the projected epic, the novel, the theoretical essays—and ended by consuming the rest of his life. Once the first "definitive" anthology had appeared, full of big names like Cavafy and Sikelianos, Seferis and Elytis, he couldn't resist undertaking the thirty-thousand-line Odyssey *of Kazantzakis. That alone* took seven or eight years. Looking up dazed from the task, he saw a new generation of poets. They clamored like dogs round a stag at bay. How could they dream of international renown without being read in English, and who could they trust to bring this about if not Kimon? Critical articles, further anthologies, medals and honors from a government keenly aware of the steps leading to those two Nobel prizes—and suddenly it was close to a half century later. Across from me sat, depressed and short of breath, the cricketlike husk of the man who had given so much to so many and taken so little for himself. If in retrospect his life gave off a paradoxical aura of self-absorption, one had to remember that, whether by accident or design, he had never found the right person to share it with.

Peter Hooten liked Kimon from the first. In 1989 we went to see him in a suburb of Athens where Kimon had moved to escape the bad air downtown. He was recovering too slowly from open-heart surgery, perhaps because his growing dependence upon sedatives left him restless at night and disoriented by day. More than once, he told us, during the past five years, since meeting my new love and seeing what we meant to each other, Peter and I had come to him in a dream, and our happy, wordless presence comforted him. Over lunch we urged him not to live alone, at least for the time being. Surely, said Peter, a student would be honored to occupy the spare bedroom, shop and cook for him, while helping with Kimon's current project, a selection of Kazantzakis's letters. But this had been tried two or three times already. And . . . ? Kimon gestured grimly at his depleted shelves. The books didn't just vanish without help. H. had come to stay with him a couple of summers ago, all friendliness, wanting to bury the hatchet. But when he left he took with him the dozens of intimate letters he had written to Kimon twenty years earlier, before his own success— for which indeed he had Kimon partly to thank—made their undestroyed existence, even at the bottom of a trunk in Kimon's storeroom, a potential threat.

"I'm surprised I still have that," said Kimon, meaning his Tsarouchis oil sketch of the tanned young sailor, cock a fat mauve daub in its inky thicket, glowering from bedsheets at a chocolate-suited buddy. Was it, I wondered, a painting we'd seen that distant morning? "When did I take you to Yanni's studio?" asked Kimon, shaking his head in amazement.

During the 1960s in Athens, when I was forever participating in life studies bold enough to have been dashed off by the master himself, I came to regret *my decision not to buy one that day in his studio. Tsarouchis had in the mean-time grown famous and changed his style. Now that he was dead, his prices, at least for such early work as this, unmarred by what its creator liked to call the bloom of decadence, were skyrocketing. "Oh, wow," said Peter, under the spell of Kimon's little canvas. "Cavafy lives! Let me take you and JM in front of it. Here we go, the flash is set—heads together now. There!"*

I I I

The Roman café is filling up. I am alone for the first time in many months, but without anxiety: my father docks in Naples tomorrow noon, and I shall meet him there. It is dark, yet not dark. Facades and fountains are lit as on the stage. Before long I shall find a restaurant and order not, thank goodness, Greek food but some perfect, undreamed-of *specialità*. Two smartly dressed Roman matrons meanwhile settle themselves at the next table. I have studied Italian at college, have read Dante in Dante's own tongue, and am now about to hear it *in bocca romana*. As the women flip silently through a newspaper, I glimpse my first headline. Thrilling, but does it count as Italian? RECITANO BAUDELAIRE VESTITI DA COWBOYS. A second headline, announcing the death of the actress Maria Montez in her bathtub, holds my neighbors' attention. The elder speaks in a richly derisive voice: *"Almeno è morta pulita."*

The following morning I'm getting dressed, when a sudden awfulness afflicts me. Dropping my pants, I peer through my legs into the hotel-room mirror—yes, there *something* is, but what? A small pedantic voice advises me to look up "haemorrhoid" in my portable (two heavy volumes) *Oxford English Dictionary*. Thus the riddle is solved by a Greek word, in memory of daily heroics in a Greek hospital. The pain, however, stays.

I find my father at the Excelsior Hotel, where a suite has been booked to rest in before we catch the afternoon boat to Capri. He kisses me affectionately. It is always a pleasure to set eyes upon him: silver-haired, his round face lightly tanned, a small, compact figure in smart clothes. I am his youngest child; he has a daughter and son by his first wife. I've come to think of him as less paternal than grandfatherly. He was after all over forty at my birth, and two or three heart attacks have added a decade to his age. Conversation is happily just now out of the question, what with the two American factotums who met his ship, the come and go of waiters with sandwiches and tea, and the excited claims of his traveling companions. On a previous crossing my father enrolled his Negro valet in the passenger list as a banker from Cairo and enjoyed with this undemanding sophisticate a quiet table for two in the first-class dining saloon. This time my sister has talked him into bringing along not only a trained nurse— Miss MacHattie, who properly coaxed could pinch-hit as valet—but Neddy, my brother-in-law's brother and the spiffy grasshopper to his ant. He and I will be sharing a room for the next month. Why Neddy of all people? The reason ought to have been clear: my father dreaded solitude as much as I did.

He also dreaded the company of his third wife, for love of whom he'd left my mother, and her absence from the scene added measurably to the charm of Naples and its bay. That was merely a smoking volcano in the distance, not Kinta with her whims and irascible vapors. After the flurry of docking at Capri and settling ourselves—where was Miss MacHattie's brown suitcase? had Mr. Merrill's caviar been consigned to the hotel's refrigerator?—high above the port in luxury that surpassed even his own arrangements in Southampton or Palm Beach, we could positively feel his blood pressure going down, day by brilliant, carefree day.

Capri. This ingenious toy amazed us by the number of its working parts. Starting from the miniature square with its mix of local and international beauty, any narrow walk led past baker and goldsmith, tinker and tailor. We gawked over fish and vegetable stalls like bumpkins in the

Louvre. Here was produce grown on the island, here monsters "which only the fisher looks grave at," hauled from waters we strolled above. Hoping to please Kinta on his return, my father had abstracted from her shoe closet one of the few pairs she spoke well of. After breakfast we sought out the shoemaker in his wee shop and asked if he could copy them. The man responded, hand to heart. Honored, overcome, he vouched in advance for the signora's perfect satisfaction. How many pairs—one? two? *Twenty pairs?* His expression, as he revised his view of us from respectable spreaders of the wealth to cartoon Americans, never changed. *Benissimo.* The shoes, at a few dollars a pair, would be finished in eight days.

Leaving the shop, we ran into Miss MacHattie, who had ordered some ready-next-day velvet slacks around the corner. Nevertheless she looked grumpy. Last night's noodles and veal in wine sauce hadn't gone down well, and she had no use for the Eyetalians. She was a plain forty-year-old with curls blonde as tin and a good figure; from the first, men crooned like doves and pinched her as she passed. She didn't see how she could stand a whole month of it. My father out of long experience with discontented women shook his head compassionately. "I know just how you feel," he said. "How soon would you like to go home?"

Two evenings later—she was catching the early morning boat—we made a little party of it. Miss MacHattie wore her new slacks, and Neddy telephoned for "Mr. Merrill's caviar" to be brought up from the kitchen along with toast, lemons, hard-boiled eggs, and a couple of bottles of champagne. No one could remember who sent the caviar to my father when he sailed, but we blessed the giver. The tin must have held a full kilo, glistening black and fresh and priceless, for our four selves to consume. We spread it lavishly on toast, washed it down with champagne, spread more, spread even a portion for the hovering waiter, who hoped it was tasty. At orgy's end we had him return the tin, two-thirds empty, to cold storage with Mr. Merrill's name on it. We saw it next on the weekly bill, where it equaled the cost of our rooms. Charged for his own caviar? my father protested. No, sir, this was the *hotel's* caviar; nothing was known of his private supply. But . . . ! (Ah!) *Un momento* . . . Whereupon a tuxedoed gentleman from the great mirrored and chandeliered dining room returned with the quite intact two-ounce glass jar given him for safekeeping on our arrival. No matter; Miss MacHattie'd had her send-off. She was promptly replaced by an Italian nurse, Miss Beltrami, who knew how to flirt and added a festive, continental note to her duties.

Donkeys bore Miss Beltrami and me to Tiberius's villa. A boatman in the Blue Grotto serenaded our gently rocking party. Neddy was already licking his lips at the prospect of a night in Rome with the Cockney divorcée he'd met in a piano bar. My father and I went by carriage to see the faience church floor at Anacapri. On our return, the driver, disapproving of our silence, pointed out a statue in a roadside niche: "*La Vergine.* The Virgin." "The only one on the island," said my father, and I laughed at his joke. A half hour alone with him could be all uphill. *His* talk flowed, the pauses companionable, the delivery frank: a business deal, an old mistress, family stories and boyhood exploits. He had played "semipro baseball" (whatever that was) and piloted a plane. Feeling his love and goodwill as we leafed, side by side, through these albums of his life, I despaired of showing him the least snapshot in return.

Young people often strike their elders as sleepwalking, drugged by youth, heads full of music no one over thirty can hear. Is that how my father saw me? Or did he guess that I was all this while quivering with awareness—of sun and sea, of the lustrous phlegm coughed into his white handkerchief, of the hairs in our coachman's ears and the chip in the Virgin's smile? A thousand details reached me, but like a primitive painter ignorant of perspective, I had no way to order them; the mosquito was the same size as the horse or the purple blossom of the artichoke. Worst of all, this awareness, which ought to have been my lifeline to the world, at present divided me from it, every detail a pane of glass. No doubt the seedling psyche needed time in the greenhouse. Yet I felt stifled, unable to express a thought, my thoughts being primarily erotic. How could I? Hadn't my mother said more than once, looking me straight in the eye, "If your father ever knew about your life it would be the death of him."

Would it? My father despised secrecy. Demystification had been the key to his own great success: no more mumbo jumbo from Harvard men in paneled rooms; let the stock market's workings henceforth be intelligible even to the small investor. I was visibly sharing in the profits of such openness. As our carriage ride ended, my father began a story I listened to with mixed feelings—gratitude for the broken silence, apprehension for the import of any given tale. "When I was about ten years old," he said, "some older boys who lived on our block ganged up on me after supper and started to push me around. I was faster than them; I made it home without getting hurt and complained to my father. He told me, 'Get back out there right now and stand up to them, son. Make them respect you. Sure, you'll get a thrashing. But you'll get an even worse one from me if you don't do what I say.'"

"So you went out?" I faintly asked, recalling that my grandfather wore "a silver plate in his skull" after having been mugged on the streets of Jacksonville. Had that old man with his terrifying white mustaches wanted my father to taste the same medicine?

"I went out," said my father. He turned to face me squarely—here came the homily—then broke into his widest, most charming grin. "And I had better sense than ever to do a damn-fool thing like that again."

The ointments and sitz baths Miss Beltrami suggested for my complaint did little good. As our next stop was Rome, she arranged for the famous English doctor who attended Orson Welles and Ingrid Bergman to see me. My father put on the scowl of a thwarted little boy—he collected doctors—and demanded an appointment of his own. Came the day to settle accounts. We found the shoemaker bent over the nineteenth pair of Kinta's identical spectator pumps; he delivered all twenty to the hotel that evening. A new suitcase was purchased to carry them. "Have you ever known anyone as thoughtful as your father?" Neddy chortled. "It'll be a red-letter day when he gets back to Southampton!" "Don't count on it," sighed my father.

Dr. Albert Simeons had a kindly face, sallowed by decades in India. There he'd run a leper colony, working to stamp out both the disease and the prejudice against its victims. His novel about this experience was soon to be published. A later book, *Man's Presumptuous Brain*, still turns up in popular-science or holistic bookstores. This work claims, as did its author when he examined me, that every physical symptom is to some degree psychological. Even my piles? Absolutely, said the doctor, warming to his theme. He unscrewed his pen to sketch first a normal, then a spastic colon, all the while describing the mental tensions likely to turn one into the other. Really difficult cases he treated in conjunction with a psychiatrist. He asked so many questions about my health and habits and self-image that, simply to keep the ball rolling, I complained of being fat. Dr. Simeons appraised with new interest my slender person (what I'd meant to say was that I had no *muscles*, that I was essentially soft flesh and bone—an endomorph, had I known the word) and told me to come back to Rome whenever I had a free month; a newly developed course of injections would change all that. As for my immediate problem, the quickest solution was surgery.

True to his theory, no sooner had Dr. Simeons finished the short operation than up to my hospital room he trotted with a couple of psychological tests. The Rorschach cards looked like watercolors by Max Ernst, and I associated freely and fluently. But lest he dismiss me as a pushover, I balked at identifying as such an obvious phallic shape; nor in the Szondi test which followed (where the patient is asked to evaluate a rogues' gallery of mad crones and elderly murderers), would I explain, for all the doctor's urging, why I distrusted the one effete young man who looked like me. My local anesthetic was wearing off. Dr. Simeons left to order a shot of morphine. Presently a girl mopping the corridor paused and, seeing me in pain, ran to my bedside with tears in her eyes. *"Ah, quanto mi dispiace!"* she breathed, beautiful as a goddess, clasping my hand before darting back to work. I returned to our hotel the next morning, well enough to take my father to a matinee. I had never heard *Zazà*—and when if ever had *he* gone to the opera?—but we both felt at home with the tuneful score and the plot's conventional characters. Husband and mistress, wife and child, how one knew them! It could have been another Szondi test.

A boy of fourteen now joined us for a weekend from his Swiss boarding school: Robin Magowan, my half sister's son (hence Neddy's nephew as well as mine) and my father's oldest grandchild. Robin was only ten years my junior. I knew in my bones how the pressures of upbringing (tennis lessons, languages, the dress codes of Southampton) had told upon him. Naturally left-handed, he'd been "encouraged" to conform to a dextral world, a shift that marred his diction—so faintly, however, that it sounded like a throwback to his father's Scotch ancestry. "I was so excited," he told us on arriving at the hotel. "I couldna eat breakfast on the train." Like my father and me, Robin was traveling equipped with the names of those tailors and restaurants without visiting which, in his parents' view, no Roman holiday was thinkable. At his shy suggestion we booked a table for that evening at Alfredo's, where the *fettuccine* were stirred by the proprietor with a fork and spoon of solid gold. Neddy had a date with his doxy from Capri, Miss Beltrami was put at liberty; the three of us sat among the music and lights, beaming in our newfound— But now what? Halfway through a story, my father, bent over, scarlet, is coughing up his dental bridge into the celebrated noodles. (It occurs to me that he's had one drink too many, yet this cannot be. Liquor makes us charming, witty, accessible, not—) In no time we are back at the hotel, and Miss Beltrami, dressed for her ruined evening, is receiving instructions from Dr. Simeons. It isn't a heart attack, he says, putting away stethoscope and hypodermic kit, just a close shave; a couple of days in bed, some further precautions . . .

So Robin ate his first Roman dinner off a table on wheels in my room (and Neddy's) at the Grand Hotel. The couch had been made up into a bed, but he wasn't sleepy. He was frightened—was Grandpa going to die? I just happened to have with me some chapters of a novel I'd begun in New York, in whose prophetic opening scene the hero's invalid father, attended by a needle-brandishing nurse, weathers a crisis similar to the one subsiding next door. Meaning, perhaps, to reassure my nephew that this sort of thing occurred regularly, I put my pages into his hands. I must have known already that he was susceptible to words. Tonight, however, it would dawn upon him that actual people, people he knew, could be written about, and not merely in the local paper's society column but in *real books*, stories contrived for the hard-to-please grown-up reader he himself was turning into under my eyes. An old man's brush with death, a boy's glimpse into the secret workshop . . . When at last Neddy stumbled in, lipstick on his jowl, the young initiate was sleeping as fast as he could.

I wasn't to learn for many months what Dr. Simeons said to my father at their consultation. Now that he was again on his feet, and Robin back in school, we undertook the full-time job of seeing Rome. A limousine appeared every morning at our hotel. Its high-spirited young driver, Marcello (who spoke ten words of English and twenty of French), whisked us to museums and churches, to lunch at Tivoli, to the Vatican. Marcello, like everything else, had been pulled from a hat by those two Americans who danced attendance on our first day in Naples. Their calling was to foresee, make feasible, make positively festive for clients such as my father, every aspect of the Italian Experience. Through their uncanny connections they could smuggle a della Robbia relief back to Tulsa as casually as they could book a private dining room. An audience with the pope? Nothing simpler. Here my father came into his own. First calling the concierge to make sure that the pope had no monopoly on white raiment, he appeared in snowy, double-breasted swank. A gold bill-clip shaped like a dollar sign held his blue silk tie conspicuously in place. "Hey, Charlie, great!" cried Neddy. "His Holiness'll kiss *your* hand when he sees that." Miss Beltrami removed it as we neared the Vatican, lowering a black veil over her smile. Nineteen fifty was the Anno Santo, and many other pilgrims lined the audience chamber, but my father and the waxen, white-robed ascetic now making his way toward him—two men who had "reached the top" in their respective fields of godliness and finance—eclipsed the rest of us, in my view, like some long-awaited conjunction of Jupiter and Pluto.

To be the son of the founder of the world's largest brokerage firm meant, among many comforts and conveniences, being liable to hear the person I was meeting for the first time say, "Merrill? Not so fast—any relation . . . ?" and having to decide in a split second whether my cross-examiner was someone I could fool by pretending to go along with the joke ("Oh sure!") or whether I must hang my head and confess. With members of the world I grew up in, it cost nothing to tell the truth. Their sense of how to live was neither mine nor, I suspected, my father's, who, as the son of a crusty but credit-extending doctor in Green Cove Springs, had taken jobs to get through college and never left a room without switching off the lights. "Thank goodness I come from poor parents," I once said, to the hilarity of my companions. But I meant that my parents' values had been formed long before they had money. Finally there was a world teeming with people who'd never heard of my father or the Firm, people like the girl from the hospital corridor or the models of Tsarouchis, and I yearned to know them, to be mistaken by them for their own kind. In these fantasies it had yet to strike me that my unlikeness to their own kind was precisely what made them look twice at me. I went on trusting that some yet-to-be achieved incognito would save me from exposure until—faint as the chances were—I should have "made a name for myself."

Florence came next. Alas, Rome had so glutted us with sights that it is more the gleams and glooms of our shuttered hotel than the Duomo or the Uffizi that evoke our week there. The Maggio Musicale was mounting, in the Boboli Gardens, two thrillingly rare operas—Gluck's *Iphigénie en Aulide* and Weber's *Oberon*—which I insisted we attend. But opera out-of-doors, it transpired to my grief and to my father's uncomplaining somnolence, gave up its strongest claims. Gone were the effects I cherished most: the dimming of pineal baubles at the auditorium's inner zenith, the gasp of stale backstage air on my face when the gold or crimson curtains parted, the sense, all evening, of sheltered communion and psychodrama. One touch of nature routed such illusions; Agamemnon's soldiery swarmed down the real hillside like a glee club of ants, and Teresa Stich-Randall as she sang swimming into view—in the moat's real water—came closer to Mack Sennett than to the naiads of folklore.

The weather turned summery. In that same heat, under the sun of this same June, I would be meeting Claude; the days were now countable on fingers. It was time to collect Tony's and my Citroën, in Venice. There for a day, I recall little but inhibitive waterways and wrong turnings. Tony had settled into a famous old *pensione* on the Zattere, his room enhanced with pictures and ornaments, a green-and-white-striped coverlet, extra pillows, a bowl of anemones. The trip to Spain had been a trial, nearly literally so. There'd been a "sort of accident" in a remote village. He'd hit someone—a child—not seriously: he'd seen it in the rearview mirror, getting to its feet. Should he have stopped? The thought of a night—or a month—in a provincial Spanish jail spurred him onward to Madrid. There the French ambassador—Martine's husband, if I remembered Martine—had said a word to the right person. But no sooner were Tony's nerves mending in Venice than a worse blow fell: a column drunkenly leaned into from a moving New York subway train had split open Bill Cannastra's head. One of the several ensuing elegies likened this death to the great god Pan's. Ah, it had been a horrendous season. . . .

But not entirely a waste. For all his languid manner, Tony had the phenomenal energy of a Cellini, able to jump six feet in air from a standing position. When I saw him he'd just had a pamphlet of poems printed by the monks on San Lazzaro in the lagoon, where Byron spent mornings learning Armenian. I had to admit the book was handsome. It looked French; motifs from a disk of black jade Tony kept on his desk decorated front and back covers; a single sonnet ran over onto the next page. There were ten short lyrics in all, too hushed and aesthetic even for me, though certain effects had a simple oddity I pondered the making of:

> *When the snow falls in a wet March*
> *And we wear our velvet collars up,*
> *Silence, a silent figure on the Marble Arch,*
> *Breaks from her broken pedestal and rises UP.*

Tony was elated that day by the perceptive things "someone" had said to him about these poems, a few nights before, in a gondola. Who? Oh, a new friend, he offered vaguely, a princess. . . . My heart sank; princesses *were* poetry if he liked, but what could they make of it on the page?

Tony had discovered photography as well. Together we picked up his latest prints, which pleased him so much he ordered them bound into a Venetian-paper album stamped with his initials. To anyone with an identity problem the camera is a godsend, each shot proving (if nothing else) that the photographer has composed *himself* for the split second needed to press the shutter. It is also a way to make quick raids on life while keeping it at arm's length; you look at things no longer quietly, for their own sake, but greedily, for the images they yield. Studied later, if the rainy day ever comes, their historical present inspires an emotion not always felt at the time. I bought my camera on the spot and before driving to France photographed my father.

It is after lunch. He is sitting in the hotel room, nicely dressed as usual. Miss Beltrami, leaning forward like a fortune-teller, is taking his blood pressure. At his elbow, half eaten, the crème caramel he orders at every meal. Beyond it, a tray of medicines: cough syrup, thyroid extract, sleeping pills, nitroglycerin, to name the few I remember. As I haven't learned to coordinate the lens opening with the light meter, these beginner's images suffer from melodrama. My father looks ancient, ravaged by shadows, deprived of natural light or a flash of humor from me. One picture, though, by accident, is of professional quality: a half-full goblet of water set on the window ledge between open shutters. Bleached and sunstruck, the city blurs off into background—but no, the glass, a lens within a lens, contains it: a tiny topsy-turvy Florence, there alone in magical focus, its values true. My next subject will be Claude.

•

Not long ago Robin gave me a fat autobiographical typescript to read. Here I found the story of his being shown, in our Roman hotel, pages from my novel—an incident otherwise forgotten. Writing more or less overtly about his life became my nephew's calling. Ever since that night? I can almost think so. Through the years I've watched him, from woman to woman, in Greek taverns, in Zen gardens, his agile frame clothed vividly as a bird's, younger than his children, his script still cramped as a boy's, taking patient, at times hallucinated, note. Poems, annals of bicycling, travels to Madagascar or Turkestan. The things one can be held answerable for . . .

My father, in 1950, had six years to live. To this day he remains an almost perversely mild and undemanding presence in my thoughts, triggering none of the imaginary confrontations I have with my mother. His company, by those last years, was an end in itself. As part of his entourage, I no longer questioned how to improve the hour. I didn't care if I ever wrote another poem; I lay back, contented, in the very arms of Time. It was a contentment I strove again and again to recapture. A risky project, since one of its elements was an almost limitless boredom. It would be the wise lover who by dint of scenes or séances kept my spirit on its toes. Surely this bland diet, this custard on the emotional menu, cost more than it was worth. My father had disciplined me conventionally as a child, here a spanking, there a blue eye darting fire, but once I no longer lived under his roof, any such showdown came to seem unthinkable. A four-page letter in his beautiful, rounded hand documents a ripple in the too-smooth surface we'd arrived at. Naturally, he wrote, it disappointed him that I didn't care to join the Amherst fraternity whose national president he was. Still, he understood and respected my choice. What left him puzzled was the violent tone of my letter saying so. Knowing how vital it was that he avoid stress after his latest heart attack, couldn't I have tempered my refusal? Evidently not. It was a stab, however ill timed, at restoring the dynamics proper to the discourse of fathers and sons, forfeited by our years of living apart.

It is 1986 and I am again in Rome. This wet Sunday morning has been uncommonly trying. I left my passport in a taxi the night before. Since Peter Hooten is tied up with the producer of the thriller he has just starred in, I've invited a dull American friend to lunch. The police station where one registers the loss of a passport is conveniently on the way to our restaurant, but the officer I speak to shakes his head. Taxi drivers don't, by and large, return lost passports; at best they drop them in a mailbox. Let the signore come back in two hours and talk to the head of that department. Once at table, it turns out that my guest takes his Sunday lunch very seriously indeed. Apertif, antipasto, piccata, salad, dessert, coffee, grappa . . . Mainly to keep him company, I too order dessert—something simple, anything, a crème caramel? But how delicious it is! I scrape my plate clean. Parting from my friend in a glow of well-being, I return to the police station, and there, on the desk of the man I was told to see, my passport awaits me. Next, it is brilliant late afternoon. Peter and I are overlooking the city from the terrace of the Aventine. Peter grew up in Florida, an easy drive from my father's birthplace; sometimes I pretend that he is my father as a young man, before my birth. The light deepens. Now only do I recall that crème caramel was my father's great weakness, often ordered twice a day, during our long-ago time in Italy. Today, moreover, this very Sunday, October 19, is his birthday. He would be one hundred and one years old.

I V

The Lovers Reunited.
Last Hours with Hans.

Homey and unremarkable by morning light, the Hôtel des Roches Blanches at Cassis on the Côte d'Azur had seemed, at the end of my fifteen hours at the wheel, a blazing palace. Claude himself, closing his Herbert or Traherne, rising so abruptly that his chair fell over, for a long moment answered fully to the ardent phantom he'd become during our separation. I gasped to see him once more in flesh and blood. He looked the way I felt: stunned with relief, at peace because we were together at last, off balance because we would now have to face the fact, not the fantasy, of being so. Was his frame limber and powerful enough to receive the likeness I'd made of him? In the lens of my new camera, his chin was weaker than I recalled, and his hands stronger; his hair less golden, his gaze more intense. Those hands and that gaze humbled me. From them had issued a flow of such letters!—pages marveled over in Paris and Poros and Rome, earlier ones wrapped in silk at the back of a drawer in my empty apartment—letters of an eloquence and spontaneity I hoped one day to rise to, though my efforts seemed a schoolboy's by comparison. No matter; the long term apart had ended. From letters I was graduating into life.

What with separate lodgings at Amherst and the rare, guilty weekend at a New York hotel, Kimon and I had hardly ever spent nights together. Now with Claude came unlimited, unprecedented bounty. For as far into the future as I could see, my lover and I were free to sleep and wake side by side. Through an infinity of days and nights ahead, each would have—what greater blessing?—open access to the other's body. So deep and pent-up was my craving for blind flesh-and-blood reassurance, it once or twice crossed my mind that almost anybody might have— No, banish the thought! It was Claude I had chosen, Claude I loved, Claude I would cleave to.

Neither of us had sunned on a shingle beach, or tasted sea urchins, or visited so many little towns in an afternoon's drive. It was early in the season—the hotels half full, the Mediterranean cold—when a walk down the empty beach at St. Tropez led us into hot water. Far off, two other bathers could be made out, squirming irritably back into their briefs at our approach. Fifty meters later, cries of amazed recognition. It was Barney Crop and his lover Hubert. Barney!—once cute and catchable as a tadpole but now, after a couple of years in Paris, painting still lifes and society women, well on his way to adult froghood. We'd lived together—how else but platonically?—during the months before his departure and had kept up; he knew all about the love of my life. I tried not to see, over the carafe we shared on the waterfront, a glaze or withheld comment settle upon his naughty, grinning face. At Claude's expense? What impudence! But no matter, I said to myself again; Barney was a shallow vessel; I was graduating from him too.

As we drove back to Cassis, after a long silence, "You were once in love with Barney," Claude said.

"Claude! I was in love with everybody! And why? Because I didn't have a lover. *I do now.* That's the difference—don't you see?"

"You'd had Kimon."

Oh dear, this was awful. "Weren't there other people in your life?" I whispered.

Claude took my hand. We both intensely hoped no more faces would loom up out of the past.

The hope wasn't to be realized. We'd planned to drive across northern Italy to Salzburg, our destination for the summer. A phone call changed our itinerary. Hans Lodeizen was dying of leukemia in Lausanne. Thus this chapter—which ought to have been, like my honeymoon with Claude, devoted to *him*—has a Dutch poet as its central figure.

Hans was a graduate student at Amherst when we met in 1946, five months after Kimon had sailed for Greece. True to form, I fell in love. Just as certain words—like "naked" or "muscular"—would leap from the page I was reading to stimulate an erotic nerve end, so this Cherubino had but to think "love" and every problem dissolved, light filled him, he knew why he'd been born. A variety of religious experience? I hadn't yet come across Borges's definition of the lover as founder of a religion with a fallible god, but I was nothing if not devout. Devout and fickle. Between my eighteenth and twenty-fourth birthdays there must have been ten or twelve young men *en fleurs*—like Barney—whom I was smitten by in succession, or two or three at a time. Of these, Hans was by far the most meaningful. The affairs, true to some grand renunciatory model, tended not to be consummated in any usual sense of the term. Rather, they gave rise to *poems* about love—a sorry substitute, I feared, for the real thing. Whether those young men divined from the start that I would be made happier by a poem than by lying in their arms, or that *they* would be, I cannot say. Perhaps it was a simple case of that curious but widespread law whereby people instinctively withhold what you want from them.

But what exactly did I want, or think I wanted, from a lover? To be undressed of my affectations, clothed afresh in passion's more convincing wardrobe? Out of childhood comes a bluntly scissored memory of paper dolls, over whose all but genderless undergarments new selves—hunter or peasant, soldier or man about town—could be affixed by tabs at shoulders and hips. If at present the garb of an aesthete seemed cut out for me, it was because poetry and grand opera were the only keys I possessed to the heart's innermost chamber and the psychic nudity permitted there. Alas, the heart's innermost chamber, to judge by the reaction of those I paid suit to, was all too often a suffocating hole.

I didn't think of *them* as paper dolls, no; but . . . postage stamps? I could spend hours, at ten or eleven, with my album, attaching new finds by means of little gummed hinges, calculating the ever-increasing value from my catalog. Not otherwise did I catch myself, at twenty or twenty-one, gloating over bygone names and faces. I took pains to distinguish between the uncanceled idealization of that year's crown prince and the far more precious rarity of a timed and dated "conquest," which (soaked in advance by one cocktail too many) had slid into my care, summoning up foreign parts, dark-skinned couriers, intimacies scrawled on lost pages addressed hardly ever to a person I knew. How thrilled I'd been to obtain my first stamp from Siam or the Orange Free State! Now, with Hans's profile already in the engraver's hands, and my presses thundering yet again into action, I could look forward to filling in my first window on the blank page of "Holland."

Hans wanted, sensibly enough, a love that kept his spirit intact. He was first of all a young man of the Old World, whose blue sunbeam eye, purling Dutch voice, and friendly sketch of a bow on meeting or parting functioned by reflex at times when my compatriots would have been tearing their hair. However vital to him the writing of poetry, good manners made him treat it as something that simply "happened," as if a tree should say with a rueful shrug, "Look, these little pink what-d'you-call-'ems have broken out all along my branches." Indeed, Hans was blossoming here in the New World, and not only as a poet. He was tasting the freedom and anonymity felt by Americans abroad. For the first time in his life he had escaped his large, influential family; the last thing he needed was to have his style cramped by a possessive friend. Yet he was drawn to me. The time I spent on poems and term papers impressed him in spite of himself. The atomic age had begun, and I still favored the cumbersome old cotton gins of Art and Scholarship? Next to mine, Hans's mental furnishings were streamlined, eclectic. He expounded the existentialists. He held forth on Plato's vision, on Nietzsche's, calling the latter "terrible, terrible" with a smile and a shiver, as if speaking of a tale by Poe. In the biology lab he showed me the scarlet pulse of a fertilized egg. He wanted me to read Chamfort's maxims, look at a mask from the Congo, hear the violin sonatas of Beethoven.

One autumn afternoon we left the music library with a borrowed album. I was coming down with a cold, and midway to my rooms, feeling a nip in the air, Hans took off his scarf and put it round my neck. I lived off campus that year, in the town barber's house. We lit a fire and sat on the floor with sherry, while the ravishing *Spring* Sonata, interrupted every four minutes by having to change the record, burgeoned around us.

When it ended, Hans asked if I knew the Henriette episodes in Casanova's *Memoirs*—of course I did not—and began to tell, delighting in every detail, that infinitely romantic story. It begins with the laugh of an unseen woman at a roadside inn; shows her to us first disguised as a soldier, then in Rome at Casanova's expense, refusing to tell him who she is but playing the cello so passionately that her lover stumbles from the room to bury his face in the lilacs outside; and ends years later with words scratched by her diamond on a windowpane in the Alps. My cold, however, just when I might have glowed with joy, was ripening fast. In the face of Hans's concern—he offered to come back with soup from the dining hall—I protested that it was nothing, that I needed no mothering, without ever pausing to reflect until the downstairs door shut quietly behind him how welcome *his* mothering would have been. The moment was like a sprain; henceforth our intimacy would limp somewhat.

I'd had another crush at Amherst, on a shy, black-haired American from Argentina named Seldon James. We roomed together the summer following my demobilization. (During my eight months in the army—basic training, then office work—the war had been virtually won. Clerks with bad eyesight, like me, were being returned to civilian life.) But Seldon left college at term's end for the navy, and I'm afraid I barely noticed his reappearance on campus a year later, so taken up was I by my feelings for Hans. There came a painful evening nevertheless. Maggie Teyte, then my favorite singer, miraculously turned up in Amherst with a program of Debussy and Fauré. Those songs were charms I tried to keep always within reach. Many of them I'd sung under my breath on marches in the army; they dissolved pain and made boredom sparkle like wine. At intermission, throwing on my Oscar Wilde overcoat, I went out into the chilly dark. Seldon stood nearby; so did Hans, wearing only a jacket and shirt. "But you're not warmly dressed; you'll catch cold," I cried. "Here—" And remembering the scarf he had once put round my neck, I took mine off and insisted that he wear it. People were watching; I felt Hans's discomfort but couldn't drop this parody of what he himself had done so gently and impulsively a few weeks earlier. He might have shamed me by handing the scarf back. Instead he sketched his little bow and moved away. Indoors, just as the lights dimmed, I noticed to my dismay that he was sitting with Seldon. They'd come to hear Maggie Teyte together;

they were friends! Pangs reserved exclusively for the gay shot through me—I was jealous of both parties at once. From the stage a third love produced her ageless, lilting summary:

> *C'est l'histoire des oiseaux*
> *Dans les arbres.*

Two years later, in New York, my heart must have been engaged elsewhere: I spent an afternoon with Hans, and even heard that he was meeting Seldon for dinner, without a trace of those old palpitations. Yet when word reached me in Cassis that he was ill and wanted to see me, I knew only how much he had always meant to me and that we must travel by way of Lausanne. Claude hugged me and agreed.

The clinic might have passed for a luxurious Swiss hotel. Pacing the corridor on Hans's floor was our college friend Ray, who had traced me to Cassis by phoning my mother in New York. He told me things I preferred not to register. Hans's parents—I'd met them once at Amherst—joined us, thanked me for coming, but added that it would be a kindness if I stayed under an hour. I went in. The large, lived-in room, full of books and records, overlooked the lake. Hans lay cranked up in bed, a picture of health thanks to his daily transfusion. He had asked, he said, blushing as if confessing to a clandestine love, to meet his principal donor, and shaken hands with that great strapping fellow whose blood was keeping him alive. But soon, he added solicitously, lest I grow too alarmed, his condition would stabilize. He'd thought of Italy for his convalescence; if I was there in the fall we could perhaps spend some weeks together? Nothing, I swore, would make me happier. (And Claude?) Among the books on the bed were George Sand's memoirs, which Hans praised in the same terms—"She sends me floating up and up like a balloon"—he used to describe the nurse's nightly injection that put him to sleep like a baby.

He then drew from the bedclothes, diffidently, his book of poems, *Het Innerlijk Behang (The Wallpaper Within)*, published just that month in Holland. A prompt reviewer had already hailed its freshness and assurance. Although I knew no Dutch, the work indeed appeared daringly up-to-date—short, unrhymed lines, free of capitals and punctuation. As we turned the pages together, I saw that Hans had inscribed the book to me and that it was dedicated to Seldon. "Seldon and I were both displaced in America," he said with a slow, candid look. "It was natural for us to gravitate toward each other. Yours was the friendship I wanted, but Seldon's the one I needed." He next found a poem whose epigraph was a line I'd written, then a few sly stanzas about a party at my mother's in New York, finally the two poems dedicated to me. One by one he read them out in English. The last of the four was no more than a quatrain, but it brought back a certain midnight amble through the campus together, an hour I'd forgotten precisely for its having unsheathed, like a Euclidean proof, the clash of temperament that divided us:

> *the stars & the incurable*
> *moment of the two crossed beams.*
> *Orion discovered & in his hand*
> *o fate in his hand the sword.*

When word of Hans's death not long afterward reached me in Salzburg, a poem began to take form—or rather, for once, *not* to. Lines varied in length, end words rhymed or didn't. The phrases, like river stones, learned their own shape and smoothness from the current of grief that swept through me. I'd had no brush with death so close as this. The experience merged for my poem's purposes with that of Europe, of Switzerland in particular, where

> *The glittering neutrality*
> *Of clock and chocolate and lake and cloud*
> *Made every morning somewhat*
> *Less than you could bear;*
>
> *And makes me cry aloud*
> *At the old masters of disease*
> *Who dangling high above you on a hair*
> *The sword that, never falling, kills*

—for it seemed to me that Hans had died cheated of his "real" death, that death to the very last remained his sword of Damocles, never falling, always out of reach. This was pure poetic double-talk, meaning, if it meant anything, that I as survivor remained incapable, and would for months and months, of deeply realizing what had befallen my poor friend. The hanging sword as an image of deferral appeared from out of the blue—or so I thought. But in a flash that winter I recognized it as the sword from Hans's quatrain, *his* image and the image of his youthful valor, which on his deathbed he had put into my hands.

We were no longer alone when I took my leave. Our friend Ray— well named, his pleasant features abeam—had returned with flowers and magazines. A nurse came in to ready Hans for his dinner tray; or was there to be a transfusion appetizer? Looking back, half out of the room, I caught my breath. A brilliant stripe of late sun ran down the left side of his glowing, rosy-brown face. Why didn't he shift, or squint? A blood vessel had burst when he bent over a few weeks earlier, and Hans was already blind in that eye.

•

My erotic activity in those early years between seeing Kimon off to Greece and saying hello to Claude at Freddy's party was rare and seldom involved the person I happened to be "in love with" at the time. Neither was it much pleasure to look back upon. This was due partly to the insecurity more or less guaranteed by the odd sexual athlete who saw in me a novel challenge, and overwhelmingly to my own naïveté. Finding someone willing to spend the night seemed of itself such a miracle that I would start before daybreak sending out tendrils to bind my companion to me forever, despite the scant affection or trust I felt. (Why did I need someone to spend the night in the first place? Because I had no Inner Resources and feared being alone. Because, as in Auden's tongue-in-cheek Utopia, what was no longer forbidden was compulsory. Because in a few years I would be an old man of thirty and no one would ever look at me again.) Needless to say, my gambits frightened off creep and charmer alike. If by any remote chance a second meeting came about, I would arrange to bring to it so much uneasiness that the rendezvous ended before it had properly begun. Some such mechanism underlay my break with Kimon. In my guilty view—for which I had, if not my mother, "society" to thank—the reprieve he offered took on the aspect of a sentence. Like the colt that, genetically programmed to be broken, nevertheless throws its first riders, I shied away from being saddled with a lover capable of seeing into my heart, for would he not then despise the confusion he saw there? Far better the unrequited pangs I knew so well, which guaranteed me "no little innocent bliss," as Tonio Kröger put it, and could always be used as fuel for a poem. Regarding those platonic crushes, it should be added that back then—before such matters were codified by the color and placement of a pocket handkerchief—I was pretty much in the dark as to sexual "roles" and "types" and may (for all I knew) have been sleepwalking on the brink of incompatibilities all too apparent to my beloved.

Long after his death, I heard that Hans, without any help from me or Seldon, had found love in America: a young Puerto Rican dancer living in a Harlem apartment crowded with family. When Hans returned to Holland he told Ignacio (if that was his name) to write him not at home but in care of a friend who knew the story. A day came when this friend had to write a letter himself, breaking the news that there would be no others. It was read in angry disbelief. Ignacio knew—knew—that Hans couldn't have died; this was all a plot, on the part of those (as he must have pictured them) cinematically bourgeois parents across the ocean, to thwart his love. It took a Dutch go-between's visit to New York, and a folder of newspaper tributes, to convince the boy.

The story, had I heard it during Hans's lifetime, would have filled me with jealousy. Forty years later—like "Tu oublieras Henriette" etched on an icy windowpane or the Spring Sonata heard by chance on public radio—it stops me in my tracks. I smile, I shake my head. With passions like that, for instinct's beautiful children, there could have been no question of competing. I am old enough to have survived one or two similar loves, know what they bring to a sedentary, overcultivated type, and am glad that life granted Hans this particular deep enchantment.

V

In Salzburg, Claude and I rented an apartment crammed with the owners' books and furniture. A tiny cement balcony permitted a view of the mountain. A great feather-quilted bed gave rise to dreams and their fulfillment. At the street door began the cafés, the chocolate shops, the souvenirs imprinted in gold with silhouettes of Mozart. Much of the town lay in ruins. Fountains, facades, sidewalks, the cathedral dome were all undergoing repairs. After dark a great night-watchman searchlight from the Café Winkler uphill checked on their progress. The festival had just begun. We'd booked a few performances in advance, but as we pored over the complete prospectus it seemed that something irresistible was being offered at every turning: tomorrow's concert of Dittersdorf trios in the salon of a genuine *Schloss*, or the next afternoon's marionette version of *Faust*. In the weeks ahead we spent hours every day wangling rehearsal passes, offering coffee and pastry to a *Frau Philharmoniker* (the wife, that is, of an orchestra member—even *she* had a title!) whose friend had tickets to sell, begging our landlady to rack her brains for another contact when the original one fell through. Reading magazine articles many years later about the agony and expense of sustaining a drug habit, I would be reminded of that summer's quest for tickets to the Salzburg Festival.

The rehearsal we attended was of the second act of *Fidelio*. That day I would be hearing Kirsten Flagstad for the first time since 1941. With our entry into the war, it became unpatriotic to admire Wagner, yet Flagstad's singing of his heroines had overwhelmed me as a boy. Single-handed she proved by her noble presence and the clarion tenderness of her voice that opera, risen above the sorrows of consumptive harlots or seamstresses, left also the Greek dramatists in the dust and Shakespeare in the shade. Here she came now, my idol, as Leonora, one of the few irreproachable roles in the entire repertoire. A matron disguised as a beardless youth, wearing homespun knee-britches and holding a little lantern, she descended the dungeon stair. Time stopped at her first, spoken words. In my emotion I simply didn't hear the other singers. Only at a later performance did Julius Patzak, the Florestan, with his sweet, tarnished tenor, emerge as a perfect wonder. To the American press many of these European artists gave off a distinct sheen of "collaboration." Flagstad herself was said to have sung for the Nazis in her native Norway; the same accusing finger pointed to Elisabeth Schwarzkopf (our Marzelline); while the festival's reigning maestro, the great Furtwängler, conducted both the orchestra and himself in visionary, white-haired disdain of such petty rumors. True, we were here on "enemy territory," an easy drive from Berchtesgaden, yet in my innocence I tried to rejoice at how much people had thrust behind them.

But was this not, Claude darkly suggested, a mere entr'acte in some nonstop theater of war? For the so-called Korean Crisis was making headlines that summer. Our mothers, never thinking international escape routes might differ from one war to the next, wrote identical letters urging us to open bank accounts in Portugal, so that if Americans were suddenly obliged, etc. We smiled, but panic was in the air. Must the world be put through it all again? Wallace Stevens had called for a poet "capable of resisting or evading the pressure of reality." Now in dead earnest Claude and I talked of moving for the rest of our lives to Liberia. Even a few years of grace were a lot to ask and would only grudgingly be wrung from Washington and the Kremlin. Our hopes and fears came back to us from the stage of the Felsenreitschule as Josef Greindl, across footlights, directly addressing an audience so musical, so sober, and so cosmopolitan that they would surely, the next morning, be able to bear his message to the heads of state it most concerned, sang Sarastro's noble plea for brotherly love.

One afternoon Claude returned excited from the post office, where he had run into a Harvard friend. We'd been asked on a picnic the following day. We were six: Claude's friend and his wife, and another young couple, recently married. The husband of this second couple, whom Claude had also known at college, was the son of the poet John Peale Bishop. Meeting friends of Claude's for the first time—he had already met most of mine—I was relieved to note that they looked and behaved like anyone else. There would have been hundreds more of us in Europe that summer—young, educated, "nice" Americans whose discovery of the Continent, in the footsteps of Hawthorne and Henry James, had been deferred by the war. Many were on grants to study abroad. In a new city we headed straight for the museum, for the churches starred in the guide, for *Schloss* and *Denkmal*. If our choice excluded, as choices will, broad realms of experience—so be it. The events of the past decade had spoiled any appetite we might have had for public life. It was Culture's turn now, and we meant to get as much as we could. With, of course, breaks for fun, like today. Claude and I having spent the past weeks wholly among foreigners, these compatriot faces, shy though I felt in their presence, refreshed us like the little meadow pond we splashed about in after the first glasses of white wine had been drunk.

Jonathan Bishop's wife, Alison, cut a striking figure in her swimsuit: blonde, white-skinned, elongated, with the cat face of a Cranach Venus. One waited for her to purr. Out came instead a voice at once hollow and assertive, like an oracle's; Claude whispered that she was a writer, and deaf in one ear. Over our sandwiches she began telling an unpleasant story. Somebody they'd known at Harvard, while driving through a Spanish village a few months earlier, had struck and killed a child. Unfeelingly, unthinkingly, this person sped on, never stopping, to Madrid, where influential friends pulled strings. I realized at once that the driver in question was Tony Harwood and, when Alison had finished, remarked loyally that hers wasn't quite the story I'd heard from him— although, even secondhand, it exhaled the airy hubris that woke my original pity and terror. Alison gave me a shrewd look. "Oh, if he's such a friend of yours," she said in her odd voice, "why didn't you stop me when I began the story?" After that, I hoped never to see her again.

The car that struck the child was of course the same black Citroën Claude and I drove away from the picnic and in which we would soon set off from Salzburg. The festival was ending. We contrived to hear a *Don Giovanni* with Ljuba Welitsch as Donna Anna, a role she'd sung in New York the previous winter. But the heroin that, unknown to her fans at the time, made for those electrifying performances—the tiny Ottavio sucked dry by his Black Widow—had taken its toll. Here in Salzburg, only months later, she was unable to get through her last great aria. Schwarzkopf sang Elvira in this production, and Irmgard Seefried Zerlina. These two sopranos had over the summer come to stand in our eyes for polar opposites: Schwarzkopf all airs and artifice, effects so fine as to be virtually detachable from the score; Seefried at her most lyrical, still somehow *speaking* the music in her human concern for directness and clarity. How could they bear one another? Yet at the end, astoundingly, they took their curtain calls hand in hand.

A high sunny road leads into Italy. "Verona, Vicenza, Padova," Claude chants in ecstasy as the road signs fly past. "Ferrara, Firenze, Ferrovia!" By evening we've returned the tainted car to Tony's Venetian garage— let it be his from now on—and settled ourselves above him in the historic *pensione*. Mosquito nets draping the beds give our room the air of a colonial hospital ward. It is rather Mrs. Humphry Ward that Tony's room, more so even than in May, evokes. White-and-red Fortuny curtains of sheer silk, weighted with colored beads, float inward from the balcony doors. A sandstone Khmer head is flanked by two pictures framed in blond tortoiseshell. I recognize his unhappy, wisecracking mother, but who on earth is that other siren, equally striking in her sultry ripeness? Is *that* his poetry-loving Princess? At my question he rolls his eyes and utters an indrawn, Jamesian "Ah . . . !"

Claude's mother has herself decided that Europe is safe enough for a month or two of sightseeing. A tough cookie, bossy and independent, Vira nevertheless warms my heart as the kind of mother—in my book there are two kinds only—who seems resigned if not indifferent to her child's private life. She knows enough to leave unsaid a number of things whose saying all but severed the lines of communication between my mother and me. Well, perhaps we're always at our best with mothers not our own. If Vira's presence strains Claude's patience, I slip happily into the role of a difficult son's "nice friend," who eases the tensions and takes up the slack—now in the sumptuous hotel at the Lido, where Vira treats us to lobster and roulette, now in shops full of costly things we despise, now in the railway carriage where, after a scene with the porter, Claude pointedly withdraws into Meister Eckhart. When we reach Florence, Vira decides to go off by herself to Capri. Whether a romantic encounter is in the back of her mind or subliminally invited by her gait and perfume, within ten days she has met a well-spoken, suitably mature Saudi Arabian businessman and revised her entire future. A grand villa with servants awaits her on the Persian Gulf. Her fiancé has already gone ahead to make the arrangements; the wedding is set for next June in Missouri, where Vira lives. Claude is presented to his prospective stepfather over lunch in Rome. What's he like? "Oh, dapper, emphatic, sure of himself . . . ," says Claude, looking troubled.

"Dependable?"

"How would I know? I've never met an Arab before. Neither has she."

"Shouldn't you—what is it the men in a family are supposed to do—have him investigated?"

"Where would one begin? Besides," Claude resumes after a silence, "what right have I to interfere? We don't let our mothers run *our* lives."

This is my good strong-minded Claude. I still picture the "rights" between parent and child as one-sided.

With Vira we proceed to Naples and sail for Barcelona in early October. A few days later we have settled—Claude and I for the winter—on Mallorca, in the Hotel Maricel, above the sea, a long walk or pleasant tram ride from Palma. The hotel is new and two-thirds empty. A few other Americans linger on, among them a Hollywood scriptwriter, bitter and broken, who late one night following our brandies at the bar taps on Vira's door, groaning her name. Over breakfast he will cringe to hear it told with a laugh in the acoustically merciless dining room. Europe has so served its purpose that Vira goes home sooner than planned. The writer departs for Rome, like the penitent Tannhäuser. We aren't lonely. In December, Freddy comes to spend a fortnight at the hotel. Thanks to our single letter of introduction, we meet the foreign colony. Lunch with Robert Graves is a failure. Claude expresses doubts about the White Goddess; shown to the bathroom, I perceive too late that I should have asked for the loo and am obliged to pee in the basin; we aren't asked back. More congenial are the Bowdens, a retired American couple who off and on throughout the winter have us for tea and music. Accompanied by her husband, Mrs. Bowden sings Schubert songs we can't hear often enough. She would have turned eighteen in the early 1900s. Beneath a club-woman's camouflage—tailored jacket of blue wool, permanent wave in her white hair—her psyche wears trailing skirts and speaks in symbols. She gives a dinner for us in town; on my plate lies a laurel wreath. But my sense is mainly of being alone with Claude. We spend mornings reading and writing in our connecting rooms, pausing to stare out at the sea or down at the little uniformed bellboys acting their age on the terrace. Late afternoons we walk along the coast, or in to Palma for an aperitif before dining back at the hotel. We've talked it over and decided not to acquire Spanish lest it "spoil our Italian." Yet something gets through, because one day the young barber who comes to our rooms with his scissors and lotions is prattling away and I break into laughter. "How marvelous that you are poets," he has just said unmistakably. "Nothing comes out of *my* head but hair!"

Mornings at work, local color, the sea . . . "It's Georgetown with plumbing and servants," said Freddy, meaning the summer we'd spent in Maine together. I nodded nostalgically. There was no need to point out the major difference, that I was now (another Spanish word slipping through the blockade) *casado*—housed; that is, "married." Yet I couldn't help noticing, alone with Freddy at his visit's end, how much more freely my tongue wagged and my mind worked than they did with Claude. It wasn't that I'd made the wrong choice. Friendship's chattering stream simply came as a relief from the uncharted waters of love, though it was to these that I'd committed myself. As other friends were doing. Returning from our walk, we were met by the little bellboy with an envelope addressed in Tony's impulsive cuneiform. He was leaving Venice for Geneva—a prolonged stay—this great change had taken place in his life—he could say no more at present. Freddy jotted down the name of our friend's hotel. He had cousins in Geneva and planned to look them up later in the spring, unless his publisher's advance ran out before then.

Freddy left behind a typescript of his new novel, *The Seasons' Difference*. He and I figured in it as a pair of secretive, inseparable teenagers. Countless touches I knew by heart brought "Harry" and "Rufus" to life and measured the inches we had grown in the seven years since our graduation from Lawrenceville. Hadn't every cell in our bodies changed? The message of Freddy's book, however, seemed to be that none of his characters, young or old, was going to change in any profound sense without the help of Christ. My head swerved aside from this spoonful of bitter syrup. If, as I kept fancying, my homosexuality was driving a wedge between us, so was Freddy's piety, and nothing either of us could do would change our ways. My eventual letter about his novel brimmed with things unsaid, and he must have felt its inadequacy as sorely as I did.

These reservations notwithstanding, on Christmas Eve Claude and I attended midnight service in the cathedral. At its climax a surpliced choirboy climbed into the pulpit and holding upright before him an angel's flashing sword sang, unaccompanied, a Catalan hymn for the Last Judgment. Mrs. Bowden tracked down words and music; I learned to play the haunting song on my recorder, which sounded almost like a boy soprano. (Recorder duets were one of Claude's and my sedate entertainments.) On Christmas morning Claude gave me a pair of *rouge-gorges*. The little brown finches—the male with a band of crimson at his throat, as if he'd just then slit it—built a nest, laid eggs, neurotically destroyed them. We named the birds Ralph and Ivy. Released from their cage, they would hover for long minutes in midair before the closet door's oval mirror, enthralled by selves they could never be sure were their own.

From my publisher in New York came a present that allowed for even greater self-absorption than the finches': my first book. I looked at it in every conceivable light. What impression would it make upon my old teachers? upon Randall Jarrell? upon the youth of Liberia? upon a future world from which English had disappeared? The edition was limited to 990 numbered copies. Had I known onto whose shelves these books would go I might well have set about examining the text afresh through the eyes of each new owner in turn. But it was life-threatening to learn that my father had ordered a hundred copies for his friends and business associates, people to whom a page of verse, were it ever to confront them, would be speckled forbiddingly with stanza-shaped reefs and treacherous, variable soundings. So—one-tenth of the tiny edition doomed to oblivion, at a single stroke! (Two years later my book had not sold out. I'd hoped for a small, select readership? I was getting my wish.)

Spring came early. One morning a taxi drove us twenty-five kilometers into the countryside, to a point from which we could hike back to the hotel through almond-blossom fragrances that buzzed and stung like bees. Another day we saw folk-dancing in an inland village. A Scarlatti-like melody for pipes and drums that sometimes comes over me in the course of a sleepless night will have to be surgically removed from my brain if I am ever to be free of it. One afternoon I let the finches out of their cage without remembering that the window was open. Before I could shut it, Ralph had flown, not for once to the mirror, but to a tree in the garden below. He and Ivy (safely behind bars) called back and forth heartrendingly. It was sadder than the *Trovatore* "Miserere." I ran downstairs with the cage, set it outdoors where he could see his mate. It did no good. His cries, as evening fell, came from farther and farther away. A bird used to captivity makes little sense of the greater world, falling prey easily to owl or hawk. We replaced Ralph, but the new finch lacked spirit, failed to ingratiate himself with Ivy or with us, and we gave them both away without bothering to name him.

•

"Isn't it lovely here?" my companion is saying. "After so many stoic winters with Jonathan in the cold. Look at those palm trees, feel the air."

Thirty years have passed since our first, unfortunate meeting. Alison Lurie and I are sitting by starlight on the steps of a boarded-up shack halfway between her house and David Jackson's. We became friends with Alison and her husband (now amicably divorced) not long after Salzburg, when I was Jonathan Bishop's colleague in the Amherst English department.

"Who would have thought we'd end up like this?" she marvels in her odd, off-key voice, which has come to delight me. "In 1950 there seemed to be thousands of other young people just like you and David, or Jonathan and me—

full of talent and ambition. But so few of us kept at it. And now those who did have readers and reputations. The rest . . ."

The rest married, raised their children, voted for the wrong candidate, sold products nobody much wanted (including ideas), took to the bottle, had heart attacks, went south for the winter. Over the years it hasn't been beyond us to do some of these things ourselves. What made the difference?

"I used to think," I say, "that deep down, all the other boys at school with me were just as clever and imaginative as I was. Even the bullies. We were Americans after all, we'd been created equal. The only difference was that they'd learned, and I hadn't, how to disguise this fact in order to be popular."

"With other clever little boys pretending to be dumb? I see," Alison laughs. "What age did the truth dawn on you?"

"Oh, thirty-five . . . forty? Has it dawned?"

"It's true," she goes on after a pause. "Back then we hadn't done anything yet. Not that we were completely interchangeable either; this was before the campgrounds and the discos. We were just young, like everyone else, and in Europe for the first time. Starry-eyed, dying to feel at home there."

"Remember Tony Harwood?"

"Of course. Jonathan liked him. He said it wasn't given to just anyone to emerge full-grown from the brain of Evelyn Waugh. He had that accident in Spain. What became of him? Are you still friends?"

"He died three years ago."

"Oh, I'm sorry," says Alison. "What of?"

I sketch in the marriage, the drugs, the delusions. The unwritten masterpieces, the Tibetan child. The life in hotels. The life his example taught me not to live. The leather, the lawsuits. One night his heart simply stopped while he was ranting. I'd kept—in spite of so much nonsense—a kind of faith in him, in his being able one day to write something amazing.

"But he went mad instead. Was he a pure product of America?" Alison muses. "The kind that Europe stains beyond redemption? Americans are meant to resist the wicked influence, like Scotchgarded fabric. Especially writers. If our novelists want to live in Paris, they've got to drink a lot and act extra tough. Have you been to the Hemingway house yet? It's worth the five dollars. Look at the faces, listen to the comments. They've never read a line he wrote, but he's Papa, he's a fertility symbol. You and I are viewed with suspicion: we're 'mid-Atlantic,' we're 'genteel.'"

"It's not fair. We're as American as lemon chiffon pie."

"Speak for yourself," Alison says. *"I just meant it must show in our sentence structure that I have a flat in London and that you spent all those years in Athens or listening to foreign operas. Perhaps we'd be taken more seriously—and Tony Harwood would be alive and famous today—if none of us had ever left home in the first place. But then who would you want to be taken seriously by, who doesn't take you seriously already?"*

I suppose she's right. She is certainly right about Key West. After "all those years in Athens," this return to a world I've known from infancy moves me in mysterious ways. It is the America that shaped my parents. Here are the same black families on porches, the same root-cracked sidewalks and giant smooth-torsoed trees I knew from visits to my grandmother in Jacksonville. Nothing surprises, everything delights. Often, before daybreak, the rooster next door utters a cry so like Norma's piteous "Io non posso!" as sung by the late Florence Foster-Jenkins that my own laughter wakes me; and down the street from us a cemetery, sugar white and wholly above ground, makes dying seem like a piece of cake.

V I

Romanesque Buildings.
The Science of Love.
My Sister in Rome.
Music in Paris.
Named by Alice.

Brick by brick, the color of dried blood, a molecular mystery took shapes that echoed the body's own. Lobes and groins stretched off into murk. Only later would come those Gothic "miracles" of engineering, psychic spaces pierced by gemlight. At St. Sernin in Toulouse, weird creatures, small as parasites, glared through drilled eyeholes from capitals supporting a weight of architectural dogma. The cold pink of cherry blossoms lightened Albi's fortress church, and the Tarn moved on tiptoe eddies. The eponymous heresy, with its "dualist doctrines" for which thousands perished, seemed harmless enough by now, like brick structures massive against clouds but, once reflected, going to pieces in the slow green river. We heard Palm Sunday service in the old church at Elne, its gloom shot through by chocolate fish, dolls, stars, all wrapped in multicolored foil and dangling from the tips of laurel boughs, so that the congregation appeared to inhabit a huge, supinely fragrant Christmas tree. Joining the

children's procession through the cloister, we mouthed the words of the
dismal anthem:

Chrétien, j'entends à haute voix:
Vive Jésus, vive Sa Croix!

Now by bus, now by local train, we and our ton of luggage zigzagged
slowly north. We went to Moissac and Carcassonne. We saw Lascaux.
After only minutes in the caves, our guide told us that our presence was
killing the wall paintings and expelled us from those numinous animal
presences to the Arcadian woodland overhead. We did well to pay for a
second look, for within a year or so the whole affair closed down, like an
injured bivalve; eventually a replica was built for tourists. But if my poor
human breath was harmful here, something in this vernal France was taking its revenge. Night after night I lay propped up in bed, gasping till daybreak. The initial thrill of being a famous asthmatic soon wore off. Like
Proust, however, once inside the *cordon sanitaire* of the great boulevards
I found my symptoms abating.

Alice Toklas had booked us into the Hôtel Récamier in Place St.
Sulpice. Our two rooms this time were small and connected by a length of
public corridor. What had happened to our great love? Back in a city after
months of isolation, we found difficulties springing into relief. Claude was
companionable but restless, taken up with other friends. In self-defense I
had lunch with Barney Crop, who then guided me through a very large,
serious shop crammed with the crystals and iridescent beetles he loved to
paint—sitters demonstrably more brilliant than Mrs. Bemberg on Christian Dior. I had dinner with the cleverest of Freddy's Princeton girls; she
hung her head to one side and said how lonely she was in Paris. I agreed.
Used to Claude's presence, I was unequal to these hours without him. The
more cripplingly dependent I grew, the more I felt him puzzled, holding
back. One cause for our troubles was plain: I hadn't learned how to love.
Like the young person who yearns to "be a writer" without putting himself through the blind alleys, the fears and rebuffs impossible to sidestep if
the lifework is to be truly accomplished, I had counted on "being a lover"
with no credentials beyond a certain expectant footlit intensity. That my
feelings were childish I might have guessed from how quickly they

changed—Cinderella slipping into her rags after the ball—into hurt feelings. But we'd invested too much in each other to dream of parting.

It troubled me most that my intensity wasn't up to Claude's. From my old "unrequited passions" I had come to believe that the lover had certain sacred privileges. In those Provençal courts we'd missed visiting by less than a millennium, the love-crazed troubadour like Peire Vidal was *owed something*—if only pity and high consideration—by the lady who listened without yielding to his suit. Yet there must have been hours when that lady would have preferred small talk to romance. Claude's love, like his taste in music or art, abashed me. Where I was content to "find myself" in a Fauré song or a Degas interior, he identified manfully with a Zen scroll or the *St. John Passion*. We weren't of course competing, yet how not to feel superficial next to him? I was enough in touch with the amateur psychology of my time to assume that the nastier the insight, the truer it was. High spirits must be downplayed; the fanged uglies of the ocean floor were more fundamental than the dolphins and flying fish.

How had Claude learned to love? For one thing, he studied the handbooks every morning: Plato, Augustine, St. Francis, Freud. (In my room I read Mallarmé—page upon page that almost completely resisted the understanding—or Bachelard's elemental, unpeopled reveries.) More to the point, Claude had learned how to live. He rose impatiently above boredom and unhappiness, the better to grasp what the world offered. He set aside hours of the day for chores, for study, for meditation. He knew the rounds of labor and diversion proper to city or countryside. The journal he'd been keeping almost since mastering the alphabet served him as both judge and guardian angel, for even the wasted day bore fruit, once confessed to at due analytical length. During seasons of solitude and introspection Claude thought nothing of leaving a party early or a concert at the intermission; by staying on he would merely have encountered more raw experience than his journal could process without fudging. Despite his example, I sat for hours inhaling the wallpaper's hypnotic poppies and thought well spent the morning given to repunctuating a poem months old.

One of that winter's poems described the implacable European hotel room—I wrote it holed up in one—among whose "six walls" a faceless traveler or a fictive "we" recurred, materializing and dissolving like the room's own dreams. It had the obligatory note of sadness struck without exception by my early poems, regardless of my state of mind during their composition. (Hadn't someone said that all poems were elegies?) In short, I was highly pleased with it. Not Claude. "Look what you've called it," he said. "'Hôtel de l'Univers et Portugal.'"

"Yes; remember," I said hastily, as over me an awful realization began to creep, "I showed you the ad on the ship to Barcelona, in a travel magazine? Such an exquisitely silly name—"

"But Portugal? What 'Portugal' meant to us last spring? Didn't you think of that when you wrote these lines?" And he read aloud:

"Bleakly with ever fewer belongings we watch
And have never, it each time seems, so coldly before

Steeped the infant membrane of our clinging
In a strange city's clear grave acids . . .

Or this," Claude added in his gentlest voice, as I hung my head. "Think what this says about our faith in one another:

The lovers' speech from cool walls peeling
To the white bed, whose dream they were."

It did not occur to me to protest that these last lines owed more to a poem Freddy had written seven years earlier than to my feelings about a real lover. Poems were made out of words, as Mallarmé told Degas—a bit of wisdom that readers like Claude kept obstinately brushing aside. But he was right about the title; why hadn't I thought to change it before showing him the poem? Now the harm was done, I'd betrayed part of our lovers' code for the sake of mere art and had nothing to offer in my defense.

My sister wrote announcing a trip to Rome in April and hoped I might feel like joining Bobby and her there for a few days. Claude urged me to go. When I made a face, he pointed out that it had been nearly a year since I'd seen any of my family. What if I was homesick, nothing else? Very well, I groaned, it was worth a try. And indeed my spirits began to lift in the plane, revived at the hotel, bubbled like *spumante* throughout dinner. Robin's spring holiday—he was the fourth at table—had given his parents a pretext, but another reason for their Roman holiday soon emerged. Our father wanted Doris to consult Dr. Simeons about her headaches.

It came out with the rueful merriment she called upon in all but the gravest emergency. Headaches were headaches, nothing more. On days when they didn't keep her prostrate in a dim room, she went on blithely about her business. Wife, mother, daughter, hostess, board member, wrapper of presents and runner of households, throughout it all as much a joy for the eyes as her midsummer flower arrangements, Doris was the wonder if not exactly the envy of her friends. One paid for a life so given over to claims and duties. If she couldn't explain her headaches, others could. My father, who returned from Italy a convert to the psychosomatic view of illness, had been dropping Dr. Simeons's name at regular intervals. "In case you haven't heard," Bobby interposed, "your father's gone through a hell of a time with Kinta these last months." Doris reached protectively for Robin's hand—wasn't he too young for these adult topics? The boy himself settled her doubts. He already knew from his younger brother that Grandpa wanted a divorce.

I made a rapid calculation: yes, it was time. Our father's first two marriages—to Doris and Charles's mother, and to mine—had each lasted thirteen years. Kinta's term had expired exactly a month ago. "Do you mean," I hazarded, "that twenty pairs of shoes from Capri failed to bring happiness?" We all began laughing, as family members will at stories lost on the outsider. Daddy might have known, said Doris, wiping her eyes, those shoes for Kinta would misfire. When the first pair she tried on didn't fit, out they were thrown, the whole lot, without further ado. "I thought she could have donated them to the Salvation Army," Doris went on, "but Kinta didn't appreciate the suggestion." "Tell Jimmy what she said." "Oh, that was funny," said Doris, putting on her idea of a vexed New Orleans accent: "'Why, Doris dear, what a thought—twenty indigents in the Hamptons, all wearin' *my shoes!*'" The episode contributed to my father's growing sense of being yoked to a perfectly impossible woman. The realization that she might survive him and inherit houses he loved, paintings and furniture he had collected, filled him with life-giving rage. Robin had been well informed: divorce was in the cards. By the same token, given the old man, so was remarriage. Past and future loves, flames not exactly pentecostal, were already descending upon the guest rooms of Palm Beach and Southampton. "Your sister and I'll have our hands full, just keeping him single for the rest of his life," and Bobby laughed, mirthlessly now, lighting his pipe.

I brought a copy of Tony's Venetian book of poems for Robin. As he read it in the next bed before we turned out our lights, his murmurs of pleasure took me by surprise. "It's so fresh, so simple!" he kept marveling. I bit my tongue. Any "simplicity" of Tony's would have to be the purest artifice, a Petit Trianon of titled milkmaids and silver churns. According to Kimon, poetry in our complex age was *meant* to be ambiguous, allusive, hard to read. Still, one had to begin somewhere, and my nephew had plenty of time to ripen—but wait. Wasn't I judging his taste with the same high-handedness that Claude, had he wished to do so, might have brought to bear upon those "lesser" writers and composers I preferred to Homer or Bach? I closed my Cocteau play with a grimace, wished Robin sweet dreams, and switched off the pink-shaded bedside lamp.

It was a pleasure to see Dr. Simeons again. After examining Doris he sat down with us both to discuss her symptoms. They were, he thought, due largely to stress. He and his psychiatrist colleague, a Dr. Detre, could do her a world of good, if she in turn would consider staying in Rome for two months. My sister went through the motions, but I knew before the question was out what her answer would be. She couldn't possibly spare the time, no matter how tempting the goal. Nor was it simply a matter of time, I understood without her saying. What of the usual mortifying incidents and feelings that everybody knew were apt to surface under the analytic eye? And if the treatment didn't work? "I guess I'll just have to make the best of it," she said with a little silvery laugh, pressing Dr. Simeons's hand and glancing my way for support. Life made claims, the glance conveyed; we had others beside ourselves to think of. But Doris's decision helped me to one of my own. Before leaving his office I asked her to wait and had a few words alone with the doctor. I mentioned my asthma attacks. As for those injections he had spoken of last year, just what would they do for me? Dr. Simeons was eloquent. Doris had slipped through his fingers; I did not. On the basis of his reply I returned to Paris glowing with anticipation.

We hear a piano recital by Solomon that wittily includes perhaps the easiest sonata by Haydn ("Why, I play *that*," says Claude) and the Beethoven

Opus 111, difficult both to play and to hear, Schnabel having omitted it
from his complete 78 r.p.m. recording. We know it largely from its
description in *Doktor Faust*. Tonight's performance—the trills of that last
variation drawing a fluttering curtain across green chasms and misty
heights—leaves us both gasping. "He is the *only* composer," Claude says,
and for once I agree. Another evening Flagstad bids farewell to the Paris
Opera. I've not heard her as Brünnhilde since 1941. Although it is sung
in German, all the elements of this French *Götterdämmerung*—scenery,
direction, the very texture of the orchestra—lend an indefinable silliness
to the sacred work, as when the Bible is read in the language of Marivaux
and Voltaire. Noble, vindictive, radiant, Flagstad alone is proof against
trivialization. "You can tell she has a very great soul," a strange voice once
proclaimed in the crush between acts of *Tristan*—meaning, I suppose, the
singer's access to feelings and actions that sprang not at all from what we
knew of her private life as a Norwegian housewife. I think of the remark
as Flagstad, making her final entrance, prepares to set heaven and earth on
fire. Is being "true to oneself" such a virtue after all? Aren't there passages
whereby the psyche climbs into far, high-ceilinged chambers, then returns
safely from the escapade? At evening's end, in any event, Brünnhilde's last
flames leapt skyward, and the good-natured log, uncharred as always,
came out to receive a standing ovation.

Claude took me, on our first arriving in Paris, to call upon Miss Toklas in rue Christine. He and Alice had corresponded for several years
before they met. That spring he'd stayed on in Vermont to hand-set,
print, and oversee the binding of Gertrude Stein's *Things as They Are*.
Plain, even governessy on the outside, all passionate turmoil within, the
finished book (Claude had given me its first numbered copy in Cassis) lay
on the drawing-room table, at one now with the Picassos, the needlepoint
chairs and plum-glossy horsehair sofa, the high windows illuminating the
clutter of two exemplary lives. It was here, Claude told me, that his hostess joined him a thoughtful half-hour late on his initial visit, allowing him
time to look through the prominently placed handful of letters I'd sent in
her care, while he was crossing the Atlantic.

Alice and Gertrude had always kept a special fondness for male couples, if literary so much the better, and Alice's welcome, when she joined
us, was the warmer for decades of practice. Many pilgrims had described

her. One knew about the tiny stature, the sandals, the mustache, the eyes. Like Max Beerbohm or the young Truman Capote, she might have been something created by a doll maker for a fastidious child. News to me, however, was the enchantment of her speaking voice—like "a viola at dusk," as a critic in the thirties had written of Flagstad's quieter moments; the phrase suited Alice equally well. She had no traceable accent, no affectation; the voice was quiet, pitched low, and of a kind of homespun suavity that kept slightly puckering her mouth, as though it, too, in its way, were savoring the charm of her diction. (Gertrude's voice was beautiful also, to judge from recordings. Imagine hearing the two antiphonally!) The big white poodle Basket, the original Basket's replacement but still the most famous animal I've ever met, lay at her feet. His manners were plain, even perfunctory, like an old countrified nobleman's; as man of the house, he clearly had his share of nonsense to put up with.

"I grew up in San Francisco," said Alice on my second visit. "My father was a Pole, an army officer. I remember being made to dance on a tabletop, at nine or ten, for a crowd of uniforms—and loving it! Ten years later music was still my passion. I and my San Francisco friends awaited the new piano pieces by Debussy much as New Yorkers had the death of Little Nell. But Gertrude decided our life was already so full of writers and painters that there was no room left for another art, so that was that."

Going with Claude to a Ravel opera had been her first musical outing in decades. I was surprised that Alice, having known (and judged so stringently) all those famous people, should be refreshed by the likes of us, until Claude pointed out the obvious: she'd buried most of the others. We were asked back, to lunch, to tea. Early on, she decided that "Jimmy," as my friends called me, wouldn't do. Neither would "Jim," my grandmother's choice, which made me sound "all boy" and was adopted without question by every Southerner I met, as well as my teachers and fund-raising classmates. No, Alice would call me Jamie. She told us which stationer to patronize and took us in person to her barber for haircuts. We were presented to the painter Francis Rose, Gertrude's and her last enthusiasm and their only mistaken one. It may well be that she thirsted for *any* company now that she was alone. Yet she gave a good account of her solitude—rereading that year the New York Edition of Henry James—and I timidly concluded, by the time we left Paris, that she'd accepted us as friends.

We were going to Rome. I'd arranged with Dr. Simeons to take his course of injections and persuaded myself (and Claude?) that this would turn me into a new and muscular person, happier, more self-reliant. We would return to Paris at summer's end, under which mistaken impression we left our two largest suitcases and some boxes of books in the Hôtel Récamier's baggage room and boarded the night train relatively disencumbered.

•

I liked Alice's calling me Jamie; it lent me the winsome air of a lover in a ballad. A decade later, also in Paris, Daryl Hine and I were strolling about after our first lunch together. He was twenty-four and wore a cape. Mended spectacles flashed beneath a forehead Victor Hugo's mother would not have disowned. "Quel joli papillon," purred a fallen woman from her doorway. "We'll pretend she means your bow tie," said Daryl, then cleared his throat hesitantly to ask, "Shall I call you James—"

"Oh, please do," said the gracious elder poet.

"—or Jimmy?" Embarrassed, I let my answer stand. But as others took up the name, I found that I quite liked it; "James" makes me sound in control of my life, as by now, surely, I am. Still others who've known me first from reading The Changing Light at Sandover *feel easier with the semifictional "JM," and I respond accordingly. The only nuisance is the hour spent unearthing a letter in order not to sign the wrong name to my reply.*

Alice also had her own fond and funny name for David Jackson, based on an initial misconception she clung to long after it was cleared up. To her he would always be David Livingstone, as though in order to find him I'd had to brave, like Stanley, some remote and uncharted "interior." Which was, after all, one way of looking at it.

Nor was it hard to hear in Alice's name for David—with his gift for good-natured, self-forgetful response—an allusion to the very timbre of life. Living's tone. Next to me, who out of fear or pride held back from experience, David greeted it with open arms. Whether responding to the quizzical looks at our first massive Stonington party (the liquor store owner's ruby anniversary) or running singing and laughing down a green mountain in Japan, he treated the whole world as a friend. Even his marriage's failure left him on happier terms with his wife than ever before; he had the golden touch.

It showed in his writing as well. When we first met, David was finishing a novel remarkable for its flexible prose and wide-ranging sensibility. There was no character, however remote from himself, to whom his quickening imagination didn't extend. His single fault as a novelist was an unwillingness either to revise or to plan ahead in more than the vaguest terms. As time passed and book after book didn't quite get accepted by a publisher, David stopped writing. The untended garden turned to peat, to tar, and eventually fueled our séances at the Ouija board. Here the problem of shaping the material into an intricate, balanced whole was out of our conscious hands. Peering like teenage grease monkeys into the celestial machinery, we had to trust it to hang together. Its revision into a poem, or play of voices, would be my affair. Of us two, David was the medium: a cinch to hypnotize, reacting with tears to messages that had yet to be spelled out. He was born with a caul—a rag of membrane, pressed stiff and brown in the family Bible—and this, according to the South Dakota midwife who attended his mother, usually meant psychic powers. Everyone who met him was drawn to the warm, eager tone of his living. For better or worse, the powers behind Sandover *were no exception.*

VII

Settling Down?
Kimon and Mina Pass Through.
A Picnic at Nemi.
Dr. Simeons Tries His Hand.

The ravishment of Rome in early summer! It must have eluded me the previous year, when my father's presence, like one of the tinted monocles I'd acquired for my camera, bathed whatever subject I focused upon in invalid yellow or a kind of harmless Oedipal crimson. Here at last was the city, if not in its true colors, then filtered capably through the eyes of Corot and Hubert Robert. Domes glowing with health rose above drowsy green thunderheads (the famous pines), walls forgave the wisteria that dragged them down, the Spanish Steps uplifted their descender, and a new light so loved the world that it edged my shadow with gold and braided itself over and over into the fountains' crystal fringes.

My euphoria came in part from those daily injections of what turned out to be the hormone ACTH, extracted from the urine of pregnant women. Dr. Simeons, summoning his only male patient from the waiting room packed with plump, voluble society women, whom the treatment allowed to subsist on a caloric pittance of 1500 a day, administered it jovially. He asked how I felt, how my work was going. And on these cool, radiant mornings, walking back to the hotel from his clinic, hearing the cries of tennis-playing monks, not quite meeting the eyes of the young flower vendor in the shadow of an ancient wall, I could imagine no place—and more to the point, no person—I would rather be.

At a fussy little writing table in the hotel, I went on with the novel I'd shown Robin the opening of. Strange as it sounds, I really believed I knew something about the human heart, as if a few romantic comeuppances (like Seldon James or Charlie Shoup), together with a taste for opera, sufficed to give me Stendhalian credentials. The project got nowhere. I kept retyping its handful of chapters, each time with fewer lines and wider margins to increase the number of pages and make it look like a book Tony would want to read. Finally it foundered and sank; the surviving characters, more dead than alive, crawled aboard my next piece of fiction. Well, I could always go back to poetry—or could I? Week after week, whatever I began led nowhere. I was reduced to dear life, dipping into it uneasily, like a widow into capital.

Claude, too, felt the diminishing returns of desk work in these new and beautiful surroundings. Before lunch he and I would visit the small, sleepy American Express office in the Piazza di Spagna, to collect our letters. Upright green-and-black taxis sailed round the fountain, and the periodic bus, leashed to a system of electric cables overhead—which spat out harmless fireworks whenever the connection broke—wheezed to a halt at the foot of the great flower-banked staircase. Some days we'd skip our prepaid lunch at the hotel in favor of a vine-roofed courtyard nearby, where the waiter let us go through our mail in peace. "Listen to this," I said, reading from my mother's letter. "'. . . I know I've reached the age where such things happen, but it's hard to believe, Son, that in the past two weeks *three* of my oldest and dearest friends have died. . . .'"

"Snap! Crackle! Pop!" Claude twinkled irreverently, quoting the classic Rice Krispies ad. I loved his rare fits of silliness. We were so young after all; I could see no connection between the deaths of my mother's sexagenarian cronies and the tears I had shed for Hans.

Hotel life wears thin. Claude decides he must go to Ravenna. Resentful of my injections, which keep me in Rome, I will myself to write a poem imagining Claude alone and happy among the mosaics I perhaps shall never see. That weekend, at least, I'm free to meet the dazzled sightseer in Florence for Haydn's recently unearthed *Orfeo ed Euridice*. (A detail missing from Gluck's version fascinates us: the death of Eurydice by snakebite. "Trust Haydn to be specific," says Claude.) Back in Rome, we move into three high, cool tiled rooms in Via Gregoriana, a perfect refuge from the summer's heat. With it comes the use, at hours when the dressmaker's fitting rooms that give on it are idle, of a verdant courtyard downstairs. At last we can cook and eat at home.

Such a refuge, I hope, will help me fend off the kind of invitation I received from some friends of my mother's. "Floyd and I just bet you're starved for a real American meal," said Eula Baker on the telephone. "Do you want to bring a friend? Fine. It'll be just us and the children." Floyd was an army major. Both he and Eula were from Jacksonville. We must have known a hundred people in common.

Their neighborhood of squat stucco villas and small gardens looked, in fact, not unlike parts of Jacksonville, minus the broken sidewalks and the Spanish moss. Their two mannerly little girls (who as our talk swirled round them greeted each surfacing name with the single question "Are they kin?") went to a Bible-oriented school for officers' children. All four gasped at how "Uncle Jimmy" lived. I had an apartment, spoke Italian, ate where the Romans themselves did? I might have gone native on some coral isle. Eula feared the salami, the shellfish, the salads. Did I realize that the Italian cheeses weren't pasteurized? Aside from a nightclub or two, they hadn't set foot in a restaurant all year; she and Floyd ate in American homes. It was amazing how quickly the Italian housekeepers learned what the family liked. The Bakers hadn't taken to pasta. "You know how we Southerners feel about rice!"

Grace was said over food of dreamlike familiarity: glazed ham with pineapple, rice, sweet potatoes, frozen string beans, biscuits, homemade coleslaw, vanilla ice cream and coconut layer cake. Plates thus laden had to be cleaned. Claude had a theory that unwanted food didn't put weight on. But Dr. Simeons's scales, the next morning, showed exactly how much the meal had meant to me. In its course I was made to realize what it had cost, in both time and taxpayers' money, to bring to table. For none of these things could be found in *Rome,* said Eula with affectionate condescension, as if talking of a small town upriver from Jacksonville. No, no; Italy still counted as a "hardship zone." Eula and some of the other wives took a military plane to Germany twice a month and shopped for food at the central PX. "They must be mad," said Claude, hearing about it. "I could eat Roman food for the rest of my life."

I savored the Bakers more than I did their dinner. Their idiom soothed my ears like once-popular songs. Henry James would have prized them as cameo performers in the comedy of Americans abroad. Still, to enjoy such evenings wasn't my reason for leaving home. I hinted as much in a letter to my mother, who wrote back that "we never know" when friends like these might come in handy. Priority seating on the last plane out before the Reds took over? The thought appalled me. Nothing must stand in the way of my expatriation.

Now Kimon and Mina arrive (on their way to New York, where I've offered them my apartment), with gifts impossible to live up to—a Byzantine wooden cross, a cigarette holder of red amber that belonged to Mina's husband, and his amber worry beads. The last two are presented in boxes of molded leather; Rome is full of them: Kimon found these in a shop near his hotel. By unhappy coincidence I've bought the same kind of box to give *him*, for cuff links or trinkets, but haven't thought to put any-thing in it. Finding it empty, he looks up, bewildered.

Kimon has never been to Rome and wants to see Keats's grave. Mina, who hasn't left Greece for thirty years, will see anything we like. Of all the art Claude and I have conscientiously "done," the piece I keep return-ing to and most care to show them is a large Etruscan sarcophagus in the Villa Giulia. Two gleaming terra-cotta figures recline on its lid, gazing off in the single direction of the afterlife—man and wife, no doubt, though they could as easily be brother and sister. Their identical smiles recall those of archaic Greece, only shyer, more full of wonder. As we study them, bewilderment again crosses Kimon's face. I know what he is think-ing. Why, with all the splendors of Rome to choose from, have I wanted him to see these hollow effigies? Do he and Mina resemble them, in my view? I wished things didn't always have to be taken so *personally*. True, the terra-cotta man, in these last moments, has begun to look dreadfully like Kimon. But what if it's the placid, sensuous accord of the couple that moves me most? And where do I fit in? I picture Kimon and Mina waking in my New York apartment next week, answering each other from room to room, raising blinds upon possessions the sunlight ransacks; it will be like the looting of a tomb. I decide on the spot to give the hero of my unfinishable novel a purpose in life. Let him be writing a monograph on Etruscan funeral sculpture.

Irma Brandeis is the next to pass through. Twenty years my senior, she made up the entire Italian department at Bard College the year I taught there. She has the lofty bearing and principles of those ladies with garlands or a musical instrument, to whom sestinas were written in the *dolce stil nuovo*, ladies quick to chastise the unvirtuous, stern in spirit, gentle in heart and speech. Though allowed to meet her mother and some of her friends—Barbara Deming, Joseph Campbell and Jean Erdman, an old Chinese gentleman—and though we talked freely about a thousand and one subjects, I divined that her story was to be heard only gradually, if at all. I matched my reticence to hers. We'd spent one of my last days in New York together, having lunch, going to see the Richard Lippold *Sun*—a huge and diaphanous rhombus of gold wires quivering in space— at the Metropolitan Museum. Before parting she said, "So I'm not to hear about that ring you're wearing?" It was a plain wedding band from Claude, engraved on the inside "J.M. from C.F." I'd given him in exchange a signet ring from my mother, flashing the Merrill crest to the world and also engraved inside, but with her initials and mine. I glanced at Claude's ring as if I had never seen it before. "Oh yes," I said, blushing. "My hand was beginning to look awfully bare, so I bought this for myself."

Irma comes to lunch in Rome, bringing us a book by a poet whose name neither Claude nor I have heard—Eugenio Montale. She reads aloud the opening poem to us before the book leaves her hands. *"Le trombe d'oro della solarità,"* it resonantly ends, calling to mind the *Sun* we saw on our last day together. Leafing through its pages, I notice that the book is dedicated "to I.B." but after all, countless people bear the same initials, and even supposing these point to my friend, it isn't for me to comment—a lapse that Irma may well find supremely tactful instead of what it is, my shyness amounting almost to indifference when faced with the treasure of someone else's life. That same shyness underlies my chronic anxiety in the realm of ideas—theology, critical theory, Plato *vs.* Aristotle, and so on. Shaped by ideas like everyone else, I nevertheless avert my eyes from them as from the sight of a nude grandparent, not presentable, indeed taboo, until robed in images. "A mind so fine that no idea could violate it"—Eliot's famous phrase, suggesting the elfin tissue from which such robes are spun—will eventually, I trust, flatter and justify my fastidiousness. Meanwhile how to get by in the company of friends like Claude and Irma, to whom ideas are paramount? Their immediate pleasure in each other lifts that burden from my shoulders; I can be silent if they want to talk about Aquinas or "difficult ornament" in medieval rhetoric.

Irma joined us for a picnic at Lake Nemi, called Diana's mirror in antiquity, whose circular beauty outshone its historical—or prehistorical—associations. With us was someone Claude knew, and I knew of, from New York: Robert Isaacson. This bizarrely handsome young man, olive-skinned and heavy-lidded, with manners derived from a close reading of Firbank, had once studied the harpsichord at Black Mountain and was now in Rome for an indefinite stay. I could see that Claude was attracted to him, and masochistically assumed the attraction to be mutual. Sure of us both, Claude led Irma into a long allusive discussion. We listened for a while; then, as counterpoint, or in order not to be silent, Robert and I discovered a number of "common friends" and made light of them while our companions went on drawing Virgil and Caligula and *The Golden Bough* up from the depths of the reputedly bottomless lake. We swam, drank our Frascati, ate our sandwiches. I took photographs, but the camera failed to catch the day's blur of fellowship; each of us looked distinctly harried, ready for a bath and another set of friends.

Irma's high-mindedness didn't prevent us from asking her an outrageous favor. Since she was on her way to Paris, and since we had decided to stay in Rome, would she mind "just stopping by" the Hôtel Récamier and arranging for the suitcases and boxes in storage there to be shipped to us? The maneuver turned out to involve their transport by taxi to a distant station, where paperwork took up most of the day, but she never reproached us, and in due time we and our tyrannical possessions were reunited.

It was now, in this charming summer apartment, with so much for once neatly unpacked and in place, that things at last fell apart. Claude, not surprisingly, had the wit to take charge of his own life. He sought out a psychiatrist—Dr. Simeons's colleague, in fact. At a joint consultation they had given him sodium amytal or, as it was popularly known, the "truth drug." Claude couldn't recall, by evening, what truths emerged, only that the doctors had exchanged glances and agreed that he should be helped.

I envied him. What would *I* do, now that my course of injections had ended? There were no flare-ups between us, just a sense of Claude's dogged need to break away and my own loveless clinging. One day I took out my recorder and started to pick out the opening theme of a late Beethoven quartet, a favorite of Claude's. He asked me curtly to stop. One evening he was going out to dinner by himself as respite from too much silent tension and the "diminishing voltage," as he put it, of our shared hours. Alone in the twilit rooms, I felt abandoned, paralyzed. I poured a drink, unable to think where to have my own meal. Forty minutes later I happened into the vine-roofed courtyard where we had gone more than once together. There sat Claude, peacefully attacking his antipasto. He didn't see me; I had time to find another table, another restaurant. But making my presence known, I croaked self-consciously, "Well, since, I'm here, can I sit down?" So the meal was a misery for us both.

Freddy wrote from Geneva about a dinner with Tony and his Princess. This lady was Russian, or Georgian, a sister of the "marrying Mdivanis"—three brothers known for their successful courtship of American heiresses. Nina herself was married to Denis Conan Doyle, Sir Arthur's son, presently in Ceylon. She appeared, said Freddy, both old and corpulent enough to be Tony's mother. Her lifestyle—the awful word might have been coined just to describe it—was grand to the point of suffocation: dachshund, chauffeur, maid, Bentley, hotel suite. Yet Tony struck him, Freddy went on, as being wholly in his element, if an element were indeed what titles and vain ornaments, Theosophy and hovering waiters, combined to make. Not that Tony's weakness for unlikely women came as a surprise—surely I remembered the *sage-femme*. How could I forget her? (As a soldier late in the war, Tony had found himself prowling the streets of a mean little Norman town. His then limited French didn't deter him from ringing a fortune-teller's doorbell and boldly extending, to the hag who opened, his palm: *lisez*—read it! It took her a while to get him off her steps, and him longer yet to grasp her calling: not a "wise woman" at all—

a midwife. Telling the story on himself, its hero struck us as exulting in this proof of an innocence never to be wholly tarnished.) Dear Tony. Now he and his Princess, figures on still another Etruscan sarcophagus, were together gazing off in a single direction, as Rilke said lovers should, and I was in no position to make fun of them.

Dr. Simeons had urged me to keep in touch. His injections left me feeling fit, if not exactly transformed in body. Where were those muscles? "Get some exercise," he suggested at our last meeting. "Go to a gym." As if the tennis and swimming urged upon me as a child hadn't been enough for a whole lifetime. Now, inspired by Claude's therapy, jealous of it as well, I made an appointment and volunteered, in reply to the doctor's usual questions, that both my life and my work left something to be desired. Dr. Simeons listened closely, then acted with undreamed-of kindness and dispatch. "Come with me," he said, in a flash ushering me out of his downtown office—was it lunch hour?—and onto the backseat of a smart little pale-green motor scooter. I put my arms, as instructed, about his stout, gray-suited person, and off we went in sunlight, through traffic, under trees, past architecture, over the muddy river, and up to "his" hospital, the Salvator Mundi on the crest of the Janiculum. Here we settled ourselves, both slightly panting, in an impersonal white cubbyhole. With Claude's experience in mind, I was looking forward to the truth drug. Instead we got right down to business. I needed psychiatric help, the doctor thought. Under normal circumstances he would have referred me to his gifted colleague, but Claude was already Dr. Detre's patient, and I could see, couldn't I, that a conflict of interests might arise? He himself (Dr. Simeons went on, a glow of anticipation overspreading his face), while not a trained psychiatrist, had sufficient clinical experience to feel sure that he could do me some good. Would I let him try? We'd know soon enough if we got into waters too deep for him. I grasped eagerly at the straw.

It was a step toward independence, if independence was what I wanted. Claude seemed to want it *for* me, and must have tried—he was too sensible and articulate not to—to bring some of our difficulties into the open. But I, like all three of the proverbial monkeys at once, cared neither to hear nor see nor speak to him about what we were going through. I presently found myself taking a second step. A young man I'd been seeing during the year at whose end I met Claude—seeing if not believing, and never bedding after the first couple of times—rose up from the pavement late one afternoon. He, too, had come to Rome for an indefinite stay. Was Via Veneto turning into MacDougal Street? With the red-gold curls, the perfect profile and spoiled mouth of a shopwindow mannequin, Wayne had remained as tenderhearted as his flighty nature permitted. When I told him my troubles he broke a date, gave me dinner, and took me back to his rented room. My blue-and-red silk neckerchief was scorched, I noted happily, from having been draped over the bedside lamp. We spent the next afternoon at Ostia, on the oily sand, in the dirty sea. A Roman boy on the train back to town caught Wayne's eye; we parted at the station without making plans. But I felt better about life in general.

•

That early novel was a self-defeating venture for two reasons. One was language itself. Given metrical facility, poems are far easier to write than prose. Shaw dashed off a three-act verse play in as many weeks; it would have taken him six months to cast it in his usual closely argued, painstakingly unmetered simulacrum of human speech. And Shaw had had the grounding in Latin that allows one to write correct prose without undue difficulty. I, on the other hand, like most American writers, must either make do without a style or patch one together from a dozen imperfectly assimilated models. The second problem was my simple youth. A young poet's ignorance of life will go unnoticed. Meter, rhyme, felicitous phrases, and whatnot mask the underlying weakness or banality. With fiction, where dissimilar characters suffer and grow and interact, there is no place to hide. One either knows what people go through or doesn't.

I'd had a brush with psychotherapy in New York four years earlier, soon after my break with Kimon. The theory in those days was that homosexuality was an illness, hence curable. At my mother's earnest wish I agreed to consult a doctor her doctor had recommended. My mother flatly dismissed the life I dreamed of living. "Society will not condone it," she more than once told me in her soft, reasonable voice; but if society meant the kind of people who, before the divorce, spent weekends with us in Southampton and Palm Beach, I longed for the day when I should be safely beyond the pale. My father had broached the forbidden topic once only, years before. He was recovering from a heart attack when I went to say good-bye on the eve of my induction into the army (and prompt surrender to an opera buff with chevrons). His advice from his hospital bed was brief and practical, more like folk wisdom than an uncanny reading of my mind: "Never let another man put his hand on you." I begged him not to worry.

As expressions of mid-twentieth-century prejudice go, these of my mother and father seem harmless enough. Hundreds of thousands of parents—not just mine—must have spent the forties and fifties urging secrecy and repression upon their queer sons. So I am surprised to hear from Jerl (a young, politically correct friend who digs me like an archaeological trench of outmoded notions) that he and his "support group" view such meddling as a form of verbal sexual abuse. He has to be joking! But no, he assures me; a single shame-producing word can be as traumatic as an incestuous caress. I nod soothingly. Jerl and I represent the difference between classic psychotherapy—that constricting and expensive underwear once made-to-order in Vienna—and its postmodern evolution toward letting our lives hang out in vivid, one-size-fits-all attitudes cheaply available at Benetton or The Gap.

However. My first psychiatrist turned out to be large and motherly, thus precluding on the spot any confessional ease. At twenty-one, did I even have a self to disclose? Still, we kept at it doggedly for several months, until my evasions and general listlessness got through to her. A year or so later I met Louise. She was my "advisee" at Bard, this bright, funny, tiny tomboy from Memphis, who brought a villanelle to our first conference. At a roadhouse one evening she asked me to dance. Back in my room she began undressing me. Any "cure" was all at once beside the point; what we found ourselves doing proved to be a thrilling discovery—at least until Louise broke off, pleading pain and fear, and fled. Like Faust upon his first glimpse of Marguerite—"O belle enfant, je t'aime!"—I was in love. In the days ahead I slipped pleading messages into her campus mailbox, bought prophylactics, sought to waylay her on the paths between dormitory and classroom. For her part she avoided me, left the notes unanswered, changed her major from contemporary literature to child psychology, and moved in with the lesbian head of that department. So much for heterosexuality. Louise and I met on my return from Europe and liked each other all over again. We even went to bed one sunny, tipsy dusk, but were by then so set in our ways that nothing came of it. Instead we made do with life-long friendship.

VIII

Mothers on Their Own.
A New Sister.
The Rings.
Scenes from Married Life.

Vira's matrimonial bubble burst. Only weeks before her wedding, with hundreds of friends invited to a reception at the country club in Missouri, came a telephone call from the bridegroom in his seagirt villa full (we indignantly fancied) of houris and loukoums. It was Vira's first clue that things were amiss. Sweet talk over the crackling wire failed to sugar the pill: he was backing out. Claude returned white-faced from the stoically brief call, his worst fears confirmed. I wondered if his mother wanted him to come home.

"I don't think so—she's too humiliated." He gave a mournful laugh. "Fifty years ago I'd have challenged the cad to a duel. Mother would have been rid of us both. . . ."

"At least she's come through in one piece," I said. "Not like the woman in your story." Our previous talks about Vira's romance had carefully skirted any mention of a fable Claude had written in Salzburg, months before the Saudi Arabian. In it a divorced American woman traveling abroad meets Death personified as a sinister foreign gentleman. I couldn't help but feel Vira's not dissimilar experience had been shaped in part by the power of her son's word.

"Remember," said Claude, "poetry makes nothing happen." His tight smile closed the subject. "Let's hope your mother's luckier."

For by the kind of counterpoint dear to Victorian novelists *my* mother was getting married at summer's end. Each week two or three letters kept me abreast of the latest arrangements. Something told me (though I refrained from passing it on to Claude) that my mother wasn't about to make Vira's kind of mistake. The snapshot I received of Colonel William Plummer in his air force uniform showed him to be lean and sandy-haired, with a look of the utmost probity. He himself had written—telling of a daughter nearly my age—and sent presents, a book he thought I'd enjoy, a two-pound box of guava paste. Although I'd never heard his name until the previous fall, he and my mother having lost touch for a quarter century, their friendship "went back" to World War I. Bill was then a young air force pilot at Pensacola. On weekends in Jacksonville, her hometown, he knew Hellen Ingram as one of the pretty girls who went to dance under the Japanese lanterns on the roof of the new George Mason Hotel.

By 1950 Bill's first wife had divorced him and his second had died; he was close to retirement. My mother, single for thirteen years, charming to her suitors but not looking for a change, suddenly letting herself be persuaded . . . ? "The sons cross the ocean," said Claude gloomily, "and leave them with no one to turn to." Whether or not he was right, I approved of this autumnal courtship. The fact that my mother and Bill remembered each other in blossom time seemed to ensure their happiness. The ocean between us, however, diluted the reality of her decision. It took a letter announcing the arrival in Rome of Bill's daughter to jolt me into full awareness. I hadn't thought so far ahead. From now on there would be these new, flesh-and-blood family members to have and to hold, to love and to lie to—for if I'd understood anything from my mother since 1946, it was that my "life," while I'd now reached legal age to pursue it, must not be rubbed in the faces of right-thinking people. Betty Plummer was coming with three friends, all of them fresh from Southern women's colleges. My mother knew *my* kind of male friend better than to suggest that I supply "dates" for the whole party. But naturally I would want, said her letter, to do as much as my schedule allowed for Betty and her friends during their brief stay.

The doing took some thought. Those sharp-eyed ambassadresses couldn't be asked to Via Gregoriana. They would want to explore every inch of the apartment. Although by July Claude was sleeping no longer in the bedroom but on an austere couch in the *salone*, the big incriminating double bed spoke for itself. It crossed my mind to dissociate Claude from the project altogether. Wayne would have thrown himself happily into a night on the town with Betty and the others. But I feared that his vivid looks and manner would give him—and by association me—away. Claude, with his intellectual dignity, plus a new mustache, which lent him the air of a young Flaubert, was the obvious choice to impersonate exactly the friend he was, for that matter, on his way to becoming: sober, reliable, a Good Influence, as Betty might say when questioned. Not that my mother was likely to change her tune where Claude was concerned. I decided to keep him offstage until the eve of Betty's departure. Before then I should have taken my new sister on a moonlit carriage ride past the Forum to the Colosseum, and the entire party for a day at Tivoli and the Villa d'Este.

Dr. Simeons pretended to think my qualms worth hearing about and advised me, not for the first time, to spare myself as much stress as I could. Lately there'd been a narrow escape. A pleasant older woman, whom we'd met the previous fall on the ship to Mallorca, asked us to Positano for a weekend. Claude declined almost angrily; I thought it might be fun to go—wasn't it time we saw a few Italians? "Don't forget," Dr. Simeons urged me, "that if you're not enjoying it you needn't stay. Come straight back to Rome and give me a call." I stayed; but it wasn't easy. Having let fly the one joke I'd prepared—something to do with my arrival from the Amalfi station in a carriage, like *mozzarella in carrozza* (a tasty Roman specialty)—I fell prey to an anxiety known till then chiefly in dreams. My hostess and her lover did their best, in vain: I might have been seated naked all evening before an instrument I could not play. Next morning, after a hushed telephone call, they deposited me at the villa of a fat expatriate American, perfectly nice, no doubt, but to me that day an evil cartoon of everything I dreaded turning into. Tense and silent, I sat with him on a concrete bathing platform, until he gave up trying to be friendly and excused himself. Why didn't I rally my forces, phone Dr. Simeons, return to Rome? A fly stung me; the sun weighed like lead. Do something, God! I implored. Whereupon a white-capped head popped out of the sea, a lipsticked mouth began chatting: "Aren't you coming in? What's the matter, can't you swim? The water's divine even if the fishermen do make ka-ka in it. Twenty years ago I had a hygiene complex, but my analyst got rid of that." Within moments I was up to my neck in intimate (if faintly shitty) sapphire. My savior was a Russian sculptor named Guitou Knoop, who lived exultantly by her wits and whose work—conventional busts and Arp-like abstractions—was collected by discerning millionaires she proceeded to name, along with the well-known artists and musicians whose mistress she had been. We dined together that night. "Well, you landed on your feet, didn't you?" said Dr. Simeons approvingly, when he heard about my weekend.

Now here I was once more *in carrozza*, clopping with Betty Plummer through the city she thought I was at home in. The other, less fortunate girls were writing postcards and "rinsing out their things" at the hotel, while before us the soot-and-silver monuments loomed and pivoted and receded beneath a full moon in "unpavilioned heaven." Nothing was easier than to like Betty. An only child who didn't act the part, relaxed yet pert, with blonde bobbed hair, slender waist, and responses that bubbled from her like an enthusiastic meadow spring, she was a young version of women I'd known from babyhood, "Aunt" Lalla or "Aunt" Mil, Jacksonville friends of my mother's, into whose laps I'd crawled, whose voices I could distinguish in the dark. From that single hour I began to guess how much Betty and my mother would come to mean, over the years, to each other, the joys and misgivings exchanged, the snapshots of children and anniversaries, the whole lifelong tissue of trust to be woven between them. She would give my mother—without even realizing she was giving—the very things I withheld. In return she would treasure the love I kept at arm's length, not to mention the sound advice on everything under the sun, from setting a luncheon table to conducting a life, that I would be following less and less in the future.

. . .

My mother's efforts to make me into a different person had led her to open letters not addressed to her, to consult lawyers and doctors—behavior that appalled her even as she confessed it. Her latest move, however, I found hard to forgive. Packing to leave New York for Atlanta, where she and Bill would live after their marriage, she came upon some boxes in the cellar, full of letters to me, and wrote asking my permission to destroy them. Time was precious, the mails slow; if I agreed, I had only to send her a couple of words by cable. Otherwise she'd have them put in my apartment, to which she had a set of keys. I recalled the boxes in question; they contained letters brought home from the army, nothing I greatly cared to save. Freddy's and Tony's letters from that period I had already stored safely in my desk, many blocks away, along with Kimon's and Claude's. I sent off my thrifty cable: DESTROY LETTERS. In due course my mother wrote saying that she knew I would be relieved to hear that *all* letters had been destroyed—those under her roof and those under mine. I wrote back in shock. Freddy's letters alone meant "an incalculable loss to posterity." In the context of Claude's and my deteriorating love, her action struck a crippling blow. It left me with little evidence of having been loved by anyone, except her. What was the poor woman thinking of? I knew well enough. As postwar vegetation overcame many an ancient stronghold, the arguments among people her age against sexual or political irregularity were shrinking to a single mean-spirited fear. Publicity would render you unemployable, a "security risk." Your former partners would come forward, with letters and so forth as evidence, to blackmail you. With so many "mysterious young men" in the picture—my mother's case went—those "awful" letters could vanish overnight, and I would live under the "threat of exposure" for the rest of my days. (Had she read the letters, or was she just imagining their awfulness? Either thought led to misery.) It never occurred to the alarmists that a person who made no secret of his life was a sorry target for blackmail. The discretion my mother urged was the *sine qua non* for the scandal she dreaded. But so fine a point eluded me at the time, as it did Dr. Simeons.

All the above figured prominently in my sessions with him. One day, feeling I'd painted too cheerless a portrait, I was inspired to illustrate my mother's lighter side with a little story. After their marriage, in February 1925, my parents lived in New York, in a brownstone on West Eleventh

Street. By autumn my mother was, as people used to say, "expecting"—
her close friends already knew the thrilling news. One of these friends, an
ex-beau named Frank Huckins, finding himself in New York prior to his
own marriage, came to tea. When the butler showed him in, my mother
rose awkwardly; Frank hadn't realized how advanced her pregnancy was.
"Oh, Frank, isn't it exciting!" she cried, taking his hand and pressing it
against her swollen belly. As his palm sank into a deep unnatural softness,
he stared at my mother in horror and concern—whereupon, mischie-
vously smiling (being barely three months pregnant at the time), she
removed the down pillow she'd stuffed into her dress as a joke. "I always
thought I'd write a Japanese 'pillow book' one day," I said, looking at Dr.
Simeons for corroboration of my mother's zany wit. His face was a study,
his laugh reluctant.

Betty and her friends, all unawares, shed a gentler light upon my mother's
nature. We had a beautiful day for our excursion, and it had been an inspiration to hire Marcello—my father's driver, whose telephone number I'd
kept—to take us. His ten words of English were now several hundred. In
his pearl-gray slacks and powder-blue sport shirt, he looked as certifiably
Roman as any tourist, dropping a coin into the Trevi Fountain's quivering reticule of light, could wish. I felt an extra degree of credit beamed
my way for having produced so genuine an article. The girls, like blossoms in the presence of a bee, seemed to grow lovelier and more animated
as the day wore on. Whatever lay in wait for us—brickwork and vista,
fountain and muddy path, the herb in the sauce and the ice in the wine—
they greeted with cries of wonder. With questions too. Who on earth
dreamed this up, and when? How in heaven's name was it built? Was
there a book on the subject? Would the cook part with his recipe? Why
was the sky so blue? Marcello, whose English was giving out, threw back
his head and laughed. After a few attempts at replying, I saw his point,
saw—from the girls' too-rapid nods of comprehension—that facts
would only clutter their lively minds unnecessarily, like a full basket on a
racing bicycle. Their Confederate pennants fluttered, their spokes flashed
and hummed. How easy life would be if my mother's curiosity were like
theirs, an aimless reflex called into play, so many laps on an oval track. But
in her view, inquiry *led somewhere*. To letters in a drawer, to the torso

among ferns. It was the cross she bore. She'd been a journalist—in this chapter we've seen her blue pencil at work—and had spent half of her life up North.

One of Betty's friends—dark-haired, magnolia-skinned Grace—struck me as holding back in a cloud of irony faint and provocative as scent. Had *she* lived up North, I wondered, or was she simply more grown up, closer to marriage, than the others? "I thought," said Betty, reading my mind and taking my arm, her words masked by the sound of plashing water, "that Grace might be fun to ask out to dinner with you and Claude. She's a little more grown up than the others. If that's all right?"—finishing on a smiling, hesitant note because Southern men must imagine, however mistakenly, that the final decision is theirs.

Everything went smoothly. We collected Betty and Grace at their hotel and gave them a Campari on Via Veneto. I cannot remember where we dined, but a photographer making the rounds of the restaurants passed through ours, so I know even today what an attractive foursome we made—the girls in their smartest dresses, Claude and I in the light-weight cotton suits that were the inexpensive height of fashion that summer. (Claude's was palest buff and mine a whitish olive, but the variety seemed endless. Robert Isaacson had found one of electric blue closely threaded with crimson.) Only late in the long and merry meal did an awkward moment arise. "I'm going to ask Jimmy about his ring," Betty announced gaily. And turning to me: "Rings have to have a story, I always think."

My fielding of the same question from Irma a year earlier stood me in good stead. "Oh, it's just a ring I wear. I've had it for ages."

"May I see it?" Betty held out her hand.

"If only I could get it off . . . !" I grimaced, making a show of trying.

"May I see yours?" said Grace to Claude with a smile, holding out *her* hand. Horrified, I watched him obediently remove his ring—my ring, rather, with my initials and my mother's on the inner band—and surrender it. By the time I collected myself enough to kick him under the table, Grace was turning the ring this way and that, trying to read the inscription. Claude gave a little pleading chuckle and got it back from her. Too late. Meeting my eyes across the empty glasses and crumpled napkins—with no trace of hostility, more as if (or so it reaches me today) we could at last, now that the All Clear had sounded, be the best of friends—she mouthed, for me alone, a petrifying two-word sentence:

"I saw."

•

Speaking of marriages, a couple of my mother's stories illustrate the lights and darks of hers to my father. On an early trip to Paris, the incorrigible man, who never hid anything from her, even the truths likeliest to cause pain, took my mother to a kind of nightclub-brothel, which he and his partner, Mr. Lynch, had patronized as bachelors. Only when seated at a table with a bottle of champagne did my father learn that "his" girl had chosen marriage and respectability far from the capital. This was reported by "Eddie's" now middle-aged playmate, in her backless dress and marcelled hair, who sat with them sipping and smoking, perfectly indifferent to my father's winning ways. Was she only pretending to remember him? He redoubled his efforts; it stung him to be seen in so bleak a light. Presently the band finished their cigarettes and struck up a sultry tango. The Frenchwoman turned to my mother and asked if she cared to dance.

"What did you do?" I gasped.

"I said I'd be delighted. You should have seen Daddy's face. That was the last time he tried to impress me with his old girlfriends."

The second story shows my parents twelve years later. They are dining at "21" in New York; once again—as Jerl nods thoughtfully in the back of my mind—my father has ordered champagne. He wants my mother to know that he means to break with Kinta and turn over a new leaf. (But Kinta's winning cards—the false pregnancy, the threatened suicide—have yet to be played.) As always, my father believes his words. So does my mother. Alas, in the car back to their apartment he goes too far. The worst is over, they're going to be closer than ever, he tells her—falling silent before the glowing embers of his unburdened spirit at last. My mother presses his hand. Then, with an amazed headshake, he breathes as if to himself:

"But God, I sure do love that little girl."

"My heart simply turned to ice," said my mother, ending her narrative. "When we got home I collapsed, I fell to the floor. He had to call a doctor."

Late in life, hearing this story, I tried to distance it by recalling a line from my poem "The Broken Home": "How intensely people used to feel!" Used to feel? In fact these parental tendencies—his to give pain by confessing, hers to suffer it in silence—were alive and well in my own nature.

At least no extremes of irony or anguish marked my mother's marriage to Bill Plummer. An incident dating from their early friendship would seem to assign it to the genre of those Hollywood screwball comedies so popular a decade later. In 1925 my mother, by then publisher of her own society news-paper, was spending a week at a new Miami Beach hotel free of charge in exchange for future mention in her columns. Bill, in town overnight, took her to a downtown restaurant. He was already safely married, and my mother safely engaged, though wearing the ring on a chain round her neck rather than on her finger. My father's divorce was still pending, and scandal, in that age of innocence, could ruin your life. Driving back from dinner, Bill failed to see the sharp, never-again-unlit left turn onto a bridge; before they knew it, both young people found themselves in deep water. They surfaced, dripping, then had to fend off a succession of Samaritan drivers stopping with offers of help. "Bill, the publicity!" my mother hissed each time he seemed to waver. (Pub-licity—dreaded with reason, now that it was hers to dispense?) Finally a taxi picked her up, leaving Bill to wait for the salvage crew. Over the telephone the next morning my father admitted that, seized by a premonition, he had fallen to his knees and prayed for her safety. "You mean last night?" marveled my mother, who all too soon would see my father's amorous antennae tuned to other wavelengths, and learned that it had been at the precise moment when the bay's water stopped her watch.

Why these compulsive vignettes? Perhaps their heroine lends herself more readily to anecdote than to any firsthand account. Or is it that her behavior—like the muse's own—keeps crystallizing into verse or narrative? Readers impatient for the real thing will be rewarded soon enough. My mother is already making plans to visit me in Rome.

Two years after our meeting in the sea at Positano, Guitou Knoop began work on a head of my father, which I had commissioned thinking they'd take to each other. The scheme misfired. Southampton wasn't equal to this "interloper," this "adventuress." In family mythology Guitou joined my ever-swelling ranks of friends "unworthy of your least attention," as both my mother and my sister, revealingly, phrased it in their letters. Still, I got a novel out of Guitou's profitable summer. And she had a crucial part to play in my life with David

Jackson, for it was her account of Stonington that led us to rent the top floor of an old building there: "You'll feel right at home—it's a tiny Mediterranean port, full of beautiful young Portuguese fishermen." In her eyes, perhaps. In ours it was a New England village on the Sound, full of clever wrinkled semi-famous people whom by the end of our second season we couldn't live without. We hardly missed Guitou when she broke with her local lover and moved away. I'm afraid my portrait of her in The Seraglio *didn't please her. But those are all different stories.*

I X

A Room of My Own.
Streetwalking.
A Literary Soirée.
Making Friends with the Natives.

Our summer lease was up. Wearily, sadly—but relieved, too, that the stale-mate had been broken—Claude and I moved into separate apartments; we'd lived together not quite fifteen months. He found a high sunny studio overlooking Piazza di Spagna. I took the first place I was shown, at the top of a big ugly turn-of-the-century building in Via Quattro Novembre. For its height it was singularly viewless, and I have never lived anywhere qui-eter: a big bare parqueted room with so generous an alcove for sleeping that it had a fireplace and could double as my study. There was a glassed-in gal-ley for cooking, and above the bathroom tub an antique *scaldabagno,* whose great roaring grid of blue flames produced hot water in a trice and a trickle. I lit it with alarm no familiarity could dispel. My actual landlord, a Count Bracci, I met when I signed the lease and saw only once again—by comic accident—at the end of my stay. I would hand my monthly envelope to his son or daughter-in-law. The young count and countess made a show of consulting me, before I moved in, as to the re-covering of the armchair and sofa, which—along with a bed and a lamp and some kitchen things—turned the bare apartment into a furnished one. From shop to shop they took me, wanting to be sure both that I liked the fabric and that it would be extremely cheap. Late in the day we agreed on something green-and-white. Praising my frugal tastes, they then sent me to a nearby carpenter for a worktable and a bookcase, which I could further economize by painting (green-and-black) myself. To get even, I bought two more lamps, expensive ones, and four elegant straight chairs. But my greatest luxury—sent by airmail at unthinkable cost from Aunt Mil in Jacksonville—was a down pillow. After the inert slabs of wadding I'd endured for months, here was such stuff as dreams were made on.

To Claude and me, on alternate days, came Quinta, a slender gray-haired *cameriera* who kept our modest lodgings as if they were palace apartments. Quinta's homemaking IQ was at genius level. In my coffin of a kitchen she cooked delicious roasts and vegetables, having begun the day by shopping for them. She braved the *scaldabagno* for my laundry, stringing sheets and shirts out of a back window before ironing them—where? And never in all her comings and goings did she cross the wide wooden floor without shuffling underfoot a collection of cloths so soft and waxy that her paths gleamed like canals at twilight.

Along with Quinta, Claude and I would be sharing another key figure: Dr. Thomas Detre. A month before we gave up Via Gregoriana I had a dream identifying Dr. Simeons with my father. The former heaved a sigh and confessed that he'd bitten off more than he could chew. He'd never pretended to be a psychiatrist. For one thing, we were already friends. For another, he had far too much personality of his own. He spent "my" hours elaborating, out of a genuine wish to help, such roseate metaphors for the therapeutic process that I left his office walking on air. Unhappily it was from what the sufferer, not the healer, found himself saying that help would come in the long run, and I was grateful to Dr. Simeons for acting on this truth as soon as it had dawned upon him. Any objection to my becoming Dr. Detre's patient seemed to have vanished with Claude's and my resolve to separate. A schedule of appointments was set up at our initial meeting—the usual fifty minutes a day, five days a week. Thus while Claude and I no longer had a common roof over our heads, we would soon (at different hours) free-associate on the same couch.

I had to wait for a departing patient to make room. "Two or three weeks at most," Dr. Detre said in his precise Hungarian voice. "We are winding up our work together." As I knew of cases where going to an analyst had become a lifetime's occupation, part of me was relieved that the doctor foresaw—he did, didn't he?—some kind of time limit to our own "work." He assured me matter-of-factly that ten months or a year would suffice for our purposes: I was young enough, and healthy enough, not to require prolonged treatment. Another part of me had been looking forward to a career as a concert psychotic. Now it emerged I needed little more than to have, as it were, my clumsy fingering of "The Happy Farmer" corrected. But of course getting on with life was the main thing. Why, by next July, I might be free!

Dr. Detre's office, actually the sitting room of his apartment, was out in Parioli. Allowing for a thirty-minute bus ride to and from our sessions, I calculated that they would take care of over two hours each day—as if time were a restless child in need of supervision, instead of the old, impassive guardian. Meanwhile how to get through the weeks before we started? I might conceivably work at something of my own, though my papers were dusty and yellowing, but who would I spend my evenings with?

I went out into the streets, hoping to find my answer there. From Via Quattro Novembre's noise and fumes I could escape to the Quirinale in one direction or (crossing Piazza Venezia) to the Campidoglio and the Forum in the other. My favorite route to Piazza di Spagna—where the American Express office or the English bookshop a few blocks away relieved the pangs of homesickness—took me down the narrow Via Pilotta, under the limestone buttresses that shored up the hanging gardens of the Palazzo Colonna, past furniture makers, junk shops, every imaginable kind of artisan. I paused longest at the "windows"—two narrow glassed cabinets taken indoors at night—of an engraver patronized, it would seem, exclusively by the College of Cardinals. His specialty was a round paper label, an inch or two across, just the thing for a debutante's bookplate or for sealing up a cellophane packet of sweets, against whose contrasting ground (red on white, red on lavender, red on paler red) a flamboyant ecclesiastical hat stood out, dripping tassels of varying lengths that forked and multiplied like antlers or a family tree. Within sat the old man, at a work space no bigger than his two huge hands, scrutinizing through a jeweler's loupe some latest triumph of two-dimensional millinery.

I hoped for courage to step inside one day. At another shop, photographs of grim old people had been transferred onto white enamel ovals, evidently a popular form of tombstone decoration. Why not go in and arrange for the photographs I'd been taking of Betty and Irma, my father and Freddy, to be made into shower-stall tiles? What better audience for my steamy renditions of "Nell" or "Le Spectre de la Rose"?

Often I lingered at these shopwindows so as not to be caught scanning faces in the street. Seeing the reflection of a jaunty young man, I took care to let him pass before turning to study his back. If ever, feeling my eyes, one of these boys looked round, ready to smile, I went through a whole charade of preoccupied indifference that sent him, smiling now for other reasons, on his way. A few further steps brought me to the Trevi Fountain, where one could appear to be idly enjoying the play of waterlight upon baroque gods and horses while peripheral vision took in the workmen already half turned by marble dust into overalled statues, seated together at a wineshop I would sooner have turned to stone myself than enter. The kind of encounter I looked for depended on acting with the speed of a camera—a "click" of intelligence between two perfect strangers. Wayne, to hear him talk, brought it off several times a day. But the people my cumbersome time exposures were set up to attract vanished into a ghostly blur, as behind sheet after sheet of water, until I was the only figure left standing among the thousands whom the great fountain refreshed.

If my wanderings lasted until evening, I took care to avoid the Colosseum, the banks of the Tiber, or the Borghese Gardens, places recommended by Wayne, where I pictured furtive persons like myself congregating in order to meet emancipated ones like him. I kept to the thronged streets. As the starlings, chirring like crickets, settled in the trees and the shopkeepers lowered their iron curtains, would there be among these crowds no single young man to be struck dumb, like Des Grieux in Act I, by my noble demeanor and sweet face? There would not. Each was headed for a meal at home. Later, perhaps, answering the call of pleasure . . . ? But I would be asleep by then. I'd found a restaurant I kept returning to. Although the food was indifferent and the lights too bright, it had the virtue of being so near my apartment that I ran no risk of attracting company on my tipsy way to bed. Some anonymous verse on the menu charmed me at first with its Da Ponte–like fluency:

Sè l'Albergo da Raimondo
Ricercato è dagli sposi,
Ciò vuol dir che deliziosi
Sanno i giorni qui passar!

Yet by the fifth or sixth visit the words had grown callous and mocking, and a night came when I walked past the unctuous proprietor with the coolest of nods. Perhaps for once I had somewhere else to go.

Two poems I'd written in Mallorca were being printed in *Botteghe Oscure*, edited in Rome by Marguerite Caetani—a princess (not as hard to come by, evidently, as Tony made them sound) and an American to boot. Soon after my move I went to a large evening party at the *palazzo* in the street that gave its name to the magazine. I knew not a soul and was about to leave when a gaunt bespectacled man with a dragging foot limped up to me. He said my name, took my hand in both of his, and introduced himself in a melodious drone: "I am Morra. We live at the same address." It was hard, in the talk-filled dimness, either to hear or to see as much as I would have liked, but I told him I had a good cook and offered to give him lunch. After agreeing on Friday he led me across the room to meet a couple of black writers and their wives. The idea had come to him that one of them, a poet named Ben Johnson, might help me translate a few poems by—had I heard of a living poet named Montale? I could say truthfully that I had. With the smile of confirmed intuition, Mr. Morra now excused himself. I stayed on talking to my fellow Americans, drank another glass or two of wine, and made a second lunch date before saying good night. No one at the princess's party resembled the kind of person I longed to meet in Rome. But anything was better than another whole day left to my own devices.

My stock went up when Quinta, who must have checked with the *portiere* downstairs, learned that she would be serving lunch to *Count* Morra. Ah, Signor Jim, this was a personage of great distinction, a Resistance hero, intimately allied with the House of Savoy! I had never known her so voluble. At the sight of my guest by daylight, in his shabby jacket and old-fashioned shoes laced above the ankle—the sole built up a good three inches beneath his lame foot—I automatically dismissed her report as gossip. ("Discounted," I nearly wrote; but he could keep his title—who *wasn't* a count in Italy?) Umberto, as I would gradually learn to call him over the months to come, accepted a finger's-breadth of wine and set about putting me at ease. His face, at once goatish and austere under a high brow from which sparse reddish hair had been slicked straight back, hardly moved as he talked; his hands, however, were restless as a satyr's. I caught myself trying to see how far up his cuffs the glinting red-gold wrist hair went. His English put mine to shame. His manners were natural, even humble, like the hut of forest boughs that shelters a great wizard. At fifty-five he seemed both very old and of no age at all; his mind kept him young, as did an adorable innocence of spirit. It wasn't just that he was a bachelor; he might have been a virgin. In his company, conversation was always taking a turn that left him blushing, whether from shock or amusement one could never say. It would then be for Umberto, fingers sinuously interlaced, to sound his characteristic drone, a deprecatory note long as a lifeline, and haul the endangered topic back to respectability.

This virginity, if that is what it was, gave him a good deal of license, especially (it seemed to me) in his friendships with young men. I didn't suppose that my being *literary* made Umberto seek me out, though it helped. Later, when he met some of my friends, I was able to tell in advance which ones he was likely to take to. Claude, for instance, with his cogitator's brow and fierce mustache, he found too deliberate, too much what he would be for the rest of his days; by contrast, Robert Isaacson's hesitant, emotional temperament drew him like a candle's glancing flame. These judgments, to be sure, were never put into words. Neither were the "ideas" he embodied. Was he a saint? a socialist? *He* wouldn't say. I thought of Kimon, unable to get through an hour without verbally reminding himself and his listeners of the meaning of Life. In Umberto, by contrast, it was the life of Meaning that showed, in his gait, in his speech, in his scholarly habits and his restless hands. Part of me longed to seduce him, part of me despaired of ever living up to him.

There was food left over for Ben Johnson and me that Sunday. After lunch we lit our cigarettes and turned to the two Montale poems he had brought along. Until that moment I had been proud of my Italian; now, faced with line after line I did well to decipher a word of, I realized my folly. I'd scarcely passed the level of fluency enjoyed in English by a youth I met years later on Crete. "English is a much simpler language than Greek," he informed me complacently. "You have only the single word 'stone,' while *we* have . . ." (proceeding to rattle off the Greek for rock, boulder, pebble, etc.). Ben suggested I get a serious dictionary before we went any further. It was a beautiful warm day, his wife had gone to the movies—why not take a walk?

We tried the Forum. I might have waxed sentimental over the ruins of Catullus's *garçonnière*, but places that "breathe history" have always left me cold. The chalk-and-blackboard ghosts of "great" (that is, ideologically inspired) human deeds deaden the very air between stroller and scene. Shakespeare's play in which I had acted Casca to Freddy's Cassius at Lawrenceville was already more than I cared to know about ancient Rome. I hoped to learn instead something about Umberto, how he and Ben had met, what form their friendship took. The tale I heard was simple to the point of drabness, involving a committee, a fellowship, an intercultural institution that Umberto helped to run. Ben made it—made culture itself— sound prosaic and depressing, like a branch of civil service. I wondered for an instant if I'd been mistaken in my enthusiasm for Umberto, then concluded that the drabness came from my companion's view of these matters, the dreary "forum" of faction and opinion I found so suffocating in American intellectual circles. Or not only American: the following year Umberto had me to lunch with a Serbian literary critic. Afterward my fellow guest and I walked as far as the Trevi Fountain. Knowing that I was a poet, he asked, *"Quelles sont vos recherches?"* I changed the subject in alarm. I didn't want to talk shop, and while I suspected that this question meant nothing more intimidating than "What are you after?" or "What are you trying to accomplish?" the word *recherches* with its overtone of "research," of archives and institutional backing, set me gasping for fresh air. Or was it, finally, that both the Serbian critic and Ben Johnson were straight and saw no point in trying to charm another male?

We had followed some of the Sunday crowds into the catacombs, the cool dim underground chambers a relief from the swelter aboveground. As we emerged I realized that we were being followed. A handsome, rather dreamy-eyed policeman in uniform had kept us in sight for some time, turning where we turned, pausing when we paused. I mentioned the fact to Ben, who reacted—like any man with a clear conscience—by looking round and establishing eye contact. The young policeman came up to us, smiling with relief, and asked if we were Americans, where we were from, how we liked Rome. He was just now off-duty; could he treat us to a coffee? Emboldened by Ben's chaperonage, I suggested we return to my apartment for a glass of wine.

Luigi Valentini came from a village fifty kilometers south of Rome. After Ben took his leave, we sat on, with our wine and, unless I was greatly mistaken, greatly liking each other. Luigi's pistol lay in its holster across the room. I'd dreamed of an Italian lover; now was the time to act. "It's child's play," Wayne had told me. "You just lean over and nuzzle them." But what would Luigi think of me then? Besides, in my fantasy, now so close to realization, it was he who leaned over. Why hadn't he? Well, no doubt his finer feelings prevented him. My operagoing self, always my guide in romantic matters, cast him in the role of a modest boy, reluctant to aspire beyond his station. Out of the question to disenchant him by making a vulgar pass. No, no, we must first become friends. Eternal friendship—duets from *Don Carlos* or *The Pearl Fishers*—rose fluently to the lips of my operagoing self. I needed to practice my Italian, a knowledge of English could lead to promotion for him. His eyes glowed, his whole face beamed at the prospect. A different person would have made hay in that sunshine, or written the hour off as a total loss. But knowing no better, I asked him to dinner on his next day off, shook his hand warmly, and sent him on his way.

•

My operagoing self. It was born in the music room at Southampton during the summer (1937) my parents separated. Picture a huge hushed space hung with red damask. Sun streams through stained-glass escutcheons and spirals up each corner column of carved and gilded wood twenty feet high. I am sitting at one of two grand pianos, next to Mrs. Longone, who has just opened the score of Pagliacci *and is explaining the dramatic appearance—through the curtains, before the action itself begins—of the hunchback Tonio. Carol Longone is a new friend of my mother's. Originally from Florida, she was once married to an impresario and has Lived Abroad. I will start piano lessons with her in the fall. Meanwhile . . .*

The score she plays from shows the singers' words in both Italian and English. Tonio warns the audience that a powerful story is about to be enacted, and not to mistake its interpreters for bloodless puppets. (It may be this morning that I outgrow, once and for all, my marionette theater.) "We have human hearts," Tonio sings, "beating with passion!" Passion? I've been, so far, a happy, sheltered child. Although something terrible is happening to our family, it hasn't been brought home to me in any profound sense. A couple of weeks ago my mother called me into her room and handed me my father's brief and no doubt handsomely phrased letter saying that he was leaving her. Having read it, I was inspired (at eleven) to let it flutter from my fingers to the carpet. "Oh, don't be dramatic," said my mother with some asperity. I knew what she meant—up to a point, beyond which I knew nothing whatever. Tonio's words, sung to a melody I find unspeakably beautiful, puts things in perspective. Just as a child cannot dream of attaining the depth of the woman's feeling as she detaches herself from his arms and goes—like the heartsick clown in Mrs. Longone's synopsis—to powder her face at the mirror, so we in the audience must feel less than the actors do; it is as simple as that. Strong feelings are the stuff of art. They belong not in the home but onstage.

Thus opera was from the start an education less musical than sentimental. During performances my eye kept straying to row upon row of us, blank-faced in stagelight, inert, waiting to be moved. We were the puppets! But weren't we learning too? Why else had we paid (or our mothers paid for us) to hear Violetta suffer, Wotan turn upon his wife, and Gilda disobey her father? Against so many all-too-human figures Flagstad's Brünnhilde stood out larger than life. Her love threw a wrench into the entire celestial machinery; when the flames died down and the Rhine subsided, nothing was left but the elemental powers that prevailed long before the gods (narrow-minded nouveaux riches, like the people we knew in Southampton) sprang up to embody them. Next to the powers of such a woman, all male activity—Siegfried's dragon slaying, Einstein's theorizing, the arcana of password and sweat lodge—seemed tame and puerile. I longed throughout adolescence to lead my own predestined hero, whose face changed every month, into music's radiant abyss.

(Such dreams die hard. "I want this to cost everything," Claude remembers my telling him during our courtship. Strange how the reckoning, when it came, asked not a groan more or less than either of us could afford, given our age, our pretensions, our resilience. At fifteen—at twenty-five, for that matter—I trusted suffering to improve the style, the lover's loss to be the artist's gain. Don't I still? In the final tableau of a recent New York Götterdämmerung, human figures have ventured forth among the wreckage to peer upstage as light *breaks over the stilled waters. The director might have illustrated my point by getting these survivors up to look like Mahler and Strauss, Debussy and Stravinsky.)*

Week by week, then, those first seasons at the old Met, I pursued my education. I learned what Thaïs inwardly suffered, what mad Lucia, what even her heartless brother and nitwit husband "felt." Surrendering to adult voices in the darkened house or singing along in my room to a drinking song whose flip side was a prayer, I found myself trying on emotions till then inconceivable, against the day when I should be old enough to wear them in public.

Long before that day dawned, I weighed the morality of interpretation. I'd heard Iago cheered and Desdemona hissed. What, after that, did "good" and "bad" mean? If, as my mother might have said in her own defense, genuine feeling kept one's responses from being dismissed as "dramatic," so did artistry. How to decide at Salzburg, for instance, between Schwarzkopf and Seefried? Their human tempers—the one's iced champagne, the other's flaky strudel— were equally products of the strictest training. Art honored both the reticence my mother recommended in life and her right—or mine, if it came to that—to fall to the floor when nothing else availed. To the degree that the aria's meaning depended on who sang it, the question of how to attack one's own high notes was in no way academic. Throughout the 1960s in Athens I off and on mourned the lengths to which Chester Kallman (Auden's beloved and our neighbor, his life, like all our lives those years, a tissue of passionate betrayals) had modeled himself in boyhood upon the Wrong Soprano—on Zinka Milanov, say, with her queenly airs and clutch-and-stagger reflexes, or on Ljuba Welitsch, incandescent and obsessed, whose last performance at Salzburg haunted me still. (It was in homage to Welitsch, I felt, that Peter Sellars, in his Harlem-slum staging of Don Giovanni, *had Donna Anna shoot up on the brink of her final, ecstatic cabaletta.)*

For my part, memories of Rosenkavalier *with Lotte Lehmann helped me to smile and shrug through the worst. Here was a bittersweet, faintly homosexual, wholly survivable alternative to my dreams of immolation and all-consuming love. Certain doubts arose belatedly when I took Peter Hooten to that opera, which had all but made me who I was, only to see him unconvinced by the Marschallin's "self-sacrifice." He blazed out at her, as we walked home, like a young Chenier or Cavaradossi attacking the corrupt regime. Manipulative, narcissistic—who could swallow such a woman? It came to me that Peter was indirectly attacking certain aspects of my relationship to him, with its own dramatic age difference and offstage Feldmarschall (David Jackson), whose prior claims made the young Octavian's position so intolerable. Listening to him without shrugging, I felt what it had cost the Marschallin to shrug. The hold of art wasn't to be broken that easily.*

X

Dr. Detre Takes Over.
The Rake *Onstage and Off.*
Luigi's Hospitality.

Out of nervousness and a desire to impress Dr. Detre at our initial interview, I brought into play the heavy red amber cigarette holder that once
belonged to Mina's husband. My psychoanalyst and I were sitting face-to-
face; the couch work would come later. To offset his youth—for he was
only a few years my senior—Dr. Detre was soberly dressed and gave out
an air of sallow, almost funereal gravity. Midway in our talk the beautiful
holder fell and broke into three pieces on his tile floor. I pocketed them.
Neither of us would ever allude to the incident. Dr. Detre finished what
he had begun to say. While in therapy the patient was urged strongly neither to marry nor get divorced. Among homosexuals, with no legal ties
between partners, distinctions tended to blur. The principle was nonetheless worth keeping in mind. The only other "rule" was relatively trivial:
if for any reason I missed an appointment without giving notice in
advance, I would be expected to pay for it.

 "One question now, if I may," he said mildly. "Why are you consulting me?" I cast about in momentary panic. Wasn't it enough to be

disturbed, or "shattered," even, like my piece of amber? Then it came to me: I didn't know how to love, I didn't know how to live, but I did know how to write a poem. Did once and didn't now—hadn't since leaving Mallorca, months before. That was my reason for seeking help. I wrote, therefore I was; if I couldn't write, I was nobody. "You must not expect that situation to change in the near future," said Dr. Detre. "Psychotherapy is a full-time job. You will have little energy left for creative work."

Three weeks later our daily sessions began. The first step was to get my "history"; the word called up a vision of the Forum downtown in all its documented dullness. Still, I did my best to keep him entertained: my parents, the divorce, my beloved Mademoiselle, my stint in the army, teachers and friends and lovers, recurrent dogs and loyal, one-man dreams. "Take your time," the doctor had said. To oblige him I dwelt upon certain climactic moments. At eleven, for instance, following a schoolmate's hint, I tracked down a story in the kind of New York newspaper "we" never saw; the caption beneath my photograph read "Pawn in Parents' Fight." I knew my custody was in dispute, but—only a pawn? I suggested to Dr. Detre, just to make things easier for him, that my sense of personal unworthiness dated from this incident. But even with such digressions my history was over in four hours, like those half-day bus tours of Rome from which the archaeologist-to-be forms his first vague suspicion of the strata, the sleeping temples and thoroughfares, that underlie the modern city. As I talked Dr. Detre sat across from me, silent and receptive as a mirror, now and then meeting my eyes or asking for clarification of a specific point. These were crucial hours. For one thing, we would never again *see* each other. Once I moved to the couch, I would be talking to the blank ceiling or to the brilliant window across the room, while he, in a chair discreetly to one side, made sense of my words.

One dream I reported dated from the summer of 1947, but it had stayed with me. In it I'd become a fish, beslimed and barnacled, making sluggish rounds in the central tank of an old-fashioned municipal aquarium. People were gazing at us—at me and the *real* fish, that is—through thick glass. Our greenish waterlight played over their faces. All at once I realized I'd caught someone's eye, a stout middle-aged man in nineteenth-century dress, whom on waking I identified as a bit player in the film *Les Enfants du Paradis,* one of the crowd assembled outside a carnival tent to see Arletty as a naked allegory of Truth. With the limited expressiveness at my command, mainly the intense focusing and flashing of my starboard eye, I tried to signal to this person: *Look! I'm not what I seem, I'm a man like you!* The message got across, but with the wrong results. The stout man broke into smiles and pointed me out to his neighbors—*voyez donc,* a fish who imagined he was human, what next! "So I guess even then," I laughed glumly, "I may have been signaling for help." Dr. Detre nodded. My museum of past dreams all at once looked small and shabby.

I never asked Dr. Detre what school he belonged to. One of his initial suggestions was that I not, during treatment, read up on psychoanalytical theory, case histories, and all the rest. One day, he hazarded, Freud's *Introductory Lectures* or Jung's *Autobiography* might interest me, but not now, please. I saw his point—it would be far more valuable to find words for our developing relations than to blunt them in advance by terms like "fixation" or "transference"—and gave thanks that our verbal dealings weren't to be overtechnical. I wondered, though, about Dr. Detre's command of English. The undertones and double meanings I sought in my poems were bound, I thought, to reappear in dreams or slips of the tongue; was he up to catching them? But where Dr. Simeons had been all nods and appreciative chuckles for the odd connection I now and then achieved, Dr. Detre's silence took me aback. He showed no interest, furthermore, in my writing, past or future. The impulses behind my poems would as a result be expertly blocked and moved, as they say in word-processing circles, into the newly opened file of our joint effort. The goal, I gathered, was to get me back on speaking terms with my psyche, for as in diplomacy, once those "talks broke down," life became progressively more dangerous.

Part of me, of course, went on as if nothing were amiss. Another part, with an energy similar to my mother's in detailing the plans for her wedding, wrote a number of long letters announcing—to both parents, my sister and brother, to Freddy, to Kimon—the contract I had entered into with Dr. Detre. The proper volume for self-assertion is hard to gauge at twenty-five; if a whisper goes ignored, try a howl of pain. Whatever the tone level of my manifesto, my correspondents expressed their alarm and affection by return mail, in letters sometimes longer than mine. Clearly I was getting through to them. Clear, too, was the wisdom of having placed myself beyond their reach. Since the "work" of psychotherapy took place subliminally, while the patient was asleep or sunbathing or making a scene at the post office, I, or what was left of me, remained free to lead an ever worldlier life.

I obtained leave from Dr. Detre to go with Claude to Venice for the premiere of *The Rake's Progress* at La Fenice. Passing by the theater on the eve, we heard the chorus rehearsing and stood transfixed by these faint, precious hints of what awaited us. We also found the libretto in a music store and within hours knew much of it by heart. Montale, in the Milan paper he wrote for, likened its spare elegance to a bamboo birdcage. The work promised to embody what most attracted us in the collaborators, Stravinsky's neoclassical vein (a cannibal in a top hat, as somebody put it) and Auden's lyrical, cabaret-haunted glamour. People assumed wrongly that Chester Kallman's contribution to the text was nominal; in fact he and Auden wrote alternate scenes. I'd met them both in New York through Kimon, once at the Algonquin bar and again at the Gotham Book Mart party for the Sitwells, whose famous group photograph has Auden perched on top of a ladder. (Chester, Kimon, and I, along with the dozens as yet unpublished in book form, were herded without apology into a back room.) But those long-ago meetings I suffered through mute with shyness weren't to be presumed upon in Venice. Claude and I made do with much loitering in the Piazza, hoping vainly to glimpse the celebrities. For the premiere the world's prettiest theater had been further titivated by a bouquet of red and white roses on the bosom of each box. The house was full; we were all in evening dress—all but a handsome young man who, lest the effect be spoiled, had been made to wait for the lights to dim before marching down the aisle. "There goes Ned Rorem," whispered Claude.

Stravinsky bowed from the podium, the applause swelled and died, the music began. Whatever I'd imagined in advance came out freshly, differently, so much so that after the first scene I suspected the composer of perversely choosing the least plausible setting for the poet's lines. But plausibility—embodied onstage by Nick Shadow—emerged as the wry familiar spirit of the *Rake*, the score, when finally recorded, grew to enchant me as much for its angelic surprise and invention as for its diabolical way with pastiche. The high point, that first evening, was Anne Truelove's solo scene, which closed Act I with a stirring cabaletta. Here Schwarzkopf came into her own, if not exactly into the role itself. Playing a village maiden unused to pomp, she appeared dressed for London in a great sleeved and cloaked magnificence of gray velvet. (The night before, as we shamelessly eavesdropped, someone in the know, two tables removed from ours, regaled his friends with an account of the dress rehearsal. Doubts had arisen as to that lavish costume; "I'll make the difference with my face," said the diva firmly. And even Stravinsky had been forced to admit, when the curtain fell on a high C bright as the full moon: "She sings well, our little Ilse Koch!") The scene was a triumph notwithstanding. We sat through the remaining acts in a glow of self-congratulation. From this pinnacle the rest of the twentieth century would be all downhill.

Although the Roman opera season hadn't begun, smaller companies were performing one-act rarities by Rossini and Donizetti. Now that Robert Isaacson had left for an October in Venice with the Carpaccios and the Tintorettos, I saw Claude more often and more amicably than I'd expected when we moved apart. He was still courting Robert, doggedly and to no avail. I knew this not from either of them but from Hubbell Pierce, the dearest and most deadpan of my MacDougal Street friends, who'd come to Italy to catch his breath before his London winter. He and Robert were also friends; he refused to believe that we'd never met in New York and scarcely knew each other in Rome. But whom didn't Hubbell know? He bedecked me for, and took me to, a Halloween headdress party at Frederick Prokosch's, introducing me to ten people in as many minutes, including the scion of Jacksonville's most prominent banking family. Here at last was something to put in a letter to my mother, even if I failed to describe my crown of chrysanthemums, Hubbell's navy-blue pillbox, whose brief, businesslike veil concealed not a trace of makeup ("the way we wanted our mothers to look on Parents' Day"), and the young Floridian's bracelet of big emeralds, worn like a bandage across his darting eyes. I began to suspect that, had my concerned friends and relations seen me amid these diversions, for which I might have seemed to give up all thought of writing poetry, they would have felt distinctly shortchanged.

Wayne, too, had left for Venice, with one of his Italian admirers; *he* didn't depend on the foreign colony for companionship. That season found him caught up in the one great winning streak of his life. He could do no wrong. He added gold to his hair and lovers to his list. He actually, like some grand courtesan of the Belle Époque, gallicized his name from Wayne Sheppard to Jean de la Bergerie. The entire world lined up for his favors, no longer because he was beautiful but because of his fame: he was known throughout Italy as the Boy from Venice. People arrived at our Roman gatherings, gasping like messengers in Sophocles, with his latest exploits on their lips. All at once it was over. He was back in Rome, sitting by my fire, a plate of leftovers on his knees. He'd fallen in love. Who was it this time, I wondered, wearily lifting my eyes—a Milanese businessman, a German prince, a gondolier? "No," said Wayne, his face a wistful rainbow. "An American, a year older than me. But so wonderful! He says he knows you—Robert Isaacson?"

That name again. They'd met just two days ago. "And you left him in Venice to come back *here*?" I asked, captivated, at the tale's end. "Why on earth?"

Wayne shook his head. It didn't make sense, did it? Perhaps they both needed a spell apart, to sort things out. Had Robert said as much? Not really, but . . .

"But you're both serious, you both feel the same way?"

"Oh, I can't tell you—!"

A great certainty filled me; I knew what *I* would do in his place. "You must return to Venice at once. Nothing keeps you here. Show him how much you care."

"You really think . . . ?" Then the light in his face died. "I don't have any money."

This was easily remedied. Wayne thanked me with tears in his eyes, hugged me to his heart, and ran off to book a berth on the midnight train. Was psychotherapy already turning me into a mature person, capable of disinterested kindness? I slept well and woke glowing with satisfaction.

"Tell me now," said Dr. Detre a few hours later, upon hearing the full story, "who among the principal characters in this drama are you hoping to impress by your show of generosity?"

I started to say Wayne, but that didn't sound right. Claude? *He* wouldn't thank me for thrusting a person he had designs on into someone else's arms. "Oh," I said aloud, after some further thought. "You mean it's Robert I want?"

"So it would appear," said the doctor.

I took my bus back to the center of town in real perplexity. My quest for a lover—my window-shopping in the streets of Rome—had shown me, if nothing else, the types that appealed to me. I knew also that peerless looks would be of no lasting interest without the invisible psychic musculature, a nervous system trained from the cradle to impart a certain frank, self-assured play to the features, a certain manly swagger to the frame, like youths in Whitman or like Gino the goalie from Trastevere—green grape-blush skin of a Simone Martini Judas and chest like a horsehair mattress ripped open—whom Hubbell had met within hours of settling into a *pensione* where no questions were asked and who was now wearing one of my cast-off shirts to their daily rendezvous. ("Angel," said Hubbell, "shall I give him your telephone number when I leave Rome? He just looks forbidding—underneath he's gentle as the family doctor." Fainting with excitement, I said no, Gino didn't interest me.) Back to Robert, I couldn't deny that Wayne's story put him in a new light. But on neither the physical nor the temperamental level was I aware of being attracted. On the contrary: His striking person was too boyish, his movements too nervous and peremptory. He smiled too quickly, as if passing off an injury or trying to placate his tormentor. I had to conclude that my supposed interest in him came from an altogether different quarter. Here my mind stopped working. Those shadowy corners were for Dr. Detre and the fullness of time to illuminate.

A couple of evenings later I lit a fire for Luigi Valentini. We'd dined and drunk; now he was describing his life in the police barracks, how at daybreak he ran from his bunk to splash himself—*torso nudo, così!*—at a barrel of icy water in the courtyard. As if his words enabled me to see him shirtless, I leaned forward and filled his glass. And was there nothing beyond the barracks? I asked. He must be very lonely in Rome, so far from his village. That was true, he replied, *ma c'è sempre la fidanzata.* A fiancée? Yes, a good girl; she had followed him from the village and found a job in Rome as a seamstress. *"La voglio bene,"* he added smoothly. (He "wished her well," did he? Bravo, so did I.) He would see that we met one day soon. I would appreciate her intelligence; she was taking a course in bookkeeping. I felt like Carmen hearing about Micaela. But why, given the *fidanzata*, had he gone out walking alone that Sunday of our meeting?

Ah, you know, he said with a wink and a grin, a man sometimes—! He'd brought me something, he went on, looking embarrassed and drawing a paper from his shirt pocket. It was a poem he'd written—long ago, he added quickly, to cover himself. Would I care to hear it?

> *Sognai—e vent' anni non eran—*
> *Sognai la libertà del corpo e dell' amore—*

it began. It was nothing I could think of as a poem, but it touched me like a declaration of love, and I decided to risk an "impulsive gesture." With a great air of—what?—sharing the sentiments of my fellow man, I grasped his hand and spoke my pleasure in our friendship. Our eyes blazed, the iron was hot, but once again Luigi failed to strike. Still hampered, clearly, by his finer feelings. Instead he invited me to come out to his village the following Sunday. After he left I fell into bed. *Torso nudo*— the words ran through my mind, splashing themselves on me until I shivered off to sleep.

Wayne telephoned the next morning. He was back in Rome; the great love had burst like a bubble. Robert had been too busy with other friends to see him, except for a coffee, and they parted acknowledging the sadness and impossibility of it all. "But you must be miserable," I said to Wayne, with equal twinges of guilt and excitement. (Was this brush-off a signal from Robert to me?) "Well, that's life, isn't it?" he said, managing a laugh. If he was free this evening, would he like . . . ? No, he already had a date. (Did I hear sharpness in his tone? Was I going to be blamed?) He thanked me sadly for all I'd done, adding that he was thinking of going to Paris as soon as a certain check arrived. We'd see each other before he left. And after Paris? Back to Rome? "Not on your life. Back to MacDougal Street!"—Wayne's laugh at last a real one of relief and anticipation.

The weather turned nasty. The little local train to Luigi's village dawdled and smelled, but I looked forward to our reunion. For one thing, I'd met his *fidanzata*. A call from Luigi a few nights after our supper by the fire announced that they were together in a coffee bar near my apartment and hoped I was free to join them for a meal. I lied, pretending to be expected at an American friend's, but would stop on my way for a glass of wine. At the sight of the *fidanzata* I didn't know whether to laugh or cry.

She was short and fat, with thinning hair and popping eyes. Her hand-shake felt like a scouring pad. How wise of her to have followed Luigi to Rome; had she stayed behind in the village, he might have let himself be snapped up by the first comer. After ten minutes as the soul of courtliness, I drained my glass and went home in high spirits: my rival posed no threat whatever. Now, from the train window, I studied a wet, hilly bleakness, enlivened here and there by huts of whitewashed stone. Perhaps Luigi lived in one of those, and after our lunch of bread and cheese washed down by some famously intoxicating local wine, we would fall back on sheepskins by *his* fire, drowsy but amorous— Ah! Here was the station. And here stood Luigi in his Sunday best, holding out an extra raincoat for me. *"Ciao,"* he beamed. *"Come stai?"* Thank you for coming. My mother and grandmother are waiting impatiently to receive you."

The house was indeed little more than a hut. Was there so much as a second room? In the one I entered, a hearth blazed and an improvised banquet table had been laid, but the space, to judge by such other furnishings as a chest of drawers, the unyielding cot drawn up to the table like a bench, and a rack of tools on the wall, lent itself to every purpose. A window transformable somehow into a second door gave onto a wee wet pasture behind the house; here two or three sheep grazed and some chickens pecked. I drank in these details avidly; it was the setting for all the fairy tales I'd ever read. Luigi's mother and grandmother, wrinkled and weathered like the perpetual black they wore, greeted me as guests were greeted in Homeric times. I was made to sit in the one chair. A volley of civilities— except that few of my returns so much as cleared the net—gave way to questions about my journey. Sensing a long afternoon ahead, I gave them my journey in a larger sense, beginning with farewells to my own mother and grandmother, or greatly humbled versions of them, and including my wanderings through Mediterranean lands before being washed up, so to speak, in Rome. Luigi listened with pride, underscoring the chance felicity or glossing, according to his lights, the many that misfired. There was now bread and wine on the table, and real food imminent. Excusing herself, the mother turned to the hearth and heaped two plates with spaghetti in a fragrant sauce for Luigi and me. "Eat, eat!" cried the grandmother. But their own plates—? Never mind, Luigi explained; the women would eat later, as a matter of course.

It was my first experience of the hospitality of the poor. Never stopping to think that pasta merely prefaces a meal, I accepted a second helping. Then—merciful heavens!—came the meat and the potatoes and beans, the salad, the fruit, and the *dolce*. Our every forkful, our every swallow of wine, was scrutinized; the grandmother cheered us on like athletes. Hours passed. There was no further question of conversation. A single joke—about the quantity of wine I'd seen their wretched paragon consume in a wholly fictive Roman tavern—"did" for the whole afternoon. *"Sì, sì, è un gran' ubriaco!"* I kept assuring them, as they rocked and crowed with delight. As man of the house, Luigi positively gleamed; but the medal's reverse side depicted a road whose deep ruts of gender it would take an ox to negotiate. He must have given a sign, for the women reluctantly served themselves, and the heavy food quieted them. Meeting my eye, Luigi rose. We would walk down to the "center" *per divertirsi* before I caught my train. My hostesses didn't protest—men had their reasons. His mother, dignified as Penelope, took my hand and thanked me for being her son's friend. His grandmother made the sign of the cross over me, nodding sagely as unexpected tears filled my eyes. Then we were walking downhill in the dusk. I was too bursting with food to think of anything but Rome and solitude and the contents of my medicine chest. One more ordeal, however, lay in store: the "club" across from the station, where somber-suited men, refugees like us from hearth and groaning board, were drinking and listening to the radio. "To divert ourselves," Luigi had said, but *we* created the diversion here. Everyone was middle-aged or old, none was good-looking, each had to verify my provenance and degree of expressiveness in his language. Whereupon deciding that I was genuine—or passably so, for surely a single glance from their expert eyes had detected the forgery—these Berensons of the community would clap for little glasses of brandy it was not permitted to refuse. When at length the train choked and staggered into the unlit station and the moment came to thank Luigi, my jaw hung open and no words came out.

•

Speaking Italian (as later Greek), I used the language at best well enough to say what I meant—a daring departure from the frills and involutions brought out in me by the mother tongue. Likewise on Dr. Detre's couch I found my English adapting itself, somewhat, to his own. Along with everything else, our sessions were teaching me to be intelligible to a foreigner. Out in the world, as my Italian progressed, I found myself learning even more easily from fellow Americans whose mistakes I heard and inwardly corrected than from monoglot Romans using expressions they were at a loss to paraphrase. (Thus, urged by my mother to seek friends worthy of me, I was glad to acquire a minimal fluency in Virtue and Honor from strangers to those tongues, instead of having to communicate solely with the often dull and respectable "natives.") Again and again I've replayed my dialogue with Luigi, that first evening by the fire. Freely rendered into Greek and moved a decade into the future, it would have run little chance of miscarrying, the preliminary understanding behind it having been arrived at through further practice on one or both sides. Yet there was always a first time, and Luigi's crumpled loose-leaf poem kept surfacing among my old manuscripts and letters for many a year.

Victims of brain damage unable to speak but asked to set their needs to a familiar tune—"Greensleeves" or "Santa Lucia"—have uttered what they couldn't otherwise. In much the same way a foreign language frees the speaker. Once he has learned his first five hundred words and mastered a few idioms and tenses, he is ready for action. He has added to his Greek Nai ("Yes") the slow headshake meaning assent, to his Italian exasperation the pursed bud of emphatic fingertips already caught in a second-century mosaic of a fishwife in the Naples museum. He is on his way to embodying, however crudely and clumsily, that local divinity, the language. The process teaches him to speak a mind far less individual than he had once thought it. Among friends we are no doubt free to be "ourselves"—giddy, vague, sullen, unforthcoming. We can say what we don't mean, and still be understood. Or we can say nothing, like couples long married who speak hardly at all. A stranger's ear and a stranger's grammar, by contrast, keep us at concert pitch. So does a stranger's garb.

In 1950, before cheap sportswear became uniform worldwide, it was harder than it is today for the American to look European (or vice versa). Yet I prided myself upon melting into the Roman pot. One morning I realized that everything I had on had been acquired in Italy—underwear, jacket, shoes—and exulted, as when I'd dressed for the Paris Party some friends and I gave in our senior year at Amherst. We held it in a romantic empty house once owned by the author of the Uncle Wiggly books. Our invitations told you who to come as.

Tom Howkins played Diaghilev to Bill Burford's Nijinsky; Ben and Helen Brower came as Mallarmé and Berthe Morisot, and Bill and Nancy Gibson as George Moore and the Folies-Bergères barmaid (both by Manet). Seldon was a hollow-eyed, dope-crazed apache. Hans, on a cane, with a bloodstained bandage round his head—in reality he still had three years to live—was Apollinaire. Greasepaint mustache and Monday-night-at-the-opera tailcoat sufficed to turn me into a Proust athletic enough to stand on a table and recite Don Pasquito's Tango from Façade. We had strong punch, a small combo, a moonlit garden. It ended badly—with Hemingway (a student none of us knew, invited for his looks) pistol-whipping our poor drunken Somerset Maugham under a blossoming tree—but what was an ointment without flies? In memory the party shimmers and resounds like a Fête by Debussy. Freedom to be oneself is all very well; the greater freedom is not to be oneself.

XI

Mademoiselle.
Claude's Dinner Party.
Robert and His Friends.
The Michelangelo Pietà.

I dreamed that night of my beloved Mademoiselle, from whom (as I reminded Dr Detre) I'd been separated at the age of eleven, just when I needed her most. She was the oldest and simplest of three all-but-generic sisters who'd somehow made it through World War I with their civilities intact. Her title was purely professional. Mademoiselle had been married and widowed. She wasn't even French but a guilty mixture of Prussian and English. Among her forebears she was proudest of the explorer Fanning: we found on my globe the specklike islands named for him. At nine and ten, when my mother's troubles gave her scant time for me, I transferred, day by day, more and more love to this good soul. Such was my need for *her* love that I drew with my compass the kind of neat statistical pie plate that embellished the financial pages my father threw aside in frustration, and each night before our prayers—I knew the Hail Mary in four languages, thanks to her—asked Mademoiselle how much more of it I'd earned that day. Whereupon the shading in of another slender wedge allowed me to fall asleep proportionately fulfilled. One night I got carried away and told her I loved her more than I did my mother. Mademoiselle recoiled, scandalized. That was the end of our chart and my first taste of a love that dared not speak its name.

The second promptly followed. When my parents separated it was felt that I could do with masculine supervision. But the rugged young Irishman my mother hired—handsome as Flash Gordon—didn't work out. It wasn't his fault. He helped me with my math, took me to a gym on weekends, slept in the next bed. Watching him undress through slitted eyes, I ached to lie in his arms, as I sometimes had in Mademoiselle's after she'd signed my forehead with a good-night cross, but of course this was unthinkable *between men*. So I spurned his efforts to be friends, teased, pouted, ran away from him in the subway until he gave up, quitting at the end of his second month. How lonely he must have been, stuck day and night with a minor who appeared to despise him, and how badly in that Depression year he must have needed the job. But if sides had to be taken, my loyalties were to the discarded, long-suffering, irreproachable woman he had supplanted—to Mademoiselle, I added, in case I wasn't being clear.

"Do not forget," said Dr. Detre, "that Mademoiselle was originally hired to supplant your mother, so that *she* would have more time to attend to your father's needs."

Say no more—I was off. My father had supplanted my mother *twice*, not only with Mademoiselle but with Kinta. By seeking custody of me, hadn't he aimed at taking my mother's place himself? ("We're getting warm!" Dr. Simeons would have exclaimed; Dr. Detre let me find my own footholds.) No wonder tears had filled my eyes when Luigi's mother thanked me for my loyalty and his grandmother made the sign of the cross over my head. This was the mothering I missed: ignorant, reliable as rock. My poor plain pious Mademoiselle, who'd boarded out her daughter in East Hampton the better to care for— But wait: didn't that turn *me* into a supplanter? According to an appendix in *Webster's Collegiate Dictionary*, my very name, James, meant "the supplanter." Luigi himself—wasn't he, in this cat's-cradle fantasy, supplanting my father? the young Irishman? any man I loved but couldn't attain? Or had I made sure, loyal to injured womanhood, that the men I loved should *be* unattainable?

Reaction set in on the bus home. How deeply, how unspeakably, such perceptions bored me. They shot up like vines overnight, a strangling jungle growth, at absolute odds with that clean spare cabin of the achieved self waiting at the heart of so much pathlessness. But maybe the achieved self wasn't clean and spare at all, was rather a sprawling temple of volcanic stone, quarried from bygone outbursts, the uppermost blocks carved with huge satisfied heads facing in every direction. Having seen friends in analysis grow into "monuments of selfishness," I very much hoped to avoid the fate. The different person I meant to become would be more receptive to others than I had been thus far, more conscious of their needs than greedy for his own fulfillment. When I reached my apartment Quinta told me to call Signor Claudio. I did; it seemed that Robert had returned from Venice, they were having dinner two nights later, would I care to join them? I hesitated over the right tone to take. "It was Robert's idea," Claude added with a trace of irony. "He said he wanted to know you better."

The weather had changed; it felt like summer again. I wore a pale cotton jacket and a green bow tie. Robert, asked elsewhere for drinks, wanted to meet us at the restaurant. So Claude and I had an hour to ourselves beforehand. Dr. Detre was never mentioned; we'd agreed from the start not to compare notes. I told him about my day with Luigi, he described the concert I'd missed as a result. What did he hear from his mother? Mine was coming to Rome—yes, yes, in less than two weeks—then taking me to Paris to meet my new stepfather. Claude shook his head sympathetically: I'd really had to face quite a parade of passers-through. Irma, Wayne, Betty, Hubbell. . . . Was no one content to stay quietly at home and let us get on with it? "With our Emancipation," I put in wryly, "our Metamorphosis." "I've been noticing, though, from keeping my journal," said Claude, "how linear, how elegant, one's experience is over here—don't you agree?—after the busy weave of life in America." (I stole a look at his tweed jacket, in which he was beginning to perspire.) "Living at such a remove," he went on, "we're able to confront these figures one by one, in the full glow of what they mean to us. They don't overlap or interact. We can see them coming from far off and prepare ourselves. It's like a marble frieze, or a Greek play. That was Creon's scene, now comes Jocasta's." I nodded, impressed by his overview; of course, Claude was further along in analysis than I was.

We dined, I seem to recall, in a kind of Hungarian basement—unless this detail is merely the product of my wish to go deeper into things, in fanciful conjunction with Dr. Detre's nationality. We were the first to arrive. We sat down, ordered wine, and said we expected *un altro signore*. Claude frowned at his watch, a trio struck up *Zigeunermusik*, at which point—and there had never been anything quite so strange—I myself came hurrying into the restaurant, wearing a pale cotton jacket and red bow tie, looking distraught without my glasses, and hoping I hadn't kept us waiting. This newcomer, that is, while plainly Robert Isaacson, was dressed like me, had the same haircut, the same turn of the head, was someone I knew with more than intimacy. I knew him from inside the skin, the way I knew myself—not that that was saying a great deal at the time. He sat down next to Claude, smiling across at me with the same mollifying smile I'd produced on such occasions from early boyhood. I looked away.

Far from being elated, I felt let down, as by some elaborate practical joke. That the joke, its sartorial aspect at least, hadn't been planned cut no ice with our host, who looked hurt and excluded. The story of Wayne that Robert and I shared—stamped though it was *for future reference*—set up vibrations Claude must have sensed without being able to identify. Or identified wrongly as sexual, since I, for my part, felt nothing of the sort. As the evening wore on, however, our complicity showed in fits of infectious silliness, and Claude's discomfiture grew; his every remark, so reasonable and intelligent, urged us back to his level, which we proceeded to deface with conversational graffiti. The meal lurched toward its end. It would still take a good half hour to finish the Tokay Claude had ordered with our pastry, but thinking the least I could do was to leave him alone with Robert, I rose and thanked him, said I'd slept badly the night before, and would have to be getting home. Like a shadow taken by surprise, Robert leapt to his feet, protesting he had to be up very early the next morning. Together we left Claude in the Hungarian basement.

Our respective ways led down the Spanish Steps, at whose foot we would part. Robert had a room in Via del Babuino. But no sooner had we begun our descent than "Ouf!" he groaned. "It was so hot in there. Could we sit here for a minute?"—dropping onto the cool stone. We smoked awhile in silence. It was nearly eleven o'clock. From where we sat, facades glowed faintly all over town, like box holders in the light from the orchestra pit, while the domes of a dozen churches, floodlit earlier in the evening, could now barely be told from purple sky. "This is very nice," said Robert softly. My heart turned over. It was no more than I'd begun to expect, but his directness caught me off guard. Before I knew it, a surpassingly naive question rose to my startled lips: "Are you in love with me?" Robert gave a murmur of protest, as if he'd been seized too roughly. Had I spoiled everything as usual? Then, *"Cosa fate qui?"* new, official voices were demanding. We blinked up into eyes inscrutable beneath visors: a pair of *carabinieri*. As we set about stringing together some few lame words, *"Stranieri,"* said the second policeman, in a contemptuous undertone. (Was no Italian capable of the iniquities he had in mind?) His partner, the bright one, put out a restraining hand. *"Somigliano,"* he observed, *"guarda. Sembrano fratelli."* And to us, indicating our upturned faces, our matching summer jackets and bow ties: "You a-re brrothers, no? *Gemelli*—touins?" Yes, yes! we excessively nodded, still trembling but relieved; amused, too, by his acumen. Or was he slyly letting us off the hook? *"Adesso a casa,"* he smiled. *"Dormire, hanno capito?"* We understood, and thanked them. The splendid figures saluted in unison—maybe *they* were twins too—and marched briskly down the steps.

"We'd better do what he said," Robert whispered. "I can't ask you to my place. The landlady's wired it for sound."

"Come to mine."

The next morning, after Robert had gone back to his room, promising to meet me for lunch, Claude telephoned. (He would already have heard from the landlady that her tenant had slept elsewhere.) "I have only one thing to say," he said in a low furious voice. "I hope never to see you again."

And for the second time in twelve hours I was startled by the words I found myself uttering: "Thank you . . . thank you . . ."

"You have been wanting to establish your independence of Claude for several months now," said Dr. Detre. "This move was long overdue."

"But *thanking* him? Thanking him for what?"

"Well, since you are as yet incapable of breaking with someone you once loved—something the rest of the world does every three weeks— you took your time and found a sure way to make him do it for you. Do not forget, you were raised in a house full of servants."

My feelings for Robert were so profuse and bewildered that I feared Dr. Detre would discourage them, or at the very least remind me of his stricture against "marrying" while in therapy. But he kept mercifully silent, and I began over the following weeks to suspect that my behavior made sense to him, if not altogether to myself. Knowing my mother's visit was imminent, Robert and I spent as much time together as we could. By comparison with Claude, who had a pronounced hermit gene, my new love was sociability itself. His friends in Rome were fun to be with, and he shared them with me—as I in turn, who had no circle to speak of, took pains to have him meet Umberto—with perfect openness. Each accordingly grew to know the other not just from intense tête-à-têtes, or sleepy ones, but from the no less telling standpoint of his behavior in company.

Robert came from St. Louis. His parents were divorced. He had been raised by his mother and grandfather. His father, remarried and living beyond the Rockies, kept his distance. There was money on his mother's side of the family—how much or how acquired I never wanted to know, since wealth robbed him of the kind of "reality" I conferred unhesitatingly upon Luigi or Gino the goalie. Love couldn't be kept in a golden bowl, said Blake. And sex, as a cynical Frenchman put it, was the theater of the poor? If so, I wanted a seat in that theater. Money was just one of the disadvantages under which Robert and I labored. That I had greatly enjoyed our lovemaking puzzled me no end. Robert himself seemed blissfully relieved to have exchanged a series of "vulgar" or "tiresome" lovers for someone whose manners and education approached his own. Wayne had been the last straw: "That day he reappeared—before breakfast!— 'Death in Venice' took on a new meaning."

"Poor Wayne. He thought you were his great love."

"Rubbish. I'd sent him packing; I didn't care if I ever saw him again."

"But you knew I'd hear about it from him?"

Robert blushed as if I were extorting a confession from him. "I told him, if he had to talk about it, I didn't mind your knowing."

Although he kept his room in Via del Babuino, my apartment allowed us greater privacy and comfort. Quinta washed and ironed his shirts along with mine. We liked to wear each other's clothes. We rented an upright piano and bought—in a shop around the corner—a cherrywood virginal made in East Germany, complete with gold-and-black label above the keyboard giving us the manufacturer's telephone number in case of emergency. For all his diffidence and airs of the salon, Robert was an accomplished musician. My great pleasure was to sit beside him, studying the brown aplomb of his hands and turning the pages as he played. Much of his repertoire was new to me: Rameau, Couperin, Scarlatti, Haydn, Byrd. I asked again and again for a grumpy little Telemann bourrée with the melody in the bass, until finally—shades of Albertine made to keep pedaling the same piano roll—there was one less piece of music in the world and one more truth. But even with pieces I did know, like Mozart sonatas or the Italian Concerto, the delight of hearing them unmediated by phonograph or concert hall never wore off. It was the difference between the bread one had baked oneself and a packaged loaf. Robert's very limitations along with the instrument's, the impurities of volume or a mordent's unexpected crunch, seemed to make the music wholesomer, less forbidding. I began to spend time alone at the keyboard, trying to approximate Robert's style by dotting the rhythm as with raisins or adding like so much ornamental sugar the trills and *appoggiature* licensed by Baroque convention. I saw that piano practice, prison fare in childhood, could become a staple of adult life.

The brightest and nicest of Robert's friends was an art historian named Marilyn Aronberg. From St. Louis like Robert, she knew, unlike him, quite clearly where she wanted her life to lead and was fully equipped to get there. Exploring Rome with the two of them, or with Marilyn alone, pausing for long minutes to analyze a fresco I wouldn't, by myself, have wasted a second glance on, seeking entry to famously inaccessible churches—San Giovanni in Restauro or Santa Maria Sempre Chiusa, as we nicknamed them in our vexation—I began to see what a given school or period might imply beyond a handful of masterpieces and a few world-famous names. The least promising picture, under Marilyn's expert eye and Robert's intuitive one, showed ways of "handling space" that a later master had learned from. Barocci's "boudoir pinks" anticipated Fragonard. Afternoon sun through Carlo Dolci's leaded windows made light of figures borrowed from Raphael. Objects told stories, drapery billowed and glistened with emotion. The stage lighting of Caravaggio, the body language of Bellini's infant Christs, the buried geometry in Piero della Francesca, revered and misunderstood by otherwise negligible men, testified to a vitality, a unity of effort, that crisscrossed the map of Italy with magnetic currents. Here was a history that didn't, for once, rise up from old, bloodthirsty stones. The power it chronicled, however warped by fashion and patronage, was comparatively clean, selfless, conferred by surrender to the craft itself, part of a proud calling and a long tradition that left me dazzled, though to a serious dilettante like Robert these were truths that went without saying.

Besides Marilyn and her circle he had two older friends: a spidery Italian art collector who knew Mario Praz—who in turn had the evil eye!—and a fat English diplomat who for next to nothing rented St. Philip Neri's vast apartment in the Palazzo Massimo. (The hitch was having to move out each year on the Saint's day—along with every last trace of tenancy: papers, clothes, toothbrush—for the pope to say mass on the spot and in the proper spirit.) These two men might have been put on earth as warnings to a tasteful young person not to overdo it. But culture, for Robert, was a lighted house full of wit and feuds and cooking smells, where he would always be welcome. The family received him, so to speak, in their dressing gowns. There was even a chapel for his worst moments. Outside that haven raged the emotional life, his previous taste of which—the year with Rolf, a German photographer in New York—had left him "all but dead from exposure. Time exposure," he added contritely when I looked startled. It was odd and not unpleasant for a change to feel stronger, more reliable, than the person I loved; and I resolved to use my advantage with caution.

Michelangelo's great abandoned *Pietà* (now in Milan) could, in those years, be seen on the last Monday of every month in a banal thirties' villa at the edge of town. We were the only callers that afternoon. The sculpture stood in the curving well of a small staircase. Inert, narrow-chested, Christ sags to his knees, utterly dependent—as to judge from his frailty, he must have been in life—upon his upright mother. Both figures are unfinished afterthoughts, scarred all over by the same chisel. But broken free, just inches to one side of them, dangles a splendid muscular arm, grimily veined under its polish: the arm of the solar god who might have towered above all comers, had the stone been sound. (When did *my* marble split? Snapshots from years before the divorce tell how something had already turned one brave, unlettered little boy astride a gigantic stallion into a sissy of six, posed, hands folded and ankles crossed, at the slide's foot.) Faced with the *Pietà* as with an athlete doomed by injury to spend his youth in a wheelchair, reading law or Sanskrit beneath photographs of a self in glorious action, the visitor feels both loss and gain. Without that flaw in the original marble, this inward, famished understudy for creative Love would never have come to light.

"The prince and I think it's an allegory of the Dark Ages," said Robert in the inane voice of a hostess. But I guessed that to us both the sculpture spoke more troublingly than either wanted to admit.

•

Therapy has its fashions, like everything else. Had my break with Claude come thirty years later, Dr. Detre might have urged me to discover and "release my aggressions." In the famously mild 1950s, however, breaking through to some idealized core of anger wasn't the obligatory gesture it later became for lovers on the outs. Toward Claude I felt no lurking ambivalence. If taking up with Robert answered to a somewhat bitchy impulse of mine to get even—why not? But there it ended. Schooled respectively by Senecan forbearance and Mimi's crystalline "senza rancor," and on both sides by a mother's dignity in the face of rejection, Claude and I spared ourselves no little fruitless havoc.

Life with Robert was a far richer immediate source of unexplored feelings. With it came a certain blurring of identity and gender, as when lovers wear each other's clothes or adopt each other's mannerisms, and the solitary reader looks up in sudden doubt as to who he or she might have become under the spell of a seductive book. Proust had broken this difficult ground for our time, but at such exhaustive analytical length as to put the entire subject off-limits. A few years after my return from Rome, however, a poem by Elizabeth Bishop appeared in a little magazine and pointed to new strategies, while summoning up with a pang those joyous months when Robert wore my jackets and I his shirts without thinking twice about it. "Exchanging Hats" was a mere eight tetrameter quatrains long, neatly rhymed, lighthearted. But like the White Rock nymph, it smiled down at its reflection in depths so refreshing that I read it a second, a third, a tenth time.

The poem begins by evoking the behavior of grown-ups—clownish uncles and spinster aunts—at a beach picnic, but through a number of delicate modulations, changes of tense and meter and tone, these figures grow ghostly, other- or underworldly, wise as that Ovidian Tiresias who at a more genital level than Miss Bishop's also explored (in her phrase) "the headgear of the other sex." The poem ends:

> unfunny uncle, you who wore a
> hat too big, or one too many,
> tell us, can't you, are there any
> stars inside your black fedora?
>
> Aunt exemplary and slim,
> with avernal eyes, we wonder
> what slow changes they see under
> their vast, shady, turned-down brim.

I never doubted that almost any poem I wrote owed some of its difficulty to the need to conceal my feelings, and their objects. Genderless as a fig leaf, the pronoun "you" served to protect the latter, but one couldn't be too careful. Whatever helped to complicate the texture—double meanings, syntax that William Empson would have approved—was all to the good. Here, though, was a poet addressing herself with open good humor to the forbidden topic of transsexual impulses, simply by having invented a familiar, "harmless" situation to dramatize them. I was enthralled.

People keep talking about man's "search for a father," the importance of a male paradigm for the growing boy. Hence the young Irishman my mother hired to teach me manhood, little dreaming he would turn out to be an object of desire instead. But how about that child's need for a female role model, lacking whom, conceivably, the grown man's psyche or anima (always envisioned as feminine) might well remain pinched and mean? To this end I've always had an eye out for "the right woman," someone my spirit could aspire to resemble or, put less ponderously, to whose turn of mind and way with emotion

I felt attuned. Neither Brünnhilde nor the Marschallin had turned out to be much of a help in day-to-day living. Over the years Elizabeth kept filling the bill. Like her I had no graduate degree, didn't feel called upon to teach, preferred to New York's literary circus the camouflage of another culture. My accord with the author of "Exchanging Hats" came to a head, as it were, one day in Brazil, when she and I were being driven through sunny red-and-green hillsides sparkling from a recent downpour. Just ahead squatted a small intense rainbow we seemed about to collide with before, leaping out of our path, it reappeared round the next bend. Something Elizabeth said in Portuguese set the fat black driver shaking with laughter. "In one of the northern provinces," she explained, "they have this superstition: if you pass under a rainbow you change your sex."

XII

Psychosomatic Behavior.
Paternal Tact and Maternal Prejudice.
Revelations.

The day before my mother arrived I lay on Dr. Detre's couch, repeating a familiar litany. She couldn't endure my "life," I must practice the utmost discretion, it would kill my father if he ever found out, and this in turn paralyzed my relations with *him* to the point where—

"If I may interrupt," said Dr. Detre, "we are wasting time. Whether you know it or not, last May your father asked Dr. Simeons and me for a joint interview. He told us then that he believed you were homosexual and asked what, if anything, he personally could do about it. We said there was nothing. He thanked us, he paid us, and that was that."

It figured. My father had always been a great one for seeking expert opinion. Dr. Detre's story, with its instant ring of truth, overwhelmed me. My mother was mistaken: my father knew! Better yet, whether as man of the world or merely as compassionate parent, he'd had the tact to keep silent. How long had he known? How did he find out? (Not that I would ever put such questions to him.) Tenderness and gratitude flooded me. He loved me intelligently, without wanting to change me into somebody I wasn't.

This revelation brought my mother—too often blurred by excessive closeness if not by the trembling of the handheld camera—into sharper focus than usual. Her dread of scandal or blackmail, which for lack of experience I was unable to dismiss, struck me next to my father's behavior as an old-fashioned, provincial reflex. She had been named for her grandmother, a formidable woman, born in the North, an educator and historian who showed her designs for an early wagon-lit at the Chicago world's fair of 1893, who "nearly" saw the connection between malaria and mosquitoes, and whose medical researches led her to publish a long paper "proving" the biological superiority of whites to blacks. The benign side of this heritage underlay my mother's intelligence and resourcefulness, her newspaper work, the maiden voyage to Europe paid for by her savings. Rather than give in to idle self-pity when my father left her, she started a small business in New York, made her own circle of friends, and attended as best she could to her mother and her increasingly operatic child. At the end of World War II—I had already been demobilized—she was serving with the Red Cross on Guam. A touchier legacy showed in a couple of passionate biases, one of which was maternal.

I was what mattered most, I was "all she had." A single look into my eyes awoke in her the blind instincts of the partridge or the she-wolf. She marked with despair my lack of protective coloring, my inability to lie low in a world rife with danger. True to the values of her time and place, my mother knew chiefly how happy she would be if my terrible tendencies were "just a phase," to be swept sooner or later under the rug for good. In practice, my father's forbearance amounted to the same unspoken wish. But as a man living more widely in it than any woman of that world could or would—hadn't his boyhood paper route included the red-light district of Jacksonville?—*his* rug was a positive Aubusson next to the sensible, narrow, braided-rag affair laid down like a law by the prettiest girl on the other side of town.

I too had instincts, and my answer to my mother's arrival in Rome was to get sick. I'd met her plane, settled her into the hotel where my flowers awaited her, taken her to a famous old restaurant at the foot of the Spanish Steps. We had plenty to eat and plenty to discuss. Untouched on the banquette beside her lay a work in progress; ever since I could remember she'd resorted to needlepoint when bored or under stress. Out instead came photographs of her wedding for study and commentary. I was shown my grandmother, Betty, *her* grandmother, friends I'd scarcely thought of for a year and a half. After dinner we climbed the steps by easy stages. Before kissing me good night in the hotel lobby, she took my face in her hands, searching it for signs of change or simple reassurance. I managed to smile and nod. Outside, I retraced our route. I sat for a moment on Robert's and my step overlooking the footlit domes and palaces; but no feelings came, and I walked home like an automaton. The next morning's first sip of tea and taste of bread and honey awoke a dry, grinding pain at the center of my being. Had my mother recovered from her ulcer only to pass it on to me? I telephoned Dr. Simeons, who told me to come right over. I broke my appointment with Dr. Detre, then called my mother to unmake our plans for the day. After examining me, Dr. Simeons, bursting with delight and interest—here, if ever he had seen one, was a classic psychosomatic complaint—declared that my gastric juices had ceased to flow and that I could digest not so much as a biscuit without first swallowing a substitute for the truant fluid, available at any pharmacy. So mine was a common complaint? Oh dear me, yes, said Dr. Simeons; one out of every five Italians had trouble stomaching family life.

"Your point is made," said Dr. Detre the next day. "She cannot fail to take you seriously now."

Or I her. Back on my feet two nights later, I escorted my mother to the opening gala (*Nabucco*) at the opera. The best seats I could get were in the second balcony. Even here our neighbors struck us as sumptuously turned out, their satins and uniforms pure Stendhal. A life in tune with the senses had burnished these Romans to perfect physical types. Peach-bloom youth and the proud ivory of age met here as equals. In her improvised evening dress, its chief elements a choker of big false pearls and a low-cut black cardigan, my mother alone emitted mixed signals, managing to look at once joyless and girlish, widowed and provocative. Had she forgotten how a married woman dressed? Yet against the intermission's chattering crush, to whom the madness of a biblical king might have been their hall porter's latest tantrum, she stood out with such mute unflinching rectitude that I led her to the bar defiantly, ready to challenge the first quizzical glance shot her way.

I invited Floyd and Eula Baker that Sunday, along with some of my new friends—Umberto, Dr. Simeons, Robert and Marilyn, Ben Johnson and his wife, three or four others—for drinks and canapés. Such occasions brought out the best in my mother. Her doctrines and sermons were little help to me nowadays; as in the churches I visited with Marilyn, it was art alone that made the excursion worthwhile. But the light of my lost faith shone brightly in the faces of other members of the congregation. Guest after guest sat beside her, drawn into the smiling communion I took, as host, some indirect credit for. Thus, after the party, by ourselves at last, I wasn't prepared for the sudden dropping of the mask. Out came her needlepoint.

"What are you working on now?" I asked cordially, as if to a fellow writer.

"Something for you," she said, meeting my eyes. "The Merrill and the Ingram crests. To remind you of the kind of people you come from. At the rate I'm going, it'll have to be for *next* Christmas. I'll have them stretched and framed in any case, and you can hang them or not, as you see fit."

"Oh, what a very . . ." The words stuck in my throat. It felt like a great burden disguised as a gift.

"Tell me just one thing, son." My mother spoke in dry, exhausted tones. "Would you have asked your father to meet these friends of yours?"

What was she getting at? "I think so; yes. Why not?"

"Do you know that this is the first time in my entire life that I've had to meet colored people socially? If I wrote home that you'd done this to me, no one would believe me. You didn't see the look on Eula Baker's face. And I can promise you that your father wouldn't have taken it as well as I did. Can you answer my question? Would you have asked the Johnsons to a party for him?"

"If I shared my friends with him as fully as I do with you," I said pointedly, "yes. Besides, I've heard all my life about parties you and he went to in New York. At one of them you met the whole cast of *Porgy and Bess*."

"Those were *entertainers*," she sighed. Was I unable to grasp this basic distinction?

"Well, Ben Johnson's creative too." It was maddening to defend a person for whom I felt so little enthusiasm. "A writer. Probably a notch above somebody who sang and danced on Broadway twenty-five years ago."

"How can I explain? People just milled around at those big parties. We never had to *sit down* with the Negroes."

Her frank distress, however conventional in a Southern woman of my mother's vintage, puzzled me, for the attacks I was used to came from a different quarter. Was it simply beyond her to cope with any "minority" at all, including the one I belonged to? "You grew up among Negroes in Jacksonville," I ventured. "Didn't you ever sit down in the kitchen with Old Jane?"

"We're not *talking* about *servants*, son. I loved Old Jane more than anyone in the whole wide world. I'd have thrown my arms around her and kissed her if she'd risen from the grave and walked in on us today. I'd have sat her down in my own place on this sofa. But never"—and here my mother's fixed gaze heightened the eerie gentleness of her tone—"never would you have seen me shake her hand."

So the Civil War continued to reverberate in odd corners of the planet, far from Antietam or Gettysburg, and a decade before Rosa Parks sat down with white folks in the front of the bus. I thought of bringing up my father and his colored valet dining peacefully at a first-class table for two on the old *Queen Elizabeth*. But I was saving his example for ammunition in a skirmish closer to home than this one. Besides, my mother would just have repeated her line: We weren't talking about servants.

And yet, thanks to her quarter century in the North, she passed for a farsighted, iconoclastic sibyl among her Jacksonville friends. One of these, lately widowed, had moved to a brick bungalow suitable for the third Little Pig and stuffed it with the suffocating furniture of her prime. One day after giving us lunch, the dear woman complained, "Hellen, no one ever sets foot in this living room. Tell me, with your good sense, how can I make it more attractive?" My mother had lots of ideas. Down with the heavy drapes, out with the silk flowers, never hang a chandelier from such a low ceiling, get rid of those glass-front whatnots full of eggcups and china puppies—oh, and while you're at it, bring the *chairs* into some sort of inviting relation to one another, not just all witlessly lined up against the wall! Our hostess, who had been looking about in wild surmise, on this last point stood her ground. "Hellen precious," she reminded her lifelong friend, "the chairs were against the wall at Versailles."

Dr. Detre asked what had been my own feelings about the Negro servants I grew up among. I painted a few rapid idealized portraits—Emma the maid, James the chauffeur. What had I especially loved about them? Well, that they had time for me, that they were physically warm, instinctive, *real*. Less fierce than the models of Tsarouchis, more relaxed than the girl from the hospital corridor. "Children themselves, in a sense?" the doctor suggested. I shook my head; it wasn't that simple. Bribed by my father's lawyers, Emma lived with us like a secret agent, reading my mother's mail, taking note of her telephone calls. All this she confessed with tear-stained dignity after the divorce. Yet I felt that Emma would have been incapable of betraying *me*. Why? Well, for one thing she'd have to *see into* me, understand what she saw—

"And you could trust her not to see," said Dr. Detre. "From the givers of physical tenderness no evaluating insight is to be feared. While from those who appreciate your creative gifts, love is the last thing you are able to accept."

Hmm. . . . But in an instant, dreamlike transition I found myself talking about my writing and defending my sense that a poem too easy to read was without value. Not that I aimed at total impenetrability. My difficult surfaces were rather a kind of . . . mask, an invitation to . . . to the right reader who would have fought through to the poem's emotional core. Could I accept love from such a reader? I wasn't at all sure that I could.

"Do you remember a fairy tale," Dr. Detre asked, "about the princess, comatose for a hundred years, closed in by thorns? What is it called in English?"

" 'Sleeping Beauty,' " I smiled, blinking up from his couch. The child put to sleep, I went on, by the prick of a woman's embroidery needle— and here we were back to my mother. I failed to make out why my poetics had to be so mixed up with her; but as Dr. Detre remarked before dismissing me, there was no hurry.

My mother and I sit in a rented car in the parking lot at Hadrian's Villa. We've walked about in the early December sunlight, admiring the brickwork, the colonnade, the vistas. No need to name Antinoüs, to call up the emperor's deifying love for a shepherd boy from Asia Minor, in order to feel how languorous, how beautiful, how secure the setting has grown over the centuries. Yet on our way back to the car a tall evergreen hedge makes me think of Southampton, and I take this idyllic moment to say

I've learned something that may surprise her: my father knows—has known for some time—about my life. From Dr. Detre's account of his reaction, it is safe to add that her worst fears have been misplaced; the knowledge hasn't killed him. The honeycomb brick glows, the high hedge sways in confirmation. Now, what has my mother to say to that?

It doesn't seem to surprise her. "How do you suppose he found out?" she asks quietly. That, I shrug, is anybody's guess. She waits for me to open the car door, slides into her seat, and seeks my gaze before proceeding: "No, son. I told him."

Thus we sit side by side in the rented Fiat, while the whole suppressed episode comes to light.

After their divorce and much to Kinta's annoyance, my mother and father stayed on friendly terms. This meant access by telephone, now and then putting their heads together over my welfare, and his rare, flattering afternoon calls upon my grandmother. At first I wanted nothing to do with him—hadn't he Destroyed Our Home? My mother took pains to keep me open-minded. She urged me to go to Southampton or Palm Beach whenever invited. If my manners and appearance gave satisfaction at court, so much the better: this showed *her* in a good light too. Over the years, my father's heart attacks and my ongoing academic honors made him less formidable and me more so. One day I might even be his equal. But when late in 1945 my mother's suspicions drove her to open a certain letter, making plain the extent of my relations with Kimon, she panicked. I was under twenty-one, she had legal custody of me—should she take me out of college, away from the tempter? (I nod grimly; all this I remember. Now comes what I haven't heard before.) Not knowing where else to turn, she went straight to Southampton with her story.

My father's reaction was appalling, my mother says, beyond anything I could imagine. Why, his first impulse, until she talked sense into him, was to have Kimon killed—"rubbed out" by Murder, Inc. (Surely Czar Lepke and his henchmen were all behind bars by 1945? The question goes unasked; I am listening in pity and terror.) At the very least, my father stormed on, he could have Kimon dismissed from Amherst—a scandal involving us all, as my mother pointed out. Later that afternoon he called a lawyer, who listened intelligently and added his voice to hers. My father simmered down. He had, after all, two other children and the Firm. Emergencies cropping up far and wide shielded me, in the long run, from the full, unwandering glare of his attention. By the time my mother left for New York, the situation had begun to modulate toward comedy: my father was thinking of hiring a prostitute to seduce me into the paradise of sex with women. (Did my mother dissuade him from this too? A little bird tells me not to ask.) Nevertheless, "I thought he was going to have another heart attack that day," says my mother in the car. "That's why I said it would be the death of Daddy if he had to go on hearing things about you. Before you judge me too harshly, please remember, son," she finishes, turning a wet, white face my way, "that I saved Kimon's life."

European parents might have seen the affair otherwise. In their view no particular harm would attend the seduction of a willing nineteen-year-old. Yet disaster (look at "Death in Venice") awaited the susceptible middle-aged man in love with a youth who didn't know his own mind.

Oblivious to his narrow escape, Kimon was summoned to New York, and we were made to promise not to see each other—a promise we didn't try to keep beyond our first twenty-four hours back at Amherst. The following June he sailed for Greece. The lawyer from Southampton who sat in on that secret parental powwow became my lifelong friend and adviser. In the same spirit that would lead him to consult Dr. Simeons on sexual matters, my father sought opinions about my poems, and on hearing from the president of Amherst that they met, or even surpassed, "professional standards," gave them from then on his full if never wholly comprehending approval. My mother developed an ulcer but was strong enough to effect the cure whose final step was her remarriage.

In our parked car at Hadrian's Villa my head spins with all she has told me; I feel that I belong to the House of Atreus, that individually programmed Furies have attended me from birth. Utter nonsense in perspective. But as Robert Frost says, the master plan of any sensible god surely entails its being just as hard at every stage in history for people to save their souls. If so, then the obstacles a fortunate young man creates for himself may—must—have some value he cannot conceive at the time. Even my parents' divorce, however painful and mistaken for them, I am already coming to read as a gift of fate. If being the product of a "broken home" means in my case that I will not risk marriage and children, the homework for future joys, some brief, some lifelong, is already being prepared. Time is a great purifier, and many all too natural wrongs that people do to one another can be used, like fortunes made by cutting forests down, by the next generation to open a school.

•

Not long ago I came upon a little book bound in pink quilted moiré and filled, in my mother's youthful hand, with sentimental lists: my week-by-week weight gain; my first words; important dates, like the day (March 25, 1926) I was brought home from the hospital to a brownstone on West Eleventh Street, which had every reason to think it would last my time. (Little did it know . . .) The most absorbing list of all went on for pages: the gifts I'd received at birth. The "five shares of stock" from my father's partner, the inevitable silver spoons (nine of them), the six pairs of "silver military brushes" and the upright masculine life these recommended, were lost in an avalanche of dainty apparel and accessories—lace and net pillows; monogrammed carriage robes; embroidered dresses; a "pink crêpe de chine coat"; a "silk shawl and sacque"; caps of organdy or lace; gold diaper pins, blue pins, pink-and-pearl pins; rattles and bootees and yet more dresses. I counted over a hundred such items. The fairy godmother at my cradle must have sported a BORN TO SHOP *T-shirt. Not listed were the genetic traits showered with equal lavishness upon the neonate, which, unlike his dresses and bonnets and diaper pins, are with him to this day.*

The miraculous gift of life we receive from our parents comes in a package almost impossible to unwrap; often it seems wiser not to try. Inside are the various clues—most of them older than time—to who we are and how we behave. The fresher the clue, the more unnerving it can be. Family stories, for instance, put me to sleep. As Southerners, both my parents had quite a stock of them, priceless no doubt to the sentimentalist, or as oral history. To my ears they wore thin from the start. Even a story originally as full of suspenseful action and as crucial to my life as the one told me at Hadrian's Villa comes, with time, to date. The poster colors of my father's initial outburst fade in the light of his subsequent civilized response. (By the same token, his prompt letter of apology to Dr. Detre for a remark made in Rome about "those goddamned Jewish psychiatrists" remains for its recipient a high-water mark of handsome, man-to-man sincerity.) Also, my mother's "it would kill your father if he knew" impresses me less powerfully now that I've heard from three or four friends that the very same words were said to them by their mothers on similar occasions. Given the poverty of the dramaturgy, I wonder at its magnetic pull upon us, who late in life start saying and doing things that remind us of our parents, and our parents of theirs. Surely (thinks many a gifted child) a different self, formed in my case by the pages of "The Snow Queen" and W. H. Hudson's A Little Boy Lost, *by passions enacted within the Metropolitan Opera's gold proscenium or the Ouija board's alphabetical one, continues to give that genetic other a run for its money. Surely those fictions draw me closer to truth than—*

Steady. For doesn't Sandover *end in a ballroom like Southampton's? And what do we hear at the opera if not the unwearying cries of personal history?* Sua madre! Padre mio! *Why does my father keep appearing in the men I've loved? Not in Kimon or Claude; they were the lovers. Life with them, however absorbing, lacked, in the long run, "theater," that invisible fourth wall of mutual desire easier to act out than to analyze. Putting it far too simply, if my beloveds saw in me a certain power and charm inherited from the old man, in them I found again his enthralling weaknesses: his fiery blue-eyed rages, his way of defusing honest grievance with a joke or an expensive gift, his emotionality like a schoolboy's ever-ready erection.*

"Your father," says my young friend Jerl, "sounds like what my group would call a Love and Relationship Addict."

"No, no," I laugh, "that's the story of my *life." But even as I speak I think of the "seraglio," as I titled my early novel about a white-haired tycoon serene in a house full of women once or presently loved.*

"Perhaps a degree of alcoholism, then?" Jerl suggests respectfully. Drawn to "adult children," he is reassured by seeing me as no less a survivor than himself.

I protest. That people drank to excess in those years between the wars was a rule of the game, and liquor blunted neither my father's professional acumen nor his sociability. For all we knew, it helped him close deal upon deal. Two or three drinks allowed him to reach others while, yes, making it harder for them to reach him. But the glass in his hand, against which he warned me—I was nine—with tears in his eyes, figures in Jerl's somberly appraising ones as a diabolic rival like Dr. Miracle in The Tales of Hoffmann, *who over the years has crossed my path in various guises and turned my loves dysfunctional. Suppose he's right. Admittedly, in each affair, a day dawns when I resort to the same aloof, injured airs with which my mother foiled—or fueled—"Daddy's temper." (I must, by the way, find the right moment to tell her that the therapist whose insight and good humor have seen me through the past couple of years is a black woman.) As Jerl talks, my father's demon grows ever realer. Is it good to be so impressionable? I glimpse the familiar hoofprint in Strato's gambling, in David's TV set jabbering till dawn, in Peter's long-buried compulsions now coming harrowingly to light. Looking back, I can read into those dear ones' first radiant smiles the promise not only of simple devotion but of an elaborate codependency, as it is known in the rooms Jerl frequents. Do I conclude that my life has been less a flight from the Broken Home than a cunning scale model of it? that my heart, far from being the wild untamable bird of Carmen's "Habanera," had its wings clipped while still in the egg?*

Let others connect neurosis with creativity. The real point is that something of the kind awaits virtually every child on earth. Call it cruelty, call it culture. These are the extremes of a broad and unbroken spectrum made visible through our being reared by other humans in the first place, rather than by wolves, like l'Enfant Sauvage. Small wonder we honor our father and mother even when we can't obey them. Without their imprint of (imperfect) love, the self is featureless, a snarl of instincts, a puff of stellar dust.

In his letter about the draft I sent him of this chapter, Freddy singles out its last sentences. (I thought he might like them. No longer a schoolmaster, he lives on the edge of a noble and unthreatened forest in Vermont.) Freddy then quotes a couple of sentences from the chapter he's been writing about a painful episode in his own past: "The fearsome blessing of that hard time continues to work itself out in my life the way we're told the universe is still hurtling through outer space under the impact of the great cosmic explosion that brought it into being in the first place. I think grace sometimes explodes into our lives like that—sending our pain, terror, astonishment hurtling through inner space until by grace they become Orion, Cassiopeia, Polaris, to give us our bearings, to bring us into something like full being at last."

I might have said that it's the gradual focus of human vision, intelligence rather than grace, whereby those traumatic stars, like their ancestors in the night sky, acquire names and stories. But why split hairs? Let the mind be, along with countless other things, a landing strip for sacred visitations. When the insurance man whose poems Freddy left unread at twenty wrote that "God and the imagination are one," I could hardly disagree. And now my friend of fifty years, having typed out my words together with his, goes on to shelve all further question of our divergence, while incidentally positing an exchange of hats not covered by Elizabeth Bishop's poem: "I was struck by how I sounded more like you in mine and you more like me in yours."

XIII

With the Plummers at the Ritz.
At the Tour d'Argent with Tony and Nina.

In the months following the liberation of Paris, Colonel William Plummer had been put in charge of the Ritz Hotel, where Allied brass and distinguished civilians were billeted. Now our turn came. Little of the personnel had changed since his heyday six years earlier, and we felt at once the grateful affection in which he was held by the assistant managers, the concierges, the maids and doormen. *"Mon colonel,"* the men called him, although upon his recent retirement from active duty Bill had been promoted to general. He, too, retained a fund of gratifying memories. The telegram from Ernest Hemingway announcing his marriage ("We've made an honest innkeeper of you"). Marlene Dietrich asking in her famous dulcet rasp who she had to sleep with in order to get a hot bath—a moment whose recounting made him flush, mouth drawn downward in sour and soundless amusement. This slight, barrel-chested man with thin blond hair and ice-blue eyes radiated dependability. As a career officer, spartan himself, Bill knew how to make things easy and comfortable for others. He'd been, for instance, assigned to Winston Churchill during the latter's visit, late in the war, to Miami and Cuba. From our first hour together in Paris I could sense his delight at having at last not a statesman or superior officer to care for, but a woman he loved. In his happiness he'd even quit smoking. In *my* happiness—wasn't she finally off my hands?—Bill struck me as answering the prayer my mother uttered each time she sat down at the piano, plaintive in lamplight, to accompany herself in what had become the theme song of those thirteen years between husbands: "Someone to Watch Over Me."

Bill calls her, instead of Hellen, by a nickname I don't catch right away. It sounds like "Was" but turns out to be the first syllable of *Oiseau*.

"That was my name for your mother long ago, in Jacksonville," he explains. "There was something birdlike about her—I don't know: soft and bright and alert. Not that she's changed in any way," he finished gallantly. "The name still fits."

Feigning to ignore us, my mother has taken from her purse a dozen postcards. Writing them between courses to friends at home is her sociable refreshment from the introspections of needlework. With the signing of each in her firm vertical script, a beaklike check mark pecks a name from the master list. Soft as a dove in Bill's eyes, stern as a hawk in mine?

"Oiseau? That was very poetic of you," I tell Bill, half to flatter, half in teasing allusion to the letter he wrote me about my book, frankly declaring it beyond his depth. The very format of verse, for Bill and my mother, suffices to obscure forever even the lyrics I've worked longest to make clear, whereas a page of my most devious and artificial prose will be greeted with relief: "Now you've written something *I* can read!"

"Poetic? If you say so." He coughs, strangled by the notion. "I wouldn't know. I certainly appreciate the time you spent with Betty in Rome."

"I'd give anything to have her with us right now," says my mother, checking off another name and passing me the card addressed to her step-daughter. "I've left room here for you to write her a line." I take out my pen. So twig by thread the nest of kinship weaves itself.

A day before I left Rome my phone rang. It was Claude. How was I, how was Robert? We were well—not that we'd seen that much of each other, with Mrs. Plummer in town. More to the point, how was *he?* (Still angry? I could tell from his voice that he wasn't.) He was well, thank you. He'd heard from Quinta about my trip and wondered if I had room for a little something—an umbrella actually—he wanted Alice to have for Christmas. Could he drop it off with my *portiere*? A weight I'd been living with floated away, I said I'd be delighted, and asked him to the Christmas party Robert and I were planning. With his little laugh of relief, Claude accepted.

A teatime fire burned in rue Christine. Alice, dressed for winter, peeped forth from a chic but bulky woolen suit. At her sandaled, wool-stockinged feet lay Basket, and Claude's vivid Roman umbrella leaned against her armchair. She was anxious, puzzled. She and Gertrude had always grieved when their favorite couples broke up. Such a waste of time and effort for all concerned! One began by knowing two people; suddenly, each having found someone else, there were four. In another year, eight, sixteen . . .

"You wouldn't have to know them all," I suggested.

"Who could!" She smiled from long experience of those evanescent family trees. But Claude and I, she went on, had seemed so well matched, so right for each other. "You would have seen that he had fun, Jamie. He would have seen that you used your mind."

I tried to reassure Alice that Claude and I would probably remain close friends, if not a couple. She was glad to hear it. Ah, but why psychotherapy? It was so Wagnerian—those hours of listening, that suffocating texture of motives. Why couldn't one conduct one's life in the concise, lighthearted spirit of French music, of Ravel or Poulenc, instead? Of the enigmatic rose-period Picasso girl, hand raised as though too much had already been said, in profile on the wall behind me? Of the dwarf Louis XV chairs whose needlepoint Alice had exquisitely worked from designs by Picasso? She named a once talented friend who after being treated by a psychiatrist no longer cared to paint. And surely that was the worst, said Alice in her honey voice, relighting a cigarette—not to use one's talents, to have beauty and intelligence at one's fingertips and not *let it out* into the world? I nodded, shamefaced, thinking how gladly I would have traded the creative life for that of the senses. It didn't escape me that Alice focused her concern upon the two realms my parents were least able to explore—my writing and my loving—and I marveled at her sound instinct. As I left she asked me to bring my mother and Bill to tea later in the week. I thought of warning her that Bill wasn't notably, how to put it, in the cultural swim. But Alice had eyes and ears; she'd find out without prompting.

A message awaited me from "la Princesse Canada," a name not even the concierge of the Ritz was able to gloss. When I called the accompanying number, however, a familiar voice answered: "Ah, there you are!" It was Tony. Yes, yes, my recent postcard had been forwarded to him in Paris. Nina—who by the way called herself the Princess Conan Doyle, a title far zanier (I thought) than its form garbled by the hotel switchboard—hoped very much I and the Plummers were free to dine that evening or the next. As it happened, Bill had been stewing over how to see some dull Americans in Neuilly without pointlessly involving us; my mother and I needed but the exchange of a glance to save him from Tony and the Princess.

The Bentley picked us up. Tony leapt out, kissing my mother's hand before settling her in the backseat next to a large dim perfumed cordiality, and off we were swept to the Tour d'Argent. "It is a vulgar restaurant," said Tony, squeezed between me and the chauffeur, "but Paris, too, has a vulgar streak, and one might as well *en profiter*." Our table overlooked the floodlit buttresses of Notre Dame. Along the black, excited river stretched a planetary system of radiant orbs. Tony wore a dinner jacket, and Princess Nina—at whom we were now getting our first good look—a loosely cut gown of tangerine silk. She was a theatrical, fleshy woman, much powdered, with red plush lips and iron-gray bangs. Over her balcony flowed a *rivière* of dime-sized diamonds, whose lights rivaled those of the Seine. "What an amazing necklace," I said without meaning to. Nina made a gesture of largess: "For you, darlings, for you!" Tony meanwhile saw to our pleasure with an easy assiduity I might have envied but didn't; to be that conversant with sauces and labels, with headwaiters and wine stewards, was surely a life's work, and I hoped I had better things to do.

Well, he was still the most insufferable boy at school, but with one immense difference: Nina. They were leaving early in the new year to join Denis in Ceylon. "Now tell me, who is Denis?" asked my mother. "Denis is my husband," said Nina. "And," Tony added, "considered by Those Who Know to be a very remarkable person." ("He would have to be," said my mother later, "to put up with *that* situation.") From Ceylon the three planned a slow move north, maharajah by maharajah, to the foothills of the Himalayas. The pure air would do Denis good, as would a certain saint in Kashmir, whose latest letter Tony just happened to be carrying. He passed it to me. The stationery was imprinted with the holy man's name and address on such and such a road, "above the tailor shop." I read that my friend was always to carry upon his person a small piece of iron and a sapphire wrapped together in silk and that he must feed bread every Thursday to a black dog. "Not so easy in Geneva or Paris," said Tony archly, "where the dogs are used to filet mignon." But he took out his magician's silk handkerchief and showed us its contents.

By comparison, Princess Nina came across as an earthy realist who understood the stock market, loved her position in the world, and wanted my honest opinion of Tony's poetry. Was he too sensitive, did I think? Was it not a pity that so rare a spirit—he'd taken to reading an act of Racine aloud to her every night before they retired—had to publish his work himself and be known only by his friends? Couldn't I give him an introduction to my New York publisher? Of course I could, but it wasn't the kind of poetry readily accepted nowadays. Nina nodded; that was Tony's line—editors were slaves to fads and trends, unable to tell the real thing from the trash they marketed. "But that is his pride talking," Nina continued. *"You* are published in New York, yet you are a true poet. I know because I am Russian, so I feel the temperament, the soul, feel it *here*." A plump crimson-tipped hand came to rest upon her diamonds. "Also my sister-in-law is a poet." "Who is your sister-in-law?" I asked, wondering if I had seen her name in the quarterlies. "No, no"—Nina shook her head—"Barbara is like Tony; she will not risk a rejection slip. But her work is pure and beautiful, like his." Here Tony, interrupting whatever he was telling my mother, identified the unhappy heiress among whose six or seven husbands had been one of the "marrying Mdivanis." "Why, I remember Barbara Hutton from Palm Beach!" my mother exclaimed. "Was she writing poetry then?"—as if asking whether she'd had bobbed hair in 1931. Tony rolled his eyes my way. Was this the kind of talk our work would inspire twenty years hence?

As we left the restaurant he took charge: "Dearest, Jimmy and I thought we might walk a half hour by the river—if you don't mind dropping Hellen at the Ritz?" Whereupon he again kissed my mother's hand, then Nina's, which stayed extended in my direction. Though I did no better than to shake it, "You have a friend in me," she said with gracious emphasis. Then the Bentley purred off into the night. Sighing, relaxing, our topcoat collars upturned, Tony and I walked in silence through the mild moist glistening leaf-plastered dark. The evening's wines had made me giddy, and when an old Eddie Cantor song—from a record Tony'd had at school—floated into mind, I began to sing under my breath:

> *"Give me a limousine*
> *And diamonds like the Queen,*
> *Give me most anything else you have to spare—"*

breaking off in embarrassment at this unthinking allusion to Nina's car and necklace. But with his old devil-may-care smile Tony took up the lyrics himself:

> *"And if my marriage should prove a phony*
> *Give me plenty of alimony—*
> [Both] *This is the Twentieth Century Maiden's Prayer!"*

Another spell of silence. Then in a new faraway voice: "I have seen a panorama that I wish to portray. Given five unbroken years of work, I am convinced that I could make the first revolution in prose fiction since Proust."

"Is something preventing you?" I asked innocently.

"What do you think? I don't complain." He shrugged. "What has one to give, in the long run, but oneself?" These were familiar words. I'd heard them week after week in New York, during that season when Bill Cannastra had glanced at the gift and waved it aside. His voice more and more like a sleepwalker's, Tony now began to relate an incident from his first weeks with Nina in Geneva. They had gone together into an elegant shop, of luggage and leather goods. "Nina's *maladie d'achat* is really a case for the specialists," he sighed. "Here in Paris I've been unable to write even a line of Poyetry. Do you like to shop? Come along! We go every morning. The car takes us to Fauchon, or the Galeries Lafayette, or the Samaritaine."

"What do you buy there?" I really wanted to know.

"Ah, you have put your finger on it." He gave up the ghost of a laugh: "Something that must be returned in the afternoon . . ." But back then in Geneva, the pattern, insofar as it involved Tony, was just beginning to take shape. They stood in the leather shop, pursuing, as people will in an unlikely place, the kind of idle, hushed, dreamlike conversation that changes the rest of their lives. As they talked, Nina kept playing with a limber riding crop she'd picked up from a display table, bending it this way and that until—"until it snapped . . . like the spine of Vronsky's horse," whispered Tony, stopping on our Parisian pavement, overcome. Nina had handed the broken crop to the startled Swiss clerk and in her grandest manner told him to put it on her bill and have it delivered to the hotel. With which she took Tony's arm and left the shop. "I knew then," he said, starting to walk again, "that I could never live without her."

It was from Tony that I first learned how effective a cliché can be at the right moment.

"You'd been looking for her a long time," I said to break the silence.

There was a sense of Tony smiling in the dark. "My *sage-femme* . . ."

"What about her husband?"

"Nina and I are twin souls. We have loved each other in many, many lives. It would be a great wickedness if we were to be kept apart in this one. In fact," Tony finished, his voice still that of a dreamer, "if you can keep a secret, we expect to marry next year. We are going to Ceylon to ask Denis for a divorce."

"What if he . . . ?"

"It is out of the question. A bond such as Nina's and mine is understood by Those Who Know."

I did not keep the secret. "He made it sound like a kind of celestial shotgun wedding," I told my mother the next morning.

"It's the end of him," she said somberly. "With a woman like that, Tony doesn't stand a chance."

"He said he's had no time for his work. His writing."

"It's her *age*, son; it's the unsuitability. She's older than his *mother*. It would be ludicrous if it weren't tragic. Just when he could have been enjoying his youth." This reversed my mother's standard line, which I had heard only a few days earlier following our lunch with Barney Crop. What was he *doing* here in Paris—painting a picture or two, having fun the rest of the time? That wasn't a life! His poor parents must be worried sick. As we pursued the subject of Nina, my mother's words called up, at a merciful remove, her first, spontaneous objection to Kimon: not, curiously, the nature of our love but the difference in our ages. The "unsuitability" of such unions was no mere formula. It had taken a diplomatic embassy from my paternal grandmother to win over my mother's parents to the dangerous notion of her marrying a divorced man fifteen years her senior. Such conventional wisdom was the *Code Napoléon* of a society, the unadorned, bedrock prose Stendhal aspired to; once *it* was set down clearly and forcefully, flightier forms would come to seem beside the point. I never fancied that "prose" of this rigor was anything but much, much harder to bring off than Barney's bachelor doggerel or the stately alexandrine couplets of Tony's liaison. Where Tony was concerned, however, I saw eye-to-eye with my mother, a state of affairs so refreshing that, instead of contradicting her out of long habit, I kissed her and went out—for, like Nina, I myself relished a morning in the shops—to buy spats for Robert, of heavy dark-gray felt with bone buttons.

The day of our tea with Alice, we had lunch by ourselves near the hotel. "There are some things Jimmy and I have to talk over," she told Bill, as my heart sank. Must I be lectured yet again about my "life"? I needn't have worried. That subject had become Dr. Detre's affair and was off-limits for the duration, perhaps forever. The closest she came was a single question, over our beet-and-celery salads in the bistro: "Have you anything to tell me?"—which I took to mean anything "reassuring," anything she could repeat to her friends without embarrassment. Excited by my imminent return to Rome, I did my best. The hours with Dr. Detre, I said, absorbed me totally. Whatever listlessness I'd felt with the motherly therapist in New York had melted away. Just as a careful reader might help me to write a better poem next time, analysis would enrich the text of the years ahead. Something Dr. Detre had emphasized at the outset came back as I spoke. I mustn't expect to be "happy ever after" when he finished with me. The problems that had sent me to him weren't going to evaporate. But when they recurred I'd know, for once, how to face them.

Who wanted the bland diet of happiness anyway? Bring on the sizzling mixed grill, the chilled and sparkling flute! *"Surtout pas le bonheur!"* as Oscar Wilde had said, though I knew better than to quote him to my mother. "The point," I did say, since we were at lunch in not only Wilde's but Lambert Strether's favorite city, "isn't that a given life be 'happy' or 'sad' but that you have the appetite to live it. It's such a waste, such a loss, if you don't." The phrases came easily; I'd written them not long ago to my father, congratulating him on his now final divorce from Kinta. "That's why your marrying Bill is so splendid. You've left your sickroom, you've taken hold of your life. You've become a new person!"

"No, I haven't," said my mother, placing her hand over mine. "Please understand one thing. Bill Plummer is a fine man. He has more gentleness and consideration in his little finger than Charlie Merrill ever showed after the first years of our marriage. That was your father's nature; don't think I'm blaming him. Bill's life hasn't been easy, but I love him and I promise you I'll make him a good wife. But, son, we're not talking about what I felt for your father. It's not only that I'm past the age. There are things I couldn't put myself through again, things I can count on Bill to spare me."

"The pain, the humiliation . . ." I echoed the words often on her lips after my father left.

"And the whatever you want to call it. Rapture? I couldn't face that again either. So don't dismiss happiness too quickly, Jimmy. It looks pretty good from where I sit."

I was sorry that rapture played no part in my mother's new marriage. The romantic in me would have liked to see her not just watched over but swept away. In any event, Bill got high marks in an unexpected quarter. When I telephoned Alice to thank her for having us all to tea, she said how pleased she was to have met my mother and how truly delighted she had been by General Plummer. "He's bound to be a blessing in your life, Jamie. So decent and sensible. Just the kind of man Gertrude Stein liked best."

•

In my father's divorce from Kinta, my mother (I learned recently) played a small but gratifying role. Soon after she and Bill were married, my father gave them lunch at a Palm Beach club. Over coffee he asked Bill, with a comradely frankness used through the years on many a husband, to grant him and the new Mrs. Plummer an hour alone. Life with Kinta, he admitted once Bill had strolled out onto Worth Avenue, was now intolerable. My father didn't know how much longer he had to live, but he'd be damned if he wanted to die while still married to that bloodsucker. He had always trusted my mother's judgment; what did she think? They discussed in some detail his provisions for children and former wives, the present state of his finances, and so forth. At last came the bittersweet, long-to-be-savored moment. He and my mother exchanged (or so I imagine it) a look brimming with something far rarer than love—with unspoken if, on her side, not wholly disinterested intelligence. "What on earth are you waiting for?" she asked in her mildest voice. The question sealed Kinta's fate. Two weeks later his divorce was under way.

Nor was my pep talk over our lunch in Paris wholly disinterested. I wanted my mother's marriage, and the freedom it promised me, to last. It did. Bill would "watch over" my mother devotedly for fifteen years, until emphysema sapped him; then her turn came. Since his death she has stayed on in Atlanta. Betty and her husband drive over from Anniston every two or three weeks, and countless local friends—younger and younger as time passes—make much of her.

A tinted oval photograph shows her at eighteen with soulful eyes and Cupid's-bow lips, her forehead ringleted, the whole wrapped in a fichu of pink tulle against a studio backdrop of plantation oaks. It bears a clear likeness to my mother even now, while giving no clue to her uncanny, lifelong vitality. (One clue, no doubt, is the daily quarter grain of thyroid extract she has taken since my birth. This emerged when she broke a hip at eighty. Hospitalized without her medication, she lapsed before our eyes, like the beautiful girl at the close of Lost Horizon, *into an old, old woman. Then she mended, and a tiny white pill again reversed the process.) Late in life, still glancing longingly at the dance floor, all animation from her first drink, her dark hair barely frosted by the years, she has not lost the ability, or the desire, to draw her companion into that old complicity of vigorous nods and knowing smiles, her slender hand coming to rest on his arm for emphasis. At ninety my mother has the smooth legs of a girl. Her breasts, glimpsed through a loose peignoir, are large and unwrinkled. The only physical sign of age is in the shoulders—giving out, as if they'd borne too much—and in the slow erosion of her once military spine to a fragile question mark.*

Last year in Atlanta I was helping to pack her latest boxful of clippings about me (reviews, interviews, magazine appearances, and the like) for mailing to the university library that collects my papers. Presently she sat back and turned my way her delicate unlined face—unlifted, too, by any surgery more drastic than her oiled fingertips as she listens to the morning news. "The articles about you always tell who your father was," she said without petulance, "but there's never any mention of me. It's as if you'd never had a mother." I reminded her of many exceptions to this new pronouncement, including how she figured in my own writing, but it didn't convince her. Peering into that open grave of paper and newsprint between us, I thought of the letters she had destroyed so long ago—my letters from Kimon and Claude, from Freddy and Tony, destroyed not to punish me but lest their evidence harm me in the eyes of the world—and for a sad, startled minute saw these already yellowing heaps of "favorable publicity" saved over the years since her rash act as a kind of penance, like a conscientious little girl's smudged apology for a blunder that had better be tenderly forgiven, once and for all: any day now it will be too late.

On the last morning of my visit my mother kept an appointment at Atlanta's most genteel funeral parlor. Made comfortable in a room full of antiques, each piece labeled with donor and date, we were duly joined by one of the firm's junior partners. I watched this bloodless youth turn human, rosy in the glow of my mother's warmth as she answered his questions and told him her requirements. Since I'd showed no eagerness to be buried in the family plot in Jacksonville— where, with Bill Plummer already settled, there was, she offered hesitantly, just enough room for her and me and, if I wished, David Jackson—she had decided to "bring" Bill to Atlanta and lie beside him in the Cathedral garden. I felt her pain, as a Christian believer, at knowing that our dust would not be mingled, and then and there considered granting her that posthumous satisfaction. After all, what earthly difference could it make? But no; I wanted a return to the elements, wanted my ashes to be scattered upon dancing waters by hands I loved, and I kept silent. We rose to take our leave. Something I'd said recently about ecology and the need for biodegradable packaging must have been in her mind, along with all the rest, for on the sunny threshold she turned to her funereal friend, resting a hand on his arm:

"One last thing. Did I make it clear that I want to be buried in a biographical *container?"*

XIV

Arrivederci, Robert.
Translating Montale.

In the Piazza Navona, its ring of Christmas booths an enchantment after dark, Robert and I bought tree decorations out of Mozart and Ariosto: eighteenth-century ladies with powdered hair, knights in quicksilver armor. Other, humbler booths evoked the *trattorie* of Elfland. Impossible to resist their little painted dishes of vegetables, spaghetti with tomato sauce, a whole roast chicken or grilled fish on a platter three centimeters long, baskets of glistening bread, bowls of tiny apples and pears. Remembering these miniature pop sculptures from childhood Christmases, I felt I'd come home. My half brother and his family arrived from Austria. Our nephew Merrill, who had replaced Robin at the famous Swiss school, joined their party. Day after day was filled with shopping, sightseeing, restaurants. My father had commissioned me to buy presents for everybody; so had my mother. A production of *The Emperor Jones* showed us—the text in Italian, the singers in blackface—the charms and pitfalls of cultural exchange. On Christmas Day nine grown-ups and six children met in Via Quattro Novembre. Dr. and Mrs. Simeons brought their sons. Robert found a recipe for eggnog; there must have been a fruitcake or a *panettone.* Claude appeared, all smiles and packages. Marilyn's red-nailed hands fluttered over the keyboard, and out came, in her hilariously high small voice,

> *"She's gotta be cool in summer, warm in fall,*
> *Hot in the winter and tha-at ain't all,*
> *In the springtime she'll be fine as wine—*
> *She's a four-season mama and she's mine, all mine!"*

while Umberto listened in suspended disbelief. A week later we drank a bottle of champagne, and it was 1952.

But no sooner had we begun to trust the steadying joys of a life shared than the blow fell. Checking back at his landlady's one morning, Robert found an urgent message. His grandfather was dead, his mother needed him at home, he had no choice but to pack up and go. The misfortune shook us both. Neither was ready to take the other for granted. Each day began and ended with naked, electric arousals and the license to satisfy them at shameless length. Over meals we talked inventively, self-delightingly—no tense misunderstandings, no restful silences. Couples more set in their ways, used to communicating in platitudes, pricked up their ears at nearby tables. One morning when our *permessi di soggiorno* needed renewing, we armed ourselves against the boredom by taking along *The Way of the World* to read aloud in the waiting room of the Questura. The other petitioners, a slow-to-dwindle crowd, lowered their newspapers as our performance gathered momentum. Mirabell and Millamant's wry declarations brought tears to our eyes. Robert got to play Lady Wishfort's scene in the last act. "Begone! begone! begone!—go! go!—That I took from washing of old gauze and weaving of dead hair, with a bleak blue nose over a chafing dish of starved embers . . ." Unable to contain myself, I cut him off in mid-tirade: did he realize that was Hopkins? I quoted from the famous sonnet, ". . . and *blue-bleak embers,* ah my dear! / Fall, gall themselves, and gash gold-vermilion." Really, it was too uncanny. —Oh? Why should Hopkins not have read Congreve? asked Robert pettishly, still in character; Jesuits were famous for liking naughty books. Yes, but to take the actual words (I said) and use them in a poem dedicated to—! Robert interrupted me to cite the reverse example of

Chabrier, who, borrowing precisely those themes from *Tristan* praised by the critics for their intrinsic loftiness, had used them in a suite of music-hall galops for two pianos. I saw his point at once: Hadn't I gone through a phase of marking passages in *Walden* that proved it beyond all doubt a clever forgery by Proust? The reclusive temperament given to worldly images, the set pieces wherein the nature is seen revolving through seasonal prisms. "Concord" itself, the fictive town nearest to the narrator's retreat, had been transparently named after a famous square in Paris. . . . We agreed then and there to collaborate on a scholarly article—"Lady Wishfort and the Windhover"—and were discussing its strategies when a scowling official called our names. No doubt our giddiness was ill-considered. But being young, we wanted to display it in public, and neither was musician enough to modulate into a more natural key.

Before Robert left we gave ourselves a weekend in Naples. The city fed our taste for the exaggerated, the bizarre, the frivolous. (For human beauty too; every other man looked like Gino the goalie.) We lingered among Pompeian frescoes of dainty gods and heroes. "Profoundly superficial," I jotted on an envelope. We saw the *Cristo Velato,* so realistic that its marble shroud was said to sweat; and, at the aquarium, a jellyfish of live, fringed crystal big as a skull, hovering over a much littler one. "Madonna and Child," Robert murmured. We heard *L'Assedio di Corinto,* our first tragic opera by Rossini. But no matter how grave a juncture had been reached in the libretto, his music was unable to keep a straight face. Like our hours together, it bubbled, winking and flushed, from some deep well of delicious amusement. Back in our room we lay exhausted, stroking each other's cheeks, exchanging reassurances. Rays from the bedside lamp barely transgressed its flounces of pink glass. I would miss all this terribly. Since I was tied to Italy by my analysis, Robert promised to return and spend the summer with me.

"It may be just as well for you to be alone for a while," said Dr. Detre. "You have been creating a duplicate self out of Robert."

"Is that bad?"

"Put yourself in his place. How would you feel?"

"If someone did that to me? Oh dear. Misunderstood, ignored . . . But if he is 'me,' then by loving him I could be learning to love myself. At least that's to the good?"

"No doubt. But there is only so much to gain from paying court to the mirror."

"None of it gained by the mirror . . ."

"Regrettably so. It is a one-sided transaction."

Robert left. In the light of Dr. Detre's comments I felt almost relieved by his departure, as though, had he stayed in Rome, I would inevitably have caused him pain. It was going to be hard, after the delights of companionship, to resume a solitary life. But I trusted my analysis would progress by leaps and bounds now that it had no rival for my attention. There was always, to be sure, the opera. Like some midwinter cold snap, a transalpine company descended upon Rome with *Siegfried* and *Elektra*—an opera my mother had forbidden me, at thirteen, to attend. Did she fear my learning what sons under stress were capable of? Now at last I was free to look and listen, tingling with expectations no performance could have lived up to. Wagner brought out a formidably serious audience who shushed for quiet throughout the first act, only to sleep, heads rolling like a seal colony, in the brilliant stagelight of the last scene. Other works unknown to me kept being mounted—*Der Freischütz, Adriana Lecouvreur, Sakuntala*. The score of this last, by the Alfano who completed *Turandot*, had been destroyed when a bomb fell on a library in Bologna. Unfortunately the composer was still alive and had nothing better to do than to recreate it from memory. He must have overlooked a few instrumental parts, for one came away giggling like an idiot from an overdose of harp, woodblock, and triangle—not to mention the old man's curtain calls after each act, hands clasped triumphantly over his head, while five or six students cheered in the half-empty house.

At last I began work on the two Montale poems Ben Johnson had given me months ago. The first, "La Casa dei Doganieri," turned out to be relatively easy, but the second, "Nuove Stanze," even after I'd looked up every other word in my new dictionary, kept resisting the intelligence, to my theoretical approval and practical dismay. Its elements were a cigarette-smoking woman, a chessboard with a game in progress, a room above the towers and bridges of a town, and various unspecified dire events looming on the horizon—which the woman's glowing gaze, her "eyes of steel," appear to challenge and oppose. Montale was clearly taking pains not to say all he knew, and to say what he did say with such mysterious force that any reader except for that ideal *tu*—the woman pondering the chessboard—would have an awed sense of eavesdropping upon a prayer. A wraith of tightly knit logic—a syntax to be followed at your own risk, for the thread might snap at any turning—marked even the least of Montale's poems, any one of which called for as much constructive guesswork as did an ode by Horace. Rhyme and assonance surfaced at tantalizing random—hazards of the medium rather than part of the blueprint. For me it was the ladles and love letters, the furniture and pets, those blessedly ordinary nouns embedded like votive plaques in its walls, that drew a reader ever deeper into the labyrinth. Their translator had to go a step further and pretend to know what dwelt at its heart.

Our short-lived collaboration behind us, Ben and I were pleased that its fruits found approval in Umberto's eyes. He, it emerged, was on good enough terms with Montale to suggest my calling upon him should I ever go to Milan. "I'm sure he would welcome you also as a friend of Miss Brandeis," Umberto added, lowering his eyelids and weaving his fingers together. I assumed a look of interest but, having recently seen in a book-shop a sullen, unprepossessing photograph of the poet, made up my mind to leave well enough alone.

"What was it you disliked about his appearance?" asked Dr. Detre.

I saw what he was getting at—Dr. Simeons had already tried the Szondi test on me, with its disturbing or lunatic faces—so there was no harm in going along with the game. "Montale? Oh, he looked, I don't know, like a hedgehog. Mean and unloving. As if he would take every-thing and give nothing. That's absurd, I know, because in his poems he's already given more to the world than most people ever do. I simply didn't want anything to do with him myself. Besides, what language would we speak? His English is bound to be awful."

"When did you see this photograph?"

"Just after Robert left. Perhaps a month ago? Just as I was getting down to those translations."

"Strange that you persisted in so antipathetic a project."

I half rose from the couch to look round. "It's no reflection on the *work*. The work is marvelous! I guess I'm just a Platonist," I said, falling back and thinking that if Dr. Detre knew anything about poetry, now would be the time to quote that stanza where Spenser asserts that the more heavenly light there is in the soul, the more physical beauty will show in the person. Not that this could possibly be the case. On the contrary, beauty was terrifying, and only a very foolish moth expected any good to come from his affair with the flame. But Dr. Detre and I had covered this ground many times. Montale's repulsiveness was the topic at hand. "So," I went on with a touch of sarcasm, "I suppose you want me to say who I've really been describing under the aspect of Montale. A rival for the muse's favor? Closer to home, an older male presence with some sort of prior claim on an important woman in my life? Bill Plummer? How many father figures can one *have*?"

"Excuse me. Mean? Unloving? That doesn't sound like General Plummer. Taking everything and giving nothing? Are you comfortable with this description of your father?"

"Montale . . . I don't know the whole story, but I somehow picture him treating Irma shabbily. Like my father when—"

"Who is it in your *present* life who does not love you, who takes everything and gives nothing in return, who has encouraged a temporary separation from your sexual partner, and whose peculiarly accented words are you condemned to translate every day as best you can?"

A dreadful silence spread through the room. "You," I managed to breathe.

•

Those early Montale translations failed in part because the poet's ambiguous textures called for the kind of judgment Ben and I might never acquire. (The pianola in a phrase from the "Motetti" could be rendered by Irma as belonging to "the people downstairs" or by Dana Gioia as part of the furniture of Hell—in either case justifiably. How to know?) Yet our essential failure lay in not yet having a full command of our own language. This is the rock on which nine out of ten translators founder and accounts for the baby talk of poets who, writing under the spell of Rilke or Neruda, have read them only in user-friendly versions geared to "accessibility."

Today "Nuove Stanze" is less opaque than it once was. Familiarity with other poems by Montale—more often than not, picked out by Irma as worth attempting in English—has no doubt helped. So have the notes in the 1980

Opera in Versi *(Einaudi) which, on my way through Italy that year, I bought for Irma. But it seemed that she'd already received those two volumes from another source; my gift was sent back to me. Here, opening it for perhaps the second time in ten years, I see that "Nuove Stanze" dates from the spring of 1939 and deals with "la guerra che matura. Ultimi giorni fiorentini di Clizia"—a name that would have meant nothing had I come across it in 1950. One poem, however, which I later undertook at Irma's behest ("L'Ombra della Magnolia"), is addressed to this enigmatic Clizia. Who was she? When I asked Umberto for help, he said he imagined she was the nymph in Ovid who was changed into a sunflower. Through my head darted the radiant last line of the poem Irma had read aloud to Claude and me before presenting us with the book dedicated to I. B.: "The golden trumpets of solarity." Yet I held back from putting a face to the sun-worshipping nymph.*

Move by move over the decades, slow as a chess game, it grew clear that she was Irma herself. One day I heard of a picnic she'd gone to with Montale. Two years later she showed me a fat biographical dictionary of European literary figures. Montale's entry was illustrated not by the usual glum portrait but the snapshot of a cat striding across a book-littered table on which rested—seen from the back, yet that tangled hair looked familiar—a woman's head. Irma's. More years passed. No single revelation marked the point at which I "knew." Somehow, one afternoon, I felt entitled to wonder why they'd parted. Ah well, Irma said without emotion, war was about to break out; as a Jew, she couldn't possibly have stayed in Italy. Montale, though—mightn't he have come to the States? Irma shook her head. She'd done everything in her power, got him the papers, secured him the university position. By then, however, the other woman—for yes, there had been, finally, another woman—had staked her claim. Montale remained in Italy. Irma returned many times. After the flood of 1966 she worked in Florence as a volunteer, salvaging the precious documents. But she and Montale never met again.

Or did they? There were always third parties to whom they could, if they wished, apply for news of each other. But only after Montale's Nobel Prize—after, too, the death of "Mosca," whom he had married—did the question of a meeting arise. Irma broached it to me one evening in New York. Suppose she wrote—the merest line, you understand, expressing pride in his fame. Then what? Gestures like that had consequences. After all this time, was there any-thing to be gained, any point, any pleasure, on either side, in the notion of

coming face-to-face? What did I think? What did I think! My eyes were shin-
ing with the romance of it. Write him, I urged her. Who knew where it would
lead! She turned upon me, if not the "eyes of steel" of the woman in "Nuove
Stanze," then surely that "hard crystal glance" of the anguished but divinely
prescient muse in "L'Orto." Would I never, said that look, act my age? Again,
months went by. One day at Casaminima, Irma's cottage near the Bard cam-
pus, she reopened the topic. "I heard from Montale, did I tell you? Oh, some-
time last winter. Here, let me show you." I looked over her shoulder as she
unfolded a page of heavy white paper. At its center was a square, not much
larger than a postage stamp, of cramped, elderly script. "Irma," it began,
"you were ever my godess [sic] *"—switching to Italian to ask where and when*
they should meet. It was signed, with no suspicion of a flourish, "Montale."

"You see," she said, managing to laugh, "this won't do. Either his mind is
gone or . . . I never called him 'Montale.' If he doesn't remember that . . . !"

"I'm always forgetting which people call me what," I said lamely.

Another mineral look. Then: "I'm flying to Milan at the end of the month.
I had thought in spite of everything to see him. But now I hear from G."—indi-
cating a second letter at her side— "that there's talk of his marrying his house-
keeper. Under those circumstances a meeting is out of the question."

Which is all I know of Irma's final trip to Italy. Meanwhile, in the wake of
Montale's worldwide fame, "Clizia" had been identified as Irma in a learned
journal. Another year, and this scoop reemerged on the front page of the New
York Times Book Review. *A flurry of interest peaked and died down. The*
woman who long ago foresaw the doomed pawns blinded by war madness, who
beneath her high room's "frightened ivory moldings" stubbed out another cig-
arette, eyes blazing with scorn and despair, turned back into words. In the notes
to "Nuove Stanze" Montale is quoted telling a friend that its latest draft has
made the poem "more Florentine, more like intarsio-work, a harder sur-
face"—phrases that turn his chessboard to inlaid marble. Above Irma's book-
case hangs (or did until her recent death) a portrait of herself done in the 1930s.
Modigliani would have liked that face—proud, pale as fire, but amused too,
and without a shred of pathos. Everything fits. Montale's poem, like the forces
behind it—the approaching cataclysm, the convulsed loyalties, the bell (la
Martinella) rung only to signal a disgrace—grows daily more alive and clear,
at the usual cost of whatever human presences brought it into being.

(David and I naturally called up Irma on the Ouija board. We like to

make sure that friends who've died aren't left cooling their heels by some minor bureaucrat but get in with the right set from the start. We needn't have worried; Irma sounded altogether at home. As death's pain and confusion ebbed away, she told us, she came to herself ECSTATICALLY SKIPPING ROPE. ENDS OF THE ROPE HELD BY MONTALE & DUSE.)

About to return those two volumes of L'Opera in Versi *to the shelf, I'm stopped in my tracks. Heavens! Did Irma mail the wrong books back to me ten years ago? Or was it more like her to have trusted this final discovery to undo me at its own sweet pace? For these I am holding came to her from the poet himself. On the flyleaf of the first volume, in that cramped elderly hand I seem to have glimpsed once before, appears the inscription "a Clizia." And beneath it is . . . a name? The name Irma called Montale by when they were both young? One would need to have known it in order to make it out today.*

A false conclusion: the books were inscribed and sent (according to Luciano Rebay, the distinguished montalista) not by their author but by their editor. Yet having basked long months in the sunset glow of fable, I'll just sit here awhile in the gloom before switching on for good the poor lamp of fact.*

XV

Broken Vows.
Nils.
Franco.
The Unlit Garden.
Good-bye to Luigi.

Dr. Detre seemed pleased by my having at last expressed, however indirectly, some feelings about him. Popular psychology had led me, at the start, to anticipate falling in love with my analyst. It turned out, however, that "transference" covered a wide spectrum of emotion and that the veiled resentment brought to light by my fantasy about Montale's photograph was a not unacceptable form for this phase of the pilgrim's progress. Although we were never to dwell long upon the moment of truth, I knew from my praise of Montale's work that—whatever coldheartedness I might project upon a Dr. Detre of flesh and blood—my faith in his professional skill had come through intact. Not long after my little breakthrough he volunteered that we were "on schedule." I felt I'd been given a prize at school.

Another early misconception had to do with dreams. Before entering analysis I fancied them to be the very meat on which patient and doctor breakfasted insatiably together. Each night therefore I set off in catlike pursuit of a new one, and next day proudly laid the dead mouse at Dr. Detre's feet. But far from praising my cunning, he let it be felt that all this dream work was an elaborate ruse to keep the real issues at arm's length. These—the real issues—were coming more and more to seem of my own devising. It was as if my life until now had been governed by certain vows that I'd made—the vow, for instance, to keep my heart open, as my father did, to anyone I'd ever loved; or the vow always to be truthful and do my "level best," in my mother's phrase; above all, never to break faith with the pure, gemlike feelings of adolescence lest I turn, like Dorian Gray, into a hideous and corrupt thirty-year-old who lived for sensual delights and treated his lovers as means to a shameful end. The crayon colors of these projects, and their iconography of stick figures, boxlike house, and all-seeing sun, ought to have ensured their removal, long before this, from a grown person's refrigerator door. My mother, after all, that day at Hadrian's Villa, had confessed her old duplicity as to an equal. In Claude's arms after hearing that Hans was dead I knew the pain my father must have caused his latest love by never quite relinquishing the bygone ones. The feelings my poems drew upon were no longer a school-boy's, but how was a reader to tell? What if my efforts to resist that reader's intelligence were masking not just the gender of my loves but the insidious onset of manhood? Heaven forbid! Sleeping Beauty hadn't been meant to age even a day during her long coma.

The task ahead was to release that wise but ignorant young person from those vows he had made to himself. This would have to be brought off—like all dealings with unhappy teenagers—patiently, amicably, diplomatically. "Look," I might say to him, "there's someone at this party who keeps glancing your way. Why not risk talking to him? You're not committing yourself to anything." Or: "We've never walked through that unlit garden on our way home. Yet other people seem to be making the detour. Why not try it tonight?" The party in question was given by a film director I'd met through Wayne, and the person looking my way was a young Swedish scene designer named Nils. The unlit garden, no distance at all from my apartment, turned out to be a hotbed of fickle silhouettes, a world that could be craved, possessed, and forsworn, all in twenty minutes.

.   .   .

Nils's beauty blinded me to his dull wits and melancholy nature. Indeed, this last may well have been caused by his beauty, or by the advantage so many people had taken of it in his short life. Blond, with dark brows, blue eyes, and meltingly chiseled lips, he had already learned—perhaps from the films of his compatriot Greta Garbo—a minimal, enigmatic play of feature. Was his deepest wish, like hers, to be left alone? On just the break with his middle-class parents Nils seemed to have squandered a whole lifetime's allowance of imagination; now it was up to the rest of the world to look out for him. But what could he hope for from his new milieu? His stage designs, when he brought them to lunch, were pitifully inept and obvious. In bed, a few nights later, he might have been a sack of potatoes. The rest of the world, that season, boiled down to me. One day he showed up in great fright and pain. I took him to Dr. Simeons, who diagnosed a duodenal ulcer, psychosomatically induced to be sure, and prescribed six weeks in hospital, where Nils could be overseen, body and soul. He had no money; I offered to take care of it. But lest he imagine that these expenses—like the settlements made by my father upon his ex-wives—in any way replaced ongoing love and interest, I ran errands for him downtown and took a bus to the hospital every afternoon. Unable to amuse him, I stayed out my hour and left, promising to come the next day.

Time passed and he was cured. One wet night soon after his leaving the hospital for a friend's apartment, he invited me to the ballet. Featured that evening was the premiere of a new work choreographed by Anton Dolin, a famous dancer then past his prime. I offered Nils a bite to eat first. He arrived carrying a single rose of an unusually vibrant red, which I put in my buttonhole. We were both rather dressy; I wore a pearl-gray waistcoat with my dark suit. After supper, when we were on the point of leaving for the theater, Nils flung his arms round me dramatically, harshly too, as if to say, *Here, this is what you expected, let's get it over with!*—waking no response in me and mangling my rose. I salvaged one brilliant petal, tucked it in my waistcoat pocket, and out we went. Why we were sitting through this inane performance became clear only at its end. Dolin himself, whom Nils had to thank for our tickets, expected us backstage. Small, trim, hair blackened and cheeks rouged, the former *premier danseur* extended both hands in welcome. I was about to mention that I'd seen him dance in New York, before the war. But Dolin now drew back, shooting me an abrupt head-to-toe look of dreadful gravity. "What is that peeking out of your pocket?" he inquired.

"Where? Oh. It's just . . . a rose petal."

Dolin's eyes kindled. So that was what the boy had done with his morning's gift of roses—given them to this young American! Moments later I was on the street, alone, having had the uncharacteristic good sense to excuse myself. I'd been shown too many things at once—Nils's weakness and banality, the famous old dancer's airs, his unloving drive to dominate, and my own contribution to the whole hothouse farce. Worse yet, how plausibly I myself could slip, over the years, into Dolin's role. Did I see Nils again after that? If so, it was with the sense of a narrow escape. Better far the photograph I'd taken of his beautiful head gazing mysteriously up from the hospital pillows.

Yet something told me that my impulse towards Nils was more than a matter of looks. On Dr. Detre's couch I recalled the afternoon at Amherst when Hans played the *Spring* Sonata on my phonograph; I was catching cold but gallantly fought off his offer to bring me soup and make me comfortable. Why? Perhaps it was less urgent for me to receive care than to dispense it. If my need was to be needed, Nils's very instability may have drawn me to him.

"Need is an infantile form of love," said Dr. Detre. "Going to bed with someone just because he or she 'needs' you might be compared to taking sexual advantage of a small child."

I thought of the years I'd languished unmolested.

"Be glad that you were not too much needed as a child," he went on. "Your father and mother had admirably full lives without you. Nurses kept the little boy clean and amused until the summons came from downstairs."

I remarked that after my parents' separation my mother seemed to need me very much. But by then it was as if—did Dr. Detre recall that caption to my picture in the newspaper, "Pawn in Parents' Fight"?—the most expendable piece on the chessboard was within a move or two of becoming a queen.

Undeterred by my wit, Dr. Detre proceeded. "The proofs of concern you received from your parents in adolescence came too late. You were already inventing your superior way of responding to an appeal—not only with money but with time and love. To this day anybody who needs you, or appears to, even for a half hour, can have you."

There were no obvious psychological pitfalls in that unlit garden near my building, where I might far more readily have consummated my desire for Nils—and *with* Nils, it belatedly occurred to me—than by troubling to invite him to lunch. Here were shrubs and benches, and one of those turn-of-the-century urinals I'd seen all over town, which looked like something fathered upon an Iron Maiden by the Beast with Two Backs. You could pretend to be relieving yourself while waiting in double obscurity, with pounding heart, for the next stranger's hand to reach round the partition that divided you from him. Sometimes, before entering his side, he would light a cigarette, allowing you to judge whether to stay put or to yield your place to another. Sporadically the striking and extinguishing of matches transformed the whole garden into a mating ground for fireflies. At first I preferred the security of my hunter's blind. But gradually realizing that everyone else was nearly as frightened and furtive as I was, I ventured out into the shrubbery. Nowhere—as far as I could tell—was there any question of all-out copulation. (One went, according to Wayne, to the Colosseum for that.) Distractable as dogs, we sniffed from partner to partner, making do with the sort of exploratory thrill a boy of fourteen is meant to have outgrown. If a climax occurred it seemed like an inadvertent disgrace, and the culprit promptly banished himself from our midst. On my fourth—and final—visit, thinking I'd found someone I liked, I urged a man to come home with me. He did, but reluctantly; once behind closed doors, he would not undress, or lie down, or meet my eyes. As Dr. Detre pointed out, I might as well have stayed in the garden.

One bright midday in late February, as I was passing the Albergo da Raimondo on my way home, a voice in my ear began singing a popular love song. I looked round into the eyes of the rather dashing man, perhaps eight years my senior, who was picking me up. But just like that, on the street, in broad daylight! Out of simple discretion I hurried him past the *portiere* and up to my apartment. In a half hour we were again dressed, and talking. His name was Franco, he worked—well, let's say that his work kept him out of Rome a lot of the time. There was really no address or telephone where I could reach him. He had a confident, bohemian air and gazed at me ardently throughout this explanation, so I saw nothing wrong with it. He told me of his good heart and sincerity as well. One indispensable phrase rose many times to his lips: *io invece*—I on the other hand—words that favorably distinguished the speaker from those thousands who were using the very same formula, wherever Italian was heard, at that exact moment. Somehow it added to Franco's credibility; had he been playacting, he'd have had a better script. I gave him my telephone number, and when he called two weeks later asked him over right away. Separation had inflamed us both. We fell into bed. *"Ti voglio bene, Dʒim, ti voglio bene,"* Franco kept breathing as he sought to turn me facedown beneath him. But this position alarmed me, for all its exciting novelty, and besides—*ti voglio bene?* That wasn't saying very much. If Franco merely "wished me well," as Luigi had his ugly fiancée, he had better go by himself to the tavern where his friends gathered and where he'd suggested on the telephone that I accompany him this evening. Obviously this Lothario had all along been trifling with an innocent boy's emotions: Why should I let myself in for a lifetime at the beck and call of such a heartless person? His clothes furthermore were shabbier than I'd remembered, and he had a blackhead on his neck.

I expected Dr. Detre to applaud my mature decision. Instead he allowed himself a youthful laugh. "You have proven to my satisfaction that the only way to learn a foreign language is in bed. Do you honestly not know what *ti voglio bene* means? It is how an Italian says 'I love you.'"

I protested. *Amo* was the verb, just as in Latin. Lovers were *amanti*. *"L'amo,"* confesses Violetta in Act III—I love him. *"M'ama"*—she loves me—sings Nemorino in *L'Elisir d'Amore*.

"I do not question your experience of nineteenth-century opera," said Dr. Detre, "only of the Italian language as it is spoken today."

I bit my lip. Franco loved me! But how would I ever find him again?

"Nevertheless," Dr. Detre pursued, "from your account of this admirer and the circumstances under which you met, I have to agree with your appraisal of his character."

Well, there was always Luigi. Over the Christmas holidays he had joined an excursion to the zoo with my brother and his family. Many of the cages were empty. Others contained domestic animals—dogs from Africa, North American poultry. Luigi himself was voted the most popular exhibit. I saw the kind of father he would make and identified wistfully with four-year-old Bruce, perched high on his shoulder. From Austria the two older girls sent him valentines in my care—wasn't Valentini his family name?—which I gave him when he came to lunch. Quinta liked him, too, and fed him well those days. If I expected him to regret our evenings by the fire, just the two of us with our leftovers, our wine, our dreams, and shake his head over What Might Have Been, I had misjudged my man. Luigi was now the friend of the family. I knew his people, he knew mine. His place at table was assured, his second helpings were forthcoming. When an idea crossed his mind he expressed it; otherwise— companionable silence, the cheerful munch, the meeting of eyes as when old friends share food. A day came when I could bear no more.

"Luigi, I must talk to you," I said in Italian. "These last months have been difficult for me. I want only to go back to my country, yet I cannot. I must stay in Rome until the therapy I am pursuing for a nervous condition comes to an end. Among Italians—even with you, my good and sincere friend—I feel an estrangement, *un disamore*, which does them, and you, a great injustice. But my one consolation is to be with my fellow Americans. Do you understand?"

"*È naturale,*" said Luigi, nodding slowly, as though my speech, which to my own ears sounded so perfidious, summed up what he had long ago come to realize. "You are a poet; your nerves are not like mine. Shall I not see you again?"

"If the mood lifts," I promised. We finished our *dolce*, drank our coffee, and parted with unfeigned affection. It was that simple.

•

It was a truth universally acknowledged in those innocent decades from 1950 to 1980 that a stable homosexual couple would safely welcome the occasional extramarital fling. David and I, still in our early thirties, found that a good deal of anxiety could be finessed by setting out together when we felt the itch, rather than carrying on behind each other's backs. We kept on the lookout for a threesome or a "double date" with some other couple on our wavelength. Like high-school buddies we compared notes afterward, laughed and commiserated, took care to smooth the plumage of any third party who felt he'd been badly treated. By and large, though, we gravitated toward the kind of exploit offered by that unlit garden in Rome, or a New York bathhouse. For me those hours were the adolescence I'd been too shy or repressed to put into action at the time. Their polymorphous abundance spilling over into our lives kept us primed and sexually alert toward each other.

The pattern takes on new colors and dimensions when we begin our annual trips to Greece. There are of course many nonlibidinous reasons for going—our delight in Tonáki and Maria, the diamond-clear air (of those first years) that dries out David's sinuses, the charm of the new culture and the new language. The fun also of being foreigners. Thus labeled, we feel a great burden of personality—individual history—lifted from our shoulders, and set about playing our parts in the ancient Athenian comedy.

And the Greek youths we take up with? Don't they have personalities themselves, and histories? No doubt; yet it seems to us that they primarily have humors, choleric or melancholy, sanguine or phlegmatic, as in pre-Renaissance psychology. Also our friends strike us as creations of their Mediterranean society far more than we are of ours; one of the surefire words in the jukebox songs is yitoniá—*the neighborhood—shaper of these young men and ongoing arbiter of their behavior. Emerging all aglisten from the gene pool, too proud to notice us just yet, the newcomer puts his coin in the slot. What will "his" song be—the exquisitely good-humored "Myrtia"? the noble lament of "Kaimos"? Something at any rate from that golden age before Theodorakis turns political, discovers Byzantine chant, and begins writing plainsong cycles too bleak and pretentious to hum or to dance to. By the mid-seventies only busboys are shameless enough to perform a floor-show* hasápiko. *But in those early days . . .*

One evening Barney Crop, who'd given up Paris for Athens, took us to a tavern near some barracks at the edge of town. Here soldiers got up to dance and a handful of civilians or foreigners sat ready to applaud, send wine, try out the phrase-book phonetics for The Rendezvous, or deftly slip a telephone number into a khaki pocket. One of the camp followers kept glancing at our table. With a show of pique, Barney addressed the ceiling: "Very fetching, but no, thanks. Not my type at all. The idea of going to bed with a 'sister' couldn't interest me less."

David protested. The young man didn't look—

"Then he's probably trade. Or still doesn't know what he wants. Don't mind me, I like my men straight."

Such pedantic taxonomy made my heart sink. Yet Barney's words shed a light that had eluded me under the Roman trees and in the New York steam, though I might well have seen it in the pages of Margaret Mead. The soldier on the dance floor, like nine out of ten from his class and culture, would count himself lucky to catch a permissive male lover—one who wouldn't appear in the yitoniá making a scene. No reflection on the dancer's masculinity. Girls weren't easy to come by in 1959, outside of marriage or the brothel; and who on a military wage of thirty shoeshines a month could afford either one? Your own fiancée, supposing she escaped her mother's eye, wouldn't go "all the way." A hussy might now and then grant access to what Barney in his racy French called the entrée des artistes—but, he grinned, "we" could do this as well as any girl and with far less fuss. The affair might last a night, a season, years. Deep affection might blossom on both sides. As Barney talked, a vague long-ing I'd felt in Luigi's presence took detailed and plausible form. That the dancing soldier hoped one day to marry and raise a family struck me as the best news yet. More than the barriers of language and background, it seemed to ensure our never going overboard in Greece. David and I could follow with no harm to him the faun incarnate in this or that young man, and without losing ourselves or each other. We were very optimistic to think so.

—Why, why does all this have to be spelled out? my mother sighs in the long conversation we never have. You're not hurting me; you're diminishing your-self. Don't imagine, son, that these are things people need to know.

—But they are things I need to tell. If they were boy-and-girl adventures no one would bat an eyelash.

—There you're wrong, said my mother. A young couple, married or living together, as you and David were, doesn't behave in the manner you describe. That's what shocks me.

—I'm sorry. The young people you have in mind have no taboos to exorcise. Society protects them when love fails to. (If you've missed seeing your values embodied, ask Betty to bring her grandchildren over.) David and I had to patch our lives together out of ethical snippets woven originally as protection in a cli-mate we chose to live as far away from as possible. Too much to keep under wraps! No wonder that in my case, over the years, the forbidden fruit of self-

disclosure grew ever more tempting. The spirit of the times ripened it like a kind of sunlight. The very language was changing. An article saying that I "lived with my lover in Athens" sickened you—what would the world think?—until I was able to point out that by 1970 "lover" denoted, as it hadn't in your girlhood, either a man or a woman. . . . Came the day when even the behavior you find so shocking, which by then lay decently buried in my past, or in my poems, was clear to anyone who still cared. As in the classic account of Sarah Bernhardt descending a spiral staircase—she stood still and it revovlved about her—my good fortune was to stay in one place while the closet simply disintegrated.

XVI

Easter in Graz.
By Myself in Ravenna.

My brother's lifelong passion for Central Europe was somewhat gratified by his year as an exchange teacher in Austria. Naturally he would rather have left his school in St. Louis for Poland or Hungary or Yugoslavia, where the history was more colorful and the intellectual life more intense, but would those hardship zones have been fair to his wife and children? Graz, where they had settled after the first months in Vienna, was an interesting compromise, a small, abashedly Germanophile city staggering back to peacetime, with its own university and an unbombed opera house. By the time I arrived to spend Easter with the family, Charles had already given several extracurricular lectures and been unnerved to see how many citizens in the intimate hall were studying him through opera glasses. I suggested that the glasses, unknown to him, might have been reversed for the sake of aesthetic distance. "Giving," he said, delighted by the joke while adapting it to his own ends, "the impression of a larger room, hence a more *hörenswürdig* lecture." Humor was our common ground. Six years apart in age, we hadn't greatly troubled to know each other until I was in college. Even then, his taste for history and politics left me cold, and I hereby erase from the record a remark he made, at twenty-four, about "The Rape of the Lock." But Charles had an appealing flamboyant side. He loved opera long before I did. At Harvard he wore an ankle-length Polish military cape and played the flute like Frederick the Great. And he took, over our father's initial, knee-jerk objections ("How can he say he loves her? She's the first girl he ever dated! The damn fool—can't he see she's just after his money?"), a wife whose wit and equanimity charmed me from the start. His marriage, like our sister's, was extremely stable. Longer than I these children *du premier lit* had seen the havoc caused by our father's restless libido. Forewarned was forearmed.

Charles and I had quite different ways of coping with the paternal menace. He'd actually taken a course in military strategy at college. Thus, while I sought to postpone or altogether avoid confrontation, my brother's breathtaking repertoire of shock tactics, diversionary movements, positions secured by verbal barbed wire, and so forth, kept the old man on the defensive and the rest of the family on the edge of our chairs. By 1950 the war had been won. Neither Charles nor I was expected to join the Firm. Hands had been washed of us; thanks to our trust funds, and to being American, we could do as we liked, live far from home in poorly furnished apartments, wear suits of burnt-orange Turkish wool tailored in Prague or cheap puce velvet too tight to sit down in, entertain left-wing ideas or moot young men—it hardly mattered which. All these parodies of luxury were made possible by our baffled, hardworking, womanizing parent in his English cambrics and cashmeres; one could hardly blame him for the hour when he saw red.

Doris meanwhile worked to restore the balance, helping the career of a smart and successful husband, naming one of their sons after the Firm, planning family holidays in attractive resorts, redecorating their three houses at frequent intervals, not to mention the enormous "beach cottage" at Southampton, which our father, once more a bachelor, now decided to move into—all this at the cost of those crippling headaches she couldn't spare time for Dr. Simeons to treat. The old man, I'm afraid, often took for granted her desire to be the perfect daughter, while yearning in the best tradition of patriarchs after his prodigal sons.

This season we were all, for once, in his good graces. With Kinta out of the picture, he wanted to draw up a new will and saw no reason to include the children whose future he'd already so handsomely assured. An old-fashioned Florida lawyer, retained more for piquancy than pertinence, spoke up: "Charlie, you can't just cut your children off. They've got every right to contest this after your death." Original to the end, my father proposed that we simply sign away any future claims upon his estate. The lawyer mopped his brow, but we naturally agreed; whereupon each received a bonus of one hundred dollars as full quittance. Charles now brought out an Easter letter from our sister. Visiting Daddy in Palm Beach (Doris wrote), she'd appeared one morning in a beautiful dressing gown, and when he teased her for being extravagant, silenced him by saying she'd used up her inheritance to buy it.

Dr. Detre gave me the whole week off for Easter—nine days counting both weekends. Charles and Mary had wanted to meet me in Yugoslavia, but one of the girls was recovering from chicken pox, so we sat tight. On Easter Eve we attended *Parsifal* at the Graz Opera. The production was old and shabby, the tenor wore brown street shoes along with his tunic of moth-eaten skins, one Flower Maiden used pince-nez in order to see the conductor, and Kundry woke at Klingsor's bidding with a shriek that sounded suspiciously like a sneeze. Yet the reverential audience willed into fitful being a performance they could leave exalted by. We ourselves slipped out after the second act. Next day, church bells, the apartment-wide egg hunt, the feast. Every so often the children—Cathy and Amy in their dirndls, little Bruce in his lederhosen—abandoned their play to overrun me like vines and come to rest heavier than a lapful of watermelons. Would they have happy lives? Would I be a father myself one day?

The best we could manage in lieu of Yugoslavia was a night in the little border town of Radkersburg. Our hotel hung over the narrow, fast-flowing river; we could see the ruins of the bridge, or keep warm in bed gazing wistfully at the Croatian landscape. Charles brought along a novel he'd just finished writing—he filled notebooks in longhand, like Sir Walter Scott—and I began reading it as dusk fell in the warm *Stube* where we would presently order a bottle of wine and, later, dinner. Radkersburg couldn't have seemed farther away from Rome, or Charles and Mary (he knitting his brows over a political biography, she placidly sewing) from the people I'd been seeing there. No less remote was the heroine of

Charles's tale, a young Austrian who'd survived the war. Worthy of the noble ideas she embodied, she shared her author's gift for discourse but fell short of his irony and prodigious floor-pacing sulks.

"How's Marilyn?" asked Mary the next time I looked up. To my surprise I felt able to follow every stitch of her thought. She'd begun wondering how the children were getting along, entrusted to a favorite baby-sitter, but still . . . She'd savored anew, as I'd been doing for the past hour, the glow of family feeling. Sensing how much Charles's and my slow evolution from wary siblings to respectful and affectionate grown-ups owed to her, hadn't she then—an only child—gone on to dream by the fire of an ally, a lively younger sister-in-law with whom she could marvel at their two impossible husbands who kept refusing to grow up, who would always . . . ? Marilyn had been a hit over Christmas; from St. Louis herself, she knew the school my brother and a friend had opened there, knew people he and Mary knew. . . . Then, too, surely the problems I was being treated for, my touchy sparks and green splinters, would begin to settle, like the blaze in the *Stube's* porcelain stove, for an overall companionable warmth, if only . . .

"Marilyn's fine," I said. "She sent love."

They saw me off on the night train. I am not, however, going straight to Rome but to Ravenna. This daring plan, wholly without precedent, leapt from my head full-grown as I was booking my tickets at American Express. I would for once do something by and for myself, unaccompanied, unsupervised. It is cool sunless midday by the time I check into a hotel and consume, standing up at a dented metal counter, my ham sandwich and Campari-soda while poring over a map of the town. Had Dr. Simeons's injections not kept me in Rome the previous June, I would no doubt have gone to Ravenna with Claude, ticked it off my list of places to see, and never found myself there now. I leave the bar and head for San Vitale. It comes over me, as never before, how dull and full of self-pity I made those two or three days in Rome. At the time, I thought I was spending them wisely, writing an anniversary poem, for it was already a year since my reunion with Claude in Cassis. But the poem—which imagined us together among the mosaics I knew merely from postcards—came out willed and sour, resentful between its lines of the carefree time he was having without me. His dry peck on the cheek was more thanks than I deserved.

As I approach San Vitale, a small brick building, squat and clumsy beside its tall domed neighbor, like an X in some architectural tick-tack-toe, catches my eye. This will be the Tomb of Galla Placidia, where the oldest mosaics are to be found. One may as well begin at the beginning; I go in. Nothing has prepared me for what I see: a midnight-blue dome, an old skull thick with gold stars; in the vaults, more stars, precise as snowflakes and big as streetlights enlarged by mist. The space, effortlessly anthropomorphic, has been created, it seems, to dramatize the inner life of a seer or a sibyl, the miracles hidden beneath weathered, baked-brick features, unpraised in thought. The means to this lavish end are simple, durable, anonymous—nothing of the "personal" brushwork that marks a square inch of canvas as the work of such and such a master. Yet instinct and initiative are everywhere at play. Thousands upon thousands of glass-paste dice—each by itself dull and worthless as a drawn tooth—have been shrewdly cast to embed a texture now matte, now coruscant, with colors fifteen hundred years have failed to dim. Through narrow alabaster panels, their art deco patterns lymph-washed and bloodless, like human tissue on a slide, comes a glow I try to resist, if I am going to make out . . . Look! There's the *buon pastore* seated among his lambs. But this young shepherd hasn't yet evolved into a Christian savior. Cross held upright like a primitive bass viol about to be played, he is still Orpheus, or Apollo; and I recall from my dictionary that "mosaic" derives from a Greek word meaning the work of the muses.

I step outside, gasping, as if having run up three flights of stairs. Tomorrow at leisure I can take it all in more sensibly; now is the time for rapid impressions. I enter San Vitale. Here is greater splendor yet, placed higher up. No night sky overhead. The old astronomer's heavenly vision gives way to quadrants of a cupola where green foliage on gold alternates with gold foliage on green, like sun filtering into a rain forest. I stand as though in the mind of some young, wide-eyed god, extravagantly in love with detail, and grieved by nothing under the sun, not even the bigotries he has already begun to foster or the self-determined faces in those two imperial retinues above my head. Here gender confronts gender, and gaze, gaze. Real people are being caught in this act; the emperor needs a shave, one of Theodora's ladies twiddles her ring. But reality throws no lasting wrench into works of such sumptuous invention. Round each panel runs a border, no, a series of borders, each a decorative *idée fixe* of the utmost plainness, which notwithstanding, when put together, become steps in an argument so daring yet so crucial to the rest of my life that I know I must get it by heart—not now, though. I have glimpsed peacocks. I've noticed that the motif of counterpoised sheaves or horns of plenty in an archway is being echoed, on pilasters elsewhere, by one of paired dolphins. The dolphins have black-and-white eye shadow, red mouths and crests and tails. Their tails are linked and their heads thrown back, as on the last chord of some ecstatic universal tango.

I walk out into sunlight. Sarcophagi lie about the churchyard, carelessly, their contents turned to tall grass; and it is true—death doesn't matter. An old coachman, recognizing my symptoms, proposes a ride to Sant'Apollinare in Classe. Here I see a mosaic meadow full of sheep; in Sant' Apollinare Nuovo, the sages whom Yeats called "the singing-masters of my soul." By evening next to nothing remains unseen. I have taken not a single photograph. I sit by myself in the hotel dining room, brimming with insights, free associations that sparkle my way from remote crevices of the past: a forest scene composed of butterfly wings from Brazil; sun rising over fish-scale wavelets; a richly iced gingerbread cottage; my grandmother's beaded evening purse, turned inside out. "Childhood is health," said Herbert, and here is mine, along with Christianity's. Merely to know that these early, glistening states are still attainable . . . ! Had Ravenna been a psychiatrist, today's hours alone would have cured me.

The next day I fill in gaps and go back to the places that struck me most. Morning light in the starry vaults of Galla Placidia show up textures piteously withered; it is like gazing upon the mummy of Ptolemy. In San Vitale, by contrast, Jesus stands waist-deep in ripples. His genitals are visible through the lucid warp. I open my notebook and begin to sketch a section of the decorative borders that, like an idealized circulatory system, here tracing a groin, there confining some pious vision to a lintel's brow, link quite a number of structural elements. Its central nerve, one golden tessera in width, bisects this blood-red passe-partout, branching at fixed intervals to create a run of alternating ovals and oblongs. These enclose perhaps a dozen tesserae apiece, just enough for the nice gradation of greens in the oblongs, blues in the ovals, to convey depth—so many gold-framed, kohl-rimmed swimming pools reduced to snuffbox size. Punctuating the spaces between pool and pool, big pearl-white colons invite the eye to pause, then move on. A second border, which parallels or diverges from this one at whim, resembles an awning of white flounces, each blazoned with a squat black cross. A third—but no matter. The profusion of motifs, their vigor by now a reflex long past thought, gives out a sense of peace and plenty in the lee of history's howling gale. It isn't the creeds or the crusades they tell of, but the relative eternity of villas, interior decoration, artisans, the centuries of intelligence in fingers not twenty years old. While empires fell offstage, these happy solutions to the timeless problems of scale and coherence stretched, like flowers to the light, wherever a patron beckoned. Palmyra lies in one direction, Addison Mizner's Palm Beach (for better or worse) in the other. Or Tiffany glass. There is no limit to the life encoded by my anthology of mosaic borders. For this morning hour in San Vitale I feel like the aborigine who can describe all the people and animals who have traveled a road, just from whatever grows along its edge.

Back in Rome, I telephoned Claude. "I'm so proud of myself," I said. "I did it!"—no sooner realizing that he might be hurt by what I was about to imply than not caring if he was. He of course, I went on, had been living that way most of his life. And while even I had been known to go to the opera by myself—did that explain why I loved it so?—I'd never believed, never trusted, never been told what rapture solitude could be in a place like Ravenna. The sheer hours on end of *seeing*, of never having to exchange remarks or keep looking around in case one's companion was bored—why, it made all the difference in the world. "Like a note struck once," I finished, "that turns suddenly into a trill. To be *alive* and *alone* . . . !"

"I know," said Claude gently. "It's so sad."

•

Scripture and fiction are full of nicely opposed brothers; why shouldn't life be? At Ravenna the decorative elements moved me to tears, whereas Charles would have exclaimed "Tiens!" on reading in the guide that Charlemagne had built a replica of San Vitale in Aachen, and agreed with those visitors who valued the basilican purity and thrust of Sant'Apollinare in Classe above the pastoral charm of its mosaics. He would have been more interested yet in what it was like to grow up in such a town, in schools and labor unions, employment rates and the chances of survival for a chamber music society. He would have gone out of his way to meet the priest or the podestà *over a lunch I'd have sat squirming through. Perhaps his being a family man, with five clever children, caused him to focus, wherever he went, upon community issues rather than the natural or artistic splendors of the place. In my view these concerns held one back; it was important to travel light. But where, if it came to that, were we all going, and what was the big hurry?*

William James once descibed Henry as his "younger and shallower and vainer brother," and that is how I tend to see myself next to Charles. A devout pragmatist, he founded a school (Commonwealth, in Boston) where the lessons of history were paramount. Here students met their opposite numbers from Poland or Ghana, sang the Lord Nelson *Mass, and learned to draw their own conclusions about Job, Mao, capitalism, and the right to die. Years later they would speak of him with reverence. He has gone on missions of mercy to far corners of the earth and worked for understanding between blacks and whites. Among countless low-profile good deeds, he helped with the renovation of the Graz state theater. (His reward? A festive luncheon at the motorcycle factory.) My brother writes voluminously still, always in longhand, the burden involved but graspable, his whole message behind every word. I have done none of these things. Low on public spirit, without "ideas" in his sense of the word, or should I say ever leerier of their frontal presentation, in writing I have resorted, after the first scrawled phrases, to keyboards of increasing complexity, moving from Olivetti to Selectric III, from Ouija to this season's electronic wizard. Now each morning, risen like Kundry in* Parsifal *with a shriek and a shudder to do my Klingsor's bidding, I make for the arcane, underworld glow of a little screen. Presently minimal bits of information, variable within strict limits, like the tesserae of a mosaic, flicker and reassemble before my eyes. As best I can— here slubbing an image, there inverting a hypothesis—I set about clothing the blindingly nude mind of my latest master. Line after line wavers in and out of sense, transpositive, loose-ended, flimsy as gossamer, until a length of text is at last woven tightly enough to resist unmaking. Then only do I see what I had to say.*

. . .

Soon after my return from Rome I settled down. With David Jackson it was easy to renounce New York and its pitfalls for the stabler routines of life in Stonington. My New York friends—like Robert or Hubbell—complained that I'd let myself be "taken out of circulation." How could I give up the music, the exhibits, the midnight suppers? In truth I asked nothing better. I'd seen so many paintings, heard so many operas—fuir, là-bas, fuir! It was time to get to work.

We were both writing novels, David on a table in the kitchen, I on a sideboard under the tin dome of the dining room we'd painted flame red, perhaps to placate the powers that one day, such was our delight in the old wooden building, might set it ablaze. (Sages standing in God's holy fire? Each time we left we shut our manuscripts in the refrigerator.) We had a record player, a rowboat, a brass bed, but few invitations and no telephone. Just then, when life had never been more fulfilling, the genetic angel, as in a parody of the Annunciation, struck. What was this—nearly thirty and not yet a father! If through childlessness I'd been spitefully putting my parents in their place, parenthood would put me in theirs; how else to make peace between the generations? But I had better act quickly lest I be too old to enjoy my children. (David's marriage, unrewarding to both parties, though his wife was now our best friend, had cured him of any such nonsense.)

In real distress I relived that Easter in Graz, with Charles and Mary, the restless play of growing limbs and minds, the heart-stopping repose of moonlit sleepers glimpsed through open doors. And now Freddy wrote that he'd fallen in love; soon he would be on his way. With no mother lined up for my child, I began to look, willy-nilly, at the local females. Was that tomboy divorcée still fertile? What about the teenage daughter of new friends, whom David was teaching how to drive? Anxiety swept me. Dr. Detre, by then conveniently in New York, felt that "settling down" was itself the issue; young men like us didn't belong in resorts for the idle or retired. He made a few suggestions (go back to teaching, don't spend so much time by yourselves), and the crisis passed. Another summer, and the house had filled up—not quite what Dr. Detre had in mind—with Ephraim and Company, who were prepared, like children, to take up as much of our time as we cared to give, but whose conversation outsparkled Ravenna, and who never had to be washed or fed or driven to their school basketball games.

XVII

Claude Plans to Leave Rome.
Visiting Umberto.
The Piero Resurrection.

Claude had me to lunch. It was a lovely spring day. His French windows, open onto tiny balconies, overlooked the Piazza di Spagna six flights below. Quinta presided in a cheerfully visible kitchen—how unlike mine—and the round table had been set for three. Above it hung a mobile of wire and wooden balls, vaguely planetary, a new addition. I'd seen his apartment just once before but felt greeted by things I recognized, above all by the serenity they achieved under his roof, which my own unruly belongings could never aspire to. The books stood in thoughtful order, a little Murano vase I'd given him held a fresh flower, the Olivetti slept like a parrot beneath its patterned kerchief next to the densely typed pages of Claude's vast, ongoing journal. Over a glass of wine we talked of Ravenna. Out came a book on the mosaics I might like to borrow. Alice had written; she was well and said I owed her a letter. They were doing *I Puritani* next month at the opera—had I ever heard it? I understood: he was treating me as a guest. I glanced again at the third table setting and waited for the doorbell to ring. Or did the new person already have his own key?

"It's gone on ten months," Claude was saying in his diffident murmur, but with a merry twinkle. "We've agreed that the end's in sight."

What had I missed? It was unlike him to talk so openly of a failed romance, but I supposed he had Dr. Detre to thank for this new, rather callous frankness. Ten months? So the affair had begun while we were still together, soon after our move to Rome. Feeling wronged in retrospect, I asked—since I had to say something—if "he" was Italian.

Claude stared. "I don't understand."

"Your friend of these last ten months . . . ?"

"I was talking about my analysis, about Tom," said Claude, still puzzled. (He called Dr. Detre Tom, just as he used *tu*, like a true Italian, when speaking to Quinta—with whom I had locked myself into the formal *Lei*.) "The year he'd originally estimated is nearly up. I forgot an appointment the other day. It's a classic sign that the patient is ready to move on. But you thought—" As the nature and implications of my mistake dawned on him, Claude broke into uneasy laughter. The doorbell rang.

Quinta admitted a frail, black-haired young man, who greeted her familiarly. Claude introduced him as Jorge, an artist from Peru. His was the assemblage of hoops and spheres that hung above us as we sat down to lunch. At once I liked it less. I found Jorge plain, his deferential manners at odds with my latest notion of table talk on a sunny day. Of course he and Claude were lovers; the lunch had been arranged to make this clear. Was he the "best Claude could do" in Rome? It pleased my vanity to think so, and to remind itself that Robert would soon be returning; the part of me that wished Claude well was depressed.

Not that I was entitled to show any of this. Love had once allowed us to read each other in the dark. Now the psychic lens opening had contracted; we must let what could be made out by friendship's plain daylight guide us, without reference to that secret nocturnal terrain we no longer stumbled through. Here a more exciting thought broke in. If Dr. Detre was planning to send Claude home—cured!—in six or eight more weeks, wouldn't my own term end shortly thereafter? I decided not to ask the doctor this question; it would have been like glancing at one's watch during the salad course. Nor did I intend to bring up my impressions of Jorge lest, like Montale, he dissolve on closer inspection into Dr. Detre himself. Whose precise, amused voice I could hear already: ". . . this yellow-faced foreigner Claude has been seeing secretively, who has replaced you at the center of his life." I didn't need to be told by my shrink that I'd been chafing under his schedule. After Ravenna, I wanted to visit new places by myself and taste the drug of solitude in each of them. And for the first time in months, at the risk of sapping the creative energy I was expected to bring to our analytical work, I found myself fiddling with a poem. It began with some negatives of photographs I'd taken of Robert and ended by returning him—or "her," as convention dictated—to the status of a perfect stranger:

> *Here where no image sinks to truth*
> *And the black sun kindles planets in noon air*
>
> *The lover leads a form eclipsed, opaque,*
> *Past a smoked-glass parterre*
> *Toward the first ghostliness he guessed in her . . .*

Quinta's *risotto primavera* was delicious. I mentioned my forthcoming weekend in Cortona. ("It is now officially spring," Umberto had said in his deep drone, "and the rooms are no longer freezing.") "You will be near Arezzo," said Jorge, "where the great Piero della Francesca frescoes are. Have you ever seen them? For me he is the supreme Italian painter." I had not; I knew Piero's works chiefly from photographs. Marilyn had visited the famous *Flagellation*—"In Urbino," said Jorge reverently, and began to enumerate the other Pieros, peasant madonnas and farmboy saints, rendered with a dispassion itself amounting to saintliness, which studded central Italy like solitary gems, while Claude gazed fondly at him, pleased that our talk was giving his friend a chance to shine. Although these things were worth hearing, Jorge's account of them struck me as wooden and impersonal. What, I wondered not without slyness, was the best book on Piero? The dim young man named it eagerly; it was the source of his passion; no more than I had he stood before the paintings themselves. Claude's eyes now met mine in a brief, intensely neutral look. "You and I may feel," the look said, "that it is pitiful to boast of secondhand knowledge; nevertheless Innocence is as precious as Experience, and I will thank you not to snub my friend." I felt the justice of a reprimand that must have been made more than once on my behalf, when Claude was my lover and I rattled mindlessly or tipsily on. So the luncheon party left a sour aftertaste.

Umberto met me at the Cortona station. A sunburnt man of forty, introduced as Mario, drove us uphill in the tiniest conceivable Fiat. Each summer of his childhood, Umberto explained, ox-drawn wagons would move the entire household—people and bedding and so forth—from the winter house in town to the purer air of the "country" place five kilometers away. Mario turned down a long tree-shaded drive and stopped on gravel in front of a facade three stories high. The house looked suitably old, of mottled gray-gold stucco, with green shutters and a quaint escutcheon: the head, in relief, of a blackamoor—for *Morra*—above a date in the 1760s. The front door, framed with green and red stained-glass panes, opened into a cool, frescoed parlor I was given no time to study. While Mario took my suitcase, Umberto led me—past (good heavens) a sedan chair and a stuffed bear rearing seven feet tall in the stairwell—to the kitchen, where a couple of children fled our approach and Mario's . . . sister? wife? mother? bowed us onward. "There is someone here who expects to meet my guests as soon as they arrive," said Umberto.

In a sunny chair outside the kitchen door sat an old party of considerable presence. His features, above a knitted cardigan, wore the noble, sclerotic bloodlessness of a bust. One big inert hand lay tucked along his thigh. The other took mine in a marble grip. Words of welcome surged from the living half of his face. "This is Tonino," said Umberto, leaving me prey, as we returned indoors, to wild conjectures. Had they been lovers long ago, when Umberto was a student and Tonino a . . . gamekeeper? E. M. Forster would have known what to make of the situation. I did not.

I'd noticed, in the kitchen garden where Tonino sat, an outbuilding on whose plaster wall trompe-l'oeil fruit trees had been painted. Back in the house similar touches came to light. A small barrel-vaulted library had been made into a tent of pale red-and-white hangings. A ceiling upstairs dissolved into the heaven of a sunbeamed attic storeroom. The dining room walls were painted with broad stripes of lime and silver, to simulate wallpaper; while those of the little parlor through which guests came and departed, and where Umberto and I sat over apertif or camomile, had been enthusiastically decorated with a ruined pyramid, a stone sphinx, a pair of lovers on a pedestal, all in a landscape of hills and lakes and blue willow trees. The chairs we sat on were covered in pretty (patriotic?) stripes of red and green and ivory cut velvet, but so old that the thread-bare, tattered fabric had now to be stitched back into place after every washing. Under a hanging lamp the round table at the center of the room was piled with books and international periodicals; I had never in my life seen such absorbing clutter—that is, until I entered the formal drawing room upstairs. Here, along with draperies, vast mirrors, sofas and chandelier, a larger round table, piled higher yet with culture, stood a seven-pedaled ottocento piano. A forest of photographs on its lid could hardly be seen for the family trees they faintly but imperiously summoned up: Savoy, Romanov, Hohenzollern. Not for me to recognize the crests on the frames, or ask—we Americans having evolved beyond all this twaddle of rank and royalty—who that tiaraed beauty was, or that fat-faced child wearing a toque of pearls.

One small room downstairs—between the parlor and the dining room—was hideous beyond description. Heavy, turn-of-the-century furniture that looked machine-made, dried grasses, glassed cabinets jammed with medals and bibelots, surrounded a full-length life-sized portrait of a man in uniform. A tapestried stool in front of it invited the guest to kneel. Curiosity at last banishing my republican feelings, I asked Umberto if this was his father. "That is the King," he replied. "Or *was* the King."

"Your family knew him?"

"My father was a general, in charge of, well, regiments, campaigns. Later, an ambassador. I believe they were on rather close terms."

"Do you remember him?"

"The King? No. I was a baby when he died."

"Was this . . . Victor Emmanuel?"

"The son of Victor Emmanuel. Umberto."

"Oh? Then you were named for him!"

Umberto gave his helpless drone of amused constraint. "Well, that is one way of putting it. In fact mine will have been, to all intents and purposes, a family name. . . ."

Mario put on a white jacket to serve our dinner: broth, an omelet with vegetables, stewed fruit, and a carafe of stunningly bad wine, which Umberto knew to pass up but for the single tablespoon stirred into his broth. We saw each other so regularly in Rome that I was no longer shy in his company, yet I still couldn't be sure what interested him or how much he wanted to know about me. At least he himself enjoyed talking, and without his in any sense holding forth, I heard a good deal about Berenson, Edith Wharton, Salvemini, and others. Here in Cortona he had quite a circle of friends, many foreign; a few were coming to dinner the following evening. We might go into town next morning to see the Signorellis; not painting of supreme interest, still ... His hands sketched a gesture of modest pride: in so rural a backwater, what could one offer but these cultural equivalents of fresh eggs and milk straight from the cow? I asked if anything by Piero della Francesca lay within a reasonable radius. "Ah," he smiled, "you give me an idea."

Back in the parlor, over our camomile, I mentioned that Robert Isaacson would be returning in a couple of weeks to stay through the summer in Via Quattro Novembre. Umberto blushed—with pleasure *for* me, I somehow felt—and said I must be sure to bring him along on my next visit. As we parted for the night he took my hand in both of his and wished me *buon riposo*. I fell asleep wondering if I could find my way to his bedroom and how my barefoot presence there would be received.

The next morning it was all arranged. Mario was driving us to Sansepolcro, where Umberto had a brief but long-deferred errand and we could see the Piero *Resurrection* before lunch. Arezzo would have been a shorter excursion, but then we'd have needed more time to study the frescoes, so it worked out. The masterpiece awaiting us at our drive's end had yet to be properly installed after spending the war in a bomb shelter; its own provisional resurrection, Umberto remarked before leaving me alone with it, was quite as moving in its way as that of the central figure. Banner in hand, one foot on the rim of his sarcophagus, Christ was climbing back into the world. I tried my best to see through Freddy's light-filled eyes, while summoning to my own lips Freddy's faint inward smile, this haggard, glaring adult. It didn't work. After the green-and-gold childhood of faith, glimpsed at Ravenna, so stark an embodiment of its maturity left me cold. Deep down I feared that Jesus and I, both, had reached our zenith as children and that I would be hard put to avoid a terminal phase shot through, like his, by showmanship and self-promotion.

Weren't those, however, among the traits I saw Jesus as sharing with the artists I most admired? Like Baudelaire he had a weakness for loose women. Like Mallarmé he enthralled and mystified his disciples; like Oscar Wilde, courted ruin at the height of his fame. Like Proust he had dipped, with miraculous consequences, a cookie into a restorative cup. These figures—themselves moved in rare, subliminal ways, by his example—moved me immoderately; why not Our Savior? Well, it is one thing for an artist to behave like a god. How many charming and eloquent young men have we not seen idealized, exploited, "crucified" at last by their power to attract a large audience? (In my youthful poems I was already taking measures to keep this from happening to me.) But when a god behaves like an artist—! I might gladly have accepted Christ as a kind of living ideogram for the imagination, a spark of godhood breathed upon in each of us. In the Sistine Chapel's *Last Judgment*, the central dancing figure, like the great marble arm detached from the same artist's unfinished *Pietà*, was pure Apollonian radiance. What chilled me was the (so to speak) movie version of that supreme fiction. Pulpits the world over urged it upon the whole family. Stills from it hung in a thousand museums, luridly fleshing out the leading man's looks and attitudes and—always the thorn in my side—history. How to disown one's mother, fulfill prophecies, hypnotize crowds, and serve oneself up to the cannibalistic instincts of the tribe weren't, I hoped, the things I lay on Dr. Detre's couch in order to learn. What then: to love my neighbor as myself? Well and good; but that meant figuring out how to love myself without, for once, a lover—human or divine—to make the difference. While these ideas hovered just out of reach, I went on studying Piero's *Resurrection* avidly, storing up the precious painterly touches that compensated, if anything did, for so grim and "significant" a subject.

Yet it was a subject that seemed to elude an American couple who had joined me in front of the Piero when Umberto returned from his errand. "Excuse me," said the husband, making signs of recognition. "Count Morra? We met last year in Basel at the XYZ conference. This picture—what does it mean? Is it a story we should know?" Umberto rose to the occasion; indeed, he said, Piero's "unidealistic" view of Christ might easily puzzle the pilgrim, and so on—assuming, as a man of the world and against all evidence, that his American acquaintances properly valued the myth at the heart of the Western world. Intelligence dawned at length upon husband and wife; yes, yes, it was all coming back: Sunday school, loaves and fishes, "on the third day," yes, thank you, they remembered now—drifting cordially away, the weight of centuries light as a feather upon them.

"That might be described as a surreal moment," Umberto said with a smile, over lunch. "Or is it a trait of the American mind to have declared its independence from Christian things? Of course Piero is a case apart; his images are not *bondieuseries*. And I am not a 'believer,'" he went on, with a headshake of self-deprecation for standing perversely outside the fold. "Even so, religion like poetry being an almost irresistible form of hearsay, it is hard to envision a world in no way nourished by these grand rumors."

I didn't mean to waste my weekend with a father figure of rare sweetness like Umberto, complaining about somebody else's son. Yet if there *was* a God, I ventured, it seemed to me that I would have to be His child no less than Jesus was, and the idea of needing an older sibling or "mediator" in order to approach my parent struck me as offensive if not absurd. Did that count as an American trait? Umberto's laugh showed his brown teeth. "Rilke," he said, blushing now for unavoidably dropping another name, "once compared it to trying to reach the Almighty by telephone, only to keep getting the operator. *Allora*." He made a sign to the waiter, and the subject was closed; neither of us cared to agree further upon matters about which it was seemlier not to have spoken at all.

The party that evening included a young French diplomat who had a house nearby, a Swiss musicologist, and a professor of history who had come down from Turin to spend a few days with Umberto. Close to him in years, the Professore looked ageless as an elf; his blue eyes sparkled in a face like a fresh rose. I joined him the next morning after breakfast for a walk up and down the long alley of trees and heard—after months of vain conjecture—a great deal about our mutual friend. For instance, he had spent his earliest years in St. Petersburg, where his father was *en poste*; the Czar was his godfather. (Would he and Mina have met at a party for diplomatic children?) Umberto had gone on to do brilliant scholarly work in his youth; had translated Voltaire and Trevelyan; been a protégé of Berenson's; was presently writing an extremely valuable memoir of the young socialist Piero Gobbetti, dead at twenty-five. Umberto's infirmity resulted *not* (my companion emphasized) from throwing himself in front of a carriage in order to avoid military service, as rumored in certain quarters, but rather from a tubercular hip in childhood. His stamina was nonetheless remarkable. In 1943, on the eve of Italy's surrender, he had gone *on foot* from Rome to Naples in order to make the vital liaison between the Italian antifascists and the Allied forces. He had stood on a balcony with General Mark Clark and megaphoned the terms of peace to the crowd below. Absorbing and admirable as these facts were, I'd hoped for something juicier, less journalistic.

"I can't get over this house," I said. "Has anything been done to it in the past fifty years?" "No," the Professore laughed. "A twinge of electricity—nothing more. And closer to one hundred years than fifty. Umberto's mother, you see, died young. This was his family's place. In the normal course of things the bride would have done it over from top to bottom. But all she got round to was that little chamber of horrors dedicated to the King. The rest is a time capsule from the preceding generation, when *I Promessi Sposi* was the best-seller and 'Eri Tu' led the Hit Parade." The Professore began humming the famous aria from *Un Ballo in Maschera.* His words set in motion a train of thought that lurched from a king's friend and his faithless wife to the old invalid, so much nobler in aspect than Umberto, sunning himself outside the kitchen door.

"And Tonino? Does he go back to the beginning too?"

"Ah, Tonino," said the Professore. "I presume he is a kind of relative. Have I been indiscreet? Hadn't we better turn back?"

•

Until his death eight years ago, Umberto's was the house I returned to most regularly in Europe, either alone or with an array of companions as dear and diverse as David Kalstone, Grace Stone, and Strato. It never occurred to me that any part of my life needed to be hidden from this kind friend. Not long after my return to America, Umberto and my father both found themselves in New York, and I asked them to dinner together. I dreamed up, for the occasion, an appetizer of shrimp with orange-garlic sauce, in whose polite rejection, if in nothing else, they were unanimous. (Alice put it in one of her cookbooks, though; to my recipe she suggested adding, before serving, a tablespoon of warmed curaçao.) On his next visit my mother gave a party for Umberto in Atlanta. Whatever his view of these meetings, they gratified me no end. My parents could hardly fail to be impressed by the priceless human antique I'd acquired abroad for next to nothing.

David Jackson and I stayed with Umberto when he ran the Italian Institute in London. He visited us in Athens. He was cordial to our lovers and courtly to the Alexandrians who'd taken us up. I can see him now at a party, bending an ear to little eye-fluttering Mika, a fifth highball clutched in her bird claw. Sudden panic crosses her face: does this Italian man of letters expect her to broach a topic? "Ah," she giggles instead, "you're so sexy—yum-yum-yum!" In an article about his trip Umberto evoked these ladies as having emerged "stanche e sfatte"—tired and unmade—from the pages of Lawrence Durrell.

His tolerance for people unlike himself—indeed, his attraction to them—underlay his friendship with Grace Stone. Grace was the most cosmopolitan of our Stonington neighbors. Formed like me by exposure to opera at a dangerously young age—open on her piano still lay a tattered score of Manon with one-word appraisals of each aria ("ravissante" ... "exquise" ... "parfaite") in her schoolgirl hand—she had gone on, as a navy wife, to break hearts from Paris to Shanghai. Umberto was an easy, platonic conquest, dating from those last Roman winters, when her sight was failing. His letters to her, which one summer afternoon I was asked to read aloud as respite from Don Juan or the Odyssey, were virtual declarations of love for her charm and courage, qualities he wrongly feared were lacking in himself. The affection was mutual, though tinged by snobbery on Grace's side. From her I learned that Umberto, according to Roman gossip, was not only the old King's namesake but his son by the wife of his trusted friend, the general and ambassador-to-be. People still spoke of our friend's uncanny resemblance to the King.

"Umberto must know—or does he?" I wondered, thinking of the portrait in that hideous parlor. Ah, Grace breathed, exhaling smoke and taking on the aspect of the famous novelist she had once been, who knew what Umberto knew?

As for Tonino, gossip had it that he was the general's son by a peasant girl.

"Umberto's half brother ... ?"

"Well, no," said Grace. "That's just the point. No relation at all. It's the world of Beaumarchais—false identities and the droit du seigneur. In our world Tonino would have been half black and Umberto a corpse at Gettysburg. They arrange these things better abroad."

If Umberto knew himself to be the subject of such unblushing speculation, he gave no sign. "*Wax to receive and marble to retain*," his friendship, once bestowed, was never withdrawn. On his last, brief trip to Washington and New York, a man in his seventies who by then navigated with extreme discomfort, he had gone hours out of his way to spend an afternoon alone with Ben Johnson in the Veterans Hospital outside Boston, where Ben was dying of lung cancer. When Umberto was dying, Mario and his family overflowed the corridors of the clinic. Umberto left the wonderful house to them.

Visiting Umberto one chilly April when he was still in his low-ceilinged "winter quarters" downstairs, I was given the master bedroom, a dim white cavern, all pillars and mirrors and hangings. A tidy brazier in a wooden frame—the "priest," as it was known—had been slipped between my sheets to warm them. Alone in the huge lumpy bed of a man I loved, I remembered the night in Southamptom when I'd insisted, at seven, on being allowed to sleep with my father. (He and my mother had lately moved into separate bedrooms.) Neither of us shut an eye; I lay awake till dawn—when Emma, peeking in, beckoned me back to my room—marveling at my situation and waiting in vain for the pajamaed form tossing and groaning at my side to place a soothing hand upon me. In Umberto's bed, finally, I slept like a child.

My bedroom wallpaper in Southampton was a hypnotic tangle of vines on which sat elves dressed in olive or puce. Above the bed hung two pictures: one, a manger scene all radiance and oxen and wise men; its companion, a Jesus no older than I, in a white nightie, alone and barefoot on a woodland path. His smile promised safe-conduct through that forest not yet Dantesque, and after my prayers I fell asleep watched over by the adorable little boy overhead.

To run Christ down in later life, as I'd done that day with Umberto, gave me no satisfaction. What prompted such talk? An intricate campaign of disenchantment, set off by the changing of my wallpaper. A romantic couple—"boy in gray" and crinolined belle—beside a cannon, the Stars and Bars unfurled above, one summer replaced the elves. Jesus ascended to the attic. No more make-believe, the message read; history would be my fate from then on. The red-blooded boys of Southampton were expected to serve unreturnably fast balls in tennis, not Our Lord. Certain white-haired English teachers in tears *over the Victorian poets confirmed the impression of a creed outworn. By the time my mother (with no justification in the Gospels that I ever found) called on Christ's teachings to straighten me out sexually, or Freddy's novels made their pitch for his gentling presence in our lives, the damage had been done. I'd thrown the baby out with the churchly bathwater. But "there is no purification without myth"—Jan Kott. Of late Peter cannot stop talking about his month in a Trappist monastery ("High time I gave myself the silent treatment"), nor Jerl about the rehabilitation center for victims of early sexual abuse, where he recently visited his lover. There the therapeutic sessions concentrated upon the Inner Child, a self-image of helpless innocence in each of us, that never deserved its rough treatment at the world's grown-up hands. Listening to Jerl, I've tried to picture my own Inner Child—and who but the smiling towheaded Jesus on the threshold of the forest springs to mind? I'm sixty-six; second childhood plucks at my sleeve. Time to make peace not only with that little boy who may, for all I know, have seen me through the glooms and forking paths of the middle years but with the man he became on its far side. Some nights I even say a prayer to him.*

XVIII

Reunion with Robert.
Regression with Rolf.
Auden Unmet.

Woken from a heavy sleep, I seem to have grown a new set of arms and legs. A voice—my own?—is murmuring my name. These novel proliferations have time to both worry and comfort me before I decode them: Robert returned yesterday, and I will never be lonely again. Rome's cup, as well, has begun to overflow. Summer's here. Hubbell is taking us to Ostia for a noon picnic. And Robert expects Rolf—his onetime lover—to pass through a month hence, on his way to photograph bright-eyed urchins in the Blue Grotto. "Such a German idea of a holiday," Robert snorted, draining his glass at the restaurant, earlier. He was groggy from the long flight but looked wonderful—tanned, flushed, eyes sparkling into mine. Now in the narrow bed I shift gingerly, inhale his skin and hair, give thanks for the weight of his head on my arm. Together we sink back into sleep.

The separation has been hard on him. His grandfather's death, the lawyers, his mother's state of mind—Robert is the only child. But he withstood every inducement to stay at home; the thought of Rome, of joining me and prolonging—as we all were doing—the magic glow of a life not fully answerable to the grown-ups' world, kept him sane. As during our first weeks, I've given in to the charm of loving "myself" in the person of another. The likeness is no longer chiefly physical, although a cluster of similar impulses and reactions, shrugs and smiles, sleights of mind and turns of phrase, once made it seem so. Hubbell as well—despite airs distinctly more mannered than ours—partakes of the family resemblance. The way fledgling artists write a manifesto and start a "movement," or like the generic movie star of the twenties—blonde, enigmatic, with a suspicion of baby fat, before fate transforms her into Garbo or Dietrich, Elisabeth Bergner or Carole Lombard—each in his fashion lends himself to an image of the elegant young gay man of the period. This composite figure has a stylish assurance none of us will attain as individuals for some time. Not that twenty or thirty years later the style in question still seems worth trying for; but we bear its scars, like an old face-lift.

The style may have derived originally from the manners of our divorced mothers at the bridge table or at dinners where it behooved them to sparkle; also from the assumption, in America at least, that a boy can do better than to grow up like his old man. Yet it's the paternal note I miss— if I miss anything—with Robert and Hubbell at Ostia, on sand so exactly the shade and texture of our mixed pepper-and-salt in its wax-paper nest that we dip our rubbery eggs more than once into the wrong condiment. Our topics are those usually classed as feminine—personalities, culture, "dirt"; our mode is telegraphic and facetious. Lacking is the restraint of sons who have looked to their fathers for emblems of conduct. Yet our flapping sallies and diamond veerings need some such centerboard to keep them on course, to remind us that the world is periodically real and life now and then a serious business. Well, I can always get back in touch with Luigi—*he* would eat that last sandwich! But no, what I dream of is what I never had from Luigi: a steadying male presence who, finding in me elements of both mate and child, would bind himself to me sexually, for a while.

"Sex between men is by its character frustrating," Dr. Detre said. "The anus is full of shit; the mouth is a well of flattery and untruth. The honest penis is left with no reliable place to go."

Embarrassed, I studied the ceiling.

"It might be worth considering," he went on, "that this masculine self you crave is available within you, only you have not accepted the power to harm that goes with it."

"Must one do harm in order to be a man?"

"You seem to have received that impression."

"From . . . ?"

"A woman who, hurt and rejected, turned to you."

A woman whom I, on the beach with Robert and Hubbell, kept echoing in spite of myself. "Are you saying it's time I went out and hurt someone?"

"Not necessarily. Is there someone you wish to hurt?"

"No, but . . ." I couldn't shake the idea. "Supposing there were, though, and that I did. Would I inflict the man's kind of harm or the woman's?"

It seemed to be the ultimate question until Dr. Detre took it a step further: "Or the child's?"

Robert bought a little car, which gave us new mobility. Collecting me on the bright noon pavement outside Dr. Detre's building, he could whisk us out of town—to the beach, to Tarquinia or Cerveteri for the afternoon, to this or that celebrated villa or garden. One weekend we drove Umberto from his house to Lake Trasimeno, where he sat in the shade and watched us in scanty swimsuits disporting ourselves, consciously athletic, to give him something to remember. That evening our host cleared dozens of princely photographs from the seven-pedaled piano so that Robert could unlid and soothsay from its entrails, mute for generations. Equally silent was our subsequent lovemaking—just a twang from the old outraged bed, and stifled giggles as we imagined Umberto's eye glued to a secret peephole.

Like figures on a clock, our former lovers retreated and advanced. Claude was sailing home, Rolf was due any day. Claude and I dined by ourselves on the eve of his departure. Inquiring for his Peruvian friend, Jorge, I learned that he'd left Rome. "He had become totally dependent upon me," said Claude. "It was a sad, unhealthy situation." The soft reluctance in his tone called to mind how dependent I'd once been on him myself.

Claude wasn't beyond bringing that out in people, through his many disciplines and convictions. The point, no doubt, would have been to develop a few of one's own. I felt a pang for poor banished Jorge, and another for Claude. Who wanted these neurotic alliances!

About his year with Dr. Detre he was sad, euphoric, silly, and wise. "Absurd as it sounds," he said, "I feel equipped for a long and complex adventure." I was close enough to gaining my own freedom to know what he meant. If his plan (to join Vira in Houston, where she'd moved after the Saudi Arabian fiasco, and help run a restaurant she had, with winning resilience, opened there) didn't quite answer to the splendor of the challenge, Claude could be trusted to make the most of it.

"The future looks possible, for a change," I suggested. "Not the sheer cliff it was last summer. We've found footholds, a way to get up there."

"The process seemed so gradual," said Claude dreamily. "Almost automatic. I hardly noticed the changes until they'd taken place. Remember Psyche's tasks in Apuleius?—having to unscramble all those different grains and seeds, the lentils and millet and poppy, into separate piles. The ants do it for her. It must be the earliest allegory of psychoanalysis. I never felt Tom 'doing' anything. What happened in our sessions, from week to week, was more like the work of time than of any human agent. Dali's pocket watch swarming with ants. I never asked him about that. Maybe you will. . . . "

We smiled and raised our glasses. Each of us had seen the other through, from start to finish—at a distance, to be sure, like mowers in neighboring fields—and those nearly parallel labors and their harvest filled us with pride. Not long ago, before Robert's return, this mutation from love to friendship had seemed to me a step down in the world. But now, "I'll really miss you," I told Claude as we wandered into the cobbled, saffron-and-indigo night. "You'll come to visit," he said. "Alone or with anyone you like." I tried to picture that house in Vermont, not as I'd seen it before, icy and stern beyond the glow of its blazing hearth, but open to all the fragrant winds of summer. We had reached my door. It was the turning point. I wouldn't have come to Europe without him; now I was here independently—alone or with anyone I liked. "I could spend the whole night wandering through Rome," Claude was saying. "I've loved it so! Good-bye, dear Jamie." We embraced. He waved from the corner and was gone.

. . .

On Rolf's first evening Robert and I picked him up at his hotel and drove to an outdoor restaurant in Trastevere. Rolf turned out to be in his late thirties: tall, pale, soft-fleshed. He had left Germany as an adolescent, before the war, and spoke with only the hint of an accent. He wasn't a "verbal type" like Robert or me. His observations, dogged and humorless, discouraged response, as did the superior airs he gave himself. "I am a serious, somber person," Rolf's manner asserted, "not above shouldering my cameras and my backpack and striding off right now into the hills in search of the nourishment I derive neither from this *saltimbocca alla romana* nor from your bright, piss-elegant behavior." What *did* nourish Rolf? I asked Robert at the evening's end.

"Oh, you know, the elements. Sunlight, the sea, boys . . . platitudes of the *Zitronenland*—"

"Boys? Were you too old—that's why he left you?"

"Whoever said he left me? After the first months I thought I'd go mad. I was twenty, he was thirty-five. He was getting older, *I* was getting *younger*. Who wanted a father, let alone a Hamburger!"

Our other guests had left. Across the room, at the piano, Hubbell sang on in a husky undertone: "There were two little babes in the wood . . ." Marilyn sat beside him, already matronly in her happiness. She'd arrived bubbling with news: date fixed for her return, plans to marry before the year was out. Her fiancé, an art historian named Irving Lavin, had thus far figured so sketchily in her talk that I half disbelieved in him. He could, however, be inferred from her conduct. The unattached American girls we knew that year were in the throes of disastrous love affairs with Italian men. Cute little Ruth from Iowa had been caught up in a ring of young doctors who drank ether and staged orgies in the X-ray room of a respectable private clinic; close-ups of skeletal hoopla were held to the morning light in coffee bars. How sensible of Marilyn to prefer the amusement, the absolute safety of *our* company. We watched our language in front of her, treated her with brotherly fondness and respect. (Robert came and went, collecting glasses, emptying ashtrays. "Two little hearts," Hubbell sang on, "two little heads . . . ") Yet it was odd to think that, all during these months, Marilyn's inner compass had been pointing toward another person—faceless to us, a mere silhouette, not unlike the self awaiting me even now at the end of the reverberating Roman tunnel.

I'd had too many cocktails. I sank down on the sofa next to Rolf.

"You've been flirting with me all afternoon," he observed quietly.

I shot him a naughty smile. "Why would I do a thing like that?"

"I don't know," he said with a look that wiped the smile from my face.

Another three days, and I thought of no one but Rolf. He spent an afternoon photographing Robert and me at the piano, then at the little skylit kitchen table, whispering behind a big palmetto fan: images of each other in our interchangeable Roman suits. His camera wooed us. Robert had learned the hard way to resist that mechanical courtship; I was powerless against it. Rolf's eye—perceiving, whichever way I turned, more new Jimmys and Jamies than a tailor's mirror—stole my soul. Qualities I'd found tiresome on our first evening I now saw as gravity, mature independence, freedom from Claude's or Kimon's bookish airs. Then, too, Rolf counted as a foreigner—better yet, my first German. "Know Your Enemy," urged posters during the war. Had I been older, had Rolf not emigrated, we might have met, soiled and battle-weary, in no-man's-land and surrendered to each other in a barbed-wire bower. The great, original attraction, I realized to my dismay, was his having been Robert's lover.

Rolf, keeping to his plan, left for Naples two nights later. At his request—and virtuously telling Robert where I was going—I dined with him before seeing him off on the night train. We went into his sleeping compartment, where Rolf put strong solemn arms round me and kissed me. "Let us meet in ten days. Give me time to get my old winter body in shape. Come with Bobby. It will be all right. You'll see." Whatever that meant.

The train pulled out, disclosing further platforms, studded with family groups. Fathers kissed their children, women wept; this, after all, was Italy. I stood by the bare tracks, unwilling to break the spell of Rolf's last look, uncertain, too, of what awaited me at home. Robert drunk and sarcastic? Robert senseless in a pool of his own blood? No; for as a train in the middle distance began pulling out, a voice I knew cried "Archie!" and a figure in nimble pursuit proffered a forgotten briefcase to a frantic golden-haired man leaning halfway from his compartment window to receive it. Mission accomplished, the sprinter turned back flushed and panting. It was Robert.

He saw me. Like mirror images, abreast but with the tracks between us, we approached a limbo where parallels dissolved, and fell into a taxi. "That was Archie Colquhoun," Robert said. He'd dropped the name in the past, but the fat old party it conjured up bore no resemblance to the Apollo on the train. "He phoned me just after you went out. I had no idea he was in Rome. He was catching the sleeper to Milan, so we had dinner. Pure opera buffa there at the station: his briefcase left behind—you saw? Five years' work on Manzoni. Well. I think he saved my life tonight. . . . How about you? Rolf got off?" "Yes." "Did he kiss you?" I nodded. "Was that all?" I promised that it was. "You were lucky"— Robert laughed, facing away from onrushing lights—"because if he'd made love to you you'd have been disgusted. Disgusted! Do you understand?" I did not; it sounded like something a writer ought to know about.

Still, it was all at a puzzling remove, like faraway things reflected in nearby glass. Dr. Detre agreed; dynamics of two or three rather different situations had come into play. In one, Robert stood for my mother. Assured of love from this quarter, I nonetheless needed a father and saw one in Rolf; had for that matter seen one in Archie, as though any man my lover ran after couldn't fail to set fantasies in motion. Or else I was my father's own son, never more loyal to an old flame than when a new one beckoned. Finally, at some level wasn't I my mother as well, and Robert the child neglected in favor of a demanding, all-too-familiar intruder? It took me two hours on the couch to figure that much out.

"Do not forget," added Dr. Detre, "that Robert has thus far been primarily an image of yourself, an innocent, vulnerable self, whom you are this week subjecting to an ingenious punishment."

"Punishing myself—him? What for . . . ?"

Time, which for the moment had run out, would tell.

Robert and I joined Rolf in Naples. He'd said it would be all right? He was wrong. We sailed for Ischia, sitting on deck in bursts of spray; the waves were gunfire-bright. Ten days of beach life had left Rolf looking handsomer than he'd been in Rome. Back and forth we talked, saying whatever came to mind, seeking each other's eyes. Robert sat between us, taking swigs from a bottle of whiskey. At one point he deliberately stubbed out a cigarette onto his bare calf. "Oh, don't!" I cried, appalled, but he looked past me and shrugged. So did Rolf, who then rose to stroll down the deck. He seemed used to Robert's self-destructive behavior; in his day he must have provoked enough of it himself. As I gazed after him desire scorched, leaving a stench of fear and distaste. The stew it had taken me all that time to prepare was suddenly inedible. I touched Robert's arm. Why didn't he and I stay on board, return to Naples, leave Rolf behind forever? But things had gone too far for easy amends. Robert stared as though a stranger had spoken. "What can you be thinking of?" he inquired in clipped, withering tones. "Are you trying to spoil our holiday?"

So we did our time on Ischia. In those years, W. H. Auden was that island's Prospero—invisible to us, though a compatriot of Rolf's, joining us for dinner on the terrace of the *pensione*, repeated this season's gossip about the increasingly eccentric genius. Many bottles of wine had glazed over the miseries of the day. "But I mean!" I cried, adopting Robert's huffiest voice under the tipsy impression that any note of solidarity would please him. "Auden really goes too far. In New York he wears his carpet slippers to the opera, with a dinner jacket. Being a great poet doesn't excuse that sort of affectation. Of course I've barely met him, so it's not for me to say . . . " (trailing off into pettish inaudibility).

Rolf was looking at me with delight. "You're a great mimic," he laughed. "You've got Bobby down to a T."

I turned to my friend in dismay. I hadn't meant—! (Or had I?) But Robert's gaze was fixed elsewhere. "I wish I could see Wystan," he said.

"You know Auden?" asked the German.

"Would I call him Wystan if I didn't? But it's not because he is famous or in order to make fun of his slovenliness behind his back that I want to see him but because he is a kind man who can put me in touch with a priest. I mean to receive communion tomorrow morning."

"Oh, no," Rolf groaned. "You're not still going through that old religious crisis? Spare us, please!"

Although I'd seen Robert's odd behavior in churches we visited for their art, I tended to dismiss his bobbings and crossings as reflexes more worldly than virtuous—when in Rome, and so forth—and secretly wished for the style to get away with them myself. But any port in a storm. Why not find Robert a priest? I'd found a psychiatrist. It was, however, too late to seek out Mr. Auden this evening; he was famous for retiring, said Rolf's friend, on the stroke of nine.

"Can't you just show up at a confessional before the service?" I asked.

"Of course he can. Anyone can." Rolf chuckled. "The Church would go bankrupt otherwise." He winked at me good-naturedly, as if his presence were sunshine.

"It all depends," said Robert, answering my question, "on the gravity of the sin you're confessing."

"Is yours so very grave?"

"No, I suppose not. A bagatelle, now that you ask." He looked into my eyes for the first time in hours. "I've wished I were dead."

"Oh, what are you saying?" I moaned.

"I'm saying that if we treated our bodies the way we treat our souls, none of us would live past twenty."

There was a circle in the Inferno for the violent against themselves. Must I confirm Robert in his misery by assenting to his theology? Sin be damned. To feel for my friend it was enough to recall my own jealousy when Hans and Seldon showed up together at Maggie Teyte's Amherst concert—only neither Hans nor Seldon had ever returned my love. That both Rolf and I had returned Robert's made his corner of the triangle—to say the least—pinch more acutely. One soprano led to another: I thought of the deranged heroine of last month's *Puritani,* so ravishingly sung by an ungainly newcomer named Callas that I went to all three performances. "Ah, rendetemi la speme o lasciatemi morire!"—give me back my hope or let me die! Over and over the piteous refrain rose and fell, while two baritones with swords and lace collars wished they had acted better. A needle on my dial registered in decibels the pain I'd caused. But on a nearby wavelength someone quite different was jazzily bewailing his lost opportunity to find out what made Rolf so "disgusting" as a lover, and blaming Robert for making a fuss.

Dr. Detre saw my behavior as "regressive"—that of the child I feared I would no longer be after therapy. "This trick," he said, "of stealing from your lovers someone to whom they are or once were attracted, you and Robert have already played on Claude. Try not to get into a rut."

In short, I wasn't as far along as he'd thought at Easter. Did he mean I wouldn't be through by August? Well, he replied, perhaps October; certainly November. Hearing this, I felt like a child indeed—kept after school—and said so.

"All the more reason to get on with the assignment," said Dr. Detre.

A stubborn silence. Then, with many pauses between one unit of insight and the next: "You said I was punishing Robert; that sounds right. . . . But why? . . . Strange how soon I lost interest—had I cared for Rolf at all? Robert was the one I . . . Perhaps I cultivated our mirror likeness because, left to myself, I'd never have attracted anyone . . . like the orchid in Proust, masquerading as a bee. . . . When Rolf lit on me, I was able to punish Robert for . . . loving me? For being like me himself?"

"Put it simply: to punish both yourself and him for being homosexual," said Dr. Detre with his flair for the last word.

•

The house I return to most regularly in America is Claude's. Its rooms remain of a gleaming, exemplary bareness, the books high-minded and intently read. The sad truth is that I shall never live up to him—he who has no more than one lover at a time; who seldom travels farther than thirty miles from home, and then only to meet his students at Bennington; who, exchanging his recorder for a shakuhachi, came back from Kyoto a Buddhist. By now he looks like one, rotund and roseate, eyes alert under heavy lids, a loose, much-mended kimono sashed round him: Zenmaster Time's favorite pupil. Visiting him is restorative. For chronic complaints like my weakness for a new face and the resulting guilty sense of

> *Love, too frequently betrayed*
> *For some plausible desire*
> *Or the world's enchanted fire*

my old friend dispenses, if not exactly comfort, a twinkling tonic all his own. "A little pain never hurt anyone," it isn't beyond him to remark, or "The fire begs to be played with"—quoting a sutra? I wouldn't know. (The lines quoted above, by the way, are Auden's, from The Rake's Progress.) *I climb the stairs to bed with a lighter heart. Waking at Claude's—alone or with David, or with Peter—I blink up at a ceiling blanker than any mirror, and slowly, peacefully calculate how old I am this year.*

It should go without saying that my early dismissal of Auden had to do with his being so openly homosexual—an impression based not so much on any active naughtiness, or the relative chastity of his voice in print, as upon the reported promiscuity of his talk. Invoking "Miss God" or referring to himself as "your mother," he must, I see now, have chosen his listeners with care. Nowadays, of course, in my young friend Jerl's eyes, letting one's hair down is a political act, a step toward reality, self-esteem, and enlightened legislation. But thirty years ago gay idiom (unless one was abroad, where it was risky fun to assume that the natives didn't understand or one's fellow tourists eavesdrop) served as a deshabille to be slipped into behind closed doors. In this it resembled shoptalk. The Wystan who held forth at blissful length about poetry and opera in a seminar would have sat mum with distaste in those literary cafés where public impersonation of the stereotype is taken for the real thing. To the artist a closet is quite as useful as it once was to the homosexual: what John Hollander calls, in the lingo of spy thrillers, a cover life, allowing us to get on with our true work as secret agents for the mother tongue—a phrase itself grown ineffably off-color, thanks to Wystan.

Athens, 1965. Auden arrives late, rumpled and wrinkled. Nelly's rooms are full of people eager to meet him. Catching sight of me, he smiles. Although we aren't yet the intimates we shall become after his death, he approves of my work and fancies that I exemplify moderation to Chester.

"What I'd really like, my dear," he says, "is to sit down somewhere and enjoy another drink."

"Follow me." I lead him to the sofa from which Maria Mitsotaki, a reclusive star, warily observes the crush. "Look sharp, Maman," I say. "Here's the guest of honor."

"Enfant, this time you've gone too far," she murmurs, even as he lowers himself beside her. Dressed in her eternal black, wreathed in the smoke of her eternal Gitane, Maria is the closest I'll ever get to having a muse. There is no one saner or more sympathetic, more in love with overtones, quicker to register

anything said or left unsaid. Her genius for listening comes across like a drop of scent dabbed behind each ear. So it hardly surprises me, returning with Wystan's full glass, to find them—ten years hence, the leading lights of San-dover—already deep in talk, eye-to-eye like accomplices.

"It's the great, great pity with Mediterranean men," Wystan is stating with his usual frankness. "They like sex, but love stumps them. Love is giving, and they simply don't know how to accept it." Intelligence flickers behind Maria's dark glasses. She has no trouble fleshing out this dictum with succulent particulars: Chester and his evzones, David and George Lazaretos, Strato and me. Wystan continues:

"They can't be bothered to learn our language, they've no conception of culture, ours or theirs. I mentioned guilt in a talk I once gave in Rome, and it was translated over the earphones as gold leaf. South of the Alps, guilt has only its legal or criminal sense. The rest is all bella figura. When you love a Mediterranean man there's nothing whatever you can give him. Except children."

"Or money," whispers childless Maria, smiling.

"Exactly."

Meanwhile my mother and I pursue our imaginary argument:

—From the age of nineteen I've been made to feel (first and foremost by you, dearest) my difference from the rest of the world, a difference laudable and literary at noon, shocking and sexual at midnight—though surely from the beginning my nights were part of the same vital process as my days. Age, however, has brought one blessing: the sense of how much like everyone else I'm becoming. Young people trust me; they never used to. Elderly taxi drivers see my gray hairs and talk to me like a brother. You wanted me to conform? I have!

—Since when? inquires my mother, intent upon her Bullshot. (I was hoping to make her smile.) And to what?

—To that composite gay young man I thought up on the beach at Ostia. To the sexagenarian poet kept young, like Wystan, by past and present indiscretions. To my type, if you like, in the human comedy.

—Anyone who lives long enough gets to be a "type." I could name plenty we both know, but I'd die before I called them that to their faces. It's no compliment and no blessing that I can see.

—You're looking in the wrong direction. In nature the type is everything, and you and I are tolerated only to the degree that we're true to it. If in the process we refine it, better yet. The first and hardest step is getting into nature's good books. One reason my behavior was "unnatural" a hundred years ago was that nature found on her shelves so few texts proving otherwise. But in our day she's had to build a whole new bookcase! Wonderful, isn't it, how she keeps working to improve her mind? Just like you.

My mother makes a helpless gesture. Compliments to our intelligence are seldom refused.

XIX

A Glimpse of Istanbul.
Second Visit to Poros.

Perhaps sixty feet underground, we had the wooden platform to ourselves. A stone forest fanned outward into gloom, inscrutably plotted; the
two or three spotlights lit only those columns nearest us. They rose from
shallow water, supporting a groined monotony of brick. The air was stale
and cool. We breathed it guardedly, as if buried alive and having to con-
serve oxygen. At length an unseen hand put out the lights; our time was
up. Back at street level, Robert checked off the great cistern in our *Guide
Bleu.*

It had been folly to dream of seeing Istanbul in two days, yet a brief
impression was better than none; better as well, I'd begun to think after
Ravenna, than a prolonged, studious one. It was mid-August. Dr. Detre
had released me for another nine days. (He himself was going to the seaside. He, too, had a "normal life"; a human heart beat beneath that white
shirtfront and funereal necktie.) Thanks to Robert's little Fiat, merely en
route to the Brindisi ferry we had seen: the octagonal gem of Castel del
Monte, the old bare church on the harbor at Trani, the fourth-century
bronze giant in the square at Barletta, the euphoric ochre baroque of

Lecce. We took care never to look at anything long enough to reduce it to a known quantity. Going through the Corinth canal we craned from our porthole at clifflike walls close enough to touch, then fell back for another hour's sleep. Our flight to Istanbul took us over Samos, Lesbos, the tiny islands in the Sea of Marmora, on one of which Kimon was born. We checked into the Pera Palas just after sunset.

This was our first non-Christian city, and we meant to drink in as much *orientalisme* as we could. A muezzin woke us at daybreak. Opening the wardrobe onto our Roman summer suits, hanging alike as two peas, I was mystified.

"Why is your suit covered with snails and not mine?"

The snails were tiny and conical. Robert's suit looked like an aerial reconnaissance photograph of the stalagmite chapels in Cappadocia.

"It's too tiresome. I never wear my decorations on holiday, but try getting that into their heads. Give it here."

He brushed them off. They knew better than to cling.

Downhill, past moribund blocks of flats, a flash of waters, distant minarets. Seen close, Istanbul illustrated all the evils of the industrial revolution. Forges roared. The air tasted of coal. Cars long extinct in other countries served as taxis. Thanks to Ataturk's reforms, the street signs were laughably intelligible. POLIS, TUVALET, KREDİ (a bank). Should the tourist go astray, Greek shopkeepers fluent in six languages peered from doorways, ready to direct him past the actual reek and noise of the streets to the true city they dreamed of reconquering; to seawalls and Hippodrome; to the handful of miraculous structures on which, a thousand years later, the upstart mosques would be modeled. Byzantium glimmered at every turn. Who could say but that the bazaar might yield a bird "of hammered gold and gold enameling"?

In 1952 the available postcards of the interior of Hagia Sophia were sorry affairs, retouched so that only the big gold-on-green calligraphic lunettes and hanging lamps like instruments of torture stood out against a dim oatmeal of pillars and bays. Not knowing what more to expect, we weren't at first thrilled on entering. Where were the mosaics promised by Yeats, by Gibbon for that matter, who described the dome as a "glittering spectacle"? Lacking these, we turned to the celebrated marble facings,

Rorschach blots in porphyry or verd antique that had once mirrored the torches and gems of Theodora's retinue. But they'd grown stagnant, unresponsive, barely giving back our shadows as we approached. Starved for ornament, we were reduced to dull immensity, and here our preference for the fleet impression helped not at all. Spaciousness implied leisure, time to expand the psyche to the height of certain prodigiously intersecting arcs, vaults within vaults, sheer walls that themselves appeared to lean back and gasp as the dome's peeling cabochon slowly floated to rest within its setting of pronged sunlight. But now we were outdoors again.

We went to Topkapi and saw the arm of John the Baptist, ostrich-plume fans and turbans Hubbell would have wanted for Christmas, jeweled dirks, a small fish tank half filled with emeralds. "Exactly like sucked candies," said Robert. "Have another, Roxane? I can't possibly finish the box by myself." A gleaming collection of celadon vases and platters, gifts from a seventeenth-century Chinese emperor, filled a further room. Their preservation, we read, was due to the sultan's pique on opening the first crate; no gold encrustations, no embedded garnets and pearls. And no reflection on him—hadn't I hoped for mosaics in Hagia Sophia?

"I met a woman," said Robert, "whose husband did business with the sultan of somewhere-or-other. Over the years she made friends with the Swiss lady in charge of the sultan's household. One day they were strolling through this endless storehouse of china and glass, you know, Limoges and Baccarat, and my friend said, 'What became of your lovely dessert service, two hundred pieces of pale-green opaline?' 'Oh well, you see,' the Swiss lady said, 'it is wicked to value things for themselves. By strict Moslem law, any household possession that hasn't been used in a given year must be destroyed. We called in the men and had it smashed to bits.' Like a wife past childbearing, I suppose. . . ." Robert's voice trailed off.

Beyond the Hippodrome a steep path led down to the "little Hagia Sophia," as the Turks called the old church of Sts Sergius and Bacchus. It was closed. A child with shaved head saw us, cried out, and ran off—in dread? No—to fetch the custodian. Leaving our shoes on the porch, we entered a space perfectly scaled to the play of human attention. Again, no mosaics. Calligraphy in bolts of ultramarine lightning lit the shabby whitewash overhead. The dome's marble rim was solid with Greek. Were we allowed upstairs? Our host gestured like a pasha. A wide gallery paved with rosy stone led round to an overview of threadbare blues and crimsons that carpeted the church—the mosque, rather; for from this vantage we could also see the apse reoriented, by an oblique dais, toward Mecca. Next to it a flight of narrow marble steps led nowhere. Members of the congregation had left slippers and prayer beads roundabout. An artisan's cotton smock hung, limp with wear, one pocket torn, from a row of five wooden pegs painted orange.

While Robert sniffs at so much adulteration of past splendors, I find myself drinking in those humble objects the tide of daily use has filled brimful. Such visions were denied me as a child. I was told to look away from the broken bedstead on a curb or the eyeless doll in an old woman's lap. At home we had "nice things." There I could learn the difference between good and bad, with respect at least to silver and china and furniture. But the lesson of our Meissen plates and Sheraton chairs intimidated me. They kept their own counsel; our postures and hungers affected them hardly at all. The chair shrugged us off, each careful washing rinsed the dish of us, and the objects resumed, like heroines in Henry James, a gleaming, inviolable fineness their uncouth admirers could only fall short of. By contrast the smock on its peg, the beads and slippers I gaze down upon in this hushed corner of Byzantium or Islam, move me in mysterious ways. They belong. They shine with a proud, illiterate life given over to their users. True, they've seen better days. I picture my mother throwing these things out to make room for new ones, or ridding herself of them without quite seeming to, the way she sends me Aunt Mil's latest letter marked "Destroy—have answered." But I am weak. I side with Mademoiselle, with Luigi's grandmother, whose instinct is piously to mend the smock, polish the slippers, add the letter to a cache of others. It comes to me for a rare, unselfish moment that Lambert Strether's may not be the last word, that what one wants in this world isn't so much to "live" as to . . . *be* lived, to be used by life for its own purposes. What has one to give but oneself?—as Tony himself asked from within his gilded cage. The willingness of the beads to be held and numbered, of the slippers to be worn and scuffed—or, put more sensibly, the continuing honor in which they are held and worn—leaves these objects proud and mindful in subjugation, old dogs on a warm hearth.

We glimpse their masters as we pass the Blue Mosque on our way back to the hotel. Prayers have ended. A huge congregation is disbanding—all men. This in itself is worth remarking after a year in Italy and a lifetime in

America, where the churchgoing male more often than not wears the look of having been dragged there by his wife. Surely, with less than fifty years to the next millennium, such militant belief is old-fashioned, out of step with the times. Yet the eyes of these Turks blaze with doctrine. In dark trousers, cheap striped shirts, a collar button in lieu of a tie, here and there a uniform jacket from the Great War, they could be an army streaming past us. I try to imagine myself part of a society fueled by such monotheistic carbons. As a scribe, the very way I form my letters—regardless of the word they spell—would express some aspect of my faith; the same phrase can be rendered as a dish of sweetmeats or a nest of scorpions. After seeing the intricate gold-and-black squid-shaped *tugras* and *firmans* on display in the calligraphy rooms at Topkapi, I can't approve Ataturk's decision to romanize the written language. Inflammatory as Beethoven, hieratic as Mallarmé, the Arabic script gives a thrilling, godlike primacy to the most banal slogan. Well, the milk is spilt; now, less than three decades after the reform, only scholars are able to read the archives and the sacred texts in their original glory. A few more generations brought up on roman minuscules, and perhaps these men melting wild-eyed into the dusk will simmer down.

We crossed the bridge to Pera, the old foreign colony—hotels and embassies, restaurants and shops. Looking back across the Golden Horn, we tried to decipher, from so many domes and minarets, where we'd been that day. But the skyline, too, had grown unreadable. We dined on staid "European" food at the Rejans (Régence!), its dingy elegance overseen by a life-sized oil of Ataturk in white tie and tails. Between courses Robert fished out the notes given him by the fat English diplomat he knew in Rome. The Rejans was starred on a little handmade map, with the following scholium: "Set up by Ataturk for a White Russian mistress; scene of riotous drinking parties; at one of them Kemal's wolfhounds ate the belly dancer." That heyday was long past. For good measure our informant listed two or three louche hamams—recommendations Robert flung aside: by what right had such interests been attributed to us? Sanctimoniously I agreed although, truth to tell, I fancied that lovemaking from country to country—from class to class, if it came to that—could hardly fail to yield a treasury of ethnic and professional variations. In the spirit of disinterested research I might have enjoyed comparing the courtship dance of a Turkish blacksmith to Franco's or Wayne's. Another indelibly surcharged stamp for my album . . . But the recent drama with Rolf, and its effect on Robert, had for the time being cramped my style.

Next morning at the bazaar—a warren of blazing bulbs, coffee smells, exhortations edged in dental gold—we found its one quiet shop and bought rings, not as love gifts but each for himself. Robert's was bronze, a circlet of verdigris flattened to a seal at the crest. Mine, of soft gold, wore a half-effaced bunch of grapes; a child's jewel, it fitted just above the second knuckle of my ring finger, making the hand look paintable by Memling. We also bought a backgammon board and played with gusto throughout the wait at the airport, the next day's long bus ride from Athens to Delphi, and on the afternoon boat to Poros the day after that— always to nods of the greatest friendliness. It was one of the approved male pastimes.

Back in Athens after Delphi, we walked barefoot over the burning bald marble of the Acropolis, until a guard ("Kyrii! sivouplé!") made us put our sandals on. It gave visiting diplomats, he explained in what might be called Freek, the wrong impression. We drank a can of retsina under vine leaves and philosophized until it was time to collect our baggage. On the way we found a dry goods shop and bought meters of cheap local cotton—dark chalk blue, a turmeric orange—to have made into shirts that wouldn't last a dozen washings. One kept an eye out for the perfect souvenir. We stood at the rail, counting islands. The brilliant warm dry wind carved our faces into archaic smiles.

Poros wasn't the same without Mina. She had stayed in New York that summer. For a year now, she and Kimon had occupied my apartment. It was deeply gratifying to shelter these grown-ups from afar, like the porcelain parents in a doll's house. Their being under my roof implied acceptance of countless choices made by me in the past. If above my bed hung Blake's engraving of Job affrighted by visions, or if (as Kimon wrote, genuinely puzzled) I owned neither a toaster nor an ironing board, these pluses and minuses were as much part of the package as my personal mannerisms; friends would have to take them or leave them. But just before I left Rome a letter had come from my New York landlord. He and his wife wanted my floor of the old brownstone for their newlywed son, and to that end, with many apologies, weren't renewing the lease. Kimon and Mina would therefore have to move out earlier than expected, and everything go into storage—on the virtual eve of my return. "It must be symbolic, don't you agree?" I laughed crossly. "I mean, now that I've been made over by analysis, my former life washes its hands of me. Does this throw a terrible wrench in your plans?"

Kimon was smiling and shaking his head. "On the contrary. I, too, have some news. Mina and I are to be married."

My face snatched one of my mother's smiles to cover its nakedness.

"Next month, as soon as I get back," Kimon went on. "My classes start right after Labor Day. Mina's already looking at apartments. She's become a real New Yorker; she rides the subway! Can't you arrange to be home by then, Jimmy? I want you to be my best man!"

Quick as Kimon was to explain his marriage as one of convenience, enabling Mina to stay in America or to come and go as she pleased, a dozen gratifications not wholly beside the point fluttered round him like putti as he spoke. The homosexual's desire for a conventional life. The slum child's dream of marrying "above" him. The exile's newfound world embodied in a lover. Elements, too, no doubt, of real tenderness, devotion, gratitude. My heart sank nonetheless. If Kimon of all people was taking a wife, what hopes had I of resisting the undertow of generations? I noticed Robert listening attentively, his large eyes lowered. When they met mine he blushed.

That afternoon I opened a door into Mina's room—tidy, austere, more a space to wake and get dressed in than a shrine to her personality. Yet a shelf under the window seat held certain children's books I recognized, books from which Mademoiselle had taught me nineteenth-century French and nineteenth-century virtues. Their dark-pink bindings brought a lump to my throat. Where was my copy of *Le Pauvre Blaise* or *Les Malheurs de Sophie*? Had I outlived their precepts, could my lips still form their birdlike vowels? I missed childhood, I missed Mina. Gone were the wildflowers; the hills looked parched, the sea dusty. Our silver-haired Persephone was doing time in the New York subway system. Mitso had gained weight, and this year's baby cried a lot. Too late I remembered how little there was locally to admire—no freestanding column, no pretty Hellenistic theater, just the sun and moon and Kimon's discourse. I'd been wondering, after Ravenna, if I didn't prefer places to people; a scene can mirror more expressively than a friend the confusions we bring to it. Poros, though, was a place that recalled what it would have been kindness, in a friend, to forget. Here was the tree I'd dozed beneath, the table where Mina brought me tea. At every turn I met my listless, enfeebled self of two years before.

Leaving his cottage, with the Medusa above the door, to Robert and me, Kimon had moved into the main house. "That way you'll have privacy," he said. But we were together for meals, walks, talks, swims in the cove. Like the setting, without Mina's transforming presence Kimon showed at a disadvantage, by turns gushy and sententious. "He's as bad as Rolf," Robert sighed at our second evening's end. "What a taste you have for the serious-type queen." Robert had undressed and was pensively draping his tanned body, this way and that, with meters of blue. I shook out the long folds of orange and followed suit. We found straw hats and wore them at smart angles, like Tanagra figurines. Woken by Kimon for the early boat to Athens, we were still entangled in the vivid lengths we'd gone to.

While Dr. Detre listened I expressed Oedipal petulance. Kimon was joining a frieze of vital figures moving into the sunset with their Minas and Ninas. Months of silence from Tony—still in Ceylon?—told as much, in their way, as my mother's irrepressible bulletins from Atlanta. Two perfectly unheard-of women had entered my father's life. Could people never stay put? Much as my grown-up self understood, the neglected child in me was pouting.

"I thought we outgrew our useless old feelings," I complained.

"Why? The horseshoe crab is an ancient creature—ugly, obsolete by human standards. Yet it continues to thrive and multiply."

I silently congratulated Dr. Detre on having returned from his seaside holiday with a metaphor.

•

Robert also, within two years of his return to New York, marries a delightful woman older than himself. He opens a gallery and buys his first Gérôme. As with Kimon, I feel obscurely to blame. Did my shortcomings drive him into the arms of women?

"Angel," says Hubbell, "you can't have been the easiest act to follow. Après toi they take the pledge, if not the veil. Try to be flattered."

. . .

That first winter Mina enrolled at Columbia to study Chinese. Even married life might seem easy by comparison. They found an apartment uptown. Instructed by Kimon, the doorman called her Baroness. Kimon taught his classes; Mina gave lessons in English and Italian to the young daughters of a diplomat. Money remained a problem. Later came the phase, freely dramatized in my second novel, when the two began to think with real bitterness of each other; yet there was no reason to divorce. The bitterness passed and, with it, the intimacy. All at once Mina was very old, back on Poros for good. "They no longer say 'Live to be a hundred' on my name day," she said, laughing, when I saw her for the last time, "since that's just a few years off." She stayed alone in the big house; her cats filled Kimon's cottage; Mitso, a grandfather, had moved to his daughter's in Patras. "People look in every so often," said Mina vaguely, "but they bore me." She had decided to publish her translation of Lao-tzu into modern Greek, but whom to trust with the project? It had absorbed her for nearly three decades, ensuring a sophistication and purity of spirit that might otherwise have rubbed away. To illustrate the danger, her grandson, once a little boy crowned with water lilies, now an architect in his thirties, entered the room announcing that he and his girlfriend would after all not stay for supper but try to beat the traffic back to Athens. As she took in his words, love changed Mina before my eyes into a crooning, head-waggling peasant granny: "Eat something first, my child! Take a warm sweater with you!"—not until he was out of sight reverting to the woman I knew.

Mina was born in Istanbul, but no Greek has ever stopped calling it Constantinople, or just the City. In the popular imagination it is simply a matter of time before the City is theirs again. The years following my first visit saw the dispersal of the Greek community; before long nobody on the street spoke anything but Turkish, or a little Gastarbeiter *German, and the social give-and-take suffered accordingly. But the dream persists. Shortly after the young King Constantine was crowned, Strato assured me—for once not laughing, his green eyes lit with conviction—that here at last was the long-awaited hero.*

"The prophecy tells of a Constantine with twelve fingers who will reconquer the City," he declared.

As it happened, a recent photograph had shown the King in action: a karate leap with five-fingered hand extended. Strato had seen it too.

"My golden one, don't you know that they touch up all those pictures?" He used the word eikónes. *"But I who have seen the King on horseback, with my own eyes, know differently."*

Why argue? Thanks to the Turks, there had been no Renaissance in Strato's history. Never, I smiled to think, could such an assertion have crossed the lips of an Italian youth, with Machiavelli in his veins. These much-handled properties of Strato's mind—like the slippers and beads seen at Sts. Sergius and Bacchus—filled me with delight. Our days were numbered; his faith in long shots had already handed him over to an underworld of cardsharps that would be his ruin. His smile owed some of its brilliance to my not knowing this. We promised to go to Constantinople together for the fireworks when it became once more part of Greece.

Meanwhile I returned to Istanbul without him, with others, time after time. One winter dusk David and I tried out the louche hamam. *One June, after wishing my mother good night at our hotel, I was roughly treated in a park. By and large it was the beaten path I kept to, from Hagia Sophia to Topkapi, to the Suleymaniye, to St. Savior in Chora, to the bazaar, retracing my tracks again and again as if I'd learned nothing, or had lost something precious. (One year, at an all-night party in New York, it seemed poetic to let my gold ring fall, like Mélisande's, into a French girl's highball; I never saw it again.) On perhaps my sixth visit a street vendor's trinket caught my eye—a kind of pendant or pennant, chevron-shaped and fringed, entirely made of tiny glass beads: blue-green, white, orange, lemon-yellow, pink. At the center, on a perch of beads, a beaded bird swayed; above it, beads spelled out* MAŞALLAH *(Glory be! Praise the Lord!). No two were alike; they cost nothing; I bought several. In Stonington I hung one in the doorway between our domed red dining room and the shoe-box parlor with its huge gilt mirror and its bat-and-cloud wallpaper designed by Hubbell. The longer I lived with the bird, the more it charmed me. Istanbul was a city of birds; a vortex of birds, Wyndham Lewis might have called it: sparrows and swifts, fishwife gulls, storks on chimneys. Storks, too, made of limber Arabic letters in the Calligraphy Museum—already migrating, in what I feared was a one-way passage, from Nature's realm to that of the Mind. Chickens huddling for warmth where their tavern roost revolved above blue flames. The empire's two-headed eagle. The peacock whose cousin, Mirabell, had for one long summer at the Ouija board sung to us "of what is past, or passing, or to come." My beaded talisman could have issued from no other place in the world. I wanted all my friends to have one, which meant a seventh trip to Istanbul.*

This time, tourist buses jam the streets. Trucks at midnight unload mountains of carpets for sale the next morning. Son et lumière *fill the great cistern, and duckwalks lead to two columns at the very back, resting on heads of monumental marble half submerged in dreamlike transparence. Pretty wooden hotels have sprung up near the antiquities, with tables outside, and fountains. I wonder if the Rejans still exists. All this has happened in Greece too. No sooner does the real thing vanish than it returns, with a conniving wink, as folklore. Near our hotel we find a vendor of beaded birds. This year's model, however, comes in uniform blue and yellow, with two birds to a perch. (Two twittering pangs, the finches Ralph and Ivy, flit through me for a split second.) They look machine-made, matrimonial, not at all what I . . . Days pass; the end of our stay is in sight. I've frankly given up the search, when Peter spots a glinting mound in the bazaar, like Iris on her rubbish heap at the opera's end. We buy the lot. No need ever to travel again; it's the perfect souvenir: a translation into the demotic of Yeats's golden bird on its eternal bough. Swaying from the rearview mirror of Claude's Volkswagen or basking in the glow of my mother's bridge lamp, the talisman (readily unstrung, but who isn't) keeps up appearances, reminding us how notions such as Joy or the Imagination—the Holy Ghost Itself, if it comes to that—out of some recurrent urge to be embodied, make for a Halloween trunk full of feathers and wings.*

XX

A Game of Murder.
Leave-takings and Creative Stirrings.

Its summer-long siesta at an end, Rome began languidly making up for a new season. Out came the black pencils, the golden powders, the rouge of earlier sunsets. One evening we were invited to a party in the penthouse of a medieval brick tower near the Forum. The hosts were a blond Italian decorator, fortyish, and his handsome, serious-looking young American lover. We didn't know them and never caught their names. Our invitation came by way of Hubbell, who was himself unable to attend, having been hired to play the piano, evenings from seven till midnight, in the twinkling blue-and-gold bar at the Orso. At the party Robert and I were two of twenty-odd guests, all men, mostly young and American. It seemed there were more circles in Rome than we'd realized. Except for nice silver-templed Fritz Prokosch, we'd never laid eyes on any of them before. Or had we? One elegantly turned-out young man echoed my name in amazement when we were introduced. He was the son of our Southampton doctor; we'd last seen each other at age eight.

A game of Murder was to be the evening's entertainment, and its rules were now explained. Each player draws a slip of paper from a bowl and examines it secretly. All the slips are blank but for two—one marked with a black dot for the Murderer, the other with an X for the Cross-Examiner. In darkness the players wander from room to room. The Murderer is free to claim his victim—a gently stylized blow to the heart will do—at any juncture, hoping to be unobserved when the body cries out and drops to the floor, and at least a room away by the time it is discovered. Lights then go up, the players gather, the questions begin. In replying, the Murderer is entitled to whatever lies he can get away with; only if directly accused must he tell the truth. The person who has been falsely challenged becomes the next Cross-Examiner. We gathered round, drew our slips of paper, unfolded them privily. My heart skipped a beat—there was the big black dot! Robert looked at me, his face a question. Mine showed nothing.

Off went the lights. We fanned out into the apartment. Its several rooms linked by a long hallway were soon filled by silently milling men. The silence and near-invisibility punctuated here and there by a glowing cigarette reminded me—and many of the others, I fancied—of the unlit garden I'd explored during Robert's absence. It seemed, during the first few minutes, not impossible that our game would develop into a kind of somnambulistic orgy. I recalled a ballet conceived, but never choreographed, by Maya Deren to three playings of the overture to *The Magic Flute*. Twelve dancers would repeat the basic action, each time at a progressively higher (or deeper) level: from cocktail party to *partouze* to sacred ritual. Suppose our game . . . ? But rules were rules; I fingered the slip of paper in my pocket and kept moving, feeling like the killer my father had wanted to hire to eliminate Kimon. In the dark corridor I spotted Robert; he went by with shining eyes—a willing victim?—yet gave no sign of knowing me, as if such compromising circumstances called for tact. Here came the Southampton doctor's son; he winked without slowing his pace. Here came our host, peering into every face with that needle-threading glance of the Violent Against Nature, in Dante. Poor fussy old queen, whom I prayed I would never grow to resemble, having to give a party for people like me, Americans he didn't even know. . . . He deserved some attention. I looked swiftly in both directions and struck him dead.

When the cry went up and the lights came on we all trooped blinking into the *salone*. Out came wine and cookies, and the interrogation began.

Everyone was asked where he'd been at the fatal moment. I stuck to a simple alibi: in such and such a room, near the bookcase. In this highly polished crowd I must have cut a figure so dim that it was hardly worth anyone's while to doubt me. After weighing his evidence, the sleuth hazarded a wrong guess, stepped down, and the whole process was repeated by his successor. And *his*. . . . It was a chapter out of Kafka. Time trudged by, the wine was running out, Robert and I rolled eyes at each other. Half the party had been exculpated by the time Fritz, as Cross-Examiner, lit on me and I confessed. Everyone groaned with relief, rose, stretched, circulated. A few guests glanced at me with new interest. The victim, who'd been making lengthy telephone calls in the bedroom, returned to pinch my cheek and joke about his resurrection. "My dear," said Robert, "we must do this more often." Another half hour, and the party broke up. At the door, however—

The good-looking young American lover of the man I'd killed was seeing people out. We hadn't spoken beyond my thanking him when he filled my glass. Now, about to shake hands, he looked most meaningfully into my eyes; at the same moment a slip of paper—instructions for a new game?—was being pressed into my palm. Surprised, I took a step back. "It's nothing," he muttered, stooping to pick up the note and pocket it. Our eyes met again; he looked put out. No one else seemed to have noticed. "Wait for me!" I called to Robert on the stairs. (If only I'd gone to the party alone!) What had the handsome stranger been proposing: a tryst with his lover's murderer? a life together in Montana? I would never know. Far too shy to dream of learning his name and telephoning, I found several pretexts, in the week that followed, to walk past the scene of the crime. But he never came running out after me.

The golden days grew shorter. Marilyn put aside her studies—no less engrossing now that her future was settled—and flew to Milan with us for *Falstaff* at La Scala and a day of churches and museums. "What will it be like to meet in New York?" she wondered brightly. "What will New York have to say to us, or we to say to one another? Now, I mean, that we've all become—"

"Italicized," said Robert, and we laughed in full accord, for weren't we more elegantly slanted now, more emphatically set upon the world's page, than the blunt types of a year or two earlier, into whose midst—or "chase," as Claude had taught me to call the printer's tray—we must again face being distributed? But to what end? Marilyn at least looked forward to a life in academic circles. She'd be returning to Italy for summers and sabbaticals. Culture wasn't, in her case, the blind alley I sometimes feared it was in mine.

Well, Robert and I could always bring our trained eyes to bear on St. Patrick's or the Thomas Coles at the Historical Society. Yet Marilyn's question—what would we have to say to one another?—touched a sensitive nerve. It brought to mind my old longing to escape from New York and the people I saw there, whose friendships gave me no leeway to change and make new friends. Hadn't that been the chief reason for going abroad? And had I now reached the same point all over again, in Europe? Depressing thought. "You are once more putting the cart before the horse," said Dr. Detre. "There is no one to prevent you from changing, if you wish to."

Robert on the telephone to a customs broker: "You mean, with tourist plates I can't . . . It's cheaper than to . . . Are you serious? How much does having a car destroyed cost? . . . I see. . . . May I watch?" And so forth. Hanging up, he turned to me. "For three hundred dollars La Cenerentola will have her coach viciously dismembered at a government garage. The next of kin are not invited. Italy! Shall we go out?"

In those weeks of fine weather we took long walks every afternoon. There was so much of Rome we'd missed or wanted to revisit. Robert developed an insatiable appetite for Borromini, whose works weren't always easy to see. We bribed our way into the tiny church of San Carlo alle Quattro Fontane—its dimensions exactly those of one of the four pilasters that upheld the dome of St. Peter's—with its pearl-gray cloister no bigger than a brooch. We were obliged to attend a Sunday mass at Sant' Ivo in order to admire the bee-shaped interior's gold-and-white cupola, where concave and convex stagger forth from the corkscrew skylight as though a New England meetinghouse had drunk too much rum. (Here Robert abstained from communion.) In the facade of St. Agnes in Agony we sought qualities answering to the gestures of dread and distaste that Bernini's river gods, grouped round their obelisk, directed at his rival's work. Sure enough, along with his preciousness of scale and taste for perishable materials, Borromini could be seen as cunningly parading his hollows and undulations, like structural limp wrists and swaying hips, in order to provoke a limestone outcrop of homophobia from the robuster artist. (What? Borromini wasn't gay? The river gods weren't by Bernini? No matter. Fact could hold no candle to instinctive truth.)

These promenades were our farewell to the city and, whether or not we knew it, to each other. Robert was returning to New York in late October. He had come over for the summer, thinking I'd be free to leave with him at its end. Now pressure from his mother, and the need to find an apartment in New York—if he wasn't going to spend the rest of his life in St. Louis with her—decided him to go first. "Where will you live?" he asked diffidently, knowing I had nowhere to stay. "I could look for a place big enough for us both. Would that . . . ?" I urged him to do so. It seemed the ideal solution, didn't he agree? Somehow, though, we failed to pursue the topic. After the intimate summer trance of throbbing engines and glittering wake, my head was filling with new horizons, faces, tones of voice. I tried to disown them. Robert deserved better from me than this guilty foreknowledge of a shipboard romance coming to its end.

A shipboard romance . . .

I'd heard a story, where and from whom I was never able to recall—perhaps from some sunburnt grandchild of the tiaraed muse seated next to Henry James at dinner parties. A couple of friends charter a boat to go fishing in the Gulf Stream off the Florida coast. An argument leads to a bet. Can one of them, harnessed for once not to his chair against the pull of marlin or tarpon but to the end of the other's line, hold out for ten minutes, a fish in water himself, to be "played" with rod and reel by his sportsman friend? The idea filled me with horror. At fifteen or sixteen I wasn't past working myself into a panic over the imaginary shark in my father's swimming pool. Think of *being* the bait in an ocean teeming with ravenous monsters! All at once it was a subject I couldn't shake. Perhaps a one-act play, set in the fishing boat . . . ? Or set both "now" and "then," the scary incident coming to life as one of the characters remembers it from a safer vantage in time and space (Ravenna?). What if this character were a woman?—since words came more easily to me in a woman's voice than in a man's. What if she were the sister of one of the friends and—yes!—beloved by the other? What if she were cold and flippant, causing pain to her lover, as I had to Claude by taking up with Robert, as I had to Robert by flirting with Rolf? The climax would come when, stung by her taunts, the lover goes overboard, underwater, fighting against the friend (for these long moments his enemy) who struggles to reel him back to air and safety. He has gone deep, deep into himself, where the others can't dream of following. Back with them in the boat, he and they no longer share a language. The risk-taker is left with his solitary sense of having done all he can.

Whatever my little plot "meant" didn't detain me. I was eager to explore the form I'd chosen. Since first learning to read, I'd responded to the dreamlike immediacy of a play in print: no descriptive or analytical set pieces; rather, gesture and tone stripped to bracketed italics, allowing the reader's sedentary imagination to get into the act. Daringly the stage could encompass both the fishing boat and an Italian piazza. Best of all, thanks to there being more speakers than the single all-creating *I* of a poem, anyone who went on at too great length could be interrupted by new information in a new voice. What most excited me was this very prospect of dividing the labor of consciousness, or whatever light the murky action engendered, among reflectors at greater or lesser odds with one another. From behind a mask we tell the truth, said Oscar Wilde; and in each of my characters I saw a side of myself combined with elements of someone who mattered to me. Claude with his seriousness and intellectual courage stood behind the figure of Charles (who takes the plunge and finds himself); yet the very name Charles, my father's and my brother's, implied relative maturity and spoke for the part of me that lay, now fighting for life, now spluttering in self-pity, on Dr. Detre's couch. By the same token I associated Gilbert (who wields the fishing rod) somewhat with Dr. Detre, but also with that fussy, expendable person I felt in recurrent danger of aging into, like the host at the other night's party, whom I'd so neatly killed. Hating waste, I gave Julie (my heroine) phrases from my old unsatisfactory poem to Claude about Ravenna, plus a versified account of the mosaics, lifted from a letter to Freddy. Before grinding to a halt I'd filled quite a few pages of my long-abandoned notebook.

Revulsion followed. I was rusty, unused to holding a pencil. At first I hadn't thought the project worth mentioning to Dr. Detre—he had shown, for one thing, so little interest in my writing—but now I did. The writer's block I'd originally gone to him to get rid of was still there, I said grimly, big as life.

Dr. Detre asked what my play was about.

"It will have occurred to you," he said when I finished, "that your hero's adventure is made possible by a line attached to himself. The word 'line' suggests something besides fishing, no?"

I had to think for a moment. "You mean, like a line of poetry?" Never before had Dr. Detre acknowledged my—could I say?—calling. For him to so do after all these months thrilled and silenced me.

"If I am not mistaken," he presently went on, "in one of our first meetings you related a dream in which you were a fish trying to become human. That has now come to pass. In your scenario it is a healthy and good-hearted man who is hauled from the sea by those he loves."

My heart leapt, my eyes stung. "But they don't love *him* any longer," I pointed out.

"Perhaps," said Dr. Detre, "they loved a different person."

"The person he no longer is . . ."

"Exactly. The person who, by the way, is now free to decide whether he still loves *them*."

•

The Bait *was part of a program of one-act plays—John Ashbery and Barbara Guest wrote the other two—directed by Herbert Machiz and produced by John Myers. John, an ageless, hulking Irishman with the self-image of a pixie, had come to New York from Buffalo in the thirties, worked on* View *magazine by day and as a puppeteer and comedian in an offbeat nightclub. I'd met him through Kimon, but only now, six years later, felt proof against his flamboyant crusade for the avant-garde. During my years abroad John had become a force to reckon with; parties every other night—merry little dinners, midnight traffic jams—took place at his and Herbert's one-room apartment. A bomb falling on one of these gatherings would have set the arts in America back six weeks. Here I met my contemporaries, the founders of the (had it already been named?) New York School. John and Herbert wanted to produce Plays by P*O*E*T*S, with Sets by P*A*I*N*T*E*R*S—not that mere asterisks can render the starry-eyed emphasis John brought to the plan. "Sweetie," he cried, darting forward on tiptoe, "you must write something wonderfully, perfectly,* *divinely beautiful for our Artists Theater. Hush! Don't say a word, just let it happen!" John touched my brow with his imaginary wand. A couple of months later, back from visiting my father in his latest retreat—a handsome old house on Barbados, surrounded by cane fields—I showed them the finished playlet.*

It was a kind of closet opera. Without singing or music, there were nonetheless arias, duets, trios, and the odd prose recitative. In truth I still hadn't learned very much about writing speakable verse. Nor did the production help. The set—a café table in Venice juxtaposed with the stern of a fishing boat in the Gulf Stream—looked messy and abstract expressionist rather than spare and ambivalent. The leading lady had a German accent. At the first performance the noble (and nearly nude) hero had begun his climactic sestina in a green, "underwater" spotlight—

> *I am not one to think much about pain.*
> *I would not choose to dwell upon myself*
> *In public, sipping at a tumbler of stale water.*
> *It has never been my thought to preach to the fish.*
> *Nevertheless, if I am ever in my life*
> *To think profitably, to see with clear eyes,*

> *Let it be now*

—when a sudden commotion shook the tiny packed theater. Arthur Miller and Dylan Thomas, whom Kimon had brought to see the play, stumbled out, making remarks I'd have preferred not to hear and dragging after them the audience's attention, along with poor Kimon himself. ("What could I do?" he said next day on the phone. "Dylan wanted a drink." Years later I learned what Mr. Miller, with uncanny insight, had whispered in Dylan's ear shortly after the curtain rose: "You know, this guy's got a secret, and he's gonna keep it.") I went outside during the intermission and let a few friends comfort me. One of them introduced his companion—a slender blond man with a voice that didn't sound at all like New York, a perfectly convincing wedding ring on his finger, and the friendliest smile; if only I'd caught his name. Then back we all went to our seats for John Ashbery's play, the hit of the evening. A week or two later I'd stopped, for the first time in over three years, at my old haunt, the San Remo

on MacDougal Street, when the man with the smile and the wedding ring walked in, alone. This time I got his name: David Jackson.

The Bait *was done again thirty-five years after its premiere. The writer who lives long enough finds his youthful idiom yet more stilted than it was to start with, his view of society positively quaint. I used the occasion to liven it up a bit: Julie grows older, and her dim boyfriend, as if having passed under a Brazilian rainbow, changes sex. Peter Hooten played her brother, Gilbert, the trickster who initiates the action that enmeshes him along with the others. It was wrenching to see Peter, with his resonant voice, his profile of Apollo, impersonate a teasing, superficial character. Gilbert and Julie, as I've said, embodied aspects of myself I shrank from facing directly, like my cruelty and flightiness during Rolf's weeks in Italy. Peter brought to the role a volatile anguish which he would draw more deeply upon for the wrathful, suffering angel Gabriel in the performing version of* Sandover. *Watching him play Gilbert, I felt, in ways I couldn't easily explain to him, that these youthful sins of mine, like so many games of Murder, were being lifted into the light and forgiven. It was a catharsis overlooked in antiquity: that of a poet by the actor's uncanny grasp of his role. So* The Bait *with all its flaws and affectations, and despite the miserable situation that inspired it, remains close to my heart. Its rainbow has spanned my life, early to late, leaving a pot of gold at either end.*

XXI

End of Therapy in Sight.
Hubbell's Repertoire.
My Favorite Words.
The Pillow Book Concluded.

I wanted a Roman gift for Robert. Here at last was reason to enter the old engraver's shop near the Trevi Fountain. Among his round red or violet cardinal-hat seals I'd noted a few secular ones and wondered if he could make the bookplate I had in mind: a unicorn's head, the motto CANDOR & RARITY, and the initials R. I. The old man's eyes slowly lit up—busy as he was, a real commission. Six weeks later he greeted me with satisfaction. This very day, *proprio oggi*, he'd made a start—indicating his work space, dwarfed by an antique marble fragment, the quarter-life-sized head of a horse. It came, he smiled, from his personal collection; how else to model the rarely seen *liocorno?* The bookplates—white on tobacco brown, small as silver dollars—were ready before Robert left. He spoke his pleasure, yet I had the oddest feeling that he would never use them. Rarity and candor were a dew that dried up when one called attention to it.

Dr. Detre confirmed his summer prediction. I could go home, if I wished, at the end of November. The long-awaited news disoriented me.

Wasn't I still the anxious, unhappy person who'd dropped his amber cigarette holder at our first interview? Now a mere month remained. How
could I throw away my crutches at its end? There'd been no shattering
breakthrough, no climax out of Hitchcock.

"I often think," said Dr. Detre, "that the relatively uneventful cure is
the most lasting. Like a good dark suit." Before I could ask his opinion of
my colorful shirt and tie, he continued. "I have some news, by the way. I,
too, shall be moving to New York. I have secured my visa from your State
Department."

So! That's what *he'd* been doing these months in Rome: waiting for
clearance. His internship at an American hospital would begin next January. Thus, though our "work" was finished, any bits that came unglued
could be fixed on the spot. Dr. Detre was after all a fellow mortal, with
worries and aspirations of his own. The war's end, which found me eager
for wicked, blackened old Europe, found him—the rest of whose family
had disappeared at Auschwitz—among those millions dreaming of a
passport to Freedom. Who could blame him?

I'm not used to living alone. With Robert gone, with my life aired and
swept clean like so many rooms waiting to be furnished (rooms whose
proportions and views change daily), my ties to the present grow ever
flimsier. Hubbell persuades me to fly with him to London for a week
before sailing home from England on the new *Queen Elizabeth*. I welcome
the plan; eager as I am to start living, it seems wise to approach life indirectly, to catch it off guard. I am proud of my years away but fearful too.
If friends no longer know me, if strangers take me for a foreigner? Perhaps on docking in New York I should hire a taxi straight from the pier to
Montauk—or some such equivalent of Proust's Balbec—where, during
long hours in an empty dining room above the sea, I can glean from the
banter of busboys and waitresses the latest cultural passwords. Am I still
American? Hearing my language on the street, I look round into tourist
faces wan and apathetic from the pursuit of happiness. Out of the Grand
Hotel, with its memories of my father and Robin, steps a mink-coated
woman crying "Whoopee!" and brandishing the *Rome Daily American*
above her head. Is she drunk? A red-white-and-blue ribbon flutters from
the newspaper. It's the morning after Election Day. Eisenhower (a hero
of Bill Plummer's) has won.

As my departure draws near, I contact a packer and shipper for the things I want to keep—books, a lamp, the harpsichord. See to returning the rented piano. Give lunch to Dr. Simeons, to Marilyn, to Umberto. Join the Bakers for a farewell "feast of fat things" (Isaiah 25:6): fried chicken with gravy, rice, frozen succotash, biscuits, salad with syrupy tangerine segments and cream-cheese balls rolled in chives, butter-pecan ice cream and devil's food cake. But most evenings I manage to keep free, not for any final sowing of wild oats, rather for a kind of refresher course. Seated in the corner nearest to Hubbell's spotlit piano bench in the dark blue-and-gold bar of the Orso, I listen to Cole Porter and Richard Rodgers, Gershwin and Noël Coward, songs from an era whose afterglow plays upon my friend's impudent, lightly pitted clown face as he puts body and soul into his next selection.

These songs evoke a period more or less coinciding with the first fifteen years of my life: from just before the crash on Wall Street to Pearl Harbor. To their lilt my parents danced and I took my own first steps. They precede Actors Studio and rock stars, precede (for that matter) beboppers and jitterbuggers; agitation has yet to become the earmark of sincerity. The tunes are catchy, metropolitan, popular without being entirely of the people—you go to Nashville or New Orleans for that. The lyrics are literate but not highbrow; witness the phrase from "Smoke Gets in Your Eyes": "Now laughing friends deride . . . ," where the redundant adjective is chosen lest a listener not know what the verb means and feel left out. No; it isn't the language so much as the tone (as they called it at Amherst) that risks being misunderstood. When the hero of "I Can't Get Started with You" brags about his intimacy with FDR, his pilot's license, and his "showplace," is this a dangerous megalomania talking? a light-headed soup-line daydream? Vital discriminations I feel at work within me. If Rilke's poems, so comforting in adolescence, imply a handful of readers privileged by their fluent access to pain and solitude, the songs in Hubbell's repertoire conjure up, in another wing of the house, a Byronic elite of fox-trotters classy enough to crack jokes while their hearts are breaking.

Before closing time a stunningly handsome figure entered the bar: not Gino the goalie this year but Enrico, with his elegance, his title, his sense of humor. When the last set ended he swept my friend off to a late supper. Urged to go along, I seldom did. The streets were empty, moon-misted as I walked home, singing Hubbell's songs under my breath.

Pronouns ricocheted through their lyrics, relationships being of prime importance. The heartless She, the unempathetic They (who asked how I knew my romance was through, who threatened, evening after evening, to begin the beguine); foremost, of course, the eternal You and I. . . . Would there never be a poem purged of the whole love-addicted crowd? Clichés meanwhile rolled past like Hollywood vamps in open, vintage cars. Clever polysyllabic rhymes, allusions to remote places (Spain!), to cigarettes and exotic drinks, hinted at the vocalist's sophisti-cation, even as recurrent words like "tears" or "heart" or "Baby" con-firmed the soft spot beneath a glamorous, know-it-all veneer.

What were my recurrent words? No longer, as at sixteen, "pale" or "dim," or even the irresistible names of colors—"violet" or "rose," scented respectively by turbulence and upward movement. The words I never wearied of were rather those adverbs like "still" or "even," or adverbial phrases like "by then" or "as yet" or "no longer," which, sharp-ening a reader's sense of time, suggested a reality forever in the process of change, that had "only now" come into being or was "already" on the point of vanishing. "Still," with its triadic resonance of immobility, endurance, and intensification ("Eleanor grew still more animated"), was perhaps the hardest to resist. Deep in the pinewoods of my vocabulary, it yielded an intoxicating moonshine I would keep resorting to in small, furtive sips.

The evanescent reality mirrored in such dewdrops of syntax came as a vast refreshment after my trek through the cut-and-dried. Young people in my day—in any day?—believed that a comprehensive account of everything would presently be rendered. With the development of the hydrogen bomb, matter had begun to yield its inmost secrets. The poets we read most carefully seemed to have the last word—witness the tran-scendent certitudes of the *Four Quartets*, or Stevens when he wrote, "The prologues are over. It is a question, now, / Of final belief." But *final* belief, or ultimate truth, was the last thing I wanted. That it should be in a fiction, as Stevens went on to say, or that Eliot's vision kept rippling off into wordless radiance, was a paradox to whose height I had yet to grow. "Central man?" I saw a totem pole of rigid, glaring faces; while belief and believer—why, just to breathe the words set up a green rustling in my mind.

I'd been ravished to discover that (in English at least) "truth" and "tree" shared a single Indo-European root. Truth, then, could be felt as a living organism, varying from time to time and place to place. Now a seedling among thousands, now a gaunt trunk crowned with fire, it grew and withered in natural cycles. So did the various tongues in which it was couched. Wasn't my own psyche, cradled and fed by those out-of-date lullabies Hubbell gave gravelly voice to, night after night at his spotlit piano, already outgrowing them? Any creative spirit truly *à la page* came most to life, I hoped, by the perpetual freshening of human language—the slang of each successive decade, the gaudy breakthroughs of folk idiom, the body English explored in a new dance craze, or the latest concept in astrophysics.

These blissfully self-sufficient hours left me convinced of having changed but vague as to how deep, or how cursory, the change had been.

"Remember," said Dr. Detre, "it has been a time of breaking for you." Breaking, I understood, with my mother's stifling scenario; with Tony's exhibitionistic solutions; with Freddy's calm and conventional ones. Teaching that year at Lawrenceville, Freddy was also courting a girl whose parents and his had been friends. Such fidelity to beginnings would have been the end of me. My dream, a love flowering far from Palm Beach and Southampton, mirrored Freddy's centripetal one toward early figures and scenes. But did it truly matter—both inner and outer space being curved—which direction one set out in?

"Now I've broken faith with Robert too," I observed faintly. "Is this what I'll more and more find myself doing?"

"Robert, like Claude before him, contributed to your present freedom. Through him you explored and rejected the choices he stood for."

And having served his purpose, was he now simply to be shrugged off—Sleeping Beauty's last dream before waking? I hated seeing myself in that light.

"You were warned at the outset not to make too deep an emotional commitment while undergoing treatment."

Well, it appeared I hadn't. But henceforth I'd be free to—?

"Of course," said Dr. Detre in a fresh, amused voice, before I could decide what.

Sitting up on Dr. Detre's couch, tingling all over, I felt I'd had a rub-down with salt and oil. Was it the moment to ask Claude's question? "Tell me," I said, with a laugh part apologetic, part euphoric, "how much of this was really necessary?" How, in other words, was a patient ever to know that time mightn't have brought about the longed-for changes? Time passing normally, without all the probing and soul-searching, the cost to oneself and others.

When Dr. Detre smiled he looked like a different person. "Time," he said, "approximates with surprising accuracy the work we do. But we"—his satisfied pronoun embracing a host of colleagues—"we do it faster."

One morning I've set aside an hour, before catching the bus to Dr. Detre's, for errands. I pick up my new passport photo in Piazza di Spagna. I photograph Claude's building, the boat-shaped fountain, a policeman directing traffic like a ballet master. (For two years now I've killed time with my camera, focusing the image, making the moment stand still. But all this while, if Dr. Detre is right about "doing it faster," my inner life has been a speeded-up movie, one that the principal actor, however enriched by it, never gets to see.) Next I buy a couple of ties in a smart shop nearby. It's a short walk to the English bookstore. From there I make a detour to the Villa Giulia and say good-bye to the Etruscan couple reclining on their terra-cotta sarcophagus. They look past me, as always, with calm, enraptured smiles. I continue through the Villa Borghese Gardens, down Via Veneto to the American Embassy. Here I complete the necessary forms and submit them, with my old passport and new like-ness, to a white-haired woman full of questions. Aimed at obstructing the prodigal's return? No such luck.

"We'll have everything ready by noon tomorrow," she gloats. "VIP treatment for all our citizens!"

I step back into Roman sunlight the more precious for these minutes on American soil. Going by way of the National Museum will see me home in good time for Quinta's lunch. In the museum's cavernous brick antechamber (originally part of some great Roman bath) hangs a black-and-white mosaic of a human skeleton. The technique, after the wonders of Ravenna, is crude and cartoonish. The figure reclines, skull propped on bony forearm; above it in big capitals float the words GNOTHI SEAU-TON: Greek for "Know Thyself." Was self-knowledge, even in ancient times, a kind of death? or brooding upon one's nature a lifelong career, that carried over into the grave? Heaven forbid. Above the sober "consolations of philosophy" I'll take my constellations of peacock and seraph twinkling forth from vaults of gold. Yet the motto's starkness pleases me. Obviously for anyone undergoing psychoanalysis—oh my god!

Bells were ringing. My hour with Dr. Detre was up, and I had forgotten the appointment.

•

At my first appointment with Dr. Detre in New York I arrived on the wrong day and his jolly American wife opened the door. Confusion. Apologies. A glimpse of my confessor without necktie. What had been bothering me in the four months since my return, I said when eventually we sat face-to-face, was my calendar: black with names and numbers, lunches, cocktail parties, drinks at intermission, nightcaps after the opera. Would I, like Tony, never have time to write? True, in the odd hour between engagements I'd finished The Bait *and was at work on a second play. On a visit to my father in Barbados, I'd begun planning a novel about his life there, surrounded by former mistresses, new loves, the inevitable disapproving nurse. Poems, too, like comets at whose tails I grabbed, whistled overhead. What did it mean, I asked Dr. Detre, and where would it all end? He reminded me that I could answer such questions myself.*

On arriving in New York I stayed at the Plaza. My mother and Bill were coming to spend Christmas with my grandmother and me. Over the days ahead I planned to find an apartment and move into it by the new year. Robert phoned from St. Louis. He was eager to see me, would be returning shortly to the small flat he'd taken on Irving Place. Though I was welcome to share it as an interim measure, it seemed best at present for him to live alone.

Outside the Plaza that first evening, dusk had fallen. Before drawing the curtains of heavy hotel-green silk, I looked out into the gemlike reds and whites of traffic. Good-natured horns blew, a crystal fringe gusted and shivered beneath Karl Bitter's bathing nymph. A sleighload of gifts—I'd done my Christmas shopping in London—filled a corner of my room. As for my presents, I knew that my mother's needlepoint family crests had been framed and mounted; I would try for a suitable glow of pleasure when I unwrapped them. But here awaiting me was a package, not in Christmas paper, from Freddy. The card read: "Welcome home. You know you've always wanted one." It was a Ouija board.

Thus, while Freddy never won me to Christ, he once again—as when at fourteen he made writing a poem seem the most natural and desirable thing in the world—put me in touch with a whole further realm of language. Within a couple of years David and I, having escaped New York and its merciless cultural calendar, begin holding candlelit séances after dinner. We change to a homemade board—more spacious than Freddy's—with an overturned willowware cup as pointer. The messages are from the start arresting:

> *Originally from Cologne.*
> *Dead in his 22nd year*
> *Of cholera in Cairo, he had KNOWN*
> *NO HAPPINESS. He once met Goethe, though.*
> *Goethe had told him: PERSEVERE.*

These lines, for all their parlor-game tone, turn out to be as crucial to my poetry as Aeschylus's bringing onstage an "answerer" (the hypocritēs*) was to the development of Greek drama. Two voices—my narrative one in lower case, the young German ghost's in upper—together compound the cozy lyric capsule. A promising start; yet I am slow to draw further upon our transcripts. Dr. Detre calls the board a folie à deux and wonders if we aren't "playing with lightning." Besides, who at thirty wants to spend hours each day communing with the dead? Past fifty—our age when cold, inhuman voices usurp the Board—we shiver a bit but go along for the ride. By then we'll have guessed that the very flimsiness of the Ouija apparatus somehow protects us, obliging the lightning to articulate itself by slow degrees. So that even when flashes come from highest heaven we are seldom blinded to the fruitful suspicion that they dwell all along in a manner of speaking.*

Late in the summer of 1990 the dramatization I'd put together, for Peter, from The Changing Light at Sandover *is videotaped. Nothing in life, short of the gradual coming into being of that long poem itself, has ever thrilled me more. Peter is both actor and producer. Airline tickets, hotel suites, caterers.*

Lighting and stage crews, director, settings, a cast of nine. We have taken over the Agassiz Theater in Cambridge. Countless ganglia connect a magic truck, denser with technology than a pharaoh's tomb with hieroglyphics, to our soundstage, two flights up. Finally all is ready. I play myself, and each day now begins with the magic of having wrinkles painted out, temples darkened, eyes and lips brightened by a makeup man. Time reversed, the Princesse de Guermantes's terminal reception run backward. One by one the key figures of the poem (of my life as well, if the two can be told apart) gather round the coffee urn: Ephraim in his Greek miniskirt, Mirabell in peacock leotard; Wystan and Maria, side by side, smiling like accomplices. Here is Peter, sportshirted and sandaled, who before long will reappear in skintight archangelic silver. Too keyed up for words, we make do with a powerful hug.

Here now comes DJ—or Terry, as I'm learning to call him. Once a street clown in Paris, he is hunkier than strictly necessary. But his easy American manners and infectious smile recall the David I knew when this impostor was in nursery school, so that I almost forget the real friend left behind in Stonington—who with no one to paint out his wrinkles will be spending today in bed, chain-smoking, eyes fixed on quiz shows or sitcoms.

What worries Terry this morning is having to react to the Ouija dictation without being able to lean over and read it. He's left with nothing to do. JM at least is seen to keep transcribing. I tell him how in real life David often foreknew the messages, tears welling up on the verge of some especially poignant passage. Terry brightens at once: this means business. At noon he will bring me a present, a tiny clay pot containing a smooth miniature pinkish-gray boulder cleft in twain, like Gertrude's heart in Hamlet. *From the cleft a pink flower has opened. I've never seen the like; is it a kind of succulent? Pleased by the success of his gift, Terry himself turns a shade pinker. "It's called a living stone," he explains. Alice's name for David—Dr. Livingstone! I'm once more on her horsehair sofa in rue Christine; a cleft thirty years deep is filling with light.*

Back to 1952. There was time, that evening, to walk to my grandmother's. She lived on East Seventy-second Street, in the same building my mother and I moved to after the divorce. My grandmother, long a widow, had given up Jacksonville to cast her lot with us in New York. Having first leased this apartment, she went to buy it in 1941, when the building "went cooperative," for fifteen hundred dollars. So astonishing a bargain didn't keep her from fretting over "*tying up that kind of money in real estate.*" *She'd been poor for the first fifty years of her life, poor but genteel. She had painted on china as a girl and played the piano pieces of Grieg and MacDowell. A genuine Dresden doll—her muse?—in panniers and lace fichu perched on her dressing table. Settled now in four comfortable rooms, with a live-in maid and no friends of her own to entertain, though my mother's and mine fussed gratifyingly over her, my grandmother harbored all the reflexes of frugality. "I never thought I'd live to see the day," she said as we sat down to the coquilles of deviled crab which I'd asked to taste again, "when crabmeat would skyrocket to two dollars a pound."*

It is rare in America that a given address figures in one's life for more than a decade. The upward or downward mobility of tenants makes for turnover. Or else the house itself vanishes—as when my first home, the brownstone on West Eleventh Street, was inadvertently blown up in 1970 by student activists. Yet this apartment of my grandmother's, in a building where I lived fifty years ago, can be seen to have gradually passed into my hands since her death. The latest clue, bought in Athens for exactly what the old lady paid for her apartment, hangs on the wall: an outspread black-paper fan painted by Tsarouchis. It shows—my answer to the Dresden doll?—two swarthy, wasp-waisted soldiers in boxer shorts, winged like cabbage whites or some companionably low order of angel. A key turns in the lock. Peter enters, rosy from the chill dusk outside. But he wears a remote, melancholy face I know better than to question.

Saying he's in a hurry to change and leave for dinner, he hands me the mail I overlooked this morning on purpose: the friends who fifty years ago wrote long, eagerly awaited letters nowadays reach for the phone. Here accordingly is the usual haul of kitchen-appliance catalogs, fund-raising for AIDS, beachwear from Saks, organizations to save the planet. The unspeakably urgent coupled with the utterly inane. A far more absorbing pile awaited me on a table in this very room, the night of my return from Europe. After our crab, our stewed fruit and peanut-butter cookies, I poured myself a drink and while my grandmother readied herself for bed—immemorial pantomime of shoe trees and quilted hangers, ablutions, face cream and hairnet, the aquamarine brooch and earrings wrapped in tissue, the drawers evenly closed, the faucets ritually strangled—gave this hoard a preliminary glance. Ah! here was a 1953 calendar from Irma. Next, a fat, richly stamped letter from Tony; I put it aside to read later, along with those from my mother, my sister, and Claude. This flat parcel from Holland felt like a book. . . . Opening it, I found that Mr. and

Mrs. Lodeizen had sent me Hans's just-published second collection of poems, handsomely bound in leather, with a ("I'm late—who loves you?" Peter off so early? Faint slam) frontispiece photograph of the author.

As if I had fallen into a sudden chasm, I stumbled weeping into the next room, where my grandmother, asking no questions, held me in her arms for the moments it took to pass. Hans's immediate posthumous fame, his place today as the inventor, for Dutch poetry, of an offhand, "modern" way of seeing and putting what he saw on the page, sprang from those manners that so charmed his friends, manners at one time of a piece with his live, physical being. No longer. Between these ounces of paper and leather and print he had become— his biographical container, in my mother's phrase—and the person I'd known and loved lay all the difference in the world. It was of course myself I grieved for. I had glimpsed, through the joy of homecoming, the degree to which I was consenting to the transformation my friend had already—taking his leave with a little bow—undergone. Hungry for experience and cured of my writer's block, wouldn't I, too, turn, word by word, page by page, into books on a shelf?

•

On my last Roman morning I stand gazing about the denuded apartment while Quinta comes and goes. Hubbell will be picking me up downstairs in ten minutes; we fly to London at noon. I've already taken formal leave of Quinta, spoken the words of friendship and gratitude, given her a fat envelope for Christmas. My empty bookshelves and worktable have resigned themselves to my departure; placidly they await their next user. A studious child . . . a sick old woman . . . ? The sharpest pang comes when I look out at the mild blank blue of early December sky. Never again will I see—will anyone see—today's particular morning sun, breadth and bias of its retreating path ordained by the hour, the season, the year, the millennium, as it treads the gleaming boards I can still for a moment call mine.

"Signor Jim," cries Quinta, holding it up from the bed she is stripping. "Il guanciale! Non dimenticarlo!" The pillow—my precious down pillow—so many healing and transforming dreams have been dreamed upon. Well, such pillows are no rarity where I am going. Besides, months of heavy duty have left this one battered and limp. Would Quinta like to have it? She beams with delight. A final look round, a last embrace, and downstairs in the elevator piled with luggage. On to the new life! But reaching the door of Hubbell's waiting cab, I discover from a check of my pockets that I've left something vital, wallet or passport, behind. Up again I go. What on earth . . . ? A white blizzard—feathers everywhere— fills the

(Weeks later, the explanation. No sooner have I been seen to leave, Umberto would write in reply to my fascinated query, than the elder Count Bracci—"who believes he had the pleasure of meeting you once, at the signing of your lease"—popped in to scrutinize the premises. Had the American tenant perhaps left behind a usable ashtray, a bottle of ink? Aha! That pillow appeared to be in decent condition. . . . Sharp-witted as a Goldoni hostess, Quinta said it was now hers; did the *padrone* wish to make an offer for it? Wait: how to know, the old count countered, unwilling to be duped, that it was *piume d'oca*, genuine goosedown? Because if not . . . ! Heated words and mutual interest presently led them to rip open one corner for a peek.)

—fills the apartment. I've walked in upon two people my parents' age struggling to contain the damage. The proscenium of the sleeping alcove frames them. Quinta's eyes flash with an embattled passion never seen before. Count Bracci, white-haired but dapper in jacket and tiepin, sputters and waves his arms like a broken toy. Before either discerns me in the storm of feathers (through which I see *them* more and more clearly), I have retrieved whatever I came for and slipped away for good.

NOTES

In the following headnotes we describe, when pertinent, the further provenance of these prose pieces. In the textual notes proper we have sought to include the following items: names of JM's friends and teachers who might not be familiar to the ordinary reader or are not sufficiently characterized in this volume; names of composers, writers, and artists whose reputations are by some standards comparatively modest (Gérôme is here, Monet is not, Duparc is and Debussy is not, Rameau is and Rimbaud is not) or whose import is not inferable from context; names of composers, writers, and artists when the text indicates *only* a work (an opera or aria, poem or novel, painting or sculpture); and allusions that are not self-explanatory. Ordinarily we have glossed names only once, usually on their first appearance. We have excluded foreign words and phrases easily found in dictionaries and most of JM's allusions to his own poems, fiction, and drama. JM himself disliked a fussy scholarship, and in that spirit we have limited this apparatus. Readers in search of items not noted should consult the index.

WRITING

3   *Acoustical Chambers*

This essay was published originally under the title "Condemned to Write about Real Things," as part of the *Book Review*'s series "The Making of a Writer," a feature in which writers were invited "to comment on various aspects of their craft: their imaginative and autobiographical sources, their practices of composition, the origin of their sense of vocation."

3   Mademoiselle: Lilla Fanning Howard.

4   Carmen's "Habanera": lyric in *Carmen*, opera by French composer Georges Bizet (1838–1875).

5   St. Bernard's: boys' school (f. 1904) in Manhattan, attended by JM.
    Lawrenceville Lit: *Lawrenceville Literary Magazine*, sponsored by the Lawrenceville School (f. 1810) in Lawrenceville, NJ, a boarding school attended by JM (class of '43).
    Heredia: José Maria de Heredia (1842–1905). French poet born in Cuba, one of the Parnassian group.
    Alice Meynell: Alice Thompson Meynell (1847–1922). English poet and essayist, known especially for her religious intensity.
    Elinor Wylie: 1885–1928. American poet and novelist. See JM's essay in this volume on pp. 435–45.

6   J. M. Barrie: James Matthew Barrie (1860–1937). Scottish author of *Peter Pan* and *Dear Brutus* and other plays as well as novels.

7   Reuben Brower: 1908–1975. Professor of English at Amherst College and Harvard University, author of numerous books including *Mirror on Mirror: Translation Imitation Parody* and *The Fields of Light: An Experiment in Critical Reading* (1951), in which JM appears in a footnote on p. 43.
    Theodore Baird: 1901–1996. Literary critic and professor of English at Amherst College. See Robin Varnum, *Fencing in Words: A History of Writing Instruction at Amherst College in the Era of Theodore Baird, 1938–1966*.

9   *The Education of the Poet*
First delivered on April 12, 1988, as the annual "Education of the Poet" lecture, at the invitation of the Academy of American Poets, held at the Guggenheim Museum in New York City, this essay was subsequently published in the academy's newsletter.

10   "Evangeline": epic by American poet Henry Wadsworth Longfellow (1807–1882).

11   "I hate to see . . .": the first line of W. C. Handy's "St. Louis Blues."

12   Hugh Kenner: JM quotes *The Pound Era*, pp. 187–188.

13   Maggie Teyte: 1888–1976. English soprano.
     Alfred Cortot: 1877–1962. French pianist and conductor.

15   the extensive and the intensive, Calvino calls them: cf. *Six Memos for the Next Millennium* by Italian writer Italo Calvino (1923–1985) and especially "Exactitude," in which "the extension of the infinite into the density of the infinitesimal" is the subject and in which such of JM's favorite writers as Mallarmé, Valéry, Ponge, and Stevens appear.

17   Lady Diana Duff Cooper: Lady Diana Cooper (1892–1986). Born Diana Manners, she married Alfred Duff Cooper, Viscount Norwich. A famous beauty, socialite, and the Churchills' close friend.

19   *Jung Love*
The *Voice Literary Supplement* is a monthly feature in the New York City tabloid the *Village Voice*. As the editor explained in a prefatory comment, "We asked some current and former kids to tell us how they sharpened their intellectual milk teeth." JM's was one of many responses.

19   Wagner's Nibelungen: cf. the operatic cycle *Der Ring des Nibelungen* by German composer Richard Wagner (1813–1883).

20 Amfortas: the Fisher King, or Keeper of the Grail, in Wagner's opera *Parsifal*.
Bakst: Léon Bakst (1866–1924). Russian artist and illustrator.
Klimt: Gustav Klimt (1862–1918). Austrian painter and illustrator.

21 *On Literary Tradition*
These are excerpts from the transcript of a symposium held at George Mason University, April 4–5, 1982. The topic was "Literary Tradition," and the participants were Nadine Gordimer, David Kalstone, William Matthews, Myra Sklarew, Susan Sontag, D. M. Thomas, and JM.

22 Lytton Strachey: 1880–1932. English biographer and literary critic, member of the Bloomsbury group, author of *Eminent Victorians*.

23 famous poem: Keats's "Ode on a Grecian Urn."

24 *On "The Country of a Thousand Years of Peace"*
The poem is in JM's *Collected Poems*, p. 57.

25 Hans Lodeizen: 1924–1950. Dutch poet. He reappears in JM's work.
Barbara Deming: 1917–1984. American political activist, feminist, pacifist, and poet, author of *We Are All Part of One Another*, *Running Away from Myself: A Dream Portrait of America Drawn from the Films of the Forties*, and *Prison Notes*.
Benjamin DeMott: b. 1924. Professor of English at Amherst College and social critic, author of *Killer Woman Blues: Why Americans Can't Think Straight about Gender and Power* and other works.

26 *On "Snapshot of Adam"*
The poem is in JM's *Collected Poems*, p. 826.

28 *Foreword to* Recitative

28 *Una voce poco fa*: aria in *Il Barbieri di Siviglia* (I.ii), opera by Italian composer Gioacchino Rossini (1792–1868).
Il mio tesoro: aria in *Don Giovanni* (II.ii), opera by Wolfgang Amadeus Mozart (1756–1791).

29 *From* Pourquoi écrivez-vous?
The book included the responses of four hundred writers to the question posed.

30 *On Allusion*
A special issue devoted to "allusion," edited by Eleanor Cook, included solicited "comments" from several poets, including A. R. Ammons, Margaret Atwood, Anthony Hecht, John Hollander, Jay Macpherson, and JM.

30 *tous les livres*: JM is quoting "Brise marine," a poem by French poet Stéphane Mallarmé (1842–1898).

31   C: Chester Kallman (1921–1975). American poet and librettist and W. H. Auden's longtime lover. Kallman was JM's and DJ's neighbor in Athens and with Auden wrote the libretto for Stravinsky's *The Rake's Progress* (cf. note to p. 146).
LEADEN CASKET: cf. Shakespeare's *The Merchant of Venice* (II.vii), in which Bassanio is a character.

32   The Poet's Notebook
The editors had originally assembled notebook excerpts from poets for a special edition of *Seneca Review* in 1991. More contributors, including JM, were added for the book-length version. The editors' stated aim was "to illuminate the poet's temperament and process, to reveal the blue out of which the poetry arises."

34   The bold diction of expiring sense: cf. T. S. Eliot, *Four Quartets*, "Little Gidding," II: "the cold friction of expiring sense."
Rossini's "Musique Anodyne": in Rossini's opera *Péchés de viellesse*.
Metastasio: Pietro Metastasio (1698–1782). Italian poet and librettist.
Dolly Sister: *The Dolly Sisters*, a 1945 film starring Betty Grable and June Haver.
Bruce Chatwin: 1940–1989. Onetime director of Sotheby's, travel writer, novelist, author of *In Patagonia*, *The Songlines*, and *Utz*. His sketch of André Malraux appears in *What Am I Doing Here?*

35   Stesichoros: Greek poet (fl. sixth century BCE) whose work survives only in fragments.

36   "PH": Peter Hooten (b. 1950). American actor, JM's lover. He appears numerous times in JM's work.

37   Mary Lou: Mary Lou Aswell (d. 1984). Fiction editor for *Harper's Bazaar*, friend of JM's in New Mexico.
DMc: David McIntosh (b. 1938). Painter, friend of JM's and Georgia O'Keeffe's, longtime resident of New Mexico.
Charlotte: Charlotte Hafley. Atlanta friend of JM's, wife of artist Bruce Hafley.

38   "not waving but dronning": cf. Stevie Smith's poem, "Not Waving But Drowning." JM uses the pun in "Word Made Flesh" in the sequence "More Bits" (*Collected Poems*, p. 852).
Germaine: Germaine Nahman, JM's Alexandrian acquaintance, quoted also in his poem "The Thousand and Second Night" (*Collected Poems*, p. 182).
Christian: Christian Ayoub Sinano (1927–1989). JM's Alexandrian friend, long a resident of Montreal, author of *Artagal*, *Pola de Pera*, and *Piera de Pola*. JM's poem "Pola Diva" (*Collected Poems*, p. 271) bears the epigraph "after Christian Ayoub" and translates the latter's poem of the same name.

The two poems appear together in *Pola de Pera* (Erin, Ontario: The Porcupine's Quill, 1989), which is Maud Burnett's translation of *Proses pour Pola* (Paris: René Juillard, 1964). *Pola de Pera* is illustrated by the author and illustrator Virgil Burnett (b. 1928), a friend of JM's.

40   On Scripts for the Pageant, *The First Five Lessons*
JM wrote this introduction for the first magazine appearance of this portion of his book-length 1980 poem, the final section of the *Sandover* trilogy.

42   On "The Ballroom at Sandover"
This "word of explanation" preceded JM's reading of "The Ballroom at Sandover," the concluding section of the *Sandover* trilogy, as the 1980 Phi Beta Kappa Poem at Harvard, Sanders Theater, June 3, 1980.

42   Marius Bewley: 1916–1973. Professor at Rutgers University, author of *Masks and Mirrors: Essays in Criticism*, *The Complex Fate: Hawthorne, Henry James and Others*, and *The Eccentric Design: Form in the Classical American Novel*. Dedicatee of JM's "Mouthpiece" (*Collected Poems*, p. 815).
Maya Deren: Eleanora (Maya) Deren (1917–1961). Avant-garde filmmaker (*Meshes of the Afternoon* and others), anthropologist, author of *The Divine Horsemen: The Living Gods of Haiti*, a friend of JM's and an important figure in his *Sandover* books.

43   Mimí and Vassílis Vassilikos: Greek novelist Vassílis Vassilikos (b. 1935) and his first wife, Mimí, close friends of JM's and David Jackson's in Athens and figures in *The Changing Light at Sandover*.

44   Foreword to A Reader's Guide to James Merrill's *The Changing Light at Sandover*
Robert Polito describes his book as "a reader's handbook and alphabetical index" to JM's trilogy. In addition to extensive references, the book includes reviews and responses by critics to JM's epic.

INTERVIEWS

We have omitted several interviews whose information overlaps significantly with that in the interviews included. Any of those omitted interviews, however, might be illuminating on any given subject. They are as follows: with Jean Lunn, *Sandscript*, 1982; with Richard Jackson and Michael Pandri, *The Poetry Miscellany*, 1983; with W. S. Di Piero and Diane Middlebrook, 1984, transcribed and edited by Michael Stillman, the Archive of Recorded Sound, Stanford University; with Robert Basil and Seth Magalaner, *Sequoia*, Winter 1985; with Peggy Friedman, *Jacksonville*, June 1985; with Robert Polito, originally entitled "*The Changing Light at Sandover*: A Conversation with James Merrill," *Pequod*, 1990; with C. A. Buckley, *Twentieth Century Literature*, Winter 1992.

49   *An Interview with Donald Sheehan*

This interview was conducted on May 23, 1967, in Madison, Wisconsin, where JM was poet-in-residence for eight weeks at the University of Wisconsin.

51   A. D. Hope: 1907–2000. Australian poet, a traditionalist with a satiric flair.
history . . . I'll be condemned to repeat it: JM alludes to George Santayana's maxim, "Those who cannot remember the past are condemned to repeat it" (*The Life of Reason*, vol. I).

52   *Short Stories*: ten-page chapbook comprising JM's poems "Gothic Novel," "A View of the Burning," "The Octopus," "The Cruise," "The Wintering Weeds," "The Greenhouse," "About the Phoenix," "A Narrow Escape," and "Midas Among Goldenrod" (*Collected Poems*, pp. 810, 95, 58, 92, 71, 63, 110, 77, and 78, respectively), a limited edition of 210 numbered copies printed by Claude Fredericks at the Banyan Press in 1954.

53   Reed Whittemore: b. 1919. American poet, critic, professor at the University of Maryland.
George Johnston: b. 1913. Canadian poet, professor of English and Old Norse at Carleton University for twenty-nine years until retirement.

54   Mrs. Wix: governess in Henry James's novella *What Maisie Knew*.

55   the "Waldstein" Sonata: piano sonata, op. 53, by Ludwig van Beethoven (1770–1827).
Fauré: Gabriel Fauré (1845–1924). French composer, among whose works are settings of poems by Paul Verlaine (1844–1896).
Duparc: Henri Duparc (1848–1933). French composer whose oeuvre amounts to just thirteen songs.
Albert Samain: 1858–1900. French poet influenced by Charles Baudelaire (1821–1867) and Verlaine.
Leconte de Lisle: 1818–1894. French poet associated with the Parnassians.
De la musique avant toute chose: from Verlaine's poem "Art poétique."

59   *Little Lord Fauntleroy*: popular children's book by Francis Hodgson Burnett (1849–1924), author also of the children's classic *The Secret Garden*.

61   "The essential gaudiness of poetry": Stevens's remark about "The Emperor of Ice Cream" is in a letter to the poet William Rose Benét (1886–1950), January 6, 1933.

62   *An Interview with Ashley Brown*

In a note to this interview's original appearance, Brown mentioned that, at regular intervals during their conversation, he would leave the room and write down what he remembered of JM's answers.

62   George Whicher: George F. Whicher (1889–1954). Professor at Amherst College, literary critic, Emerson scholar, author of *This Was a Poet*, one of the standard critical biographies of Emily Dickinson.

63   G. R. Elliott: George Roy Elliott (1883–1963). Longtime friend of Robert Frost's and his colleague at Amherst, closely associated with the New Humanism, author of *The Cycle of Modern Poetry*.

64   Marjorie Kinnan Rawlings: 1896–1953. Journalist and regional novelist whose works include *The Yearling*, which won a Pulitzer Prize in 1938.

66   Ransom: John Crowe Ransom (1888–1974). American poet, novelist, and influential literary critic closely associated with New Criticism.

67   Katherine Anne Porter: 1890–1980. Pulitzer Prize–winning short story writer and novelist known for the often harsh exactness of her style.
       Anne Meacham: b. 1925. American actress, originator of several roles in plays by Tennessee Williams, and winner of two Best Actress Obie Awards.

68   Those little *données*: cf. Lowell's poems "Mother Marie Therese" and "Falling Asleep over the *Aeneid*," respectively.

69   Ferlinghetti: Lawrence Ferlinghetti (b. 1919). Leading Beat poet and co-founder of City Lights Books in San Francisco.

70   the imagination "pressing back against the pressure of reality": cf. Wallace Stevens, concluding paragraph of "The Noble Rider and the Sound of Words" in *The Necessary Angel*: "[The mind] is a violence from within that protects us from a violence without. It is the imagination pressing back against the pressure of reality." Cf. note to p. 216, and p. 504.

71   An Interview with John Boatwright and Enrique Ucelay DaCal
The interviewers were students at Hotchkiss and Bard. The interview was conducted in 1968 and published in a small interscholastic literary magazine.

72   Donizetti: Gaetano Donizetti (1797–1848). Italian composer.
       Lorca: Federico García Lorca (1898–1936). Spanish playwright and poet (*Romacero Gitano* and other works) whose social realism and leftist sympathies led to his assassination by the Fascists during the Spanish Civil War.
       Brecht: Eugen Berthold Friedrich Brecht (1898–1956). German poet and playwright who wrote (with composer Kurt Weill) the satiric operas *Die Driegroschenoper* and *Aufsteig und Fall der Stadt Mahagonny*. A Marxist, he lived in exile much of his life.
       Robert de Montesquiou: Comte Robert de Montesquiou-Fezensac (1855–1921). French poet and critic renowned for his *dandysme* and "decadence."

73 Dow Chemical man: i.e., recruiter for the chemical company that makes Saran Wrap and produced napalm during the Vietnam War.

74 *On "Yánnina": An Interview with David Kalstone*
This interview, when it first appeared in *Saturday Review,* accompanied by the text of the poem, was entitled "The Poet: Private," and was meant to provide a contrast to an interview with Rod McKuen, called "The Poet: Public." "Yánnina" is in JM's *Collected Poems,* p. 380.

75 William Plomer: 1903–1973. South African-British author of works in many genres, verse to libretti, he wrote *The Diamond of Jannina: Ali Pasha, 1741–1822.*

82 Those lines in Jarrell: JM quotes from "The End of the Rainbow" by American poet Randall Jarrell (1914–1965).

85 *An Interview with Helen Vendler*
When this interview first appeared (as "James Merrill's Myth: An Interview"), Vendler wrote in her brief introduction, "The questions it occurred to me to ask Merrill are those of a reader confronting a poem [*Mirabell: Books of Number*] unquestionably beautiful, but also baffling."

86 *The Lives of a Cell*: collection of essays, which won the National Book Award in 1974, by Lewis Thomas (1913–1993), research pathologist and medical administrator as well as author.

88 Julian Jaynes's book: *The Origin of Consciousness in the Breakdown of the Bicameral Mind.*
The Anathemata: long poem by the British poet and artist David Jones (1895–1974).
John Heath-Stubbs: b. 1918. English poet, editor, translator. His *Artorius* is subtitled *A Heroic Poem in Four Books and Eight Episodes.*

89 Castaneda: Carlos Castaneda (1925?–1998). Peruvian-born anthropologist and author of several perhaps fictional books about a Mexican Yaqui shaman, Don Juan Matus.

90 *An Interview with Ross Labrie*
The interview, originally entitled "James Merrill at Home: An Interview," took place at JM's home in Stonington, Connecticut, on June 13, 1980.

93 a poem that resists the intelligence almost successfully: JM is quoting Wallace Stevens's poem "Man Carrying Thing."

94 *Trovatore*: *Il Trovatore,* opera by Giuseppi Verdi (1813–1901).

95 *The Bacchae*: play by Euripides (c. 480–406 BCE).

97 a mind which "no idea violates": cf. T. S. Eliot on Henry James, in a review of a book by Henry Adams, in the *Little Review*, August 1918.

98 As Yeats said: JM alludes to the last paragraph of "Introduction to *A Vision*."

103 An Interview with J. D. McClatchy
This interview, part of "The Art of Poetry" series in *The Paris Review*, was conducted entirely by correspondence.

106 "You're nothing but a pack of cards!": JM quotes Alice's last words in Wonderland, spoken to the Queen of Hearts and her court, in Lewis Carroll's *Alice's Adventures in Wonderland*.

107 Stephen Orgel: b. 1933. Professor of English at Stanford University, literary critic, editor of many books including *The Complete Masques* of Ben Jonson.

112 As Shaw reminds us: George Bernard Shaw (1856–1950). English dramatist. See especially his preface to *Back to Methuselah: A Metabiological Pentateuch*.

114 eternity . . . the grain of sand: cf. William Blake, "Auguries of Innocence."

115 *Mrs. Wiggs of the Cabbage Patch* . . . out the window: in the children's book by Alice Caldwell Hegan (Rice) (1870–1942), Mrs. Wiggs gets the last word: "Looks like ever'thing in the world comes right, if we jes' wait long enough!" *St. Nicholas Magazine*: cf. JM's remark on p. 195 of this volume. We have been unable to find these lines in the *St. Nicholas Magazine* or any similar publication.

116 Stanford White: 1853–1906. Innovative American architect (a partner in McKim, Mead and White) and bon vivant whose murder and the trial following were among the most sensational events of their time.
a houseguest: Carol Longone, who became JM's childhood piano teacher.
Pagliacci: opera by Italian composer Ruggiero Leoncavallo (1858–1919).

117 Stevens . . . blue and yellow stream: JM quotes, however, not from "Notes toward a Supreme Fiction," but first from "Arrival at the Waldorf" and then from "A Lot of People Bathing in a Stream."

119 Madison Morrison: b. 1940. American writer now living in Asia, professor of English at the University of Oklahoma when JM knew him, who embarked in the 1980s on an epic project entitled *Sentence of the Gods*.

120 Da Ponte: Lorenzo Da Ponte (1749–1839). Italian poet, librettist (for three operas by Mozart), propagator of Italian culture in the United States.

121 Elizabeth's elegy: "North Haven."

123 Empson's famous ones: "Missing Dates" and "Villanelle" by William Empson (1906–1984), English literary critic and poet associated with New Criticism, author of many books, including the influential *Seven Types of Ambiguity*.

Austin Dobson: Henry Austin Dobson (1840–1921). English poet (notable for his light verse) and essayist.

126   An Interview with Jack Stewart
Review is published by the Society for the Fine Arts at the University of Alabama. This interview, conducted by a graduate student there, occurred on June 16, 1982, the morning after JM had given a reading at the university.

128   Victor Hugo transcripts: The French writer (1802–1885), along with others, engaged after 1853 in séances that involved table tapping and resulted in transcripts of communications with "the other world." In the recent edition of Hugo's *Conversations with Eternity* (trans. John Chambers with an introduction by Martin Ebon) there are several references to JM's own experiences.

129   "The only solution is to be very, very intelligent": the original source of the quotation seems to be T. S. Eliot, who wrote in his essay "The Perfect Critic" (*The Sacred Wood: Essays on Poetry and Criticism*), in the course of an appraisal of Aristotle's wider "intelligence," that "the only method is to be very intelligent."

130   "Go, lovely rose": poem by English writer Edmund Waller (1606–1687).

133   T. S. Eliot on Blake's early work: in the essay on Blake in *The Sacred Wood: Essays on Poetry and Criticism*.

134   Henri de Régnier: 1864–1936. French poet, member of Mallarmé's circle.

135   An Interview with Fred Bornhauser
This interview was conducted by correspondence during October 1981. When the interview was reprinted in *Recitative*, JM requested that, because they seemed repetitive, eight of the questions and answers be deleted and four others from the original set, not included in the published version, be restored. The version from *Recitative* is printed here.

136   Cleanth Brooks and Robert Penn Warren: editors of the influential critical anthology *Understanding Poetry* (1938, revised 1950), the cornerstone of New Criticism.
Keats had spoken: in a letter to Shelley, August 16, 1820.

138   E. F. Benson: Edward Frederick Benson (1867–1940). English biographer and novelist, the author of the six *Lucia* novels, collected in *Make Way for Lucia*.

139   Robert Polito . . . little pamphlet: in fact, it became a book (see note to p. 44). C. P. Snow's once-famous theory: cf. Snow's *The Two Cultures and the Scientific Revolution* (1959, revised 1964).

140   As Oscar Wilde said: in *The Critic as Artist*.

142   the *American Heritage Dictionary*: the appendix has since become available as a separate text, *The American Heritage Dictionary of Indo-European Roots*, ed. Calvert Watkins.

144   An Interview with Jordan Pecile

State of the Arts is a publication of the Connecticut Commission on the Arts. JM was appointed the state's first poet laureate in 1986. In an introductory note, the interviewer says: "Probably because he was a little tired of the hullabaloo and spate of gossipy articles that followed his selection as poet laureate, Merrill asked that questions for this interview be mailed to him. So perhaps it is instructive to indicate here the questions he chose not to respond to: questions about the part inspiration plays in writing poems; about personal habits or fetishes to spark the creative process; about whether a writer should be engaged in the social and political issues of his day; and about whether a writing teacher should discourage students with limited talent."

144   "Poems are made with words, not ideas," said Mallarmé to Degas: the exchange is recounted by the French poet Paul Valéry (1871–1945) in his essay "Poésie et pensée abstraite."

146   *Falstaff* or *The Rake's Progress*: operas by Verdi and Russian-born composer Igor Stravinsky (1882–1971), respectively.
Humbert Wolfe: 1885–1940. English poet.

148   "To be twenty and a poet . . ." Who said that?: French painter Eugene Delacroix (1798–1863).

149   three intrepid women: Karen Pennau Fronduti and Ann McGarrell are the Americans and the poet Marcella Massidda is the Italian. The project has since been left for Fronduti to complete. "Book 0" of *Mirabell* has been finished though not yet published.

150   a little play: "The Image Maker," included in JM's *Collected Poems*, pp. 513–26.
a volume of collected prose: *Recitative*, the contents of which are included in this volume.

151   An Interview with Thomas Bolt

The interviewer had been JM's choice for the 1989 Yale Younger Poets series. In his introductory note, Bolt says: "The subject was pursued cross-country for this written interview, by mail, fax machine, and telephone; but since Merrill's manners in his conversational verse and versatile conversation are wonderfully alike, I had no trouble imagining we were sitting down to chat before a quietly uncoiling tape."

151   a memoir of the early 1950s: *A Different Person*, included in this volume.
Kundry . . . Klingsor: characters in Wagner's opera *Parsifal*.

156   A. H. Clarendon: the "saintly human being and a superb hand at [duplicate] bridge" is fictitious, an alter ego for JM. Clarendon is quoted in JM's "The Thousand and Second Night" (*Complete Poems*, p. 176) and section Q of "The Book of Ephraim" (*Sandover*, p. 58).

158 Graves's Triple Goddess: cf. Robert Graves (1895–1985), *The White Goddess*. Ina Claire: 1892–1985. American actress featured in *Ninotchka* and *Claudia*, among other films.

159 Chardin: Jean-Baptiste-Siméon Chardin (1699–1779). French painter. Sesshu: 1420–1506. Japanese ink painter and Zen Buddhist priest.

160 Untermeyer's or Oscar Williams's: Louis Untermeyer, ed., *Modern American Poetry* (first published 1919), and Oscar Williams, ed., *A Little Treasury of Modern Poetry* (1940).
Kimon Friar and John [Malcolm] Brinnin: their anthology is *Modern Poetry: American and British* (1951). Two of JM's early poems, "Foliage of Vision" and "The Black Swan" (*Collected Poems*, pp. 27 and 3, respectively), appear in this volume.

162   An Interview with Augustin Hedberg
The Lawrentian is the alumni magazine of the Lawrenceville School, where JM was a member of the class of 1943. While visiting the campus to receive the Lawrenceville Medal in 1991, he "agreed to answer a few questions relating to his days at the school and the future of poetry."

162 school-of-Burne-Jones: Sir Edward Coley Burne-Jones (1833–1898), painter and designer, member of the Pre-Raphaelite Brotherhood (cf. note to p. 468). Tennyson—like Keats, Shakespeare, and Dante—was a frequent source of inspiration for the PRB, as it called itself.

164 *The Tale of Genji*: a Japanese novel (sometimes thought of as the earliest novel ever) written by Lady Murasaki or Murasaki Shikibu (c. 973–1025), whose real name is uncertain and about whom almost nothing is known.

166   An Interview with Roderick Townley
The Keep is the newsletter of the Writers Place in Kansas City, Missouri. The interview took place by telephone.

167 the memoir I've been working on: *A Different Person*, included in this volume.

170   An Interview with Heather White
This interview was conducted through the mail in the fall of 1993, when *A Different Person* had just been published.

171 Lord Berners: Sir Gerald Hugh Tyr Whitt-Nelson (1883–1950). English dilettante, composer, and the model for the character Lord Merlin in Nancy Mitford's novels.

174   An Interview with Justin Spring
On the occasion of the publication of *A Different Person*, JM gave this interview to the local newspaper in Southampton, New York, where he spent his summers while growing up.

175   Stendahl says: JM refers to the novel by Stendhal (Mari-Henri Beyle, 1782–1842) entitled *Le Rouge et le noir*.
Rosa Ponselle: 1897–1981. American soprano.

176   a new family friend: Carol Longone.

WRITERS

183   Divine Poem

This review of Allen Mandelbaum's translation of Dante's *Inferno* first appeared in *The New Republic* and was later revised slightly for its appearance in *Recitative*. That latter version appears here.

184   Paulus Orosius: Christian apologist and historian (fl. fourth century) who worked with St. Augustine in North Africa and St. Jerome in Palestine and wrote the first Christian universal history, *Historiarum adversus peaganos libri septem*.
the *Voyage of St. Brendan*: the Irish monk St. Brendan of Ardfert and Clonfert (484–587) is said to have made a seven-year voyage to the Land of Delight or the Promised Land, chronicled in the various *Navigatio Brendani*, which might or might not have historical foundations.
Ibn Arabi: Muhyaddin Ibn ʿArabi (1165–1240). Sufi mystic and prolific author of writings on Islam.
Irma Brandeis's *The Ladder of Vision*: A study of Dante. Cf. note to p. 222.

185   Akhmatova: Anna Akhmatova (1889–1966). Russian poet. JM refers to her short poem "Dante."

188   *Adventures of a Hole*: cf. Peter Newell, *The Hole Book*, first published 1908.

190   those sonnets to Forese: Dante and Forese Donati (d. 1296), his friend and relative by marriage, exchanged sonnets of insult *(tenzone)* in their youth. Forese appears in *Purgatorio*, Canto XXIII.
the Malebolge: The eighth circle of Dante's *Inferno*, Canto XVIII.
the Jongleur de Notre-Dame: title role in the opera by French composer Jules Massenet (1842–1912).

193   Unreal Citizen

Originally published under the title "Marvelous Poet," this was a review of *Cavafy: A Critical Biography* by Robert Liddell and *C. P. Cavafy: Collected Poems*, trans. by Edmund Keeley and Philip Sherrard, ed. George Savidis. "Unreal Citizen," the title on JM's manuscript, must derive from Robert Liddell's fictional account of Cavafy in his book about Alexandria, *Unreal City*, which takes its title from T. S. Eliot (*The Waste Land*, l.60), who in turn referred his reader to Baudelaire's "cité pleine de rêves" (in "Les Sept Vieillards").

Constantine Cavafy (1863–1933), the Greek (or "Hellenic," to use the term he preferred) early modernist, born in Alexandria, was the first poet to write seriously in a mixture of demotic Greek and *katherevousa,* and that he often wrote about explicitly homoerotic subjects and about the Hellenistic era makes him all the more remarkable. Thanks to E. M. Forster (in *Pharos and Pharillon,* 1923), Lawrence Durrell (*The Alexandria Quartet,* 1957–1960), W. H. Auden (introduction to Rae Dalven's translations, *The Complete Poems of Cavafy,* 1961), and such fine translators as Keeley and Sherrard, Cavafy, whose works were not published in a book in his lifetime, has been influential in English and American letters at least as long as he has been a major figure in Greek literature. Liddell's dedication to his book reads *"à Bernard de Zogheb et aux autres amis alexandrins."* On Bernard de Zogheb, JM's friend, see the note to p. 357. (JM's translations of three poems by Cavafy and his poem "After Cavafy" appear in the *Collected Poems,* pp. 801–804 and 853, respectively.)

197　the German baron who spent his adult life in Taormina: Wilhelm von Gloeden (1856–1931), who took such photographs in the 1880s, and sold copies profitably by mail order.
　　Casca: in Shakespeare's *Julius Caesar.*

198　Stratis Tsirkas: 1911–1980. Greek novelist, born in Egypt, best known in the English-speaking world as the author of the trilogy *Drifting Cities.*

200　Marguerite Yourcenar: 1903–1987. Franco-Belgian novelist, essayist, translator, the first woman elected to the Académie Française, author of *Présentation critique de Constantin Cavafy.*
　　Agostinelli: Alfredo Agostinelli (1887–1914). Marcel Proust's chauffeur, secretary, and lover on numerous excursions in Normandy, which inspired the "Impressions de route en automobile," published in *Le Figaro.*

207　Object Lessons
Francis Ponge (1899–1988), a major midcentury French poet, resisted fashionable trends and concentrated his poetic attention on the assiduous, clarifying description of quotidian objects. JM's essay was a review of two selections of Ponge's work: *The Voice of Things,* translated by Beth Archer Brombert, and *Things,* translated and selected by Cid Corman.

207　René Char: 1907–1988. French poet.
　　Rameau: Jean-Philippe Rameau (1683–1764). French musicologist and composer.

208　Gautier: Théophile Gautier (1811–1872). French poet, critic, novelist, and journalist.
　　Michaux: Henri Michaux (1899–1984). Franco-Belgian artist, writer of diverse experimental prose, documenter of drug experience.

210　"There is no wing like meaning": Wallace Stevens, "Adagia" in *Opus Posthumous.*

216   On Wallace Stevens's Centenary

On April 18, 1979, JM gave a poetry reading at the University of Connecticut at Storrs as part of its celebration of the centennial of Wallace Stevens (1879–1955). He was asked to open with some words about what the example of Stevens had meant to his own work. "The Green Eye" originally appeared in *First Poems* (1951), "Charles on Fire" in *Nights and Days* (1966); both poems can now be found in JM's *Collected Poems* (pp. 5 and 195, respectively). On October 2, 1954—Stevens's seventy-fifth birthday and the publication day of his *Collected Poems*—his publisher, Alfred Knopf, held a luncheon in Manhattan for seventy-five guests to celebrate the occasion. One of those guests was JM, then the house's promising young poet. He was seated at the head table with the guest of honor. A couple of months later Stevens wrote to his old friend Witter Bynner about the party: "There were a lot of people there whom you would have enjoyed quite as much as I did, including young James Merrill, who is about the age which you and I were when we were in New York."

216   elephants in Ceylon: JM has in mind a stanza in part V of "It Must Be Abstract" in "Notes toward a Supreme Fiction."

218   poor Fräulein von Kulp, frozen forever: in Eliot's poem "Gerontion."
John Adams wound like a mummy: in Pound's *Cantos LXII–LXXI.*
Vuillard: Edouard Vuillard (1868–1940). French postimpressionist painter.

219   Theatre / Of Trope: JM quotes "Notes toward a Supreme Fiction," the tenth section of "It Must Change."
"like a French translation of a Russian poet": in Stevens's "Variations on a Summer Day," XI.

220   On "The Love Song of J. Alfred Prufrock"

As part of the Centennial Conference on T. S. Eliot (1888–1965) held at Washington University in St. Louis, Missouri, in September 1988, several poets were asked to read an Eliot poem and preface it with some remarks. The poets were Amy Clampitt, Anthony Hecht, Gjertrud Schnackenberg, Richard Wilbur, and JM. His reading of "The Love Song of J. Alfred Prufrock" is included in the audiobook *The Classic Hundred Poems*, ed. William Harmon (Columbia University Press, 1998; HBP 59239, CD five).

221   Mrs. Willy Loman's words: in *Death of a Salesman*, the play by American writer Arthur Miller (b.1915), Linda Loman's judgment is that "Attention— attention must finally be paid to such a man."

222   On Montale's "Mottetti VII"

For a special issue of *Field* devoted to "Poets Reading," JM provided this brief commentary on one of Italian poet Eugenio Montale's *Motets*. The translation he cited was by his friend Irma Brandeis (1905–1990), herself an important figure in Montale's life and imagination, the dedicatee of JM's "The Thousand and Second Night" (*Collected Poems*, p. 176) and the "muse" of his "Syrinx" (*Collected Poems*, p. 355). Montale (1896–1981) was awarded the Nobel Prize in 1975.

224   Foreword to Nineteen Poems

Robert Morse (1906–1976) was JM's Stonington neighbor and friend. He and his wife Isabel are two of the dedicatees of *Water Street,* as well as models for characters in "The Summer People" (*Collected Poems,* p. 272). He also figures prominently in "The Higher Keys," the coda of *The Changing Light at Sandover.* After Morse's death, JM had this small edition of his poems printed for his family and friends.

224   Joseph Cotton: undersecretary of state for President Herbert Hoover.
the "Dolly" Suite: op. 246 by Fauré.
Pulcinella: suite by Stravinsky, based on music in his 1919 ballet.

225   Eileen Garrett: 1893–1970. Irish-born medium and author of several books including the autobiography *The Skeptical Medium.*

227   Hugh Kenner: cf. Kenner's book *The Pound Era,* especially pp. 76–191, where the idea that "words exchange dynamisms in the ecology of language" is a motif.

229   On Elizabeth Bishop

The newsletter of the Academy of American Poets asked JM to choose several poems by Elizabeth Bishop for a memorial issue, and to add a few words about her.

231   Elizabeth Bishop (1911–1979)

Elizabeth Bishop had died on October 6, 1979, and this elegiac memoir was written soon afterward.

231   Charles Olson: 1910–1970. American poet, leader of the Black Mountain poets. Robert Duncan: 1919–1988. American poet. Because he was always associated with the avant-garde (the New York circle of Anaïs Nin and Henry Miller; the San Francisco Renaissance; and Black Mountain College), to have initiated him in this respect might seem a coup.

232   Frank Bidart: b. 1939. American poet, longtime friend also of Robert Lowell (cf. note to p. 243), whose *Collected Poems* he has co-edited with David Gewanter. that early prose piece: Bishop's story "In Prison."

233   The young painter: José Alberto Nemer, Linda Nemer's brother.

234   The Transparent Eye

Published first under the title "The Clear Eye of Elizabeth Bishop," this essay was a review of her posthumous *The Complete Poems 1927–1979.* When it was reprinted in *Recitative,* JM asked that its brief discussion of the poem "Exchanging Hats" be deleted because it is substantially repeated in "A Class Day Talk" (pp. 350–56 in this volume). That later version is printed here.

234   Mary McCarthy: see note to p. 260.
Eleanor Clark: 1913–1996. American writer, author of *Rome and a Villa,* the National Book Award–winning *The Oysters of Locmariaquer,* and novels including *Baldur's Gate.* Married to the American man of letters Robert Penn Warren.

237 in the early 1950s: in fact, Pound was in St. Elizabeths from 1946 until 1958.

241 *624 White Street*
At a ceremony on January 4, 1993, sponsored by the Florida Center for the Book, a literary landmark plaque was unveiled on the house in Key West where Elizabeth Bishop lived from 1938 to 1946. JM was the speaker at the event.

243 *Memories of Elizabeth Bishop*
For this composite oral biography of Bishop, JM was interviewed by Peter Brazeau on May 10, 1984, at his Stonington home.

243 Joe Summers and his wife, U. T.: Joseph Summers (1919–2003), professor at the University of Rochester and an authority on George Herbert and John Milton; and U. T. Miller Summers, writer and professor at the Rochester Institute of Technology.
Cal Lowell: Robert Lowell (1917–1977). American poet (cf. note p. 256).
Lizzie Hardwick: Elizabeth Hardwick (b. 1916). American novelist and journalist, Lowell's second wife.

244 Linda Nemer: b. 1931. Friend of Bishop's when the latter lived in Ouro Prêto, Brazil.
Lota: Lota de Macedo Soares (1910?–1967). Brazilian architect, political activist, and Elizabeth Bishop's lover during her years in Brazil.

245 a little tin stove: Bishop's painting of this stove or one very like it appears on the cover of her posthumous book of watercolors, *Exchanging Hats.*

246 Jane Carlyle: Jane Welsh Carlyle (1801–1866). Scottish wife of the Victorian man of letters Thomas Carlyle (1795–1881) and famously witty hostess whose letters have been published with those of her husband.
George Jackson: 1941–1971. African-American radical who spent most of the last half of his life in prison, where he founded the Black Guerilla Family, wrote *Soledad Brother: The Letters of George Jackson from Prison*, and was killed in an attempt to escape.
Lady Mary Wortley Montagu: 1689–1762. English poet, prose writer, and feminist, first a friend and then an archenemy of Alexander Pope, and author of *Embassy Letters*, much admired by Samuel Johnson, Edward Gibbon, and other readers ever since their publication at the end of her life.

247 *Afterword to* Becoming a Poet
When he died in 1986, David Kalstone had in manuscript the bulk of a study of contemporary poetry he had been working on for some years. Robert Hemenway was then asked (by Kalstone's literary executors, JM and Richard Poirier) to edit the manuscript, filling in gaps, narrowing the focus, polishing the drafts. See note to p. 364.

251 whose island leaves not a wrack behind: cf. Shakespeare, *The Tempest* (IV.i.146ff).

256   Cal: his friends' nickname for Robert Lowell (see note to p. 243).

258   Memories of Truman Capote

Truman Capote (1924–1984), American writer (*Breakfast at Tiffany's* and *In Cold Blood*), rented a house in Stonington for the summer of 1956, a time that JM recalls for this oral biography of the novelist.

258   Jack Dunphy: 1915–1992. American novelist and memoirist (*Dear Genius: A Memoir of My Life with Truman Capote*), Truman Capote's companion of thirty-five years.

260   Memories of Mary McCarthy

Mary McCarthy (1912–1989), the novelist and critic, was a friend of JM's and David Jackson's. In fact, they loaned their Stonington house to McCarthy and James West for their honeymoon. Throughout Kiernan's biography, direct excerpts from transcribed interviews are tipped into the narrative. JM's memories begin with the award to McCarthy of the 1984 MacDowell Colony Medal, presented by her old friend and Castine, Maine, neighbor Elizabeth Hardwick. He next moves to her teaching at Bard, beginning in 1945. Then follow comments on her novels, her personality, and her dispute with Lillian Hellman. On McCarthy's *Memories of a Catholic Girlhood*, cf. p. 177.

260   Lizzie: Elizabeth Hardwick (see note p. 243).

261   Eleanor Perényi: b. 1918. JM's Stonington neighbor, author of *Green Thoughts: A Writer in the Garden*, *Liszt: The Artist as Romantic Hero*, and other prose works.
       that woman who married Gorky: in 1941 Agnes Magruder, a twenty-year-old New England socialite, married Arshile Gorky (1904–1948), the Armenian-born painter who lived mostly in the United States, and separated from him five years later, two years before he committed suicide.
       Jim: James Raymond West (1914–1999). Mary McCarthy's fourth husband.
       Bowden: Bowden Broadwater (b. 1926). Mary McCarthy's third husband.
       Grace: Grace Zaring Stone (1891–1991). JM's Stonington neighbor, novelist, Eleanor Perényi's mother and like her one of the four dedicatees of JM's *Water Street* (1962).
       Harry and Elizabeth Ford: JM's friend and editor at Atheneum and Alfred A. Knopf (1919–1999) and his first wife.

262   Hellman's writing: Lillian Hellman (1905–1984), American memoirist and playwright whose work included *The Little Foxes* and *The Children's Hour*. Her long quarrel with McCarthy was itself the subject of several literary works.
       My little foundation: the Ingram Merrill Foundation.

263   Introducing Richard Wilbur

On December 7, 1989, Richard Wilbur (b. 1921) read at the Pierpont Morgan Library in New York City. The occasion was the annual invitational poetry reading sponsored by the Academy of American Poets. JM introduced Wilbur, one of his oldest friends.

266   Howard Moss

For its forty-fifth edition, published February 28, 1992, *Collier's Encyclopedia* had commissioned JM to write about the poet Howard Moss (1922–1987), longtime friend and poetry editor of the *New Yorker*.

268   On W. S. Merwin

Remarks written for delivery on September 29, 1994, at a ceremony in the Library of Congress where the first Tanning Prize (now the Wallace Stevens Award) for mastery in the art of poetry was presented to W. S. Merwin (b. 1927). The occasion was part of the sixtieth-anniversary celebration of the Academy of American Poets, one of whose chancellors JM then was. JM had served as a judge of the award, along with Carolyn Kizer and J. D. McClatchy, but was unable to attend the ceremony.

270   Preface to Burning the Knife

Poet and prose writer Robin Magowan (b. 1936) is JM's nephew. This preface to an edition of his selected poems was dated March 31, 1984.

271   "Vissi d'amore, vissi del viaggio": allusion to the heroine's aria in *Tosca*, Act II, "Vissi d'arte, vissi d'amore," by Italian composer Giacomo Puccini (1858–1924).

271   Robert Bagg: A Postscript

Robert Bagg (b. 1935), poet and translator, was an undergraduate at Amherst while JM was teaching there. A review by Ralph J. Mills of his first book of poems, *The Madonna of the Cello*, as well as a book of poems by Alan Dugan, appeared in *Poetry*, accompanied in the same issue by this response.

272   Yeats's "vast labyrinth": cf. the "great labyrinth" at the end of section II of the poem "The Tower" by W. B. Yeats (1865–1939).
Donne's roving hands: in the poem "To His Mistris Going to Bed" by John Donne (1572–1631).
Baudelaire's "La douceur qui fascine": in the poem "A une passante."

274   The Relic, Promises, and Poems

This is a review of four collections: *The Relic and Other Poems* by Robert Hillyer, *Promises* by Robert Penn Warren, *Poems 1947–1957* by William Jay Smith, and *The Open Sea and Other Poems* by William Meredith. The editor of *Voices*, poet Harold ("Beauty hurts, Mister") Vinal had asked JM to be guest editor for the issue. Having assembled the contents and sent them to Vinal—who then refused to print a poem by Robert Bagg because it used the word "urine"—JM demanded in protest that he be listed merely as "Editorial Assistant" on the issue's masthead.

275   Walker Gibson: William Walker Gibson (b. 1919). Rhetorician, critic, poet, a teacher of JM's at Amherst.

279   Gérard de Nerval: 1808–1855. French poet with an oneiric sensibility.

THE YALE YOUNGER POETS

The Yale Series of Younger Poets was begun by Yale University Press in 1919 and has ever since been a prestigious poetry competition in this country. Manuscripts are accepted from poets under forty who have not yet published a book; those manuscripts are vetted by in-house readers, and a dozen or so finalists are sent on to the presiding judge who then selects and introduces the year's winning volume. JM served from 1983 until 1989. He was the eleventh judge in the series; he followed Richard Hugo and was succeeded by James Dickey.

287 *Foreword to* The Evolution of the Flightless Bird

289 word golf: Nabokov's term for the word game invented by Lewis Carroll, who called it "doublets," exemplified in Nabokov's novel *Pale Fire* and here in Kenney's poem.
Bachelard: Gaston Bachelard (1884–1962). French philosopher, author of *La Poétique de la reverie*.

291 *Foreword to* Navigable Waterways

292 God Lurks in the Details: often attributed to architect Mies van der Rohe, this maxim is also credited to German scholar Aby Warburg (1866-1929), who founded the Warburg Institute, a school for the advanced study of the classical tradition, now housed in the University of London. Its distinguished scholars have included Gertrud Bing, E. H. Gombrich, and Francis A. Yates. Cf. p. 136.

297 *Foreword to* Terms to Be Met

300 Camus: Albert Camus (1913–1960). French novelist and existentialist philosopher. JM is quoting an entry near the end of Camus's *Carnets 1935–1942* (translated under the title *Notebooks 1935–1942*), April 1939–February 1942.

307 *Foreword to* To the Place of Trumpets

307 "Man is only man superficially": JM is quoting Paul Valéry: "L'homme n'est l'homme qu'à surface. Lève la peau, dissèque: ici commencement les machines. Puis, tu te perds dans une substance inexplicable, étrangère à tout ce qui tu sais et qui est pourtant l'essentielle" (*Homo* section of the Pleiade ed. of the *Cahiers*, vol. II).

312 *Foreword to* Out of the Woods

313 another poet: perhaps an enthusiast of T. S. Eliot's *The Waste Land*.

316 *Foreword to* Hermit with Landscape

316 Richard Howard: b. 1929. American poet, translator, critic, and poetry editor. Chamfort: see p. 411 and note.

318 Satie: Erik Satie (1866–1925). French composer.

OCCASIONS

323   The Beaten Path
JM and David Jackson went to the Far East in the fall of 1956, the first leg of a nearly yearlong around-the-world trip. In lieu of travel diaries they kept carbons of their letters home. These impressions—all but the poem—were worked up by JM from letters at the request of John Bernard Myers, the editor of *Semi-Colon* (cf. note to p. 367).

330   Congreve: William Congreve (1670–1729). English playwright, notably of comedies of manners, including *The Way of the World*.
Couperin: François Couperin (1668–1733). French composer chiefly of music for harpsichord.
Borromini: Francesco Borromini (1599–1667). Italian architect of the baroque era.
Gaudí: Antoni Gaudí i Cornet (1852–1926). Spanish architect and designer, pioneer of art nouveau.

332   Garlic Soup
The publication of this recipe in volume 8 of the magazine *Contact* was a prelude to the appearance in October 1961 of the book *The Artists' and Writers' Cookbook*, eds. Beryl Barr and Barbara Turner Sachs (Sausalito, California: Contact Editions), with a foreword by Alice B. Toklas, and dedicated "to the art of imperfection in the kitchen." Other contributors included Man Ray, Lawrence Durrell, Katherine Anne Porter, Lillian Hellman, Caresse Crosby, Isak Dinesen, Marcel Duchamp, Georges Simenon, Anthony Powell, Richard Wilbur, Upton Sinclair, Harper Lee, Marcel Pagnol, and Marianne Moore.

In her 1958 cookbook, *Aromas and Flavors of Past and Present*, Alice B. Toklas includes a recipe for "Shrimps with Oranges à la James Merril [sic]." In *A Different Person*, he recalls a dinner he served to his father and Umberto Morra with "an appetizer of shrimp with orange-garlic sauce, in whose polite rejection, if in nothing else, they were unanimous. (Alice put it in one of her cookbooks, though; to my recipe she suggested adding, before serving, a tablespoon of warmed curaçao.)" JM contributed a recipe for tsatziki, the Greek dip made chiefly of yogurt and cucumber, to *Food in Vogue*, ed. Maxime de La Falaise (1980).

334   Notes on Corot
JM's friend John Maxon had recently been appointed curator of paintings at the Art Institute and had requested this essay for the catalogue to accompany the October 6–November 13 exhibition of paintings and graphic works by French artist Jean-Baptiste-Camille Corot (1796–1875).

335   Rousseau: Jean-Jacques Rousseau (1712–1778). Prolific French man of letters whose work famously endorses the natural in contradistinction to the civilized.
Chateaubriand: François-René, Vicomte de Chateaubriand (1768–1848). French romantic author.

Claude: Claude Lorrain (1600–1682). French classical landscape painter.
Poussin: Nicolas Poussin (1594–1665). French painter associated with the classical style.

337   Arkel to Mélisande: characters in Debussy's opera *Pelléas et Mélisande*.
L'Arlésienne: painting by Van Gogh.

338   Bougival: cf. Renoir's painting *Bal à Bougival*.
Barbizon: a town in France, eponymous center of the mid-nineteenth-century school of landscape painters.

340   Hubert Robert: 1733–1808. French painter associated with the rococo style.
Watteau: Jean Antoine Watteau (1684–1721). French painter associated with the rococo and known especially for his *fêtes galantes*.

341   Millet's peasant scenes: the paintings of Jean-François Millet (1814–1875) are often thought of as social realism.

342   *Ten More*

For a special issue of *Intransit* ("The Andy Warhol–Gerard Malanga Monster Issue"), published by Toad Press in Eugene, Oregon, editor Gerard Malanga had written to JM requesting a contribution. "I seem not to have much on hand this season," JM replied from Athens, on April 27, 1966. "Here is something from a few years ago." JM's manuscript is dated 1959. Among the more than one hundred contributors to the issue were John Ashbery, Charles Henri Ford, Jean Garrigue, Allen Ginsberg, John Hollander, Howard Moss, Phil Ochs, Lou Reed, May Swenson, and John Wieners.

344   *Yannis Tsarouchis*

Found among JM's papers, and now in the Merrill archive at the Beinecke Library at Yale, this appreciation seems never to have been published, and probably dates from the mid-1960s. Yannis Tsarouchis (1910–1989) is generally considered one of the greatest and most popular painters in modern Greece. JM owned one of his prints, a portrait of a sailor, which hung in his dining room in Stonington.

346   *Acceptance Speech, National Book Awards, 1967*

The award was made to JM's *Nights and Days* by judges W. H. Auden, James Dickey, and Howard Nemerov. The ceremony took place in New York City, at Lincoln Center's Philharmonic Hall, on March 8, 1967. The citation read: "The 1967 National Book Award in Poetry is awarded to *Nights and Days* by James Merrill, for his scrupulous and uncompromising cultivation of the poetic art, evidenced in his refusal to settle for an easy and profitable stance; for his insistence on taking the kind of tough, poetic chances which make the difference between aesthetic success or failure." The other books nominated for the poetry award were John Ashbery's *Rivers and Mountains*, Barbara Howes's *Looking Up at Leaves*, Marianne Moore's *Tell Me, Tell Me*, Adrienne Rich's *Necessities of Life*, and William Jay Smith's *The Tin Can and Other Poems*.

348   Acceptance Speech, National Book Awards, 1979
The award was made to JM's *Mirabell: Books of Number* by judges Elizabeth Bishop,
Michael S. Harper, and Anthony Hecht. The ceremony took place on April 25, 1979,
at Carnegie Hall in New York City. The citation, written by Hecht, read: *"Mirabell:
Books of Number*, by James Merrill, is the second volume of a work in progress that
is nothing less than monumental in scale and invention. It is without precedent in
the poetry of our century, for though large-scale works have been attempted before, none
has shown the architectural and formal coherence of Merrill's. It is a work profoundly
serious, resolutely comic, a visionary linking not only of this world and the next but of
particle physics, evolutionary science, and the generations of the soul. It is a vast poem
crammed with imaginative riches and a warmth of personal affection. It is, quite simply,
without match." The other books nominated were Robert Hayden's *American Journal*,
John Hollander's *Spectral Emanations*, Sandra McPherson's *The Year of Our Birth*, Philip
Schultz's *Like Wings*, and May Swenson's *New & Selected Things Taking Place*.

350   A Class Day Talk
JM had been invited by the graduating class of 1980 to give the annual Class Day talk.
JM's connections with the college are close: he graduated from Amherst in 1947 (the college his father also attended), he taught there in 1955–1956, and he was awarded an honorary degree in 1968. He was honored by the college in a symposium in 2004, which
celebrated the acquisition of his letters to the American poet and translator William Burford (b. 1927).

350   "If they tried rhomboids . . .": Wallace Stevens, "Six Significant Landscapes."

351   "aigrette of vertigo": i.e., "aigrette de vertige" in Mallarmé's "Un coup de
dés."
our late President Cole: Charles W. Cole (1906–1978), president of Amherst
from 1946 until 1960.

353   "new, tender, quick": Bishop was quoting the last words of George Herbert's
"Love-unknowne." JM quotes the same phrase at the end of the Wallace
Stevens segment in the *Voices and Visions* program videotaped for television
(Annenberg/CPB, 1988).

357   Foreword to Le Sorelle Brontë
One of the home entertainments concocted by the Alexandrian artist and writer Bernard de
Zogheb (1924–1999) to amuse his first American friends, *Le Sorelle Brontë* was often performed by The Little Players at their private puppet theater in New York City. Whenever
they performed this "opera," or others by de Zogheb (notably *Vacanze a Parigi* and *Phae-
dra*), a variant of JM's essay served as a program note.

358   "La Fille du Bédouin": a *chanson paillarde*, a bawdy popular French song ("La
fille du Bédouin / se branlait dans un coin / avec une banane, / et moi dans
l'autre coin, / en voyant son vagin, / je bandais comme un ane . . .").

360 *Ravel's* Mother Goose

Summer Music, an annual outdoor music festival in Waterford, Connecticut, commissioned JM to write and perform a text to accompany Maurice Ravel's *Mother Goose* Suite. The concert, called "A Touch of the Poet," took place on August 1, 1987, in Harkness Memorial State Park; the Harkness Festival Orchestra was conducted by Peter Sacco. Maurice Ravel (1875–1937) first wrote his *Ma mère l'oye* as a suite of piano duets for the two children of his friend Cipa Godebski between 1908 and 1910. His publisher thought they should be orchestrated for a ballet score, and the composer produced a revised version in 1911. Following a prelude, there are five movements and a finale. For this concert, the order of the movements was as follows:

Pavane de la Belle au bois dormant

Petit Poucet

Laideronnette, impératrice des pagodes

Les Entretiens de la Belle et de la Bête

Le Jardin féerique.

362 *Barbara Kassel*

JM's appreciation appeared in a catalogue accompanying an exhibition of paintings by Barbara Kassel (b. 1952) held at the Maxwell Davidson Gallery in Manhattan April 28–May 30, 1987. JM owned work by Kassell, and one of her paintings appears on the cover of his 1988 collection *The Inner Room*.

363 The author of *Invisible Cities*: Italo Calvino (cf. note to p. 15).

364 *Memorial Tribute to David Kalstone*

David Kalstone (1932–1986) was a literary critic and professor at Rutgers University, the author of *Five Temperaments*, which includes a chapter on JM. He was also one of JM's closest friends and readers, and makes his first appearance in a JM poem as "caro" in "Matinées" (*Collected Poems*, p. 267). The memorial ceremony in his honor took place on September 20, 1986, at the New York Public Library. The speakers were J. D. McClatchy, Richard Poirier, Maxine Groffsky, Edmund White, Charles Kalstone, Alfred Corn, and JM. Their remarks were later privately printed as a chapbook for distribution to Kalstone's friends. Kalstone's death figured in several poems by JM of this period, including "Investiture at Cecconi's," "Farewell Performance," and "Prose of Departure" (*Collected Poems*, pp. 580, 581, and 541, respectively).

364 Maxine Groffsky: b. 1936. New York literary agent.

Win Knowlton: Winthrop Knowlton (b. 1930). Author, investment banker, former president of the New York City Ballet and former chairman of Harper & Row, husband of Maxine Groffsky.

George Smith: American businessman, long a resident of Italy and a member of David Kalstone's summer circle of friends in Venice.

365   David's edition of Sidney: Sir Philip Sidney's *Selected Prose and Poetry*, edited by Kalstone, who was also the author of *Sidney's Poetry*. See also JM's essay "Afterword to *Becoming a Poet*," pp. 247–57 in this volume.

367   *Memorial Tribute to John Bernard Myers*

John Bernard Myers (1919–1987), who first met JM in 1949, was an art dealer and critic, editor and publisher of little magazines and chapbooks, theater producer and puppeteer. He and his lover, director Herbert Machiz, had an important role in the production of JM's plays. Myers's book of memoirs, *Tracking the Marvelous* (1983), is dedicated to JM. A memorial service was held for him at the Grey Art Gallery in New York City on October 15, 1987. The speakers were Thomas Sokolowski, Hilton Kramer, Grace Hartigan, and JM. Their remarks were printed in a chapbook published by Sea Cliff Press in 1988 for distribution to Myers's friends.

367   Alan Ansen: b. 1922. American poet associated with the Beats, friend of W. H. Auden's as well as JM's, author of *Contact Highs: Selected Poems 1957–1987*.

369   *Memorial Tribute to Irma Brandeis*

JM spoke at a memorial service for Irma Brandeis (1905–1990) on March 14, 1990. The service was held in the Chapel of the Holy Innocents at Bard College, where she had been on the faculty from 1944 until 1969 and where she continued to teach and assist on an interim basis after her retirement. (JM's poem "Syrinx" is in the *Collected Poems*, p. 355.)

371   *A Tribute to Marie Bullock*

On September 30, 1980, at New York University's Tishman Auditorium, JM gave the Marie Bullock Poetry Reading for the Academy of American Poets. Before reading his own poems, JM offered this tribute to Marie Bullock (1911–1986), who had founded the academy in 1934 and, until her death, had served as its president. *Poetry Pilot* was the academy's newsletter.

372   *M. F. K. Fisher (1908–1992)*

Memorial tributes to recently deceased members of The American Academy of Arts and Letters are written and read by fellow members at private academy meetings. This tribute to Fisher, written by JM, was delivered by William Gaddis on November 4, 1992.

374   *Memorial Tribute to John Hersey*

Novelist John Hersey (1914–1993) was JM's friend and Key West neighbor. At a gathering to inter his ashes at the West Chop Village Cemetery in Vineyard Haven, Massachusetts, on June 19, 1993, JM spoke—along with several of Hersey's children, and Virginia Mazer, Jules Feiffer, Felicia Kaplan, Robert Brustein, Margaret Lang, Daniel Mueller, and Peter Feibleman. A booklet containing the speeches was later printed for distribution to Hersey's friends.

376   Patmos

This portfolio was printed in an edition of one hundred copies on the occasion of David Jackson's seventy-second birthday. It reproduces fourteen drawings and watercolors by Jackson, each accompanied by a text, either by JM or Jackson. JM's contributions include reprintings of his poems "Manos Karastefanís" and "David's Watercolor" (*Collected Poems*, pp. 379 and 503, respectively), excerpts from "Words for Maria" and "Bronze" (*Collected Poems*, pp. 235 and 449, respectively), and an excerpt from his novel *The (Diblos) Notebook*. "Patmos" is the only original selection.

STORIES

381   Rose

The story was written in 1946 and appeared three years later in *Glass Hill*, a mimeographed literary magazine published in Buffalo. The issue also had contributions from Richard Wilbur, John Frederick Nims, Paul Fussell, Byron Vazakas, and James Schevill.

385   Driver

392   "And if thy mistress": Muriel read from John Keats's "Ode on Melancholy."

401   Peru: The Landscape Game

JM was to accompany his brother and sister-in-law to Machu Picchu and wrote this story before embarking.

401   the Offenbach score: of *La Périchole,* operetta by Franco-German composer Jacques Offenbach (1819–1890).

404   sentence from Prescott: William Hickling Prescott (1796–1859), author of *History of the Conquest of Peru.*

406   the *Nuits d'été*: song sequence composed by French composer Hector Berlioz (1803–1869) based on texts by Gautier (cf. note to p. 208).

TRANSLATIONS

411   Selections from Chamfort

Sebastien-Roch-Nicolas Chamfort (1741–1794), French wit, aphorist, and man of letters, was the son of a provincial grocer. The charm of his ironic conversation helped him rise in society and enter the court. He wrote comedies, criticism, and poems, but it was his *Maximes et pensées* that secured his fame. Along with La Rochefoucauld's, his adages are the most brilliant and audacious of the era. After the Revolution (he was among the first to storm the Bastille), his famous tongue caused him political trouble; having once been arrested, he determined to commit suicide rather than be confined again. His final witticism is among his most renowned: "Je m'en vais enfin de ce monde où il faut que le coeur se brise ou se bronze." JM's translations appeared in the first issue of *Semi-Colon*, along with work by John Ashbery, Frank O'Hara, Harold Rosenberg, Edwin Denby, and Paul Goodman.

411   Coypel: Charles-Antoine Coypel (1694–1752). French painter, First Painter to the King.

412   Fontenelle: Bernard le Bovier de Fontenelle (1657–1757). French philosopher and mathematician.

413   *C. P. Cavafy, "In Broad Daylight"*
See earlier note to "Unreal Citizen," pp. 193–206. This short story is the only one Cavafy wrote.

421   *Vassílis Vassilikos, "The Three T's"*
In the acknowledgments included in the 1968 English translation (by Marilyn Calmann) of his best-known novel, *Z* (written in Greek and first published in 1966), Vassílis Vassilikos (cf. note to p. 43) thanks JM (along with Mary Manheim, Mary McCarthy, Joseph Frank, and Ralph Manheim) for "inestimable help with the English version of my book."

JUVENILIA

429   *Madonna*
Reprinted in *Jim's Book* (1942).

430   the Happy Shade from *Orfeo*: i.e., *Orfeo ed Euridice* (Act II), opera by German composer Christoph Willibald Gluck (1714–1787).

435   *Angel or Earthly Creature*
Reprinted in *Jim's Book*. In later years, JM often singled out Elinor Wylie as a strong influence on his early poetry. JM's own footnotes appear at the bottoms of the pages.

446   *Undergraduate Comment*
JM, class of '47, contributed this comment to an issue largely devoted to articles about the effect of war on Amherst undergraduate life. Articles about the Civil War and World War I precede JM's account of the campus in the midst of World War II.

446   Winter being necessarily the season of intellectuality: JM is paraphrasing a passage from Mallarmé's "Réponses a des enquêtes" (*Echo de Paris*, March 24, 1891) that he quotes in the French as an epigraph to his poem "The Summer People" (*Collected Poems*, p. 272).

449   *The Transformation of Rilke*

449   George: Stefan George (1868–1933). German poet. George made it a point not to capitalize nouns in his verse.

454   C. M. Bowra: Cecil Maurice Bowra (1898–1971). English classical scholar and literary critic, whose chapter on Rilke appears in *The Heritage of Symbolism* (1943).

Miss Butler: Eliza (Elsie) Marian Butler (1885–1959). Irish-born scholar of German studies whose *Rainer Maria Rilke* (1941) was the first biography of the poet.

Rilke's epitaph: As a whole, it reads, "Rose, oh reiner Widerspruch, Lust, / Niemandes Schlaf zu sein unter soviel Lidern."

455   Eliot's phrase: in the last verse paragraph of "Little Gidding" in *Four Quartets*.

A DIFFERENT PERSON: A MEMOIR (1993)

460   two older children: Charles E. Merrill Jr. (b. 1920) and Doris Merrill Magowan (1914–2001), children of Charles E. Merrill and his first wife, and JM's only siblings.

461   *Rigoletto*: opera by Verdi.

463   Stein's . . . early novella: *Q.E.D.*, published posthumously as *Things As They Are*.

Elisabeth Schumann: 1888–1952. German soprano.

464   Havelock Ellis: 1859–1939. English psychologist and spokesman for sexual liberation, author of the once banned six-volume *Studies of the Psychology of Sex*.

468   the Pre-Raphaelites: a "brotherhood" of British writers and artists (including the Rossettis, Holman Hunt, Edward Burne-Jones, and William Morris) in existence from 1848 until the mid-1850s, who disdained contemporary vulgarity, emulated the art of the Italian quattrocento, and often favored religious symbolism and mystical subject matter. Their main apologist was John Ruskin.

Louis Untermeyer's anthology: *Modern American Poetry*, first edition 1919.

a *Yellow Book* fever: the *Yellow Book* (1894–1897), the major journal of the Aesthetic Movement, itself influenced by the Pre-Raphaelite Brotherhood, featured writing by Max Beerbohm, Ernest Dowson, Henry James, and others along with illustrations by Aubrey Beardsley.

469   one of my teachers: G. R. Elliott (cf. note to p. 63).

470   *"Amants, heureux amants"*: in La Fontaine's *Fables*, IX, "Les Deux Pigeons."

473   "a little anthology": *The Poetry Center Presents: An Anthology*, edited with an introduction by Kimon Friar (New York: Gotham Book Mart, 1947).

478   Scarpia's gruesome *"Insistiamo!"*: in Puccini's opera *Tosca* (Act II).

Louis MacNiece: Frederick Louis MacNiece (1907–1963). English poet and acquaintance of W. H. Auden and Stephen Spender, whom he met at Oxford, and the other "thirties poets."

The Playboy of the Western World: play by Irish playwright John Millington Synge (1871–1909).

479   Maria: Maria Demertzi Mitsotáki (1907–1974). JM's and DJ's friend in Athens, subject of "Words for Maria" in JM's *Collected Poems*, p. 235, and figure in *The Changing Light at Sandover*.

Tonáki (our darling Alexandrian Tony): Tony Parigory (1925–1991). JM's and DJ's friend in Athens, the subject of JM's elegy "Tony: Ending the Life" (*Collected Poems*, p. 642).

482   Maria Montez: Maria Africa Antonia Gracia Vidal de Santo Silas (1912–1951). Dominican-born film actress, "The Queen of Technicolor," who despite a lack of formal training became a pinup favorite and a star in Hollywood and Europe, especially after performances in *Arabian Nights* and *Ali Baba and the Forty Thieves*.

487   Max Ernst: 1891–1976. German artist at the forefront of the movements of Dada, surrealism, and expressionism.

Zazà: opera by Leoncavallo.

489   della Robbia: the name of a Florentine family that produced several notable sculptors and ceramicists in the fifteenth and sixteenth centuries.

490   Teresa Stich-Randall: b. 1927. American soprano, remembered here in Gluck's *Iphigénie en Aulide*, she made her European debut in the other opera JM attended at that time, *Oberon*, by German composer Carl Maria von Weber (1786–1826).

Mack Sennett: 1880–1960. "The King of Comedy," Sennett directed over thirty films starring Charlie Chaplin and founded Keystone Studios, which produced the slapstick chase films featuring the Keystone Kops.

Cellini: Benvenuto Cellini (1500–1571). Florentine sculptor and goldsmith.

495   Barney Crop: a fictitious name, a rare occurrence in *A Different Person*.

497   "Spring" Sonata: sonata for violin and piano, op. 24, by Beethoven.

502   Tonio Kröger: eponymous figure in the novella by Thomas Mann (1875–1955).

504   *Fidelio*: opera by Beethoven.

Kirsten Flagstad: Kirsten Malfrid Flagstad (1895–1962). Norwegian soprano.

Elisabeth Schwarzkopf: b. 1915. German-born English soprano. Schwarzkopf had been a member of the Nazi Party in Germany.

Berchtesgaden: town in the Alps near the German-Austrian border where Hitler had his retreat, a mountaintop house known as Eagle's Nest.

505 Sarastro: character in Mozart's opera *Die Zauberflöte*.

506 Ljuba Welitsch: 1913–1966. Bulgarian soprano, emigrated to Vienna in 1940. Schwarzkopf... and Irmgard Seefried... polar opposites: cf. JM's "rival sopranos who sang on alternate evenings" in his poem "The Opera Company" (*Collected Poems*, p. 263).
Mrs. Humphry Ward: Maria Augusta Arnold Ward (1851–1920). Victorian novelist and social activist.

507 Meister Eckhart: 1260–1328. German Dominican mystic.

508 Tannhäuser: eponymous hero of the opera by Wagner.

512 Norma: eponymous heroine of the opera by Italian composer Vincenzo Bellini (1801–1835).

515 Mallarmé... Bachelard's elemental, unpeopled reveries: JM implicitly contrasts Plato et al. with Mallarmé and Wallace Stevens, as well as Bachelard, author of *L'Eaux et les rêves*, *La Poétique de la reverie*, and other works (cf. note to p. 289).

518 Solomon: professional name of Solomon Cutner (1902–1988). English pianist.

519 Schnabel: Artur Schnabel (1882–1951). Austrian composer and pianist, known especially for his interpretations of Beethoven.
Doktor Faust: opera by Italian composer Ferruccio Busoni (1866–1924).
Gertrude Stein's *Things As They Are*: cf. p. 463 and note.

520 Max Beerbohm: 1872–1956. "The incomparable Max," English essayist and caricaturist.

527 Joseph Campbell: 1904–1987. Eminent American comparative mythologist, author of many books including *The Hero with a Thousand Faces* and *The Masks of God* (four volumes) and co-author of *A Skeleton Key to Finnegans Wake*.
Jean Erdman: b. 1916. Joseph Campbell's wife, a dancer with the Martha Graham Dance Company and later a solo artist who collaborated on occasion with John Cage, Merce Cunningham, and Maya Deren.
"Le trombe d'oro della solarità": Brandeis read Montale's poem "I Limoni."

528 "A mind so fine... violate it": T. S. Eliot's phrase (cf. note to p. 97).
Firbank: Ronald Firbank (1886–1926). English novelist, extravagant prose stylist, and famous aesthete.

The Golden Bough: major work of comparative mythology by Sir James George Frazer (1854–1941) which influenced T. S. Eliot and other modernists.

532   Jerl: Jerl Surratt (b. 1949). Writer, researcher, and strategist for nonprofit organizations.

Louise: Louise Fitzhugh (1928–1974). Author and illustrator of young adult novels, including the award-winning classic *Harriet the Spy*.

534   "poetry makes nothing happen": Claude is quoting W. H. Auden's "In Memory of W. B. Yeats."

Betty Plummer: Beatrice Choate Plummer (Potts) Woodruff (b. 1930). Daughter of William Plummer, second husband of JM's mother, Hellen Ingram Merrill.

546   "Nell" or "Le Spectre de la Rose": respectively, song for voice and piano in G-flat major, op. 18/1 by Fauré and song by Weber based on the poem by Gautier (cf. note to p. 208).

Des Grieux: either the character in Massenet's opera *Manon* or the character in Puccini's opera *Manon Lescaut*, who are comparably affected by Manon's beauty.

547   Count Morra: Umberto Morra di Lavriano. Italian intellectual, friend of Balthus, Bernard Berenson, Alberto Moravia, and others. Cf. JM's poem "Bronze" in *Collected Poems*, p. 449.

549   Shakespeare's play: *Julius Caesar*.

550   *Don Carlos*: opera by Verdi.

The Pearl Fishers: i.e., *Les Pecheurs de perles*, opera by Bizet.

551   Violetta: character in Verdi's opera *La Traviata*.

Wotan: character in Wagner's opera *Die Walküre*.

Gilda: character in Verdi's opera *Rigoletto*.

Siegfried: character in Wagner's opera *Die Götterdämmerung*.

to cost everything: cf. the last verse paragraph of T. S. Eliot's "Little Gidding" in *Four Quartets*.

552   Thaïs: title character in the opera by Massenet.

Lucia: title character in Donizetti's opera *Lucia di Lammermoor*.

Iago and Desdemona: characters in Verdi's opera *Otello*.

Zinka Milanov: 1906–1989. Diva born in Zagreb, she made her debut at the Metropolitan Opera in 1937, had differences with management, and returned in 1950.

Peter Sellars: b. 1957. American opera director.

Rosenkavalier: opera by German composer Richard Strauss (1864–1949).

Lotte Lehmann: 1888–1976. German-born American soprano.

Chenier: character in *Andrea Chenier*, opera by Italian composer Umberto Giordano (1867–1948).

Cavaradossi: Tosca's lover in Puccini's opera *Tosca*.

556   *Les Enfants du Paradis*: classic film written by Jacques Prévert and directed by Marcel Carné.

557   Ned Rorem: b. 1923. American composer and author.

558   Ilse Koch: 1906–1967. "The bitch of Buchenwald," sadistic wife of the infamous camp's commandant, Karl Koch.

Frederic Prokosch: 1906–1989. Colorful novelist, poet, printer, and forger.

560   Carmen . . . Micaela: characters in Bizet's opera *Carmen*.

563   Berensons: i.e., connoisseurs, à la American art historian Bernard Berenson (1865–1959).

565   Berthe Morisot: 1841–1895. French impressionist painter. Fragonard's granddaughter, Manet's sister-in-law, and Corot's student.

George Moore: George Augustus Moore (1852–1933). Anglo-Irish novelist who studied painting and literature in Paris.

Don Pasquito's Tango from *Façade*: a part of the 1922 musical "entertainment" by English composer William Walton (1902–1983) with lyrics by English poet Edith Sitwell (1887–1964).

571   sex . . . was the theater of the poor: after an aphorism sometimes attributed to Oscar Wilde.

572   Scarlatti: Domenico Scarlatti (1685–1757). Italian composer.

Byrd: William Byrd (1543–1623). Foremost English composer of his era.

Telemann: Georg Philipp Telemann (1681–1767). German composer.

the Italian Concerto: BWV 971 by J. S. Bach (1685–1750).

Marilyn Aronberg: Marilyn Aronberg Lavin (b. 1925). Art historian, author of *Piero della Francesca: The Flagellation* among other works, wife of art historian Irving Lavin.

Barocci: Federigo (or Federico) Barroci (or Barrocio) (1530–1612). Italian painter whose later works show traces of the baroque mode.

573   Fragonard: Jean-Honoré Fragonard (1732–1806). French painter who studied with Chardin and Boucher. Noted for his delectably painted erotic and pastoral scenes (many done for the court of Louis XV) which sometimes verged on the sentimental.

Carlo Dolci: 1616–1686. Florentine painter and designer of stained glass.

Raphael: Raffaello Santi or Sanzio (1483–1520). Italian painter of the High Renaissance.

Caravaggio: Michelangelo Merisi da Caravaggio (1573–1610). Revolutionary painter and *enfant terrible* of his day, noted for his dramatic use of chiaroscuro and the baroque structures of his paintings.

Bellini: Giovanni Bellini (c. 1430–1516). Italian painter of the High Renaissance, whose students included Giorgione and Titian.

Piero della Francesca: c. 1420–1492. Early Italian Renaissance painter, whose students included Luca Signorelli.

Mario Praz: 1896–1982. Italian scholar, literary critic, and art critic.

574   Mimi's crystalline *"senza rancor"*: in Puccini's opera *La Bohème* (Act III).

575   the White Rock nymph: the icon for White Rock Sparkling Beverages indeed pictures a nymph on a rock.

579   *Nabucco*: opera by Verdi.

580   *Porgy and Bess*: 1935 "folk opera" with African-American cast composed by George Gershwin based on the novel by DuBose Heyward with libretto by Heyward and Ira Gershwin.

581   Rosa Parks: Rosa Louise McAuley Parks (b. 1913). African-American woman who refused to give up her seat to a white man on a bus in Montgomery, Alabama, on December 1, 1955, and in so doing sparked the desegregation movement in the United States led by Martin Luther King Jr.

583   Murder, Inc. . . . Czar Lepke: Lepke ("Little Louis" in Yiddish) Buchalter, born Louis Bookhouse (1897–1944). Head of Murder, Inc., mobster organization created by Lucky Luciano, Lepke was eventually convicted and executed by electrocution.

584   House of Atreus: descendants of Tantalus, cursed thenceforth and doomed to commit hideous intrafamilial sins. Atreus murdered children of his brother, Thyestes, who had seduced Atreus's wife, and served them to him at dinner. Thyestes's son killed Atreus and so on.

585   a brownstone on West Eleventh: JM's first home, 18 West 11th Street, later a bomb factory for the Weather Underground, a radical political group, unintentionally blown up by them in 1971 (cf. p. 537 and JM's poem "18 West 11th Street" in his *Collected Poems*, p. 314).

586   *The Tales of Hoffmann*: opera by Offenbach based on stories by E. T. A. Hoffmann (1776–1822). Dr. Miracle is the form that Hoffmann's evil genius takes in the act set in Munich.

587   *l'Enfant Sauvage*: 1970 French film by director Francois Truffaut (1932–1984) based on a case history of the French physician Jean Itard.

      the insurance man: Wallace Stevens, whose quoted hypothesis is set forth in "Adagia" in *Opus Posthumous*.

592 Barbara Hutton: 1912–1979. The shy poet was the granddaughter of F. W. Woolworth, the daughter of E. F. Hutton, and one of the world's richest and most flamboyant women, many times married, once to Prince Mdivani of Russia—and to Count Cort Revenlow of Austria, Cary Grant, and others.

593 Eddie Cantor: Edward Israel Iskovitz (1892–1964). American songwriter, singer, comedian.

594 Vronsky's horse: in Tolstoy's *Anna Karenina*.

596 Lambert Strether: character in Henry James's *The Ambassadors*.

597 *Lost Horizon*: also known as *Lost Horizon of Shangri-La*, 1937 American film directed by Frank Capra based on the best-selling novel by James Hilton.

599 *The Emperor Jones*: play by American writer Eugene O'Neill (1888–1953).

600 *The Way of the World*: play by Congreve (cf. note to p. 330).
Hopkins . . . famous sonnet: "The Windover" by English poet Gerard Manley Hopkins (1884–1889).

601 Chabrier: Emmanuel Chabrier (1841–1894). French composer.
Tristan: the opera *Tristan und Isolde* by Wagner.
Walden . . . a clever forgery by Proust: Indeed, Proust in a letter to the Comtesse de Noailles had advised her "Lisez . . . les pages admirables de *Walden*. Il me semble qu'on les lise en soi-même tant elles sortent du fond de nôtre expérience intime."

602 *Elektra*: opera by Richard Strauss.
Der Freischütz: opera by Weber.
Adriana Lecouvreur: opera by Italian composer Francesco Cilea (1866–1950).
Sakuntala: *La Leggenda di Sakuntala*, opera by Italian composer Franco Alfano (1876–1954), who completed Puccini's opera *Turandot*, left unfinished at Puccini's death.

604 that stanza where Spenser asserts: stanza 19 of "An Hymne to Beautie" by English poet Edmund Spenser (1552–1599): "So every spirit, as it is most pure, / And hath in it the more of heavenly light, / So it the fairer bodie doth procure / To habit in . . ."
Dana Gioia: b. 1950. American poet and translator.

605 the book dedicated to I. B.: i.e., Irma Brandeis.

610 Anton Dolin: born Patrick Healey-Kay (1904–1983). English ballet dancer and choreographer, at different times premier dancer for Diaghilev's company and frequent partner of Alicia Markova.

613 *L'Elisir d'Amore*: opera by Donizetti.

615 Theodorakis: Mikis Theodorakis (b. 1925). Greek composer of all genres of music, advocate of Greek popular music and progressive politics.

hasápiko: Greek popular dance done customarily by two (or more) men, arms on one another's shoulders.

620 *Parsifal*: opera by Wagner.

623 "the singing-masters of my soul": Yeats, "Sailing to Byzantium."

"Childhood is health" said Herbert: English poet George Herbert (1593–1633), in "Holy Baptisme (II)."

624 Addison Mizner's Palm Beach: Addison Mizner (1872–1933) was a self-taught Florida architect, famous for his luxurious Mediterranean-style resorts.

625 "younger and shallower and vainer brother": American philosopher William James (1842–1910) in his simultaneous resignation from the National Institute of Arts and Letters and his declination of an invitation to join the American Academy (letter of June 17, 1905).

the *Lord Nelson* Mass: Mass in D, also known as the *Missa in augustiis*, by Franz Joseph Haydn (1732–1809).

626 *fuir, là-bas, fuir*: allusion to Mallarmé's "Brise marine."

Sages standing in God's holy fire: Yeats, "Sailing to Byzantium."

627 *I Puritani*: opera by Bellini.

629 Here where no image: from JM's poem "Some Negatives: X at the Château" (*Collected Poems*, p. 65).

Marilyn had visited the famous *Flagellation*: cf. p. 572 and note.

632 Salvemini: Gaetano Salvemini (1873–1957). Italian historian and vehement opponent of Mussolini's Fascism.

635 *I Promessi Sposi*: novel by Italian novelist and statesman Alessandro Manzoni (1785–1873).

Un Ballo in Maschera: opera by Verdi.

636 *Manon*: opera by Massenet.

Beaumarchais: Pierre Augustin Caron de Beaumarchais (1732–1799). French playwright known especially for *Le Barbier de Seville* and *Le Mariage de Figaro*.

637 "Wax to receive and marble to retain": Byron, *Beppo*, stanza 34.

638 Jan Kott: 1914–2001. Polish theoretician, critic, poet, and essayist who lived and taught in the United States after 1966.

640 Elisabeth Bergner: professional name of Elisabeth Ettel (1898–1986). Austrian-born dramatic actress and film star.

Carole Lombard: born Jane Alice Peters (1908–1942). American film star.

642 Psyche's tasks in Apuleius: i.e., in the *Metamorphoses* or *The Golden Ass*, by Apuleius (c. 125–c. 170), North African conveyor of Greek tales to readers of Latin (most notably *Cupid and Psyche*).

647 ungainly newcomer named Callas: Maria Callas (1923–1977). Greek-American soprano, perhaps the most famous opera diva of the twentieth century.

649 John Hollander: b. 1929. American poet. Cf. Hollander's long *poème à clef*, *Reflections on Espionage* (1976).

653 "of hammered gold and gold enameling": Yeats, "Sailing to Byzantium."

658 *Le Pauvre Blaise* or *Les Malheurs de Sophie*: young adult novels by Sophie Rostopchine, la Comtesse de Segur (1797–1874).

659 Gérôme: Jean-Léon Gérôme (1824–1904). French painter and sculptor.

661 Wyndham Lewis: 1882–1957. American-born novelist, artist, and critic who emigrated as a child to England.

665 *Falstaff*: opera by Verdi.

666 the Thomas Coles: paintings by Thomas Cole (1801–1848), American allegorical and landscape painter, sometimes viewed as the originator of the Hudson River School of art, founder of the National Academy of Design.

675 "The prologues are over": from Wallace Stevens's poem "Asides on the Oboe."
"Central man": one of Stevens's terms for the most evolved human being.

679 the dramatization I'd put together, for Peter, from *The Changing Light at Sandover*: the film, called *Voices from Sandover*, was produced by Peter Hooten (Poetry Works, Inc.) and directed by Joan Darling. The cast included Hooten, William Ball, Elzbieta Czyzewska, Keith David, Leah Doyle, Terry Layman, James Morrison, and David Neumann. JM played himself.

680 Princesse de Guermantes's terminal reception: in the last volume of Proust's novel *A la Recherche du temps perdu*.
Terry: Terry Layman (b. 1948). American actor who played David Jackson in *Voices from Sandover*.

BIOGRAPHICAL NOTE

James Merrill was born in New York City on March 3, 1926, the son of the financier and philanthropist Charles E. Merrill, one of the founders of the brokerage firm Merrill Lynch & Co., and his second wife, Hellen Ingram. Merrill, who attended St. Bernard's School, was raised in Manhattan and Southampton, Long Island, where his family had a country house that was designed by Stanford White, and in Palm Beach, Florida. His parents divorced in 1939, and the reverberations of the "broken home" can be heard throughout his poetry. After attending the Lawrenceville School, Merrill enrolled at Amherst College, his father's alma mater, took a year off to serve in the army, and graduated summa cum laude with the class of 1947. He taught at Bard College in 1948–1949, and although he fought shy of academe in the following years he did accept short appointments at Amherst, the University of Wisconsin, Washington University, and Yale University. In 1954 he moved with his companion, David Jackson, a writer and painter, to a house in Stonington, Connecticut, which is still maintained by Stonington Village and houses an artist-in-residence every year.

In 1957 Merrill and Jackson undertook a trip around the world, and for two decades beginning in 1964 they spent a part of each year in Greece. They owned a house in Athens at the foot of Mt. Lycabettus and were famous among the local literati for the terrace parties they threw. Beginning in 1979 Merrill spent winters in Key West, Florida, where he and Jackson acquired another house. Key West was a place he had an affinity for partly because it had previously attracted two of his favorite poets, Wallace Stevens and Elizabeth Bishop, the latter his close friend for decades. Merrill, a gifted linguist and a lover of different cultures, always traveled widely, and the displacements and discoveries of his travels, along with the routines of his life in his different homes, are the stuff of many of his poems. He died away from home, in Tucson, Arizona, on February 6, 1995.

A selection of Merrill's earliest writings, taken from his contributions to the *Lawrenceville Literary Magazine,* was privately printed by his father as a sixteenth-birthday gift in 1942, under the title *Jim's Book.* The young writer proudly distributed most of the one hundred copies as soon as possible—and before long began to retrieve as many of those copies as he could. A group of his poems appeared in *Poetry* in March 1946, the same year that saw the publication in Athens, Greece, of a limited edition of poems entitled *The Black Swan.* He published his first full-fledged book, *First Poems,* when he was twenty-five, in 1951. He next tried his hand at playwriting: *The Bait* was produced at the Comedy Club in 1953 (and published in a journal in 1955 and in a book in 1960), and *The Immortal Husband* was performed at the Theater de Lys in 1955 (and published in 1956). Meanwhile, his first novel, *The Seraglio,* a Jamesian roman à clef, appeared in 1957 (it was reissued in 1987), and his second commercial volume of poems, *The Country of a Thousand Years of Peace,* in 1959 (revised edition, 1970). His third volume of poems, *Water Street*—its title refers to the street Merrill lived on in Stonington—came out in 1962, and his second, experimental novel, *The (Diblos) Notebook,* based in part on his first experiences in Greece, in 1965 (reissued in 1994).

His 1966 collection *Nights and Days* received the National Book Award. The judges for that year, W. H. Auden, James Dickey, and Howard Nemerov, cited the book for its author's "scrupulous and uncompromising cultivation of the poetic art evidenced in his refusal to settle for an easy and profitable stance; for his insistence on taking the kind of tough, poetic chances which make the difference between aesthetic success or failure." *The Fire Screen* appeared in 1969, followed in 1972 by *Braving the Elements,* which was awarded the Bollingen Prize for Poetry, and in 1974 by a selection of previously uncollected poems, *The Yellow Pages.* When *Divine Comedies* came out in 1976, it won the Pulitzer Prize.

The narrative poem "The Book of Ephraim," which was originally included in *Divine Comedies,* later served as the first installment of an epic visionary poem based in large part on Merrill and Jackson's communications with the Other World by way of the Ouija board. The subsequent two parts were *Mirabell: Books of Number,* which appeared in 1978 and received the National Book Award for Poetry, and *Scripts for the Pageant,* published in 1980. In 1982 Merrill brought together these three long poems and "Coda: The Higher Keys" in a comprehensive edition of the work he now called *The Changing Light at Sandover.* That landmark volume won the National Book Critics Circle Award. The same year, Merrill published his first selected poems, *From the First Nine: Poems 1946–1976.* His book of poems *Late Settings* was published in 1985, and a collection of essays, interviews, and reviews entitled *Recitative* appeared in 1986. In 1988 *The Inner Room* was honored with the first Bobbitt National Prize for Poetry, awarded by the Library of Congress. *Selected Poems 1946–1985* appeared in 1992, and his memoir, *A Different Person,* came out in 1993. *A Scattering of Salts,* the last book of poems that he saw through production, was published posthumously in 1995. His *Collected Poems* appeared in 2001 and his *Collected Novels and Plays* in 2002.

INDEX

A NOTE ON THE TYPE

Pierre Simon Fournier *le jeune,* who designed the type used in this book, was both an originator and a collector of types. His services to the art of printing were his design of letters, his creation of ornaments and initials, and his standardization of type sizes. His types are old style in character and sharply cut. In 1764 and 1766 he published his *Manuel typographique,* a treatise on the history of French types and printing, on typefounding in all its details, and on what many consider his most important contribution to typography—the measurement of type by the point system.

Composed by NK Graphics, Keene, New Hampshire
Printed and bound by R. R. Donnelley & Sons, Crawfordsville, Indiana
Designed by Chip Kidd